# A GRAMMAR OF THE
# PALESTINIAN TARGUM FRAGMENTS
# FROM THE CAIRO GENIZAH

# HARVARD SEMITIC MUSEUM
# *HARVARD SEMITIC STUDIES*

### Frank Moore Cross, editor

# A GRAMMAR OF THE PALESTINIAN TARGUM FRAGMENTS FROM THE CAIRO GENIZAH

by

Steven E. Fassberg

Scholars Press
Atlanta, Georgia

# A GRAMMAR OF THE
# PALESTINIAN TARGUM FRAGMENTS
# FROM THE CAIRO GENIZAH

by
Steven E. Fassberg

© 1990
The President and Fellows of Harvard University

**Library of Congress Cataloging in Publication Data**

Fassberg, Steven E.
    A grammar of the Palestinian Targum fragments from the Cairo
    Genizah / by Steven E. Fassberg.
    p. cm. — (Harvard Semitic studies ; no. 38)
    Includes bibliographical references and indexes.
    ISBN 1-55540-569-X (acid-free paper)
    1. Aramaic language—Grammar. 2. Bible. O.T. Pentateuch.
Aramaic—Versions, Palestinian—Language, style. 3. Cairo Genizah.
I. Title. II. Series.
PJ5252.F37 1991
492'.29—dc20                                         90-23362
                                                     CIP

Printed in the United States of America
on acid-free paper

*For my parents*

# PREFACE

This book is a revision and expansion of my dissertation submitted to Harvard University in 1983. I should like to express my appreciation to the following institutions for the help extended to me at an early stage of this study: the Lady Davis Trust, the Memorial Foundation for Jewish Culture, the Bodleian Library, the Taylor-Schechter Collection of the Cambridge University Library, the Jewish Theological Seminary Library and the National and University Library, Jerusalem. I wish to express my gratitude to Professors F. M. Cross, T. O. Lambdin, J. Huehnergard, M. L. Klein, and M. Bar-Asher for their aid and advice. Finally, I should like to give special thanks to my wife, Celia, for her patience, and to Carol Cross for her amazing and painstaking work on the manuscript.

Steven E. Fassberg
Jerusalem 1988

# TABLE OF CONTENTS

^ reading differs from that in Klein, *Genizah Manuscripts of Palestinian Targum*

\* unattested, reconstructed form

/ / phonemic transcription

/?/ phonemic transcription based on unpointed or partially pointed evidence, or the phonemic transcription is uncertain

/\* ?/ reconstructed and uncertain phonemic transcription

[ ] phonetic transcription

∅ zero morpheme

# word boundary

בֺ legible letter, although not fully preserved

[בֺ] legible letter, although poorly preserved

[ב] illegible letter

(2x) the word or root is attested two times in the same verse

(+2x) the word or root is attested two additional times in all of the fragments

| | | | |
|---|---|---|---|
| abs. | absolute state | Imperf. | Imperfect |
| Act. | Active | Inf. | Infinitive |
| c. | common | m. | masculine |
| C | consonant | pl. | plural |
| cst. | construct | Pss. | Passive |
| det. | determined (emphatic) state | Ptc. | Participle |
| f. | feminine | s. | singular |
| G | Guttural | V | vowel |
| Imper. | Imperative | | |

*Verbal Conjugations*

| | |
|---|---|
| G | Peal |
| D | Pael |
| C | Aphel |
| Gt | Ithpeel |
| Dt | Ithpaal |
| Ct | Ittaphal |
| Q | Quadriliteral |
| Qt | Quadriliteral medio-passive |
| Š | Shaphel |
| Št | Ishtaphel |

*Books of the Bible*

| | |
|---|---|
| MT | Masoretic text |
| Gn | Genesis |
| Ex | Exodus |
| Lv | Leviticus |
| Nu | Numbers |
| Dt | Deuteronomy |
| Jos | Joshua |
| Sa | Samuel |
| Is | Isaiah |
| Je | Jeremiah |
| Mi | Micah |
| Jb | Job |
| Dn | Daniel |
| Ezr | Ezra |
| Ch | Chronicles |

*Editions Cited*

Cairo Genizah
fragments

M. L. Klein, *Genizah Manuscripts of Palestinian Targum*, 2 vols. Cincinnati: Hebrew Union College Press, 1986.

Masoretic text

K. Elliger and W. Rudolph, *Biblia Hebraica Stuttgartensia.* Stuttgart: Deutsche Bibelstiftung, 1967-1977.

Targum Onqelos,
Targum Jonathan,
Hagiographa

A. Sperber, *The Bible in Aramaic*, I-IV. Leiden: E. J. Brill, 1959-1977.

Targum Pseudo-
Jonathan

E. G. Clarke et al., *Targum Pseudo-Jonathan of the Pentateuch: Text and Concordance.* Hoboken, NJ: Ktav, 1984.

Targum Neophyti

A. Díez Macho, *Neophyti 1: Targum Palestinense MS de la Biblioteca Vaticana*, 6 vols. Madrid-Barcelona: Consejo Superior de Investigaciones Científicas, 1968-1979.

Fragment Targum

M. L. Klein, *The Fragment-Targums of the Pentateuch According to Their Extant Sources*, 2 vols. Analecta Biblica 76. Rome: Biblical Institute Press, 1980.

Samaritan Targum

A. Tal, *The Samaritan Targum: A Critical Edition*, 3 vols. Tel-Aviv: Tel-Aviv University, 1980-1983.
For a list of errata, see A. Tal *apud* G. Sixdenier, "La langue du targum samaritain," *Journal Asiatique*, 272 (1984), 231-234.

Peshiṭta

Peshiṭta Institute, *The Old Testament in Syriac According to the Peshiṭta Version.* Leiden: E. J. Brill, 1977—; A. M. Ceriani, *Translatio syra pescitto Veteris Testamenti ex codice Ambrosiano*, I-II. Milan: 1876-1883.

Note:
Mandaic transcribed as in E. S. Drower, R. Macuch, *A Mandaic Dictionary.* Oxford: Clarendon Press, 1963.

Ma'lula transcribed as in A. Spitaler, *Grammatik des neuaramäischens Dialekts von Ma'lula (Antilibanon).* AKM 23,1. Leipzig: Deutsche Morgenländische Gesellschaft, 1938.

Samaritan Aramaic transcribed as in Z. Ben-Ḥayyim, *The Literary and Oral Tradition of Hebrew and Aramaic Amongst the Samaritans*, 5 vols. Jerusalem: The Academy of the Hebrew Language, 1957-1977 (see I, pp. 13-17;

also R. Macuch, *Grammatik des samaritanischen Aramäisch.* Berlin: Walter de Gruyter, 1982, p. 69).

Syriac transcribed according to a reconstructed state of language containing *shewa mobile* and gemination.

Targum Onqelos transcribed according to Yemenite supralinear pointing.

| | |
|---|---|
| *AJBA* | Australian Journal of Biblical Archaeology |
| *AJSL* | American Journal of Semitic Languages and Literatures |
| *AKM* | Abhandlungen für die Kunde des Morgenlandes |
| *ArOr* | Archiv Orientální |
| *Aug* | Augustinianum |
| *Bibl* | Biblica |
| *EI* | Eretz Israel |
| *EJ* | Encyclopaedia Judaica |
| *HUCA* | Hebrew Union College Annual |
| *IEJ* | Israel Exploration Journal |
| *IOS* | Israel Oriental Studies |
| *JA* | Journal Asiatique |
| *JAOS* | Journal of the American Oriental Society |
| *JBL* | Journal of Biblical Literature |
| *JJS* | Journal of Jewish Studies |
| *JNES* | Journal of Near Eastern Studies |
| *JQR* | Jewish Quarterly Review |
| *JSS* | Journal of Semitic Studies |
| *JTS* | Journal of Theological Studies |
| *KirSef* | Kiryat Sefer |
| *Lesh* | Leshonenu |
| *Mass* | Massorot |
| *MélPhLJ* | Mélanges de Philosophie et de la Littérature Juives |
| *MGWJ* | Monatschrift für Geschichte und Wissenschaft des Judentums |
| *Mus* | Le Muséon |
| *OLZ* | Orientalistische Literaturzeitung |
| *REJ* | Revue des Études Juives |
| *ScrHier* | Scripta Hierosolymitana |
| *Sef* | Sefarad |
| *SVT* | Supplements to Vetus Testamentum |
| *UF* | Ugarit Forschungen |
| *VT* | Vetus Testamentum |
| *ZAW* | Zeitschrift für die Alttestamentliche Wissenschaft |
| *ZDMG* | Zeitschrift der Deutschen Morgenländischen Gesellschaft |
| *ZNW* | Zeitschrift für die Neutestamentliche Wissenschaft und die Kunde der älteren Kirche |

# I. INTRODUCTION

**§1**

**§1a**  Until 1930 only three Jewish Targumim to the Pentateuch were known. The official Rabbinic Targum, and hence the most prestigious, was Targum Onqelos.[1] It is, on the whole, a literal translation of the Masoretic text.[2] The classical position concerning the origin of this Targum, as expressed by Th. Nöldeke, is that it was written in Palestine, but that it underwent final redaction in Babylonia. Its language reflects the Aramaic of Palestine with secondary Babylonian influences.[3] There were many proponents of this view, although they often disagreed among themselves as to the degree of the Babylonian influences.[4] Opponents of this position, notably A. Geiger[5] and P. Kahle,[6] maintained that Targum Onqelos was written and edited in Babylonia. The discovery of Aramaic documents at Qumran[7] and of the Bar Kochba letters[8] has provided additional evidence of the Palestinian origin of Targum Onqelos. Today the language of its original composition is generally thought to belong to the period of Middle Aramaic,[9] sometimes referred to as Standard Literary Aramaic.[10]

**§1b**  The two other Jewish Targumim were called Palestinian Targumim or Jerusalem Targumim.[11] G. Dalman described them as "die Sprachdenkmäler mit gemischtem Sprachtypus."[12] He considered them a mixture of Galilean Aramaic and the language of Targum Onqelos in which features of Babylonian Talmudic Aramaic could be identified. The first of these two Targumim, Targum Pseudo-Jonathan (Targum Yerushalmi I),[13] is an almost complete translation of the Pentateuch,[14] containing considerable Aggadic material. Much has been written on the constitutive elements of this Targum. There are two main schools of thought. The first school argues that the Targum is essentially Targum Onqelos, to which additions were made from a Palestinian Targum.[15] The second holds that it is an essentially Palestinian Targum, edited under the influence of Targum Onqelos.[16] This latter view is widely accepted today. It is clear that the final redaction of Targum Pseudo-Jonathan took place no earlier than in the 7th century C.E. since historical personalities of that period are mentioned in the text.[17] The name of this Targum is thought to originate in a 14th century misreading of the initials ת״י

2

(תרגום ירושלמי) as תרגום יונתן. As a result of this misreading, authorship of the text was erroneously ascribed to Jonathan ben Uzziel.

§1c   The Fragment Targum (Targum Yerushalmi II),[18] in contrast, contains only verses, partial verses, and, occasionally, single words. It was thought by some to be a collection of variant readings to Targum Pseudo-Jonathan;[19] others contended that it was a list of variants to Targum Onqelos.[20] W. Bacher[21] and Kahle[22] were of the opinion that the Fragment Targum was a collection of readings from an old Palestinian Targum, at times predating Targum Onqelos and Targum Pseudo-Jonathan. Modern scholars generally regard it as a selection of readings representing a Palestinian Targum tradition. They are, however, unable to explain why it was preserved only in fragmentary form. The Fragment Targum resembles the Targum Pseudo-Jonathan in that it contains many Aggadic interpolations; it differs, however, in its language. Dalman did not distinguish the language of Targum Pseudo-Jonathan from that of the Fragment Targum and classified them both as a *Mischsprache*. More recent works have argued that the language of the Fragment Targum is distinct. Targum Onqelos and the Babylonian Talmud seem to have had less of an influence on the language of the Fragment Targum than on that of Targum Pseudo-Jonathan.[23] No comprehensive linguistic analysis of the differences has, however, been made.[24] There are six primary sources of the Fragment Targum containing, all in all, about 1000 verses.[25] The selection of verses is not identical in all the manuscripts and it is not clear how or why they were chosen. The date of compilation of the Targum is difficult to determine and the manuscripts seem to belong to four different recensions.[26]

§1d   In 1930 some 600 verses of Aramaic were published by Kahle in *Masoreten des Westens, II*. They belonged to different fragments found in the Cairo Genizah and appeared to be part of a complete Targum to the Pentateuch, written in a dialect similar to that of the Fragment Targum.[27] Some of the fragments were poorly preserved while others contained several continuous chapters. They did not belong to one codex; Kahle assigned them to six manuscripts which he labelled MSS A-F.[28] Two of the manuscripts contain some of the same passages but differ in text and orthography.[29] One linguistic tradition seems, however, to characterize the language of all these texts.[30] Just under half of the verses are vocalized, shedding light on the pronunciation of the language.[31] Unlike Targum Pseudo-Jonathan and the Fragment Targum, the consonantal text of these manuscripts seems to be free of features which characterize the language of Targum Onqelos and Babylonian Talmudic Aramaic. Kahle's texts were pointed by vocalizers who, in general, used Tiberian vowel signs to represent a Palestinian vocalization.[32] At times, however, their familiarity with the Tiberian pointing of Biblical Aramaic led them to point, at times deliberately and at times unconsciously, according to the norms of that dialect.[33] Despite this occasional influence in pointing, the Cairo Genizah manuscripts were acclaimed as an authentic reflection of the language of the Palestinian Targum.

§1e Since the publication of *Masoreten des Westens II*, another 270 verses of this Targum from the Cairo Genizah have been published by W. Baars,[34] A. Díez Macho,[35] and M. L. Klein.[36] Klein has recently re-edited all Genizah manuscripts of Palestinian Targum to the Pentateuch.[37]

§1f The discovery of Codex Neophyti 1 in 1956[38] confirmed the existence of a complete Palestinian Targum whose language resembled that of the Cairo Genizah manuscripts and the Fragment Targum.[39] Targum Neophyti and the Cairo Genizah manuscripts parallel one another closely, although there are differences in text and language. It has been noted that where Targum Neophyti has marginal and interlinear glosses, these correspond with the Cairo Genizah manuscripts more closely than does the Targum Neophyti text.[40] The linguistic differences can be accounted for by the fact that Neophyti is an early 16th century copy of the Targum.[41] During the course of its transmission, scribes occasionally altered the language (as they must have done in the case of Targum Pseudo-Jonathan and the Fragment Targum). Consequently, although Targum Neophyti preserves a complete Palestinian Targum, the language of the Cairo Genizah manuscripts seems to be a more accurate reflection of the type of language in which Targum Neophyti must have originally been written.

§1g The language of the Cairo Genizah manuscripts and of Targum Neophyti has been a subject of controversy.[42] Although Kahle thought that the Cairo Genizah manuscripts must have been written between the 7th and the 11th centuries,[43] he argued that the language of these manuscripts was one "which we can say...is very similar to that spoken by the earliest Christians."[44] He called it Palestinian Aramaic. E. Y. Kutscher preferred to call it "a type of Aramaic which is slightly different from the Galilean type."[45] He strongly rejected the view that it was the language of the 1st century C.E. and favored a date closer to ca. 500 C.E.[46] Others, such as F. Rosenthal[47] and J. A. Fitzmyer[48] have called it Jewish Palestinian Aramaic, preferring to categorize it together with Targum Onqelos and Targum Jonathan to the Prophets, Targum Pseudo-Jonathan, the Fragment Targum, and the Palestinian Midrashim and Palestinian Talmud. A. Tal[49] has proposed the term Palestinian Targumic Aramaic. He sees a natural, linear evolution from Qumran Aramaic through Palestinian Targumic Aramaic to Palestinian Talmudic Aramaic. Recently, K. Beyer[50] has used the term Galilean Targumic Aramaic.

§1h The Cairo Genizah manuscripts, regarded as the most reliable representation of the dialect in which the Fragment Targum and Targum Neophyti were written, have frequently been used as a basis for comparison with other Aramaic dialects. The language reflected in these manuscripts has, however, never been systematically described. Only select features and isolated lexical items have been discussed by various scholars.

§1i  The first to comment on the language of these manuscripts was H. L. Ginsberg. In a short article, "Notes on a Palestinian Targum,"[51] he discussed some of the outstanding features of the dialect, such as the reflexes of Proto-Aramaic *i and *u as e and o, and the 1 s. Imperf. נקטול. In many of his articles Kutscher commented, in passing, on lexical items from the manuscripts. His most significant contributions, however, are his discussion of the reflexes of *i and *u in "Articulation of the Vowels u, i in Transcriptions of Biblical Hebrew, in Galilean Aramaic, and in Mishnaic Hebrew" and his short sketch of Galilean Aramaic in the *Encyclopedia Judaica.*[52] The discussion of phonology in this sketch is based largely on the pointing found in the Cairo Genizah fragments. Y. Peri studied the morphology of the language of these fragments in an unpublished dissertation. His treatment is, however, limited to the noun and is based on Kahle's reading of the manuscripts, which is not always reliable.[53] A. Tal has dealt with the demonstrative pronouns and the Infinitive in these fragments, as well as what he considers to be a paragogic /n/; in his study of Targum Jonathan to the Former Prophets he frequently discusses lexical items.[54] Z. Ben-Ḥayyim has also dealt with lexical items and isolated grammatical featuares in passing in his work on Samaritan Aramaic and in *Studies in the Traditions of the Hebrew Language.*[55] Mention should also be made of the works of Beyer[56] and T. Muraoka,[57] as well as the textual studies of A. Marmorstein,[58], J. Teicher,[59] R. Bloch,[60] and G. Schelbert,[61] which include remarks on the language of these fragments. The grammar of the Cairo Genizah fragments promised by Kahle, in collaboration with W. Stevenson, never appeared.[62]

§1j  The language of these fragments has also been treated indirectly in works on Targum Neophyti. Some of these studies are a grammar of Targum Neophyti by B. Levy,[63] a syntax of the non-translational portions in Targum Neophyti by J. Lund,[64] the introductions to the published volumes of Targum Neophyti by Díez Macho,[65] and the unpublished doctoral theses of G. Cowling,[66] G. Lasry,[67] and J. Foster.[68] Works on the marginal glosses to Targum Neophyti have also touched on the Cairo Genizah manuscripts. The most important study is by S. Lund and J. Foster,[69] who identified two distinct linguistic traditions in the glosses and devoted some attention to the tradition resembling that of the Cairo Genizah fragments.

§1k  In the absence of any comprehensive treatment of these manuscripts, the study presented here has two objectives. The first is to present a complete and systematic analysis of the orthography, phonology, and morphology of the language of the Cairo Genizah manuscripts, as well as to note some syntactic features. Two different pointing systems were employed in the fragments, each of which contains more signs than the number of vocalic phonemes in the language, making it difficult to identify each phoneme.

5

Consequently, special attention will be devoted to the relationship between the vocalic phonemes and their graphic representation. This relationship is also important for an understanding of the morphology of the language.

**§ll** The second objective of this study is to compare the cardinal features of the language of the Cairo Genizah fragments with those of the language of other Palestinian Targumim and with those of other Aramaic dialects. This comparison will concentrate on the language of Targum Pseudo-Jonathan, the Fragment Targum, and the Targum Neophyti, and on the following dialects: Biblical Aramaic, Targum Onqelos, Syriac, and dialects from Syria-Palestine (Palestinian Syriac, Samaritan Aramaic, Galilean Aramaic, and Ma'lula). Where relevant, other dialects have been included. Features of Rabbinic Hebrew, a language with which the Jewish scribes were familiar, will also be described where pertinent.

**§lm** The language of the Cairo Genizah fragments seems to be similar to, but not identical with, Galilean Aramaic.[70] It must, however, be remembered that little is known of the vocalic phonemes of Galilean Aramaic. Therefore, it is difficult to examine the relationship between the two dialects on a phonological level. It should also be stressed that this dialect shares many features with other dialects from the Syro-Palestinian area, including Syriac. The isoglosses will be noted in the course of the study.

**§ln** The readings presented in this study are based on the examination of the original manuscripts[71] and frequently differ from those of Kahle, Díez Macho, Baars, and Klein. Readings which differ from those found in Klein's *Genizah Manuscripts* will be indicated by the sign ⌒, e.g., בדיפלה A Ex 22:6.⌒

6

## Footnotes — Chapter I

[1]The *editio princeps* of Targum Onqelos appeared in Bologna in 1482. The most recent and reliable edition is A. Sperber, ed., *The Bible in Aramaic, I: The Pentateuch according to Targum Onqelos* (Leiden: E. J. Brill, 1959). In the Babylonian Talmud (Tractate Qiddushin 49a) it is called תרגום דידן. The 9th century Gaon Natronai (in Seder Rav Amram, 29a) refers to it as תרגום־דרבנן.

Non-Jewish Targumim to the Pentateuch include the Peshiṭta and the Samaritan Targum.

[2]For a discussion of the literal and non-literal aspects of the translation, see B. J. Roberts, *The Old Testament Text and Versions* (Cardiff: University of Wales Press, 1951), pp. 206-207.

[3]Th. Nöldeke, *Die semitischen Sprachen*, 2nd ed. (Leipzig: Tauchnitz, 1889), pp. 37-38.

[4]E.g., A. Berliner, *Targum Onkelos*, II (Berlin: Gorzelanczyk, 1884), p. 110; E. Y. Kutscher, "The Language of the Genesis Apocryphon: A Preliminary Study," *ScrHier*, 4 (1958), pp. 9-10. G. Dalman in particular downplayed the degree of Babylonian influence. See Dalman, *Grammatik des jüdisch-palästinischen Aramäisch*, 2nd ed. (Leipzig: J. C. Hinrichs, 1905; reprint Darmstadt: Wissenschaftliche Buchgesellschaft, 1960), pp. 12-13.

[5]A. Geiger, *Urschrift und Übersetzung der Bibel in ihrer Abhängigkeit von den inneren Entwicklung des Judenthums* (Breslau: Hainauer, 1857), pp. 163ff.

[6]P. Kahle, *Masoreten des Westens*, II (Stuttgart: W. Kohlhammer, 1930: reprint Hildesheim: Georg Olms, 1967), pp. 1*-12*, and Kahle, *The Cairo Geniza*, 2nd ed. (Oxford: Basil Blackwell, 1959), p. 195.

For an up-to-date and comprehensive summary of the controversy, see M. H. Goshen-Gottstein, "The Language of Targum Onqelos and the Model of Literary Diglossia in Aramaic," *JNES* 7 (1978), 169-179.

[7]For a convenient collection of texts and bibliography, see J. A. Fitzmyer and D. Harrington, *A Manual of Palestinian Aramaic Texts* (Rome: Biblical Institute Press, 1978), and K. Beyer, *Die aramäischen Texte vom Toten Meer* (Göttingen: Vandenhoeck & Ruprecht, 1984).

[8]See Kutscher, "The Language of the Hebrew and Aramaic Letters of Bar Koseba and his Contemporaries. Part I: The Aramaic Letters," *Lesh* 25 (1961), 117-133 (in Hebrew).

[9]This period stretches from ca. 200 B.C.E. to 200 C.E. The term Middle Aramaic was first proposed by Fitzmyer in *The Genesis Apocryphon of Qumran Cave I: A Commentary* (Rome: Biblical Institute Press, 1966), pp. 19-20, n.60. He elaborated on it in "The Phases of the Aramaic Language," *A Wandering Aramean: Collected Aramaic Essays* (Missoula: Scholars Press, 1979), pp. 61-62. Kutscher originally proposed a different division of Aramaic in "Language of the Genesis Apocryphon," pp. 1-11, but later accepted Fitzmyer's classification in "Aramaic," in *Current Trends in Linguistics*: Vol. 6, *Linguistics in South West Asia and North Africa*, ed. T. A. Sebeok (The Hague: Mouton, 1970), pp. 347-348.

[10]J. C. Greenfield, "Standard Literary Aramaic" in *Actes du premier congrès international de linguistique sémitique et chamito-sémitique*, Paris, 1974, eds. A. Caquot

and D. Cohen (The Hague: Mouton, 1974), p. 287, and Goshen-Gottstein, "Literary Diglossia," p. 178. Mention should also be made of the language of Targum Jonathan to the Former Prophets. A. Tal has demonstrated that it represents the same tradition as Targum Onqelos. See Tal, *The Language of the Targum of the Former Prophets and its Position within the Aramaic Dialects* (Tel Aviv: Tel Aviv University, 1975; in Hebrew).

[11]The earliest mention of such a Targum occurs in a *responsum* of Hai Gaon (d. 1038 C.E.) where he refers to תרגום ארץ ישראל, which he has heard of, but with which he is not familiar. In the Rabbinic Bibles one finds the term תרגום ירושלמי. For a discussion of the history of these terms, see Dalman, *Grammatik*, pp. 27-29; G. Kuiper, *The Pseudo-Jonathan Targum and its Relationship to Targum Onkelos* (Rome: Institutum Patristicum Augustinianum, 1972), pp. 7-34; S. Lund and J. Foster, *Variant Versions of Targumic Traditions within Codex Neofiti I* (Society of Biblical Literature Aramaic Studies, No. 2; Missoula: Scholars Press, 1977), pp. 1-13.

[12]Dalman, *Grammatik*, pp. 27-33. S. A. Kaufman has recently suggested the term "Late Standard Literary Aramaic."

[13]The terms Targum Yerushalmi I and Targum Yerushalmi II were first introduced by L. Zunz, *Die gottesdienstlichen Vorträge der Juden*, 2nd ed. (Frankfurt a. Main: Kaufmann, 1892), p. 75. Dalman adopted the terminology and popularized it. The *editio princeps* of this Targum appeared in 1591 in Venice with the title תרגום הקדוש יונתן בן עוזיאל. In 1903, M. Ginsburger edited the Targum based on the London manuscript, in *Pseudo-Jonathan: Thargum Jonathan ben Usiël zum Pentateuch* (Berlin: Calvary, 1903). His edition, however, contains many incorrect readings. The Targum was re-edited by D. Rieder, *Pseudo-Jonathan: Targum Jonathan ben Uziel on the Pentateuch Copied from the London MS* (Jerusalem: Salomon, 1974), and most recently by E. G. Clarke, *Targum Pseudo-Jonathan of the Pentateuch: Text and Concordance* (Ktav: Hoboken, New Jersey, 1984).

[14]15 verses are missing from Targum Pseudo-Jonathan.

[15]For example, Dalman, *Grammatik*, pp. 32-33; Kahle, *Masoreten des Westens*, II, p. 12*, and *Cairo Geniza*, p. 202.

[16]Ginsburger, *Pseudo-Jonathan*, p. 21; A. Díez Macho, "The Recently Discovered Palestinian Targum: Its Antiquity and Relationship with the Other Targums," *SVT*, 7 (1959), 222-245.

Kuiper (*Pseudo-Jonathan Targum*, p. 103), argues "that PJ is essentially a strand of the Pal. tg. tradition...and that the minor contacts with O in this tradition, apart from those due to the transmission of the mss., are examples of the dependence of O on this Pal. tradition."

[17]In Gn 21:21 Muhammad's wife A'isha and his daughter Fatima are mentioned by name. Other indications of a late date are the allusions to Byzantium (or Christian Europe) and Islam in Gn 49:26 and Dt. 33:2. For a discussion of the date of compilation and redaction, see B. Grossfeld, "Bible: Translations," *EJ* (Jerusalem: Keter, 1971), 4, cols. 845-846; Dalman, *Grammatik*, pp. 30-31.

[18]The *editio princeps* of the Fragment Targum appeared in the first Rabbinic Bible (Venice, 1517-1518) and was based on MS Nürnberg. In 1889, M. Ginsburger published the text of MS Paris Heb 110 along with variants from MS Vatican Ebr 440 and MS Leipzig to the *editio princeps* in *Das Fragmententhargum* (Berlin: Calvary, 1899). M. C. Doubles identified many errors in Ginsburger's list of variants in an

8

unpublished dissertation, "The Fragment Targum: A Critical Re-examination of the Edition Princeps, *Das Fragmententhargum* by Moses Ginsburger, in the Light of Recent Discoveries," (Ph.D. thesis, University of St. Andrews, 1962). This thesis is cited and discussed in the most recent edition of the Targum by M. L. Klein, *The Fragment-Targums of the Pentateuch Accordiing to their Extant Sources*, 2 vols. (Analecta Biblica 76; Rome: Biblical Institute Press, 1980) which is based on a re-reading of all the extant manuscripts. Introductory essays on the history and nature of the Targum are included.

In addition to the terms Fragment Targum and Targum Yerushalmi II, one also finds Fragment Targums and Fragmentary Targum.

Dalman's Targum Yerushalmi III *(Grammatik*, p. 29) consists of small fragments of Targum that appeared in printed editions of the Bible and in some mediaeval manuscripts with the notation תוספתא, נוסחא אחרינא, or תרגום ירושלמי. These were included in Ginsburger's *Das Fragmententhargum*, p. 71-74.

[19]See Zunz, *Die gottesdientslichen Vorträge*, p. 74.

[20]See J. Bassfreund, "Das Fragmenten-Targum zum Pentateuch, sein Ursprung und Charakter und sein verhältnis zu den anderen pentateuchischen Targumim," *MGWJ*, 40 (1896), 97.

[21]W. Bacher, "Targum," *The Jewish Encyclopedia*, 12 (New York: Funk and Wagnalls, 1906), p. 60.

[22]Kahle, *Masoreten des Westens*, II, p. 9*, and *Cairo Geniza*, p. 202. For the most recent discussion of the question, see Klein, *Fragment-Targums*, I, pp. 12-19.

[23]See R. Le Déaut, *Introduction à la littérature targumique*, première partie (Rome: Institut Biblique Pontifical, 1966), p. 106; Lund and Foster, *Variant Versions*, p. 3; J. Lund, "A Descriptive Syntax of the Non-Translational Passages According to Codex Neofiti 1," (M.A. thesis, Hebrew University of Jerusalem, 1981), p. 2 (in Hebrew).

[24]Foster drew up a chart of contrasting forms (using the list prepared by Dalman in his *Grammatik*, pp. 44-51) that included the forms in Targum Pseudo-Jonathan and the Fragment Targum. There is, however, no systematic discussion of the different forms. Moreover, her comparisons are based on editions of the two Targumim which have been shown to contain many misreadings. See J. Foster, "The Language and Text of Codex Neofiti 1 in the Light of other Palestinian Aramaic Sources" (Ph.D. thesis, Boston University, 1969). The most recent investigation of Targum Pseudo-Jonathan is that of E. M. Cook, "Rewriting the Bible: The Text and Language of the Pseudo-Jonathan Targum" (Ph.D. thesis, University of California at Los Angeles, 1986).

[25]For a description of the manuscripts, see Klein, *Fragment-Targums*, I, pp. 26-37. For an index of verses preserved in the Targum, see I, pp. 242-249.

[26]Klein, "The Extant Sources of the Fragmentary Targum to the Pentateuch," *HUCA*, 46 (1975), 115-137. An additional manuscript of the Fragment Targum has only recently been published. See MS DD in Klein, *Genizah Manuscripts of Palestinian Targum to the Pentateuch*, 2 vols. (Cincinnati: Hebrew Union College Press, 1986). It is the oldest known manuscript of the Fragment Targum; M. Beit-Arié *(apud* Klein, vol. I, p. XXXVII) dates it to the period from the 9th or 10th century to the mid-11th century.

[27]Foster, "Language," pp. iii-iv; Kahle, *Masoreten des Westens*, II, p. 10*. A. Marmorstein pointed out textual affinities with the Fragment Targum in "Einige

vorläufige Bemerkungen zu den neuentdeckten Fragmente des jerusalemischen (palästinensischen) Targums," *ZAW*, 49 (1931), 231-242.

[28]Kahle, *Masoreten des Westens*, II, p. 1-62. The language of MS G differs considerably from that of MSS A-F and does not reflect the same dialect.

[29]MS D Gn 43:20—44:15 and MS E Gn 43:23—44:5; MS D Gn 38:16-26 and MS E Gn 38:16—39:10. The number of parallel passages has increased with the identification of new manuscripts. For a list of parallel passages, see §2f.

[30]This is not, however, the opinion of Foster ("Language," p. iv) and of G. Cowling, "The Palestinian Targum: Textual and Linguistic Investigations in Codex Neofiti 1 and Allied Manuscripts" (Ph.D. thesis, University of Aberdeen, 1968), p. 8. Cowling's thesis is discussed in detail by Foster.

[31]MS Vatican of the Fragment Targum is fully vocalized. The vocalization has not, however, been studied because it is "unfortunately...inaccurate, internally inconsistent and probably not original to the consonantal text" (Klein, *Fragment-Targums*, I, pp. 29-30).

The pronunciation of a related dialect can be gleaned, on occasion, from the sporadic vocalization in Palestinian Talmud fragments from the Cairo Genizah, edited by L. Ginzberg in *Yerushalmi Fragments from the Genizah* (New York: Jewish Theological Seminary, 1909), and Ginzberg, *Genizah Studies in Memory of Dr. Solomon Schechter*, I (New York: Jewish Theological Seminary, 1928). These Aramaic portions have been re-edited in L. Svedlund, *Selected Passages in Galilean Aramaic* (Jerusalem: Academon, 1967).

Indirect evidence can be gathered from place names. See Kutscher, *Studies in Galilean Aramaic* (Ramat Gan: Bar Ilan University, 1976), translated by M. Sokoloff. This evidence must, however, be treated with extreme caution. The same is true of the transcribed Aramaic words in Josephus and in the New Testament. For examples of these transcriptions, see E. Kautzsch, *Grammatik des Biblisch-Aramäischen mit einer kritischen Erörterung der aramäischen Wörter im Neuen Testament* (Leipzig: Vogel, 1884), pp. 6-12.

[32]The term vowel sign is used in this study to refer to the graphic representation of the vowel. Vocalization refers to the actual phonetic system. Some of the manuscripts have Palestinian supralinear pointing.

[33]Kutscher claimed that these manuscripts "are the most reliable text. Except for ordinary scribal errors, they have no fault" (*Studies*, p. 3). In a later article, he expressed the opinion that the vocalization of these manuscripts occasionally betrays the influence of Biblical Aramaic and Targum Onqelos ("Articulation of the Vowels u,i in Transcriptions of Biblical Hebrew, in Galilean Aramaic, and in Mishnaic Hebrew," *Benjamin de Vries Memorial Volume*, ed. E. Melamad (Jerusalem: Tel Aviv University and Stichting Fronika Sanders Fonds, 1968) pp. 227-232 (in Hebrew).

Cowling ("Palestinian Targum," p. 81) considers MSS A and E to be the best texts and thinks that the other manuscripts have been influenced, in varying degrees, by Targum Onqelos. Foster also claims that MSS A and E are the purest texts ("Language," p. iv). She argues that the other manuscripts were not revised under the influence of Targum Onqelos, but are rather later versions which "can be understood as conscious and deliberate revisions which maintained the language in conformity with a still living and changing Palestinian Aramaic."

10

Mediaeval Jewish scribes also emended manuscripts of Mishnaic Hebrew to conform to the norms of Biblical Hebrew. See Kutscher, "Mishnaic Hebrew," *Henoch Yalon Jubilee Volume*, ed. S. Lieberman, et al. (Jerusalem: Kiryat Sefer, 1963), pp. 246-280 (in Hebrew).

[34]W. Baars, "A Targum on Exod. XV 7-21 from the Cairo Genizah," *VT*, 11 (1961), 340-342.

[35]A. Diez Macho, "Nuevos fragmentos del Targum Palestinense," *Sef*, 15 (1955), 31-39; "Deux nouveaux fragments du Targum palestinien à New York," in *Studi sull'Oriente e la Bibbia offerti a P. Giovani Rinaldi* (Genova: Studio e Vita, 1967), Part II, pp. 175-178. He has also included the Cairo Genizah fragments in his edition of *Biblia Polyglotta Matritensia, Series IV Targum Palestinense in Pentateuchum* (Madrid: Consejo Superior de Investigaciones Científicas), 2: Exodus (1980), 3: Leviticus (1980), 4: Numeri (1977), 5: Deuteronomium (1980). T. Martínez presents a re-reading of Kahle's fragments in this edition.

[36]Klein, "A Genizah Fragment of Palestinian Targum to Genesis 15:1-4," *HUCA*, 49 (1978), 73-87 (Klein points out that this fragment may instead belong to the Fragment Targum); "Nine Fragments of Palestinian Targum to the Pentateuch from the Cairo Genizah," *HUCA*, 50 (1979), 149-164; Klein publishes for the first time MSS Y, Z, AA, HH, and additional fragments of MSS A, B, and D in *Genizah Manuscripts*.

[37]Klein includes manuscripts of straight Targum, Targumic Tosephta, Targumic poetry, and Fragment Targum in his edition, See below §2a, n.1.

[38]Diez Macho, ed., *Neophyti 1, Targum Palestinense MS de la Biblioteca Vaticana*, 6 vols. (Madrid: Consejo Superior de Investigaciones Científicas), I: Génesis (1968), II: Éxodo (1970), III: Levítico (1971), IV: Números (1974), V: Deuteronomio (1978), VI: Apéndices (1979). For bibliography on the text and language of Targum Neophyti, see the Introduction to each volume.

[39]Despite the similarities between these texts, they demonstrate that there was no standard Palestinian Targum. Palestinian Targum traditions can now be said to include Targum Pseudo-Jonathan, the Fragment Targum, the Cairo Genizah manuscripts, the body of Targum Neophyti and the marginal and interlinear glosses of Neophyti. Mention should also be made of bits of Palestinian Targumim embedded in Rabbinic and mediaeval sources and recently published in Goshen-Gottstein, *Fragments of Lost Targumim*, I (Ramat-Gan: Bar-Ilan University, 1983; in Hebrew). The term Palestinian Targum is also used by some to include a proto-Targum Onqelos and the Peshiṭta. See Le Déaut, *Introduction*, pp. 121-123.

[40]Le Déaut, "Lévitique XXII 26—XXIII 44 dans le Targum Palestinien. De l'importance des gloses du Codex Neofiti 1," *VT*, 18 (1968), 458-471; E. G. Clarke, "The Neofiti 1 Marginal Glosses and the Fragmentary Targum Witnesses to Gen VI-IX," *VT*, 22 (1972), 257-265; Lund and Foster, *Variant Versions*, passim; Diez Macho, "Valoración de las Glosas de Neofiti 2," Introduction to *Neophyti*, II: Éxodo, pp. 23-24.

For a discussion of the relation of the glosses to the body of Neophyti, see Goshen-Gottstein, "The 'Third Targum' on Esther and Ms. Neofiti 1," *Bibl*, 56 (1975), 301-329.

[41]See A. Tal, "Ms. Neophyti 1: the Palestinian Targum to the Pentateuch, Observations on the Artistry of a Scribe," *IOS*, 4 (1974), 31-43.

11

[42]For a summary and bibliography of the controversy, see Lund and Foster, *Variant Versions*, pp. 10-11.

[43]Kahle, *Masoreten des Westens, II*, pp. 2*-3*.

[44]Kahle, *Cairo Geniza*, p. 208.

[45]Kutscher, *Studies*, p. 4. See also Kutscher, "Aramaic," *EJ*, 3, col. 270. ·

[46]Kutscher, "Das zur Zeit Jesu gesprochene Aramäisch," *ZNW*, 51 (1960), 46-54. Kutscher remarks in "Language of the Genesis Apocryphon" (p. 3, n.10): "The fragments edited by Kahle are dated by him to 700-900 C.E....They certainly reflect the language spoken a few hundred years earlier. But the exact date cannot be established."

[47]F. Rosenthal, *Die aramäistische Forschung seit Th. Nöldeke's Veröffentlichungen* (Leiden: E. J. Brill, 1939), pp. 106-132, and, more recently, Rosenthal, ed., *An Aramaic Handbook* I/1-2, II/1-2 (Wiesbaden: Harrassowitz, 1967).

[48]Fitzmyer, "Phases of the Aramaic Language," p. 78, n.38.

[49]Tal, "Layers in the Jewish Aramaic of Palestine: The Appended Nun as a Criterion," *Lesh*, 43 (1979), 165-184 (in Hebrew).

[50]See n.56 below.

[51]H. L. Ginsberg, "Notes on a Palestinian Targum," *Tarbiz*, 5 (1934), 381-383 (in Hebrew).

[52]See nn.31 and 46 above. See also Kutscher's *Studies*; "Jewish Palestinian Aramaic," F. Rosenthal, ed., *An Aramaic Handbook*, Vol. II/1-2, particularly the Glossary in Vol. II/2; "Das zur Zeit Jesu gesprochene Aramäisch," and "Language of the Genesis Apocryphon."

[53]Y. Peri, "The Morphology of Galilean Aramaic according to the Palestinian Targum Fragments" (M.A. thesis, Tel Aviv University, 1977; in Hebrew). Peri's study is presented as one based on a re-reading of the microfilms of these fragments. The readings, however, concur with those of Kahle, many of whose readings differ from those presented in this study. Peri's readings do, however, differ from those of Díez Macho in "Deux nouveaux fragments."

[54]Tal, "Layers in the Jewish Aramaic of Palestine"; "Studies in Palestinian Aramaic: Demonstrative Pronouns," *Lesh*, 44 (1980), 43-65 (in Hebrew); "The Forms of the Infinitive in Jewish Aramaic" in *Hebrew Language Studies Presented to Professor Ze'ev Ben-Ḥayyim*, ed. M. Bar-Asher et al. (Jerusalem: Magnes Press, 1983), pp. 201-218 (in Hebrew); *Language of the Targum of the Former Prophets*.

[55]Ben-Ḥayyim, *The Literary and Oral Tradition of Hebrew and Aramaic amongst the Samaritans*, 5 vols., especially II and III.2 (Jerusalem: The Academy of the Hebrew Language, 1957-1977, in Hebrew); *Studies in the Traditions of the Hebrew Language* (Madrid-Barcelona: Consejo Superior de Investigaciones Científicas, 1954).

[56]Beyer, *Die aramäischen Texte*, pp. 37-40; *The Aramaic Language: Its Distribution and Subdivisions* (Göttingen: Vandenhoeck & Ruprecht, 1986), pp. 23-25; "The Pronunciation of Galilean Aramaic according to Geniza Fragments with Palestinian and Tiberian Pointing," *Proceedings of the Ninth World Congress of Jewish Studies* (Jerusalem, 1985), Division D, Vol. 1, 17-22.

[57]T. Muraoka, "A Study on the Aramaic of the Palestinian Targum Fragments Published by P. Kahle," *Jubilee Volume for Professor M. Sekine* (Tokyo, 1972), pp. 203-222 (in Japanese) and the English translation of the article, "A Study in Palestinian Aramaic," *Sef*, 45 (1985), 3-21; "Concerning שני לוחות," *Lesh*, 40 (1976),

12

290; and "On the Morphosyntax of the Infinitive in Targumic Aramaic," in *Arameans, Aramaic and the Aramaic Literary Tradition*, ed. M. Sokoloff (Ramat-Gan: Bar Ilan University Press, 1983),pp. 75-79.

[58]See n.27 above.

[59]J. Teicher, "A Sixth Century Fragment of the Palestinian Targum?" *VT*, 1 (1951), 125-129.

[60]R. Bloch, "Note sur l'utilisation des fragments de la Geniza du Caïre pour l'étude du Targum Palestinien," *REJ*, 14 (1955), 5-35.

[61]G. Schelbert, "Exodus XXII 4 im palästinischen Targum," *VT*, 8 (1958), 253-263. Kahle announced that Schelbert was re-editing the Cairo Genizah manuscripts (*Cairo Geniza*, p. 201). No new addition, however, appeared.

[62]Kahle, *Masoreten des Westens*, II, p. 11\*, n.3.

[63]B. Levy, "The Language of Neofiti 1: A Descriptive and Comparative Grammar of the Palestinian Targum" (Ph.D. thesis, New York University, 1974). The most recent grammar of Targum Neophyti, by D. Golomb, *A Grammar of Targum Neofiti* (Harvard Semitic Monographs 34; Chico: Scholars Press, 1985), does not make use of the Cairo Genizah material.

[64]Lund, "Descriptive Syntax"; "The Syntax of the Numeral 'One' as a Noun Modifier in Jewish Palestinian Aramaic of the Amoraic Period," *JAOS* 106 (1986), 413-423; "On the Interpretation of the Palestinian Targumic Reading *WQHT* in GEN 32:25," *JBL* 105 (1986), 99-103; "The First Person Singular Past Tense of the Verb מהה in Jewish Palestinian Aramaic," *Maarav* 4 (1987), 191-199; "The Problem of Expressing 'Three Hundred' and the Like in the Language of Codex Neofiti 1," *Sef* 47 (1987), 149-157.

[65]See n.38 above.

[66]See n.30 above. See also "Notes, Mainly Orthographical, on the Galilaean Targum and 1Q Genesis Apocryphon," *AJBA*, 2 (1972), 35-49.

[67]G. Lasry, "Gramatica del arameo dialectal de Palestina en tiempo de Jesus según el ms. Neofiti I (Deuteronomio)" (Ph.D. thesis, University of Barcelona, 1964, mentioned in Díez Macho, *Neophyti*, Genesis, p. 32 of Introduction). See also "Some Remarks on the Jewish Dialectal Aramaic of Palestine during the 1st Centuries of the Christian Era," *Aug*, 8 (1965), 468-476.

[68]See n.24 above.

[69]See n.11 above.

[70]As noted by Kutscher. See n.45 above.

[71]The only fragments not examined were those housed in Leningrad and in Cincinnati. Because of the difficulties involved in reading vowel signs from a photograph rather than from the original manuscript (e.g., in photographs one often cannot tell whether a dot is an intentional vowel sign, an unintential ink spot, a speck of dust, a defect in the parchment, or a mark from the reverse of the manuscript), and because the vowel signs in the photographs of the Leningrad and Cincinnati fragments published in Klein's *Genizah Manuscripts* are not perfectly clear, Kahle's reading of the Leningrad material and Klein's reading of the Cincinnati manuscript have been followed, except in those cases where the published photographs clearly show a different reading.

§2 II  DESCRIPTION AND CLASSIFICATION OF MANUSCRIPTS

§2a  The Cairo Genizah manuscripts of Palestinian Targum[1] may be divided into three general groups:

1. Manuscripts with alternating verses of Masoretic text and Targum (and occasional *masorah marginalis*)

2. Manuscripts with *lemmata* (of Masoretic text) followed by verses of Targum.

3. Manuscripts with festival-liturgical readings consisting of *lemmata*[2] (of Masoretic text) followed by verses of Targum and introduced by a rubric.[3]

Manuscripts of the first category, in which complete verses of Masoretic text and Targum alternate, are almost fully pointed[4] with Tiberian vowel signs and Tiberian accents. Manuscripts of the second and third categories are either sporadically pointed with Tiberian and/or Palestinian vowel signs,[5] or not pointed at all. One of these manuscripts is almost completely pointed with Palestinian supralinear vowel signs. Some of the manuscripts possess Tiberian accents; others have Palestinian accents. Not all vowel and accent signs are, however, contemporaneous with the consonantal text,[6] and occasionally there is a difference between the *qere* and the *kethibh*.[7]

§2b  Most of the manuscripts are written on parchment in an Oriental square script[8] and may be dated roughly to between the 9th and 11th centuries; some fragments appear to belong to a period between the 11th and 14th centuries. Because the paleographic typology of the Cairo Genizah material is not yet fully worked out, precise dating of these manuscripts is impossible.[9] One manuscript is part of a parchment scroll. A few of the fragments are written on paper.[10]

§2c  To avoid confusion, the manuscripts are designated by the same letters, with some modification, as in Kahle's *Masoreten des Westens, II* (MSS A-F) and Klein's *Genizah Manuscripts* (which is based on Kahle's classification).[11] The information concerning each manuscript is presented in the following order:[12]

14

1. Location of fragments and classmarks.
2. Place of publication or description.
3. Biblical verses covered.
4. Type of text: Masoretic text and Targum, *lemmata* and Targum, or festival-liturgical readings.
5. Form and material: scroll or leaves of codex; parchment or paper.
6. Script.
7. Vowel and accent signs: Tiberian or Palestinian.
8. Distinctive orthographic features.

§2d The following notation is used in referring to the libraries and collections in which the fragments are stored:

Ant     Antonin Collection of the M.E. Saltykov-Schedrin State Public Library, Leningrad.
Bod     Bodleian Library, Oxford.
CUL T-S Cambridge University Library, Taylor-Schechter Collection.
CUL Or  Cambridge University Library, Oriental Collection.
HUC     Hebrew Union College—Jewish Institute of Religion, Cincinnati.
JTS     Jewish Theological Seminary of America, New York.
JTS ENA Jewish Theological Seminary of America, Elkan Nathan Adler Collection.

§2e The following manuscripts are treated in this study:
MS A  1. CUL T-S 20.155; CUL T-S AS 63.24,51,72,85,95,96,117,129,153; CUL T-S AS 69.241; CUL T-S NS 286.1.
2. CUL T-S 20.155 published by Kahle;[13] fragments published by Klein;[14] described by Revell[15] and Birnbaum.[16]
3. Ex 4:7-11; Ex 20:24—23:3, 8-14.
4. *Lemmata* and Targum.
5. Parchment scroll and fragments which belong to it.
6. Oriental square script.
7. Palestinian vowel signs and Tiberian accents; occasional Tiberian vowel signs.
8. *He* is predominant *mater lectionis* for final /a/; consonantal *yodh* written double.
MS B  1. Ant 739; CUL T-S B6.6; JTS 501 (ENA 2107) f.1.
2. Ant 739 published by Kahle;[17] CUL T-S B6.6[18] and JTS 501[19] published by Diez Macho. Klein assigns CUL T-S B6.6 to MS D.
3. Gn 2:17—3:6; Gn 4:4-16; Ex 39:23-37.
4. Masoretic text and Targum.
5. 6 leaves of parchment.
6. Oriental square script.
7. Tiberian vowel signs and Tiberian accents.

8. *Aleph* and *he* are *matres lectionis* for final /a/; Tetragrammaton written אדני; consistent pointing of word וַאֲמַר.

MS Bd  Although Kahle assigned CUL T-S B8.11 (Gn 7:17—8:8, 2 leaves of parchment) to MS D, it clearly belongs to MS B, based on paleography and orthography. It will be referred to as Bd. Klein assigns these leaves to MS B.[20]

MS C  1. Ant 542, ff.1,2; Bod Heb b4, ff.18,19.
2. Published by Kahle.[21]
3. Gn 31:38-54; Gn 32:13-29; Gn 34:9-25.
4. Masoretic text and Targum.
5. 4 leaves of parchment.
6. Oriental square script.
7. Tiberian vowel signs and Tiberian accents; one Palestinian vowel sign?[22]
8. *Aleph* is predominant *mater lectionis* for final /a/; frequent pointing of words וַאֲמַר, אֲרוּם; Tetragrammaton written יי.

MS Cd  A strong similarity in paleography and orthography between MS C and some fragments of Kahle's MS D suggests that the following fragments belong to MS C. Note that Kahle's MS C and MS D do not overlap. These fragments will be referred to as Cd. Klein designates them as MS D.
1. CUL T-S B8.3; CUL T-S B8.5; CUL T-S B8.10; CUL T-S B 8.12; CUL T-S Misc. 27.1.4; CUL T-S NS 76.1r.
2. Published by Kahle;[23] CUL T-S Misc. 27.1.4 published by Klein;[24] CUL T-S Ns 76.1r published by Díez Macho.[25]
3. Gn 37:19-34; Gn 38:16-26; Gn 41:32-41; Gn 43:7—44:23; Gn 46:26—47:6; Gn 47:29—48:21; Ex 5:20—6:10; Ex 7:10-22; Ex 9:21-33.
4. As in MS C.
5. 24 leaves of parchment.
6. As in MS C.
7. As in MS C.
8. As in MS C.

MS D  The two fragments listed here are all that remain of Kahle's original MS D. The paleography and orthography of these are clearly different from those of MS Bd and MS Cd.
1. CUL T-S B8.1; CUL T-S B8.8; CUL T-S NS 161.262.
2. Published by Kahle.[26]
3. Dt 5:19-26; Dt 26:18-27:11; Dt 28:15-18, 21-25, 27-29.
4. Masoretic text and Targum.
5. 4 leaves of parchment.
6. Oriental square script.
7. Tiberian vowel signs and Tiberian accents.

8. *He* is *mater lectionis* for final /a/; Tetragrammaton written אדני and יי; infrequency of *ḥateph pathaḥ*; absence of other *ḥateph* vowels.

MS E   1. Ant 111; Ant 120; Bod Heb d 26, ff.15,16; Bod Heb d49 ff.47,48; Bod Heb e43, ff.66,67; CUL T-S B8.4; JTS ENA 2755, ff.1,2; JTS ENA 2578, ff.20,21.

2. Ant, Bod, and CUL fragments published by Kahle;[27] JTS fragments published by Diez Macho;[28] Bod Heb d49 described by Revell.[29]

3. Gn 6:18—7:15; Gn 9:5-23; Gn 28:17—31:32; Gn 37:15-33; Gn 38:16—39:10; Gn 40:4-18; Gn 41:6-26; 43-57; Gn 42:34—43:10.

4. *Lemmata* and Targum.

5. 26 leaves of parchment.

6. Oriental square script.

7. Ant 111, f.1 and Ant 120, ff.1, 2a; Tiberian accents and occasional Tiberian vowel signs; in Ant 120, f.2a also occasional Palestinian vowel signs; Ant 111, f.2a and Ant 120, f.2b: no vowel signs, no accents; Ant 111 f.2b: no vowels, occasional Palestinian accents.

Bod Heb d26: Tiberian accents, occasional Tiberian vowel signs, occasional Palestinian vowel signs; vowel signs in different color ink from that of consonantal text.

Bod Heb d49: Palestinian accents in different color ink from that of consonantal text.

Bod Heb e43: Tiberian accents, occasional Tiberian vowel signs, occasional Palestinian vowel signs in different color ink from that of consonantal text.

CUL T-S B8.4, ff.1a, 1b: Tiberian accents, occasional Tiberian vowel signs; ff.2a, 2b: no vowel signs or accents.

JTS ENA 2755 and JTS ENA 2578: Tiberian accents, occasional Tiberian vowel signs, occasional Palestinian vowel signs.

8. *He* is *mater lectionis* for final /a/.

MS F   1. Bod Heb 43, ff.57-65.

2. Published by Kahle.[30]

3. Ex 19:1—20:13; Lv 22:26—23:44; Nu 28:16-31; Dt 34:5-12.

4. Festival-liturgical readings.[31]

5. 16 leaves of parchment.

6. Oriental square script; Dt 34:5-12 on f.65a was written by a different hand. (Klein designates it F$_2$.)

7. Occasional Tiberian vowel signs in different color ink from that of consonantal text.

8. *He* and *aleph* are *matres lectionis* for final /a/.

MS H   1. HUC Genizah 1134r.

2. Published by Klein.[32]

3. Gn 15:1-4.

4. *Lemmata* and Targum.
5. Single leaf of paper.
6. Oriental semi-square script (11th-14th centuries).
7. Occasional Tiberian pointing,[33] infrequent Palestinian pointing.
8. *He* is predominant *mater lectionis* for final /a/; Tetragrammaton written אדני.

MS W  1. Bod Heb f102, f.5.
2. Published by Baars.[34]
3. Ex 15:7-21.
4. *Lemmata* and Targum.
5. Single leaf of parchment.
6. Oriental square script.
7. Tiberian vowel signs on one word.
8. *Aleph* is predominant *mater lectionis* for final /a/.

MS Y  1. CUL T-S AS 70.206, ff.1, 2.
2. Published by Klein.[35]
3. Gn 21:4-7; Ex 19:5-10; Nu 28:23-30.
4. Festival-liturgical readings.
5. 2 leaves of paper.
6. Oriental square script.
7. No vowel signs or accents.
8. *He* is *mater lectionis* for final /a/.

MS Z  1. CUL T-S AS 70.176, 209-213; CUL T-S AS 71:1-5, 214-217, 281.
2. Published by Klein.[36]
3. Gn 44:16-19; Gn 47:26-49:10.
4. *Lemmata* and Targum.
5. Fragments of paper leaves.
6. Oriental semi-square script (11th-14th centuries).
7. Occasional Tiberian vowel signs.
8. *He* and *aleph* are *mater lectionis* for final /a/; Tetragrammaton written אדני and יי.

MS AA 1. CUL Or 1080.B18.1, ff.1-6; CUL T-S B13.4.
2. Published by Klein.[37]
3. Ex 12:1-42; Ex 17:8-16; Nu 19:1—21:13; Dt 26:2, 8-12, 15-27:8. Note that MS AA contains two accounts of Ex 12 which differ from one another slightly in orthography and text. Ex 12:1-42 in CUL Or 1080 B18.1 will be referred to as AA₁, and Ex 12:21-34 in CUL T-S B13.4 will be referred to as AA₂.[38]
4. Festival-liturgical readings.
5. 14 leaves of parchment.
6. Oriental square script.
7. Occasional Tiberian vowel signs in different color ink from that of consonantal text.

8. *He* is predominant *mater lectionis* for final /a/.

MS HH 1. CUL T-S H11.51, f.1.

    2. Published by Klein.[39]

    3. Ex 12:1-3.

    4. Festival-liturgical reading.

    5. Single leaf of parchment.

    6. Oriental square script.

    7. Tiberian vowel signs.

    8. *He* is *mater lectionis* for final /a/.

§2f  The following manuscripts contain passages of Targum which overlap:

    MS Cd  Gn 37:19-34; Gn 38:16-26; Gn 42:34—43:10; Gn 43:20—44:15.

    MS E   Gn 37:15-33; Gn 38:16—39:10; Gn 43:7-18; Gn 43:23—44:5.

    MS Cd  Gn 44:16-23.

    MS Z   Gn 44:18-19

    MS Cd  Gn 37:29-48:10.

    MS Z   Gn 47:28-49:17.

    MS AA₁ Ex 12:21-34.

    MS AA₂ Ex 12:1-42.

    MS HH Ex 12:1-3

    MS F   Ex 19:1-20:23.

    MS Y   Ex 19:5-10.

    MS F   Nu 28:16-31.

    MS Y   Nu 28:22-31.

    MS D   Dt 26:18-27:11.

    MS AA  Dt 26:15-27:8.

§2g  The following are the largest Midrashic interpolations:

    MS B   Gn 4:8.

    MS C   Gn 35:9.

    MS Cd  Gn 37:33.

    MS Cd  Gn 38:25-26, paralleled in MS E Gn 38:25-26.

    MS Cd  Gn 44:18.

    MS E   Gn 40:12.

    MS E   Gn 42:36.

    MS F   Lv 22:27.

    MS F   Ex 20:2.

    MS H   Gn 15:1.

    MS Z   Gn 44:18.

## Footnotes — Chapter II

[1]For methodological reasons, only manuscripts containing Targum, *stricto sensu* (including passages of straight Targum found in festival-liturgical selections) are analyzed in this study. Manuscripts of poetry, Targumic Tosephta (expansive Targum) and Fragment Targum have been excluded: poetry, because of the problems of poetic license and in the case of acrostics, the special constraints imposed by the form; Targumic Tosephta, because their aim was not to translate, but rather to serve as a framework for Midrashic material; and the Fragment Targum, because it does not constitute a continuous, complete Targum. It should be noted, however, that even manuscripts of straight Targum often have lengthy Midrashic interpolations.

JTS 605 (ENA 2587), ff. 6, 7, 26b, 30 (= MS J in Klein, *Genizah Manuscripts)* is not included since it displays characteristics of both festival-liturgical collections and the Fragment Targum (see Klein, *Genizah Manuscripts,* I, p. XXIV; Klein, *Fragment-Targums,* I, pp. 19-23).

Palestinian Targum fragments from the Cairo Genizah whose language is clearly influenced by Targum Onqelos are also excluded, e.g., JTS 608 (ENA 656), ff. 1,2 containing Ex 15:3-8, 19:7-14 (published in Diéz Macho, *Biblia Polyglotta Matritensia* = MS U in Klein, *Genizah Manuscripts)*—יומא דין (for Palestinian יומא הדין), כַּפָן (for Palestinian כַּפִּין), גברוהי (for Palestinian גברוי), and תליתאה (for Palestinian תליתייה); Bibliothèque Nationale et Universitaire, Strasbourg MS 4017, ff. 1,2 containing Ex 19:25-20:13 (= MS S in Klein, *Genizah Manuscripts)*—פום (for Palestinian פּיס/פּים), אפיקית (for Palestinian אפקת ['apqet]), [שבי]עאה (for Palestinian שביעייה); MS Mosseri (Paris) VI,59 containing Ex 19:25-20:2 (= MS BB in Klein, *Genizah Manuscripts)*—קדמאה (for Palestinian קדמייה).

Finally, it should be added that CUL T-S NS 10.17,18 containing Ex 40:9-27, which is published for the first time by Klein and assigned to MS D, does not belong to a Palestinian Targum, but rather to Targum Onqelos. This is evident from both the text and its language, in addition to the non-Palestinian (and correct!) use of the Tiberian vowel signs, cf. יהי (for Palestinian יהוי), עברוהי,מנוהי,בנוהי (for Palestinian בנוי, עברוי, מנוי), קדמאה (for Palestinian קדמייה), תנייתא (for Palestinian תנייתה).

[2]On occasion the *lemma* is omitted. The same is true of the manuscripts of Group 2. The *lemma* usually consists of the first word of the Masoretic text. In MS HH there are no *lemmata.*

[3]The following rubrics are attested: MS F - מוסף פסח, מוסף עצר, לשבועות; MS AA - תרגום אלפסח, תרגום אלפור, תרגום החדש; MS Y - תרגום בחדש השלישי.

[4]Parts of words, whole words, and entire verses are left unpointed. Because of the poor condition of some of the fragments, it is often impossible to decide when there was originally pointing. Frequently, proper names and common words are left unpointed.

In the Babylonian manuscripts of Targum Onqelos from the Cairo Genizah, which are, in general, only partially pointed, one can discern three degrees of pointing. In the most fully pointed manuscripts, prepositions are left unpointed. In less fully pointed manuscripts, common words are left unpointed. In the third type of pointed manuscripts, many words are unpointed, and those which are pointed usually have only one vowel sign. See A. Dodi, "The Grammar of Targum Onqelos according to Geniza Fragments" (Ph.D. thesis, Bar-Ilan University, 1981), p. 81 (in Hebrew).

In a study of the Palestinian pointing of liturgical poems known as *qedushtot*, Y. Yahalom shows that the most commonly omitted vowel signs are ⨪ and ⨪, which represent the phoneme /a/. This omission often occurs in the middle of a word. Yahalom suggests that /a/ was often unmarked because, in the light of its frequency in the language, the scribes saw no need to mark it. See Y. Yahalom, "The Palestinian Pointing in the קדושתות הדרותה למשמרת and the Linguistic Phenomena Reflected in it," *Lesh*, 34 (1969-1970), 25-60 (in Hebrew).

In mediaeval Rabbinic manuscripts, foreign words, rare words, and uncommon proper names were sometimes left unpointed by a vocalizer whose language differed from that reflected in the consonantal text, and who, as a result, was unsure how to point such difficult words. For a discussion, see M. Bar-Asher, *The Traditions of Mishnaic Hebrew in the Communities of Italy According to Ms. Paris 328-329* (Jerusalem: Hebrew University Language Traditions Project, VI, 1980), pp. 9-10, 53-54 (in Hebrew).

[5]In a few of the manuscripts, some words are pointed with both Tiberian and Palestinian vowel signs, e.g., וְיִגְנֹֿזוֹ A Ex 22:6, "and they will steal."

[6]In some manuscripts, one can see a difference between the color of ink and thickness of pen used in writing the consonants and those used in pointing the vowels.

[7]Any difference between the *qere* and the *kethibh* in the fragments will be noted.

[8]Birnbaum uses the term Palestinian square script in his paleographic discussion of MS A in S. A. Birnbaum, *The Hebrew Scripts*, I (Leiden: E. J. Brill, 1954), pp. 164-167.

[9]Kahle's dating of the manuscripts remains conjectural *(Masoreten des Westens*, II, pp. 2*-3*): MS A (end of 7th—beginning of 8th centuries), MS E (second half of 8th century), MSS B,C,D (second half of 9th century), MS F (10th—11th centuries). For the most recent dating of all the fragments, see Beit-Arié *apud* Klein, *Genizah Manuscripts,* I, pp. XXXVII-XXXVIII.

[10]The use of paper is significant for dating. The earliest extant Hebrew manuscript written on paper comes from the Cairo Genizah and is dated to 1005 C.E. For a discussion, see Beit-Arie, *Hebrew Codicology* (Jerusalem: The Israel Academy of Sciences and Humanities, 1981), p. 20.

[11]Klein uses the latters H-RR to designate fragments discovered after the publication of Kahle's *Masoreten des Westens*, II, which do not belong to one of the MSS A-F. One should note that Kahle's MS G is a Targumic poem and MSS H-N are Hebrew manuscripts.

[12]This is a modified form of the format in E. J. Revell, *Biblical Texts with Palestinian Pointing and their Accents* (Society of Biblical Literature Masoretic Studies No. 4; Missoula: Scholars Press, 1977).

[13]Kahle, *Masoreten des Westens*, II, pp. 1-5. MS A is generally thought to be the oldest of the manuscripts because it was part of a parchment scroll and is almost fully pointed with Palestinian vowel signs. In addition, the notations יה and יו of the triennial Torah reading cycle have not been replaced by the later notations טו and וט.

[14]Klein, "Nine Fragments," pp. 149-163.

[15]Revell, *Biblical Texts*, p. 10, listed as P110T.

[16]Birnbaum, *Hebrew Scripts*, I, pp. 164-167, listed as 91A.

[17]Kahle, *Masoreten des Westens*, II, pp. 6-7.

[18]Diez Macho, *Biblia Polyglotta Matritensia*, II, pp. 303, 305. Diez Macho published Ex 39:23-29; Klein (*Genizah Manuscripts*, I, pp. 229-301) published for the first time vs. 30-37.

[19]Diez Macho, "Deux nouveaux fragments," p. 175-178.

[20]Kahle, *Masoreten des Westens*, II, pp. 15-16; Klein, *Genizah Manuscripts,* I, p. XV.

[21]Kahle, *Masoreten des Westens*, II, pp. 8-14.

[22]See §13a, n.163.

[23]Kahle, *Masoreten des Westens*, II, p. 16-26.

[24]Klein, *Genizah Manuscripts,*I, pp. 145-151.

[25]Diez Macho, "Un nuevo fragmento de Targum palestinense a Genesis," *Aug*, 9 (1969) 120-123.

[26]Kahle, *Masoreten des Westens*, II, pp. 26-28.

[27]Kahle, *Masoreten des Westens*, II, 29-48,

[28]Diez Macho, "Nuevos Fragmentos," pp. 31-39.

[29]Revell, *Biblical Texts*, pp. 15, 133-136, listed as P163T.

[30]Kahle, *Masoreten des Westens*, II, pp. 49-62.

[31]This manuscript has the heading:
יש בו תרגום מוספים שלכל המועדים ותרגום לחנוכה.
See Kahle, *Masoreten des Westens*, II, p. 49; Klein, *Genizah Manuscripts*, I, p. XXIII.

[32]Klein, "Genizah Fragment," pp. 73-87. Klein points out the possibility that this fragment may be a part of the Fragment Targum. He prefers to explain the omission of verse 3 *ex homioteleuton*, rather than as an intentional selection of verses.

[33]Klein is of the opinion that there are "traces of a sparse Palestinian vocalization, but most of the signs are barely visible" ("Genizah Fragment, " p. 74). Examination of the published photograph reveals some Palestinian signs, but others make little sense, e.g. מֻלכִּין for expected מַלכִּין "kings" (/malkin/).

[34]Baars, "Targum on Exodus XV 7-21," pp. 340-342.

[35]Klein, *Genizah Manuscripts*, I, pp. 32-33, 272, 327, 329.

[36]Klein, *Genizah Manuscripts*, I, pp. 138-141, 156-169.

[37]Klein, *Genizah Manuscripts*, I, pp. 208-219, 252-253, 320-325, 342-347.

[38]Although there are two slightly different accounts of Ex 12, there is little doubt that CUL Or 1080.B18.1 and CUL T-S B13.4 belong to the same manuscript. The passage in CUL Or 1080.B18.1 is preceded by the heading תרגום החחד"ש and is the reading for the Sabbath which occurs before the new moon of Nisan; the passage in CUL T-S B13.4 is preceded by the heading תרגום אלפסח. See Klein, *Genizah Manuscripts,*I, p. XXV.

[39]Klein, *Genizah Manuscripts*, I, pp. 208-209. This selection is the beginning of a festival reading for *Shabbat Ha-ḥodesh*, and is followed by a series of poems. See Klein, pp. XXV-XXVI.

## III. ORTHOGRAPHY AND PHONOLOGY

§3          A. *Graphic Signs Used in Fragments*

The following is a listing of the graphic signs used in the fragments. For a discussion and examples of each sign, see the footnotes for the relevant paragraphs.

§3a   *Vowel Signs*[1]

All of the Tiberian vowel signs are attested: ⌐, ⌐, ⌐, ⌐, ⌐, ⌐, ⌐, ⌐, ⌐, ⌐. The following Palestinian vowel signs are attested: ⌐, ⌐, ⌐, ⌐, ⌐, ⌐, ⌐.[2] ⌐ also serves as a vowel sign in the Palestinian pointed fragments in addition to its other functions.

§3b   *Signs Marking the Stops /bgdkpt/ and Their Spirantized Allophones*[3]

| | Tiberian | | Palestinian |
|---|---|---|---|
| stop | בּ | *(daghesh lene)* | בּ |
| spirant | בֿ | *(raphe)* | בֿ |

§3c   *Signs Marking Gemination*[4]

| Tiberian | | Palestinian |
|---|---|---|
| בּ | *(daghesh forte)* | בּ |

§3d   *Sign Marking Consonantal He*[5]

| Tiberian | | Palestinian |
|---|---|---|
| ה, הֶ | *(mappiq)* | זֶה? הֹ |

§3e   *Sign Marking Quiescence of Aleph*[6]

| Tiberian | | Palestinian |
|---|---|---|
| אֿ | *(raphe)* | — |

§3f   *Sign Marking Absence of Gemination on Waw and Yodh*[7]

| Tiberian | | Palestinian |
|---|---|---|
| וֿ, יֿ | *(raphe)* | — |

§3g   *Signs Marking the Accents* (טעמים)[8]

Both Tiberian and Palestinian accent signs appear in these texts. Accent signs which are identical with vowel and other signs and which may cause confusion are

| a. *Tiberian accent* | = | *Palestinian vowel sign* |
|---|---|---|
| seghol ⌐ | = | ⌐ (/o/) |
| zaqeph ⌐ | = | ⌐ (/i/) |

24

| b. *Palestinian accent* | = | *Palestinian vowel sign* |
|---|---|---|
| pashṭa ⸜ | = | ⸜ (/u/) |
| c. *Palestinian accent* | = | *Tiberian vowel sign* |
| ṭippeḥa ⹁ | | |
| atnaḥ ⹁ | = | ⹁ *(ḥireq)* |
| silluq ⹁ | | |
| tebir ⹁ | = | ⹁ *(ṣere)* |

d. *Pal. accent = Pal. vowel sign = deletion mark = Tib. raphe*

rebiʿa ⸝ = ⸝ (/a/)  =  ⸛  =  ⸛

**§3h  *Metheg***

The Tiberian sign *metheg* is attested, e.g., in דְּי־נְסַב B Gn 2:22, "which he took"; קְטִילָא C Gn 31:39, "a dead thing"; בִּידֵי C Gn 32:17, "in the hands of."

**§3i  *Maqqeph***

This sign is more frequent in these fragments than in the Masoretic text. In interpolated passages it sometimes strings together several words, e.g., עַל־ דְּנָסֵבִית־כֻּתָּנְתֵּיהּ־דְּיוֹסֵף־אָחִי Cd Gn 38:26, "because I took the shirt of Joseph, my brother."

**§3j  *Abbreviations***

a. The following supralinear marks of abbreviation are found in these fragments: ⸜, ⸰, ⸙, ⸛.

b. The Tetragrammaton is abbreviated in the following ways: יְ, יָי, יֹ, יוֹ, יֹ, יי, יוי, יֹי, יוֹי, יֻ, יֵ.[9]

c. מאמרה "His Word" is sometimes abbreviated ממ, ממ, and מֹ in MSS E and F.

d. Other abbreviations are also attested in MS F: ישׂ for ישראל, "Israel" (also in MS W); שכנ for שכנתא, "the Shekhina"; שותפ for שותפין, "partners"; אינ for אינון, "they" (m.pl.); בכנ for בכנשתא, "in the assembly."

**§3k  *Signs Marking Deletion of Letter***

a. The use of supralinear ⸛ marking the deletion of a letter is usually attested with two consecutive *waws* or *yodhs*, indicating that one of the two letters is superfluous,[10] e.g., הֲוֵויתוֹן A Ex 22:20, "you were" (m.pl.), and אַיְיתוֹן Cd Gn 46:32, "you brought" (m.pl.). It is also attested once on a single letter, נְחָתْ Cd Ex 9:33,[11] suggesting the G Perfect /nəḥat/, "it descended," as opposed to the consonantal text, which suggests either a G Perfect /naḥet/ or Participle /naḥet/.

b. There is one example of a dot above and below a letter marking deletion, תִּשְׁעֶבְדוּן F Lv 23:28, "you shall enslave" (m.pl.) for תעבדון "you shall make."

**§4**  B. *Consonantal Phonemes*

**§4a**  The consonantal phonemes are

labials: /b/, /p/, /m/, /w/;

dentals: /t/, /d/, /s/, /z/, /n/, /ṭ/, /ṣ/;

liquids: /l/, /r/;

prepalatal: /y/, /š/;

palatal: /k/, /g/;
velar: /q/;
gutturals: glottal /ʾ/, /h/; pharyngeal /ʿ/, /ḥ/

**§4b** The phonemes /bgdkpt/ appear to have had both a plosive and spirantized realization, as in Tiberian Biblical Aramaic and Syriac. These conditioned allophones were [b] and [w] or [v], [g] and [ɣ], [d] and [ð], [k] and [x], [p] and [f], and [t] and [θ].

**§4c** In the Tiberian pointed manuscripts, the plosive allophones are usually marked by *daghesh lene*, e.g., בְּרַעֲוָה B Gn 4:4, "with pleasure"; גָּלָא B Gn 4:12,ˆ "wanderer"; דּוֹרוֹן־ B Gn 4:4, "gift"; לְמֶיזְכֵּי B Gn 4:7, "to be innocent"; פֵּירָין B Gn 4:16, "fruits"; תְּרֵינַן B Gn 4:8, "the two of us." Spirantization is usually represented by the ómission of the *daghesh*. On occasion, however, a *raphe*, _ֿ, is also used, particularly in MS B, e.g., אַיְתֵי B Gn 4:4,ˆ"he brought"; וּשֲׁדַכֿוּ Bd Gn 8:1,ˆ"and they subsided"; עֲתִידִֿין B Gn 4:10, "destined"; נָפַֿקוּ־ B Gn 4:8,ˆ "they went out"; וּסְגֿוֹן Bd Gn 7:17, "and they increased."

**§4d** Both the plosive and spirantized allophones are usually unmarked in the Palestinian pointed manuscripts.[1] There is, however, one example in which _᷆ appears to mark a plosive pronunciation: מִלָּֽלָת A Ex 4:10, "you spoke."[2] There are four examples in which _᷆ may mark the plosive pronunciation of /bgdkpt/ and/or *shewa mobile:*[3] בֳּנַֽי A Ex 21:5, "my sons"; וִישְׁתְּֽכֿח A Ex 21:15, "and it will be found"; בְּעִיר A Ex 22:18, "cattle"; וְשֻׁתְּֽבִֿי A Ex 22:9, "he is taken captive." In the Greek loanword בְּדִיּֽפְלָה A Ex 22:3, "double" (cf. בדיפלה A Ex 22:6), _᷆ might have been intended to mark the plosive pronunciation of the Greek π (< διπλᾶ).[4] The sign _᷆ clearly marks spirantization in only one example:[5] וְיִֽגְנְבֿוֹן A Ex 22:6,ˆ "and they will be stolen."[6]

**§4e** The graphic evidence indicates that the spirantized allophone of /b/ was realized no differently from /w/, as seen in the following examples in which one finds *beth* where *waw* is expected: אַצְבָּתְכֿוֹן D Dt 28:17, "your troughs"; ורבה E Gn 9:21, "and he was drunk"; הבת E Gn 31:8,ˆ"she was"[6] (cf. הוֹת E Gn 29:17); ורבּון E Gn 43:34, "and they were drunk"; רצבחו E Gn 41:55, "and they shouted"; בירוע קדיש AA₁ Ex 12:16, "and a holy meeting" (2x; cf. ואירע F Lv 23:3);[7] לְבָֿת HH Ex 12:3,ˆ"towards" (cf. ולוֶת HH Ex 12:1). There is one example where one finds *waw* instead of *beth*: ודלווי E Gn 30:37, "and of plane-tree."[8]

It is not possible on the basis of this evidence to determine whether /w/ and the spirantized allophone of /b/ were realized as [w] or [v].[9]

**§4f** There are some exceptional pointings with *daghesh* and *raphe* that do not occur with the phonemes /bgdkpt/ and do not seem to represent plosion or spirantization. The examples with *daghesh* are מִשְׁרוֹי Cd Gn 46:28, "his dwellings"; רֹוגֿזִּי A Ex 22:23,ˆ"my anger," עַרְטְלָיִּֽן B Gn 2:25,ˆ"naked"; לַחֲדָּה B Gn 4:5, "very"; אֶתְקַבַּל B Gn 4:8,ˆ"it was accepted"; דְּתָכְלָא B Ex 39:31,ˆ"of bluish-purple";[10] לְמִגזֹּר C Gn 35:9,ˆ"to circumcise"; לְמֶשְׁבַּק Cd Gn 44:22, "to

26

leave"; תַחְמָא Cd Gn 46:29, "and he saw"; עָצֵין D Dt 28:29,̊ "oppressed" (m.pl.); מְמַשְׁשִׁין D Dt 28:29,̊ "groping"; שָׁרְיָה F Ex 20:18,̊ "dwelling"; קֻדְמָיָה Z Gn 48:22, "the first": קֻדְשִׁין -D Dt 27:7, "consecrated offerings"; נִגְרוֹי B Ex 39:33,̊ "its bars." The examples with *raphe* are בָּסִימָא -B Gn 2:21,̊ "sweet"; וּדְלֻחִין Cd Gn 43:11, "and of almonds." In תְקִיפוּ Cd Gn 48:10, "they grew hard," the *raphe* may have been intended for the preceding *taw*.

§4g   Although the use of the *daghesh* in some of the above examples may be due to scribal error or to misreading,[11] not all examples can be explained away in this manner. It appears that the *daghesh* in most of these examples[12] occurs either initially or medially after a closed syllable and thus marks a syllable boundary. Whereas this *daghes* seems to indicate that a preceding syllable is closed (and that a preceding _ marks a *shewa quiescens* and not a *shewa mobile*), the *raphe* seems to occur after a vowel, perhaps indicating that the preceding syllable is open.[13]

§4h   There are, however, also a few exceptional pointings with *daghesh* and *raphe* which occur with the phonemes /bgdkpt/ and which do not correspond to the rules of plosion/spirantization known from Tiberian Biblical Aramaic and Syriac: עֲבִידַת -B Ex 39:32, "the work of";[14] דְּאִית־בְנַהְרָא Cd Ex 7:18, "which are in the river";[15] יְדַי -Cd Ex 9:29, "my hands"; בּוּכְּרַת Cd Gn 48:7, "first, beginning,"[16] בָּכְּרַת Z Gn 48:7,̊ בְּכוֹרוּתֵ[ה] Z Gn 49:3,̊ "[the] birthright";[17] מַשְׁכִּין B Ex 39:34,̊ "hides, skins," מַשְׁכִּין B Ex 39:34.

§4i   There are a few examples in which a *daghesh lene* in /bgdkpt/ indicates that the preceding open syllable has become closed. For the examples, see §32.[18]

§4j   There is only one *s*-phoneme in these fragments. /s/ < *ś is represented graphically by both *samekh* and *sin,* which often interchange, e.g., /basar/, "flesh" occurs 11 times with *sin* and 10 times with *samekh*. Cf. בְּשָׂרֵן -Cd Gn 37:27, "our flesh," but בִּיסרה E Gn 9:17, "the flesh"; /sahed/, "witness" occurs 14 times with *samekh* and 9 times with *sin*. Cf. לְסָהֵד C Gn 31:44, "as a witness," but שָׂהֵיד C Gn 31:48. Other words containing *ś appear with either *samekh* or *sin*. All occurrences of the root *śr "ten" and derived forms are written with *sin*, but the frequent occurrences of *śbr, "countenance"; *śyb, "hoary"; *śgy, "many"; *śdr, "order" all are written with *samekh*, e.g., סְבַר -C Gn 32:21 (2x); סָב Cd Gn 44:20; וְסָגֵי Cd Ex 9:28; סדר F Lv 22:27.

All Greek loanwords[19] are transcribed with *samekh*, e.g., סְפִּיקְלַטְרַיּה E Gn 39:1,̊ "the executioners"; אפיטרופוס E Gn 39:4, "guardian."

§4k   The gutturals are preserved in this dialect, although /ʾ/[20] and /h/[21] are elided in certain environments. Consonantal *he* is sometimes marked in Tiberian pointed texts by *mappiq*, ה, e.g., יָתַהּ C Gn 31:39, "her"; קַרְתֵּהּ C Gn 34:24, "his city." It is infrequently marked by ה, e.g., לֵיהּ F Ex 19:3, "to him"; אדמה AA Nu 19:5, "her blood." There are two examples in MS A in which consonantal *he* is marked by ־ֵהּ:[22] יְקֵידְתֵהּ A Ex 22:4, "his burning"; בְּאָבְסָדֵהּ A Ex 22:14,̊ "in his loss."[23] There is one Palestinian pointed example in which ־ֻ seems to mark consonantal *he:*[24] מרה דבַיִיתה A Ex 22:7, "the master of the house" (literally "his master").

The quiescence of *aleph* is infrequently marked by ⸚ *(raphe)* in Tiberian pointed manuscripts, e.g., עָאנֵיה B Gn 4:4, "his small cattle."

*Consonantal Phonemes—Comparative Discussion*

**s4l** The inventory of consonantal phonemes in this dialect corresponds to that of the dialects of Official and Middle Aramaic.

**s4m** The spirantization of /bgdkpt/ corresponds to that known in Tiberian Biblical Aramaic, the Tiberian tradition of Targum Onqelos, and Western Syriac.[25]

**s4n** The graphic interchange of *beth* and *waw* reflecting one pronunciation for /w/ and the spirantized /b/ is known from other Targumim and dialects of Syria-Palestine: Targum Pseudo-Jonathan[26] the Fragment Targum,[27] Targum Neophyti,[28] Galilean Aramaic,[29] Samaritan Aramaic,[30] and Rabbinic Hebrew.[31]

**s4o** The extension of the *daghesh* and *raphe* to mark syllable boundaries in consonants other than /bgdkpt/ is one of the salient features of the Palestinian-Tiberian system of pointing,[32] as exemplified in the Codex Reuchlinianus[33] and the Pre-Ashkenazi *maḥzorim.*[34] The examples in the Cairo Genizah fragments, although few in number, seem to indicate that the vocalizers were familiar with the Palestinian-Tiberian system. As for the handful of examples in which *daghesh* occurs unexpectedly in /bgdkpt/, there does not appear to be any satisfactory solution.[35]

**s4p** The merger of *ś and *s to /s/ and its representation by the two letters *sin* and *samekh* (which is more frequent) is attested in Targum Onqelos,[36] Targum Pseudo-Jonathan,[37] the Fragment Targum,[38] Targum Neophyti,[39] Galilean Aramaic,[40] and Rabbinic Hebrew.[41] In Samaritan Aramaic, Palestinian Syriac, and Syriac, *ś and *s have merged to /s/, which is represented by *samekh* alone.[42] The merger of these two Proto-Aramaic phonemes can already be seen in Biblical Aramaic.[43]

**s4q** The preservation of the gutturals in these fragments—there is loss only of /'/ and /h/ in certain environments—stands in contrast with the Aramaic of Galilean Aramaic,[44] Targum Pseudo-Jonathan,[45] the Fragment Targum,[46] and Targum Neophyti,[47] in which it appears that the pronunciation of the gutturals is not always preserved. The many instances, however, of the loss of gutturals in Targum Pseudo-Jonathan, the Fragment Targum, and Targum Neophyti may be due, in large part, to the familiarity of copyists with Babylonian Talmudic Aramaic in which the gutturals were greatly weakened.[48] Thus, the status of the gutturals in the Cairo Genizah fragments more closely resembles the situation in Official and Middle Aramaic in which the gutturals are preserved. Note that the gutturals are preserved in Ma'lula and Syriac, but not in Palestinian Syriac[49] and Samaritan Aramaic.[50]

28

§5                                    C. *Vocalic Phonemes*

§5a   Despite the fact that the manuscripts of the Cairo Genizah are not all
contemporaneous, they do, on the whole, have a common inventory of
vocalic phonemes. They differ, however, in their graphic representation of
these phonemes. The Tiberian system of pointing is found in the majority of
pointed manuscripts, while in others the Palestinian system is used.
Occasionally, one finds individual words pointed with both Tiberian and
Palestinian vowel signs, each reflecting the same pronunciation. The
manuscripts differ again in the frequency with which, within a given system,
certain vowel signs are preferred to others which represent the same phoneme.
§5b   A description of the vocalic inventory is made difficult by the graphic
representation of the phonemes. There is not always a direct relationship
between phoneme and vowel sign. In other words, a phoneme is not always
represented by one vowel sign alone. For example, both the Tiberian and the
Palestinian systems have signs for two *a*-phonemes and two *e*-phonemes,
whereas the inventory of the Cairo Genizah fragments has only one *a*-
phoneme and one *e*-phoneme. The Tiberian system, with its eleven vowel
sign, permits more fluctuation, and hence confusion, in its graphic
representation than does the Palestinian system with its eight vowel signs,
seven of which are attested in these fragments.[1] The best way to identify the
phonemes and determine by which vowel signs they are represented is to
compare identical words or morphemes which appear with two, sometimes
three, different pointings. Such pairs of linguistic forms demonstrate that one
phoneme is represented by more than one vowel sign and will be referred to as
"non-contrasting minimal pairs."[2]
§5c   A methodological difficulty arises in analyzing the interchangeability of
vowel signs in certain environments and their lack of fluctuation in others. If
certain vowel signs interchange freely in environments X and Y, reflecting
only one phoneme, does the fact that in environment Z they do not fluctuate
indicate that each vowel sign represents a different phoneme or allophone, or
is this to be attributed to scribal convention? In such cases, analysis of the
vowel signs is often not sufficient, and comparative data may be helpful. For
example, although *ḥireq*, *ṣere*, and *seghol* are, in most environments,
interchangeable in these texts, the m. pl. construct morpheme /e/ is regularly
pointed with *ṣere*. Does this reflect a conditioned allophone of the one *e*-
phoneme posited in these fragments? In this example, it seems that the *ṣere* is
to be attributed to scribal convention, namely, a conscious imitation of
Tiberian pointing rules. Comparative data from other dialects in which there
is only one *e*-phoneme do not reveal a conditioned allophone in this
environment. On the other hand, does a *ḥireq* (interchanging with *shewa
mobile*) preceding *yodh*, which is never interchanged with *ṣere* or *seghol*, e.g.
בְּיִרְקָא, C Gn 34:25, reflect an allophone of *shewa* realized approximately as [ĭ],
or is it to be regarded, as in other environments, as a graphic representation of

/e/? In this case, comparative evidence supports a conclusion that, in this environment, ḥireq represents an allophone [ĭ] of *shewa mobile*.

§5d   The influence of the Tiberian school of pointing on the vocalizers of these manuscripts is clear. The prestige of the Tiberian system was so great that, even though the vocalic inventory of the vocalizers did not match the phonemic system underlying the Tiberian vowel signs, the vocalizers adopted the Tiberian system.[3] It appears that, on the whole, the vocalizers tried to follow the rules of pointing reflected in the Tiberian tradition of Biblical Aramaic. They were, to a large extent, successful in pointing qameṣ and pathaḥ according to the Tiberian Biblical Aramaic rules. The numerous deviations, however, from the historically correct forms demonstrate that the vocalizers possessed only one *a*-phoneme. In contrast, the vocalizers were less successful in using the Tiberian signs *seghol, ṣere*, and *ḥireq* (< *i) to represent their one *e*-phoneme. They seem to have pointed "phonetically," preferring the sign *seghol*, perhaps because it was the Tiberian vowel sign whose pronunciation came closest to their own pronunciation of /e/. At times they were even guilty of hypercorrection and pointed *ṣere* for Tiberian *ḥireq*, and *ḥireq* for Tiberian *ṣere*. They knew that, in addition to *seghol*, there were two other signs representing *e*-vowels; however, they did not know how they were used.[4]

§5e   The correct Tiberian pointing of most proper names which occur in the Masoretic text underscores the fact that the vocalizers knew, respected, and tried to imitate the Tiberian system. The few proper names that are pointed incorrectly demonstrate that, even when vocalizers tried to imitate the system, they did not master it completely.[5] It is interesting to note that, in those manuscripts in which the Masoretic text alternates with the Targum, the vocalizers deviate from the Tiberian rules of pointing in the Aramaic portions far more than in the Masoretic text. The few errors that occur in the Masoretic text are similar to those found in the Aramaic text.[6]

§5f   Tiberian influence may also be discerned in the Palestinan pointing used in these texts. The use of the signs ⟂ and ⟂ corresponds to the Tiberian use of qameṣ and pathaḥ in more than 90% of their occurrences.[7] It is possible that ⟂, which usually represents /a/, is also used to represent /o/ (cf. Tiberian qameṣ qaṭan).[8] If ⟂ is used to represent /o/, it is an additional indication of Tiberian influence.

§5g   In addition to the information supplied by the two systems of vowel signs, evidence of the vocalic phonemes can often be gleaned from the use of the *matres lectionis*. This evidence alone, however, provides only limited information. For example, the *waw* in קודם E Gn 30:41 "before, in the presence of," reveals that there is some grade of *o*- or *u*- vowel, but it does not indicate anything more precise. In theory, this orthography could represent the phonetic realizations [o], [u], [ŏ], or [ŭ]. Similarly, the *yodh* of איך A Ex 22:7, "if," indicates that an e-vowel is present, but it does not indicate whether that vowel was realized as [e], [ɛ], or [i].

§5h  The Tiberian and Palestinian vowel signs, as well as comparative data, are helpful in approximating the phonetic realization of the phonemes and their allophones. It must, however, be noted that, since the language reflected in these texts has been preserved only in writing, it is impossible to ascertain their precise phonetic realizations. Consequently, in discussing the inventory of vocalic phonemes, it is desirable to emphasize the interrelationships of the phonemes and their relation to the system as a whole.

§5i  The Tiberian tradition of Biblical Aramaic serves as a basis for comparison in analyzing the use of vowel signs in these manuscripts because it is apparent from a number of features that the vocalizers tried to imitate the Tiberian Biblical Aramaic tradition. The Tiberian pointing of Targum Onqelos is a later tradition whose most reliable exemplars belie transcription from a Babylonian *Vorlage*.[9] For comparative purposes, reference will also be made to the pointing tradition of Targum Onqelos found in Yemenite manuscripts.[10]

§5j  Although the Cairo Genizah fragments are closer in language to Targum Pseudo-Jonathan and the Fragment Targum than to Biblical Aramaic, the Tiberian pointing found in the printed editions of these two Targumim is a late, unauthentic representation of their vocalic inventories. Their redactors were unfamiliar with the dialects in which they were originally written. As a result, they attempted to vocalize the Targumim in accordance with the norms of the more familiar dialects of Biblical Aramaic and Targum Onqelos,[11] but were not wholly successful. Furthermore, the pointing of these two Targumim demonstrates a broad application of the rules of Hebrew tonic and pretonic lengthening, as well as the rules governing shortening of vowels in closed syllables.[12]

§5k  Before proceeding, one may well ask if the pointing tradition in these manuscripts is the same tradition as that of the consonantal text. Apart from a handful of divergences that will be noted in the course of this study, there is nothing to suggest that the vocalized text and the consonantal text represent two distinct traditions. On the contrary, the *scriptio plena* often confirms the evidence in the pointed text.

§6  *Inventory of Vocalic Phonemes*

§6a  There appear to be six vocalic phonemes in the language of the Cairo Genizah fragments: /a/, /e/, /i/, /o/, /u/, and /ə/.

§6b  Despite the limited number of pointed manuscripts, the following contrasting minimal pairs can be found: /a/ vs. /e/, מַן- D Dt 5:26, "who" (/man/), מֵן- D Dt 5:20, "from" (/men/); /a/ vs. /i/ הָא B Gn 4:14, "behold" (/ha/), -הִיא B Gn 4:10, "she" (/hi/); /a/ vs. /o/, חֲכַם E Gn 39:8, "he knew" (/ḥakam/), אֲכ[ח]ום Cd Gn 38:26, "recognize!" (/ḥəkom/); /a/ vs. /ə/, סְלֵק C Gn 32:27, "it ascended" (/səleq/), סָלֵיק Z Gn 49:11, "he ascends" (/saleq/);

/e/ vs. /i/, ־דֵין C Gn 31:41, "this" (/den/), דִּינָה B Gn 4:7, "the judgment" (/din/); /e/ vs. /o/, וּקְרֵיב C Gn 32:26, "he drew near" (/qəreb/), קָרוֹב D Dt 5:24, "draw near!" (/qərob/); /i/ vs. /u/, הִיא C Gn 32:19, "she" (/hi/), הוּא - C Gn 32:19, "he" (/hu/).

**§7  Graphic Representation of Vocalic Phonemes**

§7a  The graphic representation of the vocalic phonemes is presented according to phoneme rather than by manuscript. This format was chosen in order to highlight the common scribal conventions followed by the vocalizers of the different manuscripts, be they fully pointed or sporadically pointed. In order to correlate vowel signs with phonemes and prove that a phoneme may be represented by more than one vowel sign, non-contrasting minimal pairs will be cited for the different environments[13] in which the phoneme occurs. Parentheses contain words which, together with the preceding word, constitute a non-contrasting minimal pair. In addition, selected examples of pointings that deviate from the expected Tiberian pointing will be given. At the end of each discussion one can find a count of the frequency with which the vowel signs correspond to and deviate from the use of the same signs in the Tiberian pointing of Biblical Aramaic. By listing the number of occurrences, an accurate picture emerges of the way in which the vowel signs are used. This helps to determine which deviating pointings represent significant features of phonology and which are probably mere slips of the scribe's quill. Excluded from the frequency counts are cases in which the morphological patterning of Biblical Aramaic and the language of these fragments clearly differ; in these environments, the vocalizers did not have a Masoretic tradition which they were trying to imitate.

**§8  /a/**

§8a  /a/ is represented graphically by Palestinian ⌐ and ⌐, and by Tiberian ⌐ and ⌐. Although the use of the signs follows, in general, the Tiberian rules for *qameṣ* and *pathaḥ*, the many examples of incorrect usage and fluctuation testify that there is only one a-phoneme. There are many more examples of ⌐ and ⌐ where one expects Tiberian *qameṣ* than there are of ⌐ and ⌐ where one expects Tiberian *pathaḥ* (except in MS A). Two reasons come to mind. The first is that the predominance of vowel signs corresponding to Tiberian *pathaḥ* suggests that the phonetic realization of /a/ was closer to the Tiberian realization of *pathaḥ* than to the Tiberian realization of *qameṣ*. The second is that ⌐ and ⌐ are less ambiguous than ⌐ and ⌐ in representing /a/. They carry a lighter functional load than do ⌐ and ⌐, which also represent /o/.[14]

§8b  *non-final, closed, unstressed syllables.*

Some examples of non-contrasting minimal pairs are חֻברה A Ex 21:18, "his friend" (cf. לְחֻברֵה A Ex 22:6; דְּחֻברה A Ex 22:7, לְחֻברֵה A Ex 22:8, לְחֻברֵה A Ex 22:9, חֻברֵה A Ex 22:10); חֻקְלֵה A Ex 22:5, "the field" (cf. חֻקְלֵה A Ex 22:4, בְּחֻקְלֵה A Ex 22:4); תְּמַשְׁכָּן A Ex 22:25, "you take as a pledge" (cf. מְמַשְׁכְּנֵה A Ex 22:25);

32

Cd בָּאַרְעֹה C Gn 31:51); יַגְרָא C Gn 31:48, יַגְרָא C Gn 31:52, "the heap" (cf. יָגְרָא-
Gn 47:4, "in the land" (cf. בְּאַרְעָא Cd Gn 47:4); פַּרְעֹה Cd Ex 5:20; "Pharoah"
(cf. דְּפַרְעֹה Cd Ex 7:14); אָעֵיל Cd Gn 43:16, "he brought in" (cf. וְאָעֵלּוֹן Cd Gn
43:25).

A few additional examples of pointings which deviate from Tiberian rules
are דַּיִּינָא -A Ex 22:7, "the judges"; חַרְכָּה Bd Gn 8:6; "the window"; עָרְבוֹנָא Cd
Gn 38:20; "the pledge"; אָעֶלּתוּן AA Nu 20:5, "you brought up"; לְמַעֲלָה AA Nu
20:5, "to bring up."

A note of caution, however, must be added. It is possible that in some of
these examples, particularly where ֻ and ָ are preceded by a labial or /r/,
these two signs represent /o/.[15]

§8c   *non-final, open, stressed syllables*

/a/ is attested in this environment in forms of the Perfect 3 m.pl. and the
Imperative m.pl.[16] With the exception of וְנָפְלוּ H Gn 15:1, "they fell," all
examples are pointed with ָ, e.g., חָזָרוּ Bd Gn 8:3; "and they returned"; וּנְסָבוּ
Cd Gn 37:24, "and they took"; וְאִתְגַּבָּרוּBd Gn 7:19, "they prevailed"; וּשְׁמַע D
Dt 27:9; "and hear!"

§8d   *non-final, open, unstressed syllables*

Examples of non-contrasting minimal pairs are לַחֲדָהBd Gn 7:18; "very"
(cf. לַחֲדָה B Gn 4:5); קָדָמִי C Gn 32:17, "before me" (cf. קָדְמַךְ-C Gn 32:18); דְּנָפִיק
H Gn 15:4, "going forth" (cf. נָפִיק H Gn 15:2).

Some additional examples of pointings which deviate from the Tiberian
rules are [בַּעֲשִׂירָיה Bd Gn 8:5; "on the tenth"; יַהֵיב D Dt 27:2, "giving"; וְאַנָשֵׁי E
Gn 30:30; "and the men of"; כָּסֵה E Gn 40:13; "his cup"; וּפָתֹר E Gn 41:15,
"and interpreting"; שְׁלָמֵה E Gn 41:16; "his well-being"; לַחֲמָרֵידְהוֹן E Gn 43:24,
"to their he-asses"; הָדֵין H Gn 15:1, "this"; אֲבָהָתֵה HH Ex 12:3; "the fathers."

§8e   *final, closed, stressed syllables*

Some examples of non-contrasting minimal pairs are חֹרֵשׁ A Ex 22:17,
"sorcerer" (cf. וֹחֹרֵשָׁה A Ex 22:17); לָךְ B Gn 4:12, "to you" (cf. לָךְ- B Gn 4:7);
יָת- B Gn 4:11 (cf. יָת- B Ex 39:31); קָדָם B Gn 4:13, "before" (cf. קָדָם- B Gn 4:16);
לְוָתָךְ C Gn 31:39, "towards you" (cf. לְוָתָךְ C Gn 31:52); בָּתְרָן C Gn 32:19,
"after us" (cf. בָּתְרָן C Gn 32:21); לְוָת Cd Gn 37:30, "towards" (cf. לְוָת- Cd Gn
37:30); דַּהֲוַת Cd Ex 9:24, "she was" (cf. הֲוַת- Cd Gn 38:21); אָב Cd Gn 44:19,
"father" (cf. אָב Cd Gn 44:20); יָתָךְ Cd Gn 48:4, "you" (cf. יָתָךְ Cd Gn 48:4);
לִשְׁמָךְ Cd Gn 48:6, "to your name" (cf. שְׁמָךְ-C Gn 35:9); וּבְיָד Cd Ex 6:1, "and
with a hand" (cf. בְּיַד Cd Gn 38:20); אֲדָם Cd Ex 7:19, "blood" (cf. אֲדַם Cd Ex
7:19); עָן AA₁ Ex 12:21, "small cattle" (cf. עָנכון AA₁ Ex 12:32).

Some additional examples of pointings which deviate from Tiberian rules
are דְאִתְמֹל A Ex 21:36, "of yesterday"; חֲמֹר A Ex 22:3; "he-ass"; וִישַׁלֹח A Ex
22:4; "and he will send"; לְמְקָם B Gn 4:10, "to arise"; צַיָּיר Bd Ex 39:29,
"embroiderer"; בְּקָל D Dt 27:10, "to the voice of"; תְּלִיתָיִי F Ex 20:5, "third";
דָּר F Ex 20:5, "generation" (2x); טָב F Nu 28:26, "good"; דְּכָר F Nu 28:27, "and
a ram"; צְרִירָן AA₁ Ex 12:34, "bound" (f.pl.); כְּלָתָר Z Gn 49:9, "your daughter-

in-law"; חֹלֶק H Gn 15:1, "portion"; פתגם H Gn 15:1, "word"; לוֹנֻת HH Ex 12:1, "towards"; לַמִנְיָן HH Ex 12:2, "to the number of."

The vocalizers have consistently preferred ⁻ and ₋ in representing /a/ in final, closed, stressed syllables. This writing convention stands out clearly in morphemes which, in the Tiberian tradition, are pointed with *qames*, such as the 2 m.s. pronominal suffix, the Perfect 3 f.s.[17] and 3 f.pl.[18] of verbs III-w/y, and f.pl. absolute nouns,[19] e.g., מִיֻנֵּ B Gn 4:8, "from you" וּקָהַת C Gn 32:26, "and it was dislocated? benumbed?";[20] יֶתְפַּתְחַן B Gn 3:5, "they will be opened"; נקבָן C Gn 32:16, "females." As might be expected, morphemes which are pointed according to Tiberian rules with *pathah* rarely deviate from the Tiberian pointing. For example, the 3 f.s. pronominal suffix is regularly pointed with ₋, e.g., יָתַהּ Cd Gn 38:22, "her." There is only one exception: רְדִידָהּ Cd Gn 38:19, "her veil".[21]

§8f    *final, open, stressed syllables*

The examples of non-contrasting minimal pairs are מָא⁻ Cd Gn 43:12, "what" (cf. ⁻מָה C Gn 32:21);[22] מָה⁻ Cd Gn 47:3 (cf. ⁻מָה Cd Gn 44:15); אָנָה⁻ D Dt 27:1, "I" (cf. ⁻אָנָה D Dt 27:10); בְּיוֹמָה D Dt 27:11, "on the day" (cf. יוֹמָה D Dt 27:1,10).

/a/ in final, open, stressed syllables is almost always represented by ⁻ or ₋. The following examples, half of which come from MS E, are the only exceptions: גְּנֵבָּתָה A Ex 22:3, "the theft"; מְאֹרָסָה A Ex 22:15, "betrothed"; גּוּבַיָּא Cd Gn 37:19, "the pits"; אָתָה E Gn 30:11, "he came"; וְשַׂעֲבָה E Gn 37:25, "balsam";[23] דְּחלמָה E Gn 40:12, "of the dream"; דחלמָה E Gn 40:18, בְּרִיָּתָה E Gn 41:7, "healthy" (f.pl); קָרָא E Gn 41:52, "he called"; מָה E Gn 42:36.

§8g    *final, closed, unstressed syllables*

The only certain example of /a/ in this environment is רְבָיֵע B Gn 4:7, "lying."[24]

§8h    /a/ is not attested in these fragments in final, open, unstressed syllables.[25]

§8i    There are a few examples in Tiberian pointed texts in which /a/ is represented by the sign ₋ and ₋. If ₋ could represent /a/ as well as /ə/,[26] it is possible that ₋ could represent /ə/ as well as /a/. An extension of the function of ₋ could have been followed by an extension of the function of ₋. The examples with ₋ are מְיָא Bd Gn 8:3, "the waters";[27] עָקָתְהוֹן Cd Gn 38:25, "their distress'; עָלָלְתֵהּ Cd Gn 48:7, "her harvest";[28] אתכְּסִי Z Gn 49:1, "he was covered";[29] דמְחֵי Z Gn 49:17, "strikes";[30] וּקָלִיל Cd Gn 43:11, "little." Examples with ₋ are עַבְדִין Cd Gn 44:16, "servants"; עַל Cd Ex 7:19, "on"; חַיָּבֵייָה F Ex 20:7, "the guilty"; וְעַבדֵּיכון F Ex 20:10, "and your servants"; וְאַמְהָתְכון F Ex 20:10, "and your handmaidens."[31]

§8j    Some of the confusion in signs may be attributable to the application of Hebrew rules of tonic and pretonic lengthening, pausal lengthening, and the tendency to shorten vowels in syllables felt to be closed.[32] Thus, for example, the ⁻ of בָּנַי A Ex 21:5, "my children" and ₋ of דְּכַנְעַן Cd Gn 48:3, "of

34

Canaan" may have been influenced by the Hebrew rules of pausal lengthening. Similarly, the ‗ of אָזְלִין E Gn 37:25, "going" and of לְעָלְמָא H Gn 15:1, "the world" may have been influenced by the shortening of long vowels in closed syllables.[33] The large number of inconsistencies and counter-examples, however, makes it difficult to attribute all examples to these explanations. These rules, for example, cannot account for the shortening in הַדֵּין H Gn 15:1, "this" or the pausal לָךְ B Gn 4:12, "to you."

§8k  The following chart shows the frequency of the graphic signs representing /a/ and their correspondence to the Tiberian Biblical Aramaic rules of pointing.[34]

| | Tiberian *qameṣ* | Tiberian *pathaḥ* |
|---|---|---|
| Palestinian Vowel Signs | | |
| MS A | ⌐ 92x, ⌐ 11x | ⌐ 92x, ⌐ 15x |
| MS E | ⌐ 2x | — |
| MS H | — | ⌐ 1x, ⌐ 1x |
| Tiberian Vowel Signs | | |
| MS A | ⌐ 1x, ⌐ 2x | ⌐ 4x |
| MS B | ⌐ 153x, ⌐ 42x | ⌐ 324x, ⌐ 3x, ⌐ 1x |
| MS C | ⌐ 832x, ⌐ 165x | ⌐ 804x, ⌐ 14x, ⌐ 3x, ⌐ 2x |
| MS D | ⌐ 135x, ⌐ 42x | ⌐ 107x |
| MS E | ⌐ 5x, ⌐ 42x | ⌐ 26x |
| MS F | ⌐ 87x, ⌐ 16x | ⌐ 49x, ⌐ 1x, ⌐ 3x |
| MS H | ⌐ 9x, ⌐ 11x | ⌐ 34x |
| MS W | ⌐ 1x, ⌐ 1x | — |
| MS Y | ⌐ — | — |
| MS Z | ⌐ 44x, ⌐ 5x, ⌐ 1x | ⌐ 49x, ⌐ 1x, ⌐ 2x |
| MS AA | ⌐ 43x, ⌐ 2x | ⌐ 12x, ⌐ 1x |
| MS HH | ⌐ 10x, ⌐ 8x | ⌐ 15x |

§9  /e/

§9a  The phoneme /e/ is represented by three vowel signs in the Palestinian pointing system: by ⌐ in 93% of the examples, by ⌐ in 6% of the examples, and by ⌐ in 2% of the examples. The use of three vowel signs seems to be the result of Tiberian influence, paralleling the three Tiberian vowel signs *ṣere, seghol,* and *ḥireq*. In some Palestinian pointed Hebrew manuscripts, ⌐ consistently corresponds to Tiberian *ṣere,* ⌐ to Tiberian *seghol,* and ⌐ to Tiberian *ḥireq*. In the Cairo Genizah fragments, however, ⌐ and ⌐ interchange freely, and ⌐ interchanges with them both. Apart from the five examples of ⌐ representing /e/, this sign consistently represents /i/ (< *ī) in these texts.

§9b  In the Tiberian pointed texts, ⌐, ⌐, and ⌐ all represent /e/ and are interchangeable with one another.[35] ⌐ is the most frequent of these vowel signs in the fully pointed manuscripts, suggesting that this phoneme was realized as [ɛ] like the presumed realization of the Tiberian *seghol*. ⸱ usually corresponds to Tiberian *ḥireq* (< *i), less often to *ṣere*, as well as to *seghol*. Pointings with ⸱ are relatively infrequent in the fully pointed manuscripts, but increase as ⸱ decreases in sporadically pointed manuscripts.[36] In MSS H and HH, however, there is no confusion in the use of the vowel signs ⸱ and ⸫, nor are there any examples of ⸱ (both are sporadically pointed manuscripts).

**§9c** One finds the following correspondences between Palestinian and Tiberian vowel signs representing /e/ in the few words which are pointed with vowel signs from both systems:

*MS A*

⸱ = ⸱   בְּגֻנֻבְתֵה Ex 22:2⸢ "for his theft"; לְחֹבְרֵה Ex 22:6⸢ "to his friend"; וְיֻגְנֻבֹן Ex 22:6⸣ "and they will be stolen";[37] אֹסטְלִי Ex 22:8, "garment."[38]

⸱ = ⸱   יַשְׂרְתֵה Ex 22:4⸣ "his burning"; יֻתקֻנֻס Ex 21:22⸢ "he will be punished"; עוֹבֹה A Ex 4:7, "his breast."[39]

⸱ = ⸱   וְנֻבְתֵה Ex 22:3⸢ "the theft."

⸱ = ⸱   יַשְׂרְתֵה Ex 22:4⸢ "his burning."

*MS E*

⸱ = ⸱   בֹרֵיוֵה Gn 39:6, "his appearance"; וַיֻתֵה Gn 41:13, "him"; לֻגֻהֻך Gn 41:21⸢ "in their midst"; עֻלֵיך Gn 43:29⸢ "upon you" (m.s.); בֵיתֵה Gn 44:4, "his house."[40]

**§9d**   *non-final, closed, unstressed syllables*

Some examples of non-contrasting minimal pairs are חֻוְיֻא B Gn 3:4⸢ "the serpent" (cf. לְחֻוְיֻא B Gn 3:2)⸢ הֻכְרִין C Gn 32:15, "males" (cf. דֻכְרִין⸢ C Gn 32:16); חֻיְתֻא Cd Gn 37:20, "the animal" (cf. חֻיְתֻא Cd Gn 37:33); אִיתֻא Cd Gn 37:33, "woman" (cf. דְאֻתְתֻא Cd Gn 38:20); נֻהֻוֵי Cd Gn 38:23, "we shall be" (cf. נֻהֵי Cd Gn 44:9); תֻסֻב Cd Gn 38:23, "you will take" (cf. תֻסֻב⸢ Cd Gn 31:50); אֻנֻן Cd Gn 48:8, "they" (cf. אֻנֻן⸢ Cd Gn 47:1); יֻהֻוֵי⸢ Cd Gn 48:19, "he will be" (cf. יֻהֵוֵי C Gn 35:10); לְמֻתֵן Cd Ex 6:8, "to give" (cf. לְמִיהֻן C Gn 34:14), לֻבֵיה Cd Ex 7:22, "his heart" (cf. בְּלֻבֵה Cd Gn 38:25); מֻלֵי D Dt 5:25, "words of" (cf. מְלִיכֻון D Dt 5:25); הֻאֻלֵין D Dt 28:15, "these" (cf. הֻאֻלֵין D Dt 5:19); תֻהֻוון F Nu 28:29⸢ "you will be" (cf. יֻהֵוֵי F Nu 28:26).

Some additional examples of pointings which deviate from Tiberian rules are מֻתקֻנֻסֵה A Ex 21:20⸢ "being punished"; מֻלִי A Ex 22:8⸢ "words of"; יֻתֵן A Ex 22:9⸢ "he will give"; סֹדרֵי H Gn 15:1⸢ "rows of";[41] אֻתְתֻא B Gn 3:6, "the woman"; לֻבֻא B Gn 4:7, "the heart"; אֻתְגֻבְרוּ Bd Gn 7:19, "they prevailed"; שֻבטֵיכֻון D Dt 5:20, "your tribes"; אֻישֻתֵה D Dt 5:21, "the fire"; לֻשֻן -D Dt 27:8, "language"; מֻתקְרֻא D Dt 27:8, "is read"; דֻאֻמֵה E Gn 29:10, "of his mother"; וְנֻתְבֻני E Gn 30:3, "and I shall be built up"; מֻנֵה E Gn 30:3,[42] "from her"; אֻשֻתמֻעֻת E Gn 30:8, "I was heard"; תֻסֻב E Gn 38:23⸢ "you will take"; עֻבְרֻי E Gn 41:12, "Hebrew"; דְאֻשֻא F Ex 20:2, "of fire"; וְאֻידֵינו AA Nu 20:3, "and they contested"; מֻתְמֻני Z Gn 44:18, "is numbered"; לְמֻתכנֻשֵׂה Z Gn 47:29⸢ "to be

36

gathered"; כְּמֶלֶךְ Z Gn 47:30, "according to your (m.s.) words"; בְּמִלָּתִי Z Gn 48:7, "in my coming."

§9e Kutcher suggested that there was a positional allophone [i] in non-final, closed, unstressed syllables when followed by a syllable with *yodh*. He cited three examples: מִנְיָנָא C Gn 31:39, "the number"; תִּינְיָנָה C Gn 32:20, "the second one"; and וְקִנְיָנְהוֹן C Gn 34:23, "and their possessions." He ignored, however, תֵּינִיָה Cd Gn 44:18, "his second"[43] and the non-contrasting minimal pair בְּמֵתִיָּה C Gn 35:9, "in his coming" (בְּמֵתִיָה C Gn 35:9). The paucity of examples containing ֶ and the counter-examples with ֵ weaken Kutscher's conjecture.[44]

§9f *non-final, open, stressed syllables*

Only ֵ is attested in this environment.[45] The examples can be found in G intransitive verbs and verbs I-y, D verbs, C verbs, and Gt verbs. The pointed examples are תְּקֵיפוּ Cd Gn 48:10, "they became hard";[46] דְּחֵלוּ Cd Gn 43:18, "and they feared"; וּקְרֵבוּ Cd Gn 47:29, "and they drew near"; וְהֵיבוּ C Gn 34:12, "and give!"; תֵּיבוּ C Gn 34:10, "sit!"; וִיתֵיבוּ Cd Gn 37:25, "and they sat down"; וִיתֵבוּ Cd Gn 43:33; סָאֵיבוּ C Gn 34:13, "they made impure"; קְבֵּילוּ Cd Gn 38:26, "receive!"; וְכַבֵּישׁוּ C Gn 35:9, "and conquer!"; קְטֵּלוּ Cd Gn 44:18, "and they killed"; וְטַלְקוּ Cd Ex 7:12, "and they threw"; וּמְלֵילוּ C Gn 34:13, "and they spoke"; וּמְלֵילוּ C Gn 34:20; מַלֵּילוּ D Dt 5:25; מַלֵּילוּ D Dt 5:25; וְאִשְׁלַמוּ E Gn 41:53, "and they were completed";[47] אֶתְיַלְדוּ Cd Gn 48:5, "they were born." The exclusive use of ֵ in these forms could be interpreted to suggest that there was a conditioned allophone similar to Tiberian *sere* ([e]?) in this environment.[48] In Tiberian Biblical Aramaic *hireq* is regularly attested in this environment in these verbal categories.[49]

§9g *non-final, open, unstressed syllables*

The only non-contrasting minimal pair which occurs in the same manuscript is חֵיוְתָא Cd Gn 37:20, "the animal" (cf. חֵיוְתָא Cd Gn 37:33).[50] Another non-contrasting minimal pair which comes, however, from two different manuscripts is דִּבֵּירַיָּה D Dt 5:19, "the Commandments" (cf. דְּבִירַיָה F Ex 20:1).

The only other example with ֵ is דִּבֵּירֵי D Dt 5:21, "his Commandments." ֶ occurs in all other examples. Representative examples are תֵּאכַל B Gn 2:17, "you will eat"; וִידֵינַן Cd Gn 37:27, "and our hands"; מֵימְהוֹן Cd Ex 7:19, "their waters"; מֵלֵיכוֹן D Dt 5:25, "your words." In Palestinian pointed texts one finds ֱ, ֵ, and ֶ, e.g., הֱוֵיתוֹן A Ex 22:20, "you were"; יְקֵידְתֵהּ A Ex 22:4, "his burning"; יְבֵידָה A Ex 22:8, "loss." Before heavy pronominal suffixes on pl. nouns one finds ֵ, e.g., וּבְנֵיכוֹן A Ex 22:23, "and your sons"; לְגוֹאֵהֶן E Gn 41:21, "in their midst."

§9h *final, closed, stressed syllables*

Some representative examples of non-contrasting minimal pairs in this environment are לְרִבּוֹנֵהּ A Ex 21:4, "to his master" (cf. רִבּוֹנֵהּ A Ex 21:4); מֵנֵּהּ B Gn 2:17, "from him" (cf. מֵנֵּהּ B Gn 3:3); יְדֵךְ B Gn 4:11, "your (m.s.) hands" (cf. וּבִידֵךְ B Gn 4:7); וּבָרֵךְ C Gn 35:9, "and he blessed" (cf. וּבָרֵךְ C Gn 35:9); אַלֵּיפְתָּ C Gn 35:9, "you taught" (cf. אלֵּיפת C Gn 35:9); אֶתְגְּלֵית C Gn 35:9, "you revealed yourself" (cf. אֶתְגְּלִית C Gn 35:9); אֶתֵּן Cd Gn 38:18, "I will give" (cf. אֶתֵּן C Gn 35:12); לְחֵם Cd Gn 43:25, "bread" (cf. לְחֵם Cd Gn 37:25); חֲסִיד Cd Gn 47:29, "grace" (cf. וַחֲסֵד Cd Gn 47:29); מֵימְרֵיה D Dt 5:25, "His Word" (cf. מֵימְרֵיה D Dt 5:25); הָדֵין D Dt 26:18, "this" (cf. הָדֵין D Dt 27:1).

A few additional examples of pointings which deviate from expected Tiberian forms are יְשַׁרְגֵג A Ex 22:15, "he will violate"; נְפֵק B Gn 2:20, "going forth"; יִפְרֵשׁ B Gn 2:24, "let him separate"; דְשֵׁיזֵב Cd Gn 48:16, "who saved"; וְנַעְבֵּיד D Dt 5:24, "and we shall do"; ותתחֵם F Ex 19:12, "and you will mark a boundary"; אַפֵּסְתְּ F Ex 20:22, "you desecrated."

§9i    *final, open, stressed syllables*

Three non-contrasting minimal pairs are attested in this environment: יְשַׁוֵי A Ex 21:30, "he will place" (cf. תשַׁוֵּי A Ex 21:1); מָארֵי בְעִיר Cd Gn 46:34, "cattle owners" (cf. מָארֵי־בְעִיר Cd Gn 46:32); מֵי הַדְיָא AA Nu 19:20, "waters of sprinkling" (cf. מֵי הַדְיָא AA Nu 19:13); יִמְחֵה D Dt 28:28 "he will strike (cf. יִמְחֵא D Dt 28:22).[51] Another non-contrasting minimal pair whose members come from two different manuscripts is לְדָרֵי AA₁ Ex 17:16, "for generations of" (cf. לְדָרֵי C Gn 35:9).

The only other examples which deviate from Tiberian rules of pointing are גְּלֵא B Gn 3:5, "revealed"; וַאֲתַנֵּי Cd Gn 46:31, "I shall tell'; סֵדְרֵי H Gn 15:1, "rows of."[52] יְהֵי C Gn 35:9, "may he be...!"[53] (and גְּדֵי Cd Gn 38:17, גְּדֵי Cd Gn 38:20, "kid" for /gəde/?[54]; סֵוגֵי C Gn 32:13, "multitude" for /soge/?)[55]

§9j    *final, closed, unstressed syllables*

There is only one pointed example in all of the manuscripts, אַקֵימֶת C Gn 31:51, "I set up."

§9k    It is possible that imitation of the Tiberian rule of vowel shortening in closed, unstressed syllables[56] is responsible for many of the examples in which one finds ֶ for expected ֵ, e.g., וְשֶׁם Cd Gn 48:16, "and the name of" vs. בְשֵׁם Cd Ex 5:23. This explanation, however, cannot account for all of the fluctuation in this environment, e.g., אֶין C Gn 31:52, "if" vs. אֵין Cd Gn 46:30, much less so in other environments, e.g., בְּתַקְיָפֵיה C Gn 31:53, "and by his mighty one" vs. וְתַקִיפֵיה C Gn 31:42. There is little evidence that the fluctuation between *sere* and *hireq* in closed, stressed syllables in the verb in Tiberian Biblical Aramaic influenced the vocalizers of these manuscripts, since one usually finds ֵ in this environment.[57] Only in MS H is there an example of an alternation of ֵ and ִ: נָפֵיק H Gn 15:2, "going forth" vs. דנָפִיק H Gn 15:4 (but note the interchange of *pathah* and *qames*). The fluctuation between the vowel signs ֵ, ֶ, and ִ in all but one of the environments (non-final, open, stressed syllables—allophone [e]?) suggests the existence of one *e*-phoneme.

§9l    The following chart shows the frequency of the graphic signs representing /e/ and their correspondence to the Tiberian Biblical Aramaic rules of pointing.[58]

| | Tiberian *ḥireq* | Tiberian *ṣere* | Tiberian *seghol* |
|---|---|---|---|
| **Palestinian Vowel Signs** | | | |
| MS A | ᤛ60x, ᤛ2x | ᤛ83x, ᤛ10x, ᤛ2x | ᤛ1x |
| MS E | ᤛ1x | ᤛ14x, ᤛ1x | |
| MS H | ᤛ1x | | |
| **Tiberian Vowel Signs** | | | |
| MS A | —3x, —5x, —1x | —1x, —6x | —1x |
| MS B | —119x, —13x, —4x | —116x, —34x | —31x |
| MS C | —240x, —73x, —12x | —434x, —19x, —5x | —41x, —8x, —5x |
| MS D | —39x, —8x, —3x | —49x, —19x | —13x |
| MS E | —1x, —1x, —4x | —40x | —2x |
| MS F | —1x, —13x | —41x, —1x | —5x, —1x |
| MS H | —8x | —11x, —1x | |
| MS W | -- | -- | |
| MS Y | -- | -- | |
| MS Z | —4x, —13x, —2x | —27x, —1x | |
| MS AA | —3x, —3x | —27x, —3x | |
| MS HH | —9x | —10x | |

**§10 /i/**

**§10a** The phoneme /i/ in the Cairo Genizah fragments corresponds to the /i/ of Biblical Aramaic, Targum Onqelos, and Syriac which is the reflex of *ī.[59] It is represented by — in Tiberian pointed texts and by ᤛ in Palestinian pointed texts.

**§10b** /i/ occurs in the following environments (with representative examples):

*non-final, open, unstressed syllables*

וּקְטִילָה A Ex 21:36, "and the dead one"; קָטִילָא C Gn 31:39.

*non-final, open, stressed syllables*

־אַקִימֵת C Gn 31:51, "I set up"; מִיתוּ Cd Ex 7:21, "they died." There are no examples with ᤛ.

*final, closed, stressed syllables*

גוּבְרִין A Ex 21:22, "men"; גברין C Gn 32:29.

*final, open, stressed syllables*

חֹבּרֹי A Ex 21:25, "wound";[60] חָבְרֵי A Ex 21:25, "wound."

**§10c** This phoneme is almost always represented in the consonantal text by *yodh*.[61]

**§10d** /i/ is represented by — 240 times in Tiberian pointed texts and by ᤛ 17 times in Palestinian pointed texts. There are only a few examples in which one finds other vowel signs that suggest a realization of /e/:

1. פִּירֵין B Gn 4:16, "fruits."[62]
2. עֲבִידְתְּכְוּן Cd Gn 47:3, "your occupation." The other pointed examples of this word are עֲבִידַת B Ex 39:32,[63] ־עֲבִידְתָּא Cd Gn 44:15, and דַעֲבִדְכְוּן Cd Gn 46:33. The pointing with — suggests that the syllable with *ī was

treated as a closed syllable and *ī > i > /e/. The closing of this syllable is attested also in Tiberian Biblical Aramaic, e.g., עֲבִידְתָּא Dn 2:49.[64] Cf. Targum Onqelos /'əbidətā/ Lv 11:32 (but עִיבִידְתָּא in the *Editio Sabbioneta*).

3. [קָבְלָתְ]הוֹן Cd Ex 6:5, "[their] cry." It appears that here, too, the syllable with *ī was treated as a closed syllable with the shortening of *ī > i > /e/. Cf. Targum Onqelos /qəbilətā/ and Syriac /qəvilθā/ (< /qəvilθā/).[65]

4. וְשֵׁיצֵי Bd Gn 7:23, "and he destroyed" (cf. שֵׁיצֵי Cd Ex 9:25, and וּשֵׁיצִיא Cd Ex 9:25)[66] and וְאֶשְׁתֵּיצִי Bd Gn 7:21, "and it was destroyed."[67] The final phoneme of the Perfect of verbs III-w/y/' in the derived conjugations is always represented by __ in these fragments.[68]

5. משׁרֵיתה AA Nu 19:3 "the camp" (cf. משׁרִיתא AA Nu 19:7).

6. אִילְנֵי B Gn 3:1, "trees of" (cf. אִילָנָא B Gn 3:6).[69]

These few examples are not sufficient to conclude that there was a general shift of *ī > /e/ in these fragments.[70]

§10e     Tiberian *ḥireq* (< *-ī)

Palestinian Vowel Signs

| | |
|---|---|
| MS A | __ 16x |
| MS E | __ 1x |
| MS H | – – |

Tiberian Vowel Signs

| | |
|---|---|
| MS A | – – |
| MS B | __ 66x, __ 3x, __ 1x |
| MS C | __ 187x, __ 2x |
| MS D | __ 10x |
| MS E | __ 6x |
| MS F | __ 13x |
| MS H | __ 6x |
| MS W | __ 1x |
| MS Y | – – |
| MS Z | __ 5x |
| MS AA | __ 14x, __ 1x |
| MS HH | __ 3x |

§11     /o/, /u/

§11a     In Tiberian pointed manuscripts, *o* and *u* appear to be two separate phonemes. /o/ is represented by ו, although in non-final, closed, unstressed syllables it is also represented by __ and ו. /u/ is represented by ו, less frequently by __. In addition to the well-attested fluctuation of vowel signs in non-final, closed, unstressed syllables, there are some pointings in other environments which deviate from the expected Tiberian distribution of *ḥolem* and *shureq/qibbuṣ*.

40

**§11b** In the Palestinian pointed MSS A and E, on the whole, ֹ corresponds to Tiberian *ḥolem* and ֻ corresponds to Tiberian *shureq/qibbuṣ*. The number of exceptional pointings in MS A, however, relative to the total number of pointings in this manuscript is puzzling. Yet there are not enough data in this manuscript to allow one to conclude that *o* and *u* are not distinct phonemes. **§11c** A discussion of the environments in which *o* and *u* occur is presented below, together with a frequency count of each vowel sign in each environment, in addition to the frequency count of vowel signs by manuscript and their correspondence to the Tiberian Biblical Aramaic rules of pointing found at the end of this discussion. Unlike the fluctuation in the graphic representation of the phonemes /a/ and /e/, which is widespread and, on the whole, does not vary significantly in different environments, the fluctuation of the graphic signs representing *o* and *u* is much more limited. In the light of the related Aramaic dialects of Samaritan Aramaic and Palestinian Syriac in which *o* and *u* are positional allophones of one phoneme ([o] in closed syllables, [u] in open syllables), it seems necessary to examine by means of this extra count whether the same phenomenon is found in this dialect. All examples of the fluctuation of *o*- and *u*- vowel signs, except for those well-attested fluctuations in non-final, closed, unstressed syllables, will be listed and analyzed following the discussion of the environments.

/o/ is attested in the following environments:

**§11d** *non-final, closed, unstressed syllables*

Kutscher noted that the majority of vowel signs in this environment were *o*-signs and not *u*-signs and deduced from the examples of non-contrasting minimal pairs that *u > /o/ in this environment.[71] ֹ is the most frequently attested vowel sign in this environment in Tiberian pointed texts. It occurs 70 times, as against 31 occurrences of ו, 11 of ֹו, and 6 of ֻ. Examples of non-contrasting minimal pairs are קָרְבָּנִי B Gn 4:8, "my sacrifice" (cf. קוּרְבָּנֵהּ B Gn 4:8); כָּלָן C Gn 34:22, "all of us" (cf. כּוּלַן C Gn 34:16);[72] בָּאָרְחָא Cd Gn 48:7, "on the way" (cf. ־אוֹרְחֵיהּ C Gn 35:9); חָטְרֵיהּ־ Cd Ex 7:12, "his staff" (cf. חוֹטְרָךְ Cd Ex 7:19); ־גוּבָּא Cd Gn 37:28, "the pit" (cf. בגוּבָּא Cd Gn 37:30) גוּבְרַיָא C Gn 34:22, "the men" (cf. וּגְבְרַיָא Cd Gn 46:32). Other non-contrasting minimal pairs from different manuscripts are וְתָקְפָּךְ C Gn 35:9, "and your power" (cf. תּוֹקְפָּיהּ־ D Dt 5:21); אוּמָא C Gn 35:11, "nation" (cf. ־אוּמָּה D Dt 5:23). The pointings with ו are phonetic spellings; those with ֹ are in imitation of the pointing of this environment in Tiberian Biblical Aramaic.[73] The examples with ֹו, ֻ, however, also appear to be imitating Tiberian Biblical Aramaic pointings: 14 of the 17 occurrences are found in words which are pointed with *shureq/qibbuṣ* in Tiberian Biblical Aramaic—אומא (3x), גובא (4x), גוברין (8x).[74] The three other occurrences are in MS F: כְּלֵיהּ F Ex 19:2, "in its entirety" (is ֻ Targum Onqelos influence or Tiberian Hebrew influence?; cf. Tiberian Biblical Aramaic כָּלְהוֹן); שׁוּבָּה F Ex 20:10, "Sabbath" (cf. Targum Onqelos

/šabbətā/); שׁוּבְעָה F Nu 28:27, "seven" (cf. שְׁבְעָה- B Gn 4:15, but Tiberian Biblical Aramaic שִׁבְעָה).

**§11e** In Palestinian pointed manuscripts, there are seven examples pointed with ⸚ in this environment: קוּרייא A Ex 21:13, "the cities";[75] חוֹטרֵהּ A Ex 21:19, "his staff"; גּוֹבְרִין A Ex 21:22, "men"; בֹּחתוֹרְתהּ A Ex 22:1, "in the breach";[76] אוֹסטְלֵי A Ex 22:8, "garment";[77] רוּגזִי A Ex 22:23, "my anger";[78] שֹׁבעה E Gn 7:2, "seven." ⸜ could represent /a/ or /o/ in the following examples: חקלה A Ex 22:5, "the field";[79] פּדעָא A Ex 21:25, "wound";[80] כוִיֵּיהּ A Ex 21:25, "burn,"[81] כוּתְיֵּיהּ A Ex 21:25, דּוּברָהּ A Ex 22:6, "of the man";[82] בָּחרְבָּה A Ex 22:23, "by the sword."[83] If ⸜ represents /o/ in these examples, the use of this sign reflects Tiberian Biblical Aramaic influence. The following two examples with ⸚ should also be included here: עוֹבֵּהּ A Ex 4:7, "his breast";[84] דְ[גֹ]וּבֵהּ A Ex 21:34, "of the pit." The pointings with a *u*-sign may also result from Tiberian Biblical Aramaic influence.

**§11f** There are a few examples in both the Tiberian and the Palestinian pointed manuscripts in which /o/ might be represented by the signs that normally represent /a/, namely ⸛ and ⸝: בְּעֶבְדָא C Gn 34:21, "by the deed";[85] כָּל- C Gn 34:24, "all"; אַחרִייא A Ex 4:8, "the last";[86] דְאָחֳרֶן A Ex 22:4, "of another";[87] אָ[ו]חֳ[ר]נִין A Ex 22:19, "others." The unusual use of these signs in representing /o/ could follow from the bivalent use of ⸛ and ⸜ to mark both /a/ and /o/. If ⸛ and ⸜ could represent both /a/ and /o/, and if ⸛ and ⸝ represent /a/, the function of ⸛ and ⸝ could also be extended to represent /o/.

**§11g** *non-final open, stressed syllables*

The few pointed examples that are attested in this environment are סׂגֵי- C Gn 32:13, "multitude";[88] עֲבוֹרוּ C Gn 32:17, "pass!";[89] תְּקוֹפוּ C Gn 35:9, "be strong!"; טוֹרוּ D Dt 27:1, "keep!"; טוֹרוּ AA Dt 27:1, "keep!" There are also five pointed examples of the place name "Goshen," e.g., דּגשׁן Cd Gn 46:28.

**§11h** *non-final, open, unstressed syllables*

There are 88 examples in this environment pointed with וֹ, e.g., עוֹפָא- B Gn 2:19, "the fowl"; אוּלֵידְת-Cd Gn 48:6, "you begat"; מָרוֹדִין F Ex 20:5, "rebels." There are 13 examples with ⸚, e.g., וּתוֹרָה A Ex 21:32, "and the ox"; צְלוֹתהּ A Ex 22:22, "his prayer"; מְזוֹנה E Gn 41:48, "the food."

**§11i** *final, closed, stressed syllables*

There are 241 examples pointed with וֹ, e.g., עֵינֵיכוֹן B Gn 3:5, "your eyes" (m.pl.); יִקטוֹל- B Gn 4:14, "he will kill";[90] יָתהוֹן C Gn 35:9, "them." There are 28 examples pointed with ⸚, e.g., תפֹּק A Ex 22:5, "it will go forth"; וּבנֵיכוֹן A Ex 22:23, "and your children"; וּנמֹר E Gn 30:32, "and speckled."

**§11j** *final, open, stressed syllables*

The Tiberian pointed examples are קָרְדוּ Bd Gn 8:4, "Ararat";[91] 11 examples of the preposition /go/, "midst," e.g., בְּגוֹ B Gn 4:12; and 7 examples of the conjunction /'o/, "or," e.g., אוֹ C Gn 31:43. There is only one Palestinian pointed example: צלֹו E Gn 28:17, "prayer."

42

**§11k** /u/ is generally represented by ו in the Tiberian pointed manuscripts;
◌ֻ is rare since /u/ is usually marked by the *mater lectionis waw* in the
consonantal text. The examples with ◌ֻ are בְּתֻחֻמֶּהּ C Gn 34:21, "in her
borders"; וְיֻשְׁרָתֶךְ C Gn 35:9, "and your honesty"; טֻעֲנֻה־ Cd Gn 44:12, "his
load"; טֻעֲנֵיהּ־ Cd Gn 44:11 (cf. טֻעוּנֵיהּ־ Cd Gn 44:11); בְּקַבֻרְתְּהֹן Cd Gn 47:30, "in
their burial place";[92] וְיִתְהַפֻּכָן Cd Ex 7:17, "and they will turn into"; שֻׁוּבָה F Ex
20:10, "Sabbath."

/u/ is attested in the following environments:

**§11l** *non-final, open, unstressed syllables*
There are 51 examples with ו in Tiberian pointed manuscripts, e.g., יְדוּנוּן C
Gn 31:53, "they will judge"; יְמוּתוּן Cd Ex 7:18, "they will die"; ולבושין AA₁ Ex
12:35, "and clothes." There are only three examples pointed with ◌ֻ in
Palestinian pointed manuscripts:[93] רֻבּוֹנהּ A Ex 21:4, "his master"; לרֻבּוֹנהּ A Ex
21:4, לרֻבּוֹנהּ A Ex 21:32.

**§11m** *final, closed, stressed syllables*
There are 85 examples of ו in this environment, e.g., אֲרֻם B Gn 2:23,
"because"; עַמּוּד־ C Gn 32:27, "column"; קְפִידֻּוֹת־ Cd Ex 6:9, "shortness of."
There are four examples with ◌ֻ: יְקֻם A Ex 21:19, "he will arise"; וִיקֻם A Ex
21:21, יְמֻּוֹת A Ex 21:20, "and he will die"; זְבִינֻּוֹת A Ex 21:21, "purchasing of."

**§11n** *final, open, stressed syllables*
There are only seven pointed examples in this environment: סִיבוּ Cd Gn
48:10, "old age";[94] וְיֻ[רֻ]יתוּ Cd Ex 6:8, "inheritance";[95] אָסוּ D Dt 28:27,
"healing"; דמוּ F Ex 20:4, "likeness"; וטבו F Ex 20:6, "and goodness"; דנבו H
Gn 15:1, "of prophecy"; דַּנְבוּ H Gn 15:4.

**§11o** *final, open, unstressed syllables*
There are 59 examples with ו in this environment, e.g., נְפָקוּ־ B Gn 4:8, "they
went out"; וּשְׁפָרוּ C Gn 34:18, "and they were pleasing"; סָבוּ Cd Gn 43:12,
"take!" There are no pointed examples in Palestinian pointed manuscripts.
**§11p** /u/ presumably occurs also in non-final, open, stressed syllables.
There are, however, no pointed examples in this environment. Unpointed
examples are קומו AA₁ Ex 12:31, "arise!"; קומו AA₂ Ex 12:31; פוקו A₁ Ex 12:31,
"go forth!"
**§11q** There are, however, some non-contrasting minimal pairs of words
pointed with both o- and u- vowel signs. There are also certain lexical items
whose pointing deviates from their attested Tiberian Biblical Aramaic
counterparts, as well as from forms which are unattested in Biblical Aramaic
but known from Targum Onqelos, Targum Jonathan to the Former
Prophets, Syriac, Biblical Hebrew, or Rabbinic Hebrew (these traditions do
not always agree with one another).
**§11r** The pointings which appear exceptional are presented according to
noun class and verbal category:
    \**qull* גֹּוּב A Ex 21:33, "pit." Cf. MT לְגוֹב Dn 6:13, but Syriac /gub/.
Other absolute/construct forms of this noun class are attested in the

form כל "all" and are pointed with ־ֶ 36 times and ־ֶ 4 times.[96] One finds a fluctuation of ־ָ, ו, and ־ָ in the determined forms of nouns belonging to this class.[97]

*qūl בְּשׁוּקָה A Ex 21:19, "in the market."[98] Cf. Targum Onqelos and Syriac /šuqā/. There are 15 other pointed examples of *qūl nouns all with u- vowel signs (8 examples when the syllable containing the vowel sign is open and 7 examples when it is closed).

*qatūl בְּתוּלְתֵּה A Ex 22:16, "the virgin(s?)."[99] Cf. Targum Onqelos /bətulātā/ Ex 22:16 (MS i /bətulətā/) and Syriac /bəθultā/ (< /bəθuləθā/). There are 12 other examples with u-vowel signs belonging to this class, all of which occur in open syllables.

qātōl[100] דַּקְטוּלִין Cd Gn 37:22, "of killers." Cf. MT וְכָרוֹזָא Dn 3:4, "and the herald." There are seven other examples of this noun class (three examples when the syllable containing the vowel sign is open, and four examples when it is closed).

*qittūl < *quttūl?[101] The unexpected pointings are סִקּוֹל־ A Ex 21:23, "mishap" (cf. סִקֹל A Ex 21:22); סֶתּוּר B Ex 39:36, "arrangement"; בְּפַלּוּג Cd Gn 44:18, "in the division"; בְּפַלּוּג Cd Gn 48:5 (cf. בְּפִילּוּג Z Gn 44:18); בְּשִׁיגּוּעָה D Dt 28:28, "with madness"; שְׁבֹּחָה E Gn 30:13, "o praise!"; שֵׁרוּיָה E Gn 28:19, "the beginning"; וְאַרְעַ F Nu 28:26, "and a festive meeting." The nouns pointed with the expected ו are נִיסוּכִין C Gn 35:14, "libations";[102] בִּכּוּרֵיכוֹן D Dt 28:17, "your first fruits"; דְּבִכּוּרֵיהּ F Nu 28:26. Note also the three examples of פקוד "command": פִּקּוֹדִין C Gn 35:9; וּפִקּוֹדֵי AA Dt 26:17; פִּקּוֹדֵי AA Dt 26:18. This noun belongs to the qittōl class in the Yemenite manuscripts of Targum Onqelos, e.g., /piqqodohi/ Dt 26:18, but to the qittūl in the Editio Sabbioneta, e.g., פִּקּוֹדוֹהִי Dt 26:18.

*maqtūl? The pointed examples of this noun class are מַבּוּלָה Bd Gn 7:17, "the flood"; דְּמַבּוּלָה Bd Gn 8:2, מַבּוּעֵי Bd Gn 8:2, "the springs of"; מַבּוּעֵיהוֹן, Cd Ex 7:19. Cf. Targum Onqelos /mabbulā/ and /mabbu'ā/, and Syriac /mabbo'ā/.[103]

*šiqtūl < *šaqtūl?[104] The only examples in this noun class are שִׁעְבְּדְהוֹן־ Cd Ex 6:7, "their enslavement"; שעבוד F Ex 20:2. Cf. Targum Onqelos /ši'budā/ and Rabbinic Hebrew /ši'bud/.

*taqtūl? The only examples in this noun class are תַשְׁלוֹמֵי A Ex 21:23, "as payment for"; תַשְׁלוֹמֵי A Ex 21:24; תַשְׁלוֹמֵיn A Ex 21:25. Cf. Targum Jonathan /tašlumətā/ 2 Sa 19:37, Rabbinic Hebrew /tašlum/.

§11s Note the unexpected pointings in the following loanwords:[105]
Hebrew: סוּלֶת F Nu 28:28, "fine flour" and סלת F Lv 23:17. Cf. Targum Onqelos /solat/ Ex 29:2, but /sultā/ Gn 18:6.
Akkadian?[106] וְשׁוֹשְׁפָא Cd Gn 38:25, "and the cloak" and וְשִׁוְשַׁפָּךְ Cd Gn 38:18. Cf. Targum Onqelos /šošippāk/ Gn 38:18, but Syriac /šušeppā/.

*Persian* דְסַעְסָגּונִין B Ex 39:34, "multicolored."[107] Cf. Targum Onqelos /sasgonā/ Nu 4:6 and Syriac /sasgawnā/.

*cultural loanword:* וּלטוֹם E Gn 37:25, "and ladanum;[108] וּלטוֹם Cd Gn 37:25; וּלטוֹם Cd Gn 43:11. Cf. Targum Onqelos /lɔṭom/ Gn 37:25.

§11t   There is fluctuation in the following verbal categories:

*Perfect 2 m.pl.*   There is one example pointed with a *u*- sign: וּקְרַבְתּוּן D Dt 5:20, "and you drew near"; all other examples have *o*- vowel signs: הַעֲבָדְתּוֹן Cd Gn 44:5, "which you did"; אַפְּקְתּוֹן־ Cd Ex 5:21, "you brought out"; וַאֲמַרְתּוֹן D Dt 5:21, "and you said"; אֶתְחַשַּׁבְתּוֹן D Dt 27:9, "you were considered"; אעלתון AA Nu 20:4, "you brought up"; אֲעֶלְתּוֹן AA Nu 20:5; אמלכתון AA Dt 26:17, "you enthroned." There is only one example of a verb III-w/y/': הֲוֵיתוֹן A Ex 22:20, "you were."

*Perfect 3 m.pl. (verbs III-w/y/')*   There is one example with a *u*- vowel sign: אֶתְגְּלוּ C Gn 35:7, "they revealed themselves." There are 29 other examples with *o*- vowel signs, e.g., וְאֶתְכַּסּוֹן Bd Gn 7:19, "and they were covered."

*Imperfect 2 m.pl. and 3 m.pl.*   There are three examples in this category with *o*- vowel signs: יֶתְמַנְעוֹן Cd Ex 9:29, "they will be held back"; ותחתון E Gn 42:38, "and you will bring down"; ויסבון AA Nu 19:17, "and they will take." There are 40 examples of this morpheme pointed with *u*- vowel signs, e.g., תשפכוּן Cd Gn 37:22, "you will pour out." In verbs III-w/y/', on the other hand, only *o*- vowel signs are attested, e.g., וְיֶהֱוֹן Cd Ex 7:19, "and they will be."

§11u   Do these exceptional pointings indicate that *o* and *u* were not phonemes but rather allophones of one phoneme? Do these few examples reflect a situation parallel to that in Samaritan Aramaic and Palestinian Syriac where *o* and *u* merged and were then redistributed as positional allophones—[o] in closed syllables and [u] in open syllables? The data do not seem to support such a conclusion. The exceptional pointings in the Cairo Genizah fragments are not related to open or closed syllables.

§11v   Note, for example, the pointed occurrences of רבון "master."[109] All pointings of this word are with *u*-vowel signs. A *u*-vowel sign occurs five times in a final, closed, stressed syllable, e.g., רְבֻּן Cd Gn 38:25, and seven times in a non-final, open, unstressed syllable, e.g., רַבּוּנִי Cd Gn 44:18.[110] If *o* and *u* were positional allophones in these fragments, because this word is unattested in Tiberian Biblical Aramaic, one would have expected some phonetic spellings since the vocalizers would not have been bound by the Biblical tradition.

§11w   It appears that the examples in which one finds *o* for expected *u* in the nominal system all occur in the environment of either a guttural, a liquid (/r/ or /l/), or /q/. A parallel sporadic shift of *u* >*o* before gutturals is attested in Eastern Syriac,[111] and more significantly, in Arabic dialects, since one may safely assume that the vocalizers of these fragments spoke Arabic.[112]

§11x  It must, however, be added that morphological conditioning may also be a reason for some of the pointings with *o* in the nominal forms. It is possible that a mixing of noun classes is partially responsible. The examples of /qettol/ nouns, which are usually assigned to the *qittūl class, suggest a merger of *qittūl and *qittul (> *qittol) nouns. Cf., e.g., /piqqod/ in the Yemenite manuscripts of Targum Onqelos as against פִּקּוּד in the *Editio Sabbioneta* (due to Tiberian Hebrew influence?) and in Tiberian Hebrew. It is possible that a merger of these two classes was initiated by a sporadic shift of *u* > *o* before certain consonants. The pointings with *u*-vowel signs found in these fragments (e.g., בְּכוּרֵיכָן) might reflect the influence of the /qittul/ form of Biblical Hebrew and Rabbinic Hebrew (/qittul/ is not attested in Biblical Aramaic).

As regards the /maqtol/, /šeqtol/, and /taqtol/ forms, it is also possible that morphological factors are partially responsible. One cannot be certain whether these forms are reflexes of *maqtul, *šiqtul, *taqtul or *maqtūl, *šiqtūl, *taqtūl, or if these classes have merged. Cf. Targum Onqelos /mabbu'/ "spring" (< *manbū'), but Eastern Syriac /mabbo'/(< *manbu'?); Tiberian Biblical Hebrew מַפֻּחַ "bellows" (< *manpūḥ?) and מִקְצָעוֹת "woodscrapers?" (< *maqṣū'), but Rabbinic Hebrew מַפּוּחַ (< *manpuḥ?) and מַקְצוּעוֹת (< *maqṣu'?).[113]

§11y  The exceptional pointings in the verbal system suggest morphological conditioning. In the Perfect 2 m.pl. of strong verbs, the one pointing with *u*, וּקְרַבְתּוּן, appears to reflect the pointing of this morpheme in Tiberian Biblical Aramaic,[114] whereas the pointings with *o*-vowel signs seem to be phonetic spellings. In the case of the Imperfect 2 m.pl. and 3 m.pl. forms וּתְחַתוּן, יְתַמְנְעוּן, וְיֵסֹון, the fact that these three examples with *on* in place of *un* occur in weak verbs suggests that this morpheme was extended from verbs III-w/y/', e.g., /hawon/, "they were," or /tehwon/, "you will be." The pointing of אֶתְגְּלֹון was certainly transferred from the pl. morpheme /-un/ of the strong verb.

§11z  The following charts the frequency of vowels in the different manuscripts that correspond to the Tiberian Biblical Aramaic rules of pointing.[115]

|  | Tiberian *ḥolem* | Tiberian *qameṣ qaṭan* | Tiberian *shureq/qibbuṣ* |
|---|---|---|---|
| Palestinian Vowel Signs | | | |
| MS A | ֹ 15x | ֻ 4x? ֻ 3x? | ֻ 17x |
| MS E | ֹ 16x | - - | ֻ 1x |
| MS H | - - | - - | - - |
| Tiberian Vowel Signs | | | |
| MS A | ו 1x | ָ 1x | ו 2x |
| MS B | ו 79x | ָ 17x, ו 2x | ו 48x |
| MS C | ו 215x | ָ 36x, ו 5x, ֻ 2x? | ו 167x ֻ 9x |
| MS D | ו 72x | ָ 8x, ו 2x | ו 21x |
| MS E | | ָ | ו 1x |

| | | | |
|---|---|---|---|
| MS F | ׀ 25x | ֫ 2x | ׀ 8x, — 2x |
| MS H | ׀ 2x | ֫ 1x | ׀ 4x |
| MS W | - - | - - | - - |
| MS Y | - - | - - | - - |
| MS Z | ׀ 11x | ׀ 5x | ׀ 7x |
| MS AA | ׀ 27x | ׀ 3x | ׀ 8x |
| MS HH | ׀ 3x | ֫ 1x | ׀ 2x |

§12 /ə/ (Reduced vowel)

§12a  In MS A, ֒ is the most frequent graphic sign with non-gutturals that corresponds to the Tiberian *shewa mobile*. Representative examples are גֹּבֹר A Ex 21:26; "man"; יֹזֹבֹן A Ex 21:37; "he will sell"; דֹּגֹבֹרֹה A Ex 22:6, "of the man"; יֹשֹׁלֹם A Ex 22:14, "he will pay"; צֹלֹוֹתֹה A Ex 22:22, "his prayer." Other vowel signs with non-gutturals in MS A corresponding to *shewa mobile* are ֒: מֹמֹשֹׁכֹנֹה A Ex 22:25 "taking as a pledge"; and ֒: יֹקוֹם A Ex 21:19; "he will arise";[116] שֹׁפֹּר A Ex 22:4; "the best of."[117] In the infrequently pointed MSS E and H, one finds the following examples with non-gutturals: ֒ in בֹּגֹין E Gn 38:26, "on account of"; דֹחֹלֹמֹה E Gn 40:12; "of the dream"; תֹּשֹׁע H Gn 15:1, "nine."

§12b  There are not many pointed examples with gutturals corresponding to Tiberian *hateph* vowels. The examples are ֒ in אֹגֹרֹה A Ex 21:19, "wage of"; וֹאֹגֹר A Ex 21:19; "and the wage of"; הֹוֹיֹתֹן A Ex 22:20, "you were"; חֹשֹׁבֹן H Gn 15:1, "he thought";[118] ֒ in וֹידֹחֹפֹן A Ex 21:22; "and they will push"; חֹקֹל A Ex 22:4, "a field"; and ֒ in אֹמֹתֹה A Ex 21:26, "his handmaiden."

§12c  There is also, however, another sign in MS A (found once in MS E) corresponding to the Tiberian reduced vowel, ֓, which occurs with both non-gutturals and gutturals. The examples correspond to 1) initial *shewa mobile:* יֹזֹד A Ex 21:14, "he will harm"; קֹנֹס A Ex 21:30, "fine, penalty"; קֹטֹילֹה A Ex 21:35, "dead"; יֹקֹידֹתֹה A Ex 22:4; "his burning"; נֹשֹׁיכֹון A Ex 22:23, "your wives"; 2) initial *hateph pathah:* עֹבֹד A Ex 21:2; "slave"; 3) initial *hateph qames:* קֹדֹמֹיי A Ex 22:26; "before me"; 4) medial *shewa mobile:*[119] יֹהֹיֹמֹנֹון A Ex 4:8, "they will believe"; בֹמֹרֹצֹעֹה A Ex 21:6, "with the awl"; יֹתֹקֹנֹס A Ex 21:20, "he will be punished"; יֹתֹקֹנֹס A Ex 21:21; מֹתֹקֹנֹסֹה A Ex 21:22; "being punished"; אֹוֹסֹטֹלֹי A Ex 22:8, "garment"; יֹתֹקֹטֹל A Ex 22:12, "he will be killed"; בֹּאֹפֹסֹדֹה A Ex 22:14; "in his loss";[120] מֹתֹקֹטֹילֹה A Ex 22:18; "being killed"; אֹרֹמֹלֹן A Ex 22:23, "widows"; 5) medial *hateph pathah:* לֹאֹבֹן A Ex 21:18, "by a stone";[121] יֹתֹאֹכֹל A Ex 21:28; "it will be eaten"; יֹתֹעֹבֹד A Ex 21:31, "it will be done"; תֹּדֹחֹקֹן A Ex 22:20, "you will push"; יֹאֹקֹטֹל A Ex 22:23, "and I shall kill." ֓ is also used in these fragments to mark gemination and the plosive pronunciation of /bgdkpt/.[122] Because of the multivalence of the sign, one cannot be certain whether ֓ was intended to mark a reduced vowel and/or gemination in the following examples: תֹּסֹבֹון A Ex 21:14, "you will take"; מֹעֹבֹרֹה A Ex 21:22, "pregnant"; יֹפֹקֹן A Ex 21:22; "and they will go forth"; דֹאֹתֹתֹה A Ex 21:22, "of the woman"; יֹפֹלֹגֹון A Ex 21:35; "they will divide"; גְנֻבָּתַהּ A Ex 22:3, "the theft";[123] דּבעֹמֹכֹן A Ex 22:24, "of your people"; תעבּרת E Gn 38:18, "and she conceived." Similarly, one cannot be certain whether ⳥ was intended to mark a reduced vowel and/or the plosive pronunciation of /bgdkpt/ in the following examples: בֹּנֵי A Ex 21:5, "my sons"; וִישֹתֹבַּח A Ex 21:16, "and it will be found"; בֹעִיר A Ex 22:18, "cattle"; ]וִישֹתֹבִּי[ A Ex 22:9, "he is taken captive." ⳥ in בֹּדִיפֹלֹה A Ex 22:3, "double" may have been intended to mark only one or any combination of the following: reduced vowel, plosive pronunciation of /p/, gemination.[124]

§12d The preponderant use of ⳥ in MS A where one finds Tiberian reduced vowels and its relation to the use of the sign ⳥ raises questions. Did the reduced vowels merge with the phoneme /e/? Was there a reduced vowel in these positions whose realization came closest to that of /e/? Or was the use of the sign ⳥ a completely arbitrary choice on the part of the vocalizers, who adopted it as a scribal convention? In the light of the examples in which both ⳥ and ⳥ occur with the same consonant, it seems that ⳥ in this position was realized as a reduced vowel and not as a full vowel.[125] And what of the relationship between ⳥ and ⳥? It appears that these two signs do not interchange freely in all environments. ⳥ corresponding to a reduced vowel occurs only in initial syllables where it interchanges with ⳥. A non-contrasting minimal pair may be בֹעִיר A Ex 22:9, "cattle" and בֹעִיר A Ex 22:18 (although ⳥ may have been intended to mark the plosive pronunciation of /b/). ⳥ is not attested with the prefixed particles /bV-/, /kV-/, /lV-/, or /dV-/. This may, however, be coincidental. ⳥ alone occurs medially.[126]

§12e In Palestinian pointed Hebrew manuscripts, ⳥ and ⳥ usually correspond to *shewa mobile*.[127] The use of ⳥ in the Cairo Genizah fragments agrees with that practice and suggests that the vocalizers realized the reduced vowel as [ĕ] (the reduced vowel appears to have been realized as [ă] in Tiberian pointed mss). The use of ⳥ in these fragments, however, is unattested in Palestinian pointed Hebrew manuscripts.[128] It seems to be a deliberate attempt to imitate the Tiberian use of a special sign to mark the reduced vowel, perhaps because ⳥ was bivalent and could represent both a full vowel and a reduced vowel.

§12f In the Tiberian pointed manuscripts, one finds ⳥ with non-gutturals where *shewa mobile* is expected, e.g., לְכֹן C Gn 34:9, "to you." The many examples demonstrate that there was a reduced vowel in these manuscripts. There are, however, a few examples with ⳥ in MS C (2% of the examples in this manuscript), as well as one in MS F and three in MS HH, which hint that this reduced vowel was realized as [ă]. The examples[129] are יְתֹמַנֻן C Gn 32:13, "they will be counted"; מִינֹקן C Gn 32:16, "nursing"; וֹאֹסֹתֹלֹקֹת C Gn 35:13, "it went away";[130] בֹּרֹיֹה C Gn 34:24, "his son" (cf. בֹּרֹיֹה C Gn 34:20); עֹזֹקֹתֹן Cd Gn 38:18, "your signet ring" (cf. עֹזֹקֹתֹא Cd Gn 38:25); וֹבֹרֹכֹתֹא C Gn 35:9, "and the blessing"; וֹאֹתֹרֹכֹין Cd Gn 46:29, "and he bent down"; וֹאֹתֹכֹּנֹיֹשֹ Cd Gn 47:30, "he was gathered"; וֹאֹמֹרֹין Cd Gn 47:3, "saying"; אֹתֹיֹלֹדֹו Cd Gn 48:5, "they were born"; בְּמִדְבְּרָא Cd Ex 7:16, "in the desert"; בְּמִשְׁמַעֵיהּ Cd Gn 44:18, "in his hearing"; וְאִתְמְנַעוּ Cd Ex 9:33, "they were held back"; שְׂמָאלֵיהּ F Ex 20:2, "his left hand";[131] וִישְׁתְּכַח Cd Gn 44:9, "he will be found"; לְמִנְיָן HH Ex 12:2, "number"; יִתְמְנֵה HH Ex 12:2, "he will be counted"; וִיסַבוּן HH Ex 12:3, "they will take." There are four examples with ָ: דַּמְהַלְכָה Cd Gn 32:21, "which goes";[132] וְיָכִלְתָּ C Gn 32:29,ׂ "you were able";[133] וברֻכָתֵיהּ Z Gn 48:20, "his blessing": שְׁמַיָּא H Gn 15:1, "the heavens."[134] Note that these exceptional pointings do not occur in the sequence $C\bar{V}C\partial C$. One also finds the unique pointings: 1) ָ, in וְקִירוּשָׁא C Gn 31:40, "and the frost"; [135] דִּינְפַלוּ H Gn 15:1, "that they fell"; 2) ָ, in בְּרַעֲוָה B Gn 4:8, "with pleasure" (cf. בְּרַעֲוָה B Gn 4:8); מְקַבְּלָא Cd Gn 44:18, "receive"; 3) ָ, in כְּדֵין Z Gn 44:19, "so, thus.'

**§12g** One usually finds ֳ in the Tiberian pointed manuscripts where *haṭeph pathaḥ* is expected.[136] There are, however, many examples with ֲ. In MS C, e.g., the ratio of ֳ to ֲ is 1.4:1. Representative examples are אֲרוּם ֿ B Gn 4:12, "because" (cf.- אֲרוּם B Gn 3:6); עֲלִי C Gn 34:12,ׂ"upon me"; דַּאֲבֶן C Gn 35:14, "of stone"; אֲנָא ֿ Cd Gn 38:25, "I" (cf. אֲנָא ֿ Cd Gn 38:25); אֲתַר Cd Gn 46:28, "place of"; חֲמֵית Cd Gn 46:30, "I saw"; אֲבוּךְ Cd Gn 47:5, "your father"; עֲלַלְתַּהּ Cd Gn 48:7, "her harvest";[137] תֶּרְחֲלוּן Cd Ex 9:30, "you will fear"; הֲוֵית E Gn 40:13, "I was"; אֲרוּם F Ex 19:5, "because"; הֲוָה H Gn 15:1, "he was"; עֲלִי H Gn 15:1, "upon me"; אֲהָרֹן HH Ex 12:1, "Aaron"; אֲבָהָתֵהּ HH Ex 12:3,ׂ"his fathers." Occasionally one finds ֲ in place of ֳ.[138] The examples are חֲקַל A Ex 22:4, "field"; עֲבֶד A Ex 21:32, "servant";[139] תִּיצְעֲרוּן A Ex 22:20,ׂ "you will trouble";[140] תִּצְעֲרוּן A Ex 22:21; תִּצְעֲרוּן A Ex 22:22; הֲוֵית C Gn 31:39, "I was"; אֲמַר D Dt 5:25, "he said"; אֲרַבָּה E Gn 30:3, "I shall raise";[141] אֲתָה E Gn 30:11, "he came"; חֲכַם E Gn 39:8, "he knew"; עֲבֵד E Gn 41:12, "servant"; עֲלֶיךָ E Gn 43:29,ׂ"upon you."[142] There is one example in which one finds ֲ: אֲנָה Cd Gn 46:30 (cf.- אֲנָא Cd Gn 38:25; אֲנָא ֿ Cd Gn 38:25); one example with ֲ: אֲלַע] B Gn 2:21,ׂ "rib"; and one example with ֲ: וְחֶסַד- C Gn 34:11,ׂ "and grace" (cf. חֲסַד F Ex 20:6).

**§12h** Three different vowel signs are attested where one expects Tiberian Biblical Aramaic *ḥaṭeph seghol*:[143] 1) ֱ: חֱמִי C Gn 31:50,ׂ "see!";[144] אֱלָהֵיהּ C Gn 31:53, "his God"; אֱמַר Cd Ex 7:19, "say!";[145] 2) ֶ: אֶתָא B Gn 4:8,ׂ "come!";[146] אֶתָא C Gn 31:44, "come!"; אֶנָשׁ- Cd Gn 38:26,ׂ"man";[147] אֶלָהּ Cd Gn 48:3, "God"; אֶלָהַן D Dt 5:21, "our God"; אֱלָהּ F Ex 20:3, "God"; אֶלָהְכוֹן F Ex 20:10, "your God"; תֶּהֱווֹן F Nu 28:29,ׂ"you will be";[148] חֱמִי Cd Gn 41:41, "see!"; 3) ֵ:[149] אֵלָהֵיהּ C Gn 31:42, "his God"; אֵלָהֵיהּ ֿ C Gn 35:9, "his God"; אֵלָהְכוֹן Cd Gn 43:23, "your God"; אֵלָהְהוֹן Cd Ex 7:16, "their God"; אֵלָהָן Cd Ex 9:30, "our God"; אֵלָהָן D Dt 5:24, "our God"; אֵלָהְכוֹן D Dt 27:2, "your God"; אֵלָהְכוֹן] D Dt 27:3;ׂ אֵלָהְכוֹן D Dt 27:7; אֵלָהְכוֹן D Dt 27:9; אֵלָהְהוֹן ֿ D Dt 28:15.

**§12i** According to the Tiberian Biblical Aramaic rules of pointing, one expects a *ḥaṭeph qameṣ* in the words[150] אָחֳרָן "another"[151] and קֳדָם "before." One finds, however, five different vowel signs: 1) ֳ: אָחֳרָנַיָּין] Z Gn 49:2; קֳדַם- B Gn 3:5; קֳדָמַי B Gn 4:10; קֳדַם B Gn 4:13; קֳדָמַיךְ- B Gn 4:13;ׂ קֳדָמַיךְ ֿ B Gn 4:14;ׂ

קָדָמַי C Gn 34:21; קָדָמְהוֹן C Gn 34:11; קָדָמְכוֹן C Gn 34:10; קָדְמֵיכוֹן C Gn 34:10; קְדָמִי -B Gn 4:16;
D Dt 5:25; קָדָמַי- D Dt 5:26; קָדָם D Dt 27:7; 2) וּ: -קֳדָם C Gn 31:42; קֳדָם- Cd Gn
38:25; קֳדָם- Cd Gn 44:18; קֳדָם C Gn 48:20; קוֹדָם AA Dt 27:7; קֳדְמַי H Gn 15:1; 3)
-ָ: אָחֳרָא C Gn 43:14; קֳדָמָיך Cd Gn 44:18; קֳדָמַי Cd Ex 7:16; קֳדָמַי F Nu 28:29; 4)
-ָ: קֳדָמַי C Gn 32:17; -קֳדָמָך C Gn 32:18; אָחֳרן F Ex 20:3; קוֹדם F Ex 20:10; קוֹדם F
Nu 28:26.[152] 5) -ָ: אוֹחֳרן C Gn 31:50. In addition, although unattested in
Biblical Aramaic, one expects to find חֳלַף "instead"[153] and עֳבַד "deed"[154]
according to Tiberian Biblical Aramaic rules of pointing. Cf., however, חֳלַף B
Gn 3:1 (but 7x unpointed written *plene*, e.g., חולף A Ex 21:27), and עבד
pointed with five different vowel signs: 1) -ָ: עֳבָדֵיך B Gn 4:7; עֳבָדִי B Gn 4:8;[155]
עֳבַד B Ex 39:29; 2) וּ: עוֹבָדֵיך B Gn 4:7; עוֹבָדֵין B Gn 4:8; עֳבָדֵיך H Gn 15:1; 3) -ָ:
בַעֳבָדֵיך Z Gn 49:4; 4) -ָ: בַּעֳבָדָא C Gn 34:21; 5) -ָ: וּבָעֳבַד Z Gn 48:22.

§12j    The fluctuation of vowel signs where one expects *ḥateph seghol* and
*ḥateph qameṣ* probably reflects a lack of scribal skill due to the low frequency
of these two vowel signs in Tiberian Biblical Aramaic. The many examples
with — and the fluctuation with o- and e- vowel signs suggest that these two
vowels were realized as the reduced vowels [ĕ] and [ŏ].

§12k    There is a significant number of examples of — preceding *yodh*, as well
as a few with *yodh* where one expects a *shewa mobile*. These pointings suggest
that the *shewa mobile* was realized as [ĭ] in these environments. The examples
before *yodh* are קְיָם C Gn 31:44, "covenant"; בְּיוֹמָא C Gn 34:25, "on the day";
מְרַבְּיָנִיתַהּ C Gn 35:9, "her nurse" (cf. מְרַבְּיָנִיתַהּ C Gn 35:8); -אַיְתֵיתִיהּ C Gn
31:39, "I brought"; אֶתְנְיֵהּ C Gn 35:9, "he rested";[156] מְפַרְסְיָא- Cd Gn 38:25,
"make known";[157] דְּיוֹסֵף Cd Gn 48:8, "of Joseph" (cf. -דְּיוֹסֵף- Cd Gn 38:26);
בְּיָמִינֵיהּ Cd Gn 48:13, "with his right hand"; וְיָת Cd Ex 9:25 (cf. -וְיָת C Gn
31:39, and -וְיַת C Gn 31:42); -קְיָמוֹי D Dt 27:10, "his laws" (cf. וּקְיָמוֹי D Dt
28:15); קְיָמַי Cd Gn 47:29, "my covenant"; בְּיוֹמָה D Dt 27:11, "on the day" (cf.
בְּיוֹמַה D Dt 27:2); וְיֵתְיָן D Dt 28:15, "and they will come" (f.pl.); וְיָאיֵין E Gn
41:18, "and pleasant" (m.pl.); וּבִיצִיבַהּ AA₁ Ex 12:19, "and of her citizens"[158]
לְסוּסִיהּ Z Gn 49:17, "horse." The examples with *yodh* are קַיְימָא C Gn 31:45,
"pillar"; -בָּיְישִׁיָּא C Gn 35:9, "the sick" (m.pl.); קַיְימָא C Gn 35:14, "pillar" (cf.
קַיְימָא C Gn 35:14). There are also five examples in which *Cəyi > Ciyi > /Ci/*.[159]
§12l    One also finds — preceding *yodh* where one expects a *ḥateph pathaḥ*:
-לְזַרְעִית Cd Gn 48:4, "to the families of" and -זַרְעִיַּת Cd Gn 48:11. Cf. Targum
Onqelos זֻרְעִיֹן (Gn 4:10 = Tiberian זַרְעֶיךָ).

§12m    Finally, note the correspondences between the Palestinian signs
marking *shewa mobile* and those of the Tiberian system as seen in the few
examples in which words are pointed with signs from both systems:

*non-gutturals* (֞ = —): קְנָס A Ex 21:31, "fine, penalty"; גְּנֵבְתָּהּ A Ex 22:3,
"the theft"; בְּאַבְסְדֵהּ A Ex 22:14 "in his loss";[160] נְשֵׁיכוֹן A Ex 22:23, "your
wives."

*non-gutturals* (֞ = —): כְּסַף A Ex 21:34,[161] "silver"; גְּנֵבְתָּהּ A Ex 22:3,
"the theft"; וְיִגְנְבוּן A Ex 22:6, "and they will steal"; בְּאַבְסְדֵהּ A Ex 22:14,
"in his loss."

*gutturals* ($\dot{-} = \_$): עֶבֶד A Ex 21:32, "servant."
*gutturals* ($\dot{-} = \_$): חֲקַל A Ex 22:4, "field."
*gutturals* ($\dot{-} = \_$): חֲשַׁב H Gn 15:1, "he thought."[162]

**§12n** The following chart shows the frequency of vowel signs which correspond to the Tiberian *shewa mobile* and to the Tiberian *hateph* vowels:

| | Tiberian shewa mobile | Tiberian hateph pathah | Tiberian hateph seghol | Tiberian hateph qames |
|---|---|---|---|---|
| | Palestinian Vowel Signs | | | |
| A | ⸴70x, ⸴17x, ⸴1x | ⸴5x, ⸴3x, ⸴2x | | |
| | ⸴2x | ⸴1x | | |
| E | ⸴2x | | | |
| H | ⸴1x, ⸴1x | ⸴1x | | |
| | Tiberian Vowel Signs | | | |
| A | _15x | _5x | | |
| B | _246x, _1x, _1x | _58x, _2x, _1x, _2x, _1x | | _9x, _2x |
| C | _433x, _13x, _2x | _168x, _82x | _8x, _5x, _3x _4x, _3x, _3x | |
| | _1x | _1x, _1x, _1x | | _2x, _1x, _1x |
| D | _77x | _21x, _1x | _7x, _1x | _3x |
| E | _9x, | _5x, _2x | – – | – – |
| F | _42x, _1x | _14x, _1x | _2x | |
| H | _1x, _1x | _6x, _4x | | _3x, _1x _2x |
| W | – – | | | |
| Y | – – | | | |
| Z | _26x, _1x, _1x | _5x | | _2x, _1x |
| AA | _3x | | | |
| HH | _10x, _3x | _2x | | |

Tiberian *shewa mobile* before *yodh*: MS A: ⸴7x, _1x; MS B: _18x; MS C: _44x, _10x; MS D: _7x, _3x; MS E: _2x, _1x; MS F: _2x; MS Z: _1x, _1x; MS AA: _1x, _1x; MS HH _1x.
Tiberian *shewa mobile* with *yodh*: MS C: _7x, _3x; MS D: _4x; MS F: _1x; MS H: _1x; MS AA: _1x.

**§13 *Zero Vowel***

**§13a** The zero vowel (represented by *shewa quiescens* in Tiberian Biblical Aramaic) is unmarked in the Palestinian pointed fragments, e.g., לתרֵע A Ex 21:6, "to the door of"; חוטרה A Ex 21:19, "his staff"; ותשׁכֹח A Ex 22:5, "and it will find." There is, however, one example in which one finds a vowel sign where a zero vowel is expected: אעֱבֹד E Gn 39:9, "I shall do."[163]

**§13b** In Tiberian pointed manuscripts, the zero vowel is regularly represented by _. There is one example in which one finds _ where _ is expected: בְּמִגְזַר C Gn 34:15, "in circumcising" (cf. בְּמִגְזַר C Gn 34:22) and one example in which _ occurs: בְּשַׁבְעַת־עֶשְׂרֵ Bd Gn 8:4, "on the seventeenth." It is noteworthy that one finds _ with gutturals in forms of the Imperfect and Infinitive where Tiberian Biblical Aramaic shows a fluctuation of *shewa* *quiescens* and *ḥateph* vowels.[164] There are 55 examples of ‗ with gutturals, e.g., יֶהְוֵי B Gn 4:12, "he will be"; לְמֶחְמֵי Bd Gn 8:8, "to see"; אֶעְבֵּיד־ C Gn 31:43, "I shall do"; יֵעְנֵי E Gn 41:16, "he will answer." The only exceptional verbal pointing is תֶהֱוֹן F Nu 28:29ˆ (cf. וְתֶהֱוֹן D Dt 28:29).[165] In nouns, on the other hand, both ‗ and *ḥateph* vowels are found with gutturals as in Tiberian Biblical Aramaic.[166] ‗, however, is the more frequent sign. There are 29 examples with ‗ and 14 examples with ‗. Note the following pairs: בְּרַעְוָה B Gn 4:8, "with pleasure" and דְּרַעֲוָה F Nu 28:27; וַאֲחֳסָנָה Cd Gn 48:5, "and an inheritance" and וְאַחְסָנָה Cd Gn 44:18; וּשְׂעָבָה E Gn 37:25,[167] "and balsam" and שְׂעֲבָא Cd Gn 37:25. Other representative examples with ‗ are דְּרַחֲמִין B Gn 4:8, "of mercy"; בְּסַעֲדִּי C Gn 31:42, "to my aid"; נַחְלָא־ C Gn 32:24, "the wadi"; שַׁחְרָא־ C Gn 32:27, "the dawn." Other representative examples with ‗ are צַעֲרַהּ־ C Gn 35:9, "her pain"; בְּנַהֲרָא Cd Ex 7:17, "in the river"; לַהֲבֵי־ D Dt 5:19, "the flames of."

**s13c** There is one noun in which one expects a *ḥateph qameṣ* according to the rules of Tiberian Biblical Aramaic (for Proto-Aramaic zero vowel):[168] אָחֳרָן (cf. Dn 2:44); however, one does not find a zero vowel sign *(shewa quiescens)* with any of the pointed examples.[169]

**s13d** Infrequently one finds ‗ apparently representing a zero vowel in sequences involving gutturals in which, according to the Tiberian Rule of Shewa, one expects either ‗[170] or ‗[171].

**s13e** For a possible example of ‗ involving a sequence of non-gutturals, where, according to the Tiberian Rule of *Shewa*, one expects ‗, see s33j.

**s13f** The following chart shows the frequency of vowel signs with non-gutturals which correspond to the Tiberian *shewa quiescens*, as well as the frequency of vowel signs with gutturals where a Tiberian *shewa quiescens* might have been expected:

| | non-gutturals | gutturals |
|---|---|---|
| | (Tiberian *shewa quiescens*) | |
| Palestinian pointed manuscripts | no marking of zero vowel (MS C ‗ 1x?) | no marking of zero vowel (MS E ‗ 1x?) |
| Tiberian pointed manuscripts | | |
| MS A | ‗23x | |
| MS B | ‗140x, ‗1x | ‗25x |
| MS C | ‗29x, ‗1x | ‗44x, ‗12x, ‗ 1x, ‗ 1x |
| MS D | ‗43x | ‗16x, ‗2x |
| MS E | ‗21x | ‗2x |
| MS F | ‗30x | ‗2x, ‗1x, ‗1x |
| MS H | ‗13x | ‗- |
| MS W | - - | - - |
| MS Y | - - | - - |
| MS Z | ‗25x | ‗1x, ‗1x |

52

MS AA   —1x            - -

MS HH   —9x            - -

**§14**   *Vocalic Phonemes—Historical and Comparative Discussion*

**§14a**   The vocalic inventory of the Cairo Genizah fragments should be viewed in the light of the vocalic inventories of other Aramaic dialects from the Syria-Palestine region. Some of the features of the vocalic system are shared by other dialects in the area and may represent either a common heritage from one parent tongue or the influence of geographically neighboring dialects. Just as important in understanding the background of the Cairo Genizah fragments are the different Jewish Targumim as well as the different traditions of Hebrew that stem from this area. The following dialects and traditions are included in this discussion: the Jewish Targumim: Targum Onqelos, Targum Pseudo-Jonathan, the Fragment Targum, Targum Neophyti; Syriac; the Western Aramaic dialects of Galilean Aramaic, Palestinian Syriac, Samaritan Aramaic, Ma'lula; the traditional pronunciations of Hebrew: Palestinian, Pre-Ashkenazi, Sephardi, Tiberian, and transliterations in Greek and Latin. For the sake of comparison, reference will also be made to the Babylonian traditions of Hebrew and Aramaic. A sketch of the different vocalic systems has been included in order to present a more complete picture of the features common to the Cairo Genizah fragments and the other Aramaic dialects and Hebrew traditions.

*Jewish Targumim: Onqelos, Pseudo-Jonathan, Fragment Targum, Neophyti*

**§14b**   The vocalic inventory of Targum Onqelos as reflected in supra-linear pointed manuscripts is /ā/, /a/, /i/, /e/, /o/, /u/, and /ə/.[172]

**§14c**   In discussing the vocalic inventories of Targum Pseudo-Jonathan and the Fragment Targum, one must clearly distinguish between the pointings found in the printed editions of these Targumim and the little knowledge that can be gleaned from the consonantal text of manuscripts.

The pointings found in printed editions are inconsistent and hence of little use.[173] The redactors of these editions were not familiar with the Aramaic dialect in which the Targumim were written. Instead, they attempted to point the texts according to the dialects with which they were familiar, namely Biblical Aramaic and Targum Onqelos. There is also evidence of the application of Biblical Hebrew rules of lengthening and reduction.[174]

In the consonantal text of the manuscripts, the only knowledge that can be gathered comes from the occurrence of *matres lectionis*, which often point to sporadic changes, such as /a/ > /o/.

**§14d**   Targum Neophyti is unpointed except for isolated passages that were most probably pointed by later vocalizers.[175] It is interesting to note that these few pointed verses demonstrate a *qames/pathah* confusion as well as the pointing of *seghol* in place of *ḥireq*, suggesting that the vocalizer had only one *a*-phoneme in his dialect, and that *i > /e/, e.g., צָמְחִין Gn 41:6, "growing"; וּבְלָעוּן Gn 41:6, "and they swallowed"; לְמִסתכלא Gn 3:6, "to look at."

*Syriac*[176]

**§14e**  Western Syriac has a vocalic inventory which resembles that of the
Cairo Genizah fragments in that /e/ is a reflex of *i (and *ay) and /i/ is a
reflex of *ī.[177] The other phonemes of Western Syriac are /ā/,[178] /a/, /u/. The
phonemes of Eastern Syriac are /a/, /ā/, /e/, /ē/, /i/, /o/, /u/. There was
also a reduced vowel /ə/ at an early stage of the language.[179]

*Western Aramaic Dialects*

**§14f**  1) *Galilean Aramaic*

The consonantal texts of Galilean Aramaic yield little information about
the vocalic inventory of the dialect. Occasional *scriptio plena* demonstrates
the presence of a *u*- or *o*-vowel and of an *i*- or *e*-vowel but does not reveal the
phonemic realizaton of these vowels. Some information can, nonetheless, be
gleaned from vocalizers who pointed words sporadically,[180] although it is
possible that the pointings were added to the consonantal text and reflect a
later pronunciation. The few pointed words suggest that the inventory
included one *a*-phoneme, as indicated by the confusion of *qames* and *pathah*,
and one *e*-phoneme, as indicated by the confusion of *seghol, sere*, and *hireq*.
They also suggest that the *shewa mobile* preceding *yodh* was realized as [ī]. See,
for example:[181] אֶלָּא, "rather"; יְהַב, "he gave"; לְמָפְרַשׁ, "to set sail"; מֶן,
"from"; דְּאִיתְרְחֵץ, "who trusted in"; דִּיַפֵּל, "that he should fell."

2) *Palestinian Syriac*

**§14g**  The analysis of the vocalic inventory is made difficult by a graphic
system in which there is no direct relationship between vowel sign and
phoneme. A detailed analysis of the pointing of the second hand in the
Evangeliarium Hierosolymitanum by M. Bar-Asher[182] shows that the
phonemic inventory consisted of one *a*-phoneme, a phoneme with the
conditioned allophones [u] in open syllables and [o] in closed syllables, and
another phoneme with possibly conditioned allophones of [i] in open syllables
and [e] in closed syllables.[183]

Nöldeke and Schulthess argued that the *shewa mobile* was realized as a
reduced vowel in this dialect.[184] Bar-Asher, on the other hand, maintains that
the *shewa mobile* (including *shewa medium*) was realized as a full vowel.

3) *Samaritan Aramaic*

**§14h**  The vocalic inventory of Samaritan Aramaic as reconstructed from
manuscripts and confirmed in the oral tradition of the liturgy of the
Samaritans contains the following phonemes:[185] /a/, /ā/, /e/, and /i/, as well
as one phoneme made up of the positional variants [u] and [o]. [u] occurs in
open syllables before the stress, and [o] occurs in closed syllables and in open
syllables after the stress. There is a similar rule for the distribution of /i/ and
/e/ when the latter is a reflex of a long vowel or of a contracted diphthong.
The *shewa mobile* and *hateph vowels* merged with the full vowels.

4) *Ma'lula*

**§14i**  The vocalic inventory of Ma'lula is made up of /a/, /ā/, /i/, /e/, /o/,
and /u/.[186] Of relevance to the Cairo Genizah fragments is the fact that *i >
/e/, *u > /o/, and *ū > /o/ in closed syllables.[187]

54

*Traditional Pronunciations of Hebrew*

§14j    Because this Targum was used by Jews, it is not unusual to find Hebrew influences in it. It is not surprising to find that the graphic system used in the Cairo Genizah fragments was the same as that used in Hebrew texts. Consequently, an examination of the various Hebrew pronunciations and the graphic systems which represent them is instructive.

1) *The Palestinian Tradition*

§14k    The closest parallel to the vocalic inventory of the Cairo Genizah fragments is the Palestinian tradition of Hebrew as reflected in Palestinian pointed Hebrew texts (also found in the Cairo Genizah). The manuscripts reflect one general tradition, but sometimes differ from one another in detail.[188] The vocalic inventory generally representative of this tradition is as follows:

|  Palestinian Hebrew | Tiberian Hebrew[189] |
|---|---|
| /a/———————————/ā/ | |
| | /a/ |
| /e/———————————/ē/ | |
| ———————————/e/ | |
| /i/———————————/i/ | |
| /o/———————————/o/ | |
| /u/———————————/u/ | |

In some texts, however, [o] and [u] are positional allophones of one phoneme, and there are two *e*-phonemes rather than one. The pointing of the קדושת הדוותה[190] e.g., reveals the following phonemic inventory: /a/, /e/ and /i/, and the conditioned allophones [o] in closed syllables and [u] in open syllables, as in Samaritan Aramaic and Palestinian Syriac. In these *piyyuṭim* *i > /i/, whereas in the Cairo Genizah fragments *i > /e/.

The representation of *shewa mobile* varies in the different Palestinian manuscripts. In some manuscripts, one finds the *e*-vowel sign where a *shewa* is expected; in others one finds *a*-vowel signs. *Shewa* preceding *yodh* seems to be realized as [i]. As for the *ḥaṭeph* vowels, the signs suggest a realization of [ă] where a Tiberian *ḥaṭeph pathaḥ* is expected, [ŏ], where a Tiberian *ḥaṭeph qameṣ* is expected, and [ĕ] where a Tiberian *ḥaṭeph seghol* is expected.[191] The scheme resembles that of the Palestinian Targum fragments of the Cairo Genizah.

§14l    The Palestinian pronunciation of Hebrew is represented graphically in two ways: i) by the Palestinian pointing system; ii) by the Palestinian-Tiberian pointing system.

§14m    i) The Palestinian pointing system is known from manuscripts of Bible, *piyyuṭim*, Mishnah, Talmud, Midrash, and Halacha.[192] Both the vowel signs and the vowels they represent have been analyzed in detail by Dietrich,[193] Revell,[194] Yahalom,[195] Kahle,[196] Murtonen,[197] and Chiesa.[198] The influence of the Tiberian system of vocalization is often evident in the Palestinian pointing system. It manifests itself in the use of the two *a*-vowel signs, ‗ and ‗, which often correspond to Tiberian ‗ and ‗,[199] the use of both of these signs (the use of ‗ is extremely limited) to represent /o/, and signs serving as *raphe* and *mappiq*.[200] In some Palestinian pointed texts, the signs ‗ and ‗ imitate the use of Tiberian *ṣere* and *seghol*. The use of ‗ follows the use of the Tiberian *daghesh* and marks both gemination and the plosive pronunciation of /bgdkpt/.[201] This Palestinian pointing system is also known as the "Simple Palestinian" system.[202]

§14n   ii) The system generally known today as "Palestinian-Tiberian"[203] consists of Tiberian signs representing a Palestinian vocalic inventory. This system has also been called "Fuller Palestinian,"[204] "Pre-Masoretic Tradition,"[205] "Proto-Tiberian,"[206] "Non-Receptus Tiberian Punctuation,"[207] and, most recently, "Tiberian Non-Conventional System."[208] As the names indicate, the system was claimed to be either a pre-Masoretic system that was pushed aside with the emergence of the Ben-Asher system, or a parallel Masoretic system which gradually disappeared only later. Kahle associated this system with that of Ben Naphtali. This theory has been disproved by Morag and Díez Macho.[209] As Morag points out, the Palestinian-Tiberian system was an attempt to give a full phonetic notation, and must then have been post-Masoretic rather than pre-Masoretic.

This pointing system differs from the standard Tiberian system in that it reflects a Palestinian vocalic inventory: the *qameṣ* and *pathaḥ*, representing /a/, interchange freely, as do the *ṣere* and *seghol*, representing /e/. Also *daghesh* and *raphe* are extended to letters other than /bgdkpt/ to mark syllable boundaries.[210]

There is one Aramaic text pointed in accordance with this system: the Targum to the Prophets in the Codex Reuchlinianus.

The Tiberian pointed texts of the Cairo Genizah fragments cannot be classified as belonging to this Palestinian-Tiberian tradition. They do both have only one /a/, but the /e/ in each reflects a different historical merging. In texts pointed in the Palestinian-Tiberian tradition, /e/ corresponds to Tiberian *ṣere* and *seghol*, whereas in the Cairo Genizah fragments, /e/ corresponds to Tiberian *ṣere, seghol,* and *ḥireq* (< *i). Moreover, the *daghesh* and *raphe* are used far more extensively in the Palestinian-Tiberian pointed texts than in the Cairo Genizah fragments. A salient feature of the Palestinian-Tiberian system which is attested in the Cairo Genizah fragments is the *mappiq/ḥireq* on the final *yodh* of a diphthong. A second salient feature, *Cəyi > Ci*, appears only rarely in the Cairo Genizah fragments.

*Descendants of the Palestinian Tradition: Pre-Ashkenazi and Sephardi Pronunciations*

§14o   i) *Pre-Ashkenazi Hebrew Pronunciation*

The Palestinian tradition of pronunciation was carried by Jews from the Syria-Palestine region to other parts of the world. Before the prestige of the

Tiberian system led to its adoption in Mediaeval Ashkenaz (Europe), pre-Ashkenazi prayer books (ca. 950-1350 C.E.) reveal that the Palestinian pronunciation was in use. The fluctuation of *qameṣ* and *pathaḥ* reflecting /a/, and of *ṣere* and *seghol* reflecting /e/ are apparent. Although most of the prayer books are written in the normal Tiberian pointing system, there are some which show clear traces of the Palestinian-Tiberian system.[211] There are also a few examples of *i > /e/, but almost all occur before *resh* (some occur before *kaph* and *gimel*), unlike in the Cairo Genizah fragments, in which the shift is complete.

§14p    ii) *Sephardi Hebrew Pronunciation*

The Palestinian pronunciation of Hebrew may have been transferred to Spain from Palestine via Italy.[212] The term Sephardi is used to describe a number of pronunciations which are alike in that they all have one *a*-phoneme and one *e*-phoneme, and that most of them realize the *shewa mobile* as [e] or [ɛ].[213] This descendant of the Palestinian pronunciation parallels the vocalic inventory of the Genizah fragments in the first respect, namely, that they both have only one *a*-phoneme and one *e*-phoneme. In the Cairo Genizah fragments, however, the *e*-phoneme includes *i. In North African Sephardi communities, Tiberian *holem* and *shureq/qibbuṣ* seem to have merged into one phoneme with two allophones, apparently under the influence of Arabic dialects.[214]

§14q    2) *The Tiberian Tradition*

The vocalic inventory of the Cairo Genizah fragments seems to parallel that of the Masoretes in the assumed realization of the *shewa* and *ḥateph* vowels, as elaborated by mediaeval grammarians.[215] In essence, the Tiberian system agrees with the Cairo Genizah fragments in the following respects: a) *shewa* was realized as [ă]; b) *shewa* before *yodh* was realized as [ĭ]; c) *ḥateph* vowels corresponding to *shewa* were realized as [ă], [ĕ], and [ŏ].

3) *The Babylonian Hebrew and Aramaic Traditions*

§14r    One feature of the Yemenite traditions of Babylonian Aramaic and Babylonian Hebrew that is similar to the language of the Cairo Genizah fragments is the realization of *shewa mobile* with non-gutturals as [ă][216] and before *yodh* as [ĭ].[217] It is noteworthy that a merger of /ā/ and /a/ takes place in certain environments in Babylonian Talmudic Aramaic,[218] and Díez Macho has argued that /ā/ and /a/ merged in the Babylonian tradition of Targum Onqelos.[219]

*Transliterations of Hebrew into Greek and Latin*

§14s    As has been noted by many scholars,[220] the transcriptions of Hebrew[221] in the Septuagint, in works by Josephus, in the New Testament, in the Hexapla, and in the works of Jerome, all seem to indicate that Tiberian *hireq* (< *i) was realized as [ɛ] and Tiberian *shureq/qibbuṣ* (< *u) was realized as [o].

*Summary*

**§14t** A comparative look at other dialects and traditions indicates that the vocalic inventory of the Cairo Genizah fragments share many common features with Aramaic dialects and Hebrew traditions from the Syria-Palestine area. A complicated map of isoglosses emerges. While it is difficult to reconstruct one model of a proto-West Aramaic which could generate all the distinct features of each dialect, it is clear that these dialects are related and in geographic proximity. In general the vocalic inventory of the Cairo Genizah fragments comes closest to that of the Palestinian traditions of Hebrew.

It is possible to derive the vocalic inventory of these fragments from the Tiberian tradition of Biblical Aramaic:

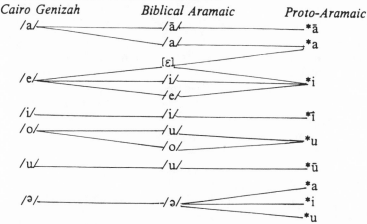

In the light of other evidence, however, such as the transcriptions of Hebrew, and Western Syriac, it seems preferable to conjecture a different line of reconstruction for the vocalic inventory of the Cairo Genizah fragments:

**§15**                                     D. *Diphthongs*

**§15a** The diphthongs /ay/, /oy/, /uy/ are attested in the Cairo Genizah fragments.

  *non-final, unstressed syllables:*

  1) *qayl nouns, e.g., בֵּיתֹה A Ex 22:6, "his house"; עֵינֵיכוֹן B Gn 3:5, "your eyes" (m.pl.).[1]

58

2) C verbs I-y/', e.g., תֵּיטִיב B Gn 4:7, "you do well";[2] אֵיְתוּן Cd Gn 46:32, "you brought."

3) interrogative pronouns: וּבְהֵילָן Cd Gn 37:30, "which?"; הֵידָה D Dt 5:23, "which?"

*final, stressed syllables:*

1) 1 s. suffix on m.pl. nouns, e.g., בְּנֵיי A Ex 21:5, "my sons"; יְדֵיי C Gn 31:39, "my hands."

2) gentilic nouns, e.g., מצריי E Gn 39:1, "Egyptian."

3) ordinal numbers, e.g., תליתיי F Ex 20:5, "third."

§15c Proto-Aramaic *ayn > /ayin/ in these fragments in:

*final, stressed syllables:*

1) *qayl nouns: עֵין A Ex 21:24, "eye."[3]

2) "two" (m.s. absolute), e.g., תריֵין Cd Gn 43:10, תְּרֵין F Nu 28:27.[4]

3) demonstrative pronoun "these," e.g., הָאֵלֵּין C Gn 34:21, הָאֵלֵּין D Dt 5:19.

4) participles of verbs III-w/y/',[5] e.g., רָעֵיין Cd Gn 47:3, "grazing"; שָׁרֵיין Z Gn 49:7, "dwelling."

§15d *ay > /e/ before pronominal suffixes on m.pl. (and dual) nouns,[6] e.g., בְּנֵיך C Gn 35:12, "your children"; יְדֵיהוֹן-Cd Gn 37:22, "their hands"; and in *qaylat nouns (§67g).

§15e /oy/ occurs in the following environment:

*final, stressed syllables:*

1) 3 m.s. suffix on m.pl. (and dual) nouns, e.g., לְעַבְדוֹי C Gn 32:17, "his servants"; וְעֵינוֹי Cd Gn 48:10, "and his eyes."

2) 1 s. suffix on m.pl. (and dual) nouns,[7] e.g., אַפּוֹי C Gn 32:21, "my face"; קודמוֹי E Gn 30:29, "before me."

§15f /uy/ occurs in the following environment:

*final, stressed syllables:*

1) 3 m.s. suffix on s. of אב "father" and אח "brother," e.g., דַאֲבוּי C Gn 31:53; אֲחוּי B Gn 4:16.

If /w/ was realized as [w],[8] then the diphthong /aw/ occurs in יַוְנָה Bd Gn 8:8, "the dove"; טַוְרַיָּא Bd Gn 7:19, "the mountains"; טַוְרַיָּא Bd Gn 7:20; טַוְרַיָּא Bd Gn 8:5 (cf. טוּרֵי Bd Gn 8:4; בְּטוּרָה D Dt 5:19; וְטוּרָה D Dt 5:20); לַוְחֵי F Ex 20:2, "the tablets of." There would then also be an example of the diphthong /ew/ in לְיוְחֵי D Dt 5:19.

§15g *aw > /o/ in these fragments in all environments, e.g., תּוֹר A Ex 21:36, "ox"; במוֹתָנָא AA Nu 20:3, "by the plague."

§15h The diphthong /ay/ is frequently represented in the consonantal text by double *yodh*. Some examples are יהיימנן A Ex 4:9, "they will believe"; לבייתה E Gn 29:13, "to his house"; עייניי E Gn 31:10, "my eyes";[9] קדמיי F Lv 22:27, "first." /ay/ is represented once by *aleph* and *yodh*, וְחָט[אֵי] Cd Gn 44:18, "sinner"; and once by *aleph* and two *yodhs*, וָאיי H Gn 15:1, "woe!" /oy/ is usually represented by *waw* and *yodh*; however, there are three examples with *waw* and two *yodhs:* בנ֫וֹיי Cd Gn 48:1, "his sons"; דקוּדמוֹיי E Gn 31:2,5, "before him." /uy/ is represented only by *waw* and *yodh*.

§15i An unusual graphic practice is the placing of *mappiq* and/or *shewa* under the *yodh* of final /ay/ and /oy/. The few examples are

/ay/: זֹבֵ֫י A Ex 21:28, "innocent"; אָחַ֫י Cd Gn 38:26, "my brethren"; חמישֵׁ֫יי E Gn 30:17, "fifth"; חסָדַ֫יי E Gn 30:23, "my shameful acts"; עברָ֫יי E Gn 41:12, "Hebrew"; בְדֽיִי E Gn 42:38, "in illness"; אתֵ֫יי־ E Gn 30:2, "come!" (f.s.); קֳדָמֵ֫יי HH Ex 12:2, "first"; לוֹיִ E Gn 30:34, "if only."

/oy/: לְמרוֹ֫יִ A Ex 22:11, "to his masters": עַבְדוֹ֫יִ C Gn 32:17, "his servants"; וְטֹֹֽוֹבֹֹֽה Cd Gn 38:26, "happy is he"; לבלחוֹדוֹי AA₁ Ex 12:16, "alone"; מוֹיִ AA Nu 20:8, "its waters"; ופקוֹדוֹיִ AA Dt 26:17, "and his commandments"; קִימוֹיִ AA Dt 26:17, "his laws." There may be one example with *sere* מוֹ֗יִ AA Nu 20:11, "its waters."[10]

It is also possible, however, to interpret ⟶ in these examples not as *mappiq* marking the consonantal nature of the *yodh*, but rather as a *hireq* in which case the pointings with ⟶ could reflect a triphthongization which was realized as /ayi/, /oyi/. Similarly, one could claim that the pointings with *shewa* reflect a triphthongization that was realized as /ayə/, /oyə/.

*Diphthongs—Historical and Comparative Discussion*

§15j The diphthong /ay/ in the Cairo Genizah fragments comes from two different sources: *ay and *āy.

§15k The diphthong /oy/ of the 3 m.s. pronominal suffix on m.pl. and dual nouns is clearly a reflex of /ohi/ (attested in Biblical Aramaic and Targum Onqelos; cf. also the Syriac *kethibh* /awhi/). According to the traditional school of thought, *ayhū > *ayu > *aw > *o + *hū > *ohu > /ohi/.[11] Recently, however, W. R. Garr has convincingly argued for a reconstruction of *ayhū (regressive assimilation) > *awhū (dissimilation) > /awhi/ > /ohi/.[12]

For the origin of the 1 s. /oy/, see §37k.

§15l /uy/ in the nouns אב and אח developed from *'abū + *hū > /'əbuhi/ > /'əbuy/ and *'ahū + *hū > /'əhuhi/ > /'əhuy/. The parent form of /uy/ is identifiable in /uhi/ of Biblical Aramaic, Targum Onqelos, and the *kethibh* of Syriac.

§15m The examples in which there may have been a diphthong /aw/—/yawna/, /tawra/, and /lawha/—are open to different explanations. The assumed Proto-Aramaic forms of these three words are *yawn, *tur, and *luh /cf. Targum Onqelos /yonā/, /turā/, /luhā/; Syriac /yawnā/, /turā/, /luhā/). In order to explain the forms with /aw/ in the Cairo Genizah fragments, one must assume that there were by-forms *tawr and *lawh (cf. Arabic /lawh/)[13] and that 1) there was irregular preservation of *aw in these forms; or 2) *aw > /o/ followed by sporadic diphthongization of /o/ in /yona/, /tor/, and /loh/. It is also possible that these words were borrowed from a dialect in which *aw was preserved (cf. e.g., Ma'lula [yawna] and Syriac /yawnā/).[14]

60

Although the origin of these three forms is not certain, it appears that these exceptional forms were common to the Palestine area. The realizations [ṭibra] alongside [ṭor], [lēbîn], and [yåbånå] in Samaritan Aramaic[15] and writings such as טוורא in Targum Pseudo-Jonathan and the Fragment Targum,[16] לווחין and יוונה in Targum Neophyti[17] and Rabbinic Hebrew[18] לווחים all point to a common geographic area. It must, however, be stressed that these forms are exceptional in all these sources, and in the Palestinian Targumim *aw regularly contracts to /o/, and in Samaritan Aramaic *aw regularly contracts to [o], [u].

§15n   The graphic representation of /ay/ by means of a double *yodh* is a scribal convention used by Jewish scribes in Palestine in both Hebrew and Aramaic texts, as evidenced in reliable manuscripts of Galilean Aramaic, Rabbinic Hebrew, and Hebrew *piyyuṭim*.[19] In Biblical Aramaic and Targum Onqelos, on the other hand, final /ay/ is marked in the consonantal text by one *yodh*. Final /ay/ is marked by both double *yodh* (יי), and *aleph* and *yodh* (אי) in Targum Pseudo-Jonathan, the Fragment Targum, and Targum Neophyti, the latter orthography in imitation usually of Babylonian scribal practices.

§15o   The use of a final dot, _, under the *yodh* of diphthongs in final position is known from manuscripts of Rabbinic Hebrew (both in Tiberian and Babylonian pointed manuscripts),[20] from Codex Reuchlinianus (in both the Hebrew and the Aramaic sections),[21] and from pre-Ashkenazi prayer books (e.g., the Worms *Maḥzor*).[22] There are two interpretations of the meaning of this sign. One school of thought holds that the dot is a *mappiq* and was placed beneath a final *yodh* in order to emphasize that the *yodh* functioned as a consonant and not as a *mater lectionis* for /i/ or /e/.[23] In some manuscripts, e.g., MS Parma (de Rossi 138) it alternates with *shewa*.[24] A second school of thought interprets the dot as a *ḥireq* and takes this pointing to represent a triphthongization of the diphthong.[25] Supporting evidence of contemporaneous triphthongization is adduced from Samaritan Hebrew where some final diphthongs were resolved into separate syllables, e.g., [iyyu], [uwwi].[26]

The following is a brief comparison of the diphthongs of the Cairo Genizah fragments with other Targumim and dialects:

§15p   *Biblical Aramaic:* As in the Cairo Genizah fragments, *ay has reflexes /ay/, /e/, and *ayn > /ayin/. *aw > /o/ in all environments.[27]

§15q   *Targum Onqelos:* *ay tends to contract to /e/ in all environments, and *ayn > /an/.[28] *aw > /o/, although there are some examples of the preservation of the diphthong.[29]

§15r   *Targum Pseudo-Jonathan, Fragment Targum, Targum Neophyti:* From the consonantal text, it appears that *ay and *aw have the same reflexes as those in the Cairo Genizah fragments, including *ayn > /ayin/.[30] These

Targumim also share with the Cairo Genizah fragments the diphthongs /oy/ and /uy/.[31]

**§15s** *Galilean Aramaic:* From the consonantal text, it appears that the situation is the same as that in Targum Pseudo-Jonathan, the Fragment Targum, and Targum Neophyti,[32] including the existence of the diphthongs /oy/ and /uy/.[33]

**§15t** *Palestinian Syriac:* *ay and *aw have contracted to /e/ and /o/ in this dialect.[34] Examples in which no contraction has taken place are due to Syriac influence.[35] The diphthongs /oy/ and /uy/ also exist.[36]

**§15u** *Samaritan Aramaic:* *ay and *aw have contracted.[37] Both [oy] and [uy] have contracted to [o].[38]

**§15v** *Ma'lula:* *ay and *aw are preserved in this dialect.[39] [ay] is also a reflex of *āy.[40] [ōy] also occurs.[41]

**§15w** *Syriac:* *ay and *aw are generally preserved in open syllables and contract in originally closed syllables.[42] *ayn > /en/.[43]

**§16**

### E. *Matres Lectionis*

The letters *aleph, he, yodh,* and *waw* serve as *matres lectionis* in these texts. For the frequency of these *matres lectionis* in the different manuscripts, see §16j.

**§16a** *Final /a/*

Final /a/ is represented by either *he* or *aleph*.[1] *He* is preferred in some manuscripts, *aleph* in others, and at times one finds the same word spelled two different ways in the same manuscript, e.g., אֲנָה C Gn 31:52, "I" vs. אֲנָא C Gn 31:44. Both *he* and *aleph* are used to mark final /a/ in determined nouns and absolute feminine singular nouns depending on the manuscript. Cf. בְרָא A Ex 21:31, "a daughter" vs. ברה E Gn 30:21, and עָלְמָא C Gn 35:9, "the world" vs. עָלְמָה C Gn 35:9. In verbs originally III-w/y, both *he* and *aleph* are used to represent final /a/, e.g., וַהֲוָה Cd Gn 37:23, "and it was" vs. הֲוָא Cd Gn 37:23. In the originally III-' verbs *qr'* "call" and *br'* "create," *aleph* alone is attested, e.g., קְרָא C Gn 31:48 (+ 6x) and וּבְרָא B Gn 2:19 (+ 5x), perhaps under the influence of Hebrew orthography.

In Tiberian pointed manuscripts, one occasionally finds a *raphe*, ⌐, indicating that a final *he* functions as a *mater lectionis* and not as a consonant, e.g., וְאַחְסָנָה Cd Gn 48:5, "and an inheritance." In the Palestinian pointed manuscripts, there is one example in which ⌐ indicates that a final *he* serves as a *mater lectionis:* וִיקִידְתֹה A Ex 22:5, "the burning."[2]

**§16b** *Medial /a/*

Medial /a/ which is the reflex of *a' is often marked by a historical *aleph*, e.g., עָאנִי C Gn 31:43, "my small cattle" (cf. עָנָא C Gn 31:43).

Medial /a/ which is the reflex of *ā or *a is infrequently represented by *aleph*: תּוֹמָאיִן E Gn 38:27, "twins"; עֲלָאיִן D Dt 26:19, "high" (written *defective* 2x);[3] עָאנֵי B Gn 4:8, "answering" (written *plene* 2x, but *defective* 5x); עֲלָאמֵי Bd

Gn 8:7, "over" (written *plene* 5x, but *defective* 9x); מָאעֵּן ‑Cd Gn 37:28, "coins"; תְּלָאתָא Cd Gn 38:25, "three" (stem /təlat-/ written *defective* 32x); וְעָאל Cd Gn 43:26, "and he entered" (G Perfect forms written *plene* 5x, but *defective* 12x); מָארֵי‑ Cd Gn 46:32, "masters of" (and מָארֵה Cd Gn 46:34, but other forms of *mr' *defective* 12x); בְּאָרָא Cd Ex 9:21, "the field" (but written *defective* 23x); וּלְרוֹמָאנֻמָךְ D Dt 26:19, "and to raise you up";⁴ דְטָאיֵּס E Gn 7:14, "which flies"; דְמָאני E Gn 39:5, "that he appointed" (and וּמָאני E Gn 39:4, but other D and Dt forms of *mny written *defective* 10x); רָאמְתָה AA₁ Ex 17:10ᵗ "the hill" (but adj. *defective* 3x), מָאֻן A Ex 21:19ᵗ "who" (but written *defective* 12x);⁵ וְאָנוﬣ]ת Bd Gn 8:4, "she rested"; וְאֻזﬥﻍﻋﻋﻋﻋ F Ex 20:15 "and they were shaken" (cf. וְזﬠﻋﻋﻋ F Ex 19:16).

The use of *aleph* in the following words may have been an attempt to distinguish between homographs:⁶ בְּאָרָא /bara/, "the field" vs. בְּרָא /bəra/, "the son"; עָאל /'al/, "he entered" vs. עַל /'al/, "on, upon"; עַלָאוי /'ellawe/, "on, upon" vs. עֲלוֹי /'əloy/, "on him"; מָאן /man/ "who" vs. מֵן /men/ "from"; מָאני /manni/ "he appointed" vs. מֵני /menni/ "from me."

**§16c** *Final /e/*

Final /e/ is overwhelmingly represented by *yodh* in these fragments, e.g., יְהוֵי B Gn 4:12, "he will be" and סַלֵי D Dt 28:17, "baskets of."

Final /e/ is infrequently represented by *aleph* in the Participle and Imperfect of verbs III-w/y/⁷ and in the m.pl.det. form of gentilic nouns. Some representative examples are קָרָא‑ B Gn 2:19, "he calls"; (cf. קָרֵי‑ B Gn 2:19); וְיִתְקְרָא Z Gn 48:16, "and he will be called" (cf. יִתְקְרֵה‑ C Gn 35:10); גָּלָא B Gn 4:12ᵗ "wanderer"; דְעֶבְרָיָא E Gn 40:15ᵗ "of the Hebrews"; מִצְרָיא AA₁ Ex 12:35, "the Egyptians" (cf. דְמִצְרָיֵי Cd Ex 7:11); וּלֵיוָיא AA Dt 26:11, "and the Levites."

*He* is rarely used to represent final /e/.⁸ The examples are חֲמַשׁ עֶשְׂרֵה Bd Gn 7:20ᵗ "fifteen"; אַרְבַּע‑עֶשְׂרֵה C Gn 31:41, "fourteen"; יְמֵחָה‑ D Dt 28:28, "he will strike" (cf. יְמְחֵא‑ D Dt 28:22); אוֹדֵה E Gn 29:35, "I will thank"; נְהוֵיה E Gn 38:23ᵗ "we shall be"⁹ (cf. יְהוֵי E Gn 28:22); שׁוֹבַעְתָה אַמְרַיֵּיה F Nu 28:21, "the seven lambs"¹⁰ (cf. שׁוֹבַעְתֵּי אִימְרַיָּיה F Nu 28:29); לְמִשְׁתָּה AA Nu 20:5, "to drink" (cf. לְמִשְׁתֵּי E Gn 30:38); שׁוֹבַעְתָה יוֹמַיֵּיה Y Nu 28:24, "the seven days";¹¹ שְׁבַע עֶשְׂרֵה Z Gn 47:28, "seventeen"; וְיִתְגָּאה Z Gn 49:17ᵗ "and he will be proud"; יִתְמְנֶה HH Ex 12:2 "he will be counted."

**§16d** *Medial /e/*

Medial /e/ which results from the quiescence of a syllable closing *aleph* can be represented by either *aleph* or *yodh*,¹² e.g., וְתֵאכְלוֹן D Dt 27:7, "you will eat" vs. וְתֵיכְלוֹן AA Dt 27:7; and לְמֵאמַר C Gn 34:20ᵗ "saying" vs. לְמֵימַר C Gn 32:20. It is represented by both in יָאיזְלוֹן H Gn 15:1, "they will go."

Medial /e/ is represented by *yodh* frequently in both open and closed syllables, although it seems to be less frequent in closed syllables when it is a reflex of *i. A few examples are אֵיתָא Cd Gn 37:33, "woman" (cf. דְאִתְּתָא Cd Gn 38:20); וּמֵיני B Gn 4:8, "and from me" (cf. מֵני‑ B Gn 4:8); שֵׁינָה A Ex 21:27, "his tooth." The particle אִין, "if," is usually written *plene*, e.g., ־אָין C Gn 31:52[13] (cf. ־וְאָן C Gn 31:50).

*Yodh* rarely occurs as a *mater lectionis* in the prefixes of the verbal conjugations. Some exceptions are וְנִיסַב C Gn 34:17,̂ "and we shall take" (cf. ־נֵסַב C Gn 34:16); לְמֵיסַב Cd Gn 38:20, "to take" (cf. למסב E Gn 30:15); וְאִיתְקַיָּמֶן D Dt 5:23, "and we endured" (cf. ואתקיימין H Gn 15:1).

**§16e   Final and medial /i/**

Final and medial /i/ (< *ī) are represented graphically by *yodh*, e.g., דְּאָחִי B Gn 4:9, "of my brother" and דִּינָה B Gn 4:7, "the judgment." There are a few examples, however, in which /i/ is not represented by *yodh*:[14] זֵהֵן B Gn 4:6, "their countenance" (cf. זִיהֵן B Gn 4:5);[15] גְזְרֵן C Gn 34:22, "circumcised";[16] דְשַׁלְטָן C Gn 35:11, "who rule";[17] בְעֵרֵה Cd Ex 9:21, "his cattle" (cf. ־בְּעִירָא Bd Gn 8:1); צדקים E Gn 38:25, "righteous" (cf. צַדִּיקָן B Gn 4:10); בסם F Ex 19:19, "sweet" (cf. ־בָּסִיקָא B Gn 2:21).[18]

There are two examples in which final /i/ is represented by both *yodh* and *aleph*: אִתְבְּרִיא B Gn 4:8, "it was created" (cf. אִתְבְּרִי B Gn 4:8);[19] וּשִׁיצִיא Cd Ex 9:25,[20] "and it destroyed" (cf. שֵׁיצִי Cd Ex 9:25).

It seems unlikely that final /i/ is represented by *he* in חוה E Gn 31:20, "he told" (/ḥawwī?/); this form appears to be a Hebraism (/ḥiwwā/).[21]

**§16f   Final /o/, /u/**

Final /o/ and /u/ are represented by *waw*,[22] e.g., בְּגוֹ B Gn 4:12, "in the midst of"; צלו E Gn 28:17,̂ "prayer"; אָסוּ D Dt 28:27, "healing"; טְבוּ F Ex 20:6, "and goodness."

There are two examples in which final /o/ is represented by both *waw* and *aleph*: בְגוֹא Cd Gn 48:16,̂ "in the midst of"; בגוא E Gn 41:18.[23]

**§16g   Medial /o/, /u/**

Medial /o/ and /u/ are more often than not represented by *waw*,[24] e.g., תחות C Gn 35:8, "under" (cf. תְּחֹת Cd Gn 47:29); וְתוֹרֵהוֹן Cd Gn 46:32, "and their oxen" (cf. וּתֹרֵיהוֹן Cd Gn 47:1); אבוהון E Gn 9:22, "their father" (cf. אבהון E Gn 9:18); אחוכֹן E Gn 42:34, "your brother" (cf. אחכון E Gn 43:3).

**§16h   /ə/**

/ə/ appears to be represented by *yodh* in the following examples: תִּעְצְעֵרוֹן A Ex 22:20,̂ "you will trouble" (cf. תִּעְצְעֵרוֹן A Ex 22:22); וְקִירוּשָׁא C Gn 31:40, "and the frost";[25] כאיברא W Ex 15:10, "like lead";[26] וּבַחֲצֵדִיכֹן F Lv 23:22,̂ "and in your harvesting";[27] בבישריהֵין E Gn 41:18, "in their flesh" (cf. בבשרהֵן E Gn 41:19).

For examples in which /ə/ ([ŏ]) is represented by *waw*, see §12i.

**§16i**   The use of *matres lectionis* in the following proper nouns differs from the orthography of the Tiberian Hebrew Masoretic text: לְאָפְרָתָא Cd Gn 48:7, "to Ephrath"[28] (MT אֶפְרָתָה); בדֹתן E Gn 37:17, "in Dothan" (MT בְּדֹתָ); לדֹתָיִנה E Gn 37:17,̂ "to Dothan"[29] (MT דֹּתָיְנָה); וֹאֹהֲרֹן F Ex 19:24, "and Aaron" (MT וְאַהֲרֹן); פרעא W Ex 15:9,̂ "Pharoah" (does not occur in this verse in the MT, but always written in MT פַּרְעֹה).

64

§16j    The following chart summarizes the use of the *matres lectionis* in these fragments:

Chart of *Matres Lectionis** 

| | Final /a/ he:aleph | Medial /e/ plene: defective | Medial /o/, /u/ plene: defective | Final /e/ yodh: aleph:he |
|---|---|---|---|---|
| MS A | 53:10 | 40:118 | 69:5 | 21:1:0 |
| MS B | 81:105 | 80:154 | 61:29 | 42:6:1 |
| MS C | 70:263 | 406:565 | 234:115 | 184:3:1 |
| MS D | 56:2 | 83:77 | 62:22 | 11:1:1 |
| MS E | 598:18 | 346:545 | 361:102 | 127:4:2 |
| MS F | 252:112 | 171:326 | 357:54 | 93:0:1 |
| MS H | 3:22 | 28:16 | 8:4 | 4:0:0 |
| MS W | 3:48 | 33:26 | 48:3 | 10:0:0 |
| MS Y | 37:1 | 12:21 | 12:6 | 2:0:1 |
| MS Z | 61:29 | 64:50 | 47:18 | 14:1:2 |
| MS AA | 297:80 | 70:262 | 129:25 | 39:16:1 |
| MS HH | 6:0 | 8:2 | 4:1 | 3:0:1 |

*The frequency counts of *yodh* representing final and medial /i/, and of *waw* representing final /o/, /u/ have not been included since the exceptions are rare. See §§16e-f.

*Matres Lectionis—Comparative Discussion*

§16k    One of the salient features of the use of *matres lectionis* in these texts is the frequent use of *he* to represent final /a/. The scribal practice by which the feminine morpheme is marked by *he*, while other cases of final /a/ are marked by historical *aleph*, common to Old Aramaic, Elephantine Aramaic, and, to some extent, Biblical Aramaic and Qumran Aramaic, no longer obtains.[30] The use of *he* to represent final /a/ has parallels in the other dialects of the Syria-Palestine region. This is the regular usage in reliable manuscripts of Galilean Aramaic, and it is the rule in Samaritan Aramaic.[31] Curiously, final /a/ is also regularly spelled with *he* in the Hermopolis papyri.[32] In Targum Onqelos and Targum Pseudo-Jonathan, on the other hand, *aleph* is used throughout. It has been suggested[33] that the predominant use of *aleph* in some fragments is due to Targum Onqelos influence. It seems more likely, however, that Biblical Aramaic orthography is responsible.[34] In the Fragment Targum, *aleph* is much more frequent than *he*. In Targum Neophyti, both *aleph* and *he* appear.[35] Both Syriac and Palestinian Syriac, which uses the Syriac alphabet, represent final /a/ by *aleph*.

§16l    The extensive use of *he*, and its parallel usage in Galilean Aramaic and Samaritan Aramaic, suggest Hebrew influence. The use of *he* at Hermopolis does not fit the data known from Official Aramaic. Kutscher tried to explain it by suggesting that these papyri originated in Palestine.[36]

**s16m** The extensive medial use of *waw* to represent /o/ and /u/ (and to a considerably lesser extent the use of *yodh* to represent medial /e/) is also known from Galilean Aramaic and the Palestinian Targumim,[37] Syriac,[38] Samaritan Aramaic,[39] Palestinian Syriac,[40] and Rabbinic Hebrew.[41]

## F. Phonetic Processes

**s17** *Sound Changes*

*Labials*

**s17a** *\*p* > /b/: This shift is attested in קָטָב E Gn 37:25, "balsam," but קָטִיף Cd Gn 37:25. One finds קטף in Gn 37:25 in Targum Onqelos, Targum Pseudo-Jonathan, Targum Neophyti, and the Samaritan Targum. Cf. also Rabbinic Hebrew /qāṭāp/.

**s17b** *\*b* > /p/: Examples of this shift are תפשילוי F Lv 22:27, "his cooked food" and תפשילין F Lv 22:27. Cf. תבשילין Lv 22:27 in Targum Pseudo-Jonathan and the Fragment Targum (MSS P,V), Targum Onqelos /tabšilā/ Gn 25:29, Samaritan Targum (MS A) תבשיל Gn 25:29, and Rabbinic Hebrew /tabšil/.

**s17c** *\*p* > /w/?: Cf. שפיין E Gn 31:5, "favorable" and שוין E Gn 31:2.[1] Targum Pseudo-Jonathan and Targum Neophyti have *špy forms (*šwy in margin of Neophyti). Cf. also קלופיין E Gn 30:37, "husks, peels" and קלוותיה E Gn 30:37.[2]

**s17d** /b/ - /p/ - /w/?: Note the forms of "balsam" with *beth* שְׁעַבָא Cd Gn 37:25´ and וּשַׁעֲבָה E Gn 31:25´ (see s8f, n.23), but Targum Onqelos /šaʿap/ Gn 37:25 (and the personal name /šaʿap/ in the MT 1 Ch 2:47,49). Cf. also שעבה in the Samaritan Targum, but שעוה in Targum Pseudo-Jonathan, שעווה in Targum Neophyti, /šaʿuθā/ in Syriac, and /šaʿawā/ in Rabbinic Hebrew.

*Gutturals*

**s17e** *\*h* > /h/: This shift is attested in /ləhod/, "only, also" e.g., לְהוד־ Cd Gn 47:3 (+ 44x, but 19x with /ḥ/, e.g., לְחוד־ Cd Gn 46:34). This shift is not found in compound forms such as לבלחודוי E Gn 42:38, "alone." It is also attested in Targum Neophyti, e.g., להוד Gn 47:3 (cf. לחוד Gn 47:3).

**s17f** *\*ḥ* > /h/: This shift is limited to the five occurrences of /zehori/, "crimson," e.g., זיהורי E Gn 38:28. This lexical item appears with /h/ in Targum Onqelos, Targum Pseudo-Jonathan, and Targum Neophyti (Gn 38:28), but with /ḥ/ in Syriac[3] and Palestinian Syriac.[4] Cf. also Rabbinic Hebrew /zəhorit/.[5]

**s17g** *\*ḥ* > /ʿ/: This shift appears in the word עוֹבָה A Ex 4:7, "his breast." It appears in Targum Pseudo-Jonathan, the Fragment Targum, and Targum Neophyti (Ex 4:6) with /ḥ/, as well as in Biblical Hebrew (בְּחֻבִּי Jb 31:33). This word is unattested in Targum Onqelos. The form with /ʿ/ appears in Galilean Aramaic,[6] Palestinian Syriac,[7] Maʿlula,[8] and Syriac.[9] In manuscripts of the Samaritan Targum, one finds עובה (MS A) as well as חובה (MS J).[10] This is the only example of *ḥ > /ʿ/, a shift known in Galilean Aramaic[11] and Samaritan Aramaic.[12]

66

§17h **✻'** > /'/: This shift is attested in the root *l'y: לְמִלְעֵי Z Gn 49:15, "to labor," and לְעוּת˃ C Gn 31:42, "labor of." There are no examples with *aleph*. This root also appears with *ayin* in the Fragment Targum,[13] Targum Pseudo-Jonathan (also with *aleph*),[14] Targum Neophyti,[15] and Galilean Aramaic.[16] *Aleph* is attested in Targum Onqelos,[17] Syriac, [18] and Palestinian Syriac.[19]

§17i **✻'/** > /y/: This shift is attested in יְבִידֵּה˃ A Ex 22:8, "loss"[20] and וּפְלִין W Ex 15:11, "miracles."[21] There are no other attestations of either root.

§18 *Conditioned Vowel Changes* (Occasional)

§18a *a > /e/ in closed unstressed syllables?* A sporadic shift *a > *i is generally thought to have occurred early in Aramaic (as well as in Hebrew—the so-called "attenuation of a to i"),[22] although it has been argued that many of the examples of *a > *i result from the confusion caused by the falling together of different noun classes in certain states (e.g., *qitl, *qatl, *qital, *qatal > qǝtal in the absolute and construct states) and a subsequent extension of *i to forms in which *a was the original vowel (e.g., baśar "flesh" from *qatal may have been mistaken as the absolute and construct form of *qital, yielding the form biśrā').[23] Examples in the Cairo Genizah fragments with /e/ which are also attested in Biblical Aramaic, Targum Onqelos, and Syriac are וּבְרָכְתָא˃ C Gn 35:9, "and the blessing" (+ 1x); בְּשֵׁם˃- Cd Gn 37:27, "our flesh" (+ 7x); וְדִכְרִין C Gn 32:15, "and males" (+ 5x); נִשְׁמַת˃- Bd Gn 7:22, "the soul of "; עִזְקָתָא Cd Gn 38:25, "the signet ring" (+ 1x); עֶשְׂרֵה˃-C Gn 31:41, "teen" (+ 1x); עֶשְׂרִין C Gn 31:41, "twenty" (+ 3x); שִׁמְשָׁה A Ex 22:2, "the sun" (+ 2x). Other examples in which it is commonly held that *a > *i in certain Aramaic dialects[24] are the Akkadian loanword זִמְנִין C Gn 31:41, "times" (+ 4x); אִתָּה B Gn 2:23, "woman" (+ 18x); בִּיזָא W Ex 15:9, "booty"; סִיטְרָה AA₁ Ex 17:12, "the side"; פִּיסְחָה F Nu 28:16, "Passover" (+ 5x).

§18b It must, however, be stressed that it is not at all certain that each of these forms had a Proto-Aramaic *a, nor is it certain in those cases in which there was a Proto-Aramaic *a that the examples with *i* or *e* are the result of a sporadic sound shift and not the result of individual analogies in each dialect. Caution must be exercised.[25]

§18c The following forms with /e/ are not attested with either an *i-* or *e-* vowel in Biblical Aramaic, Targum Onqelos, or Syriac. Some of these forms, however, are paralleled in dialects from Syria-Palestine: אֵיבָּא˃- Cd Gn 38:26, "father"[26] (+ 7x, but אַבּוּי Cd Gn 48:19); דְּיֵמָּא C Gn 32:13, "of the sea" (cf. יַמְיֵה F Ex 20:11); כְּפָנָא Cd Gn 47:4, "the famine" (and 2x written כיפנה); סְגִין B Gn 4:10, "many" (+ 4x, but סַגִּין Z Gn 48:4).[27]

§18d In the following examples, *a > /e/ before /s/ and /š/: וְאִתְאָסְהַד A Ex 21:29, "he has been warned";[28] וְתִשְׁכַּח A Ex 22:5, "it will find" (C verb, but 10x with /a/, e.g., אַשְׁכַּח Cd Gn 38:20, "he found"); בְּיֵבֶּשְׁתָּא Bd Gn 7:22, "on the dry land";[29] מִשְׁכְּנָה B Ex 39:33, "the tent" (+

2x);[30] אֶסְגּוֹן C Gn 34:12, "increase!" (C verb, m.pl.); and the s. forms of "head," e.g., רֵאשׁ C Gn 32:27.[31]

A sporadic shift before sibilants is attested in Tiberian Biblical Aramaic,[32] Syriac,[33] Galilean Aramaic,[34] Palestinian Syriac,[35] and Ma'lula.[36]

**§18e**  Note the following occurrences before gutturals and *resh:* בְּהִתְתָה B Gn 2:25,* "shame"; בְּרֵיחֲמָךְ C Gn 35:9, "and in your mercy" (+ 6x, but רַחֲמֶיךָ C Gn 35:9);[37] רֵיחֵלָן C Gn 32:15, "ewes"; בְּרַתֵּהּ C Gn 34:19, "his daughter" (+ 1x);[38] נֶהֲרוּ Cd Gn 38:25, "they shone."

**§18f**  This shift is also found in the Greek loanword פָּרְגּוֹדָא Cd Gn 37:23, "the garment (+ 2x)[39] and in the originally Persian (with Aramaic suffix) זִיגּוֹן B Ex 39:26 "bell" (2x).[40] See also /šedpana/ "blight" (§110a, n.348).

**§18g**  A shift of *a > /e/ is attested in a closed stressed syllable in the noun בֵּיר E Gn 30:10, "son" (+ 10x, but בַּר־ Cd Gn 38:17 and בַר H Gn 15:2).[41] בֵּיר is also found in Targum Pseudo-Jonathan and the Fragment Targum,[42] Targum Neophyti,[43] Samaritan Aramaic,[44] Palestinian Syriac,[45] and the base /ber-/ also occurs in Syriac.[46]

**§18h**  Note three more possible examples of this sporadic sound shift: אִיתָּן C Gn 32:16, "she-asses" (the *daghesh* in the *taw* points to *'attānān > /'ettanan/, although the reconstructed Proto-Semitic form is *qatāl),[47] בִּידְכוֹן Cd Gn 43:12, "in your hand" (in imitation of Biblical Aramaic בְּיֶדְהֹם Ezra 5:8[48] or Biblical Hebrew יֶדְכֶם, יֶדְכֶן?), and הֵדְרָךְ C Gn 35:9 "your glory" (< *qatal; see §72a, n.173).

**§18i**  The examples with /e/ which are also attested with /i/ or /e/ in Biblical Aramaic, Targum Onqelos, and Syriac reflect a Proto-Aramaic development. The shift of *a > /e/. in other words, however, particularly those before a syllable closing guttural or before *resh* (and in the loanwords?)[49], appears to have been a later shift. The examples in which /a/ appear in these texts, e.g., רַחֲמֶיךָ and סָגִין, may be explained either as older forms in the language or, perhaps, as the influence of Biblical Aramaic (and Targum Onqelos?) on the vocalizers.

**§18j**  One of the most frequently cited examples of *a > i/e in Biblical Aramaic and Syriac does not occur in the Cairo Genizah fragments, viz., *qataltu > *qatalt > Biblical Aramaic /qitlet/, Syriac /qeθleθ/ "I killed" and *qatalat > Biblical Aramaic /qitlat/, Syriac /qeθlaθ/ "she killed."[50]

**§18k**  The shift of *a > /e/ is not restricted to the Aramaic of the Syria-Palestine region. It also appears in Hebrew sources. The Greek transliterations of Hebrew in the Hexapla and the Latin transliterations by Jerome show that, outside the Tiberian tradition, *a occasionally became /e/ in closed, unstressed syllables, as opposed to *a > /i/ in the Tiberian tradition.[51]

**§18l**  *u > /e/ in closed, unstressed syllables? There may be an occasional shift of *u > /e/ in closed, unstressed syllables.[52]

68

*qutlān:* בְּטלוֹנֻה A Ex 21:19,ˆ "his idleness"; פֻּרְקֹוֹן A Ex 21:30,ˆ "redemption" (cf. פורקנה Z Gn 49:1); פָּרְֿקְנֻה] Z Gn 49:2; פְּלָחָנְהֹון Cd Ex 6:6, "their service" (cf. פָֿולְחַן F Nu 28:26)ˊ.

*quttāl:* ־חֵיפָֿיי B Ex 39:34, "covering"; חֵיפָֿי B Ex 39:34; וְרָמֹון B Ex 39:26, "pomegranate"; רְמֹונֻˊ B Ex 39:24.[53] ˋ

§18m The examples וְחֵילָֿדֻותֶֿך Cd Gn 48:6, "and your offspring," and תָלָֿדֻותֶֿה Z Gn 48:6, "the offspring,"[54] may show a shift of *o* > /e/ (cf. Syriac /tawleðtā/), although both the geminated /l/ and the /e/ vowel may have been extended from the Imperfect.[55]

§18n *u > [e] or [i] in Samaritan Aramaic in all environments, however, in *qutlān* nouns, [e] is the rule.[56] In Ma'lula, *u has two reflexes, [u] and [i], which interchange freely in closed, unstressed syllables.[57]

§19 *Assimilation*

§19a *Total assimilation of consonants:* *nC > /CC/

Syllable closing /n/ assimilates to the following consonant in verbs I-n, e.g., לְמִתֶּֿן A Ex 22:16, "to give." /n/ is preserved only in the examples of the root *nhr. See §137a.

Syllable closing /n/ assimilates in all of the many examples of the nouns שתה "year" and אפין "face," e.g., שַׁתָּה HH Ex 12:2; אַפֵּֿין Cd Gn 37:30. It also assimilates regularly in the 2 person independent pronouns, e.g., ־וְאַתּ C Gn 35:9 (m.s.); ואת E Gn 30:2 (f.s.); אתון F Ex 20:19 (m.pl.); ואתן E Gn 31:6 (f.pl.).

In the noun אנתתא, "woman," historical /n/ appears in 10 examples, e.g., אנתתֶֿה E Gn 39:9; in 21 examples, the word appears without /n/, e.g., דְֿאָתּֿתָא Cd Gn 38:20.

/n/ in the preposition /men/ usually does not assimilate to the following word, e.g., מן כל E Gn 6:19, "from every." Some exceptions are ומכל E Gn 6:19; מעלוי E Gn 29:8, "from above"; מכל F Ex 19:5; מֻֿדם Z Gn 49:11,ˆ "from the blood of." מכל generally parallels ־מִכָּֿל in the Masoretic text.

§19b *Total assimilation of consonants:* *dt > /tt/

*dt > /tt/ is attested in *hadta > /hatta/ "the one," e.g., חַתָּה F Nu 28:28 (+ 4x, but חַֿדְתה Y Nu 28:28);[58] *sidt > *sitt > /set/ "towards" עד צית E Gn 28:17.[59]

§19c *Total assimilation of consonants:* *tC > /CC/

The regressive assimilation of *t of the Gt and Dt conjugations to following dentals occurs regularly in the Cairo Genizah fragments. Representative examples are 1) *tt > /tt/: לְמֶעֲמִירֶה B Gn 4:14,ˆ "to be hidden"; ואטרפת E Gn 41:8, "and it was troubled"; 2) *dt > /dd/: מְדַֿיְנִין B Gn 4:8, "arguing"; ידכי AA Nu 19:12,ˆ "he will be purified." Although the consonantal text דתתדכר F Lv 22:27, "that you will remember" appears to reflect /dətetdəkar/, this may be only a hyper-correct orthography (the scribe wanted to indicate that this was a Gt form) which masks the realization /dəteddəkar/.[60] Note also examples in which the first letter of the root begins with /t/, e.g., ־יִתְֿלֵֿא B Gn 4:15, "it will be suspended"; וֻמִתַּֿרְגַֿם D Dt 27:8, "and translated."

There are two possible examples of the regressive assimilation of /t/ of Gt/Dt to other letters (or scribal errors?):[61] 1) *tb > /bb/: איבהלו W Ex 15:15, "they were agitated" (cf. ואתבהלו W Ex 15:14); 2) *tg > /gg/: וְיִגְנְבוֹן A Ex 22:6, "they will be stolen."[62] Conservative orthography probably hides additional examples.

**§19d** *Total assimilation of consonants:* *št > /tt/?

It is possible that *št > /tt/ is reflected in תִּשְׁדַּח [חהו]מִשְׁכ A Ex 22:3 if a Gt verb is intended (as in Targum Onqelos, Targum Pseudo-Jonathan, Targum Neophyti, the Samaritan Targum, and the Peshiṭta).[63] Cf. יִשְׁתְּכַח A Ex 22:1. There are, however, two other plausible explanations of this form: 1) a G verb with passive meaning is intended, although the few attestations of this verb in other dialects in G all point to a transitive meaning "to find" and not a passive meaning of "to be found"; 2) a C 2 m.s. verb is intended, "you will find"; the scribe and/or vocalizer has interpreted the consonantal Masoretic text תמצא as a G verb "you will find" and not as a Niphal "it will be found."

**§19e** *Total assimilation of consonants in sandhi*

אם משמע F Ex 19:5, "if you obey" (for אן משמע).[64]

**§19f** *Total assimilation of consonants to vowels:* *yɔ > *yi > /i/

This phenomenon is limited to three lexical items: אִיד A Ex 21:24, "hand" (+ 1x, but 80x יד, e.g., בְּיַד Cd Gn 38:20); איקרה E Gn 31:1, "honor" (+ 3x, but 8x יקר, e.g., יְקָר C Gn 35:13); בְּאִימָמָא C Gn 31:39, "during the daytime" (+ 1x).

This phonetic development is also attested (often in these lexical items) in the other Palestinian Targumim,[65] Galilean Aramaic,[66] Palestinian Syriac,[67] Samaritan Aramaic,[68] Ma'lula,[69] and Syriac.[70] It is not attested in either Biblical Aramaic or Targum Onqelos.

**§19g** *Total assimilation of vowels to vowels:* *ā > o following *u?

The progressive assimilation of *ā > o following *u has been argued in reconstructing the Proto-Aramaic form of the following nouns:[71] /ḥəšok/ "darkness" ([חה]וכשׁחַ D Dt 5:20), /*tom/ "twin" (תומאיין E Gn 38:27), /təḥot/ "under" (e.g., תחות A Ex 21:20). Different reconstructions, however, are possible for each of these forms.[72]

Progressive assimilation of *ā > o following *u may or may not be attested in nouns of the class *qutlān > *qutlon (assimilation) > *qitlun (dissimilation) > /qetlon/,[73] and the noun *rummān > *rummon (assimilation) > *rimmon (dissimilation) > /remmon/ "pomegranate."[74]

**§19h** *Partial assimilation of vowels to consonants:* *a > /o/ before labials, /r/ (and /n/?)

This assimilation can be found in the following examples:[75] גּוּבְרִין A Ex 21:22, "men" (+ 15x, but with /a/ גַּבְרַיָּא C Gn 34:21);[76] יוֹרְדְּנָה D Dt 27:2, "the Jordan" (+ 3x); בְּקוּרְיֵיכוֹן F Ex 20:10, "in your cities" (+ 2x); רובתה E Gn 39:9, "great" (f.s.); שׁוּבִּכוֹן F Lv 23:32, "your Sabbaths, weeks" (+ 5x);[77] שׁוּבְעָה F Nu 28:27, "seven" (+ 22x);[78] אוּף AA Nu 20:5, "also" (+ 7x, but 3x with /a/); בֹּחתּוֹרְתֵּה A Ex 22:1, "in the breach";[79] גופנין AA Nu 20:5, "grapes" (+ 1x); לגוֹּהֵֶן E Gn 41:21, "in their midst" (+ 12x),[80] במורכיוותיה E Gn 30:38, "in his troughs?"[81] (+ 1x).

The partial assimilation of *a > o, u, is a frequent shift in the other Palestinian Targumim,[82] Palestinian Syriac,[83] and Galilean Aramaic.[84] There is evidence of this shift in Targum Onqelos in only a few lexical items, e.g., גופנא, גוברין.[85] The shift of *a > /u/ is attested in the Tiberian tradition of Biblical Aramaic only in גֻּבְרִין.[86] Infrequent examples of this partial assimilation are attested in Samaritan Aramaic[87] and Syriac.[88] This shift is also attested in Rabbinic Hebrew, although not always in the same lexical items as in Aramaic.[89]

Nöldeke and Brockelmann argued that *ā > o/‗n in Syriac, Mandaic, and Nabatean.[90] Such a shift is possible in the following forms בְּטְלוּנֵהּ A Ex 21:19, "idleness,"[91] בעידוני F Ex 19:16 "at the time of"; פֻּרְקָן A Ex 21:30, "redemption";[92] וְרִמּוֹן B Ex 39:26, "pomegranate." Other explanations of these forms, however, are also plausible.[93]

**§19i** *Partial assimilation of consonants to consonants: *tz > /zd/, *tṣ > /ṣṭ/*

The partial assimilation of *t to sibilants (and methathesis)[94] in the Gt and Dt conjugations occurs regularly, e.g., אזדהרו F Ex 19:12, "be careful!"; ויצטרפון H Gn 15:1, "and they will join."

**§19j** *Partial assimilation of consonants to vowels in sandhi*

Examples of partial assimilation of consonants in sandhi: 1) להות טפלינן E Gn 43:8, "also, our children" for להוד טפלינן;[95] 2) ובחמש דעשר F Nu 28:17, "and on the fifteenth" (cf. ובחמשת עשר F Lv 23:6);[96] 3) כמסד למתמנְיָה AA₁ Ex 12:4, "in order to be counted" for כמסת למתמניה.[97]

**§19l** *Partial assimilation of consonants to vowels: /bgdkpt/*

For a discussion of the partial assimilation of the consonants /bgdkpt/ to vowels, see §§4b-d.

**§20** *Dissimilation*

**§20a** *Dissimilation of consonants: *'C' > /'C'/*

The dissimilation of two /'/ in one word occurs regularly in אלע "rib" and ארע "meeting," e.g. אֶלְעָא B Gn 2:22; וארע F Nu 28:18 (and in occurrences of the related verb). There is only one example in which the initial /'/ does not dissimilate, perhaps in order to avoid two consecutive /'/: אערע H Ex 15:9, "I shall come upon" (cf. יְאָרַע‑ Cd Gn 32:18).

Reflexes of the Proto-Semitic roots *ḏl' and *'rḍ are עלע in Biblical Aramaic,[98] ערע, עלע in Targum Onqelos,[99] ארע, עלע in Targum Pseudo-Jonathan,[100] אלע, ארע in Targum Neophyti[101] and Syriac,[102] ארע, עלע in Palestinian Syriac,[103] ארע in the Fragment Targum[104] and Galilean Aramaic,[105] and 'rḍ (Arabic influence) and 'l' in Ma'lula.[106]

**§20b** *Apparent dissimilation of gemination: *CC > /nC/, *CC > /rC/?*

The dissimilation of gemination by the insertion of /n/ is attested in these fragments in one lexical item: כל מן דעם, "anything" from *madda', "knowledge," e.g. כל מן דעם, E Gn 30:31 (+ 3x, but כל מנדעם E Gn 39:8).[107]

**§20c** *Apparent dissimilation of gemination: *CC > /rC/?*

It is possible that the dissimilation of gemination by the insertion of /r/ is attested in four lexical items:[108] בדרמָסֶק H Gn 15:2, "in Damascus";[109] כורסי

AA₁ ₂ Ex 12:29, 17:16 "chair":[110] בְּשַׁרְבִיטֹה A Ex 21:20, "with his staff" (+ 2x);[111] יְשַׁרְגָּג A Ex 22:15, "he will violate."[112]

**§21 Gemination**

**§21a** In Tiberian pointed manuscripts gemination is marked regularly by daghesh if the manuscript is fully pointed, and is marked sporadically if the manuscript is only sporadically pointed. Examples of daghesh are וְנִפּוֹק B Gn 4:8, "and let us go out" and גַּנָּבַיָּא C Gn 31:39, "the thieves."

**§21b** Gemination is usually unmarked in Palestinian pointed manuscripts. There are two examples, however, in which ـ clearly marks gemination:[113] וְיִתֵּן A Ex 21:23, "and he will give" and יֹבַקֵּר A Ex 22:4, "he will clear (with fire)"[114] In addition there are eight examples in which ـ can be interpreted as marking gemination and/or shewa mobile:[115] תִּסְבּוֹן A Ex 21:14, "you will take"; מְעֻבְּרָה A Ex 21:22, "pregnant"; וְיִפְּקוֹן A Ex 21:22, "and they will go forth"; דְּאִתְּתָה A Ex 21:22, "of the woman"; יְפַלְּגוֹן A Ex 21:35, "they will divide"; גְּנֻבְּתָה A Ex 22:3, "the theft"; דְּבַעַמְּכוֹן A Ex 22:24, "of your people"; וְעֻבְּרָת E Gn 38:18, "and she conceived." ـ can be interpreted as marking gemination, a reduced vowel, a plosive realization of /p/ or all of the above in בְּדִיפְלָה A Ex 22:3, "double."[116]

**§21c** Note that the lack of gemination of waw and yodh in Tiberian pointed manuscripts is infrequently marked with ـ, e.g., וַהֲוָה Bd Gn 7:17, "and it was"; עֲשִׂירָה Bd Gn 8:5, "the tenth."

**§22 #C₁V₁C₂C₂V̲ₓ > #C₁əC₂V₂**

It appears that #C₁V₁C₂C₂V̲ₓ > #C₁əC₂V₂ in בְּשִׁפּוֹלוֹ F Ex 19:17, "in its extremities"[117] (cf. שִׁפּוֹלוֹ- B Ex 39:24, שִׁפּוֹלוֹ B Ex 39:26) . This phenomenon is known from Rabbinic Hebrew manuscripts, particularly in the environment of sibilants.[118]

**§23 Metathesis**

The Proto-Semitic metathesis of dentals and sibilants in Gt and Dt regularly takes place in these fragments, with one possible exception: דתתדכר F Lv 22:27, "that you will remember."[119] Representative examples of metathesis are 1) *tz > /zd/:[120] וְיִזְדַּבַּן A Ex 22:2, "and he will be sold"; אזדהרו F Ex 19:12, "be careful!"; 2) *ts > /st/, *tš > /št/: וְאִסְתְּכָרוּ Bd Gn 8:2, "and they were closed"; וְיִשְׁתְּבֵק B Gn 4:7, "and it will be forgiven"; 3) *tṣ > /ṣṭ/:[121] וִיצְטַרְפוּן H Gn 15:1, "and they will join."

**§24 Glides**

There are a few examples of the furtive pathaḥ and the development of the glides /w/ and /y/: רְבִיעַ B Gn 4:6, "lying"; תֹּחַ Cd Ex 6:9, "wind"; שְׁמְעַ D Dt 5:25, "heard"; וְאַרְעַ F Nu 28:26, "and a meeting."

There are, however, other examples in which there is neither a furtive pathaḥ nor a glide: נֹח-Bd Gn 7:23, "Noah"; נֹח- Bd Gn 8:1; נֹח Bd Gn 8:6; רוֹח- Bd Gn 7:22, "wind"; רוֹח- Bd Gn 8:1; ברוֹח Cd Gn 48:1; בְּרוֹח Cd Gn 48:2; לְרֹיח F Nu 28:27, "smell"; קְרוֹח E Gn 30:32, "spotted"; וְקְרוֹח E Gn 30:32. It is not clear in this last group of examples whether the vocalizer simply did not point the

72

furtive *pathaḥ* and the glide, which existed in speech,[122] or whether the furtive *pathaḥ* and the glide were not realized.

Neither the furtive *pathaḥ* nor a glide is marked in the Palestinian pointed examples תִּבֵּע A Ex 22:2, "claimant," וְתָבֹע A Ex 22:1; קָרֹח E Gn 30:32, "spotted," וּקְרֹח E Gn 30:32; נָח E Gn 7:5.

The creation of a /w/ or /y/ glide in this environment is well documented in manuscripts of the Masoretic text[123] and in manuscripts of Rabbinic Hebrew.[124] It is also found in Codex Reuchlinianus (the Hebrew and Aramaic portions),[125] pre-Ashkenazi *maḥzorim,*[126] and in Samaritan Aramaic (e.g., [ruwwå] "wind").[127]

## §25 Elision

§25a *Elision of /'/*: Syllable closing /'/ was regularly elided in speech as indicated by its frequent omission in orthography,[128] e.g., וְסָגֹּי Cd Ex 9:28, "and many" (all 30 occurrences of the root *śgy are written without *aleph*); רַנְבוּ H Gn 15:1, "of prophecy" (+ 1x, but 2x with *aleph,* e.g., בנבואתך F Ex 19:9); דָּתֶק D Dt 28:23, "vegetation."[129] Note also the elision of /'/ in the following examples: בירוע AA₁ Ex 12:16, "and a meeting"[130] (2x; but 13x with *aleph,* e.g., וארוע F Nu 28:18); וַאמַר Cd Gn 37:22, "and he said" (there are no spellings without *aleph;*[131] cf. also וַאמַר B Gn 4:15; וַאמַר C Gn 32:17; and וַאמַר Cd Gn 38:25); דמלפן AA Nu 20:10, "who teach" (without *aleph* 5x in D Imperfect and 2x in D Participle); מן לרע F Ex 20:4, "from below" (< מן לארע).

§25b *Elision of /h/*: Initial /h/ is dropped in the interrogative particle /ha/ in אלית E Gn 39:9, "Is he not?" (< הלית).[132]

Intervocalic /h/ is regularly syncopated in the 3 m.s. suffixes *ohi* and *uhi* > /oy/ and /uy/, e.g., אָחוֹי Cd Gn 37:27, "his brethren," and אֲחוּי B Gn 4:8, "his brother." There is one example in which /h/ of the 3 m.pl. pronominal suffix on nouns is syncopated (*hon* > /on/): לוותֹן E Gn 37:18, "towards them."

It appears that /h/ of the 3 m.s. suffix /eh/ was apocopated in MS Z. There are four examples (out of 28) in which the *he* is not written (note that all of the examples occur before /dV-/): במשמעֵי ודרבוני Z Gn 44:18, "in the hearing of my master"; דרישי דאבא Z Gn 44:18, "my father's head"; מֵמַר דאדני Z Gn 48:15, "the Word of the Lord"; בעֻמקי דיָמָּה Z Gn 48:16, "in the depths of the sea."

There may be one example in MS E: בחזווי ודליליה E Gn 31:24, "in a vision of the night" (literally, "its vision of the night"? or is this the m.pl. cst."visions of"?).[133]

§25c *Syncope of /a/ in sandhi:*

It is possible that the orthography of the following examples reflects the syncope of /a/ in sandhi (with resulting assimilation and junctural doubling?): בְּשַׁלְהֶבִית דָּאִשָּׁה F Ex 19:18, "in a flame of fire"[134] *bašalhabita dašša* > /bašalhabittašša?/ or /bašalhabiddašša?/; וּמִן־שָׁעָת דִּי־עַלֵּית Cd Ex 5:23, "and from the moment I entered"[135] *ša'ata di* > /ša'atti?/ or /ša'addi?/; נפשת די הוון AA Nu 19:18 "the souls that were," *napšata di* > /napšatti?/ or /napšaddi?/.[136]

§26 *Prothesis*

A prothetic *aleph* is found in the following lexical items: [137]

אדם *"blood"*: In the absolute state one finds ‗ 4x, e.g.,אֲדַם֮ Cd Ex 7:19; ‗ 1x, אָדֵם A Ex 22:2; and ֠ 1x, אֹדֵם A Ex 22:1. One finds ‗ 3x in the determined state, e.g., אֲדְמָה Cd Ex 7:21. In addition there are 17 unpointed examples with prothetic *aleph*. This word occurs only once without *aleph*: מֹדם Z Gn 49:11, "from the blood of."

אסטלי *"garment"*: There are three attestations of this loanword, two of which are pointed with different prothetic vowels: אוֹסטֹלִי A Ex 22:8,[138] אֶסְטֹלִיתה A Ex 22:26, אסטליתה E Gn 9:23.

אשתה *"six"*: There are four occurrences of this number with prothesis, e.g., אִישְׁתָה F Ex 20:9, as opposed to seven occurrences without, e.g., שֵׁת A Ex 21:2.[139]

אדרע *"arm"*: Both occurrences of this lexical item occur with prothetic *aleph*: בְּאֶדְרַע Cd Ex 6:6, and אֻנְֿרֹ֫ע W Ex 15:16.

אמצע *"middle"*: Both occurrences are with prothesis, בְּאֶמְצַע- B Gn 3:3, בְּאֶמְצַעְיָה B Ex 39:23.

ארתך *'wagon"*: Both occurrences appear with prothetic *aleph*:[140] אַרְתַּכֵּיה Cd Gn 46:29, and דאונֿרֹתכֿֿוי W Ex 15:19.[141]

אתמל *"yesterday"*: The five occurrences all have a prothetic *aleph*, e.g., דֿאתמל- A Ex 4:10, דאתמֹל-A Ex 21:36, דאתמל E Gn 31:5.

§27 *Anaptyxis*

Anaptyxis is attested in the reflexes of *qVtl nouns,[142] בְּמשְׁרִיתה F Ex 19:16, "in his camps,"[143] and the *kethibh* of מָשִׁירְיֵן H Gn 15:1.[144]

§28 *Metanalysis*

1) general Aramaic misanalysis of consonantal /t/ of אשת "fire" (< *'iššāt) and שבת "Sabbath" as the f. marker;[145]

2) ובחמש דעשר F Nu 28:17, "and on the fifteenth"[146] (cf. ובחמשת עשר F Lv 23:6);

3) כל מן דעם E Gn 31:30, "anything" (+ 3x, but כל מנדעם E Gn 39:8);[147]

4) פטיר בולי F Lv 22:27, "head of council" (< πατροβουλή).[148]

5) מיֹ גו H Gn 15:2, "from the midst" (/meggo/);[149]

6) למקבל אגרי E Gn 30:33, "to receive my wage" is a misanalysis of the sandhi pronunciation *lamqabbəla 'agri* > *lamqabbəlagri as* /lamqabbəl 'agri/.[150]

§29 *Appended /n/*

There are a few lexical items and grammatical categories in which one finds an appended /n/ or /an/. Although one can ascribe all such occurrences to a phonetic process whereby /n/ is suffixed to final, open syllables, an examination of the different occurrences leads one to conclude that what seems to be a single phonetic process is, in reality, the result of diverse, independent developments.[151]

§29a The adverb וְכַדּוּן C Gn 31:44, "now" (+ 31x) has an appended /n/,[152] as does תַּמָּן C Gn 32:14, "there" (+ 40x).[153] ותובן F Lv 22:27, "again" (but 5x, תוב,

e.g., תּוּב D Dt 5:22) has an appended /an/.[154] Elsewhere in the dialects of the Syria-Palestine region,[155]one finds כדין in the other Palestinian Targumim and in Galilean Aramaic, but כדו in Palestinian Syriac, Samaritan Aramaic, and Syriac. תובן occurs in Galilean Aramaic, Palestinian Syriac (alongside תוב) and Syriac (alongside תוב), but only תוב occurs in the Palestinian Targumim. תמן, on the other hand, can be found in Targum Onqelos, in the Palestinian Targumim, the Genesis Apocryphon, Galilean Aramaic, Palestinian Syriac, and Syriac, but תמה is attested in Biblical Aramaic. The appended /n/ and /an/ on these three adverbs in the Cairo Genizah fragments as well as in other dialects do not seem to be the result of a process of final nasalization, for, if that were the case, one could not explain the /an/ of תובן. Rather, a more likely explanation is that the /n/ of כדין could be the result of contamination with its synonym כען,[156] whereas the /an/ of תובן and תמן possibly be the old adverbial ending *ān,[157] which has been preserved in these dialects.

§29b   The pl. adjective סגין (< *śg') "many" is attested 15x in the Cairo Genizah fragments, e.g., עו סגין E Gn 30:43, "many cattle." There is only one example of the sg., וְסָגִּי Cd Ex 9:28. It has been argued that some of the occurrences of סגין in these fragments are, in reality, the sg. סגי + /n/, e.g., סָגִין־אֲנַת חוֹבִּי מֶן־לְמִטְעֹון וְסַגִּין אִית־קָדָמָיךְ לְמִשְׁרָא וּלְמִשְׁבּוּק B Gn 4:13, "My sins are too numerous to bear and there is much to forgive."[158] One may, however, interpret סגין in this verse as a pl. adjective/noun—"many things" = "much."[159] The adverbial use of סגין in Galilean Aramaic may also have arisen from the use of the pl. adjective *śaggî'în > /saggin/ (cf. סגי as an adverb in Biblical Aramaic, Palestinian Syriac, Samaritan Aramaic, and Syriac).

§29c   There may be an appended /n/ on שבתן, "rest," which occurs in these fragments in the expression שבת שבתן, "a Sabbath of rest," e.g., F Lv 23:32 (+ 3x). Cf. שבת שבתה in Targum Neophyti (Lv 23:32) and /šabbā šabbātā/ in Targum Onqelos (Lv 16:31). However, rather than assuming this to be the result of a phonetic process, it seems more likely that the /n/ reflects an /an/ suffix which was added under the influence of the Hebrew שַׁבָּתוֹן.[160]

§29d   The /n/ of the 1 pl. independent pronoun אנן and the 1 pl. pronominal suffix /nan/ are not the result of a phonetic process, but rather were extended from other forms within the pronominal system.[161]

§29e   In the verbal system, /n/ is regularly added to the 1 pl. Perf. /qətalnan/, and to the 3 m.pl. and f.pl. Perf. of verbs III-w/y/', e.g., דַּהֲווֹן C Gn 31:39, "who were" (m.pl.), and הֲוֵין Cd Ex 9:32, "they were" (f.pl.). This /n/, too, has been extended from elsewhere in the verbal paradigm and is not the result of a phonetic process.[162]

§29f   It should be noted that there are no examples of an appended /n/ on proper nouns or place names, as there are in Galilean Aramaic and in Hebrew names which appear in the Septuagint, the Dead Sea Scrolls, and inscriptional material.[163]

§30   *Anomalous Forms*

The following is a list of some anomalous forms. It is not clear whether these are errors on the part of the scribes or whether they reflect phonetic processes.

/'/ > /'/?: אמה AA₁ Ex 12:4, "the people?, his people?" (but with *ayin* 101x).[164]

/dš/ > /šš/? /dš/ > /š/?: בּקושׁא W Ex 15:11, "in holiness' (but 17x with *daleth*, e.g., קודשׁך W Ex 15:17).

/ḥ/ > ∅?: תשׁבן W Ex 15:11, "in praise" (but 2x with *ḥeth*, e.g., לתשׁבחה AA Dt 26:19).

/mp/ > /pp/?: In F Ex 20:2 there are three occurrences of לפד, "torch": ולפד דּאֵשׁה, לפד דּנוֹר, לפדין דנור. A fourth occurrence of this word in F Ex 20:15ᵃhas a *mem* added above the line: לפּ֫דּיה. It is possible that the orthography לפד reflects /lappad/ from the Greek λαμπάδος with assimilation of /m/ to the following /p/, perhaps under the influence of the Hebrew לפיד.[165] Cf. למפדין Ex 20:3 in Targum Neophyti,[166] ולמפד Ex 20:2,3 in Targum Pseudo-Jonathan, and לפדין in Ex 20:2 of the Fragment Targum (MS P). Note also Syriac /lampiδā/[167] and Palestinian Syriac למפד.[168]

C₁VC₁ > C₁VC₂ (dissimilation)?: מול AA₁ Ex 12:5, "blemish" (cf. מום AA Nu 19:2, + 3x).

§31

## G. Stress

The pattern of word-stress in these fragments appears, in general, to be that of Biblical Aramaic, Targum Onqelos, and Syriac: stress is penultimate when the final syllable is a vowel, except in the case of vowels which are reflexes of original diphthongs or originally closed syllables; otherwise it is ultimate.[1] Evidence for the stress pattern comes from three sources: the consonantal text, the vocalized text, and the position of the accent signs.

§31a The consonantal and vocalized texts support the classical Aramaic stress pattern. The only forms in the consonantal text whose orthography could be interpreted as reflecting a different stress pattern are the two absolute forms of the noun חטר "staff"[2] and three forms of the cardinal number שבע "seven":[3] חוטר E Gn 30:37, וחוטר AA₁ Ex 17:9, and שובעE Gn 29:22 (2x), שובע F Lv 23:15. The orthography of these forms could be taken as reflecting [ḥóṭɛr] or [ḥóṭar] and [šóva']; it is also possible, however, that this orthography was intended to reflect either [ḥŏṭár] and [šŏvá'] or [ḥoṭár] and [šová'].[4] Pointings in the vocalized text which could possibly hint of a stress pattern different from that of Biblical Aramaic and Targum Onqelos are the occasional signs for full vowels which occur where one expects either a *shewa mobile* or a *ḥateph* vowel,[5] e.g., בָּרֵיהּ C Gn 34:24, "his son" (cf. בְּרֵיהּ C Gn 34:20) קֳדָם C Gn 31:42, "before" (cf. קדָם B Gn 4:13). There is, however, no internal evidence that, even if the *shewa mobile* were realized as a full vowel(which does not seem to be the case), this realization was caused by a retraction of the stress.[6] Note that the consonantal text, the pointing, and the positioning of the accent sign indicate a retraction of the stress in סֻוגֵי C Gn 32:13, "multitude."[7]

76

§31b   The Tiberian accent signs in these manuscripts are almost always positioned on syllables which are stressed in Biblical Aramaic and Targum Onqelos, even in the interpolated passages[8] where there is no Masoretic text from which to copy the accent signs. There are, however, a few examples in which the accents are placed on syllables in which one does not expect the stress. Almost all of these examples show a shift of the stress to the penultimate syllable. It is possible that the shift of the stress in some of the examples is due to an imitation of the Masoretic rules of retraction of stress in pause and *nesighah*. Examples of penultimate stress are נָפֵק־ B Gn 2:20, "going forth";[9] סוֹגִי־ C Gn 32:13, "multitude";[10] סֵיבוּ Cd Gn 48:10, "old age";[11] נֶקְבָה E Gn 30:21, "female"; פֻּלְחָנִי E Gn 30:26, "my service"; דְּרִבּוֹנֵהּ E Gn 40:7, "of his master."

§31c   There is one category, however, in which the accent seems to have shifted to the ultimate syllable from an original penultimate stress. In all of the pointed examples of the 3 f.s. Perfect of verbs II-w/y, one finds ultimate stress, unlike in Biblical Aramaic[12] and Targum Onqelos:[13] the examples are וּמִיתַת C Gn 35:8, "and she died"; דְּמִיתַת C Gn 35:9; וְקָמַת Cd Gn 38:19, "and she arose." There are two additional examples which are pointed with the postpositive accent *telisha qeṭanna*—מִיתַת̃ C Gn 35:9, מִיתַת̃ Cd Gn 48:7—and hence cannot serve as evidence of the shift.

§31d   The positioning of the Palestinian accent signs is problematic. It is generally held that the position of these accent signs varies and that the signs do not mark stress.[14] Cf. the apparently random positioning of the accent signs on the word למינה, "of its kind" in MS E: לְמִינָה E Gn 6:20, לְמִינָה E Gn 7:14, and לְמִינֹה E Gn 7:14.

§31e   It should be noted that Samaritan Aramaic,[15] Palestinian Syriac,[16] and Ma'lula,[17] have a stress pattern which is basically penultimate, unlike the basically ultimate stress pattern found in Biblical Aramaic, Targum Onqelos, and Syriac.[18] It is assumed that stress is ultimate in Galilean Aramaic.[19]

Footnotes — Chapter III

## A. Graphic Signs Used in Fragments

[1]See §§7-13 for a discussion of how the Tiberian and Palestinian vowel signs are used and what vocalic phonemes they represent. For a discussion of the use of the Palestinian vowel signs in Hebrew manuscripts, see M. Dietrich, *Neue palästinisch punktierte Bibelfragmente* (Leiden: E. J. Brill, 1968); E. J. Revell, *Hebrew Texts with Palestinian Vocalization* (Toronto: University of Toronto Press, 1970); B. Chiesa, *L'Antico Testamento Ebraico secondo la tradizione palestinese* (Torino: Bottega d'Erasmo, 1978).

[2]The only Palestinian vowel sign which is unattested is ֺֺ. This sign appears in place of ֺֺ in some Hebrew manuscripts.

[3]See §§4b–4d.

[4]See §21.

[5]See §4k.

[6]Ibid.

[7]See §21c.

[8]For a discussion of Palestinian accent signs in general, as well as their use in some of these fragments, see Revell, *Biblical Texts*, pp. 133-136. Occasionally one finds two Tiberian accent signs with one word, e.g., וַיֵּצֵא Cd Gn 43:31, "and he went out" (MT וַיֵּצֵא).

[9]Note that in MSS B and H one finds אֲדֹנִי. See §2e.

[10]The double writing of these letters is used by scribes to indicate that the letters are functioning as consonants and not as *matres lectionis*. This supralinear sign, on the other hand, is used by vocalizers who regard this *scriptio plena* as unnecessary in a vocalized text.

## B. Consonantal Phonemes

[1]In some Palestinian pointed Hebrew manuscripts ֿ marks a plosive pronunciation of /bgdkpt/ and ֿ marks a spirantized realization. Cf. e.g., Dietrich, *Neue palästinisch punktierte Bibelfragmente*, pp. 123-124.

[2]See §12c. One could argue, however, as has been argued for the second of two final *shewas* in the Tiberian system, e.g., כָּתַבְתְּ, that this sign may have been intended to reflect an anaptyctic vowel /ə/. On this *shewa* in the Tiberian system, see Morag, *Vocalization Systems of Arabic, Hebrew, and Aramaic: Their Phonetic and Phonemic Principles* ('s-Gravenhage: Mouton, 1962), p. 71, n.20.

[3]See §12c.

[4]Cf. the treatment of Greek loanwords in Syriac in which the rules of *rukkakha* and *quššaya* are not applied. See Nöldeke, *Compendious Syriac Grammar*, trans. J. Crichton (London: Williams and Norgate, 1904), pp. 19-20. It is conceivable, however, that ֿ was intended to mark gemination and/or *shewa mobile*, i.e. /deppəla?/. See §§12c, 21b.

[5]For another possible example, see §12c, n.120.

[6]Klein reads הֵבֵ. Although two dots appear in the published photograph (*Genizah Manuscripts*, II, Plate 63), an examination of the manuscript does not reveal a vowel sign.

78

[7]On the elision of /'/, see §25a.

[8]Cf. Targum Onqelos /dəlub/, Targum Neophyti דלוב (margin דלבוי), Syriac /dulbā/, Arabic /dulb/, Akkadian /tulbu/. It is difficult to ascertain the noun pattern of the Cairo Genizah form. See also §17d.

[9]Ben-Hayyim believes that the realization was [v] in Jewish Aramaic and in Samaritan Aramaic. See his *Studies in the Traditions of the Hebrew Language*, pp. 104-105. See also Kutscher, *A History of the Hebrew Language*, ed. R. Kutscher (Jerusalem: Magnes Press; Leiden: E. J. Brill, 1982), p. 121.

[10]See §77b.

[11]Kahle notes other possible examples in *Masoreten des Westens*, II, p. 7, nn.4-5, and p. 2, n.6. Klein frequently reads a *daghesh* in *Genizah Manuscripts*; however, the dots he reads seem often not to be pointed by vocalizers.

[12]The exceptions are קדְמִיה, עַצִּין, וְחַמְיָא. For another example with *daghesh*, which, however, might reflect gemination, see §142c.

[13]Were the *raphe* to occur following ֽ, one would assume that it would indicate that the preceding sign is a *shewa mobile* and not a *shewa quiescens*.

[14]See §32b.

[15]Does this *daghesh* reflect the assimilation in the non-voicing of θ > t∠b?

[16]From *bukrat? See §76b. The vocalizer may have confused this word with בְּכוֹר.

[17]Cf. Targum Onqelos /bəkerutā/ Dt 21:17 (בכורתא in printed editions). Here, too, the vocalizer may have confused this word with בְּכוֹר.

[18]See also §10d.

[19]See §§116, 153.

[20]See §25.

[21]Ibid. For exceptional forms, see §30.

[22]The placing of the *mappiq* beneath the *he* is a feature common to both the Tiberian and the Palestinian pointing systems. For Tiberian pointed manuscripts in which this pointing occurs, see H. Bauer—P. Leander, *Historische Grammatik der hebräischen Sprache* (Halle: Max Niemeyer, 1922; reprint Hildesheim: Georg Olms, 1965), p. 127. For Palestinian pointed manuscripts, see Dietrich, *Neue palästinisch punktierte Bibelfragmente*, pp. 87*-88*.

[23]See §12c, n.120.

[24]In this same manuscript ֺ is also used to indicate that *he* is a *mater lectionis*, a function which is attested elsewhere in Palestinian pointed manuscripts. See §16a and Bauer—Leander, *Historische Grammatik*, p. 122. ֺ is probably an error for ֺ (= *mappiq* as in some Palestinian pointed Hebrew manuscripts) since the *he* and the vowel sign reflect a 3 m.s. suffix. It is less likely that מרֹה reflects a construct form /mare/. See §§88d, n.262, 161d.

[25]/p/ is realized as [p] in all environments in Eastern Syriac. See Nöldeke, *Syriac Grammar*, p. 15. In the modern pronunciation of Samaritan Aramaic, there are only traces of spirantization of /b/, although Ben-Hayyim's reconstruction of Samaritan Aramaic reveals spirantization of /bgdt/. See Ben-Hayyim, *Studies*, p. 109. In Ma'lula, spirantization is generally preserved, although some shifting of sounds has taken place (e.g., there is no spirantization of /b/, and plosive /p/ is realized as [f]). See A. Spitaler, *Grammatik des neuaramäischens Dialekts von Ma'lula* [Antilibanon] (*AKM*, 23,1; Leipzig: Deutsche Morgenländische Gesellschaft, 1938), p. 13. For the situation

in Palestinian Syriac, see F. Schulthess, *Grammatik des christlisch-palästinischen Aramäisch* (Tübingen: J. C. Mohr, 1924), pp. 5-6.

[26]See Dalman, *Grammatik*, p. 105.

[27]Ibid.

[28]See Levy, "Language," pp. 31-32.

[29]See Kutscher, *Studies*, pp. 16-17.

[30]See Ben-Ḥayyim, *Studies*, p. 104; Tal, *The Samaritan Targum: A Critical Edition*, III (Tel-Aviv: Tel-Aviv University, 1983), p. 128.

[31]See M. H. Segal, *A Grammar of Mishnaic Hebrew* (Oxford: Clarendon Press, 1923), pp. 34-35; J. N. Epstein, *Introduction to the Text of the Mishnah* (Jerusalem: Magnes Press, 1948), pp. 1223-1226 (in Hebrew).

[32]See §14n.

[33]See S. Morag, "The Vocalization of Codex Reuchlinianus: Is the 'Pre-Masoretic' Bible Pre-Masoretic?" *JSS*, 4 (1959), 226-227.

[34]See I. Eldar, *The Hebrew Language Tradition in Medieval Ashkenaz (ca. 950-1350 C.E.)*, I: *Phonology and Vocalization* (Jerusalem: Hebrew University Language Traditions Project, IV, 1978), pp. 125-143 (in Hebrew). The extended use of *daghesh* is also attested in MS Parma (de Rossi 138) of the Mishnah. See G. Haneman, *A Morphology of Mishnaic Hebrew According to the Tradition of the Parma Manuscript [de Rossi 138]* (Tel-Aviv: Tel-Aviv University, 1980), pp. 19-21 (in Hebrew).

[35]The use of the *daghesh* to indicate the nature of a medial *shewa* (and thus, if a preceding syllable is open or closed) is attested also in certain Masoretic manuscripts after gutturals. See C. D. Ginsburg, *Introduction to the Massoretico-Critical Edition of the Hebrew Bible* (London: Trinitarian Bible Society, 1897), pp. 123ff.

[36]See Dalman, *Grammatik*, pp. 53, 104.

[37]Ibid.

[38]Ibid.

[39]See Levy, "Language," p. 35.

[40]See Dalman, *Grammatik*, pp. 53, 104.

[41]See Segal, *Grammar*, p. 32, who explains the examples with *samekh* as the result of Aramaic influence. See also Ben-Ḥayyim, *Literary and Oral Traditions*, V, pp. 23-24. For the view that it was the Hebrew which influenced the Aramaic, see Kutscher, *A History of Aramaic*, I (Jerusalem: Academon, 1972-1973), p. 19 (in Hebrew).

[42]*š and *s have merged to /s/ in Ma'lula. See Spitaler, *Grammatik*, p. 12.

[43]See F. Rosenthal, *A Grammar of Biblical Aramaic* (Porta Linguarum Orientalium 5; Wiesbaden: Harrassowitz, 1974), p. 16: "In BA times, this process was in its incipient stages."

[44]See Kutscher, *Studies*, p. 84: "The sum total of the loss of the gutturals as it is reflected in the actual vocabulary is not great. Just the opposite is true; their number is quite small. The indications, however, are certain...."

[45]See Dalman, *Grammatik*, pp. 96-99.

[46]Ibid.

[47]See Levy, "Language," pp. 23-30.

[48]See Kutscher, "Aramaic," *EJ*, 3, col. 279.

[49]See M. Bar-Asher, *Palestinian Syriac Studies: Source-Texts, Tradition and Grammatical Problems* (Jerusalem, 1977), pp. 367-420 (in Hebrew).

80

[50]See R. Macuch, *Grammatik des samaritanischen Aramäisch* (Berlin: Walter de Gruyter, 1982), pp. 76-78.

## C. Vocalic Phonemes

[1] ֗ is not attested.

[2]This term is used to express the opposite of "minimal pairs" used in phonemic analysis, which are "sets of linguistic forms (words or morphemes) which are different in meaning, but are identical in sound except for one item." See A. Arlotto,*Introduction to Historical Linguistics* (Boston: Houghton Mifflin, 1972), p. 73. "Non-contrasting minimal pairs" are pairs of words or morphemes which differ from one another graphically, but are identical in meaning and sound, e.g., אָנֶה- D Dt 27:1, "I," and אָנָה- D Dt 27:10.

[3]Not, however, in all the manuscripts. See MS A and the sporadic Palestinian vowel signs in MSS E and H.

[4]Kutscher explains the use of some of the Tiberian vowel signs differently. Instead of assuming that both the "correct" and the "incorrect" Tiberian pointings are the work of the original vocalizers of these manuscripts, he argues that words pointed with *ḥireq* and *shureq/qibbuṣ* were pointed by later copyists who attempted to make the pointing of these texts correspond to the pointing of Biblical Aramaic and Targum Onqelos. He maintained that the original vocalizers represented *i by *seghol* and *u by *ḥolem*. See Kutscher, "Articulation of the Vowels u,i," p. 230.

If that were the case, why were only a few words re-pointed, and why relatively unimportant words such as מִן? It is surely not necessary to resort to an explanation which relies solely on later scribal redaction. It seems preferable to assume that most of the confusion in vowel signs can be explained by the fact that the original vocalizers of these manuscripts pointed at times phonetically and at times historically.

Kutscher is right in noting that, on the whole, the sporadically pointed manuscripts agree more closely with the Tiberian rules of pointing than do the fully vocalized fragments. It should, however, be emphasized that, while these sporadic pointings do suggest a predominant Tiberian influence, they do, nonetheless, exhibit the interchange of vowel signs found in those texts which are fully vocalized. Even MSS H and HH, which come closest to being "properly" pointed with Tiberian vowel signs, reveal fluctuation between *qameṣ* and *pathaḥ*.

According to Kutscher, it was the prestige of the Tiberian Biblical forms which led copyists of mediaeval manuscripts of Rabbinic Hebrew (e.g., MS Kaufmann) to point, according to their Biblical forms, words which occurred frequently in the Bible. Rare or less frequent words, with which the copyists were less familiar, were copied with the vulgar pointing of earlier vocalizers. Here, too, one wonders whether later redactors are to be held responsible for all the "corrections," and whether the original vocalizers might not have pointed words with which they were familiar from the Bible according to their Biblical forms and words which did not occur in the Bible, or which occurred infrequently, according to their vulgar pronunciation. See Kutscher, "Articulation of the Vowels u,i," p. 234, and "Mishnaic Hebrew," *Henoch Yalon Jubilee Volume*, p. 257.

[5]E.g., וּשְׁכֶם C Gn 34:20, "and Shechem" (MT וּשְׁכֶם), and אַהֲרֹן HH Ex 12:1, "Aaron" (MT אַהֲרֹן-).

[6]Examples of "errors" include *sere* for *seghol* וִילֶד Cd Gn 44:20, "and a child of" (MT וִילֶד), and *pathaḥ* for *shewa mobile*, בָכָל- Cd Ex 9:22, "and all of" (MT בְּכָל-).

⁷Also to be noted is the use of two signs for /e/. In the oldest Palestinian pointed Hebrew manuscripts, there is only one vowel sign for this phoneme, ⸚. In later texts, the sign ⸚ appears representing *seghol*, leaving ⸚ to represent *sere*. In the Cairo Genizah fragments, as in some Palestinian pointed Hebrew manuscripts, the two signs interchange freely.

It is generally assumed that the Palestinian pointing system underwent a process of "Tiberianization," and that from an original system of five vowel signs representing five phonemes (/a/, /e/, /i/, /o/, /u/—however, even in the earliest manuscripts, there are two vowel signs for /a/ which fluctuate, leading some scholars to posit an original system of six signs for six phonemes), developed a Tiberianized system of seven vowel signs, corresponding to the Tiberian system with seven qualities of vowels (excluding the *shewa* and the *ḥateph* vowels). See, for example, A. Dotan, "Masorah," *EJ*, 16, cols. 1433-1435; Morag, *Vocalization Systems*, p. 37. For a different view of the Palestinian system, see E. J. Revell, "Studies in the Palestinian Vocalization of Hebrew," in *Essays on the Ancient Semitic World*, ed. J. W. Wevers and D. B. Redford (Toronto: University of Toronto Press, 1970), pp. 51-100; and Revell, *Hebrew Texts*, pp. 109ff.

⁸See §11e.

⁹E.g., MS Eb. 448 and the *Editio Sabbioneta*. See Díez Macho, "Onqelos Manuscript with Babylonian Transliterated Vocalization in the Vatican Library (MS. Eb 448)," *VT*, 8 (1958), 113-133; Berliner, *Targum Onkelos*, II, pp. 133ff.

¹⁰Such as MS Or 2363, which is the main text used by Sperber in his edition of Targum Onqelos, and Codex Socin 84, which is one of the sources for Dalman's *Grammatik* and his *Aramäisch-neuhebräisches Handwörterbuch zu Targum, Talmud und Midrasch*, 2nd ed. (Göttingen: Vandenhoeck und Ruprecht, 1938; reprint Hildesheim: Georg Olms, 1967). The supralinear Babylonian pointing found in these Yemenite manuscripts reflects a consistent, reliable tradition, unlike the Tiberian pointing found in mediaeval manuscripts of Targum Onqelos or mediaeval printed editions, which are internally inconsistent, resulting in part from the applicaton of rules of Hebrew tonic and pretonic lengthening (see Dalman, *Grammatik*, p. 73) and from attempts to bring their pointing in line with Biblical Aramaic. A more recent and reliable transcription from Babylonian vowel signs into Tiberian vowel signs is that done from Yemenite supralinear manuscripts, which appears in the ספר כתר תורה (more commonly known as the תאג). See Dalman, *Grammatik*, pp. 13, 14, 75.

¹¹See Roberts, *Old Testament*, p. 212, and Dalman, *Grammatik*, pp. 72-74.

¹²See Dalman, *Grammatik*, p. 73. For an extensive discussion of the conscious attempts to bring order into Targum texts in general, see A. Merx, "Bemerkungen über die Vocalisation der Targume," *Verhandlungen des fünften Internationalen Orientalisten-Congresses* (Berlin: Asher, 1882), pp. 142-225. See also R. H. Melamed, "The Targum to Canticles According to Six Yemen Mss. Compared with the 'Textus Receptus' (ed. de Lagarde)," *JQR n.s.*, 10 (1919-1920), 387ff, A Merx, *Chrestomathia Targumica* (Berlin: Reuther, 1888), pp. viiiff.

¹³For a discussion of stress in these fragments, see §31.

¹⁴See §11d-§11e.

¹⁵The shift of /a/ to /o/ before /r/ and labials is attested in Aramaic dialects and in Rabbinic Hebrew. See §19h. In the case of דּגֻבְרָה A Ex 22:6, "of the man," it is impossible to determine whether the graphic representation reflects /gobra/ (cf. גּוּבְרִין

82

A Ex 21:22) or /gabra/ (cf. גִּבְרַיָא C Gn 34:21). Comparative evidence from other dialects allows for both forms.

[16]It is also attested in the proper noun /kəna'an/, "Canaan," דִּכְנַעַן Cd Gn 46:31. The pointing found in דִּכְנָעַן Cd Gn 48:3 certainly is in imitation of the pausal lengthening in the Masoretic text. See §8j.

[17]There is only one example with ֶ, הֲוָת Cd Gn 38:21, "she was." This form is usually pointed in Biblical Aramaic with qameṣ, although pathaḥ is also attested in the Tiberian tradition, See Bauer-Leander, Grammatik, p. 174.

[18]There are no pointings with ֵ or ֶ. Kahle's reading וְיָהֲווֹן A Ex 22:23 is incorrect and should be read וְיֶהֱווֹן, as read by Klein.

[19]There are only two exceptions: טעוון Z Gn 49:2, "idols," and אֻחֲרָנִיִּן A Ex 22:19, "others."

[20]On the translation of this word, see Lund, "Interpretation," pp. 99-103.

[21]See §37b.

[22]Although the pointing of מה occasionally corresponds to the Tiberian Hebrew rules of pointing this interrogative, the majority of examples do not show any correspondence. See also §43a, n.201.

[23]It appears that the ayin was written over an aleph.

[24]One expects /a/ in this environment in 3 f.s. Perfect of verbs II-w/y. The stress pattern in this category, however, differs in these fragments from that of Biblical Aramaic and Targum Onqelos. See §31c.

[25]Unlike in Biblical Aramaic and Targum Onqelos. Cf. the Tiberian Biblical Aramaic and Targum Onqelos forms /'ənáḥnā/ "we," /qətálnā/ "we killed," /qəṭálā/ "they killed" (f.pl.), /qədāmáhā/ (Targum Onqelos) "before her" with their Cairo Genizah counterparts /'ənán/, /qətalnán/, /qatlen?/, and /qədaméh/. There are no examples of adverbs with final, unstressed /a/, as there are in Biblical Aramaic and Targum Onqelos with /ā/ (see Dalman, Grammatik, pp. 55, 56).

[26]Realized as [ă]. See §12f.

[27]Note the daghesh forte suggesting /mayya/. Cf. מָיָא Bd Gn 7:17. ֶ for expected ֶ before a daghesh forte is a prominent feature in the pointing of Maimonides' commentary to the Mishna (autograph). According to T. Zurawel, it reflects a realization of [ă], which is supported by the Hebrew reading traditions of Djerba and Aleppo. See Zurawel, "The Sheva in Maimonides' Commentary to the Mishna (Autograph)," in M. Bar-Asher, ed., LanguageStudies II-III (Jerusalem: 1987), p. 218 (Hebrew).

[28]See §72b.

[29]Note the daghesh forte suggesting /'etkassi/, a Dt form. Cf. וְאִתְכַּסּוֹן Bd Gn 7:19.

[30]This seems to be a G Participle (cf. MT הַנֹּשֵׁךְ, "who bites"). Were this a G Perfect, one would expect to find דמחה. If this form is interepreted as a D Perfect /maḥḥi/, then ֶ must still be analyzed as representing /a/.

[31]Did the vocalizer intend to point וְאָמַהְתְכוֹן (and in the previous example וְעַבְדֵּיכוֹן)?

[32]As is the case in the Editio Sabbioneta and in the printed editions of Targum Pseudo-Jonathan and the Fragment Targum. See Dalman, Grammatik, pp. 72-73.

[33]See §32.

[34]Features not included in the vowel sign counts are: 1) the consistent pointing of /a/ with ֶ (23x) in the verbal inflections /qatlet/ "I killed" and /qatlat/ "she killed" as against the Tiberian Biblical Aramaic forms /qitlet/ and /qitlat/ (although /qatlet/

is attested in verbs I-guttural); 2) the consistent pointing of /a/ of the Rule of Shewa with ‗ (67x) as against the Biblical Aramaic form with /i/ (although /a/ is attested in Biblical Aramaic in sequences involving gutturals); 3) the forms of אח "brother" with pronominal suffixes, which is attested only once in Biblical Aramaic and which has different base forms before pronominal suffixes in Targum Onqelos (in both the Yemenite manuscripts and the printed editions).

[35]There is one non-contrasting minimal triplet, מִן־ C Gn 35:9, "from" (cf. מֶן־ Cd Gn 47:1, וּמִין־ Cd Gn 47:2).

[36]See Kutscher, "Articulation of the Vowels u,i," pp. 227-232.

[37]See §§4d, 19c.

[38]Cf. אֶסְטֹלִּיתה A Ex 22:26.

[39]See §17g.

[40]‗ is the Tiberian accent zaqeph.

[41]Klein reads סֹדְרִי. The photograph shows ‗ above the samekh and not the daleth. The ḥireq beneath the daleth is puzzling if the reading is correct. For other examples of final ḥireq in place of ṣere, see §9i.

[42]As noted by Kahle, מֶניה has been corrected to מֶנֵּה.

[43]Kahle reads [וּבְבְזָעֵניה.

[44]See Kutscher, "Articulation of the Vowels u,i," p. 228. One can also add examples which Kutscher did not know of: בְּמְתֵי Cd Gn 48:7; במְתֵי Z Gn 48:7, and לְמְנְיָן HH Ex 12:2 (seghol, however, is not attested in MS HH). He neglected to add למניִן F Nu 28:29.

[45]There are no pointed examples of this environment in the Palestinian pointed manuscripts.

[46]See §4f.

[47]See §130b.

[48]There are also three poorly preserved examples: וְאָעֵלוֹן Cd Gn 37:28, "and they brought in"; וְאָ[עֵילוֹ Cd Gn 37:32; וְאַחֵתוּן Cd Gn 44:11, "and they brought down."

[49]In Targum Onqelos, one finds either ḥireq or ṣere, depending on the verbal category, e.g., סְלִיקוּ "they went up" as opposed to סְלֵיקַת "she went up."

[50]It is possible, however, that this word was realized as /ḥewta/ and not /ḥewəta/. See §32.

[51]The use of he as a mater lectionis and the pointing probably reflect Hebrew influence. See §§16c, 155c.

[52]See n.41 above.

[53]See §§151b, 155c.

[54]See §67h, n.104.

[55]See §69d, n.143. If Klein's reading כְּפִירֵי־ B Gn 4:16 is correct, then there is another example which deviates from the Tiberian rules of pointing. The published photograph (Plate 7), however, seems to confirm Kahle's reading כְּפִירֵי־.

[56]See Bauer-Leander, Grammatik, p. 31.

[57]See Bauer-Leander, Grammatik, p. 30. The fluctuation of vowel signs in these manuscripts in no way reflects the fluctuation of ṣere and ḥireq found occasionally in pausal position in Yemenite manuscripts of Targum Onqelos and frequently in the Editio Sabbioneta. See Dalman, Grammatik, pp. 54-55.

[58]Features not included in these frequency counts are 1) /e/ of G *qatila, D, C, Gt, and Dt, which is predominantly pointed with ‗ in these manuscripts (‗ 127x, ‗ 26x,

84

___ 2x, and ___ 20x) where in Tiberian Biblical Aramaic one finds *ḥireq*, except in closed, stressed syllables where one also finds *ṣere*, or *seghol* in final, closed, unstressed syllables (in Targum Onqelos *ṣere*); 2) /e/ which arises from the contraction of \*ay in m.pl. nouns with s. pronominal suffixes, e.g., /bənek/ "your sons" (pointed ___ 30x, ___ 5x) as against the *qere* of Biblical Aramaic /bənāk/; 3) /e/ of the 3 f.pl. Perfect morpheme /-en/, e.g., /həwen/ "they were" (pointed ___ 7x) as against the *qere* of Biblical Aramaic /-ā/ (/-ān/ in Targum Onqelos).

The one example in which one finds ___ where /e/ is expected is also excluded—יִגֹּ֫ח A Ex 21:31, "he will butt" since it may reflect /yəgoḥ/. See §137g.

⁵⁹\*i > /e/. See §14t.

⁶⁰See §115b.

⁶¹For the rare examples with *scriptio defectiva*, see §16e.

⁶²This is the only occurrence of this word in the m.pl. absolute. It is unlikely that this pointing was the result of confusion with /pəren/, "dowry," from the Greek φερνή (cf. פֶּרֶן C Gn 34:12). The pointing of "fruit" with *seghol* is also attested in MS Kaufmann of the Mishnah (Prof. M. Bar-Asher has collected four such examples).

⁶³See §4h.

⁶⁴For a possible explanation of the surprising use of the *metheg* in the Biblical Aramaic form, see Bauer-Leander, *Grammatik*, p. 22.

⁶⁵There are no other attestations of this word in the Cairo Genizah fragments. The evidence from Targum Onqelos and Syriac suggests a \*qatīlat formation. See §83b.

⁶⁶On the orthography, see §16e, n.20.

⁶⁷One expects וְאָשְׁתִּיצִי. Cf. however, Targum Onqelos /wə'išteṣe/ Gn 34:30.

⁶⁸All 23 examples are pointed with ___. One also expects /i/ in the Imperative (there are only two pointed examples, both with ___). It must be kept in mind, however, that שיצי is not native to Aramaic. See §130f.

⁶⁹From \*qīlān? Cf. Biblical Hebrew /'ēlā/, /'ēlon/. The e-vowel of the Hebrew forms may have influenced the vocalizer.

⁷⁰There may be an additional example, although the reading of the vowel sign is not certain: שבלין E Gn 41:22, "ears of corn." Kahle reads שֻבְּלִין; Klein reads שֻבְלִין. There is another example according to Kahle and Klein, בְּעִירָא֖ Bd Gn 7:23, "cattle." A re-reading of the manuscript, however, shows בְּעִירָא֖. Klein's reading קָטִילָא C Gn 31:39, "dead thing" is not confirmed by an examination of the published photograph (Plate 10), which shows Kahle's reading קְטִילָא֖.

⁷¹See Kutscher, "Articulation of the Vowels u,i," pp. 232-233.

⁷²On the pointing of כל, see §11r.

⁷³See Bauer-Leander, *Grammatik*, p. 32. ___ could reflect /a/ or /o/ in יְגְרָא C Gn 31:46, although /a/ is clearly attested in other examples and in other dialects. בְּרַמְשָׁא C Gn 31:42, "in the evening" could reflect /ramša/ or /romša/ (as in Galilean Aramaic and Palestinian Syriac).

⁷⁴As noted by Kutscher. See n.71 above.

⁷⁵/qorayya/? The manuscript seems to show קוֹרִיּא, although the final two signs (vowel signs?) make little sense if this is a correct reading. Klein reads קוֹרִיא. Cf. Targum Onqelos /qirwayyā/.

⁷⁶See §19h, n.79.

⁷⁷See §9c, n.38.

⁷⁸See §4f.

[79]An o-vowel is unattested in this noun in other dialects. A realization of /a/, however, is attested in these fragments See §67a.

[80]See §70b, n.162.

[81]See §82e, n.237.

[82]Cf. גּוֹבְרִין A Ex 21:22.

[83]It is possible that a > o/‗r in this example. This word is not attested, however, with o in any other Targumim or cognate dialects.

[84]See §17g.

[85]For expected בְּעֶבְדָּא. See §81a.

[86]The only other occurrence of this word is unpointed and gives no clue as to the vocalization: אחרייא F Lv 23:22. This word is unattested in Biblical Aramaic and Targum Onqelos. See §113b.

[87]In the Tiberian pointed fragments, the first vocalic phoneme is /o/. See §12i.

It is possible that ﹘ is a *raphe* sign marking the quiescence of the *aleph*. For similar forms in other dialects, see §46b. This, however, seems less likely since there are no other examples of *raphe* marking the quiescence of *aleph* in the Palestinian pointed manuscripts. One might have expected ﹍, which marks the quiescence of *aleph* in Palestinian pointed Hebrew manuscripts.

[88]On the basis of Targum Onqelos one expects סְגֵי. See, however, §69d n.137. Golomb *(Grammar,* p. 81) cites a form *soge* for Targum Neophyti (see Dt. 10:22) and explains the o vowel as assimilation to the velar.

[89]The characteristic vowel of the Imperative is /o/ and not /u/ as in Tiberian Biblical Aramaic. See Bauer-Leander, *Grammatik,* pp. 31, 99. See §131.

[90]The characteristic vowel of the Imperfect is /o/ in this dialect not /u/ as in Tiberian Biblical Aramaic. See Bauer-Leander, *Grammatik,* pp. 31, 97-98. See §131.

[91]Dalman notes in his *Handwörterbuch,* p. 388, that /qardo/ is found in manuscripts, but קָרְדּוּ is attested in the printed editions of Targum Onqelos.

[92]See §32c.

[93]See §121.

[94]One expects סִיבוּ. Perhaps the retraction of stress is in imitation of the Masoretic text מִזֹּן. See §31b.

[95]Kahle and Martínez read יְרִיתוּ. Klein reads וִירֹזֹתוּ. There may be a *ṣere* or a *ḥireq* beneath the *resh*.

[96]And once with ﹍. See §§11f; 66 n.75.

[97]See §46a, 66.

[98]< *qawl in this dialect? Cf. s. *lawḥ and *ṭawr. See §15f.

[99]Because the vocalizer of this manuscript does not always point words fully, it is impossible to determine if the s. or the pl. form is intended. Cf. בְּתולָה A Ex 22:15.

[100]The origin of this class is uncertain as is the origin of the o vowel. See §89, n.267.

[101]For other possible reconstructions, see Bauer-Leander, *Historische Grammatik,* pp. 480-481.

[102]It is possible, although less likely, that the published photograph (Plate 17) shows גִּיסוּבִין.

[103]מַבּוּל and מַבּוּעַ both belong to the *maqtūl class in Biblical Hebrew.

[104]Šaphel nouns and verbs are borrowed from either Akkadian, Amorite, or a third Semitic language. See S. Kaufman, *The Akkadian Influences on Aramaic* (Chicago: The University of Chicago Press, 1974; Assyriological Studies No.19), pp. 123-124; C.

86

Rabin, "The Nature and Origin of the Shaf'el in Hebrew and Aramaic," *EI*, 9 (1969), 148-158 (in Hebrew).

[105]See §§117-120.

[106]See §118.

[107]An unetymological *ayin* is found, on occasion, in Aramaic words of Iranian origin. See S. Shaked, "Iranian Loanwords in Middle Aramaic," *Encyclopaedia Iranica*, II, 3 (London: Routledge & Kegan Paul, 1986), p. 261.

[108]On this cultural loanword, see W. Baumgartner, et al., *Hebräisches und aramäisches Lexikon zum alten Testament*, 3rd ed., II (Leiden: E. J. Brill, 1974), p. 501.

[109]See §121.

[110]Stress appears to be on the ultima in words with the 1 s. pronominal suffix as is the rule in Tiberian Biblical Aramaic (Bauer-Leander, *Grammatik*, p. 23; but cf. אֲבִי Dn 5:13).

[111]See Nöldeke, *Syriac Grammar*, pp. 33-34.

[112]See W. Wright, *A Grammar of the Arabic Language*, revised by W. Roberston Smith and M. J. de Goeje, 3rd ed., I (Cambridge: University Press, 1896; reprint 1971), p. 9.

[113]Although the sporadic shift of *u > o* before gutturals can explain the Eastern Syriac forms, such a shift is not attested in Rabbinic Hebrew. See also P. Joüon, *Grammaire de l'hébreu biblique* (Rome: Institut Biblique Pontifical, 1923; reprint 1965), p. 206.

[114]One finds /-un/ in verbs III-w/y/' (but /-on/ in the Babylonian tradition). In Targum Onqelos one finds /-un/ in strong verbs but /-on/ in verbs III-w/y/'. One finds /-on/ in both strong verbs and verbs III-w/y/' in Syriac. See §123d.

[115]All the exceptional pointings have been excluded since one cannot be certain if the vocalizers tried and failed to imitate the Tiberian Biblical Aramaic rules of pointing, or if their pointings reflect different traditions of morphological patterning. Loanwords and words which clearly reflect a different morphological patterning have also been excuded, e.g., the Imperfect /yeqtol/ (as opposed to Tiberian Biblical Aramaic /yiqtul/) which is pointed with ֹ 88x and ֻ 12x.

[116]The pointing with ֹ could also be interpreted as imitating the Hebrew יְקוֹם. See §155c.

[117]This seems to be the noun /šəpar/ (Targum Onqelos /šəpar/, /šuprā/) in construct. It is conceivable, however, that this is the Active Participle *qātil in construct. שֹפֵר A Ex 22:4 presents the same possibilities.

[118]Klein reads חֲשׁוֹב. The published photograph (Plate 100), however, shows חֲשׁוּב. It makes more sense to take the dots ֻ as an intentional vowel sign since the Perfect /həšab/ is intended.

[119]Kahle's reading יִתְקְנֹס A Ex 21:22 is incorrect. See §9c.

[120]Kahle reads בְּאָפְטָרֵה. Klein reads בְּאָפְסְדֵה. There is a sign above the *pe*, but one cannot tell whether it is ֻ or ֹ. Kahle's reading of ֹ makes good sense. See §26, n.137.

[121]For expected בֵּאבֶן. See §156bb.

[122]See §§4d, 21b. For the possibility that ֻ reflects a final reduced vowel and/or a plosive pronunciation, see §4d, n.2.

[123]See §9c.

[124]See §§4d, 21b.

[125]See §12m below.

[126]Yahalom has argued that this sign marks syllabification. He bases this on some exceptional uses of this sign in Palestinian pointed Hebrew manuscripts and in light of the use of the *daghesh* and *raphe* signs in Codex Reuchlinianus and in some Masoretic manuscripts of the Bible. See Yahalom, review of Dietrich, *Neue palästinisch punktierte Bibelfragmente*, in *KirSef*, 45 (1970), 388-389 (in Hebrew). It is true that the *shewa mobile* does mark syllabification in the sense that the *shewa mobile* together with its consonant constitute a syllable. Were Yahalom's suggestion correct, however, one would expect to find ــٴ not only where a *shewa mobile* is expected, but also where one should find a full vowel, e.g., in a form like יקטׂל. Those few examples in which one finds this sign with a full vowel are, however, clear examples of its use as a *daghesh lene* and *daghesh forte*—functions of this sign which are well attested in Palestinian pointed Hebrew manuscripts.

[127]See Dietrich, *Neue palästinisch punktierte Bibelfragmente*, pp. *87-*88.

[128]In Palestinian pointed Hebrew manuscripts ــٴ can have several functions depending on the manuscript. It can mark gemination *(daghesh forte)*, the plosive pronunciation of /bgdkpt/ *(daghesh lene)*; consonantal *he (mappiq)*, and *sin* (as opposed to *shin)*. There are also several poorly attested functions.

[129]A poorly preserved example is חַד־כַּ(מָה) Cd Gn 44:18, "how much more so" unless the Hebrew /kammā/ is intended.

[130]See §152b, n.282.

[131]Is the first vowel influenced by the form /yammin/ "right hand"?

[132]Did the vocalizer mistake the D Participle for the D Infinitive?

[133]See §155c.

[134]See §119h.

[135]Cf. Syriac /qərušā/. Dalman *(Handwörterbuch*, p. 389) cites קְרוֹשָׁא; Jastrow *(A Dictionary of the Targumim, the Talmud Babli and Yerushalmi, and the Midrashic Literature* [London: Luzac & Co./New York: G. P. Putnam's Sons, 1903; reprint, New York: Judaica Press, 1975], p. 1415) cites קְרוֹשָׁא. It is difficult to determine the noun class to which this form belongs. Does the pointing in the Cairo Genizah fragments reflect a *qittūl class? See also §16h.

[136]ــ predominates in MS H. The sample group, however, is limited.

[137]See §§8i, 72b.

[138]There are some additional examples of ــ (where one expects *ḥaṭeph pathaḥ)* that were probably intended to represent a zero vowel. See §13.

[139]See §71a.

[140]See §16h.

[141]One expects the reading אַרְבֵּה. The *pathah* is either a scribal error or a misreading.

[142]See §9c.

[143]Not included in the examples is הֲווֹ F Ex 20:8, "be!" (m.pl.) (cf. Tiberian Biblical Aramaic הֱוֵי Ezr 4:22, but also הֱוֹו Ezr 6:6).

[144]Klein reads חֱמִי. One cannot tell from the published photograph (Plate 11) if the final vowel is *hireq* or *sere*. This word is not attested in Biblical Aramaic. Cf. however, Tiberian Biblical Aramaic I-guttural Imperatives אֱמַר, אֱמַרוּ, אֱתוֹ, חֱיִי. (See n.143 above.)

[145]This need not be taken as a Hebrew form. One finds אמור also in Targum Neophyti (Ex 7:19) and in Galilean Aramaic (see Svedlund, *Selected Passages*, p. 10. On the extension of /o/ to the Imperative and Imperfect where Classical Aramaic has /a/, see §§131n, 155c.

88

[146]Cf. Tiberian Biblical Aramaic וְאַתְּ Dn 3:26.

[147]Cf. the "correct" determined form אֲנְשָׁא Bd Gn 7:21 and אֲנְשָׁא־ Bd Gn 7:23. See also §13d.

[148]In the 30 other examples of Imperfect forms of /həwa/ where one expects a *ḥaṭeph seghol*, one finds a *shewa quiescens*. Cf. Tiberian Biblical Aramaic תֶּהֱוֵא Dn 2:40. Note the "correct" Tiberian pointing of וִיהֱוְיָן A Ex 22:23, "and they will be." Cf. Tiberian Biblical Aramaic לֶהֱוֹן Dn 5:17.

[149]For additional examples of ⎯ (where one expects *ḥaṭeph seghol*) that were probably intended to represent a zero vowel, see §13.

[150]The preposition כלקבל "in front of" (cf. Tiberian Biblical Aramaic כָּל־קֳבֵל [qolqŏvel] is excluded from this discussion since the pointed examples appear to reflect /qəloqbal/. See §156w.

[151]For the Palestinian pointed forms of this word, see §11f.

[152]The scribe and vocalizer are not the same person in this and the previous example.

[153]Cf. Syriac /ḥəlāf/ but with suffix /ḥulāf-/, Palestinian Syriac חלף, Targum Onqelos /ḥəlāp/, and Targum Neophyti חולף. One finds חֹלוֹפֵי bound by suffixes in Targum Jonathan (see Tal, *Language*, p. 26).

[154]Cf. Syriac /ʿəvāðā/, Palestinian Syriac עובדא, Samaritan Aramaic [ūbåd] (Macuch, *Grammatik*, p. 250), Targum Onqelos /ʿobād/, Mandaic *'ubada*, and Arabic /'ubād/.

[155]One expects עֶבְדַי "my deeds." The *ṣere* is either a scribal error or a mis-reading.

[156]See §§1411; 147a.

[157]See §153.

[158]See §96a, n.292.

[159]For the examples, see §33d. The majority of examples in which one expects *Cəyi* do not undergo this shift: MS A: 7x (Palestinian pointing), 1x (Tiberian pointing); MS B: 3x; MS C: 19x; MS D: 4x; MS Z: 1x; MS AA: 1x.

[160]See n.120 above.

[161]See §71a.

[162]See n.118 above.

[163]Reflecting ['ɛ'ɛveð] in imitation of the Tiberian echo vowel in אֲעֲבֵד? Or is this a scribal error for אֶעֱבד? There may be another example וּנְפֵּשׁ C Gn 32:17, "and a space," if ⸰ is intended as the Palestinian vowel sign ⸰ (the only Palestinian vowel sign in MS C!). According to Tiberian rules, one expects a realization of /unpeš/. This pointing may reflect either the realization /unəpeš/ or is in imitation of the bivalent function of the sign ⎯ (representing both a reduced vowel and a zero vowel). Or does ⸰ reflect /u/ in this example and was it meant to be over the *waw*?

[164]E.g., תֶּהֱוֵא Dn 2:40, but תֶעְדָּא Dn 6:9. See Bauer-Leander, *Grammatik*, p. 44–45.

[165]See n.148 above.

[166]E.g., דַהֲבָה Ezr 5:14, but טַעְמָא Ezr 4:21. See Bauer-Leander, *Grammatik*, pp. 44–45.

[167]See n.23 above.

[168]Perhaps, however, also בְּטִיהֳרָה D Dt 28:29, "at noon" if the *qere* is meant to reflect /ṭohra/. See §70a, n.146.

[169]For the examples, see §12i.

[170]For the examples, see §33f.

[171]There is only one example. See §33g.

[172]The Targum Onqelos manuscripts with Tiberian vowel signs have an additional vowel [ɛ], which appears in supralinear pointed manuscripts as /a/.

[173]There are also some pointed manuscripts of the Fragment Targum. See Klein, *Fragment-Targum*, I, pp. 29-30, 33. The inconsistency in the pointing of these manuscripts is due to the Sephardi pronunciation of the vocalizers. See ●1d, n.31.

[174]See ●5j.

[175]E.g., Gn 2:19; Gn 3:5-6; Gn 40:23-41:8.

[176]See Morag, *Vocalization Systems*, pp. 45-59.

[177]Some cases of /i/ do ultimately come from *i when followed by syllable closing /ʼ/, e.g., /riša/ < /reša/ < *riʼša'. See Nöldeke, *Syriac Grammar*, pp. 32-33. See also H. Birkeland, "The Syriac Phonematic Vowel Systems" in *Festskrift til Professor Olaf Broch* (Avhandlinger utgitt av det norsek videnskaps-Akademi i Oslo, II. Historik-Filosofisk Klasse, 1947), pp. 13-39.

[178]Realized as [o].

[179]See Birkeland, "Syriac," pp. 33-35.

[180]For examples of sporadic pointings see Svedlund, *Selected Passages, passim*; Ginzberg, *Yerushalmi Fragments, passim*; Kutscher, "Articulation of the Vowels u,i," p. 233. C. Levias made some use of these pointings in his *A Grammar of Galilean Aramaic* (New York: The Jewish Theological Seminary of America, 1986).

[181]With the exception of the first example (Svedlund, p. 132), all of the following examples can be found in Svedlund, *Selected Passages*, p. 136.

[182]See Bar-Asher, *Palestinian Syriac Studies*. This work brings up to date F. Schulthess' *Grammatik*. Bar-Asher's work includes corrections of many readings of previously published texts. See also Muraoka, review of Bar-Asher, *Palestinian Syriac Studies* in *JSS*, 24 (1979), 287-290, and most recently, Bar-Asher, "Le syro-palestinien-études grammaticales," *JA* 276 (1988), 27-59.

[183]See Bar-Asher, *Palestinian Syriac Studies*, p. 265, n.519, and p. 266, n.527. Bar-Asher believes that *i was shortened in originally final closed syllables, as in Samaritan Aramaic and Ma'lula ("Le syro-palestinien," pp. 44-46).

[184]For a complete discussion of the subject including a summary of other views, see Bar-Asher, *Palestinian Syriac Studies*, pp. 426-430.

[185]For analyses of the phonology of Samaritan Aramaic, see Ben-Ḥayyim, "The Samaritan Vowel-System and Its Graphic Representation," *ArOr*, 22(1954), 515-530; *Literary and Oral Tradition*, II, III.2, and V. Although this last volume deals with the grammar of Samaritan Hebrew, the phonology of Samaritan Hebrew and of Samaritan Aramaic closely resemble one another and Ben-Ḥayyim has included comments on Aramaic. See also Kutscher's review of Ben-Ḥayyim, *Literary and Oral Tradition*, III.2 in *Tarbiz*, 37 (1968), 379-419 (in Hebrew); Macuch, *Grammatik*; L. H. Vilsker, *Manuel d'araméen samaritain*, trans. J. Margain (Paris: Centre National de la Recherche Scientifique, 1981).

[186]Spitaler does not present a phonemic analysis in his *Grammatik*, yet a glance through his grammar presents the following vocalic minimal pairs: /o/ vs. /u/: [aqom] "stand up!" (m.s.) vs. [aqum] "stand up!" (f.s.), p. 161; /i/ vs. /e/ vs. /a/: ['ainōji] "my eyes" vs. ['ainōje] "his eyes" vs. ['ainōja] "her eyes," p. 53; /u/ vs. /e/: [lēlun] "to them" (m.pl.) vs. [lēlen] "to them" (f.pl.), p. 54; /a/ vs. /ā/: [la] "not" vs. [lā] "no!" p. 2 (the distribution of /ā/ is limited).

[187]Spitaler, *Grammatik*, pp. 2-3, 7 (/e/ is a reflex of *i in certain environments).

[188]See Dietrich, *Neue palästinisch punktierte Bibelfragmente, passim*; Revell, *Hebrew Texts, passim*; Chiesa, *L'Antico Testamento Ebraico, passim*.

[189]For a discussion of the relationship of the Palestinian tradition to the Tiberian and Babylonian Hebrew traditions, see Ben-Ḥayyim, "Reflections on the Hebrew

90

Vowel System" in *Studies in Bible and the Ancient Near East Presented to Samuel E. Loewenstamm on His 70th Birthday*, ed. J. Blau and Y. Avishur (Jerusalem: E. Rubinstein, 1968), pp. 95-105 (in Hebrew).

[190]See Yahalom, "Palestinian Pointing," pp. 32-56.

[191]One could also argue that these vowels were realized as full vowels and not reduced vowels.

[192]The manuscripts of Rabbinic literature have been collected by N. Allony in *Geniza Fragments of Rabbinic Literature: Mishna, Talmud and Midrash with Palestinian Vocalization*. Facsimile Edition (Jerusalem: Makor, 1973, in Hebrew).

[193]See Dietrich, *Neue palästinisch punktierte Bibelfragmente, passim*.

[194]See Revell, "Studies in the Palestinian Vocalization of Hebrew," *passim; Hebrew Texts with Palestinian Vocalization, passim.*

[195]See Yahalom, "Palestinian Pointing," and M. Sokoloff and Y. Yahalom, *Palestinian Vocalized Piyyuṭ Manuscripts in the Cambridge Geniza Collections* (Cambridge University Press, in press).

[196]E.g., Kahle, *Cairo Genizah, passim*; also Kahle *apud* Bauer-Leander, *Historische Grammatik*, pp. 71-162.

[197]See A. Murtonen, *Materials for a Non-Masoretic Hebrew Grammar*, I (Helsinki, 1958), *passim.*

[198]See Chiesa, *L'Antico Testamento Ebraico, passim.*

[199]Revell disagrees with this generally accepted view. See *Hebrew Texts with Palestinian Vocalization*, pp. 101-102.

[200]For a list of manuscripts in which the signs for *raphe* and *mappiq* occur, see Dietrich, *Neue palästinisch punktierte Bibelfragmente*, pp. *87-*88.

[201]‿ is also used to mark *consonantal he* and to distinguish *sin* from *shin.*

[202]See Morag, *Vocalization Systems*, pp. 34-38.

[203]This appellation was proposed by Allony in "What is הנקד שלנו in the Vitri Mahzor?" *Beit Miqra*, 17 (1964), 135-144 (in Hebrew).

[204]See Morag, *Vocalization Systems*, pp. 34-40. He later preferred, however, the name "Palestinian-Tiberian" in "Notes on the Description of the Pointing System of the Worms Mahzor," *Lesh*, 29 (1965), 209, n.30 (in Hebrew).

[205]See A Sperber, *A Grammar of Masoretic Hebrew: A General Introduction to the Pre-Masoretic Bible* (Copenhagen: Ejnar Munksgaard, 1959). He used this term to describe the Codex Reuchlinianus.

[206]See Diez Macho, "A New List of So-called 'Ben Naftali' Manuscripts Preceded by an Inquiry into the True Character of These Manuscripts," in *Hebrew and Semitic Studies Presented to G. R. Driver*, ed. D. Winton Thomas and W. D. McHardy (Oxford: Clarendon Press, 1963), p. 26.

[207]See M. H. Goshen-Gottstein, "The Rise of the Tiberian Bible Text," in *Biblical and Other Studies*, ed. A. Altmann (Cambridge: Harvard University Press, 1963; Philip A. Lown Institute of Advanced Judaic Studies, Brandeis University, Studies and Texts, Vol. 1), pp. 79-122.

[208]See Dotan, "Masorah," cols. 1461-1466.

[209]See Morag, "Vocalization of Codex Reuchlinianus," *passim*; Diez Macho, "New List," *passim.*

[210]For a list of other features, see Morag, "Vocalization of Codex Reuchlinianus," pp. 235-236.

91

[211]For an exhaustive analysis and bibliography of these texts, see Eldar, *Hebrew Language Tradition, passim.*

[212]See Morag, "Pronunciations of Hebrew," *EJ*, 13, col. 1125; and, more recently, "On Processes of Transformation and Transplantation in the Traditions of Hebrew," *Proceedings of the Sixth World Congress of Jewish Studies*, Jerusalem 1980, Division D, pp. 141-156 (in Hebrew); T. Harviainen, on the other hand, proposes that the Palestinian tradition and the Sephardi reading traditions reflect similar, although independent developments. See Harviainen, *On the Vocalism of the Closed Unstressed Syllables in Hebrew: A Study Based on the Evidence Provided by the Transcriptions of St. Jerome and Palestinian Punctuations* (Studia Orientalia 48:1; Helsinki, 1977), p. 116. See also Morag, review of Harviainen, *On the Vocalism of the Closed Unstressed Syllables in Hebrew*, in *JSS*, 27 (1982), 288-291.

[213]See Morag, "Pronunciations of Hebrew," col. 1142. The Sephardi reading traditions of Biblical and Mishnaic Hebrew are in the process of being described in detail by the Hebrew University Language Traditions Project. The following traditions have already been analyzed: Morag, *The Hebrew Language Tradition of the Baghdadi Community: Phonology* (Jerusalem: Hebrew University Language Traditions Project, I, 1977, in Hebrew); K. Katz, *The Hebrew Language Tradition of the Community of Djerba (Tunisia)* (Jerusalem: Hebrew University Language Traditions Project, II, 1977, in Hebrew); K. Katz, *The Hebrew Language Tradition of the Aleppo Community: Phonology* (Jerusalem: Hebrew University Language Traditions Project, VI, 1981, in Hebrew); and, most recently, A. Maman, "The Reading Tradition of the Jews of Tetouan: Phonology of Biblical and Mishnaic Hebrew," *Mass* 1 (1984), 51-120 (in Hebrew), and Maman, "La position de l'hébreu des juifs de Tétouan parmi les traditions dites séfarades," *Mass*, 2 (1986), 93-102.

[214]See Morag, "Pronunciations of Hebrew," col. 1142, nn.7-8. See also Katz, *Hebrew Language Tradition*, pp. 93-95, for a survey of the *holem* and *shureq* in Sephardi communities.

[215]See Dalman, *Grammatik*, pp. 81-86; G. Bergsträsser, *Hebräische Grammatik*, I (Leipzig: Vogel, 1918), pp. 61-62; Morag, *The Hebrew Tradition of the Yemenite Jews* (Jerusalem: The Academy of the Hebrew Language, 1963), pp. 160-178 (in Hebrew).

[216]See Morag, "Pronunciations of Hebrew," col. 1142; Morag, "The Babylonian Aramaic Traditions of the Yemenite Jews," *Tarbiz*, 30 (1961), 125 (in Hebrew); Y. Kara, *Babylonian Aramaic in the Yemenite Manuscripts of the Talmud: Orthography, Phonology, and Morphology of the Verb* (Jerusalem: Hebrew University Language Traditions Project, X, 1983), pp. 117-119 (in Hebrew).

[217]See Morag, "Pronunciations of Hebrew," col. 1142; Morag, "Biblical Aramaic in Geonic Babylonia," in *Studies in Egyptology and Linguistics in Honour of H. J. Polotsky*, ed. H. B. Rosén (Jerusalem: Israel Exploration Society, 1964), p. 120.

[218]See Morag, "The Phonology of Babylonian Aramaic According to the Pointing of MS Sasson הלכות פסוקות," *Lesh* 32 (1968), 71-78 (in Hebrew); "Processes of Transformation,' p. 154, n.61; and most recently *Babylonian Aramaic: The Yemenite Tradition* (Jerusalem: Ben Zvi Institute, 1988; in Hebrew).

[219]Díez Macho bases this on the existence of one Babylonian pointed ms. of Targum Onqelos in which *qames* and *pathah* interchange and on the Tiberian pointed manuscripts transcribed from Babylonian *Vorlagen* in which *qames* and *pathah* fluctuate. See Díez Macho, "Onqelos Manuscript with Babylonian Transliterated Vocalization in the Vatican Library (MS Eb 448)," *VT*, 8 (1958), 113-133; "Un

92

manuscrito babilonico de Onqelos en el que se confunden los timbres vocalicos Pataḥ y Qameṣ," *Sef*, 19 (1959), 273-282. The fluctuation of *qameṣ* and *pathaḥ* in these transcribed texts, however, is usually attributed to the Sephardi pronunciation of the copyists. Morag attributes the fluctuation of *qameṣ* and *pathaḥ* in the Babylonian pointed manuscript of Targum Onqelos to the influence of Babylonian Talmudic Aramaic. See Morag, "Processes of Transformation," p. 153, n.61.

[220]See Dalman, *Grammatik*, pp. 81-86; Kutscher, "Articulation of the Vowels u,i," pp. 218-227; Sperber, "Hebrew Based Upon Greek and Latin Transliterations," *HUCA*, 12-13 (1937-1938), 103-274; J. Barr, "St Jerome and the Sounds of Hebrew," *JSS*, 12 (1967), 1-30; C. Siegfried, "Die Aussprache des Hebräischen bei Hieronymus," *ZAW* 4 (1884), 34-83; C. Schlatter, *Die hebräischen Namen bei Josephus* (Gütersloh: Bertelsmann, 1913); G. Lisowsky, "Die Transkription der Eigennamen des Pentateuch in der Septuaginta" (Ph.D. thesis, Basel, 1940). E. Bronno, *Studien über hebräische Morphologie und Vokalismus auf Grundlage der mercatischen Fragmente der zweiten Kolumn der Hexapla des Origens* (AKM 28; Leipzig: Deutsche Morgenländische Gesellschaft, 1943); G. Janssens, *Studies in Hebrew Historical Linguistics Based on Origen's Secunda* (Orientali Gandensia 9; Leuven: Peeters, 1982).

Harviainen, however, has challenged the view that *i > [ɛ] and *u > [o] in the Greek and Latin transcriptions. He believes that the transcriptions do not reflect phonemic or phonetic change, but rather reflect the inadequacy of the Greek and Latin scripts in representing different vowel qualities. See Harviainen, *Vocalism*, p. 148.

One should also note that in some of the Greek and Latin sources one also finds the Hebrew *shewa mobile* transcribed as *a* (see, e.g., Siegfried, pp. 79-80), although in the same sources one also finds different transcriptions. These transcriptions must, in general, be treated with great caution.

[221]There are also some transcribed Aramaic words. See Kautzsch, *Grammatik*, pp. 6-12.

## D. Diphthongs

[1]*ay, however, contracts to /e/ in עֵנוֹ F Dt 34:7, "his eyes" (/'enoy/), and לְשָׁהֹן AA₁ Ex 12:34, "their dough" (the *pathaḥ* is an error), לְשָׁהוֹ AA₁ Ex 12:39, חלַתְכֹון AA₁ Ex 12:17, "the forces," but חֵילְוָתה AA₁ Ex 12:41, and in *qayl nouns with a f. ending. See §§67f-g.

[2]Klein reads תֵּחְיֵֽ֫יָה. The published photograph (Plate 6) shows תֵּחְיֵיָ֫ב. The two dots above the *beth*, however, make no sense.

For explanations of this form, see Bauer-Leander, *Grammatik*, p. 64, 233; Kutscher, *Studies*, p. 43, n.1.

[3]There is only one other example of a *qayl noun in the absolute state: חֵיל AA₁ Ex 17:9 "force." See §67f.

[4]The pointing of these forms could also be interpreted as reflecting /tərayn/ (or did the vocalizer only partially point the word?).

[5]For explanations of the origin of *ayn on verbs III-w/y/', see Bauer-Leander, *Grammatik*, pp. 64, 233; Kutscher, *Studies*, p. 43, n.1.

[6]See n.1 above.

[7]See §37k.

[8]See §4e.

[9]Klein reads עֵיְיֵֽ֫יָ. The published photograph (Plate 63) shows עֵיְיֵי, but the dots do not appear to belong to the scribe who wrote the consonantal text and make little sense.

93

[10] In מוי. סגין AA Nu 20:11, "its waters" (for expected מיין סגין "many waters?"). Cf. Targum Neophyti מיין סגין (marginal gloss מין סגי), Samaritan Targum מים סגים (MSS A,J), Targum Pseudo-Jonathan מיין סגיאין, Targum Onqelos and Peshiṭta /mayyā saggi'e/. Or is this form the same as Targum Pseudo-Jonathan מוי, מיין, מייא = מוי?

[11] See Bauer-Leander, *Grammatik*, pp. 60-61, 78-79; Fitzmyer, "Phases of the Aramaic Language," pp. 82-83.

[12] See W. R. Garr, *Dialect Geography of Syria-Palestine, 1000-586 B.C.E.* (Philadelphia: University of Pennsylvania Press, 1985), p. 107.

[13] In Rabbinic Hebrew the pl. לְוָחִים, suggesting a sg. *לָח, can be found in addition to the more common לוחות, s. לוֹחַ. The former has the meanings "tablets, boards, plates," whereas the latter has acquired the specialized meaning of "Tablets of the Covenant." See E. Kimron, "לוחות, לוחים," *Lesh*, 30 (1976), 147 (in Hebrew); Muraoka, "Concerning שני לוחות," p. 290. According to R. Steiner, *aw > ū/l__ in Hebrew and Aramaic and is responsible for Proto-Semitic *lawḥ > lūᵃḥ. See Steiner, "Lulav versus *lu/law: A Note on the Conditioning of *aw > ū in Hebrew and Aramaic," *JAOS*, 107 (1987), 121-122.

[14] Beyer suggests that these are "hyper-correct forms under Arabic influence" ("Pronunciation," p. 20).

[15] See Ben-Ḥayyim, *Literary and Oral Tradition*, III.2, p. 190, n.35, p. 97, n.45. See also Macuch, *Grammatik*, p. 48. In Samaritan Aramaic [ṭura] has the meaning "mountain" whereas [ṭibra] has acquired the specialized meaning "Mount Gerizim." For other examples of *aw > [b] in Samaritan Aramaic, see Macuch, pp. 118-119.

[16] See Clarke, *Concordance*, pp. 243-244, for Targum Pseudo-Jonathan, and in the Fragment Targum Ex 19:3 (MS P).

[17] See Gn 8:8, Dt 5:22(19). It seems likely that these two forms were realized /lawḥa/, /yawna/ in Targum Pseudo-Jonathan and the Fragment Targum. There are, however, no writings with double *waw* that can verify this assumption.

[18] See n.13 above.

[19] See Kutscher, "Mishnaic Hebrew," *Henoch Yalon Jubilee Volume*, pp. 251-255; Sokoloff, *The Geniza Fragments of Bereshit Rabba* (Jerusalem: The Academy of Sciences and Humanities, 1982), pp. 70-71 (in Hebrew).

[20] Tiberian pointed manuscripts include the MS Kaufmann (see Kutscher, "Mishnaic Hebrew," p. 252), MS Paris 328-329 (Bar-Asher, *Traditions*, pp. 43-45), MS Parma [de Rossi 138] (Haneman, *Morphology of Mishnaic Hebrew*, p. 15). For Babylonian pointed manuscripts, see E. Porath, *Mishnaic Hebrew as Vocalized in the Early Manuscripts of the Babylonian Jews* (Jerusalem: Bialik Institute, 1938), pp. 49, 122 (in Hebrew), and Kahle, *Masoreten des Ostens* (Leipzig: J. C. Hinrichs, 1913; reprint Hildesheim: Georg Olms, 1984), p. 164.

[21] See Morag, "Vocalization of Codex Reuchlinianus," p. 232. In this codex final *yodh* is accompanied by both a *mappiq* and a *raphe*.

[22] See Eldar, *Hebrew Language Tradition*, pp. 158-165; Beit-Arié, "The Vocalization of the Worms Mahzor," *Lesh*, 29 (1965), 27-46, 80-102 (in Hebrew); Morag, "Comments on the Description of the System of Vocalization of the Worms Maḥzor," *Lesh*, 30 (1965), 203-209 (in Hebrew).

[23] E.g., Morag, "Vocalization of Codex Reuchlinianus," p. 232.

[24] See Haneman, *Morphology*, p. 15.

[25] See Ben-Ḥayyim, "Concerning the Originality of the Penultimate Stress in Hebrew," in *Henoch Yalon Jubilee Volume*, pp. 158-159; Beit-Arié, "Vocalization,"

94

pp. 39-40; Eldar, *Hebrew Language Tradition*, p. 164.

Bar-Asher suggests that manuscripts with *mappiq/ḥireq* under final *yodh* of a diphthong should be treated separately from those manuscripts in which final and medial *yodh* are pointed with *mappiq/ḥireq* and interchange with *shewa*. In the former, Bar-Asher believes that a triphthongization is intended; in the latter, the diphthong is intended by the vocalizers. See Bar-Asher, *Traditions*, pp. 43-45.

[26]See Ben-Ḥayyim, "Penultimate Stress," pp. 158-159, and *Literary and Oral Tradition*, V, pp. 44-47, especially n.88.

[27]See Bauer-Leander, *Grammatik*, p. 37-38.

[28]See Dalman, *Grammatik*, p. 91..

[29]Ibid., p. 140.

[30]See Dalman, *Grammatik*, p. 340. There are also examples of /-an/, which are most likely the result of Targum Onqelos influence.

[31]See Dalman, *Grammatik*, p. 109; Levy, "Language," p. 64; Tal, "Ms. Neophyti 1," p. 41.

[32]*ayn > /ayin/, however, as in the Cairo Genizah fragments. See Kutscher, *Studies*, pp. 19, 43-51. See also Dalman, *Grammatik*, pp. 87-88, 340. Final /n/, however, is elided following /ayi/ in the Participles of verbs III-w/y/'.

[33]See Dalman, *Grammatik*, pp. 109-110, 198. The writing אחוה and אבוה for expected אחוי and אבוי, "his brother" and "his father," could be interpreted as reflecting a contraction of the diphthong /uy/ to /u/, i.e., /'aḥu/ and /'abu/, but one could also argue that the final /y/ was taken as the marker of the 1 person and clipped off, leaving /u/. See Fassberg, "Miscellanea in Western Aramaic," *Language Studies* II-III, pp. 202-204 (in Hebrew).

[34]See Schulthess, *Grammatik*, pp. 25-26.

[35]See Bar-Asher, *Palestinian Syriac Studies*, pp. 318-319, 248 n.416, and 498 n.111.

[36]There are examples in which /oy/ is replaced by /o/ (Schulthess, *Grammatik*, pp. 33, 50). This may be contraction of the diphthong, although other explanations are also possible. See n.33 above.

[37]See Macuch, *Grammatik*, p. 86. *aw > [b], however, sporadically. See pp. 118-119.

[38]See Ben-Ḥayyim, "Penultimate Stress," p. 158. Macuch, on the other hand, interprets spellings such as אבואה, אבוה, "his father" and אחוה "his brother" as graphic representations of ['abu'e] and ['a'uwwe]. He does not think that they represent the contraction of the diphthong /uy/. See *Grammatik*, p. 308.

[39]See Spitaler, *Grammatik*, pp. 11-12. There are, however, a few exceptions, all frequent words, e.g., [yoma], "day."

[40]See Spitaler, *Grammatik*, p. 90.

[41][ōy] does not occur in the same grammatical categories in which it occurs in the Cairo Genizah fragments. See Spitaler, *Grammatik*, p. 105.

[42]See Nöldeke, *Syriac Grammar*, pp. 34-35.

[43]Ibid., p. 123.

E. Matres Lectionis

[1]Based on the pointed text, it would appear that final /a/ is not represented by a *mater lectionis* in וּמָן־שָׁעָת דִּי־עֲלָלִית Cd Ex 5:23. The consonantal text, however, appears to reflect either a cst. s. form before /dV-/ or a vulgar pronunciation of *ša'ata di* > /ša'atti/ or /ša'addi/ with the elision of /a/. For other possible examples in the consonantal text, see §§25c, 161d.

[2]For מרה דביתה A Ex 22:7, "the master of the house," see §4k.

[3]Does the consonantal text reflect /'ella'in/? If so, the *aleph* is not a *mater lectionis;* intervocalic /y/, however, is usually preserved in these fragments. Cf. עלין AA Dt 26:19.

[4]See §§38a, 130e, 155c, 162c.

[5]Kahle reads מדין; Klein reads מֺאֺן in *HUCA* 1978, but דֺין in *Genizah Manuscripts.*

[6]Cf. Dalman, *Grammatik,* p. 71.

[7]*Aleph* is not limited, however, to verbs which are originally III-', e.g., יֶתלָא- B Gn 4:15, "it will be suspended."

[8]The use of *he* in some of these examples is in imitation of Hebrew orthography, e.g., in verbs III-w/y and the numbers 11-19.

[9]Note the use of both *yodh* and *he.*

[10]See §47g.

[11]Ibid.

[12]It is interesting to note that 20 out of 21 occurrences of /reš/ "head" (*ri'š < *ra'š) are written with *aleph,* and only one is written with *yodh. See* §68c.

[13]This *plene* writing might have been intended to distinguish אן /'en/ "if" from the interrogative אן /'an/ "where?"

[14]For a possible example, see §83a, n.240.

[15]This is an Akkadian loanword. See §118.

[16]Prof. M. Bar-Asher points out that the spelling גִזרין is found in manuscripts of Rabbinic Hebrew where גִזירין is expected and suggests that the *kethibh* here may reflect the same realization.

[17]The orthography of this form was influenced by the *defective* orthography of שֵׁלטן Dn 4:23.

[18]See §4f.

[19]Note that this verb is originally III-'.

[20]The orthography of this verb was influenced by וּשׁיצֿיא Ezr 6:15. See n.17 above.

[21]See §155c. *He* representing final /i/ is attested infrequently (and with *yodh*)in Galilean Aramaic (cf. ליה "to me" in Svedlund, *Selected Passages,* p. 10, and in Samaritan Aramaic (Macuch. *Grammatik,* pp. 5, 207-209).

[22]For the limited number of examples with final /o/, see §11j.

[23]Cf. Biblical Aramaic בְּגוֹא- Dn 3:25. This is the source of the Cairo Genizah orthography.

[24]For examples of *defective* orthorgraphy pointed with *qibbuṣ,* see §11k. As in other manuscripts, Jewish scribes sometimes avoided marking two consecutive o/u vowels with *matres lectionis.*

[25]See §12f, n.135.

[26]<*qatāl (cf. Targum Onqelos /'əbārā/, Rabbinic Hebrew /'əbār/, but Syriac /'abbārā/). If the Cairo Genizah form goes back to a *qattāl base, then the orthography reflects a shift of *a > /i/. See §18h, n.47.

[27]See §80a.

[28]The Hebrew *he locale* (< *ah)has been misunderstood by the translator, who treats it as part of the place name.

[29]Idem.

[30]For a discussion and bibliography on the use of *aleph* and *he* as *matres lectionis* in these Aramaic sources, see Kutscher, "The Hermopolis Papyri," *IOS,* 1 (1971), 103. See also Sokoloff, *Geniza Fragments,* p. 61.

96

[31]See Kutscher, "Hermopolis Papyri," p. 105. See also *Studies*, p. 16. In Samaritan Aramaic, *aleph* occasionally represents final /a/ in verbs III-w/y/'. See Macuch, *Grammatik*, p. 205, where he suggests Hebrew orthographic influence.

[32]See E. Bresciani and M. Kamil, *Le lettere aramaiche di Hermopoli* (Rome: Atti della Accademia Nazionale dei Lincei, Memorie, classe di Scienze morali, storiche e filologiche, ser. VIII, Vol XII, 5, 361-428, and more recently B. Porten and A. Yardeni, *Textbook of Aramaic Documents from Ancient Egypt, I: Letters* (Jerusalem, 1986), pp. 9-23. See also B. Porten and J. Greenfield, "The Aramaic Papyri from Hermopolis," *ZAW*, 80 (1968), 220.

[33]See Cowling, "Notes," p. 39.

[34]Targum Onqelos influence is doubtful elsewhere in these fragments, whereas Biblical Aramaic influence is certain.

[35]See Cowling, "Notes," p. 39.

[36]See Kutscher, "Hermopolis Papyri," 103-105.

[37]See Dalman, *Grammatik*, p. 71.

[38]See Nöldeke, *Syriac Grammar*, p. 5.

[39]See Macuch, *Grammatik*, p. 3.

[40]See Schulthess, *Grammatik*, pp. 7-9.

[41]See Segal, *Grammar*, pp. 25-26.

F. Phonetic Processes

[1]See Klein, *Genizah Manuscripts*, I, p. XXXIV. One wonders, however, if שוו E Gn 31:2 does not come from the root *šwy, yielding a meaning here of "same, equal," which would fit the context just as nicely as שפיין from the general Aramaic *špy "calm, clear."

[2]According to Peri ("Morphology," p. 69), the difficult form קלוותיה is the result of metathesis and *p > /w/ (קלופיתה < קלוויתה). The interchange of /p/ and /w/, however, may be due to attraction to the modifying adjective חוורתה "white," just as, in the same verse, the suffix ־יין of חווריין is due to attraction to פירוכין.

[3]See Gn 38:28 in the Peshiṭta.

[4]See Schulthess, *Lexicon Syropalaestinum* (Berlin: Reimer, 1903), pp. 55-56.

[5]The basic meaning of the root /zhr/ in Hebrew, Arabic, and Aramaic is "bright," "shining."

[6]See Kutscher, *Studies*, p. 74.

[7]See Schulthess, *Lexicon*, p. 140

[8]See Bergsträsser, *Glossar des neuaramäischen Dialekts von Ma'lula* (AKM 15,4. Leipzig: Deutschen Morgenländischen Gesellschaft, 1921; reprint Nendeln: Krauss, 1966), p. 1.

[9]See Ex 4:6 in the Peshiṭta.

[10]See Ex 4:6,7. MSS A and J represent two different strata of the Samaritan language, MS A representing the younger. For a discussion of the two manuscripts, see Tal, "The Samaritan Targum to the Pentateuch, Its Distinctive Characteristics and Its Metamorphosis," *JSS*, 21 (1976), 26-38; Tal, *Samaritan Targum*, III, pp. 17-28, 53-92; G. Sixdenier, "La langue du targum samaritain," *JA* 272 (1984), 223-231.

[11]See Kutscher, *Studies*, pp. 70-78.

[12]On the shift *ḥ > /'/ before the total disappearance of the gutturals in Samaritan Aramaic, see Kutscher, *Studies*, p. 76.

[13]E.g., Gn 49:15 (MSS P,V).

[14]E.g., למלעי Gn 49:15, but ליאות Gn 31:42.

97

[15]E.g., Gn 19:11.

[16]See Kutscher, *Studies,* p. 81.

[17]E.g., Gn 31:42.

[18]Ibid.

[19]See Schulthess, *Lexicon,* p. 100.

[20]Cf. Dt. 22:3 in Targum Onqelos, Targum Pseudo-Jonathan, Targum Neophyti, and Syriac where one finds the root *ʾbd. יבידה is found in Targum Neophyti in the marginal gloss to Lv 5:22; ייבידת is found in the marginal gloss to Dt 22:3.

[21]/pelyin/? (partial assimilation to the vowel /i/?). From the root *plʾ. Cf. פלאין in Targum Pseudo-Jonathan Ex 8:18, Targum Neophyti Ex 15:11, and Fragment Targum MS V Ex 15:8.

[22]See Brockelmann, *Grundriss,* I, p. 147; Bauer-Leander, *Grammatik,* pp. 29-30.

[23]See F. R. Blake, "The Apparent Interchange Between a and i in Hebrew," *JNES,* 9 (1950), 83.

[24]See Brockelmann, *Grundriss,* I, p. 147; Dalman, *Grammatik,* p. 88; Schulthess, *Grammatik,* p. 20.

[25]See §57.

[26]Schulthess *(Grammatik,* p. 43) believes that the e-vowel of *'ebbā* has been extended along with the gemination from "mother" *'emmā.* The orthography איבא is also attested in Targum Pseudo-Jonathan and the Fragment Targum. See Dalman, *Grammatik,* p. 88. Cf. §59a.

[27]Cf. Galilean Aramaic סיגין and Samaritan Aramaic [siggi]. See Kutscher, review of Ben-Ḥayyim, *Literary and Oral Tradition,* III.2, p. 408.

[28]See §136, n.144.

[29]Cf. Biblical Aramaic יַבֶּשְׁתָּא־ Dn 2:10. The Cairo Genizah pointing may be in imitation of the Biblical pointing.

[30]Targum Onqelos, Syriac, and Samaritan Aramaic all have /a/ in the first syllable pointing to *maqtal.

[31]*a > /e/ in both closed and open syllables in the s. of this word. One finds /a/, however, in the pl. (Hebraism). See §119b. *raʾš > *riʾš is a Proto-Aramaic shift. See Bauer-Leander, *Grammatik,* p. 60.

[32]See Bauer-Leander, *Grammatik,* p. 41.

[33]See Nöldeke, *Syriac Grammar,* p. 32.

[34]See Dalman, *Grammatik,* p. 88.

[35]See Schulthess, *Grammatik,* pp. 26-27; Bar-Asher, *Palestinian Syriac Studies,* pp. 423-424, 434.

[36]See Spitaler, *Grammatik,* p. 39.

[37]Cf. Samaritan Aramaic [remmək]. See Macuch, *Grammatik,* p. 106.

[38]There are five unpointed examples of the f.s. form bound by pronominal suffixes. See §60b. Kahle's reading בָּרְתִי Cd Gn 38:26 is corrected by Klein to כַלָּתִי "my bride."

[39]Cf. Syriac /pargawdin/. See §116.

[40]Cf. Syriac /zaggon/. See §§111a, 117.

[41]One cannot determine the vowel in eight other occurrences which are unpointed and written *scriptio defectiva.* This shift might have taken place first in the construct form (closed, unstressed syllable) and then been extended to the absolute and determined forms. It is, however, possible that /ber/ is a direct reflex of *bir. See §60a, n.48.

[42]See Dalman, *Grammatik,* p. 88.

98

⁴³E.g., in the marginal note to Gn 30:12, ביר.

⁴⁴See Macuch, *Grammatik*, p. 240.

⁴⁵See Schulthess, *Grammatik*, p. 43.

⁴⁶See Nöldeke, *Syriac Grammar*, p. 91. Cf. absolute /bar/, "son," but /berhon/, "their son."

⁴⁷Cf. Tiberian Hebrew /'əton/, Arabic /'atān/, Akkadian /'atānu/, Targum Onqelos /'ətān/. The Editio Sabbioneta /'attānā/ and Syriac /'attānā/ (note, however, that gemination in Syriac is often secondary; see Nöldeke, *Syriac Grammar*, pp. 13-14) suggest an Aramaic by-form of *qattāl. Another possible example is כאיברא H Ex 15:10, "like lead" if the parent form is *'abbār and not *'abār. See §16h, n.26.

⁴⁸This Biblical Aramaic form is in imitation of the Biblical Hebrew forms. See Bauer-Leander, *Grammatik*, p. 81.

⁴⁹Or did Aramaic speakers hear the Greek α as [ε]?

⁵⁰Note that *a > /i/ in Biblical Aramaic and Targum Onqelos, but *a > /e/ in Syriac. It is possible that *a > /e/ in the Cairo Genizah fragments (and not *a > *i > /e/).

⁵¹Bronno, *Studien, passim*; Siegfried, "Die Aussprache des Hebräisachen bei Hieronymus," *passim*; Harviainen, *Vocalism, passim*.

⁵²For a different explanation of the following forms, see §19g.

⁵³See §119b for a different explanation of this form.

⁵⁴ The *mappiq* is unexpected.

⁵⁵As suggested by Prof. T. O. Lambdin.

⁵⁶See Kutscher, review of Ben-Ḥayyim, *Literary and Oral Tradition*, III.2, p. 400.

⁵⁷See Spitaler, *Grammatik*, pp. 8-9.

⁵⁸See §52a.

⁵⁹This process is attested in the other Palestinian Targumim and Galilean Aramaic. See Dalman, *Grammatik*, pp. 103, 232.

⁶⁰Cf. Targum Pseudo-Jonathan תידכר, Fragment Targum (MS P) תידכר, (MS V) תדכר, and Targum Neophyti תדכר, all of which may reflect either a G or Gt verb. The Cairo Genizah form may also be a scribal error for the G דתדכר.

⁶¹This assimilation is also attested sporadically in the other Palestinian Targumim and Galilean Aramaic (see Dalman, *Grammatik*, p. 252), in Samaritan Aramaic (see Ben-Ḥayyim, *Literary and Oral Tradition*, III.2, p. 54, n.19; Macuch, *Grammatik*, pp. 89-90), and in Palestinian Syriac (Bar-Asher believes /t/ was regularly assimilated in this position—*Palestinian Syriac Studies*, p. 225, n.287, and "Two Grammatical Phenomena in Palestinian Syriac," *Languages Studies*, II-III, pp. 111-117 [in Hebrew]). /t/ of Gt and Dt assimilates frequently in Mandaic (Nöldeke, *Mandäische Grammatik* [Halle: Waisenhaus, 1875; reprint Darmstadt: Wissenschaftlich Buchgesellschaft, 1974, p. 213]) and Babylonian Aramaic (Epstein, *Grammar*, p. 50).

⁶²Targum Onqelos, Targum Pseudo-Jonathan, Targum Neophyti (margin), the Samaritan Targum (MS A), and the Peshitta have a t-conjugation verb. One could also argue that the Cairo Genizah form is a G verb (3 pl. functioning as passive).

⁶³Assimilation to a sibilant is attested infrequently in Palestinian Syriac (see Bar-Asher, *Palestinian Syriac Studies*, p. 472, n.376) and Galilean Aramaic (Svedlund, *Selected Passages*, p. 12 [יצרף = ויצטרף]).

⁶⁴See §157d, n.19.

⁶⁵E.g., Targum Pseudo-Jonathan אידיהון Gn 37:21; Fragment Targum (MS P) דאיממא Gn 31:39; Targum Neophyti באיממא Gn 31:39. This phenomenon appears to be less frequent in Targum Pseudo-Jonathan than in the other two Targumim.

[66]See Dalman, *Grammatik*, p. 100.

[67]See Schulthess, *Grammatik*, p. 24.

[68]See, e.g., Macuch, *Grammatik*, pp. 309-310.

[69]See Spitaler, *Grammatik*, p. 45.

[70]Initial יɔ > /i/ regularly in Syriac. See Nöldeke, *Syriac Grammar*, p. 27.

[71]See Brockelmann, *Grundriss*, I, pp. 185, 351.

[72]E.g., Barth assigns both חשוך and תחות to the *qatul class *(Die Nominalbildung in den semitischen Sprachen*, 2nd ed. [Leipzig: J. C. Hinrichs, 1894], pp. 14, 313; Dalman also assigns חשוך to *qatul in *Grammatik*, p. 151). Bauer-Leander consider חשוך to be a Canaanism in Biblical Aramaic (*Grammatik*, p. 188). Cf. Targum Onqelos /ḥəšok/, Tiberian Biblical Aramaic /ḥəšokā/, and Syriac /ḥəššoxā/ (with secondary gemination). Note the difficulty in reconstructing a Proto-Semitic form of /toma/: Syriac /tāmā/, Targum Onqelos /təyomā/, Akkadian /tū'amu/, Arabic /taw'am, tu'ām/, Tiberian Hebrew /tə'omim/, /tomim/, and Palestinian Syriac תומא (Schulthess, *Lexicon*, p. 217). Is /tom/ a Hebraism in the Cairo Genizah fragments?

[73]On this noun class, see also §§18l, 119e.

[74]On this form, see also §§18l, 19h, 119b.

[75]For possible additional examples, see §§11d, n.73, and 11e.

[76]There are four occurrences of this word with *qameṣ*, probably representing /o/. The *pathaḥ*, however, could also represent /o/. See §§11d-e.

[77]See §§28, 119a.

[78]Including the occurrences of "seventy." See §47k.

[79]Or did *i (*ī) > /o/ in this noun? One finds both חתירתה and חתרתה in Galilean Aramaic texts. Does this noun belong to *qatalat, *qatilat, or *qatīlat? Cf. Rabbinic Hebrew /ḥətirā/ and Targum Onqelos /maḥtartā/. See also §11e.

[80]< *gaww. See §156i.

[81]See §104m, n.338.

[82]See Dalman, *Grammatik*, p. 89, for examples in Targum Pseudo-Jonathan and the Fragment Targum. For representative examples in Targum Neophyti, see Nu 20:5.

[83]See Schulthess, *Grammatik*, p. 26.

[84]See Dalman, *Grammatik*, p. 89; H. L. Ginsberg, "Zu den Dialekten des Talmudisch-Hebräischen," *MGWJ*, 77 (1933), 423-475.

[85]See Dalman, *Grammatik*, p. 89.

[86]See Bauer-Leander, *Grammatik*, p. 41.

[87]See, e.g., Samaritan Targum (MS A) קורייה Gn 19:29, "the cities."

[88]See, e.g., /'of/ "also, moreover" in Nöldeke, *Syriac Grammar*, p. 32.

[89]See Kutscher, *The Language and Linguistic Background of the Isaiah Scroll* [I Q Isaᵃ] (Leiden: E. J. Brill, 1974), pp. 496-497; Bar-Asher, "The Mishnah of Ms. Parma B of the Order Ṭoharot"; Introduction to the *Facsimile Edition of Ms. Parma B* (Jerusalem: Makor, 1971), pp. 6-7 (in Hebrew).

[90]See Nöldeke, *Syriac Grammar*, pp. 31-32; Nöldeke, *Mandäische Grammatik*, p. 21; Brockelmann, *Grundriss*, I, p. 201.

[91]See §§18l, 19g.

[92]Idem.

[93]See §§18l, 19g, 119b,e.

[94]See §23.

[95]There are two other examples of להות in these fragments. See §§17e, 158e.

100

[96]θ > d/_‘ (partial assimilation in point of articulation and/or voicing). One finds a different partial assimilation, e.g., in Damascus Arabic /xamṣṭa'š/. See *Handbuch der arabischen Dialekte*, eds. W. Fischer and O. Jastrow (Wiesbaden: Harrassowitz, 1980), pp. 98-99. See also §28.

[97]θ > δ/_l (partial assimilation in point of articulation and/or voicing).

[98]עֲלָיִן Dn 7:5.

[99]Cf. Gn 2:21 and Lv 23:4.

[100]E.g., Gn 2:21 and Gn 32:18.

[101]E.g., Gn 2:21 and Gn 32:20 (but also ערע in Gn 32:18).

[102]E.g., Gn 2:21 and Dt 31:29 in the Peshiṭta.

[103]See Schulthess, *Lexicon*, pp. 19, 147, but also ערע p. 153.

[104]E.g., Gn 35:9 (MS V).

[105]See Dalman, *Grammatik*, p. 99.

[106]See Bergsträsser, *Glossar*, p. 3. Note also the orthographies עליו Gn 2:21, עלעתה Gn 2:22 in the Samaritan Targum, and עריה in Ben-Ḥayyim, *Literary and Oral Tradition*, II.2, p. 140.

[107]There are no pointed examples of this form. On the metanalysis, see §28.

[108]It must, however, be stressed that the origin of these four words is uncertain.

[109]Cf. the gemination in Biblical Hebrew /dammeseq/. On the form with /r/ in Hebrew and Aramaic, see Kutscher, *Isaiah Scroll*, pp. 3-4.

[110]Cf. the gemination in Biblical Hebrew /kissē/ and Akkadian /kussū/. On the possible origins of this noun, see Kaufman, *Akkadian Influences*, pp. 28-29.

[111]Generally thought to be from *šabbîṭ (see Bauer-Leander, *Historische Grammatik*, p. 484, or from *šibṭ with insertion of /r/ (see W. Gesenius, E. Kautzsch, A. E. Cowley, *Hebrew Grammar* [Oxford: Clarendon Press, 1910], p. 239). J. S. Sasson has suggested that this is a noun from the root *rbṭ with preformative š- ("A Note on šarbîṭ," *VT*, 22 (1972), 111.

[112]According to Dalman (*Grammatik*, p. 251), this is a Š verb; according to Jastrow (*Dictionary*, p. 1628), this verb is related to Hebrew /šāgag/.

[113]For examples in which _̲ marks a plosive pronunciation of /bgdkpt/ and a reduced vowel, see §§4d, 12c.

[114]On the meaning of this verb, see Schelbert, "Ex XXII 4," pp. 256-259.

[115]It can also represent the plosive pronunciation of /bgdkpt/ in five of the examples.

[116]See §§4d, 12c.

[117]Because of the Rule of Shewa, bə + šəpoloy > /bešpoloy/. See §33.

[118]E.g., /sakkin/ > /səkin/ "knife." See Kutscher, "Marginal Notes to the Mishnaic Lexicon and a Grammatical Note," *Lesh*, 31 (1967), 112 (in Hebrew); Bar-Asher, "The Mishnah of Ms. Parma B," p. 16; Morag, "Bamme Madliqin in Two Cairo Geniza Manuscripts," in *Studia Orientalia Memoriae D. H. Baneth Dedicata* (Jerusalem: Magnes Press, 1979), p. 114 (in Hebrew).

[119]See §19c.

[120]On *t > /d/, see §19i.

[121]On *t > /ṭ/, see §19i.

[122]One must keep in mind that the vocalizers of these fragments did not always point each word completely even in manuscripts which are, on the whole, fully pointed.

[123]See Bauer-Leander, *Historische Grammatik*, pp. 113-114.

[124]See H. Yalon, *Introduction to the Vocalization of the Mishnah* (Jerusalem: Bialik Institute, 1964), p. 217 (in Hebrew).

[125]See Morag, "Vocalization of Codex Reuchlinianus," p. 233. A glide is more frequent after /i/ than /u/.

[126]See Eldar, *Hebrew Language Tradition*, pp. 84-88.

[127]See Macuch, *Grammatik*, p. 245.

[128]The following shows the number of spellings which preserve the syllable closing *aleph* as against the number of phonetic spellings which do not:

| MSS | A | B | C | D | E | F | H | W | Y | Z | AA | HH |
|-----|---|---|---|---|---|---|---|---|---|---|----|----|
| Hist. | 6 | 13 | 18 | 2 | 10 | 6 | - | - | - | 4 | 16 | 2 |
| Phon. | 6 | 4 | 48 | 9 | 63 | 36 | 2 | 4 | 4 | 4 | 36 | 1 |

On the elision of the *aleph* in sequences involving /'əlah/ "God," see §33i.

[129]See §68e, n.127. Cf. Targum Neophyti דתין.

[130]See §4e.

[131]As in Galilean Aramaic ומר "and he said" (see Dalman, *Grammatik*, p. 299). It is also possible, however, that the vocalizer has merely not pointed the entire word and that this word was realized as /wa'əmar/ or even /wa'mar/. There are 22 similar pointings, all in MS C. There are 13 other examples of וַאֲמַר, 2 additional examples of וַאֲמַר, but no other examples of וַאֲמָר.

[132]Klein takes the *aleph* to be an error which ought to be deleted (under the influence of Hebrew איננו).

[133]See §68e, n.121.

[134]For another possible explanation, see §161d.

[135]See §§16a, n.1; 161d.

[136]See §161d.

[137]Other possible examples are a) בְּאָפְסְדֵהּ A Ex 22:14, "in his loss" (see §4k; 12c, n.120). Cf. פסידה in Targum Pseudo-Jonathan (Ex 22:14) and פסידי in the margin of Targum Neophyti (Ex 22:14), which suggest that the *aleph* in the Cairo Genizah fragments is prothetic. Cf., however, the Rabbinic Hebrew הֶפְסֵד(*heqṭēl* noun class—see Segal, *Grammar*, pp. 113-114). Perhaps the form in the Cairo Genizah fragments is the Rabbinic form with /h/ > /'/; b) אֶפְשַׁר- B Gn 4:14, "possible" in which the *aleph* may be prothetic (from root *pšr*) if the word is not a loan from Persian (also occurs in Targum Onqelos, Galilean Aramaic, Rabbinic Hebrew). See E. Ben Yehuda, *Thesaurus totius hebraitatis et veteris et recentioris* (New York: Thomas Yoseloff, 1959), I, pp. 362-364 (in Hebrew) for a discussion of the origin. The general Semitic forms *'ṣb' "finger," *'lmnt "widow," and *'rb' "four" are also attested, e.g., באצבעה AA Nu 19:4, אֲרְמָלָן A Ex 22:23, וארבע A Ex 21:37. On prothetic *aleph* in general, see E. A. Speiser, "Secondary Developments in Semitic Phonology: Application of the Principal of Sonority," *AJSL*, 42 (1926), 145-169. For possible examples of prothesis on verbs, see §130b.

[138]See §9c.

[139]A prothetic *aleph* is not attested in the one occurrence of "sixty," שְׁתִּין Cd Gn 46:26, nor in the one occurrence of "sixth," שתייי E Gn 30:19.

[140]Note that the prothetic vowel is /a/ before /r/.

[141]Klein reads רתיכוי, which, admittedly, is grammatically preferable. Cf. however, Fragment Targum (MS P) בארתיכוי, Targum Neophyti בארתכוי (but Targum Pseudo-Jonathan ברתיכוי).

102

[142]See §§67-71.

[143]One expects /mašrəyateh/.

[144]The *kethibh* reflects a realization of /mašeryan/; the *qere* reflects expected /mašrəyan/. See Dalman, *Grammatik*, p. 94, for this phenomenon in Galilean Aramaic and Targum Onqelos (note that /maširyān/ is attested in Targum Onqelos, e.g., Gn 35:3). For another possible example of anaptyxis, see §134c, n.138.

[145]See §§99a, n.303, and 119c.

[146]See §19j.

[147]This metanalysis is also attested in Targum Neophyti. See Tal, *Language*, p. 16.

[148]פטיר בולי is attested in Lv 22:27 in Targum Pseudo-Jonathan and the Fragment Targum (MS V). פטיר כלי is attested in Targum Neophyti (marginal gloss). One also finds פטיר בלי/פטיר בולי in Galilean Aramaic (see Jastrow, *Dictionary*, p. 1158).

[149]Since the ink is poorly preserved, this may be a mis-reading of מן.

[150]See §126c.

[151]Tal argues that this is a phonetic process which is attested throughout the Palestine region. See Tal, "Layers," pp. 171-172. The argument against a phonetic process is based on the fact that this appended /n/ seems to be grammatically and lexically conditioned. Tal relates this final /n/ to the nasalization of final vowels which Ben-Hayyim posits in Samaritan Aramaic, Samaritan Hebrew, and Rabbinic Hebrew. See Ben-Hayyim, "La tradition samaritaine et sa parenté avec les autres traditions de la langage hebräique," *MélPhLJ*, 3-5 (1962), 105-107. See also E. Qimron, *The Hebrew of the Dead Sea Scrolls* (Harvard Semitic Studies 29; Atlanta: Scholars Press, 1986), pp. 27-28. Dalman (*Grammatik*, p. 102) also attributes this final /n/ to a phonetic process.

[152]כדו + ן. The form כדו is explained as a contraction of כד + הוא. See Dalman, *Grammatik*, p. 212.

[153]תמה + ן. Cf. Biblical Aramaic /tammā /.

[154]The form תובה is unattested in Aramaic.

[155]For a detailed discussion of the distribution of these adverbs in the dialects of Syria-Palestine, see Tal, "Layers," pp. 179-183; see also Tal, *Language, passim*; Dalman, *Grammatik*, pp. 45, 102, 208-224; Foster, "Language," pp. 75-80.

[156]Note that one finds כדון in sources in which כען occurs (with the exception of Galilean Aramaic in which כען is not attested, but which could have been influenced by the Biblical Aramaic כען), whereas one finds כדו in dialects in which כען is not attested (and are not "Jewish" dialects which were influenced by Biblical Aramaic).

[157]Cf. Hebrew /ām/ in יומָם, רִיקָם, חִנָּם.

[158]See Tal, "Layers," p. 180.

[159]See also H Gn 15:2, סגין יְהַבְת לי וסגין אית קדמיך לְמְתן לי "you have given me much (lit. many things) and there is much for you to give me."

[160]It seems unlikely that שבתן is the Hebrew form שְׁבָתוֹן. /o/ is usually represented by the *mater lectionis* waw in this manuscript. See §§16g,j.

[161]See §§34g and 37h,m.

[162]As claimed by Dalman and Tal. See Tal, "Layers," pp. 166-177; Dalman, *Grammatik*, p. 102. See §§123d-e,g.

[163]See Dalman, *Grammatik*, p. 102; Kutscher, *Studies*, p. 61; Kutscher, "Language of the Genesis Apocryphon," pp. 23-24; Qimron, *Dead Sea Scrolls*, pp. 27-28.

[164]As noted by Klein (*Genizah Manuscripts*, I, p. XXXV, n.4), the *aleph* may be due to contamination with אומה "nation."

[165]It seems less likely that לפד represents /lappid/ as in Hebrew לַפִּיד since /i/ is almost always represented by *yodh* in this manuscript. See §16e. S. P. Brock ("Greek Words in the Syriac Gospels [VET and PE]," *Mus*, 80 [1967], 405) comments on the Syriac /lampiδā/ that "It is uncertain whether the Syriac form is due to the Greek, or dissimilation of לפיד."

[166]The interlinear gloss is לפידין.

[167]See Brockelmann, *Lexicon Syriacum*, 2nd ed. (Halle: Max Niemeyer, 1928; reprint Hildesheim: Georg Olms, 1982), p. 368, and Brock, "Greek Words," p. 405.

[168]See Schulthess, *Lexicon*, p. 104. לפד, however, is also attested.

## G. Stress

[1]See Bauer-Leander, *Grammatik*, pp. 17-22; Dalman, *Grammatik*, pp. 55-56. At an early stage of Syriac, final vowels after the stressed syllable fell away. See Nöldeke, *Syriac Grammar*, pp. 35-36.

[2]Is the form חוטר a Hebraism (cf. חֹטֶר Is 11:1)? The examples of the determined form and the construct form are clearly Aramaic. See §69a.

[3]One finds שבע 11x, e.g., שבע E Gn 29:18.

[4]Cf. Kaufmann, "Aramaic Vowel Reduction," in *Arameans, Aramaic and the Aramaic Literary Tradition*, p. 49, who holds that the orthographies עולים "youth" and פורת "Euphrates" in Qumran and Murabba'at reflect an ultra short u-vowel.

Qimron (*Dead Sea Scrolls*, p. 37, n.45) takes Qumran Aramaic קוטל/קטל to reflect [qŏṭól]. On the positioning of the stress in Qumran Hebrew forms such as יקטולו ([yiqtólu] or [yiqtŏlú]), see, e.g., Goshen-Gottstein, "Linguistic Structure and Tradition in the Qumran Documents," *ScrHier*, 4 (1965), p. 124; Qimron, pp. 40-42.

[5]See §12.

[6]As is the case in Samaritan Aramaic, Palestinian Syriac, and Ma'lula, where the general penultimate accent was responsible for the lengthening of reduced vowels. See Bar-Asher, *Palestinian Syriac Studies*, pp. 421-439.

[7]See §11g, n.88.

[8]E.g., B Gn 4:8, C Gn 35:9, Cd Gn 38:25-26, and Cd Gn 44:18.

[9]עֵמֶק בֹּה-. Is this in imitation of Masoretic *nesighah*?

[10]Is this a pausal form for סָגֵי? The Western Aramaic evidence suggests it is not. See §§11g, n.88, 69d, n.143.

[11]Is the retraction of stress in imitation of the MT penultimate stressed form מִזֶּן, which is in pausal position?

[12]Cf. סָפַת Dn 4:30.

[13]Cf. וְקָמְת Gn 38:19 in MS Eb. 448.

[14]This is the view proposed by Kahle in Bauer-Leander, *Historische Grammatik*, pp. 139-140. Against this view of the randomness of positioning is Revell in "Placing of the Accent Signs," pp. 34-45.

[15]See Ben-Ḥayyim, "Penultimate Stress," pp. 150-160, and *Literary and Oral Tradition*, V, pp. 48-53; Macuch, *Grammatik*, pp. 122-125.

[16]See Bar-Asher, *Palestinian Syriac Studies*, pp. 433-439.

[17]See Spitaler, *Grammatik*, pp. 48-50.

[18]See §31 above.

[19]See Dalman, *Grammatik*, pp. 55-56. The consonantal text in reliable manuscripts of Galilean Aramaic gives no reason to assume a stress pattern different from that of Biblical Aramaic and Targum Onqelos. Note also that an ultimate stress pattern is

generally assumed for Rabbinic Hebrew. Cf., however, Kutscher ("Mishnaic Hebrew," *Henoch Yalon Jubilee Volume*, pp. 277-280) who argues for the existence of penultimate stress.

**§32** IV. SYLLABLE STRUCTURE

**§32a** One might expect a change in syllable structure in this dialect as a result of the shift of *ā > /a/: originally open syllables containing /a/ would become closed syllables, and *shewa mobile* would become *shewa quiescens*, e.g., נֹפְקֵי C Gn 34:24, "those going forth" (m.pl. construct) in which *nāpəqe > /napqe/. There are five examples in which the occurrence of a *daghesh lene* suggests such a change: בְּמִכְלְתָּא Cd Gn 38:26, "of the measure"; יָתְכוֹן D Dt 27:10, "you"; פָּרְתּה AA Nu 19:5, "the cow"; שָׁרְיָה F Ex 20:18, "dwelling";[1] וְשַׂהְדָּא C Gn 31:52, "witnessing."

**§32b** There are six examples in which it appears that an originally open syllable containing *ī became closed and the *shewa mobile* became *shewa quiescens*. This is evidenced by the pointings of *daghesh lene* or the shortening of originally long *ī to short *i in the closed syllable and the subsequent shift of *i > /e/:[2] עֲבִידְתָּא Cd Gn 44:15, "the work"; דָּעֲבְדְּמְכוֹן Cd Gn 46:33; עֲבִידְתְּכוֹן Cd Gn 47:3; קָבְלֹתְּהוֹן Cd Ex 6:5, "[their] cry"; בִישְׁתָּא Cd Gn 37:20, "evil"; בִּישְׁתָּא Cd Gn 37:33. Cf. the Tiberian Biblical Aramaic pointings עֲבִידְתָּא Ezr 5:8, Dn 2:49 and וּבָאִישְׁתָּא Ezr 4:12, which may have influenced the pointings in the Cairo Genizah fragments.

**§32c** There is only one example in which an originally open syllable containing *ū has become closed, as evidenced by the *daghesh lene:* בְּקַבְרָתְּהוֹן Cd Gn 47:30, "in their burial place."[3]

**§32d** The closing of originally open syllables containing long vowels (following *shewa mobile* becomes *shewa quiescens*) is attested in Tiberian Biblical Aramaic[4] and is the rule in Syriac, where a subsequent shortening of long vowels is particularly common in the Eastern tradition.[5]

**§32e** The shift of *ā > /a/ and the change in the syllable structure C̄VCəC > CVCC are attested in some Sephardi reading traditions of the Mishnah (along with penultimate accent), whereas in the reading of the Bible the syllable structure C̄VCəC is preserved (with ultimate accent).[6] Thus, for example, one finds שָׁמְרָה "she guarded" realized as [ˈšamra] in some reading traditions of the Mishnah, but [šamĕˈra] in some reading traditions of the Bible.[7]

Footnotes — Chapter IV

[1]Note that the *daghesh* occurs with a *yodh*. See §4f.
[2]On the following examples, see §10d.
[3]Cf. Targum Onqelos /qəburətā/ Gn 35:20.
[4]See Bauer-Leander, *Grammatik*, pp. 16-17.
[5]See Nöldeke, *Syriac Grammar*, p. 29.
[6]See Morag, "Pronunciations of Hebrew," col. 1126, and *Hebrew Language Tradition of the Baghdadi Community*, pp. 64-83; Katz, *Hebrew Language Tradition of Djerba*, pp. 102-164; Katz, *Hebrew Language Tradition of Aleppo*, pp. 71-83; Maman, "Reading Tradition of Tetouan," pp. 91-102, especially p. 100. See also Morag, "De la tradition au dialecte: problèmes d'enquête linguistique," *Mass*, 2 (1986), 103-110.

[7]See Morag, "Pronunciations of Hebrew," col. 1126. One might speculate that the reason for this difference is the comparative importance of the two texts. In transmitting the Biblical tradition, great emphasis was put on preserving the Masoretic system. With the Mishnah, on the other hand, the pronunciation of the text was never of paramount concern.

§33                    V. RULE OF SHEWA

The Rule of *Shewa* is a synchronic description of the vowel which results from the sequence of two consecutive *shewa mobile*.[1]

§33a   In the Cairo Genizah fragments the vowel of the Rule of *Shewa* in sequences of non-gutturals is usually realized as /a/, e.g., לְבְשׂר B Gn 2:24, "to the flesh of"; דְשְׁמַיָּא Bd Gn 7:23, "of the heavens"; לְמְנַחָמָא C Gn 35:9, "to console"; וּלְמְשַׁוָּיָה D Dt 26:19, "and to place."

§33b   Realizations of /e/ are less frequent, e.g., לְמַרֵי A Ex 22:11, "to his master"; לְתְרַע C Gn 34:20, "to the door"; לְקְהַל Cd Gn 48:4, "to the congregation of"; דִּבְנֵי HH Ex 12:3, "of the children of."

§33c   Occasionally one finds the same word with two different realizations of the Rule of *Shewa*. Examples are בִּדְמוּת C Gn 32:25, "in the image of" vs. בְּדָמוּת C Gn 32:29; לִמְשַׁבְּחַיָּיא C Gn 32:27, "of those who praise" vs. לְמַשַׁבָּחָא C Gn 32:27, "to praise"; לְשְׁמִי Cd Ex 6:7, "to my name" vs. לְשְׁמִי Cd Gn 48:5; בִּשְׁבוּעָה Cd Ex 6:8, "in an oath"; vs. בַּשְׁבוּעָה Cd Gn 47:31; לִשְׁמֵיהּ D Dt 27:9, "to his name" vs. לְשְׁמֵיהּ D Dt 26:18. Note the pointing of לְמְנַטוּרֵהּ A Ex 22:6, "to guard" (cf. לְמְנַטוּרֵהּ A Ex 22:9) in which the realization of the Rule of *Shewa* is different in the Tiberian pointing from that in the Palestinian pointing.

§33d   In sequences of two *shewa mobile* in which the second consonant is a *yodh*, *Cəyə* > /Ci/, e.g., וִיקוֹם A Ex 21:21, "and he will arise"; וִיתֵב C Gn 35:9, "and he sat down." On occasion, however, one finds the /a/ of sequences involving non-gutturals extended to this sequence in the forms of יַד, "hand,"[2] e.g., בִּידֵהּ A Ex 22:3, "in his hand"; בַּיְדֵיהּ Cd Gn 44:16 (cf. בִּידֵיהּ Cd Gn 48:17); בַּיְדִי H Gn 15:1, "in my hand."[3] Note also that there are five examples in which *Cəyi* > *Ciyi* > /Ci/:[4] וְישְׁתְּבַח A Ex 21:16, "and it will be found"; וִיהַלֵּךְ A Ex 21:19, "and he will walk around"; וִיפְּקוּן A Ex 21:22, "and they will go forth"; וִידְחֲפוּן A Ex 21:22, "and they will push"; דְישְׂרָאֵל Cd Gn 48:13, "of Israel."

§33e   In sequences involving the conjunction /wə/ and a non-guttural with *shewa mobile*, *wəCə* > /uC/,[5] e.g., וּנְפָק B Gn 4:16, "and he went forth."

§33f   When the second letter of a sequence of two reduced vowels is a guttural and one expects [CaGǎ] in Tiberian Aramaic, on the whole, one finds

108

the same pointing in the Cairo Genizah fragments, e.g., וַהֲוָה Bd Gn 7:17, "and it was"; חֲזַר Cd Gn 37:30,"and he returned"; חֲמָא Cd Gn 48:8, "and he saw." Infrequently, however, one finds a *pathaḥ* in place of *ḥaṭeph pathaḥ* in MS C: דַהֲוֹן C Gn 31:39, "which were"; לְעַדַּר C Gn 32:17, "to the flock" עֲבַר C Gn 32:23, "and he crossed"; דַחֲרְב Cd Gn 44:18, "of the sword." There are five examples in which one finds a *shewa quiescens* in place of *ḥaṭeph pathaḥ* apparently reflecting a pronunciation of [CaGC]:[6] וְהְוָה Bd Gn 8:6, "and it was"; וַאֲמַר- Cd Gn 38:25, "and he said"; חֲזַר Cd Ex 5:22, "and he returned"; הֲוָה D Dt 5:20, "and it was"; וַאֲנְשֵׁי- Cd Gn 38:26, "and the men of." Because the vocalizers of these fragments did not always fully point each word, one cannot tell whether pointings such as דַהֲוַת C Gn 31:39, "which was" (cf. דַהֲוַת C Gn 31:39) and חֲמָא C Gn 32:26, "and he saw" also reflect [CaCG].[7] There are four examples in which the /e/ from sequences involving non-gutturals seems to have been extended to the gutturals for expected [CaGă]: וְחֲמָרֵיהוֹן Cd Gn 44:3, "and their he-asses"; וְחֲסָד- Cd Gn 47:29, "and grace" (cf. וְחֲסָד- C Gn 34:11); וְאֲנְשֵׁי- Cd Gn 46:31, "and the men of"; וְלֶאֲנְשֵׁי Cd Gn 46:31.

§33g There is only one pointed example in the Cairo Genizah fragments in which one expects a sequence corresponding to Tiberian Biblical Aramaic [CeGĕ]: דְאֲנָשׁ Cd Gn 38:26, "of the men" (reflecting [dɛ'naš]?).[8]

§33h There are three examples in which one expects [CoGŏ] as in Tiberian Biblical Aramaic: בַּעֲבָדָא C Gn 34:21, "in the work"; וּבַעֲבִד Z Gn 48:22; בַּעֲבָדֵיך Z Gn 49:4.[9]

§33i As is the case with the Tiberian pointing of the Hebrew אֱלֹהִים, in sequences involving אֱלָה, "God," *aleph* always quiesces, and one finds an *e*-vowel, e.g., וְאֵלָהֵיה Cd Gn 43:23, "and his God."

§33j The pointing of דִבְנָעַן Cd Gn 47:1, "of Canaan" is puzzling. Was the *pathaḥ* misplaced and intended for the *daleth* (/dakna'an/)?

§33k /a/ of the Rule of *Shewa* in these fragments in sequences of non-gutturals parallels that of Syriac (/a/), rather than /i/ of Tiberian Biblical Aramaic and Targum Onqelos.[10] The occurrences of /e/ in the Cairo Genizah fragments may represent an attempt to imitate the Rule of *Shewa* in Biblical Aramaic (Cairo Genizah /e/ = Tiberian /i/ < *i). /a/ is the original vowel of the conjunction ו and the preposition ל and has been preserved in the Cairo Genizah fragments in this environment and extended to the preposition ב and the particle ד.[11] In Tiberian Biblical Aramaic and Targum Onqelos, on the other hand, /i/ of the Rule of *Shewa* was generalized from *bi and *di and perhaps from *qatqat > qitqat.[12] In sequences involving labials (*wəLə> /uL/), these fragments agree with the Tiberian tradition of Biblical Aramaic[13] and Targum Onqelos, as against Syriac in which one finds /a/. Cəyə > /Ci/ is paralleled in Tiberian Biblical Aramaic, Targum Onqelos, and Syriac, although /Cay/ is attested in Eastern Syriac.[14]

§33l The following chart summarizes the realizations of the Rule of *Shewa* by manuscript:

109

|  | $C\partial C\partial$ /a/, /e/ | $C\partial y\partial$ /Ci/, /Cay/ | $C\partial G\partial$ [CaGǎ], [CaGa]?, [CaGC] |
|---|---|---|---|
| Palestinian pointed manuscripts | | | |
| MS A | 1x, 3x | 2x, 1x | 1x, -, - |
| Tiberian pointed manuscripts | | | |
| MS A | -, 3x | -, - | -, -, - |
| MS B | 13x, - | 1x, - | 8x, -, 1x |
| MS C | 36x, 11x | 12x, 3x | 52x, 4x, 2x |
| MS D | 4x, 11x | 2x, - | 2x, -, 1x |
| MS E | 1x, - | -, - | -, -, - |
| MS F | -, - | -, - | -, -, - |
| MS H | 6x, 1x | -, 3x | -, -, - |
| MS W | -, - | -, - | -, -, - |
| MS Y | -, - | -, - | -, -, - |
| MS Z | 6x, - | -, - | 2x, -, - |
| MS AA | -, - | -, - | -, -, - |
| MS HH | -, 1x | -, - | -, -, - |

110

[1]For the term Rule of *Shewa*, see T. O. Lambdin, *Introduction to Biblical Hebrew* (New York: Charles Scribner's Sons, 1971), pp. XX-XXI. For a diachronic analysis of the feature, see Nöldeke, *Syriac Grammar*, p. 30, n.1; Blake, "Apparent Interchange," p. 76.

[2]The Rule of *Shewa* yields /a/ 7x in sequences involving ד as against /i/ 5x.

[3]According to Klein and the published photograph, the manuscript reads בְּיָדִין מְצַוֶּן, which must be either a scribal error or result from a metanalysis of a sandhi pronunciation /baydimmeṣwan/ < *baydi meṣwan* (junctural doubling?) and a re-interpretation of /mm/ as /n# + #m/

[4]See §12k.

[5]There are no pointed examples of this sequence in Palestinian pointed manuscripts.

[6]See §13d.

[7]On the possible realization of forms such as וַאמֶר C Gn 34:11 ([wamar]?), see §25a, n.131. It should be added that there is only one fully pointed sequence of two *shewas* with a guttural in the Palestinian pointed manuscripts: וּאֵגֹ A Ex 21:19; "and the wage of."

[8]See §13d.

[9]See §§11f, 12i-j.

[10]/a/ is preserved, however, before gutturals in Biblical Aramaic and Targum Onqelos.

[11]As in Syriac. See Nöldeke, *Syriac Grammar*, p. 30, n.1.

[12]More commonly known as the "attenuation of the a vowel." See Blake, "Apparent Interchange," pp. 77-79.

[13]Cf. /wi/ in the Babylonian tradition. See Morag, "Biblical Aramaic," p. 121; Bauer-Leander, *Grammatik*, p. 36.

[14]See Nöldeke, *Syriac Grammar*, p. 31. It is limited to the lexical items /yəhuðā/ "Judah" and /yəhuðāyā/ "Jew," e.g. /layhuðā/, /layhuðāyā/.

# VI MORPHOLOGY

The syntactic use of particular forms will also be discussed.

## A. *Pronouns*

**§34**

*Singular*

1    /'əna/: אֲנָא־ C Gn 31:39, אֲנָא C Gn 31:44, אֲנָה־ Cd Gn 44:18;

2 m.  /'att/: אַתְּ־ C Gn 31:52, אַתְּ C Gn 46:30;

2 f.  /'att?/: וְאַתְּ E Gn 30:2, אַתְּ E Gn 39:9

3 m.  /hu/: הוּא A Ex 21:21, הוּא־ C Gn 32:19;

3 f.  /hi/: הִיא C Gn 32:19, הִיא C Gn 34:14

*Plural*

1    /'ənan/: אֲנַן־ C Gn 34:14, אֲנַן Cd Gn 44:16, אנן AA Nu 20:4;

2 m.  /'atton/: אתן F Ex 19:4, אתן AA₁ Ex 12:13, אַתּוּן D Dt 28:21;

2 f.  /'atten?/: וְאַתֵּן E Gn 31:6;

3 m.  /'ennun?, hennun?/:[1] אִנּוּן־ C Gn 32:18, אִנּוּן־ Cd Gn 47:1;
       הִנּוּן E Gn 7:14, הנון F Lv 23:17;

3 f.  /'ennin?, hennin?/:[2] אנין E Gn 31:2, אִינִין Z Gn 49:12, הינין E Gn 31:5.

**§34a** The 3 s. and pl. independent pronouns also serve as a copula, e.g., אֲנָא הוּא יי F Lv 22:32. "I am the Lord"; מָה־הִיא־דָא הַעֲבָדְתְּ B Gn 4:10, "What is this you have done?"; מַן־אִנּוּן אִלֵּין Cd Gn 48:8, "Who are these?"; ]מָא יִ[אַיִן אֵינִין עַיְנוֹי Z Gn 49:12, "How beautiful are his eyes!"; דמן הנון עזקתה ושושפה וחוטרה האליין E Gn 38:26, "Whose signet ring, cloak, and staff are these?

**§34b** *Independent Personal Pronouns—Historical and Comparative Discussion*

**§34c** The inventory of independent personal pronouns has much in common with other dialects in Syria-Palestine as can be seen in the chart on p. 112.[3]

**§34d** The initial *aleph* of the pronouns אנה (1 s.), את (2 m.s. and 2 f.s.), אנן (1 pl.), אתן (2 m.pl.), אתן (2 f.pl.), אנון (3 m.pl.), and אנין (3 f.pl.) is never elided in the consonantal text in the Cairo Genizah fragments, even following a proclitic particle (cf. Galilean Aramaic אנן + ו > ואנן > ונן). Nor are there any pointings such as וַאֲנַן "and we" which might indicate the elision of the *aleph* in

## INDEPENDENT PERSONAL PRONOUNS

| | Cairo Gen. | Bib. Aram.[4] | Targ. Onq.[6] | Gal. Aram.[8] | Pal. Targ.[11] | Pal. Syr.[17] | Sam. Aram.[18] | Syriac[20] | Ma'lula[28] |
|---|---|---|---|---|---|---|---|---|---|
| 1 s. | /ˀəna/ | /ˀ ənā/ | /ˀ ənā/ | אנא,אנה, (אנ),(אנ־) | אנא,אנה (אנ) | אנא,אנ | [ằnā] | /ˀenā/ /-nā/ | [ana] |
| 2 m.s. | /ˀatt/ | /ˀant/[5] | /ˀatt/ | את,(אנת)? (אָתּ־) | את,אנת[12] | אנ | [āttā],[at] | /ˀatt/[21] | [haččị],[haččị] [-aččị][29] |
| 2 f.s. | /ˀatt?/ | — | /ˀatt/ | את,(אנת)[10] | את,אנת[13] | את,אנ | [atti] | /ˀatt/[22] | [hašị],[haši] |
| 3 m.s. | /hu/ | /hu/ | /hu/ | הו,(הי) | הו,(הא),(הו) | הו,(הי) | [ū] | /hu/,/-u/ | [hū] |
| 3 f.s. | /hi/ | /hi/ | /hi/ | הי,(הו) (הי) | הי,(הא),(הו) | הי,(הי) | [ī] | /hi/,/-i/ | [hī] |
| 1 pl. | /ˀənan/ | /ˀənahnā/ | /ˀ ənahnā/ (/naḥnā/) | אנן (אנ־) | אנן,אנחנא, (אנחנ),(אנחנ), (אנא)[14] | אנן,אנחנ | [ằnằnan] (ằnằn)[19] | /ḥənan/ (/ˀanaḥnan/)[23] (/-nan/) | [anaḥ] |
| 2 m.pl. | /ˀatton/ | /ˀantun/ | /ˀattun/ | אתון,(אתן) | אתון (אתן),[15](אתנון)[16] | אתון,(אתנ) | [atton] | /ˀatton/[24] | [haččun] |
| 2 f.pl. | /ˀatten?/ | — | /ˀattin/ | — | אתן,(אתן) | אתן,(אתנ) | [atten] | /ˀatten/[25] | [haččen] |
| 3 m.pl. | /ˀennun?/, ˀennon?/ /hennun?/, hennon?/ | /ˀinnun/, /himmo/, /himmon/ | /ˀinnun/ | הנון,אנון אנון,הנון (הנון),(הנ־) | אנון,הנון אנון,הנון | אנון,הנון (אנון) | [innon] | /hennon/ /ˀennon/[26] | [hinnun], [hinn] |
| 3 f.pl. | /ˀenni̇n?/, /hennin?/ /ˀennen?/, /hennen?/ | /ˀinnin/ | /ˀinnin/ | הנין,אנין | אנין,הנין אנין,הנין | הנין,הנין (אנין) | [innən] | /hennen/ /ˀennen/[27] | [thinnen], [hinn] |

( ) contain infrequent forms
— indicate the form is unattested
- indicates the form is enclitic or follows a proclitic particle[30]

pronunciation.[31] Nevertheless, it is possible that the *aleph* may have been elided in pronunciation when non-initial.

**§34e** Historical *\*n* is never attested in the pronouns את (2 m.s. and 2 f.s.), אתן (2 m.pl.), or אתן (2 f.pl.).

**§34f** Although the final *aleph* of הוא (3 m.s.) and היא (3 f.s.) always appears in the consonantal text, it was probably elided in pronunciation.[32]

**§34g** אנן (1 pl.) is also attested in Babylonian Talmudic Aramaic and Mandaic where it is explained as developing from *\*'anaḥnă > \*'anaḥn > 'ənan*.[33] Although this reconstruction is satisfactory for those dialects in which the gutturals were weakened and lost, it is unsatisfactory for those dialects in Syria-Palestine in which the gutturals were preserved. An alternative reconstruction, which does not suppose the loss of the guttural /ḥ/, would be to view אנן as a new form based on the 1 s. independent pronoun *'əna* + 1 pl. pronominal suffix *-an*.[34]

**§35** *Enclitic Pronouns*

**§35a** There are four certain examples of enclitic pronouns suffixed to a Participle, all of the 1 s. independent pronoun /'əna/ joined to the Participle הוי:[35] הַוֵינָא מְשַׁלֵּם C Gn 31:39, "I used to pay";[36] הַוֵינָא מְשַׁלֵּם C Gn 31:39; בְּאִימָמָא אָכִיל־יָתִי שַׁרְבָּא C Gn 31:40, "the heat used to consume me during the daytime";[37] לָא הֲוֵינָה רְחִימֹה E Gn 29:33, "I was not loved."

**§35b** It is possible that there are examples of the suffixing of the 2 m.s. pronoun /'att/ to the Participle הוי as well as the suffixing of the 1 pl. pronoun /'ənan/. Possible examples with /'att/ are הֲוֵיתְ תָּבַע C Gn 31:39, "you used to demand," הֲוֵית מְשֵׁיזֵב Z Gn 49:9, "you used to save," both with *daghesh*,[38] and הֲוֵית־אָמַר Cd Gn 44:18, "you used to say," הֲוֵית מַשְׁקֵ E Gn 40:13, "you used to give drink," both without *daghesh*. A possible example of the suffixing of /'ənan/ is הֲוֵינָן נַחְתִין Cd Gn 44:18, "we used to descend." הוית and הוינן can also be taken, however, as Perfect forms.

**§35c** Enclitic pronouns on Participles are a feature of Targum Onqelos,[39] the Palestinian Targumim,[40] Galilean Aramaic,[41] Palestinian Syriac,[42] and Syriac (where they are frequent).[43] It is noteworthy that enclitic pronouns are not attested on Participles in Biblical Aramaic, Samaritan Aramaic, or Ma'lula. Enclitic pronouns are a salient feature of Mandaic[44] and Babylonian Talmudic Aramaic.[45]

**§36** *Proclitic Pronouns*

Kutscher suggested the existence of an independent pronoun prefixed to a Participle,[46] and cited as an example אַתאָזֵל־ C Gn 32:18, "you go." It seems more likely, however, that this unique form is due to lack of spacing on the part of the scribe.

**§37** *Pronominal Suffixes on Nouns*

**§37a** The possessive pronouns added to m.s., f.s., and f.pl. nouns are

|         | Singular | Plural  |
|---------|----------|---------|
| 1       | /-i/     | /-an/   |
| 2 m.    | /-ak/    | /-kon/  |

114

| 2 f. | /-ek/ | /*-ken/ |
| 3 m. | /-eh-/ (/e/ - 5x) | /-hon/ (/-on/ - 1x) |
| 3 f. | /-ah/ | /-hen/ |

**§37b** Representative examples are

*1 s.:*

*1 s.* : לְרַבּוּנִי C Gn 32:19, "to my master"; אֲבָהָתִי Cd Gn 47:30, "my fathers"; לִשְׁמִי Cd Gn 48:5, "to my name"; יְדִי Cd Ex 6:8, "my hand."

*2 m.s.:*[47] עבדך C Gn 32:21, "your servant"; בְּרָך Cd Gn 48:2, "your son"; חוטרך Cd Ex 7:19, "your staff"; יְדָך Cd Ex 9:22, "your hand."

*2 f.s.:*[48] לִיךְ Cd Gn 38:18, "to you"; ליך E Gn 30:2;[49] מניך E Gn 30:2, "from you"; עמיך E Gn 30:15, "with you"; לוותיך E Gn 38:16, "to you"; דבריך E Gn 30:15, "of your son."

*3 m.s.:*[50] לְרֹבּוֹנֹה A Ex 21:4, "to his master"; כספה A Ex 21:21, "his silver"; רְשׁוּתֵיהּ B Gn 4:7, "his authority"; לְבֵּיהּ Cd Ex 7:22, "his heart"; במשמעי [דרבוני] Z Gn 44:18, "in the hearing of my master"; דרישי דאבא Z Gn 44:18, "my father's head"; מֵּמַר דאדני Z Gn 48:15, "the Word of the Lord"; בעֳמְקִי דִימָה Z Gn 48:16, "in the depths of the sea."

*3 f.s.:*[51] צַעֲרַהּ C Gn 35:9, "her pain"; מרבִּיָינִיתַהּ C Gn 35:9, "her nurse"; אַרְמְלוּתַהּ Cd Gn 38:19, "her widowhood"; רְדִידַהּ Cd Gn 38:19, "her veil."

*1 pl.:* בִּשְׂרָן Cd Gn 37:27, "our flesh"; לרבנון Cd Gn 44:16, "to our master"; טַלְיוּתַן Cd Gn 46:34, "our youth"; אֱלָהָן Cd Ex 9:30, "our God."

*2 m.pl.:* כַּסְפְּכוֹן Cd Gn 43:23, "your silver"; אֱלָהֲכוֹן Cd Gn 43:23, "your God"; אַרְעֲכוֹן D Dt 28:18, "your land"; נפשתכן F Lv 23:32, "your souls."

*3 m.pl.:*[52] חוֹבַּתְהוֹן Cd Gn 44:16, "their guilt"; וְעָנְהוֹן Cd Gn 46:32, "and their small cattle"; בְּקָבָרְתְּהוֹן Cd Gn 47:30, "in their burial place"; ומנחתהון F Nu 28:28, "and their meal offering"; לוותהון E Gn 37:18, "towards them."[53]

*3 f.pl.:* וִיהֵן B Gn 4:5, "their countenance"; זִיהֵין B Gn 4:6; חצדהין E Gn 30:14, "their reaping."

**§37c** The possessive pronouns added to m.pl. and dual nouns are

| | Singular | Plural |
| --- | --- | --- |
| 1 | /-ay/ (/-oy/ - 3x) | /-enan/ |
| 2 m. | /-ek/ | /-ekon/ |
| 2 f. | /*-ek/ | /*-eken/ |
| 3 m. | /-oy/ | /-ehon/ |
| 3 f. | /-eh/ | /-ehen/ |

**§37d** Representative examples are

*1 s.:* גַּרְמִיי ־B Gn 2:23, "my bones"; חוֹבַי "my sins"; יְדִיי־ Cd Ex 9:29, "my hands";⁵⁴ סורחנוּיי E Gn 41:9;ׂ "my offenses"; אַפּוֹי C Gn 32:21, "my face";⁵⁵ קודמוי E Gn 30:29, "before me"; קודמוי E Gn 31:12.⁵⁶

*2 m.s.:* עוֹבָדָיך B Gn 4:7, "your deeds"; יְדָיך־ B Gn 4:11, "your hands";ׂ וְעִזָּיך C Gn 31:38, "your goats"; אַפָּיך Cd Gn 46:30, "your face."

*3 m.s.:* לְמרוֹיׂ A Ex 22:11,ׂ "to his master";⁵⁷ בְּאַפּוֹי Bd Gn 7:22, "in his face"; חֶלְמוֹי Cd Gn 37:20, "his dreams"; רחמוֹיׂ E Gn 43:30, "his mercy."

*3 f.s.:* בִּתְחָמָהּ C Gn 34:21, "in her borders"; יְדֵיהַ־ Cd Gn 38:20, "her hands"; במעיהּ E Gn 38:27, "in her womb";ׂ סגוליהּ E Gn 40:10, "her bunches of grapes."

*1 pl.:* וִידֵינָן Cd Gn 37:27, "and our hands"; טְעוּנֵּינָן־ Cd Gn 43:18, "our loads"; חלמֵינָן E Gn 41:12;ׂ "our dreams"; קורבנין F Lv 22:27, "our sacrifices."

*2 m.pl.:* נְשׁיכוֹן A Ex 22:23, "your women"; טעוּניכוֹן־ Cd Gn 43:12,ׂ "your loads"; מְלֵּיכוֹן D Dt 5:25, "your words"; לדריכוֹן F Lv 23:14, "of your generations."

*3 m.pl.:*⁵⁸ וְתוֹרֵהן Cd Gn 46:32, "and their oxen"; חָרָשֵׁהן Cd Ex 7:11;ׂ "their sorcerers"; מֵימֵיהוֹן Cd Ex 7:19, "their waters"; רגליהן E Gn 38:25, "their feet."ׂ

*3 f.pl.:* בבישריהין E Gn 41:18, "in their body";⁵⁹ בבשרהן E Gn 41:19.

§37e There are four examples in which the pointing of the pronominal suffixes on m.pl. and dual nouns clearly imitates the *qere* of Biblical Aramaic;⁶⁰ the consonantal text, on the other hand, may reflect the forms of the pronominal suffixes which are regularly attested in these fragments (in which \*ay > /e/): יְדֵיהּ- Cd Gn 37:33,ׂ "her hands" (consonantal text /yədeh/?); ידיך Z Gn 47:29, "your (m.) hands" (consonantal text /yədek/?);⁶¹ תְּלַת עֵינַהּ Cd Gn 38:25;ׂ"she lifted up her eyes" (consonantal text /'ayneh/?);⁶² הֲהַךְ־עֵינָאָ- Cd Gn 38:25, "her eyes shone" (consonantal text /'ayne/?).⁶³ There are two additional examples of the Tiberian Biblical Aramaic *qere* with prepositions: עֲלָוַיהּ- Cd Gn 38:19, "upon her"⁶⁴ (consonantal text /'ellaweh/?); עֲלָיך H Gn 15:1, "upon you (m.)" (cf. עֲלָיך Z H Gn 15:1).

*Pronominal Suffixes—Historical and Comparative Discussion*

§37f Cf. the inventory of the possessive pronominal suffixes in the Cairo Genizah fragments with the inventories of Targum Onqelos, Galilean Aramaic, the Palestinian Targumim, Palestinian Syriac, Samaritan Aramaic, Syriac, and Maʻlula:

POSSESSIVE PRONOMINAL SUFFIXES

on m.s., f.s., and f.pl. nouns[65]

| | Cairo Gen. | Bib. Aram.[66] | Targ. Onq.[68] | Gal. Aram.[69] | Pal. Targ.[72] | Pal. Syr.[76] | Sam. Aram.[79] | Syriac[80] | Ma'lula[83] |
|---|---|---|---|---|---|---|---|---|---|
| 1 s. | /-i/ | /-i/ | /-i/ | ‏י־(יי־)[70] | ‏ר־ | ‏ר־,יØ[77] | [-i] | Ø[81] | [-i],Ø |
| 2 m.s. | /-ak/ | /-āk/ | /-āk/ | ‏ך־ | ‏ך־ | ‏ך־,ןא־ | [-å̄k] | /-āx/ | [-ah] |
| 2 f.s. | /-ek/ | — | /-ek/ | ‏יך־,ך־ | ‏יך־,ך־ | ‏יב־,יב־[78] | [-ek] | /-ex/[82] | [-iš] |
| 3 m.s. | /-eh/(/-e/) | /-eh/ | /-eh/ | ‏ה־,יה־(וי־)[71] | ‏יה־,ה־(וי־)[73] | ‏הי־,הני־ | [-e] | /-eh/ | [-e] |
| 3 f.s. | /-ah/ | /-ah/ | /-ah/ | ‏ה־ | ‏ה־ | ‏ה־ | [-å̄] | /-āh/ | [-a] |
| 1 pl. | /-an/ | /-anā/ | /-anā/ | ‏ן־ | ‏ן־,נא־[74],יןי־[75] | ‏ין־,ין־,ןב־,ןב־ | [-å̄n],[-nå̄n] | /-an/ | [-ah] |
| 2 m.pl. | /-kon/ | /-kon/,/-kom/ | /-kon/ | ‏כן־ | ‏כם־,כון־ | ‏כון־(סכן־) | [-kon] | /-xon/ | [-ḥun] |
| 2 f.pl. | — | — | /-ken/ | ‏כן־ | ‏כן־ | ‏כן־ | [-ken] | /-xen/ | [-ḥen] |
| 3 m.pl. | /-hon/(/-on/) | /-hon/,/-hom/ | /-hon/ | ‏הון־,ין־ | ‏הון־,הין־ | ‏הן־ | [-on] | /-hon/ | [-ḥun],[-un] |
| 3 f.pl. | /-hen/ | /-hen/[67] | /-hen/ | ‏הין־,ן־ | ‏הין־,ין־ | ‏הין־,אזה־ | [-ən] | /-hen/ | [-hen],[-en] |

( ) contain infrequent forms

— indicate the form is unattested

## POSSESSIVE PRONOMINAL SUFFIXES
### on m.pl. and dual nouns

| | Cairo Gen. | Bib. Aram. | Targ. Onq. | Gal. Aram.[89] | Pal. Targ.[91] | Pal. Syr.[99] | Sam. Aram.[103] | Syriac | Ma'lula |
|---|---|---|---|---|---|---|---|---|---|
| 1 s. | /-ay/(/-oy/) | /-ay/ | /-ay/ | יי,י,(יי)[90] | יי,ין[92] | יי,,יי(יי)[100] | [-i] | /-ay/ | [-ōyi],[-ōy] |
| 2 m.s. | /-ek/ | /-āk/[84] | /-āk/ | יך,ך, | יך,ןי[93] | יך | [-ak] | /-āyk/ | [-ōḫ] |
| 2 f.s. | --- | --- | /-ak/[88] | יך,ך, | יכי,ין[94],יכן[95] | יכי | [-ak] | /-ayk/[104] | [-ōš] |
| 3 m.s. | /-oy/ | /-ohi/ | /-ohi/ | יהי,הי | יוי,הי | יוי,יהי(יהי)[101](יי)[102] | [-o] | /-aw/[105] | [-ōye] |
| 3 f.s. | /-eh/ | /-ah/[85] | /-ahā/ | הי,הָ | הי,ית,אתי,אתה[96] | יה | [*-iyyā] | /-eh/ | [-ōya] |
| 1 pl. | /-enən/ | /-anā/[86] | /-anā/ | ין | אנן | יין,ין(יןי) | [-inān] | /-ayn/ | [-ainah] |
| 2 m.pl. | /-ekon/ | /-ekon/ | /-ekon/ | יכון | יכון,כום[97] | יכון | [-ikon] | /-aykon/ | [aiḫun] |
| 2 f.pl. | --- | --- | /-eken/ | יכון | יכן | יכן | [-ikən] | /-ayken/ | [aiḥen] |
| 3 m.pl. | /-ehon/ | /-ehon/ | /-ehon/ | יהון | יהון,הום[98] | יהון,יון | [-iyyon] | /-ayhon/ | [-aihun] [-ain],[-ai] |
| 3 f.pl. | /-ehen/ | /-ehen/[87] | /-ehen/ | יהין | יהין | יהין | [-iyyən] | /-ayhen/ | [-aihen] [-ain],[-ai] |

( ) contain infrequent forms
— indicate the form is unattested

The following pronominal suffixes deserve special comment:

*on s. nouns*

§37g   *3 m.s. /-e/:* Although four of the five examples of /-e/ occur in MS Z, it is likely that conservative orthography masks the similar realization of this pronominal suffix in other manuscripts. *-e* is the rule in Samaritan Aramaic and Ma'lula and is also attested in Galilean Aramaic, the Palestinian Targumim, and Palestinian Syriac.

§37h   *1 pl. /-an/:* Final \*a has been apocopated, \*aná > /-an/ as is the case in Galilean Aramaic, the Palestinian Targumim, Palestinian Syriac, Samaritan Aramaic, and Syriac.

§37i   *3 m.pl. /-on/:* The syncopation of /h/ is the rule in Samaritan Aramaic and is also attested in Galilean Aramaic, the Palestinian Targumim and Ma'lula.

*on pl. nouns*

§37j   Proto-Aramaic \*ay > /e/[106] before the pronominal suffixes of the 2 m.s., 3 f.s., and all the f. and m.pl. forms (presumably also before the 2 f.s. suffix, which is unattested). This is a salient feature of the Cairo Genizah fragments. The contraction of \*ay before the pronominal suffixes is also attested in Samaritan Aramaic, presumably in Galilean Aramaic, the Palestinian Targumim, and Palestinian Syriac, and is attested before the 3 f.s. suffix in Syriac and before the 2 and 3 pl. suffixes in Biblical Aramaic and Targum Onqelos. It is possible that the *kethibh* of Biblical Aramaic also reflects the contraction \*ay > /e/ before the 2 m.s., 3 f.s., and 1 pl. pronominal suffixes.[107]

§37k   *1 s. /-oy/:* The few examples with /-oy/ in these fragments are paralleled by a limited number of examples in the other Palestinian Targumim, in Galilean Aramaic, and in Palestinian Syriac In Ma'lula, on the other hand, [-ōy] (in free variation with [-ōyi]) is the regular 1 s. suffix. [-ōy] is also the regular 1 s. suffix in Baḫ'a.[108]

It seems unlikely that the 1 s. /-oy/ is the result of a sound shift /ay/ > /oy/, since such a shift is restricted to the 1 s. pronominal suffix on m.pl. and dual nouns.[109] Nor is it likely that the 3 m.s. pronominal suffix /-oy/ has been substituted for the 1 s. suffix /-ay/ because of a feeling of impropriety in using the 1 s. suffix when reading from the Targum.[110] Rather, comparative data suggest that /-oy/ as a 1 s. form arose from the misanalysis of the 3 m.s. suffix /-y/ as *o* (pl. marker) + *i* (1 s. marker).

Cf. the pronominal suffixes found on nouns in Ma'lula:

|        | *on s. nouns* | *on pl. nouns* |
|--------|---------------|----------------|
| 1 s.   | [-i], ∅       | [-ōyi], [-ōy]  |
| 2 m.s. | [-aḫ]         | [-ōḫ]          |
| 2 f.s. | [-oš]         | [-ōš]          |
| 3 m.s. | [-e]          | [-ōye]         |
| 3 f.s. | [-a]          | [-ōya]         |

| 1 pl. | [-aḥ] | [-ainaḥ] |
| 2 m.pl. | [-ḫun] | [-aiḫun] |
| 2 f.pl. | [-ḫen] | [-aiḫen] |
| 3 m.pl. | [-hun], [-un] | [-aihun], [-ain], [-ai] |
| 3 f.pl. | [-hen], [-en] | [-aihen], [-ain], [-ai] |

The source of the *o*-vowel in the pronominal system of Ma'lula may have been the 3 m.s. pronominal suffix, which presumably was *oy at an earlier, unattested stage of the language. The pronominal suffix *oy might have been misanalyzed as *o* + *i*, i.e., *o* as the marker of the pl.[111] and *i* as the marker of the 1 s. This led to a situation in which the 3 m.s. pronominal suffix and the 1 s. suffix were identical—*oy*. In order to differentiate the 3 m.s. *oy* from the new 1 s. *oy*, the pronominal suffixes on s. nouns were added: 3 m.s. *oy* + *e* > [ōye]; 1 s. *oy* + *i* > [ōyi] (final [i] and $\emptyset$ are in free variation in Ma'lula and thus [ōyi] ~[ōy]). The 3 f.s. suffix on pl. nouns was then re-formed on the analogy *i:e:a::oyi:oye:*x, x = *oya*. In the final stage, *oyi, oye, oya* were analyzed as *o* + *yi*, *o* + *ye*, *o* + *ya*, which led to the re-formation of the 2 m.s. *o* + *ḥ* > [ōḥ] and 2 f.s. *o* + *š* > [ōš].[112]

This process, which spread to all the s. pronominal suffixes in Ma'lula, seems to have been in an initial stage in the Cairo Genizah fragments, the other Palestinian Targumim, and Palestinian Syriac,[113] spreading only to the 1 s. suffix. This created a situation in which the 1 s. and 3 s. suffixes were identical.

**§371** *3 m.s. /-oy/:* This form of the pronominal suffix is attested in Galilean Aramaic, the Palestinian Targumim, and Palestinian Syriac. In these dialects it occurs alongside its parent form, *-ohi*.[114]

**§37m** *1 pl. /-enan/:* This suffix is also attested in Galilean Aramaic, the Palestinian Targumim, Palestinian Syriac, and Samaritan Aramaic. *ayná > *en with the addition of the 1 pl. suffix on s. nouns, /-an/.

**§38** *Object Pronominal Suffixes*

**§38a** A salient feature of this dialect is the absence of objective pronouns suffixed to the verb,[115] with the exception of one example of a pronominal suffix added to the Imperfect, יְשַׁוִּּיךְ־יָתָךְ Cd Gn 48:20, "he will place you" (with independent object pronoun!), as well as one example of a pronominal suffix on a Hebrew infinitival form, וּלְרוֹמָמָ[ה]ֹ D Dt 26:19, "to raise you up"[116]

The place of the object pronominal suffixes is taken by the independent object pronouns.

**§38b** The infrequency of object pronominal suffixes on verbs is a salient feature of the other Palestinian Targumim, particularly the Fragment Targum and Targum Neophyti.[117] It is also a characteristic of Palestinian Syriac.[118]

**§39** *Independent Object Pronouns*

**§39a** These pronouns are made up of the *nota accusativi* ית /yat/ and pronominal suffixes. Representative examples are:

120

| | Singular | | Plural | |
|---|---|---|---|---|
| 1 | /yati/ יָתִי | C Gn 32:27 | /yatan/ יָתַן | C Gn 35:9 |
| 2 m. | /yatak/ יָתָךְ | C Gn 32:18 | /yatəkon/[120] יָתְכֹן | Cd Ex 6:6 |
| 2 f. | /*yatek/ | | /*yatəken/ | |
| 3 m. | /yateh/ יָתֵיהּ | C Gn 32:20 | /yatəhon/ יָתְהוֹן | B Gn 2:19 |
| 3 f. | /yatah/ יָתַהּ | C Gn 31:45 | /yatəhen?/ יתהן | G Dt 27:4 |

יָת is pointed יָת in Tiberian pointed manuscripts and יֹת in Palestinian pointed manuscripts when bound by pronominal suffixes.[120]

§39b These independent object pronouns[121] are characteristic of Targum Onqelos,[122] the Palestinian Targumim,[123] Palestinian Syriac,[124] Samaritan Aramaic,[125] and Galilean Aramaic.[126] They can also be found in Old Aramaic[127] and in the Bar Kochba letters.[128]

§40 *Independent Possessive Pronouns*

§40a The independent possessive pronoun דיד /did-/ occurs 15x in the Genizah fragments. Representative examples of the attested pronominal suffixes are:

| | Singular | | Plural | |
|---|---|---|---|---|
| 1 | /didi/ דִּידִי | C Gn 31:43 | /didan/ דִּידָן | C Gn 34:23 |
| 2 m. | /didak/ דִּידָךְ | B Gn 4:8 | /*didəkon/ | |
| 2 f. | /*didek/ | | /*didəken/ | |
| 3 m. | /dideh/ דִּידֵיהּ | Cd Gn 38:25 | /*didəhon/ | |
| 3 f. | /*didah/ | | /*didəhen/ | |

§40b This pronoun occurs in the Palestinian Targumim,[129] Galilean Aramaic,[130] Ma'lula,[131] and Babylonian Talmudic Aramaic.[132] One finds דיל, on the other hand, in Targum Onqelos,[133] Palestinian Syriac,[134] Samaritan Aramaic,[135] and Mandaic.[136] דיל, however, is also infrequently attested in Galilean Aramaic,[137] the Palestinian Targumim,[138] and Babylonian Tarlmudic Aramaic.[139] A reflex of דיד is also attested in Samaritan Aramaic.[140]

§40c דיד is generally thought to have developed from די + יד,[141] although it has been suggested that דיל[142] > דיד.[143]

§41 *Demonstrative Pronouns*

There are two sets of demonstrative pronouns, corresponding to "this, these" and "that, those."

§41a *Demonstratives corresponding to "this, these"*

a) *Functioning as pronouns* (represenative examples):

m.s. /den/:[144] דֵּין Cd Gn 48:18; דין E Gn 9:12; דן E Gn 29:33.
f.s. /da/:[145] דָא B Gn 4:10; דָא Cd Gn 38:26; דא E Gn 92:27.
pl. /'ellen/: אִלֵּין C Gn 32:18; אִלֵּין C Gn 32:20; אֵלֵין Cd Gn 48:8.
/'ellayin/: אליין F Lv 23:2; אליין F Lv 23:4; אליין F Nu 28:23.

§41b Some examples of the use of these demonstratives are as follows: לְדָא יָאֵי לְמִתְקְרָא B Gn 2:23, "it is fitting that this one should be called...";
ואתן לך להוד ית דא בפלחנה E Gn 29:27, "and I shall give you also this one for the

work"; אֲרוּם־ E Gn 38:28; "saying, 'this one came out first'"; קְדָמַי נְפַק דֵּן לְמֵמַר work"; בְּכוֹרָא הוּא־דֵּין Cd Gn 48:18, "because this one is the first-born"; אִלֵּין וּלְמַן־אַנּוּן דְּאִית־קָדָמָךְ C Gn 32:18, "and whose are these who are before you?"; אִלֵּין תְּמַלֵּל דִּי דִּבֵּירַיָּא R Ex 19:6, "these are the commandments which you shall speak."

§41c b) *Functioning as adjectives* (representative examples):

*m.s.* /haden/: הָדֵין B Gn 4:7, הָרֵין C Gn 31:48, יָהָרֵין D Dt 26:18.

*f.s.* /hada/: הָדָה D Dt 27:8, הָדָא Cd Gn 48:7, הדא AA Dt 27:3.

*pl.* /ha'ellayin/: הָאֲלַיִן Cd Gn 44:6; הָאֲלֵין D Dt 5:19; האליין F Ex 20:1.

§41d Some examples of these demonstratives functioning as adjectives are יַגְרָא הָדֵין C Gn 31:52, "this heap"; בעלמה הדן E Gn 39:10, "in this world"; אַרְעָא הָרָא- Cd Gn 48:4, "this land"; אורייתה הדא AA Dt 27:8, "this law"; פתגמייה האליין E Gn 39:7, "these words"; דבירייה האליין Y Ex 19:7, "these commandments."

§41e When functioning as adjectives, this set of demonstratives follows the modified noun, except in the expressions of time בההדה זמנה E Gn 30:20, "now" (+ 5x) and בההדה שעתה E Gn 38:25 "now" (+ 1x), both translating Hebrew הַפַּעַם.[146] In other expressions of time, such as יומה הדן E Gn 7:13, "today" (+ 13x) and ירחה הדן AA₁ Ex 12:2, "this month," the regular word order obtains.[147]

§41f There are three exceptions to the distinction between independent pronominal and adjectival forms: לְהוֹד־בְּהָדָא נִשְׁתָּתֵּי לְכוֹן C Gn 34:15, "only on this condition will we agree with you"; להוד־בְּהָדָא יִתְעָרְבוֹן עִימָן גּוּבְרַיָּא C Gn 34:22; "only on this condition may the men intermingle with us"; דִּין סִטְרַ[ה] AA₁ Ex 17:12, "this side" (note the inverted word order).

§41g In the forms of the pl. demonstrative pronoun, *ay[148] regularly contracts to /e/ in the form which functions as a pronoun, /'ellen/, whereas the diphthong is triphthongized in the form which functions as an adjective, /ha'ellayin/. Only in MS F does one find /'ellayin/ in place of /'ellen/.[149] Cf. אליין F Ex 19:6; Lv 23:2,4,37; Nu 28:23. In unpointed manuscripts the distinction between /'ellen/, /ha'ellayin/ is almost always preserved in the consonantal text, e.g., אלין E Gn 9:18, but האליין E Gn 29:13.[150]

§41h *Demonstratives corresponding to "that, those"*

The following demonstratives function only as adjectives (representative examples):

*m.s.* /hahu/: ההוא־ C Gn 32:22; ההוא D Dt 27:11; ההוא Z Gn 48:20.

*f.s.* /hahi/: ההיא E Gn 29:2; ההיא F Lv 23:30; ההיא AA Nu 19:20.

*pl.* unattested

§41h These forms follow the modified noun, e.g., בְּלֵילְיָא הַהוּא C Gn 32:14, "that night"; ביומה ההוא E Gn 30:35, "on that day"; נפשה ההיא AA Nu 19:13, "that soul." ההיא precedes the modified noun in בההיא שעתה E Gn 38:25, "at that time."

§41i The demonstrative /dəna/ functions as an adverb in these fragments. See §158b.

122

*Demonstrative Pronouns—Historical and Comparative Discussion*

**§41j** Compare the inventory of demonstrative pronouns in the Cairo Genizah fragments with other dialects in Syria-Palestine and with Biblical Aramaic and Targum Onqelos (see p.123).[151]

**§41k** The inventory and use of the demonstrative pronouns in the Cairo Genizah fragments parallels basically that of Targum Onqelos—both Targumim have similar pronouns, some of which are used pronominally and some of which are used adjectivally. Samaritan Aramaic, too, preserves the distinction between pronouns which are used pronominally and those which are used adjectivally. In the Palestinian Targumim, the distinction between the pronominal forms and the adjectival forms is beginning to blur[170]—a process which is characteristic of Galilean Aramaic and Palestinian Syriac. In Biblical Aramaic and Syriac, on the other hand, the forms of the demonstratives are used both pronominally and adjectivally.

**§411** The positioning of the demonstrative before the modified noun in בהדה שעתה, בהדה זמנה, דין סיטרה is also found in the other Palestinian Targumim in the same expressions, although the demonstrative usually follows the noun it modifies in these Targumim.[171] In Galilean Aramaic, however, the adjectival demonstrative usually precedes the noun it modifies; in Palestinian Syriac the word order is free, as is the case in Biblical Aramaic and Syriac. The demonstrative functioning as an adjective occurs before the modified noun in the Samaritan Targum, but appears to follow the noun in later Samaritan Aramaic sources.

**§41m** The inverted word order of בהדה שעתה and בהדה זמנה in the Cairo Genizah fragments may well be due to the influence of the Biblical Aramaic syntagms בַּהּ־שַׁעֲתָא, "at once," בֵּהּ־זִמְנָא, "at once," etc.[172] The former syntagm occurs in these fragments: בַּהּ־שָׁעֲתָהּ Cd Gn 38:25.^[173]

**§42** *Relative Pronouns*

There are two relative pronouns, די /di/ and prefixed ד /dV-/. The interrogative pronoun מה /ma/ functions on two occasions as a relative pronoun. The interrogative pronoun אידא /'ayda/ serves once as a relative pronoun.

Cowling has identified the different distributions of ד and ד in the translation and non-translation portions of these fragments.[174]

**§42a** a) *Translation Portions*

In these sections, די and ד are usually in complementary distribution as determined by the Masoretic text.

1) די translates

a) אֲשֶׁר in the Masoretic text when a preposition does not follow, e.g, די תשׁוֹ A Ex 21:1 (MT אֲשֶׁר תָּשִׂים); דִּי־נְסַב B Gn 2:22^ (MT אֲשֶׁר־לָקַח); די אולידת Cd Gn 48:6 (MT אֲשֶׁר־הוֹלַדְתָּ); די בְרָא D Dt 26:19 (MT אֲשֶׁר עָשָׂה); די יתאכל E Gn 6:21^ (MT אֲשֶׁר יֵאָכֵל).

b) בַּאֲשֶׁר in the Masoretic text when introducing a temporal clause in the conjunction כיון די, "as soon as, when," or a comparative clause in the

## DEMONSTRATIVE PRONOUNS

| | Cairo Gen. | Bib. Aram.[152] | Targ. Onq.[153] | Gal. Aram.[155] | Pal. Targ.[159] | Pal. Syr.[161] | Sam. Aram.[162] | Syriac[168] | Ma'lula[169] |
|---|---|---|---|---|---|---|---|---|---|
| "this" (m.) | /den/,/haden/ /haden/ | /dənā/ | /den/(/dənan/) /hāden/ | הדין,(הדא) הדין,הדא,דין הדין,הדא,דין | הדין,(הדא) הדין | הד,הדין, (הדין) הדי,(הד) | [danIādən] [ā'ənIze]163 [azze]164 | /hān/ /hānā/ | [hanna] |
| "this" (f.) | /da/,/hada/ /hada/ | /dā/ | /dā/ /hādā/ | הדא,הדין,הדא הדא | הדא,הדין (הדא) | הדא,(הדא) | [ā'da],[dā] [ā'ənIdā'a] [zē'ot]165[azzē'ot]166 | /hāδe/ (/hāδ/) | [hōdi] [hōdi] |
| "these" | /'ellen/ /'ellayin/ /ha'ellayin/ | /'el/ /'elle/ /'illen/ | /'illen/ /hā'illen/ | הלין,אלין (אלין)156 | אלין,הלין הלין,הדאלין | הלין | [āllən] | /hālen/ (/hān/) | [hannun] [hannen] [hann] |
| "that" (m.) | /hahu/ | /dek/ /dikken/ | /hahu/ (/deki/) | הההוא, הו, ההן ההן (ההוא) | ההוא (ההן)160 | ההן,ההוא,הה (ההן) | [ā'u] [yāte] | /haw/ | [hōte] |
| "that" (f.) | /hahi/ | /dak/ /dikken/ | /hahi/ (/yātah/)154 | הההיא,היא, (ההי),הההיא157 | ההיא | ההיא,ההיא,הה (ההי) | [ā'iIyāta] | /hāy/ | [hōta] |
| "those" | -- | /'illēk/ | /hā'innun/ | הההנין,הן (הההינ)(אנון)158 | הנאהן | הלין,ההנ(הלין) (ההינ) | [āllən] [yāton] [ā'imma]167 | /hānon/ /hānen/ (/hālox/) (/hālex/) (/hānoxi/) | [hatinnun] [hatinnen] [hatinn] — |

( ) contain infrequent forms

-- indicate the form is unattested

124

conjunction הָיך מה די "as," e.g., E Gn 29:10 (MT רָאָה כַּאֲשֶׁר וַיְהִי);
E Gn 43:2 והוה כיוון די אשלמו (MT יָלְדָה כַּאֲשֶׁר וַיְהִי); E Gn 30:25 (MT הַיך די ילדת
הָיך־בְּה דִי־יְמַשְׁמֵשׁ (כַּאֲשֶׁר דִּבֶּר; AA Dt 26:18 (MT הָיך מה די מלל (וַיְהִי כַּאֲשֶׁר כִּלּוּ (MT
D Dt 28:29ˆ(MT יְמַשֵּׁשׁ כַּאֲשֶׁר).

**§42b** 2) ד translates:

a) the definite article /ha-/-הַ before a Participle, e.g., דְּרָחֵם Bd Gn 7:21ˆ
דְּמַהְלְכָה C Gn 32:21 (MT הַהֹלֶכֶת);[175] דְּמַהְלְכִין C Gn 32:20 (MT הַהֹלֶכֶת
דסלקק E Gn 31:10 (MT הָעֹלִים); דקיימין F Ex 19:22 (MT הַנִּגָּשִׁים); (הַהֹלְכִים־דִי).

b) a construction which could be interpreted as an asyndetic relative clause,
כָּל־ Cd Gn 46:34 (MT כָּל־דְּרָעֵי עָאן (וְאֵין מוֹשִׁיעַ; D Dt 28:29 (MT (וְלֵית) דְּפָרֵק, e.g.,
(כָּל־נֶפֶשׁ חַיָּה E Gn 9:12ˆ(MT כל נפש דחייה (וְרֹעֵה צֹאן.

c) the genitive expressed in a construct chain,[176] e.g., מִן־אַרְעָא דִכְנַעַן Cd Gn
47:1 (MT מֵאֶרֶץ כְּנַעַן).[177]

**§42c** 3) דָאִית = אִית + ד regularly translates אֲשֶׁר followed by a preposition in
the Masoretic text, e.g., דְאִית בְּאַרְעָא (אֲשֶׁר־תַּחַת; Bd Gn 7:19 (MT דְאִית תְּחוֹת Cd
Gn 46:31 (MT אֲשֶׁר בְּאֶרֶץ־כְּנַעַן); דאית לאבוה E Gn 29:9 (MT אֲשֶׁר לְאָבִיהָ);
(אֲשֶׁר עַל־פְּנֵי הָאֲדָמָה Bd Gn 7:23ˆ (MT דְאִית אַפֵּי אַרְעָא.

**§42d** ד + הוה (/həwa/) is less frequently found as a translation of אֲשֶׁר
followed by a preposition, e.g, דַהֲוָה עִמֵּיהּ Bd Gn 8:1ˆ(MT אֲשֶׁר אִתּוֹ (דַהֲוָה־עִמְּמַנִּי;
Cd Gn 44:1 (MT אֶת־אֲשֶׁר עַל־). This latter construction also occurs with the
interrogative pronoun מה /ma/, e.g, וּמַה־דַהֲוָה עִמֵּיהּ Bd Gn 7:23ˆ(MT
(וַאֲשֶׁר אִתּוֹ).

**§42e** Examples of deviation from this distribution are rare, e.g., דִּי אֶתְיְלִדוּ Cd
Gn 48:5 (MT הַנּוֹלָדִים). In the following two instances, deviations were
"corrected" by the scribe to make them conform to the general translation
technique applied: כָּל־דִּי קָטֵל B Gn 4:15 (MT כָּל־הֹרֵג) was corrected to כָּל־
דְקָטֵל;[178] דִּי־עָאלוּ Cd Gn 46:26 (MT הַבָּאָה) was corrected to דְעָאלוּ.[179]

**§42f** The indefinite relative pronouns, which are frequent in these
fragments, also follow the rules of distribution outlined above: מן ד
"whoever, whomever"; כל מן ד "whoever, whomever"; מה ד "whatever"; כל
מה דהוה "whatever," e.g. כָּל־אֲשֶׁר יֹאמַר; D Dt 5:24 (MT כָּל־מָה דִי־יֵאמַר);
וּפְתַר (MT E Gn 40:8ˆ[180] ולית לן מן דפתר יתהן (כָּל־אֲשֶׁר־לוֹ); E Gn 39:6 (MT לֵיהּ
(אֶת אֲשֶׁר־יֵשָׁא F Ex 20:7[181] (MT כל מן דמשתבע (אֵין אִתּוֹ.

b) *Non-Translation Portions*

**§42g** In these portions, as well as in short interpolated passages in the
translation portions, the form of the relative pronoun is ד. Apart from MS H
in which ד occurs 6x and די 4x, there are only two occurrences of די: וְכֵיוָן דִּי־קְטַל
B Gn 4:16,ˆ "and as soon as he killed" and אמרת די E Gn 40:12, "which you
said." The occurrences of די in MS H are דינפלו H Gn 15:1, "that fell"; דִינְפְּלוּ H
Gn 15:1;[182] and אף על גב די מסרית H Gn 15:1, "even though I have handed over"
(cf. אף על גב דמתכנשין H Gn 15:1, "even if many gather").[183]

**§42h** A feature of the non-translation portions is the combination of the
relative pronoun ד and the independent pronouns הוא and היא, e.g., אִיתְּא
בִּישָׁה...דְהִיא מְתִילָה Cd Gn 37:33, "an evil woman...who is like"; בְּרַבֶּךְ...(וְד)הוּא־
מְשֵׁיזִיב Cd Gn 37:33,ˆ "in the master...who saves"; בְּרַבֶּךְ...דְהוּא־יַהֵיב Cd Gn

38:25, "in the master...who gives"; לבאירה דהיא ט[ויפה] E Gn 31:22 "of the well which floods"; בהדה שעתה דהיא שעת אנינקִי E Gn 38:25 "at this hour which is my hour of distress."[184]

§42i   There are two instances of מה /ma/ functioning as a relative pronoun in MS E Gn 42:36: לית אנה ידע מָה הווה בסופה, "I do not know what his end was," and לית אנה ידע מה הווה [ב]סופה.

§42j   The originally interrogative pronoun אידא serves as a relative pronoun in the short interpolated paraphrase in C Gn 31:39: וְאַיְלָא־דַּהֲוַת טָעֲיָא מֶן־מִנְיָינָא "and that which used to stray from the group."

§42k   The relative pronouns די/ד also function as part of compound conjunctions.[185] The list includes: די, ד־ "because, in order to"; דלא "in order not to"; אף על גב די / ד־ "even though"; בגין ד־ "because": בתר "if not"; אלולי ד־ "if not"; בגין ד־ "because": בתר די "after"; דלמא ד־, "lest"; היך מה די/ד־ "just as"; כין די/ד־ "when"; בזמנה די/ד־ "when"; מן בגלל די/ד־ "in order to"; מן ד־, "in order to"; כמסת ד־ "in order to"; מן בגלל די/ד־ "as soon as, when"; עד ד־ "until"; עד עידן די "until"; עד עיין די "until"; עד זמן די/ד־ "until"; עד כיוון די "until"; קדם עד ד־ "before"; על די/ד־ "because"; מן שעתה ד־, "since."

§42l   The distribution of the conjunctions כד and כדי "when" shows that כד is slightly more frequent in the translation sections (5x, as against כדי 3x), but only כד is found in the non-translation portions (8x). Cf., e.g., in the translation sections וַהֲוָה כַּד (MT וַיְהִי כַּאֲשֶׁר־בָּא) Cd Gn 37:23 and וַהֲוָה כְּדִ־מְטָה כַּד־חֲמַת־Cd Gn 43:21 (MT וַיְהִי כִּי־בָאנוּ מְטִיעֶן), but in the non-translation portions-Cd Gn 38:25, "when she saw" and כד הַוָה נָפֵק F Ex 20:2 "when it was going forth."

§42m   *Relative Pronouns—Historical and Comparative Discussion*

It has been suggested that the distribution of די/ד־ attested in the translation sections of the Cairo Genizah fragments is also found, to a certain extent, in Targum Neophyti.[186]

The relative pronoun is זי in Old Aramaic[187] and די/זי in Official Aramaic[188] (די) in Biblical Aramaic).[189] די is more frequent than ד־ at Qumran.[190] In Targum Onqelos,[191] Palestinian Syriac,[192] Samaritan Aramaic,[193] and Syriac,[194] the form of the relative pronoun is ד־. In Galilean Aramaic,[195] ד־ is more frequent than די. One finds [ti] in Ma'lula.[196]

The syntagms דהוא, דהיא are salient features of both Galilean Aramaic[197] and Samaritan Aramaic.[198]

The frequency of the indefinite relative pronouns מה ד־, כל מן ד־, מן ד־, and כל מה ד־ is a salient feature of the Palestinian Targumim;[199] they occur less frequently in other dialects.

§43   *Interrogative Pronouns*

§43a   The inventory of interrogative pronouns consists of:

"what?" /ma/[200] מָא Cd Gn 38:18, מָה־ B Gn 2:25, מָא־ B Gn 4:8[201]

"who? whom?" /man/[202] מָן Cd Gn 48:8, מָן־ D Dt 5:26 מָאן A Ex 21:19 [203]

"which?" (m.) unattested

"which?" (f.) /hayda/ הַיְדָה־ D Dt 5:23^

126

*"which?" (pl.) /haylen/* וּבְהֵילֵין Cd Gn 37:30

**§43b** /ma/ combines with לְ and כ to form the adverbial interrogatives למה, "why?" and כמה, "how much?" (see §158d). /man/ combines with לְ to form למן, "to whom?" e.g., לְמַן־אַתְּ C Gn 32:18, "to whom do you belong?"

**§43c** The examples above of "which?" are the only ones which occur in these fragments: וַהֲלָא הֲוָת אוּמָה...כְּנַתַן וְאִיתְקַיָּמַע D Dt 5:23,[204] "and because which nation...like us and endured?"; לֵית־אֲנָה יָדַע...וּבְהֵילִין אַפִּין אִיעַל לְוַת־אַבָּא Cd Gn 37:30, "I do not know..., and with which countenance should I enter to my father?" /'ayda/ functions as a relative pronoun in these fragments (see §42j).

**§43d** *Interrogative Pronouns—Historical and Comparative Discussion*

Cognates of the interrogative pronouns /man/ and /ma/ are found in Old Aramaic, Official Aramaic, and the dialects of Syria-Palestine.[205] The fusion of these pronouns with the following independent pronouns (הוא and היא) is a feature of other dialects of Syria-Palestine.[206] The interrogative pronouns היידא, אידא, היידא, היילין and איילין are characteristic of Galilean Aramaic, where one also finds: היי דין and היי לין.[207] They are also found in the other Palestinian Targumim.[208] Palestinian Syriac has הידין, הידא, and הילין.[209] Samaritan Aramaic has only [īdən].[210] Syriac has the forms: /'aynā/, /'ayðā/ and /'aylen/.[211] These interrogative pronouns are unattested in Targum Onqelos. Targum Jonathan, however, has the forms /'edā/ (f.s.) and /'eden/ (pl.).[212]

**§44** *Reflexive Pronouns*

There are no examples of nouns functioning as reflexive pronouns (cf. ‑נפש and ‑גרמ in the other Palestinian Targumim and Galilean Aramaic).[213]

**§45** *Reciprocal Pronouns*

**§45a** The nouns גבר...חבריה serve as the reciprocal pronouns "one...another" (lit., "a man...his friend") in these fragments. These words are a literal translation of the Masoretic איש...רֵעֵהוּ. Some examples are גְבַר ית חֹברֹה A Ex 21:18 (MT אִישׁ אֶת־רֵעֵהוּ‑); גְבַר מֶן־חַבְרֵיהּ C Gn 31:49 (MT אִישׁ מֵרֵעֵהוּ); גבר לחבריה E Gn 43:33 (MT אִישׁ אֶל־רֵעֵהוּ).

**§45b** "One...another" is attested twice in non-translation passages: גבר ית חבריה Z Gn 48:20, and in the parallel section in Cd Gn 48:20 גְבַר יָת־חַבְרֵיהּ. One finds גבר לאחוי E Gn 37:19 in imitation of אִישׁ אֶל־אָחִיו.[214]

**§45c** *Reciprocal Pronouns—Historical and Comparative Discussion*

Targum Onqelos and the Palestinian Targumim often imitate the Masoretic constructions איש...רֵעֵהוּ and אִישׁ...אָחִיו with גבר...חבריה and גבר...אחור. These Targumim also use the cardinal number חד "one" in the expression חד...חד, and the demonstrative pronouns, e.g., דין...דין, and אליין...אליין.[215] Galilean Aramaic uses the demonstrative pronouns, the cardinal number חד, and חברתה, חברתה to express "one another."[216] In the Samaritan Targum one finds אנש/גבר...חברה/עברה in imitation of the Hebrew (e.g., Ex 22:6). In Biblical Aramaic one finds the demonstrative pronouns used, e.g., דָּא לְדָא.[217] The reciprocal pronouns in Syriac are /haδ/.../haδ/; the second member is often replaced by /havrā/, /həvarθā/.[218]

## §46 Indefinite Pronouns

§46a The following indefinite pronouns are attested:

1) /'oḥran/, /'oḥəran/ "another".[219] בְּחִקְלָה דְאחֳרֵן A Ex 22:4 (MT בִּשְׂדֵה אַחֵר).

2) /'ənaš/ "someone": אֱנָשׁ Cd Gn 38:26 (interpolated).

3) /barnaš/ "someone": לְבַרְנַשׁ B Gn 4:14; מן יד ברנשה E Gn 9:5 (MT וּמִיַּד הָאָדָם); נפש דברנש E Gn 9:5 (MT נֶפֶשׁ הָאָדָם); יד ברנש F Ex 19:13 (MT יָ֫ד); נפשיה דברנשה AA Nu 19:13 (MT נֶפֶשׁ הָאָדָם).

4) /gəbar/ "someone": גבֹר A Ex 21:18 (MT אִישׁ), גְבַר Cd Gn 44:11 (MT אִישׁ), גבר AA Nu 19:18 (MT אִישׁ).

5) /kol-/[220] "any" before an undetermined s. noun: כל יבידה A Ex 22:8 (MT כָּל־אֲבֵידָה); כל גבר F Ex 20:12 (interpolated); "entire, whole" before a determined s.noun: בכל ארעה E Gn 41:19 (MT בְּכָל־אֶרֶץ); כל בית ישראל AA₁ Ex 17:11 (interpolated); "all" before a det. pl. noun or collective s. noun: כָּל־עָלְמַיָּא C Gn 35:9 (interpolated); כל עדריה E Gn 29:2 (MT הָעֲדָרִים); כל ביסרה E Gn 9:17 (MT כָּל־בָּשָׂר).

כל is found before מן, מה, and ד functioning as indefinite relative pronouns, e.g., כל מן ד[221] "whoever," כל מן דמשתבע F Ex 20:7 (MT אֲשֶׁר־יִשָּׂא); כָּל־מָה דִי D Dt "whatever," כל מה דאית לאבונן E Gn 31:1 (MT כָּל־אֲשֶׁר לְאָבִינוּ); כל ד B Gn 4:15 (MT כָּל־אֲשֶׁר); "whoever, whomever," כָּל־דְּמַשְׁכַּח 5:24 (MT כָּל־מְצָאוֹ); כל די לית הוא E Gn 30:33 (MT כֹּל אֲשֶׁר־אֵינֶנּוּ). כל also occurs with מנדעם "anything, something":[222] כל מנדעם E Gn 39:8; מן דעם E Gn 30:31; 39:6,9; 40:15.

§46b Noteworthy from a comparative point of view are

/'oḥran/, /'oḥəran/: חורן in Palestinian Syriac (חורין in later manuscripts),[223] Galilean Aramaic (also אחרן),[224] the Palestinian Targumim (also אוחרן);[225] אָחֳרָן in Biblical Aramaic;[226] אָחֳרָן, אָחֳרָן, אָחֳרָן in Targum Onqelos;[227] [ūrån] in Samaritan Aramaic (graphically עורן, חורן);[228] [ḥrēna] in Ma'lula,[229] [ḥəren] in Syriac (graphically חרין, אחרין).[230]

/barnaš/: בר נשא in Galilean Aramaic;[231] בר נש in the Palestinian Targumim;[232] [barnaš], [barš] in Ma'lula.[233]

/kol men da'am/: מידי in Galilean Aramaic;[234] כל מן דעם, כל מדעם, מדעם in the Palestinian Targumim (also מידי);[235] בֹּל מִדְעָם, מִדְעָם in Targum Onqelos;[236] [middåm] in Samaritan Aramaic (graphically מדאם, מדעם);[237] /meddem/ in Syriac;[238] [mette], [mett] in Ma'lula.[239]

Indefinite pronouns which are common in other dialects but not attested in the Cairo Genizah fragments are חד, כלום, and פלן.

## B. Numerals

## §47 Cardinal Numbers

§47a The numerals from one to ten, with representative examples, are

1 m. abs. /had/ חַד C Gn 34:16, חַד C Gn 34:22, חד F Nu 28:27;

1.f. abs. /həda/ חֲדָה B Gn 2:21, חֲדָא Cd Gn 44:22, חֹדָא AA Dt 26:13;

128

*1 c. det.* /ḥatta/ חתא F Nu 28:20, חַתָּא F Nu 28:28, חַתָּה F Nu 28:28; /ḥadta/ חדתה Y Nu 28:28;

*2 m. abs.* /tərayin/ [1] תריך A Ex 21:21, תְּרֵין Cd Gn 43:10, תְּרֵין F Nu 28:27;

*2 m. cst.* /təren/ תְּרֵין Cd Gn 48:1; תְּרֵין־ Cd Gn 48:5; תרֵיהֹן A Ex 22:10;

*2 m. cst.* /təre‑/ תְּרֵין B Gn 4:8, תְּרֵיהוֹן־ Cd Gn 48:13;

*2 f.* /tarten/ בְּתַרְתֵּין C Gn 31:41, תַּרְתֵּין־ C Gn 32:23, תרתין W Ex 15:17;

*3 m. abs.* /təlata/ תְּלָאתָא Cd Gn 38:25, תלתה E Gn 29:34; תְּלָתה F Nu 28:28;

*3 m. cst.* /talte?/ [2] תַלָתֵי Cd Gn 38:25; תלתֵי־ Cd Gn 38:26;^

*4 m. abs.* /'arbə‘a?/ ארבעה H Gn 15:1;

*4 f. abs.* /'arba'?/ [3] וארבע A Ex 21:37;

*5 m. abs.* /ḥamša/ חַמְשָׁה Cd Gn 47:2, חמשה E Gn 43:34;

*6 m. abs.* /'ešta/ אישתה E Gn 30:20, אִישְׁתָה F Ex 20:9, אִישְׁתָה F Ex 20:11;

*6 f. abs.* /šet/ שֵׁת A Ex 21:2, וְשֵׁת C Gn 31:41;

*7 m. abs.* /šob'a/ שִׁבְעָה־ B Gn 4:15; שֻׁבעה E Gn 7:2, שובעה F Nu 28:17;

*7 f. abs.* /šəba'?/ [4] שבע E Gn 29:18, שבע E Gn 29:20, שובע E Gn 29:22 (2x);

*7 c.cst.* /šəba'te?/ [5] שובעתי E Gn 29:27, שבעתי E Gn 41:54, שֻׁובעֻתי F Nu 28:29;

*8 m. abs.* /təmanəya?/ ותמַניֵה Y Gn 21:4;

*9 m. abs.* /teš'a?/ בתשעה F Lv 23:32;

*9 f. abs.* /təša'?/ תֵּשַׁע H Gn 15:1;

*10 m. abs.* /'asra/ עָשְׂרָא C Gn 31:41, עשרה E Gn 28:22, בְּעֶשְׂרָה HH Ex 12:3;

*10 c. cst.* /'əsarte?/ [6] עשרתי F Ex 19:25.

**§47b** The numeral חד "one" generally follows the object counted, e.g., לִבְשַׁר חַד B Gn 2:24; "one flesh"; לְעַם חָד C Gn 34:16, "one people" שָׁעָה־חֲדָא Cd Gn 44:22, "one hour."[7] There are, however, exceptions to this word order: חֲדָה אֶלַע B Gn 2:21; "one rib"[8] (MT אַחַת מִצַּלְעֹתָיו); בְּחַד־יוֹם לְיַרְחָה Bd Gn 8:5, "on the first of the month" (MT אֶחָד לַחֹדֶשׁ); בְּחַד־לְשָׁן D Dt 27:8; "one language" (interpolated) and בחד לשן AA Dt 27:8.

**§47c** A determined form of "one" is attested in the following examples: תורה חתא F Nu 28:20, "the one ox" (MT לַפָּר); דכרה חתא F Nu 28:20, "the one ram" (MT לָאַיִל); אמרא חתה F Nu 28:21, "the one lamb" (MT הָאֶחָד); תורה חתא F תורה הַאֶחָד); דִּיכְרָה חתה F Nu 28:28; (MT לַפָּר הָאֶחָד); לתורה חֹדתה Y Nu 28:28 (MT הָאֶחָד); אימרא חתה F Nu 28:29 (MT הָאֶחָד לְאַיִל); לִכְבֶשׂ).

**§47d** The m. form תרין[9] precedes the object counted when the object is undetermined, e.g., תרין זמנין Cd Gn 43:10, "two times" תרין עשרונין F Lv 23:17, "two-tenths"; ותרין אמרין F Lv 23:19, "and two lambs." There is one exception, which is in imitation of the Masoretic text: דכרין תרין F Lv 23:18, "two rams" (MT וְאֵילִם שְׁנָיִם). תרן (with contracted diphthong)[10] precedes a determined noun, e.g., תְּרֵין לוּחֵי קְיָמָה־ D Dt 5:19, "the two tablets of the Covenant";[11] תרן אמריא F Lv 23:20, "the two lambs"; תְּרֵין־בְּנָיךְ Cd Gn 48:5, "your two sons." The final /n/ is apocopated when pronominal suffixes are added, e.g., תְּרֵיהוֹן B Gn 2:25, "the two of them."[12] תרתין is found before both undetermined nouns and determined nouns,[13] e.g., תרתין נפשן Cd Gn 46:27, "two souls"; תרתין מזחיתה AA₁ Ex 12:7, "the two doorposts." There are no examples of pronominal suffixes on this form.

**§47e** The numerals from three to ten are in the absolute state when preceding an undetermined noun, e.g., תְּלָאתָא צַדִּיקִין Cd Gn 38:25, "three righteous men"; ארבעה מֹלבֹין H Gn 15:1, "four kings";[14] חמשה חולקין E Gn 43:34, "five portions"; אישתה בנין E Gn 30:20, "six sons"; שבע שנין E Gn 41:26, "seven years"; ותמֹנֵייה יומין Y Gn 21:4, "eight days"; בתשעה יומין F Lv 23:32, "nine days"; עֲשָׂרָא זְמְנִין C Gn 31:41, "ten times." Before determined nouns (m. and f.), however, a construct form of the numeral occurs. Construct forms are attested with the numerals "three," "seven," and "ten." The examples are

**§47f** *"the three"*: תַּלְתֵּי שָׂהֲדַיָּיה Cd Gn 38:25, "the three witnesses"; תלתי־סָהֲדֹוי Cd Gn 38:26, "his three witnesses"; ותלתי נשי בְנֹי E Gn 7:13, "and the three wives of his sons"; תלתי שהֹדייה E Gn 38:25; תלתי שרביטייה E Gn 40:12, "the three staffs"[15] (cf. before an undetermined noun תלתה שרביטין E Gn 40:10, "three staffs"); תלתי אבהת עלמה E Gn 40:12, "the three forefathers of old"; תלתי שעבֹדייה E Gn 40:18, "the three oppressions"; תלתה סלייה E Gn 40:18, "the three baskets."

**§47g** *"the seven"*: שובעתי יומי משתותה E Gn 29:27, "the seven days of the feast"; שובעתי יומי משתותיה E Gn 29:28;[16] שבעתי שבלייֹה E Gn 41:7, "the seven ears of corn" (cf. before an undetermined noun שבע שבלֹין E Gn 41:22);[17] שבעתי שבלייה E Gn 41:24; שבעתי תֹורייה E Gn 41:26, "the seven cows";[18] ושבעתי [שבלייה] E Gn 41:26; בשבעתי שני שבעה E Gn 41:47, "the seven years of plenty"; שבעתי שני שבעה E Gn 41:53, שבעתי שני כיפנֹה E Gn 41:54, "the seven years of famine"; שֹובַעֲתֵי אִימְרַיָּיה F Nu 28:29, "the seven lambs" (cf. before an undetermined noun שֹובַעָה אמְרִין F Nu 28:27). There are two examples in which final /e/ is represented by *he* in the consonantal text:[19] שובעתה אמריֹיה F Nu 28:21, "the seven lambs"; שובעתה יומייה Y Nu 28:24, "the seven days."

**§47h** *"the ten"*: עשרתי דבירֹייה F Ex 19:25, "the Ten Commandments."

**§47i** The attested numerals from 11-19 are

*11 c.cst.* /had 'əsarte?/: חַד־עשרתֵּי C Gn 32:23;

*12 m. abs.* /təre 'əsar?/: תרי עשר E Gn 42:36, תרי עשר F Lv 22:27;

*12 c.cst.* /təre 'əsarte/: [תרי] עֲשַׂרתֵי Z Gn 49:1;[20]

*14 m. abs.* /'arbə'at 'əsar?/: בָּארבעת עשר F Lv 23:5, בארבעת עשר F Nu 28:16, ארבעת עשר AA₁ Ex 12:6;

*14 f. abs.* /'arba' 'esre/: אַרְבַּע־עֶשְׂרֶה C Gn 31:41;

*15 m. abs.* /ḥamšat 'əsar?/: ובחמשת עשר F Lv 23:6, בחמשת עשר F Lv 23:34, ובחמש דעשר F Nu 28:17;[21]

*15 f. abs.* /ḥəmeš 'esre/: חֲמֵשׁ עֶשְׂרֶה Bd Gn 7:20;

*17 m. abs.* /šob'at 'əsar?/: בְשָׂבְעַת עֲשַׂר Bd Gn 8:4, בשבעת עשר E Gn 7:11;

*17 f. abs.* /šəba' 'esre?/:[22] שבע עשרה Z Gn 47:28.

**§47j** Some examples of numerals before undetermined nouns are תרי עשר שבטין E Gn 42:36, "twelve tribes"; אַרְבַּע־עֶשְׂרֶה שְׁנִין C Gn 31:41, "fourteen years"; חֲמֵשׁ עֶשְׂרֶה אַמִּיֹן Bd Gn 7:20, "fifteen cubits." The construct forms occur before determined nouns: חַד־עשרתֵּי בְנֹי C Gn 32:23, "his eleven sons"; [תרי] עֲשַׂרתֵי שבטֹוי Z Gn 49:1, "his twelve tribes".[23]

130

**§47k** The attested forms of the "tens," with representative examples, are

*20 /'esrin/:* עֶשְׂרִין C Gn 31:41, עֶשְׂרִין C Gn 32:15, עֶשְׂרִין C Gn 32:16;

*30 /tǝlatin/:* תלתין A Ex 21:32, תְּלָתִין C Gn 32:16, תלתין E Gn 41:46;

*40 /'arbǝ'in/:* אַרְבְּעִין Bd Gn 7:17, אַרְבְּעִין Bd Gn 8:6, ארבעין C Gn 32:16;

*50 /ḥamšin/:* וְחַמְשִׁין Bd Gn 7:24, וְחַמְשִׁין Bd Gn 8:3;

*60 /šettin/:* שֶׁתִּין Cd Gn 46:26;

*70 /šob'in/:* בְּשַׁבְעִין D Dt 27:8, בשובעין AA Dt 27:8.

**§47l** The forms of "hundred" which are attested are s. absolute /mǝ'a/ and pl. absolute /mawan/. The examples are

*120:* מאה תעשרין F Dt 34:7;

*147:* מאה וארבעין ושבע Z Gn 47:28;

*150:* מְאָה וְחַמְשִׁין Bd Gn 7:24, מְאָה וְחַמְשִׁין Bd Gn 8:3;

*200:* תַּרְתֵּין־מְאָן C Gn 32:15, תַּרְתֵּין־מְאָן C Gn 32:15;

*400:* וארבע מאן AA₁ Ex 12:40, 41;[24]

*600:* שת מאון E Gn 7:6, שת מאה E Gn 7:11.

Note that there is no dual form. "Two hundred" is expressed by "two" + "hundreds."

**§47m** The only examples of "thousand" (pl. /'alpin?/) are לאלפין דרין F Ex 20:6, "for thousands of generations," and כשית מאה אלפין גוברין AA₁ Ex 12:37, "about six hundred thousand men."

**§48** *Ordinal Numbers*

**§48a** The attested ordinal numbers, with representative examples, are

*1st m. abs. /qadmay/:* קדמיי E Gn 38:28, קדמיי F Lv 22:27, קדמיי AA₁ Ex 12:2, קַדְמָיֵי HH Ex 12:2;[25]

*1st m. det. /qadmaya/:* קַדְמָיָא־ C Gn 32:18, קדמייה F Lv 23:35,39, קִדְמָיָה F Ex 20:2, קדמייא H Gn 15:1;

*1st f. det. /qadmayǝta/:*[26] בְּקָדְמַיְתָא Cd Gn 43:18, בְּקַדְמָיְתָא Cd Gn 43:20;

*1st f. det.pl.:* קדמייתה E Gn 41:20;

*2nd m. abs. /tenyan/:* תיניין E Gn 30:7,12, תיניין F Lv 22:27;

*2nd m. det. /tenyana/:* תִּינְיָנָא־ C Gn 32:20, תינינה E Gn 7:11, דתינינה E Gn 41:52, תניינא F Ex 20:2;

*2nd f. det. /tenyanǝta/:* תיניינתה E Gn 41:43;

*3rd m. abs. /tǝlitay/:* תליתיי F Lv 22:27, תליתיי F Ex 20:5;

*3rd m. det. /tǝlitaya/:* תליתיא־ C Gn 32:20, תליתייה E Gn 31:22, תליתיה AA Nu 19:19;

*3rd f. det. /tǝlitayǝta/:* תליתייתא AA Dt 26:12;[27]

*4th m. abs. /rǝbi'ay/:* רביעיי F Ex 20:5;

*6th m. abs. /šǝtitay?/:* שתיתיי E Gn 30:19;

*7th m. det. /šǝbi'aya/:* שביעיה F Lv 23:3, שביעייה F Lv 23:8,24,27,34,39,41;

*7th f. det. /šǝbi'ayǝta?/:* שביעייתה A Ex 23:11, שביעייתה F Lv 23:16;

*8th m. det. /tǝminaya?/:* תמינייה F Lv 22:27, תמינייה F Lv 23:36,39;

*10th m. det. /'ǝsiraya/:* עֲשִׂירָיָה Bd Gn 8:5, בַּעֲשִׂירָיָה Bd Gn 8:5.

**§48b** The f. absolute forms are not attested, nor are special ordinal forms from 11-19. The days of the month are expressed by the cardinal numbers,

e.g., באר בעת עשר יומין לירחה F Nu 28:16, "on the 14th of the month"; ובחמשת
בשבעת עשר יומין לירחה F Lv 23:6, "on the 15th of the month"; עשר יומין לירחה
הדין E Gn 7:11, "on the 17th of this month." The year is also expressed by
the cardinal number: בשנת שת מאה שנין E Gn 7:11, "in the 600th year."

**§48c** The ordinal numbers can function adverbially. See §158b.

**§49** *Fractions*

The following fractions are attested:

"half" /*palgu/: בפלגות ליליה AA₁,₂ Ex 12:29, "in the middle of the night";
"quarter" /*rab'u/: רבעות הינה F Lv 23:13, "one quarter of the *hin*";
"tenth" /'esron/: עשרון F Nu 28:21 (2x), עֶשְׂרוֹן F Nu 28:29 (2x);
"two-tenths" /tərayin 'esronim/: תרין עשרונין F Lv 23:13,17, ותרין עשרונין F Nu
28:20, ותריין עשרונין F Nu 28:28;
"three-tenths" /tǝlata 'esronim/: תלתה עשרונין F Nu 28:20, תְּלָתָה עֶשׂוֹנִין F Nu
28:28.

Note also "one tenth": חד מן עשרה E Gn 28:22.

**§50** *Adverbial Multiplicatives*

Adverbial multiplicatives are expressed by the cardinal number and
/zemnin/, "times." The examples are

"twice": תריין זמנין Cd Gn 43:10, תרין זמנין AA Nu 20:11;
"seven times": שבעה זמנין AA Nu 19:4;
"ten times": עֲשְׂרָא זְמְנִין C Gn 31:41, עשרה זמנין E Gn 31:7.

**§51** *Distributive Numerals*

There are two examples of the distributive use of numerals: תריין תריין E Gn
7:9, "two by two" (MT שְׁנָיִם שְׁנָיִם); תריין תריין E Gn 7:15 (MT שְׁנַיִם שְׁנָיִם).

**§52** *Numerals—Historical and Comparative Discussion*

**§52a** /hatta/ "the one": This determined form is not limited to the Cairo
Genizah fragments. It is also attested as a m. form in Targum Neophyti,[28] e.g.,

| Text | | Interlinear Gloss | Marginal Gloss |
|---|---|---|---|
| Nu 28:21 | אמרא חדתה (MT הָאָחָד לְכֶבֶשׂ) | חדא | חתה |
| Nu 28:28 | תורה חדתה (MT הָאָחָד לְפַר) | חדא | חתה |
| Nu 28:28 | דברא חדתה (MT הָאָחָד לָאַיִל) | חדא | חתה |
| Nu 28:29 | אמרא חדתה (MT הָאָחָד לְכֶבֶשׂ) | חדא | חתה |

Note the agreement between the marginal glosses and the Cairo Genizah
fragments.[29] /hatta/ is attested in Targum Neophyti also as a f. determined
form. Cf., e.g.,

| Text | | Interlinear Gloss | Marginal Gloss |
|---|---|---|---|
| Ex 28:10 | אבנה חדתה (MT הָאֶבֶן הָאָחָת) | חדה | -- |
| Ex 36:9 | דיריעתה חדא (MT הַיְרִיעָה הָאָחָת) | חדתה | חתה |
| Ex 36:29 | עזקתה חדא (MT הַטַּבַּעַת הָאָחָת) | וח[ד]תה | חתה |

The key to the origin of /hatta/ may lie in חדתה (/hadta?/): *had* + *tā* > *hadtā*
> /hatta/.[30] -*tā* > may be a backformation from the -*te* suffix found on

132

construct pl. numbers, and like /-te/, which is found with both masculine and feminine nouns, ḥad + tā may have also occurred with nouns of both genders. One may posit that /ḥatta/ also served as a f. determined form in the Cairo Genizah fragments but, due to the fragmentary evidence, is not attested. The other Targum Neophyti forms pose few problems: m. חדא is the determined form of ḥad : ḥad + ā';[31] f. חדא is the expected Targum Onqelos form.[32]

There are no determined forms of "one" in Targum Onqelos, Targum Pseudo-Jonathan, the Fragment Targum, or Syriac.[33]

There are determined forms of "one" in the Samaritan Targum: m.s. אחדה, חדה and f.s. אחתה, חתה, less frequently f. אחדתה, חדתה.[34] The Samaritan liturgical tradition realizes the m. form as [ˈåddå];[35] perhaps the orthographies of the f. determined forms reflect *ˈåttå and *ˈåd̥tå.[36] If one views [ˈåddå] < *ḥadtā,[37] and *ˈåttå, *ˈåd̥ta[38] < *ḥadtā, then the Samaritan determined forms, too, may be the result of a backformation from the construct pl. numbers with -te.

§52b /tərayin/, /tarten/ "two": The preservation of final /n/ in the absolute and construct states (cf., however, /təreˈəsar/ "twelve") is in striking contrast to the apocopation of /n/ in the absolute and construct forms in Maʻlula,[39] in the construct in Samaritan Aramaic,[40] and to the frequent, but not universal, apocopation in Galilean Aramaic.[41] The preservation of /n/ agrees, on the other hand, with Targum Onqelos,[42] Palestinian Syriac,[43] and Syriac.[44] The preservation of /ayi/ in the absolute state in the Cairo Genizah is in agreement with Galilean Aramaic as against the other dialects. Galilean Aramaic alone, however, preserves, on occasion, the original diphthong in the f. form. The form /tərehon/, "the two of them" stands in contrast to Targum Onqelos /tarwehon/,[45] which copyists introduced into the other Palestinian Targumim and printed editions of Galilean Aramaic texts.[46] Elsewhere in Syria-Palestine the form is תרתיהון.[47]

§52c /ˈešta/ "six": The form with prothetic aleph also occurs in Galilean Aramaic,[48] the other Palestinian Targumim,[49] Samaritan Aramaic,[50] and Syriac.[51]

§52d /šobʻa/ "seven": Forms with an o- vowel are also found in the other Palestinian Targumim,[52] Galilean Aramaic,[53] Samaritan Aramaic,[54] Palestinian Syriac,[55] and Maʻlula.[56] Cf. /šibʻā/ in Tiberian Biblical Aramaic[57] and Targum Onqelos,[58] and /šabʻā/ in Babylonian Biblical Aramaic[59] and /šavʻā/ in Syriac.[60]

§52e ארבע-עשרה, חמש עשרה, שבע עשרה: The use of he to represent final /e/[61] is attested (as well as the use of yodh) in the "teens" in Galilean Aramaic[62] and Targum Neophyti.[63]

§52f תלתי, שובעתי, חד-עשרתי: The existence of construct numerals is also attested in the other Palestinian Targumim,[64] Galilean Aramaic,[65] Palestinian Syriac,[66] Samaritan Aramaic,[67] and Syriac.[68] There is also one example in Biblical Aramaic.[69]

§52g /tarten mawan/ "two hundred": Ma'lula and Targum Neophyti are the only Syro-Palestinian Aramaic sources that no longer have a reflex of the dual form *mi'atayn. Ma'lula expresses "two hundred" by the cardinal numbers "two" + "hundred" = [tarč em'a].[70] In Targum Neophyti one finds "two" + "hundreds" (pl. absolute) as in the Cairo Genizah fragments, e.g, תרתין מאון Gn 11:19, although the Targum Onqelos form /mātan/ is also attested.[71] One finds only the Targum Onqelos form מאתן in Targum Pseudo-Jonathan.[72] One finds dual forms מאתין/מאתים (MS J, less frequently MS A) and מואנין (MS A, dual of the pl. absolute מואן) in the Samaritan Targum.[73] There is, however, an example of "two" + "hundreds"—תרי מואן MS A, Gn 32:15 (2x).

§52h m. determined ordinal numbers—/aya/ suffix: The retention of intervocalic /y/ in the m. determined form of the ordinal numbers is a salient feature of this dialect.[74] *āyā is preserved in Galilean Aramaic,[75] Palestinian Syriac,[76] Western Syriac,[77] the kethibh of Tiberian Biblical Aramaic,[78] and, to varying degrees, in the different Palestinian Targumim.[79] *āyā > ā'ā in Targum Onqelos,[80] Samaritan Aramaic,[81] Eastern Syriac,[82] and the qere of Tiberian Biblical Aramaic.[83]

§52i /qadmay/, /qadmaya/, /qadmayəta/ "first": /d/ is preserved in this ordinal number in the Cairo Genizah fragments as in Targum Onqelos,[84] Syriac,[85] and Targum Neophyti.[86] In Targum Pseudo-Jonathan and the Fragment Targum,[87] as well as Galilean Aramaic,[88] one finds forms in which /d/ is preserved; however, one also finds forms in which /d/ assimilates to the following /m/: *qadmay > קמיי or קומיי. /d/ always assimilates to the following /m/ in Palestinian Syriac.[89] In Samaritan Aramaic /d/ is sometimes retained, yet other times assimilates.[90] The Arabic ['awwal] has replaced the Aramaic form in Ma'lula.[91]

§52j /tenyanəta/ "the second": The f. form of the ordinal number "second" appears to be a reflex of *tinyāy in Targum Onqelos,[92] Targum Pseudo-Jonathan,[93] the Fragment Targum,[94] and Galilean Aramaic.[95] In Samaritan Aramaic[96] and Palestinian Syriac[97] it appears to be a reflex of *tinyān. One finds forms based on *tinyāy as well as forms based on *tinyān in Targum Neophyti.[98] A form based on *tinyān is attested rarely in Syriac; the usual form is based on the cardinal number /təren/.[99] The f. form of this ordinal number is not attested in Ma'lula.[100] If one reconstructs a Proto-Aramaic m. *tinyān, f. *tinyānat then the /-etā/[101] suffix on the f. determined form (e.g., Targum Onqelos /tinyetā/ Ex 1:15) has been extended from the other f. determined ordinal numbers (e.g., Targum Onqelos /qadmetā/ Gn 13:4). If, however, one reconstructs a Proto-Aramaic m. *tinyān, f. *tinyāy,[102] then the /-ān/ suffix on the f. determined form (e.g., Samaritan Aramaic תניאנתה MS J, Gn 41:43) has been extended from the m. *tinyān.

## C. Nouns

§53 Inflection

The forms marking gender, number, and state of nouns differ from their Official Aramaic equivalents only as a result of the sound shifts that have

134

taken place in this dialect. Note that the merger of *ā and *a to /a/ has
eliminated the distinction between the f.s. construct and the f.pl. construct.

|        | absolute        | construct | determined |
|--------|-----------------|-----------|------------|
| m.s.   | Ø               | Ø         | /-a/       |
| f.s.   | /-a/            | /-at/     | /-ta/      |
| m.pl.  | /-in/ (/-im/)   | /-e/      | /-ayya/    |
| f.pl.  | /-an/           | /-at/     | /-ata/     |

§53a  Representative examples are

m.s. absolute: עָאן Cd Gn 46:32, "small cattle"; בְּשְׁלַם Cd Gn 47:30, "in peace";
עָלַם Cd Gn 48:7, "eternity";

m.s. construct: רָאשׁ- Cd Gn 47:31, "head of"; אֱלָה Cd Gn 48:3, "God of";
לְקַהֵל Cd Gn 48:4, "of the congregation of";

m.s. determined: יוֹמָה B Gn 4:14, "the day"; כַּפְנָא Cd Gn 47:4 "the famine";
דַּרְגְשָׁא Cd Gn 47:31, "the bed";

f.s. absolute: בְּשַׁבְעָא Cd Gn 47:31, "in an oath"; אוּמָה- D Dt 5:23, "nation";
סְגֻלָה- D Dt 26:18, "property";

f.s. construct: נַשְׁמַת- Bd Gn 7:22, "the soul of"; בְּמִכְלַת C Gn 35:9 (2x),
"according to the measure of"; בְּחֵיוַת C Gn 37:33, "by an animal of";

f.s. determined: וּלְכַלְתָא C Gn 35:9, "and the bride"; חֵיוְתָא C Gn 37:20, "the
animal"; מְכָלְתָה F Nu 28:29, "the measure";

m.pl. absolute: זְמִנִין C Gn 31:41, "times"; בְּחַיִּין Cd Gn 46:30, "in life"; גֻּבְרִין- Cd
Gn 46:34, "men";

m.pl. construct: לְעָלְמֵי C Gn 35:9, "forever"; דְּמַלְאֲכֵי C Gn 32:27, "of the
messengers of"; יוֹמֵי- Cd Gn 47:29, 'the days of';

m.pl. determined:[1] גַּנָּבַיָּה C Gn 31:39, "the thieves"; וְנוּנַיָּא Cd Ex 7:18, "and the
fish"; יוֹמַיָּה- D Dt 28:29, "the days";

f.pl. absolute:[2] אַרְמְלָן A Ex 22:23, "widows"; נֻקְבָן C Gn 32:16, "females"; כְּנִישָׁן-
C Gn 35:11, "assemblies";

f.pl. construct: יוֹמַת- C Gn 35:9, "the days of"; לְזַרְעִיַת- Cd Gn 48:4, "to the
families of";[3]

f.pl. determined: אוֹרְחָתָא Cd Gn 38:21, "the ways"; נַפְשָׁתָא- Cd Gn 46:26, "the
souls"; מִצְוָתָה- D Dt 27:1, "the commandments."

§54  Gender

The gender of nouns in the Cairo Genizah fragments corresponds, on the
whole, to the gender of the cognate nouns in Official Aramaic.

§54a  A noteworthy feature in the fragments is the use of דכר /dəkar/ "male"
and נקבה /neqba/ "female" to mark gender in nominal forms which can be m.
or f., and thus ambiguous:

§54b  /ber/, /bar/ "child" (usually "son") וְבַר דְּכַר] A Ex 21:31, "male child"
(MT בֵּן-); בְּרָא נֻקְבָה A Ex 21:31, "female child" (MT בַּת-); ברה נקבה E Gn 30:21
(MT בַּת) in which /neqba/ indicates that ברא is "female child, daughter" (f.
absolute form) and not "the child, the son" (m. determined form).

§54c  /torin/ "oxen" or "cows": וְתוֹרִין דִּכְרֵין C Gn 32:16, "oxen" (MT וּפָרִים-);
תוֹרִין נֻקְבָן C Gn 32:16, "cows" (MT פָּרוֹת-). Other examples in which /torin/,
/torayya/[4] clearly refer to "cows" and not "oxen" are שבע תורין בריין E Gn

41:18, "seven healthy cows"[5] (MT שֶׁבַע פָּרוֹת בְּרִיאוֹת); (שְׁבַע פָּרוֹת אחרנין E Gn שבע תורין אחרנין
41:19, "seven other cows" (MT אֲחֵרוֹת); (שְׁבַע־פָּרָוֹת דקיקתה E Gn 41:20, תורייה דקיקתה
"the thin cows" (MT הַפָּרוֹת הָרַקּוֹת); (טבתה תורייה E Gn 41:26, "the seven שבעתי תורייה טבתה
good cows" (MT שֶׁבַע פָּרֹת הַטֹּבֹת). The gender distinction between תור "ox" and
תורה "cow" is, however, preserved, e.g., ותור בר תורין חד F Lv 23:18, "and one
ox" (MT וּפַר בֶּן־בָּקָר אֶחָד); (סמוקה AA Nu 19:2, "a red cow" (MT פָּרָה אֲדֻמָּה); תורה סמוקה
קטמה דתורתא AA Nu 19:10, "the ashes of the cow" (MT וְאֶפֶר הַפָּרָה).

**§54d** /gamlin/ "camels":[6] נקבן מיינקן C Gn 32:16, "female milch-camels" גמלין נקבן מיינקן
(MT גְּמַלִּים מֵינִיקוֹת).

## Gender—Comparative Discussion

**§54e** The use of דכר and נקבה marking gender is attested in Targum
Neophyti[7] and Targum Pseudo-Jonathan.[8] It is also attested in Elephantine
legal documents—בר דכר ונקבה "a child, male or female."[9] The Hebrew
cognate זָכָר is used similarly in Biblical Hebrew[10] to distinguish a male child
from a female child—בְּנֵי מְנַשֶּׁה בֶן־יוֹסֵף הַזְּכָרִים Jos 17:2 and בֶּן זָכָר Je 20:15.

## §55 Number

**§55a** The dual absolute form is attested only in the several occurrences of
/tərayin/ "two," e.g., תְּרֵין F Nu 28:27 and in the noun תומאיין /tomayin?/ E
Gn 38:27, "twins."[11] It is presumed to have existed with other nouns, too, e.g.,
יד "hand," רגל "foot."

**§55b** There is a handful of examples in which one finds /-im/ in place of
the regular m.pl. morpheme /-in/: אַבְנִים C Gn 31:46, "stones" (cf. אַבְנִין C Gn
31:46, + 2x); מִים Cd Gn 37:24, "water" (+ 4x, but cf. מִיין Cd Ex 7:21, + 3x);[12]
עזִים E Gn 37:31, "goats" (cf. עִזִין E Gn 38:17, + 5x); צדיקים E Gn 38:25,
"righteous" (cf. צַדִּיקִין B Gn 4:10, + 1x).

**§55c** The infix /-ah-/ is attested in two pl. nouns: /'əbahan/ "fathers" (s.
/'ab/), e.g., אֲבָהָן F Ex 20:5 (+ 11x) and /šəmahan/ "names" (s. /šem/), e.g,
שְׁמָהָן B Gn 2:19 (+ 1x).

**§55d** The infix /-an-/ is attested in two pl. nouns: קוֹצְנִין A Ex 22:5, "thorns"
(no attested s.), and רברבני W Ex 15:15, "chiefs of" (s. /rab/ "chief").

**§55e** Reduplication is attested[13] in the pl. forms of the adjectival use of /rab/
"great": רַבְרְבִין Cd Ex 6:6, רברבייה F Dt 34:12, רברבן AA Dt 27:2.

**§55f** The f.pl. markers /-awan/ (absolute), /-awat/ (construct), and
/-awata/ (determined) are found regularly on nouns ending in /-u/ (< *-ūt),
e.g., טָעוָן A Ex 22:19, "idols"; סהדוון F Ex 20:13 (2x), "testimonies"; בזכוותך E
Gn 30:27, "on account of your merits"; תלדוותך E Gn 31:3, "your offspring";
טעוותה E Gn 31:34, "the idols"; מלכוותא F Ex 20:14, "the kingdoms." These
f.pl. markers are also found on nouns that do not end in /-u/: לזרעייתכון AA₁
Ex 12:21, "of your families" (cf. cst. pl. זרעיית E Gn 9:9, + 3x);[14] חלנתבון AA₁
Ex 12:17, "your forces," חיילוותה AA₁ Ex 12:41 (s. חיל AA₁ Ex 17:9); חלין AA₁
Ex 12:39, "cakes" (cf. abs. pl. חלין F Lv 23:27);[15] חקלוות E Gn 41:48, "fields of"
(cf. בְּחַקְלֵיכוֹן D Dt 28:16, + 1x; s. חֲקַל A Ex 22:4); לילון E Gn 7:4,12, "nights" (s.
לילי AA₁ Ex 12:42); מְאָן C Gn 32:15, "hundreds," מְאָן־ C Gn 32:15, מָאוון E
Gn 7:6, מאון AA₁ Ex 12:40,41 (s. מְאָה Bd Gn 8:3); במורכיוותיה E Gn 30:38, "in
his troughs";[16] מתנוותכון F Lv 23:38, "your gifts" (abs. s. מתנה F Lv 23:20);

136

[א]סוסותא W Ex 15:19, "the horses" (s. with suffix סוֹסֵיהּ "his horse" E Gn 41:44)ʃ; עיינוֹת E Gn 7:11, "the springs of" (cf. עֵינֵיהּ B Gn 3:6, "the eyes");[17] עלוֹן F Lv 23:37, "sacrifices," עלָה AA Dt 27:6,[עלוֹתכוֹן F Ex 20:21 (abs. s. עלָה F Nu 28:27).

*Number—Historical and Comparative Discussion*

§55g The dual /tomayin/ "twins" is also attested in Targum Neophyti—תומיין Gn 38:27. Cf. the Targum Onqelos pl. /tiyomin/ and Targum Pseudo-Jonathan תיומין.

§55h The examples with the m.pl. abs. marker /-im/ can be explained either as variant forms within the dialect[18] or as Hebraisms. Cf. Samaritan Aramaic where one finds ין־ and ים־ in free variation (according to Ben-Ḥayyim[19] this indicates a realization of [ũ]; Macuch,[20] on the other hand, considers ים־ a Hebraism).

§55i The pl. forms of /ʾab/ "father" and /šem/ "name" with infix /-ah-/ as well as the pl. /rabrəbanin/ "chiefs" with infix /-an-/ are widely attested in Aramaic dialects. In contrast, קרצנין "thorns" (with infix /-an-/) is not attested elsewhere (cf. Ex 22:5 in Targum Neophyti קרצין; Biblical Hebrew קצים).

§55j The pl. markers /-awan/, /-awat/, /-awata/ on nouns ending in /-u/ as well as nouns ending in /-a/, /-e/, and even consonants is a general Aramaic feature. Of interest is the distribution of this pl. marker on the following nouns ending with consonants (with representative examples):

חילוון "forces": Targum Neophyti (Ex 12:41);

חלוון "cakes": unattested elsewhere;

חקלוון "fields": Galilean Aramaic;[21]

מורכיוון 'troughs": Targum Neophyti (Gn 30:38), Targum Pseudo-Jonathan (Gn 24:20), Fragment Targum (MS V, Gn 30:38), Samaritan Targum (MS E, Ex 2:16);[22]

מתנוון "gifts": Targum Neophyti (Lv 23:38), Samaritan Targum (MS E, Lv 23:38).[23]

§56 *State*

§56a The use of the absolute, construct, and determined forms in these fragments agrees with the use of the corresponding forms in Official Aramaic.[24] For a few problematic forms expressing the genitive relationship, see §161d.

§56b There is one example in which the Hebrew definite article is added to an Aramaic word in the determined state: הארמייה E Gn 31:24, "the Aramean."

§56c The distinction in form and use among the absolute, construct, and determined states is a feature of Palestinian Syriac,[25] Samaritan Aramaic,[26] and Galilean Aramaic.[27] The determining force of the determined form is sometimes lost in Targum Onqelos,[28] as seems to be the case in the other Palestinian Targumim.[29] The determined form expresses both determination and lack of determination in Syriac[30] and Maʿlula;[31] the use of the absolute forms is limited in both these dialects.

## §57 Noun Classes

The inventory of noun classes in the Cairo Genizah fragments differs from that of Official Aramaic and Targum Onqelos as a result of the complete merger of *ā and *a to /a/. This merger led to the partial merger of the following noun classes (in the absolute and construct states):

| absolute, const. | determined | Proto-Aramaic |
|---|---|---|
| /qal/ | /qəla/ | *qal |
| | /qala/ | *qāl |
| | /qalla/ | *qall |
| /qetal/ | /qatla/ | *qatal |
| | /qetla/ | *qital |
| | /qətala/ | *qatāl |
| | /qətala/ | *qitāl |
| | /qətala/ | *qutāl |
| /qattal/ | /qattəla/ | *qattal |
| | /qattala/ | *qattāl |
| /qettal/ | /qettəla/ | *qittal |
| | /qettala/ | *qittāl |

Nouns (and adjectives) are listed under their assumed Proto-Aramaic forms. One must, however, emphasize that often more than one reconstruction is possible for two reasons: 1) the reduction of short vowels to ə or zero in open unstressed syllables has, on the whole, obliterated any trace of the original vowels; 2) *a > *i is said to occur frequently, but not universally in closed unstressed syllables (the "attenuation of *a* to *i*"); yet, at the same time, it is argued that *i > *a in closed stressed syllables (Philippi's Law).[32] Confusion of noun classes and analogy, however, may be a better explanation for the *ad hoc* invoking of these rules.

Phonemic transcription of the absolute and determined forms is presented for each noun. At least one example of each form of each noun is presented.

## §58 Single Consonant

There are twelve occurrences of פם "mouth"[33] with /e/, e.g., ־פֿם A Ex 21:22, בְּפֵים־ Cd Gn 43:18, לפֵם AA₁ Ex 12:4, פֵּימָך Cd Gn 41:40. There is one example with a *u*-vowel: פומה W Ex 15:12, "her mouth." There are seven additional examples in which the *scriptio defectiva* does not reveal the vowel, e.g., בפמיכן F Ex 20:17, "in your mouths." The example with a *u*-vowel probably represents the influence of Targum Onqelos. In Western Aramaic dialects one finds an *e*-vowel.[34]

### Biconsonantal with Short Vowel

## §59 *qal

§59a /'ab, 'ebba/ "father": abs.s. אֲב Cd Gn 44:19; det. s.[35] דְּאֲבָּא C Gn 31:42, לאבה Z Gn 44:18; 2 m.s. דאבוך E Gn 31:29; 3 m.s. דַאֲבִּי C Gn 31:53; 3 f.s. לַאֲבוּהַ E, C Gn 34:11; 1 pl. לאבונן Cd Gn 43:28; 2 m.pl. אבוכן E Gn 43:7; 2 f.pl.[36] דאבוכין E Gn 31:9; 3 m.pl. אבהון E Gn 42:36; abs. pl. אֲבָהָן F Ex 20:5; det. pl. אבהתה AA₁

138

Ex 17:12; *1 s.* אֲבָהֳתִי Cd Gn 47:30; *2 m.s.* אבהתך E Gn 31:3; *1 pl.* לאבהתן AA Dt
26:15; *2 m.pl.* דאבהתכן AA Dt 27:3; /'aḥ, *'əha/ "brother": abs.s. אח E Gn
43:6; *1 s.* אָחִי Cd Gn 38:26; *2 m.s.* אָחוּך B Gn 4:9; *3 m.s.* אחוי E Gn 29:10 (2x);[37]
אֲחוּי B Gn 4:8; *3 f.s.* אחוה E Gn 29:10;[38] *1 pl.* אחונן E Gn 37:26; *2 m.pl.* אֲחוּכֹן E
Gn 42:34; *1 pl.* אֲחָי Cd Gn 46:31; *2 m.s.* אֲחֵיך Z Gn 48:22; *3 m.s.* אֲחוֹי Cd Gn
37:27; *3 f.s.* וּלְאֲחָהּ C Gn 34:11;[39] *1 pl.* אחינן AA Nu 20:3; *3 m.pl.* אֲחֵיהֹן Cd Gn
48:6 (because of the fluctuating use of vowel signs in these texts, it is
impossible to determine whether the base of the pl. inflected forms is /'aḥ-/ or
/'əḥ-/);[40] /'ədam, 'adma/[41] "blood": ab. *s.* אֲדַם Cd Ex 7:19; *cst. s.* מִדַּם Z Gn
49:11; *det. s.* אַדְמָא Cd Ex 7:21; *3 m.s.* בְּאַדְמֵיהּ Cd Gn 38:26; *3 f.s.* אדמה AA Nu
19:5; *2 m.pl.* אדמכֹן E Gn 9:5; /yad, 'ed,[42] yəda?/ "hand": abs. *s.* בִּיד Cd Ex 6:1;
אָיד A Ex 21:24; *cst. s.* בְּיָד Cd Gn 38:20; *1 s.* יְדִי Cd Ex 6:8; *2 m.s.* יְדָך Cd Gn
47:29; *3 m.s.* ידה E Gn 38:28; *3 f.s.* בִּידֵהּ W Ex 15:20; *2 m.pl.* בְּיָדְכֹן Cd Gn
43:12;[43] *1 s.* יְדַיָּ C Gn 31:42; *2 m.s.* וּבְיָדֵיך B Gn 4:7; *3 m.s.* יְדוֹי Cd Gn 44:18; *3
f.s.* יְדֵיהּ Cd Gn 38:20; *1 pl.* וְיִדֵּינַן Cd Gn 37:27; *2 m.pl.* בידיכון AA₁ Ex 12:11; *3
m.pl.* בִּידֵיהֹן Cd Ex 5:21;

**§59b**   with a f. ending: /*'əha, 'əhata?/ "sister": *1 s.* אחתי E Gn 30:8; *3 m.s.*
אחתה E Gn 29:13, וְאַ)חְתֵּהּ( W Ex 15:20; *3 f.s.* באחתה E Gn 30:1; *1 pl.* אֲחָתַן C Gn
34:14; *3 m.pl.* אֲחָתְהֹן C Gn 34:13; /*qəša, qašta?/ "bow": det. *s.* קשתה E Gn
9:14; *1 s.* קַשְׁתִּי E Gn 9:13; /šəna?, šatta/ "year": abs. *s.* שנה F Lv 22:27; *cst. s.*
בשנת E Gn 7:11; *det. s.* שַׁתָּה HH Ex 12:2; *3 m.s.* שתיה F Lv 23:12; *3 m.pl.* שַׁתְּהֹן F
Nu 28:27; *abs. pl.* שְׁנִין C Gn 31:41; *cst. pl.* שני E Gn 41:47; *det pl.* בשנייה E Gn
41:43;

**§59c**   Biconsonantal *'am + *at "maiden" appears as a triconsonantal root:
/'amha, 'amhəta?/: abs. *s.* אֲמְהָא A Ex 21:32, לאמהא E Gn 29:24,29; *1 s.* אמהתי E
Gn 30:3; *2 m.s.* וְ)רְ(אמהתך A Ex 23:12; *3 m.s.* אמהתיה E Gn 29:24, אֲמְהָתֵהּ A Ex
21:20; *3 f.s.* אמהתה E Gn 30:7; *ab. pl.* אמהתה E Gn 31:33; *3 m.pl.* אֲמְהָתֵיה C Gn
32:23; *2 m.pl.* וְאַמְהַתְכֹן F Ex 20:10.[44] The s. form with /h/ is also attested in
Targum Neophyti[45] and Galilean Aramaic[46] and is a backformation from the
general Aramaic plural 'amhātā'. Cf. Targum Onqelos /'āmā/ Dt 23:18, but
/'amhu/ Ex 21:7. אמהו is also attested in Targum Pseudo-Jonathan.[47] Cf.
Syriac /'amtā/.

**§60**   *qil

**§60a**   /ber, bar, *bəra/ "son, child":[48] abs. *s.* וְבֹר A Ex 21:31, ביר E Gn
30:5,10,12,17,19; *cst. s.* בר E Gn 29:13, בָּר Cd Gn 38:17, בַּר H Gn 15:2; *1 s.* בְּרִי
Cd Gn 48:19; *2 m.s.* דַּבְכָך Cd Gn 38:26; *3 m.s.* בְּרֵיהּ Cd Gn 34:20, בָּרֵהּ C Gn
34:24; *3 f.s.* ברה E Gn 29:12; *abs. pl.* בְּנִין H Gn 15:2; *cst. pl.* בְּנֵי Cd Ex 9:26; *det
pl.* בְּנַיָּא C Gn 31:43; *1 s.* בְּנַיּ A Ex 21:5; *2 m.s.* בְּנֵיך Cd Gn 48:11; *3 m.s.* בנוי Cd
Gn 48:1; *1 pl.* לבנינן E Gn 31:16; *2 m.pl.* וּבְנֵיכֹון A Ex 22:23; *3 m.pl.* וְלִבְנֵיהֹון D Dt
5:26; *3 f.pl.* לְבְנֵיהֶן C Gn 31:43; /šem,šəma?/ "name":[49] abs. *s.* שֵׁם Cd Gn 48:6,
וְשֵׁם Cd Gn 48:1; *cst. s.* בְּשֵׁם Cd Ex 5:23; *det. s. or 3 m.s.?* שמה E Gn 41:51; *1 s.*
לְשְׁמִי Cd Ex 6:7; *2 m.s.*[50] שְׁמָך C Gn 35:9, לְשְׁמָך Cd Gn 48:6; *3 m.s.* שְׁמֵהּ B Gn
2:19, שְׁמֵיה C Gn 31:48; *3 f.s.* שמה E Gn 30:21; *abs. pl.* שְׁמָהַן B Gn 2:19, שְׁמָהַן B
Gn 2:20; /nəšin, nəšayya?/ "women": abs. *s.* נְשִׁין C Gn 31:50; לַנְשִׁין C Gn 34:21;

*cst.* נְשֵׁר- Cd Gn 46:26; ֿ וּנְשִׁי E Gn 6:18; *1 s.* נשׁיִ E Gn 30:26; *3 m.s.* נשׂוּיֿ C Gn 32:23; ֿ וּנשׁוי E Gn 7:7;[51] *2 m.pl.* וֹנְשִׁיכ֗ A Ex 22:23;

**§60b** *with a f. ending:* /bəra, \*barta, \*berta/ *"daughter, child"*:[52] *abs. s.* בּרֿא A Ex 21:31, ברה E Gn 30:21; *cst. s.* ברת E Gn 41:45,50; *2 m.s.* ברתך E Gn 29:18; *3 m.s.* בְּבְרַתֶּה C Gn 34:19, ברתיֿה E Gn 29:23; *1 pl.* בְּרַתן C Gn 34:17; *det. pl.* בְּנָתֿא C Gn 31:43; *1 s.* -בְּנָתֿי C Gn 31:50; -בְּנָתֿי C Gn 31:50; *2 m.s.* בְּנַתָךֿ C Gn 31:41; *1 pl.* -בְּנָתן C Gn 34:9, בְּנָתן C Gn 34:16; *2 m.pl.* בְּנָתכון C Gn 34:9, -בְּנָתכון C Gn 34:16; *3 m.pl.* -בנתהון C Gn 34:21, בנתהן E Gn 30:13; /\*həma, \*hemta/ *"anger": 3 m.pl.* וַחֲמַתהון Z Gn 49:7; /šəna, \*šenta/ *"sleep": abs. s.* -שְׁנָא B Gn 2:21; *1 s.* שֶׁנתִי C Gn 31:40; *also* /məʾa/ *"hundred"* (§471).

## Biconsonantal with Long Vowel

### §61 *qāl

**§61a** /dar, dara?/ *"generation": abs. s.* דַּר F Ex 20:5 (2x); *det. s.* בדרה E Gn 7:1; *abs. pl.* דָרין AA₁ Ex 17:16; *cst. pl.* לְדָרֵי C Gn 35:9; *2 m.pl.* לדריכון F Lv 23:31,41; *3 m.pl.* לדֿריהון AA₁ Ex 12:42; /\*hal, hala?/ *"sand": det. s. or 3 m.s.?* כחלה E Gn 41:49; *3 m.s.* כְּחָלֵיֿה C Gn 32:13; /ṭab, ṭaba/ *"good": abs. s.* טָב F Nu 28:26; *det s.* טָבֿא C Gn 34:21; *abs. pl.* טָבין B Gn 4:8; *det. pl.* טָבַיָּא C Gn 35:9; /\*kas, kasa?/ *"cup": det. s. or 3 m.s.?* כסה E Gn 40:12; *3 m.s.* כָּסֵה E Gn 40:13; /mayin, mayim,[53] mayya/ *"water": abs.* מָיִן Cd Ex 7:21; מָים Cd Gn 37:24; *cst.* מֵי AA Nu 19:13, *det.* מַיָּא Bd Gn 7:17, מָּייה E Gn 9:15; *3 m.s.* מוי E Gn 9:11, מוי AA Nu 20:8;[54] *3 m.pl.* -מֵימְהון Cd Ex 7:19, מֵימיהֿון Cd Ex 7:19; /sab, saba?/ *"old, elder":*[55] *abs. s.* סָב Cd Gn 44:20; *det. s.* סבה E Gn 43:27, *3 m.s.* סביה F Lv 22:27; *det. pl.* סביה AA₁,₂ Ex 12:21; /\*ram, \*rama/ *"high": abs. pl.* רְמִין D Dt 26:19; *det. pl.* רְמָיָּא Bd Gn 7:19; /qal, qala/ *"voice": abs. s.* קָל D Dt 5:19; *cst. s.* -קָל B Gn 4:10, -קָל D Dt 5:25; *det. s.* קָלָֿה D Dt 5:20, *1 s.* בקלי E Gn 30:6; *3 m.s.* קלֿה E Gn 29:11, קָל F Ex 20:15; *abs. pl.* קָלִין Cd Ex 9:23; *det. pl.* קָלַיָּא Cd Ex 9:29;

**§61b** *with a f. ending:* /taba?, tabəta?/ *"good": abs. s.* טבה AA Nu 19:6; *det. s.* טבתה AA Dt 26:11, *abs. pl.* וטבן E Gn 41:22; *det. pl.* טבתה E Gn 41:24; /\*ʿaqa, \*ʿaqəta/ *"distress": 3 m.pl.* עֲקָתהֿון Cd Gn 38:25;[56] /\*rama, raməta?/ *"hill": det. s.* רָאמתָא AA₁ Ex 17:10; /\*maʿa, \*maʿəta/ *"coin": abs. pl.* -מָאעָֿן Cd Gn 37:28; /šaʿa, šaʿəta/[57] *"hour": abs. s.* -שָׁעָה Cd Gn 44:22; *cst. s.* בְּשָׁעַת Cd Gn 38:25; *det. s.* -שָּׁעֳתֿה Cd Gn 38:25.

### §62 *qīl

**§62a** /\*gir, gira?/ *"chalk": det. s.* בגירה AA Dt 27:2, בגֿירה AA Dt 27:4; /din, dina/ *"judgment": abs. s.* -דִּין Cd Gn 38:26, ֿ-דִּין Cd Gn 38:26; *det. s.* דִּינֿא A Ex 21:6, דִּינָֿה B Gn 4:7; *abs. pl.* -דִּינִין Cd Ex 6:6, דִּינִין AA₁ Ex 12:12; *det. pl.* דיניה AA Dt 26:16; *3 m.s.* דינוי AA Dt 26:17, לְדִֿינוֹ Z Gn 44:18; /\*min, mina?/ *"kind": 3 m.s.* למינה E Gn 6:20; *3 f.s.* למֿינה E Gn 7:14; *3 m.pl.* למיניהן E Gn 6:20; /nir?, \*nira/ *"yoke": abs. s.* דניר AA Nu 19:2, ניר AA Dt 27:5; /\*ziq, \*ziqa/ *"water skin, comet": abs. pl.* זיקין F Ex 20:2; *det. pl.* כזיקיא W Ex 15:8; /mit?, \*mita/ *"corpse": abs. s.* במית AA Nu 19:16,18; *det. pl.* מיתייה E Gn 30:1;

**§62b** *with a f. ending:* /siʿa, \*siʿəta/ *"group": abs. s.* סיֿע(א)ֿ Cd Gn 37:25, סיעה E Gn 37:25; /\*sima, \*siməta/ *"treasure": abs. pl.* סִימָן Cd Gn 43:23.

140

**§63** *qūl

**§63a** /buṣ, buṣa?/ "byssus": abs. s. בּוּץ B Ex 39:27, בּוּץ B Ex 39:29; det. s. וּבוּצָא] B Ex 39:28; /gur, *gura/ "cub": abs. s. לגוּר Z Gn 49:9; /*ṭub, *ṭuba/ "goodness": 3 m.s. וְטוּבוֹ Cd Gn 38:26;[58] /ṭur?, ṭura, ṭawrayya/[59] "mountain": cst. s. בטור E Gn 31:23,25; det. s. בְּטוּרָה D Dt 5:19, וְטוּרָה D Dt 5:20; cst. pl. טוּרֵי Bd Gn 8:4; det. pl. טוּרַיָּא Bd Gn 7:19, טוּרַיָּא Bd Gn 7:20, טוּרַיָּא Bd Gn 8:5; /luz?, *luza/ "almond": abs. s. ולדח E Gn 30:37; abs. pl. דְּלְחִין Cd Gn 43:11; /*luḥ, *luḥa, *lawḥa, *lewḥa/[60] "tablet": cst. pl. לְוּחֵי D Dt 5:19, לוחי F Ex 20:2; 3 m.pl. לוחוֹי B Ex 39:33; /*nun, nuna/ "fish": det. s. נוּנָא Cd Gn 48:16; det. pl. וְנוּנַיָּא Cd Ex 7:18, וְנוּנַיָּא Cd Ex 7:21; /nur?, nura?/ "fire": abs. s. דנוּר F Ex 20:2 (2x); det. s. בּנוּרָא Cd Gn 38:25; בנורה AA₁ Ex 12:8; /ruḥ,[61] *ruḥa/ "wind, spirit": abs. s. רוּח Bd Gn 7:22, רוּח Bd Gn 8:1, וּרוּחַ Cd Ex 6:9; cst. s. ברוּח Cd Gn 48:1, בְּרוּח Cd Gn 48:2; /*šoq, šoqa/[62] "market": det. s. בְּשׁוּקָה A Ex 21:19, בשוקה E Gn 9:22; /mum?, *muma/[63] "blemish": abs. s. מום F Lv 23:12,18;

**§63b** with a f. ending: /ṣura?, *ṣurəta/ "form": abs. s. צוּרְתָה F Ex 20:4; /šuma?, *šumǝta/ "mark": abs. s. שומה E Gn 30:35.

*Biconsonantal Geminated*

**§64** *qall

**§64a** /bar, barra/ "wild": abs. s. בַּר Cd Gn 38:21; det. s. בָּרָא C Gn 31:39, ברה E Gn 37:33; /*gad, gadda?/ "fate": det. s. גדה E Gn 31:11; /*ḥag, ḥagga?/ "feast": det. s. חגה F Lv 23:6, Nu 28:17; 3 m.s. חגיה F Lv 23:39; cst. pl. חַגֵּי F Nu 28:26; /ḥayyin, *ḥayyayya/ "life": abs. pl. בְּחַיִּין Cd Gn 37:33, דחין AA Nu 19:17; cst. pl. בחַיֵּי Z Gn 44:18; 3 m.s. חיוֹי Z Gn 47:28; /*yem, *yam, yemma,[64] *yamma/ "sea": det. s. דְיַמָּא C Gn 32:13; det. pl. יַמַּיה F Ex 20:11; /kap, *kappa/ "palm": cst. s. דְכָף C Gn 35:9; cst. pl. כַּפֵּר C Gn 31:42; /*saq, *saqqa/ "sack": 3 m.s. בסקֵּה E Gn 42:35; /'am, 'amma/ "people":[65] abs. s. לְעַם C Gn 34:16; cst. s. עם F Ex 20:13; det. s. עַמָּה D Dt 5:25, עמא F Ex 19:10; 1 s. עַמִּי D Dt 27:7; 2 m.s. עמך AA Dt 26:15; 3 m.s. עַמֵּה Cd Gn 38:21; 2 m.pl. וּבעַמְכוֹן A Ex 22:24; /*ṭal, *ṭalla/ "dew": abs. pl. טַלִּין D Dt 28:23; /*qaš, qašša?/ "straw": det. s. קשא W Ex 15:7; /rab, rabba/ "great, master": abs. s. רַב Cd Gn 44:15; cst. s. רַב E Gn 39:1, det. s. רַבָּא Cd Gn 43:33; 2 m.s. רַבָּך Cd Gn 44:18; abs. pl. (adj.) רַבְרְבִין Cd Ex 6:6; det. pl. (adj.) רברבייה F Dt 34:12; cst. pl. (noun) רברבני W Ex 15:15;

**§64b** with a f. ending: /*'amma, *'ammǝta/ "cubit": abs. pl. אַמְוָן Bd Gn 7:20; /*ganna, gannǝta/ "garden": det. s. גִּנְתָא B Gn 3:3, לְגִנְתָה B Gn 4:16; /ḥayya?, ḥayyǝta/[66] "living": abs. s. דחייה E Gn 9:10; det. s. חַיְתָא Bd Gn 8:1, דְחַיְתָה B Gn 2:19; /*ḥalla, *ḥallǝta/ "cake": abs. pl. חלין F Lv 23:17, חלָן AA₁ Ex 12:39;[67] /*kawwa, *kawwǝta/ "window": cst. pl. וְכַוֵּי Bd Gn 8:2; /*kalla, kallǝta/ "bride, daughter-in-law": det. s. וּלְכַלְתָא C Gn 35:9; 1 s. כַּלְתִי Cd Gn 38:26; 2 m.s. כַּלְתַך Z Gn 49:9; 3 m.s. כלתה E Gn 38:16; /*para, parta/[68] "cow": det. s. פָּרְתָה AA Nu 19:5, פרתא AA Nu 19:6; /rabba?, robba?, rabbǝta?, robbǝta?/[69] "great": abs. s. רבָה E Gn 29:2, רבא W Ex 15:9 (2x); det. s. רבתה E Gn 29:26, רובתה E Gn 39:9; abs. pl. (adj.) רברבן AA Dt 27:2.

141

§65 *qill

§65a /*'em, 'emma/ "mother": 3 m.s. אֱמֵּיה C Gn 35:9,אימיה F Lv 22:27, ואמׂה
A Ex 21:15,17; /*ger, *gera/ "arrow": abs. pl. גירין F Ex 19:13; /*ges, gessa?/
"fodder": det. s. גסה E Gn 43:24;[70] /*leb, lebba/ "heart": det. s. לֶבָּא B Gn 4:7,
לִיבָּה- D Dt 5:26; 3 m.s. לְבֵּיה Cd Ex 7:22; 2 m.pl. לבביכון AA Dt 26:16;[71] /*nes,
*neṣṣa/ "blossom": 3 f.s. נְצֵיה E Gn 40:10; /qes, *qeṣṣa/ "end": cst. s. קֵץ Z Gn
49:1; 3 m.pl. קצהון C Gn 32:27; /šen?, *šenna/ "tooth": abs. s. שֵׁן A Ex 21:24;
cst. s. שֵׁין A Ex 21:27; 3 m.s. שׁינׂה A Ex 21:27; /hen, *henna/ "grace": abs. s. חֵן-
C Gn 34:11, חֵן- Cd Gn 47;29; 3 m.pl. חנהון AA₁ Ex 12:36;

§65b with a f. ending: /*hella, helləta?/ "valley": det. s. בחלתה F Dt 34:6;
/*mella, melləta/ "word": abs. pl. מלין E Gn 43:27; cst. pl. מִלֵּי A Ex 22:8; מלֵי
AA Dt 27:8; 2 m.s. בְּמֵלֵיך Cd Gn 47:30, כְמֵלֵך Z Gn 47:30; 3 m.s. לְמֵלוֹי Cd Ex 6:9;
2 m.pl. מֵלֵיכוׂן D Dt 5:25, כמליכון AA₁ Ex 12:31; 3 m.pl. מֵלֵיהוׂן C Gn 34:18;
/bezza?, *bezzəta/[72] "booty": abs. s. ביזא W Ex 15:9; /petta?, *pettəta/[73]
"bread": abs. s. דפתה E Gn 40:16.[74]

§66 *qull[75]

§66a /gob?, gobba/ "pit": abs. s. גוׂב A Ex 21:33; det. s. גוּבָּא- Cd Gn 37:28;
בגוׂבָּא Cd Gn 37:30; det. pl. גוּבַיָא Cd Gn 37:20, גוׂבייה E Gn 37:20; /*'ob,
'obba/[76] "breast": 3 m.s. עוׂבָה A Ex 4:7; /*top, toppa?/ "drum": det.s. תופא W
Ex 15:20; abs. pl. בתופין E Gn 31:27; det. pl. בתופיא W Ex 15:20; also /kol-,
kolla/, "all, any" (§46a).

§66b with a f. ending: /'omma, *'omməta/ "nation": abs. s. אוׂמָה- D Dt 5:23,
אומָא C Gn 35:11; det. pl. אוׂמַיָה- D Dt 26:18, אוׂמַיָה- D Dt 26:19.

Triconsonantal with Short Vowel

§67 *qatl

§67a /*əgar, *'agra/ "wage": abs. s. אגר F Lv 22:31; cst. s זׂאגֿר A Ex 21:19;
אֲגַר H Gn 15:1; 1 s. -אֲגֿרִי C Gn 31:41; 2 m.s. אגרך E Gn 31:8; /'əben, 'abna?/
"stone": abs. s. לֿאבֿן A Ex 21:18, אֶבֶן C Gn 31:45, הֶאָבֶן C Gn 35:14; det. s. אבנה E
Gn 29:8, אבנה E Gn 29:10; abs. pl. אַבְנִים C Gn 31:46,[77] אבנין C Gn 31:46; det. pl.
וּבאבֿנִיא Cd Ex 7:19; -אַבֿנֵיָה D Dt 27:8; /'appin, *'appayya/ "nose, face": abs. pl.
אַפֿין Cd Gn 37:30; cst. pl. -אַפֵּי Bd Gn 7:18; 1 s. אפׂי E Gn 43:3, אפׂוי C Gn 32:21;[78]
2 m.s. דְּאַפֵּיך B Gn 4:6, -אַפֵּיך Cd Gn 48:11; 3 m.s. אפׂוי C Gn 32:21; 3 f.s. אַפַּה Bd
Gn 8:8; 2 m.pl. אפיכון E Gn 40:7; 3 m.pl. אפיהון AA Nu 20:6; /'ərez?, *'arza/
"cedar": abs. s. דארז AA Nu 19:6; /'əra'?, 'ar'a/ "land": abs. s. ארע AA
Dt 26:15,27:3; cst. s. לארע E Gn 29:1,31:13; det. s. בארעׂה A Ex 22:20, -אַרעָא B
Gn 4:10; 1 s. ולארעי E Gn 30:25; 3 m.s. אֲרעׂיה Cd Ex 6:1; 3 f.s. בְּאַרעָה HH Ex
12:1; 2 m.pl. אַרעֲכוׂן D Dt 28:18; 3 m.pl. ארעהון E Gn 40:15; det. pl. ארעייה E Gn
41:54; /*bə'el, *ba'la/ "husband, master": 1 s. בעלי E Gn 29:32; 3 f.s. בַּעֲלֵה A Ex
21:22; cst. pl. בעלי H Gn 15:1; /gəbar, gobra, gabra/[79] "man": abs. s. גֿבֿר- A Ex
22:4, גבר C Gn 31:49; det s. דֻגֿבֿרׂה A Ex 22:6, גֻּבְרָא Cd Gn 38:25; גוברא Cd Gn
43:14; לגברה E Gn 43:6, גוברה E Gn 43:7; abs. pl. גוׂבֿרֿין A Ex 21:22; גוברין Cd Gn
46:32, -גֿבֿריך Cd Gn 46:34; det. pl. גבֿרַיָא C Gn 34:21, גוׂברַיָא C Gn 34:22, דגֿבֿרַיָא
Cd Gn 44:1, גוברייה E Gn 43:33; /gəpen?, gopna?/[80] "vine": abs. s. גוׂ[נ]פֿן E Gn
40:9; det. s. ובגופנה E Gn 40:10; abs. pl. גופנין AA Nu 20:5; /gərem, *garma/

"bone": abs. s. גֶּרֶם B Gn 2:23, בגרם AA Nu 19:16,18; 1 s. גַּרְמִי־ B Gn 2:23; /*dəreg, *darga/ "step": abs. pl. בדרגין F Ex 20:23; /zəra?, *zarʿa/ "seed": abs. s. זרע E Gn 7:3; זרע AA Nu 20:5; /həmar?, hamra?/ "wine": abs. s. חמר F Lv 23:13; det. s. חמרה E Gn 9:21; /həqel, haqla/ "field": abs. s. חְקָל A Ex 22:4, det. s. חקלה A Ex 22:5;[81] 3 m.s. חקלֵה A Ex 22:4; cst. pl. חקלוות E Gn 41:48;[82] 2 m.pl. בְּחַקְלֵיכן D Dt 28:16, בחקליכון F Lv 23:22; /həreb, harba/ "sword": abs. s. חַרְבָ Cd Gn 44:18, דחרב AA Nu 19:16, det. s. בְּחֹרְבָה A Ex 22:23,[83] חרבָּא Cd Ex 5:21; 1 s. חרבֵּי W Ex 15:9; /yəgar, yagra/ "heap": cst. s. יְגַר C Gn 31:46, יְגַר C Gn 31:47; det. s. יְגָרָא C Gn 31:46,[84] יגְרָא C Gn 31:48, יגְרָא C Gn 31:51; /yərah?, yarha/ "month": abs. s. ירח E Gn 29:14; det. s. יַרְחָה Bd Gn 8:5, יַרְחָה HH Ex 12:2; abs. pl. ירחין E Gn 38:24; יַרְחִין HH Ex 12:2; cst. pl. ירחי AA₁ Ex 12:2, יַרְחֵי HH Ex 12:2; /kəsep, kaspa/ "silver": abs. s. כֹּסֵף A Ex 21:32; 22:16; כְּסֵף A Ex 21:34; דַּכְסֵף Cd Gn 37:28, וּכְסֵף Cd Gn 43:12; det. s. כספא Cd Gn 43:18, דכספה E Gn 44:2; 3 m.s. כֹּסְפֵּה A Ex 21:21; כָּסְפֵּיה־ Cd Gn 44:1, כספיה E Gn 44:1; 2 m.pl. כָּסְפְּכן Cd Gn 43:23; /kərem, *karma/ "vineyard": abs. s. כְּרֹם A Ex 22:4, כרם E Gn 9:20; 3 m.s. כַּרְמֵה A Ex 22:4; /ləhem, lahma?/ "bread, food": abs. s. לְחֵם Cd Gn 37:25, לְחֵם Cd Gn 43:25; det. s. לחמה F Lv 23:18, לחמא F Lv 23:20; /*məlek, malka/ "king": det. s. מלכה AA₁ Ex 17:16, דמלכה E Gn 41:43; abs. pl. ומלכין C Gn 35:11, מלכין F Ex 19:6; cst. pl. מלכֵי H Gn 15:1; /nəhel?, nahla/ "wadi": abs. s. נחל F Lv 23:40; det. s. נַחְלָא C Gn 32:24; abs. pl. נַחְלַוֹין Z Gn 49:4; 3 m.s. נחלוי W Ex 15:16; /*nəʾel, naʾla/ "shoe": 2 m.pl. נעליכן AA₁ Ex 12:11; /nəpeš, napša/ "soul":[85] abs. s. נַפַש A Ex 21:23 נפש B Gn 2:19; det. s. נפשה F Lv 23:30; 1 s. נַפְשִׁי W Ex 15:9; 3 m.s. נפשיה E Gn 9:5; abs. pl. נפשן Cd Gn 46:27, נפשן AA₁ Ex 12:4; det. pl. נַפְשָׁתָא־ Cd Gn 46:26; 2 m.pl. לנפשתכן E Gn 9:5, נפשתכן F Lv 23:32; /*səʿed, saʿda?/ "aid": det. s. or 3 m.s.? בסעדה E Gn 39:2; 1 s. בְּסַעְדִּ־ C Gn 31:42; 2 m.s. בסעדך E Gn 31:3; 2 m.pl. בסעדכן Z Gn 48:21; /*səlem, *salma/ "likeness, statue": cst. pl. צלמי E Gn 31:19,30; /*səʾar, *saʾra/ "pain": 1 s. צַעֲרִי Z Gn 49:3; 3 f.s. צַעֲרָה־ C Gn 35:9; /qəmah?, *qamha/ "flour": abs. s. וקמח F Lv 23:14; /rehmin, *rehmayya/[86] "mercy": abs. pl. דַּבְרַחֲמִין B Gn 4:8, דְרַחֲמִין־ Bd Gn 8:1; 2 m.s. רַחֲמֵיךְ C Gn 35:9; רֶחֱמֵךְ C Gn 35:9; בְּרֶחֱמֵךְ C Gn 35:9; 3 m.s. וּבְרַחֲמוֹי Bd Gn 8:1; רחמוֹ E Gn 43:30; /*rəmeš, ramša?, romša?/[87] "evening": det. s. בְּרַמְשָׁא C Gn 31:42, ברמשה E Gn 29:23, רמשה־ E Gn 30:16; /*šəhar, šahra/ "dawn": det s. שַׁחְרָא C Gn 32:25, שַׁחְרָא־ C Gn 32:27; /*kəpen?, kepna/[88] "famine": det. s. כָּפְנָא Cd Gn 47:4, כיפנה E Gn 41:54, וכיפנה E Gn 43:1; /*təra', tar'a?/ "door": cst. s. לתרע A Ex 21:6, תְּרַע B Gn 4:7; det. s. תרעה E Gn 28:17, תרעה AA₁ Ex 12:23; /'əbed, *'abda/ "servant, slave": abs. s. עֹבֵד A Ex 21:2, עָבֵד A Ex 21:32, עֶבֵד E Gn 41:12; 1 s. עבדי F Ex 19:9; 2 m.s. עַבְדָּךְ Cd Gn 44:18; 3 m.s. דעבדֹה A Ex 21:26; abs. pl. עַבְדִין Cd Gn 44:16;[89] det. pl. עבדֵיה F Ex 20:2; 2 m.s. לְעַבְדָּךְ Cd Gn 44:23; 3 m.s. לְעַבְדֹוֹ־ C Gn 32:17; 2 m.pl. וְעַבְדֵיכן F Ex 20:10;[90] /həsep?, *haspa?/ "clay vessel": abs. s. דחסף AA Nu 19:17; /*məšek, *maška/ "hide, skin": cst. s. משך A Ex 22:26; 3 f.s. משכה AA Nu 19:5; abs. pl. מַשְׁכִּין B Ex 39:34, משכין B Ex 39:34, משכין F Lv 22:27; /'əreş?, *arsa/ "bed": abs. s. דערש F Ex 19:15; /qəbar?, *qabra/

"grave": abs. s. בקבר AA Nu 19:16,18; also /*'ᵃlep, *'alpa/ "thousand" (§47m) and /šᵊba'?/ "seven" (§47a);

§67b   with a f. ending: /*behta, behtᵊta/⁹¹ "shame": det. s. בְּהִתָּה B Gn 2:25; /*dahla, *dahlᵊta/ "fear": 2 m.s. ודחלתך W Ex 15:16; /ra'wa, *ra'wᵊta?, *rᵊ'uta?/ "pleasure": abs. s. בְּרַעֲוָה B Gn 4:4, דְּרַעֲוָה F Nu 28:27; 2 m.s. ברעותך E Gn 43:4; 3 m.pl. וּבִרעותהון Z Gn 49:6; also /šob'a/ "seven" (§ 47a);

§67c   II-': /'an, 'ana/⁹² "small cattle": abs. s. עָאן Cd Gn 46:32, עָאןۨ Cd Gn 47:3, עֶן AA₁ Ex 12:21; det. s. עָנָא C Gn 31:43, עָנָא- Cd Gn 38:17, ענה E Gn 29:3; 1 s. עָאנِי C Gn 31:43; 2 m.s. עָאנך C Gn 31:38; 3 m.s. עָאנֵיה B Gn 4:4; 3 m.pl. וְעָאנְהֶן Cd Gn 47:1; abs. pl. עָנִין A Ex 21:37; 1 pl. עינן F Lv 22:27; 2 m.pl. עָנכן AA₁ Ex 12:32; עָלِבֹהֶן AA₁ Ex 12:32;

§67d   II-w: /*hob, *hoba/ "guilt, sin": cst. pl. בחובי F Ex 20:13,14; det. pl. חובייה F Lv 22:27; 1 s. חוֹבِי B Gn 4:13; 1 pl. חובינן F Lv 22:27; /yom, yoma/ "day": abs. s. יוֹם- Bd Gn 8:5, יום F Nu 28:26; cst. s. לְיוֹם B Gn 4:7, ביום E Gn 30:14; det. s. יוֹמָה B Gn 4:14, וּבِיוֹמָא F Nu 28:26; abs. pl. יומין Bd Gn 7:17, יומָיָן Bd Gn 8:6; cst. pl. יומֵי- Cd Gn 47:29; יומת- C Gn 35:9;⁹³ det. pl. יُוֹמַיָה- D Dt 5:26; יומייה E Gn 43:9; /*mot, mota?/ "death": det. s. מותא F Ex 20:13; /*sop, *sopa/ "end": cst. s. לְסוֹף Bd Gn 8:3, לְסוֹף Bd Gn 8:6; 3 m.s. וְ)סֹפָה] E Gn 42:36; /*'op, 'opa/ "fowl": det. s. עוֹפָא- Bd Gn 7:23, וּלְעוֹפָא B Gn 2:20, עופה E Gn 6:20; /*ṣom, *ṣoma/ "fast": cst. s. צום F Lv 23:27,30; 2 m.pl. צומיכן F Lv 23:32; /tor, tora/ "ox": abs. s. תוֹר A Ex 21:36, תור F Lv 22:27; det. s. וִתוֹרָה A Ex 21:32, תורה F Nu 28:28; 3 m.s. לתורה F Ex 20:14; abs. pl. וְתורין- C Gn 32:16, תורין F Nu 28:27; 2 m.pl. תוריכן AA₁ Ex 12:32; 3 m.pl. וְתُוֹרֵיהֶן Cd Gn 46:32, וְתُוֹרֵיהֹן Cd Gn 47:1; /*yon, yawna/⁹⁴ "dove": det. s. יُוֹנָה- Bd Gn 8:8;

§67e   with a f. ending: */hoba, *hobᵊta/ "guilt, sin": cst. s. or cst. pl.? חُוֹבַתהֹון Cd Gn 44:16; /tora, torᵊta?/ "cow":⁹⁵ abs. s. תורה AA Nu 19:2; det. s. תורתא F Lv 22:28, דתורתא AA Nu 19:9; abs. pl. תוֹרִין C Gn 32:16, תורין E Gn 41:19; det. pl. תורייה E Gn 41:20, תُוֹרַייה E Gn 41:26;

§67f   II-y:⁹⁶ /*bayit, bayta/ "house": cst. s. בֵית- C Gn 31:47, לְבֵית- Cd Gn 43:21, בית W Ex 15:13; det. s. דְבִיְתֵה A Ex 22:7, בביתה E Gn 39:9; 1 s. בייתי E Gn 30:30; 31:28; 2 m.s. בְּבֵיתְך C Gn 31:41; 3 m.s. בֵּיתה A Ex 22:6, בֵּיתה C Gn 34:19, בֵּיתֵיה Cd Gn 38:26; cst. pl. בבתי E Gn 30:13; /*zayit, *zaytᵊ/ "olive": 2 m.pl. וּלזֵיתֵיכֹן A Ex 23:11; /hayil?, *hayla/ "force": abs. s. חיל AA₁ Ex 17:9; 1 s. בְחֵילִי Cd Gn 44:18, בְחֵילִי Z Gn 44:18; 3 f.s. חֵילָה B Gn 4:12; det. pl. חיילותה AA₁ Ex 12:41; 2 m.pl. חלנתבֹן AA₁ Ex 12:17;⁹⁷ /*layiš?, *leša/⁹⁸ "dough": 3 m.pl. לַשהוֹן AA₁ Ex 12:34, לשהון AA₁ Ex 12:39; /'ayin?, 'ayna/ "eye, well":⁹⁹ abs. s. עין A Ex 21:24; cst. pl. עיינות E Gn 7:11; det. pl. עֵינֵיה- B Gn 3:6; 1 s. עֵינֵינِי C Gn 31:40, עייני E Gn 31:10;¹⁰⁰ 2 m.s. עיינך E Gn 31:12; 3 m.s. וְעֵינוֹי Cd Gn 48:10, עֵינוֹי F Dt 34:7, עֵינֵוِי Z Gn 49:12; 3 f.s. תעיינֵיה E Gn 29:17, עֵיינֵיה E Gn 38:25; 2 m.pl. עֵיינֵיכֹן B Gn 3:5; /*'ayib,*'ayba?/ "thickness": det.pl. בעֵיבֵּייה Y Ex 19:9;¹⁰¹ /*tayiš, *tayša/ "he-goat": abs.pl. וּתישין C Gn 32:15;¹⁰² det.pl. תיישייה E Gn 30:35;

§67g   with a f. ending: /*hewa, hewᵊta/¹⁰³ "animal": cst. s. חֵיוַת- C Gn 31:39, בְּחֵיוַת Cd Gn 37:33, חיוות A Ex 23:11; det. s. חֵיוְתָא Cd Gn 37:20, חֵיוְתָא- Cd Gn

144

37:33; /*seba, *sebəta/ "old age": 1 s. שֶׁבְתִּי E Gn 42:38; /*'ema, *'emǝta/ "fear": 2 m.s. אימתך W Ex 15:16;

§67h    III-y: /gədi?, gəde?,[104] gadya?/ "kid": abs. s. גְּדִי־ Cd Gn 38:17, גְּדִי־ Cd Gn 38:20; det. s. גדייה E Gn 38:23; abs. pl. דגדיין F Lv 22:27; det. pl. גדיה AA₁ Ex 12:5; /*ǝre, 'arya?/[105] "lion": det s. אריא Z Gn 44:18,49:9;

§67i    with a f. ending: /*qarya, qarta/ "town, city": det s. קַרְתָּא־ Cd Gn 44:4, קרתא Cd Ex 9:33; 3 m.s. קַרְתֵּיה C Gn 34:24, קַרְתֵּיה C Gn 34:24; 3 m.pl. קַרְתְּהוֹן C Gn 34:20; det pl. קוֹרֵיא A Ex 21:13; 2 m.pl. בְּקַרְיֵכוֹן D Dt 28:16, בְקוּרְיֵכון F Ex 20:10.[106]

§68    *qitl

§68a    /*'ǝbel?, 'ebla?/ "mourning": det. s. or 3 m.s.? אבלה F Dt 34:8; /*bərek, *berka/ "knee": 3 m.s. בָּרְכּוֹי Cd Gn 48:12; /dǝbaš, debša?/ "honey": abs. s. וּרְבָ֥שׁ Cd Gn 43:11; det. s. כדבשה AA Dt 26:15, 27:3; /ḥalem, ḥelma/ "dream": abs. s. חַלֶם E Gn 41:7, חלֶם E Gn 41:11; det. s. חֶלְמָה E Gn 40:12; חלמה E Gn 40:18; 1 s. בחלמי E Gn 41:17, בחלמי E Gn 41:22; 2 m.s. דחלמָך E Gn 40:12; 3 m.s. חלמָה E Gn 40:9, חלמָה E Gn 41:8; det. pl. חלמיה E Gn 37:19; 3 m.s. חֶלְמוֹי Cd Gn 37:20, חלמוי E Gn 37:20; 1 pl. חלמינן E Gn 41:12; /ḥased, *ḥasda/ "grace, shame":[107] abs. s. וְחֵסֶד C Gn 34:11; חסד Z Gn 47:29; חֵסֶד F Ex 20:6, וְחֵסֶד־ Cd Gn 47:29, חַסָּד Cd Gn 47:29; 1 pl. חַסְדִי E Gn 30:23; /mašah, *mešha/[108] "oil": abs. s. מְשַׁח C Gn 35:14; det s. or 3 f.s.?: משחה B Ex 39:37; /nǝdar?, *nedra/[109] "vow": abs. s. נדר E Gn 28:20, תדר E Gn 31:13; 2 m.pl. נדריכון F Lv 23:38; /*nǝšar, *nešra/[110] "eagle": abs. pl. נשרין F Ex 19:4; /*sǝdar, sadra/[111] "order, row": cst. s. כסדר A Ex 21:31, סְדַר־ Cd Gn 38:26; det. s. סָדְרָא F Nu 28:29, סדרא F Nu 28:21; cst. pl. וּבְסָדְרֵי־ Cd Ex 6:6; סדרי F Lv 22:27; /*sǝṭar, seṭra/[112] "side": det. s. סיטרה AA₁ Ex 17:12; /*ṣǝmaḥ, *ṣemḥa/ "vegetation": abs. pl. צִמְחוּן D Dt 28:23; /'ǝden/ "Eden": abs. s. עֵדֶן B Gn 4:16, עֵדֶן B Gn 4:16; עֵדֶן Z Gn 49:1; /'eder, *'edra/ "flock": abs. s. עֲדַר C Gn 32:17, עֲדַר C Gn 32:17 (2x), לְעֲדַר C Gn 32:17; abs. pl. עדרין E Gn 30:40; cst. pl. עדרי E Gn 29:22, עדרי F Lv 22:27; det. pl. עֶדְרַיָא C Gn 32:20, עדרייה E Gn 29:2; /'əla', 'el'a/ "rib": abs. s. אֶלְעָ[ו] B Gn 2:21;[113] det. s. אֶלְעָא B Gn 2:22; /*'ǝseb, 'esba?/ "grass": det. s. עשבא־ Cd Ex 9:25; /*pǝtar, petra?/[114] "interpretation": det. s. or 3 m.s.? פתרה E Gn 40:18; /*ṣǝba', *ṣeb'a/ "dye, color": cst. s. וּצְבַע־ B Ex 39:29, וַוּצבע B Ex 39:24; /*qǝṭem, *qeṭma/ "ashes": 3 f.s. קטמה AA Nu 19:9,10; /*šǝbaḥ, *šebḥa/ "praise": cst. s. שְׁבַח F Ex 20:7; /*šǝbeṭ, *šebṭa/ "tribe": abs. pl. שבטין E Gn 42:36, שבטין F Lv 22:27; det. pl. שֶׁבְטַיָּא Cd Gn 44:18, שבטיה Z Gn 44:18; 3 m.s. שבטוֹי Z Gn 49:1; 2 m.pl. שֶׁבְטֵיכוֹן D Dt 5:20; /*šǝmeš, šemša/[115] "sun": det. s. שִׁמְשָׁה A Ex 22:2, שִׁמְשָׁה AA₁ Ex 17:12; det. pl. שמשתה F Lv 23:5, שימשתא AA₁ Ex 12:18 (2x); /*šǝma', *šem'a/ "fame": 3 m.s. שמעיה E Gn 29:13; /šeqar, *šeqra/[116] "lie": abs. s. דְּשֶׁקַר F Ex 20:7; also /šet/ "six" (§47a), /tǝša'?/ "nine" (§47a), /'ǝseq/ "affair" (§156s), and /sǝpar?/ "document" (§118);

§68b    with a f. ending: /*heṭṭa, *heṭṭǝta/ "wheat": det. pl. וְחִטַּיָא Cd Ex 9:32, דחטייה E Gn 30:14; also /'ešta/ "six" (§47a) and /teš'a/ "nine" (§47a);

§68c    II-': /ber?, bǝ'er?, bera?, bǝ'era?/[117] "well": abs. s. באר E Gn 29:2; det. s. באירה E Gn 29:2,31:22, דבאה E Gn 29:8; /reš, *reša/[118] "head": abs. s. רֵאשׁ C

145

32:27; cst. s. רֵ֫אשׁ־ Cd Gn 47:31, ראש F Ex 19:20; וֺרֺׁישׁ] Z Gn 47:31; 1 s. ראשׁ E
Gn 40:16,17; 2 m.s. וֺרֺׁ֫אשָׁך] E Gn 40:13; 3 m.s. רֵאשֶׁהּ־ Cd Gn 48:14, רֵאשׁיהּ־ Cd
Gn 48:17; cst. pl. רֵאשֵׁי־ D Dt 5:20, רָאשׁי Z Gn 49:16, רָאשֵׁי HH Ex 12:2;
§68d   with a f. ending: /*tena?, tə'ena?, *tenəta?, *tə'enta?/[119] "fig": abs. pl.
תאנין AA Nu 20:5;
§68e   III-w/y/': /həṭe, ḥeṭ'a/ "sin": abs. s. חֹטֹי A Ex 22:8; det. s. חֶטָאָה B Gn
4:7; 2 m.s. חֶטְאָך B Gn 4:7; /*ḥezu,[120] ḥezwa/ "appearance": det. s. חֶזְוָא C Gn
35:9, בחזוה E Gn 29:17; 3 m.s. בחזוהּ E Gn 39:6; בחזוי E Gn 31:24;[121] 3 f.pl.
חזוריהן E Gn 41:21; det. pl. חזוריה F Dt 34:12; /*pəle, *pel'a/[122] "miracle": abs.
pl. ופלין W Ex 15:11;/perin, *perayya/[123] "fruit": abs. pl. פֵּירִין־ B Gn 4:16, פירין
AA Dt 27:3; cst. pl. בְּפֵירֵי־ B Gn 4:8;, פְּפֵירֵי־ B Gn 4:16; /*rew, rewa/[124]
"appearance": det s. or 3 f.s. בְּרִיוֵּה E Gn 29:17; 3 m.s. בְּרִיוֹה E Gn 39:6; /*šəbe,
šebya?/ "captivity": det. s. שׁבֿיא W Ex 15:9; /*šəqe, *šeqya/[125] "irrigation":
det. pl. בשקייה E Gn 30:38; /ḥewwi, ḥewya/[126] "snake, serpent": abs. s. לחֻוֿ Cd
Ex 7:10; det. s. חֶוְוֺיָא B Gn 3:1, לְחֶוְוֺיָא B Gn 3:2; abs. pl. לחיוין Cd Ex 7:12;
/*dəta, *dita?/[127] "vegetation": abs. pl. דַּתׅין D Dt 28:13;
§68f   with a f. ending: /qen'a, *qen'əta/ "jealousy": abs. s. בְּקַנְאָה F Ex 20:5.
§69   *quṭl
§69a   /*'əden?, 'udna? 'edna?/[128] "ear": 3 m.s. אֹדְנֵהּ A Ex 21:6;/*'orah?,
'orha/[129] "way": cst. s. אורח E Gn 30:36, det. s. אָרְחָא־ Cd Gn 38:21, בְּאָרְחָא Cd
Gn 48:7, באורחה E Gn 28:20; 3 m.s. אורחיה־ Cd Gn 35:9; abs. pl. באורחן AA Dt
26:17; det. pl. אורְחָתָא Cd Gn 38:21, וֺאורחתה] Z Gn 49:17; 2 m.pl. אורחתכן־ D Dt
28:29; /*bəṭom, *boṭma/ "pistachio": abs. pl. דְּבַטְמׅין Cd Gn 43:11; /həṭor?,[130]
hoṭra/ "staff": abs. s. חוטר E Gn 30:37, חוטר AA₁ Ex 17:9; det. s. חֻטְרָא Cd Gn
38:25; חוטרה E Gn 38:25, חוטרה AA Nu 20:9; 2 m.s. חוֺטְרָך Cd Gn 38:18, חוטרך
Cd Ex 7:19; 3 m.s. חוֺטֽרֵהּ A Ex 21:29, חטריה Cd Ex 7:12; det. pl. חוטרייה E Gn
30:38,39; 2 m.pl. חוטריכון AA₁ Ex 12:11; 3 m.pl. חוטריהון־ Cd Ex 7:12; /*həmor,
*homra/ "socket": 3 m.s. וְחֻמֽרֵיהּ B Ex 39:33;/*nəhor, nohra?/[131] "light": det. s.
בנהרה E Gn 44:3; /*'əmoq, *'omqa/[132] "valley": 3 m.s. בְּעַמְקׅי Z Gn 48:16;[133]
/*'əmor, 'omra?/ "sheaf": det. s. עומרה F Lv 23:11,12,15: /*'otar?,[134] 'otra?/
"wealth": det. s. עותרה E Gn 31:16; /qədoš?, qodša/ "holiness":[135] abs. s. קדש F
Lv 23:20; det. s. קֻדְשָׁא־ C Gn 31:47, קֻדשׁא Cd Gn 48:2, קדשׁא F Ex 20:2; בקושׁא W
Ex 15:11;[136] 2 m.s. קדשׁך W Ex 15:13,17, קדשׁך AA Dt 26:15; abs. pl. קֻדשׁׅין־ D
Dt 27:7;[137] det. pl. קודשׁייה F Lv 23:19, קודשׁיה AA Nu 19:7; 3 m.s. קֻדֽשׁוֺהּ־ F Lv
23:38; 2 m.pl. קדשׁיכון F Ex 20:21; /qəšoṭ?, qəšeṭ, qošṭa?/ "truth": abs. s. קשׁוֺט
Cd Gn 47:29, קשׁוט Z Gn 47:29;[138] det. s. בקושׁטא Z Gn 48:15; /rəgoz, rogza?/
"anger": abs. s. בְּרׇגְוׅן Cd Ex 9:33,[139] רגו F Ex 19:22,24; det. s. or 3 m.s.? רוגזה E
Gn 30:2, דרוגזה E Gn 40:12; [140] l.s. רוֺגֽזׅי A Ex 22:23; [141] 2 m.s. רוגזך Cd Gn 44:18,
רוגזך Z Gn 44:18; 3 m.pl. וֺרוֺגֽזֽהון] Z Gn 49:7;/*təqop?, toqpa?/ "strength": cst. s.
בתקוף W Ex 15:16; det. s. or 3 m.s.? בתוקפה F Ex 19:9; 2 m.s. וֺתׇקׇּפָּך C Gn 35:9; 3
m.s. תוקפֵּיה־ D Dt 5:21, בתוקפה E Gn 29:7;
§69b   with a f. ending: /hokma?, hokməta?/ "wisdom": abs. s. חכמה F Dt 34:9;
det. s. בחוכמתה E Gn 41:43; /'orla, *orlətə/ "foreskin": abs. s. עׇרְלָה C Gn

146

34:14; *3 m.s.* עָרְלָתֵה־ C Gn 35:9; /*'*orma, *'ormɔta/ "pile": abs. pl.* עורמן W Ex 15:8 (2x);

**§69c** *II-' with a f. ending:* /*soba?, *sɔ'oba?, *sobɔta?, *sɔ'obɔta?/*[142] "*uncleanness": 3 m.s.* סאובתה AA Nu 19:13;

**§69d** *III-': /sogi? soge?,*[143] *sogya/ "multitude: abs. s.* סוֹגִי־ C Gn 32:13; *cst. s.* סוגיי E Gn 41:47.[144]

**§70** *qatl? *qitl? *qutl?*

**§70a** /*ḥɔreš, *ḥerša/*[145] "*enchantment": 3 m.pl.* בְּחַרְשֵׁיהוֹן Cd Ex 7:11; בְחַרְשִׁיהוֹן Cd Ex 7:22; /*ṭɔhar, ṭahra?, ṭehra?, ṭohra?/*[146] "*noon": det. s.* בְטִיהְרָה D Dt 28:29; טהְתָה E Gn 43:25; /*ṭɔpel, ṭapla?, ṭepla?/*[147] "*child": det. s.* טפֿלה AA₁ Ex 12:37; *1 pl.* טפֿלינן E Gn 43:8; /*yɔṣar, yeṣra/*[148] "*inclination": det. s.* דְיָצְרָא B Gn 4:7; /*nɔgar, *negra/*[149] "*bar, bolt": 3 m.s.* גֻּרוֹ B Ex 39:33; /*sɔbar, *sabra?, *sebra?/*[150] "*countenance": cst. s.* סְבַר־ C Gn 32:21 (2x), סְבַר Cd Gn 48:11; /*sɔla', *sal'a?, sel'a?/*[151] "*coin": abs. pl.* סלעֹין A Ex 21:32; /*'ez, *'ezza/*[152] "*goat": abs. pl.* עֵזָ ׅ C Gn 32:15, עזים E Gn 37:31;[153] *det. pl.* בעזייה E Gn 30:32, עזיה AA₁ Ex 12:5; *2 m.pl.* וְעֶזָוְ ׅ C Gn 31:38; /*pesha?/*[154] "*Passover": pl.* פיסחה F Nu 28:16, פיסחה AA₁,₂ Ex 12:21; /*rɔgel?, *ragla/*[155] "*foot": abs. s.* רגל A Ex 21:24; *3 m.s.* רגליה E Gn 41:44; *cst. pl.* רַגְלֵי־ Cd Gn 38:25; *3 m.s.* רַגְלוֹ־ Cd Gn 38:26; *2 m.pl.* ברגליכן AA₁ Ex 12:11; *3 m.pl.* רגליהון E Gn 38:25; /*šɔzar, *šazra?, *šezra?/*[156] "*thread": abs. s.* שֵׁזַר B Ex 39:31; /*sɔba', sab'a?, seb'a?, sob'a?/*[157] "*satiation": det. s.* שבעה E Gn 41:47, 53; /*mɔlal?, *mella?/*[158] "*speech": abs. s.* מלל F Dt 34:10 (2x);

**§70b** *with a f. ending: /'etta, 'enta, 'ettɔta, 'entɔta?/*[159] "*woman, wife": abs. s.* אִיתה A Ex 21:22, איתה A Ex 21:28, אָתָּה B Gn 2:23, לְאָנְתָּא C Gn 34:12, לאנתה E Gn 30:4; *det. s.* דְאִתְּתֵה A Ex 21:22, אַתְּתָה B Gn 3:6, דאנתתה E Gn 38:20; *1 s.* וְאתֿ)תִי A Ex 21:5; *2 m.s.* ואתתך E Gn 6:18; *3 m.s.* בְּאִתְּתֵיה B Gn 2:24, וְאִתְּתֵה B Gn 2:25, ואנתתיה E Gn 7:13, אנתתֵה E Gn 39:9; /*beq'a, *beq'ɔta/*[160] "*valley": cst. s.* בְּבִקְעַת Cd Gn 38:25, בבקעת E Gn 38:25; /*neqba, *neqbɔta/*[161] "*female": abs. s.* נֻקְבָה A Ex 21:31, נקבה E Gn 30:21; *abs. pl.* נֻקְבָן C Gn 32:16, נֻקְבָן C Gn 32:16; /*pad'a?, pod'a?, *pad'ɔta?, *pod'ɔta?/*[162] "*wound": abs. s.* פִדְעָא A Ex 21:25;

**§70c** *III-w/y with a f. ending: /ḥɔdu?, ḥedwa?, ḥɔdwa?, *ḥeduta?, *ḥedwɔta?/*[163] "*joy": abs. s.* בחדו E Gn 31:27, בחדוה F Lv 23:32, חדוה F Lv 23:36; /*'erya?, *'eryɔta?/*[164] "*nakedness": det. s. or 3 m.s.?* עריתה E Gn 9:22.

*Discussion of *qVtl*

**§71** The following chart summarizes the main reflexes of *qVtl in the Cairo Genizah fragments with regard to the main reflexes found in Syriac, Tiberian Biblical Aramaic, and Targum Onqelos:[165]

| | *qatl | *qitl | *qutl |
|---|---|---|---|
| Cairo Genizah | /qɔtel/, /qatla/ | /qɔtel/, /qetla/ | /qɔtol/, /qotla/ |
| Syriac | /qɔtel/, /qatlā/ | /qɔtel/, /qetlā/ | /qɔtol/, /qutlā/ |
| Biblical Aramaic | /qɔtel/, /qatlā/ | /qɔtel/, /qitlā/ | /qɔtol/, /qotlā/ |
| | /qɔtal/ [qɛtɛl] | /qɔtal/ [qɛtɛl] | /qɔtal/, /qutlā/ |

Targum Onqelos/ qətal/ ,/ qatlā/    / qətal/ ,/ qitlā/    / qətol/ ,/ qutlā/
   / qətel/, / qətal/    / qetal/    / qqtal/

The reflexes of *qVtl in the Cairo Genizah fragments come closest to those of Syriac; the limited data, however, suggest that, unlike in Syriac, /qətel/ appears to be in the initial stages of replacing /qətol/ (וַקְשׁוֹט ,וְקָשׁוֹט? בְּטִיהְרָה) and /qətal/ in roots III-guttural, resh (עֲדַר, עֶדֶר).

§71a  The evidence seems to indicate that there were not Hebrew segholate-like nouns in the Cairo Genizah fragments as in Biblical Aramaic and Targum Onqelos.[166] The Palestinian pointed forms כֶּסֶף, נֶפֶשׁ, עֶבֶד could be interpreted as reflecting /késep/, /népeš/, /'ébed/; however, the positioning of the Tiberian accents on these forms as well as the corresponding Tiberian pointed forms (וּכְסַף ;נְפֶשׁ, עֲבֶד ,דַּכְסַף) suggest that the bivalent sign ֶ should be taken as reflecting the reduced vowel /ə/. The scriptio plena in the nouns שׁוֹבַע חוֹטַר could reflect the penultimate forms [ḥóṭar], [šóbaʻ]; this orthography probably, however, reflects [ḥoṭár], [šobâ] (/ ḥaṭar/, /šəbaʻ/).[167] The silluq of ־סוּגִי would seem to indicate that this is merely a pausal form, although the comparative evidence suggests that a Hebrew segholate-like noun existed in Western Aramaic sources.[168]

Of the attested abs. and cst. forms of nouns which have a Hebrew segholate-like pattern in Biblical Aramaic or Targum Onqelos, three do not appear to have a segholate form—עֲבֵד, ־עֲסֵיק, חֲלֵם (note the positioning of the accent signs); the orthography of a fourth noun could reflect penultimate stress—אוֹרַח ([ʼórah] or [ʼoráh]?).

§71b  Note that סָדְרָא and חַסְדַּי which belong to the *qitl class in other Aramaic dialects, appears as *qatl nouns in the Cairo Genizah fragments.

§71c  The three pointed examples of nouns III-w/y/ʼ—גְּדֵי (2x) and סוּגִי—may reflect a realization of final /i/, although one can also interpret the data as reflecting /e/.[169]

*Triconsonantal with Two Short Vowels*
§72  *qatal

§72a  /'əbaq, *'abqa/ "dust": abs. s. אֲבַק D Dt 28:24; /'ətar?, 'atra/ "place": abs. s. אתר E Gn 28:17, אתר AA Nu 20:5; cst. s. אֲתַר Cd Gn 46:28; det. s. ־דְּאַתְרָא C Gn 35:15, דאתרה E Gn 29:22; 1 s. לאתרי E Gn 41:13: 1 pl. באתרן E Gn 29:26; /*bərad, barda/ "hail": det. s. בְּרָדָא Cd Ex 9:22,23; /*bəraq, *barqa/ "lightning": abs. pl. וברקין F Ex 19:16, ברקין F Ex 20:2; /*gəmal, *gamla/ "camel":[170] abs. pl. גְּמָלִין C Gn 32:16; det. pl. גמלייה E Gn 31:17; 3 m.pl. וְגַמְלַיהֽוֹן Cd Gn 37:25, וגמלהון E Gn 37:25; /dəhab, dahba?/ "gold": abs. s. דְּהַב Cd Gn 44:8, דדהב F Ex 20:20; det. s. דַּהֲבה Z Gn 49:2; /ḥədat?, ḥadta?/ "new": abs. s. חדת F Lv 23:14; det. s.?[171] חדתה F Lv 23:16, חַדְתָּה F Nu 28:26; /*ḥəlab, ḥalba?/ "milk": det. s. כחלבה AA Dt 26:9;[172] כחלבה AA Dt 26:15; /*ḥətan, ḥatna/ "bridegroom": det. s. לְחַתְנָא C Gn 35:9; /*kənap, *kanpa/ "wing": cst. pl. כנפי F Ex 19:4; /*kərak, karka/ "city": det. s. כְּרָכָה Z Gn 49:7; 3 m.pl. בְּכַרֵּיהוֹן H Gn 15:1; /*nəhar, nahra/ "river": det. s. בְּנַהֲרָא Cd Ex 7:17, ־בְּנַהֲרָה Cd Ex 7:20;

148

3 m.pl. [וְנַהֲרֵיהֽוֹן] Cd Ex 7:19; /*ʾəmal?, *ʿamla/ "labor": 1 s. עמלי E Gn 41:51; /ʾəpar?, *ʿapra/ "dust": abs. s. עפר AA Nu 19:17; /*hədar, *hedra/[173] "glory": 2 m.s. וְהֶדְרָךְ C Gn 35:9; /*tənan, *tanna/[174] "smoke": cst. s. תְנַן F Ex 19:18; 3 m.s. תַנְנֵיה F Ex 19:18; also /ḥad, ḥatta/ "one" (§47a), /lamḥar?/ "tomorrow" (§158b), /ʾəsar/ "teen" (§47i);

§72b   with a f. ending:

/*ʾalla, ʾəlalta?/ "harvest": 3 f.s. עֲלַלְתַּהּ Cd Gn 49;8;[175] 3 f.s. or det. s.? עללתה F Lv 23:39, עללתה Z Gn 48:7; /ʾaqra? *ʾəqarta/[176] "barren": abs. s. עקרה E Gn 29:31; /ʾarba?, *ʾərabta/ "poplar": abs. s. תערבה F Lv 23:40;

§72c   II-w, III-y with a f. ending : /*ʾat?, *ʾata/[177] "sign": det. pl. אתייה F Dt 34:11;

§72d   III-w/y: /ṣəlo?, ṣəlota?/ "prayer": abs. s. צלו E Gn 28:17; בצלו AA₁ Ex 17:11; cst. s. or cst. pl.? צְלוֹת Cd Gn 38:25; det. s. צלותה E Gn 30:8; 3 m.s. צְלוֹתֵהּ A Ex 22:22; 3 f.s. צלותה E Gn 30:22;[178] /*qəṣa, *qəṣata/ "part, end": cst. s. קְצַת Cd Gn 47:2; /ʾla, ʾəlata?/[179] "sacrifice": abs. s. עֲלָה F Nu 28:27, cst. s. לעלת F Nu 28:23; det. s. לעלתה F Lv 22:27; abs. pl. עלוון F Lv 23:37, עלָן AA Dt 27:6.

§73   Proto-Semitic *qatal replaced by Proto-Aramaic *qital:[180]

§73a   /besar, besra?/ "flesh": abs. s. בְּשַׂר B Gn 2:21, וּבְשַׂר B Gn 2:23; det. s. בּיסרה- E Gn 6:19, בסרא AA₁ Ex 12:8; 1 s. בִּשְׂרִי- B Gn 2:23; 3 m.s. בשׂרה A Ex 21:28; 3 f.s. בשׂרה AA Nu 19:5; 1 pl. בִּשְׂרַן- Cd Gn 37:27; 3 f.pl. בבישריהין E Gn 41:18,[181] בבשרהן E Gn 41:19; /dekar, dekra/[182] "male, ram": abs. s. דְכֹר A Ex 21:31, דִכַר F Nu 28:27; det. s. דכרה F Nu 28:20, דִיכְרָה F Nu 28:28; abs. pl. דְכְרִין B Ex 39:34, וְדִכְרִין C Gn 32:15, דִּיכְרִין- C Gn 32:16; det. pl. דכריה E Gn 31:12;[183] /*meṭar, meṭra/ "rain": det. s. מִטְרָה Bd Gn 8:2; מיטרה E Gn 7:4, מיטרה E Gn 7:12; abs. pl. וּמִטְרִין D Dt 28:23; det. pl. מִטְרַיה D Dt 28:24;

§73b   with a f. ending: /*berka, berkəta/ "blessing": det. s. וּבְרַכְתָא C Gn 35:9; 3 m.s. בָּרְכָתֵיה- Cd Gn 48:20, וּברַכְתֵיה Z Gn 48:20; /*nešma, *nešməta/ "soul": cst. s. נִשְמַת- Bd Gn 7:22; /*ʿezqa, ʿezqəta/[184] "signet": det. s. עֶזְקָתָא Cd Gn 38:25, עזקתה E Gn 38:25; 2 m.s. עֶזְקָתָךְ Cd Gn 38:18.

§74   *qital: /*ʾenab, *ʾenba/ "grape": det. pl. ענבייה E Gn 40:11;

§74a   *qital—III-w/y: /*məʿayin, məʾayya?/ "womb": det.du. מעייה E Gn 30:2; 2 m.s. מְעֵיךְ H Gn 15:4; 3 f.s. במעיה E Gn 38:27.

§75   *qatl? *qatal?

§75a   /*šəʾab, šaʾba/[185] "balsam": det. s. שַׁעֲבָא Cd Gn 37:25, תשעבה E Gn 37:25; /wəlad, *walda/[186] "child": cst. s. וְלַד D Dt 28:18, וולד E Gn 30:2; det. s. ולדה E Gn 38:28; det. s. or 3 f.s.? וֹלַדָה A Ex 21:22; /*harṣayin, *harṣayya/[187] "loins": 2 m.s. חַרְצָיךְ C Gn 35:11; 3 m.s. חַרְצֵיה Cd Gn 46:26, חרציה Z Gn 49:11; 2 m.pl. חרציכון AA₁ Ex 12:11; /*səpar, ṣapra?/[188] "morning": det. s. בצפרה E Gn 28:18, צפרה F Ex 19:16, צפרה AA₁ Ex 12:10 (2x); /*qəbal, qabla/[189] "darkness": det.s. בְּקַבְלָה D Dt 28:29;

§75b   with a f. ending: /*galma, *galmərta/ "hill": det. pl. גַּלְמָתָא Z Gn 49:11.

§76   *qutul

§76a   /*bəkor, bəkora/[190] "first born": det. s. בְּכוֹרָא Cd Gn 48:14, בכורא Cd Gn 48:18; 1 s. בְּוֹכֵר Z Gn 49:3;[191] abs. pl. בכורין AA₂ Ex 12:30; det. pl. בכוריה

149

AA₁ ₂ Ex 12:29; /*šǝqop?, šǝqopa?/¹⁹² "threshold": det. s. שקופה AA₁ Ex 12:7,
שקופה AA₁ Ex 12:22,23;

§76b  with a f. ending: /*bokra, *bokrǝta/ "first fruit, first born": cst. s. or cst.
pl.? בּוּכְרַת Cd Gn 48:7,¹⁹³ בְּכֹרַת Z Gn 48:7,¹⁹⁴ בוכרת AA Dt 26:10.

§77  *qatil

§77a  /*ḥǝbar, *ḥabra/ "friend": 2 m.s. דחברך A Ex 22:25; 3 m.s. לְחֹבֳרְהּ A Ex
22:6; חֹברֹהּ A Ex 22:10; חַברֵיהּ Cd Gn 38:20, לְחַברֵהּ Cd Gn 43:33; abs. pl. חברין
F Ex 20:13 (3x); /*yǝrek, *yarka/ "thigh": 3 m.s. יַרכֵּיהּ C Gn 32:26, יְרֵכֶהּ C
Gn 32:26, יַרכֵיהּ C Gn 35:9; /*yǝtem, *yetma/¹⁹⁵ "orphan": abs. pl. וִיתֹמִין A Ex
22:21, יְתֹמִין A Ex 22:23; det. pl. ליתמיא AA Dt 26:13; /*kǝtep, *katpa/
"shoulder": 3 m.s. כתפֵיה Z Gn 49:15; 3 m.pl. כתפתהון E Gn 9:23, כתפתהון AA₁
Ex 12:34; /*ʿǝqeb?, *ʿaqba/¹⁹⁶ "heel, end": 3 m.s. בעקבה E Gn 40:12; /*rǝḥel,
reḥla?/ "ewe": det. s. רחלא F Lv 22:28;¹⁹⁷ abs. pl. רֵיחֳלִין C Gn 32:15; also
/ḥǝmeš/ "five-" (§47i);

§77b  with a f. ending *qatilat > /qatla, qǝtelta/: /takla?, tokla?,¹⁹⁸ *tǝkelta?/
"bluish-purple": abs. s. וּתכֵלָא B Ex 39:29, דְּתכֵלָא B Ex 39:31; ¹⁹⁹

§77c  with a f. ending *qatilat > /qǝtela?, qǝtelǝta/²⁰⁰: /*gǝnebba?,
gǝnebbǝta/²⁰¹ "theft": det. s. גְּנֵבָתֹהּ A Ex 22:3; 3 m.s. בְּגֵנֻבָתֹהּ A Ex 22:2;
/yǝbeda, *yǝbedǝta/²⁰² "loss": abs. s. יבֵידָה A Ex 22:8; /*yǝqeda, *yǝqedǝta/
"burning": cst. s. יקידת AA Nu 19:6; det. s. וִיקֵ֣ידְתֹהּ A Ex 22:5; 3 m.s. יְקֵידְתֶהּ A
Ex 22:4; /*kǝneša?, kǝnešta/²⁰³ "gathering": cst. s. כנישת F Lv 23:36; det. s.
כניששתה HH Ex 12:3, כנישתא AA₁ Ex 12:3; abs. pl. כנישן C Gn 35:11; cst. pl.
כְּנִישַׁת Cd Gn 48:4; 2 m.pl. בכנישתכֹן F Ex 20:13; 3 m.pl. בכנישתהון F Ex 19:3;
/*gǝzera, *gǝzerǝta/ "decree": cst. s. גזירת F Dt 34:5, AA Nu 19:14;
/nǝkesa,²⁰⁴ *nǝkesǝta/ "sacrifice": abs. s. נכֵיסָא Cd Gn 43:16; cst. s. וְנֹכְ֣ריסת D
Dt 27:7, נכיסת F Lv 22:29, נכסת F Nu 28:16; abs. pl. נכיסן F Lv 23:37; /rǝteta?,
*rǝtetǝta/²⁰⁵ "trembling": abs. s. רתיתא W Ex 15:14; also /ḥamša/ "five"
(§47a);

§77d  II-y: /*gep, *gepa/ "bank": cst. s. גף E Gn 41:17; /*kep?, kepa?/
"stone": det. s. כיפה AA Nu 20:8,10,11; /kes?, *kesa/ "wood": abs. s. קיס AA
Nu 19:6; det. pl. וּבקֵיסַיָא Cd Ex 7:19; /reḥ,²⁰⁶ *reḥa/ "smell": abs. s. לריח F Lv
23:13, לרֵח F Nu 28:27;

§77e  II-ʾ with a f. ending: /*šǝ'ela, *šǝ'elǝta/ "question": cst. s. שְׁאֵלַת Cd Gn
44:18;

§77f  III-w/y/: /tǝle?, ṭalya/ "young": abs. s. טלי E Gn 41:12; det. s. טַליָא C
Gn 34:19, טַליָא Cd Gn 37:30; det. pl. טְליָה Z Gn 48:16; /*ṭǝme, *ṭamya/²⁰⁷
"impure": cst. s. בטמא AA Nu 19:11,13; /*nǝqe, *naqya/ "clean, pure": abs. pl.
נקין AA Dt 26:9,15, 27:3; /qǝne?, *qanya/ "cane, reed": abs. s. בקנֵי E Gn 41:22;
/qǝše?, qašya?/ "hard": abs. s. קש Z Gn 44:18; det s. קַשׁיָא Cd Ex 6:9; det. pl.
קשייה E Gn 40:18; /dǝke?, dakya?/ "pure": abs. s. דכֵי AA Nu 19:9; det. s. דכייה
E Gn 7:2;

§77g  III-w/y with a f. ending: /*dakya, dǝkita/ "pure": det. s. דְּכִיתָא B Ex
39:37; /naqya?, *nǝqita/ "clean, pure": abs. s. וְנֹקִייה E Gn 40:16;²⁰⁸ /qašya?,
*qǝšita/ "hard": abs. s. קשׁוֹא Z Gn 49:7.

150

§78   *qatul?[209]

§78a   /*ḥəšok?, ḥəšoka?/[210] "darkness": det. s. [חֲשׁוֹכה] D Dt 5:20; /ləhoš, ləhoša?/[211] "reddish? blackish?": abs. s. לְחֹשׁ E Gn 30:32, ולחוש E Gn 30:33; /nəmor, *nəmora/ "speckled": abs. s. וּנְמֹר E Gn 30:32, ונמור E Gn 30:33; abs. pl. נמורין E Gn 31:8; det. pl. ונמורייה E Gn 30:35; /qəroḥ, *qəroḥa/[212] "spotted": abs. s. קְרֹח E Gn 30:32, וקרֹח E Gn 30:32; abs. pl. קרחין E Gn 30:39, 31:8; det. pl. קרחייה E Gn 30:35;

§78b   with a f. ending: /*nəmora, *nəmorta/ "speckled": det. pl. ונמורתה E Gn 30:35; /*qəroḥa, *qəroḥta/ "spotted": det. pl. קרוחתה Gn 30:35.

Triconsonantal with One Short, One Long Vowel

§79   *qatāl

§79a   /*ʾəbar?, ʾəbara?/ "lead": det. s. כאיברא W Ex 15:10;[213] /ʾənan?, ʾənana/[214] "cloud": abs. s. ענן F Ex 19:16; det. s. עֲנָנָה D Dt 5:19, דעננא F Ex 19:9; 1 s. עֲנָנִי E Gn 9:14; abs. pl. בעניין F Lv 23:43; /*ʾərad, *ʾərada/ "onager": det. pl. עֲרָדַיָּא Cd Gn 36:24; /*qərab, qəraba/[215] "battle": det. s. קְרָבָה Z Gn 49:11, קְרָבָא H Gn 15:1; /šəlam, *šəlama/ "peace, welfare": abs. s. בְּשְׁלָם Cd Gn 37:22, שְׁלָם Cd Gn 43:23; 2 m.s. בשלמך E Gn 43:9, בְּשְׁלָמָךְ Z Gn 49:8; 3 m.s. שלמה E Gn 41:16, בשלמה E Gn 43:26;

§79b   with a f. ending: /təlata/ "three" (§47a);

§79c   III-w/y: /dəway?, *dəwaya/ "illness": abs. s. בְּדְוַי E Gn 42:38;[216]

§79d   III-w/y/ʾ with a f. ending: /hanaya, *hanayəta?/[217] "pleasure": abs. s. הֲנְיָא Cd Gn 37:26, הנוֹה E Gn 37:26 הניא H Gn 15:2.[218]

§80   *qitāl

§80a   /ʾedraʿ, *ʾedraʿa/[219] "arm": abs. s. בְּאָדְרַע Cd Ex 6:6; cst. s. אֻדְרֹתֵ W Ex 15:16; /ʾəlah, ʾəlaha?/[220] "God": abs. s. אֱלַּךְ C Gn 35:11, אֱלָה F Ex 20:3; det. s. אלהה E Gn 31:13; 3 m.s. אֱלָהֵיהּ C Gn 31:42, אֱלָהֵיהּ C Gn 31:53; 1 pl. אֱלָהַן Cd Ex 9:30, אֱלָהַן D Dt 5:21; 2 m.pl. אֱלָהֲכֹן Cd Gn 43:23; 3 m.pl. אֱלָהַהֹן Cd Ex 7:16; /ḥəmar, ḥəmara/[221] "he-ass": abs. s. חֹמָר A Ex 22:3, חמור A Ex 22:8; 3 m.s. לחמרה F Ex 20:14; abs. pl. וחמרין E Gn 30:43; det. pl. [וח]מְרַיָּא Cd Gn 36:24; 3 m.pl. חֲמָרֵיהֹן Cd Gn 44:3; /*ḥəṣad, ḥəṣada?/[222] "reaping": cst. s. חצד F Lv 23:22; det. s. חצדה F Lv 23:10; 2 m.pl. חצדכן F Lv 23:10, ובחצדיכן F Lv 23:22;[223] 3 f.pl. חצדהן E Gn 30:14; /kətab, kətaba/[224] "writing": abs. s. -כְּתָב D Dt 27:8, כתב AA Dt 27:8; det. s. כְּתָבה C Gn 35:9, כתבֿה C Gn 35:9.

§81   *qutāl

§81a   /ʾənaš, ʾənaša/[225] "man": abs. s. -אֱנַשׁ Cd Gn 38:26, דְּאֱנָשׁ Cd Gn 38:26; det. s. אֱנָשָׁא Bd Gn 7:21; cst. pl. וְלֶאֱנָשֵׁי Cd Gn 46:31, -וְאֱנָשֵׁי Cd Gn 46:31; /*kəraʿ, *kəraʿa/[226] "leg": 3 m.s. כרעו AA₁ Ex 12:9; /*ʾəbad, ʾəbada/[227] "work, deed": cst. s. עֲבַד B Ex 39:29, עבד B Ex 39:27, עובד E Gn 40:17; det. s. בְּעָבְדָא C Gn 34:21; abs. pl. עוֹבְדִין B Gn 4:8; 1 s. עֲבָדִי B Gn 2:4, וְעֻבְדֵי[228] Z Gn 48:22; 2 m.s. עוּבָדֵיךְ B Gn 4:7, עֲבָדֵיךְ B Gn 4:7; 3 m.s. בעבדוֹ E Gn 30:6;[229] /*nəḥaš nəḥaša/ "copper": det. s. -נְחָשָׁה D Dt 28:23; also /ḥəlap/ "instead" (§§12i, 156k) and /qədam/ "before" (§§12i, 156x).

§82   *qatāl? qitāl? qutāl?

151

§82a /*yəqar, *'iqar, *yəqara, 'iqara?/[230] "honor": cst. s. יְקָר C Gn 35:13; det. s. איקרה E Gn 31:1; 2 m.s. וִיקָרֵך C Gn 35:9; 3 m.s. איקריה D Dt 5:21; /*ləqaṭ, *ləqaṭa/[231] "gleaning": cst s. ולקט F Lv 23:22; /*qəhal, qəhala?/[232] "congregation": cst. s. וּקְהַל־ C Gn 35:11, לְקַהַל־ Cd Gn 48:4; det. s. קהלה AA Nu 19:20, 20:6; 2 m.pl. קָהָלְכֿון D Dt 5:19;

§82b with a f. ending: /*ṣərara, *ṣərarəta/[233] "bundle": cst. s. צררת E Gn 42:35, צֶרֶרת E Gn 42:35; /*sə'ara, *sə'arəta/ "barley": det. pl. סְעָרַיָא Cd Ex 9:31;

§82c II-w/y: /*ləwaṭ, *ləwaṭa/[234] "curse": det. pl. לְוַטַיֶה-D Dt 28:15; /nəyah, *nəyaha/ "rest": abs. s. וניח F Lv 23:3, וּנְיָיח F Ex 20:10; /qəyam, qəyama/[235] "covenant, law": ab. s. קִיָּם C Gn 31:44; cst. s. לקיים E Gn 9:12; det. s. קִיָמָה D Dt 5:19, קיימה F Ex 20:2; 1 s. קְיָמִי Cd Gn 47:29, קיימי E Gn 9:9; abs. pl. וְקִיָמִין C Gn 35:9; det. pl. קימיה AA Dt 26:16; 3 m.s. קָיָמוי D Dt 27:10, וּקִיָמוֹי D Dt 28:15;

§82d II-': /*še'ar, *šə'ara/[236] "rest": cst. s. תִּשְׁאָר D Dt 28:17;

§82e II-w, III-y with a f. ending: /kawya? kowya?, *kawyəta?, *kowyəta?/[237] "burn": abs. s. כּוּיֶה A Ex 21:25, [כּוּתִיֿה] A Ex 21:25.

§83 *qaṭīl

§83a /bə'ir, bə'ira/ "cattle":[238] abs. s. בְּעִיר A Ex 22:9, בְּעִיר A Ex 22:18, בְעִיר Cd Gn 46:34; det. s. בְּעִירָא Bd Gn 8:1, בְּעִירָה-B Gn 2:20; 3 m.s. בְעִירֵיה Cd Ex 9:21;[239] 3 m.pl. בְעִירְהֿון C Gn 34:23; 1 pl. ובעירֵינן AA Nu 20:4; 2 m.pl. וּבְעִירְכון F Ex 20:10; 3 m.pl. בעירְהֿון AA Nu 20:8; ובעירהון AA Nu 20:11; /*gədiš, *gədiša/ "stack of sheaves": abs. pl. גְּדִישִׁין A Ex 22:5; /*zəbin?, *zəbina?/[240] "purchase": 3 m.s. זבניה E Gn 44:2; /hədir?, *hədira/[241] "adorned": abs. s. הדיר W Ex 15:11; /həmi'?, *həmi'a/ "leavened bread": abs. s. חמיע AA₁ Ex 12:15,19,20; /həmir?, həmira?/ "leavened bread": abs. s. חמיר AA₁ Ex 12:19; det. s. חמירה AA₁ Ex 12:15; /'ərim?, *'ərima/ "sly": abs. s. עָרִם B Gn 3:1; /ṣəpir?, ṣəpira/ "he-goat": abs. s. צפיר Cd Gn 37:31; det. s. דַצְפִילָא Cd Gn 38:26; /*rədid, *rədida/ "veil": 3 f.s. רְדִידֿה Cd Gn 38:19, רדידה E Gn 38:19; also /'ətid/ "destined, future" (§129g) and the G Passive Participle (§131v);

§83b with a f. ending: /'əbida, 'əbedta/[242] "work, occupation": abs. s. עֲבִידָה F Nu 28:26; cst. s. עֲבִידַת B Ex 39:32; det. s. עֲבִידְתָּא Cd Gn 44:15; 2 m.pl. דַעֲבַדְתַּכֿון Cd Gn 46:33, עֲבִידְתַּכן Cd Gn 47:3; /*pəriša, *pərišəta/ "wonder": abs. pl. ובפרישן AA Dt 26:8; det. pl. פרישתה F Dt 34:11; /qəbila, qəbelta/[243] "cry": det s. קָבֶלְתֿוהֿון] Cd Ex 6:5; /*nəsiba, *nəsibəta/ "free-will offering": 2 m.pl. נסיבתכן F Lv 23:38;

§83c II-': /biš, biša/[244] "evil, bad": abs. s. לְבִּישׁ B Gn 3:5, בִּישׁ- Cd Gn 48:16; det. s. בִּישֶׁה B Gn 4:7;

§83d II-' with a f. ending: /biša, bišta/[245] "evil, bad": abs. s. בִּישֶׁה Cd Gn 37:33; det. s. בִּישְׁתָּא Cd Gn 37:33; abs. pl. בישן E Gn 41:19;

§83e III-w/y/: /*nəbe?, nəbeyya?/ "prophet": det. s. נְבִייא F Lv 22:27, נבייה F Dt 34:10; det. s. or 3 m.s. ? נבייה F Dt 34:5;

§83f III-w/y/' with a f. ending: /*berya, *beryəta/[246] "creature": det. pl. בירייתה E Gn 7:4; /*nəbiyya, nəbi'əta?/ "prophetess": det. s. נביא[תא] W Ex 15:20.

152

**§84 *qatūl**

**§84a** /'*əbur, 'əbura?/[247] "grain": abs. s. עֲבוּר Cd Gn 41:35, עֲבֻּר E Gn 41:49; det. s. עֲבוּרֹה E Gn 43:2; /*təhum, *təhuma/[248] "border": 3 f.s. בִּתְחֻמַהּ C Gn 34:21;

**§84b** with a f. ending: /bətula?, bətolta?/[249] "virgin": abs. s. בְּתֻלה A Ex 22:15; det. s. or pl.? בְּתֻלֹתה A Ex 22:16; /šəbu'a?, šəbu'əta?/[250] "week": 2 m.pl. שְׁבֻעֵיכֹן F Nu 28:26; /*bəqura, bəqurəta?/[251] "herd of cattle": det. s. or 3 m.s.? לבקורתה F Lv 22:27.[252]

**§85 *qutūl**

**§85a** /*dəkur, dəkura/[253] "male": det. s. דְּכוּרָא C Gn 34:15, דְּכוּרָא- Cd Gn 44:18; /ləbuš?, *lebuša/[254] "garment": abs. s. לבוש E Gn 28:20; 3 m.s. לְבֻשֹׁה A Ex 22:25, לבושיה Z Gn 48:22; abs. pl. לבושין AA₁ Ex 12:35; cst. pl. לְבֻשׁי Cd Gn 38:19; 3 m.s. לבושוֹי Cd Gn 37:34; 3 m.pl. לבושיהון F Ex 19:10,14.

**§86 *qatūl? *qutūl?**

**§86a** /*'ašun, *'ašuna/[255] "season, time": cst. s. בְּאַשַׁן Cd Gn 43:16, אַשַׁן E Gn 29:7, בְּאַשַׁן Cd Gn 48:7; /*həbuš, həbuša?/ "imprisonment": det. s. חבושה E Gn 40:5,14; /*ṭə'un, *ṭə'una/ "load": 3 m.s. טְעֻניה- Cd Gn 44:1, טְעֻנֹה Cd Gn 44:12; 1 pl. טְעֻנַן- Cd Gn 43:21; 2 m.pl. טעוניכון Cd Gn 43:12; 3 m.pl. טְעֻנָתְהֻן- Cd Gn 44:1; /səkum?, *səkuma/[256] "sum": abs. s. סכום E Gn 41:49; cst. s. סכום F Lv 23:37; /*zəbud, zəbuda/ "gift": abs. pl. זבדין E Gn 30:20;

**§86b** with a f. ending: /*gəbura, /gəburəta/ "strength": cst. s. גבורת F Dt 34:12; 2 m.s. גבורתך W Ex 15:16; /*qəbura, *qəburta/[257] "burial-place": 3 m.pl. בְּקָבְרַתְהֻן Cd Gn 47:30; ובק[בורתהחן Z Gn 47:30; /šəbu'a, *šəbu'eta/[258] "oath": abs. s. בְּשִׁבוּעה B Gn 4:15, בְּשִׁבוּעָא Cd Gn 47:31.

**§87 *qātal**

/'alam, 'aləma/[259] "world, eternity": abs. s. עֲלַם Cd Gn 48:4, עלם E Gn 9:16; det. s. עַלְמָה B Gn 4:8, עַלְמָא C Gn 35:9; abs. pl. עלמין C Gn 35:9; cst. pl. לעלמי C Gn 35:9; det. pl. עָלְמַיָא- C Gn 35:9, עָלְמָה Cd Gn 47:29.

**§88 *qātil**

**§88a** /kahen?, kahəna?/ "priest": abs. s. כהן AA Nu 19:3; det. s. כהנא F Lv 23:10, כהנה AA Nu 19:3; abs. pl. וכהנין F Ex 19:6; det. pl. כהנייה F Ex 19:22; /sahed, *sahəda/ "witness": abs. s. לְסָהֵיד C Gn 31:44; 3 m.s. סָהֲדוֹי- Cd Gn 38:26; also the G Active Participle (§131u);

**§88b** with a f. ending: /*napəqa, *napeqta/ "whore": cst. s. נְפִקַת- Cd Gn 38:21, נפקת E Gn 38:22;

**§88c** II-w/y with a f. ending: /qayəma, qayemta/[260] "pillar": abs. s. קָיְמָא C Gn 35:14, קָיְמָא C Gn 35:14;[261] det. s. קָיְמָתָא C Gn 31:51, קָיְמְתָא C Gn 31:52;

**§88d** III-': /*mar?, *mare?, *mara?, *marəya?/[262] "master": 3 m.s. מָרֹה A Ex 21:29, מָרֹה A Ex 22:7;[263] cst. pl. מָארֵ- Cd Gn 46:32, מָאֵר Cd Gn 46:34;[264] 3 m.s. לְמַרֹה- A Ex 22:11;[265] /*sane, sanə'a?/ "enemy": det. s. שנאה[ס] W Ex 15:9; 1 pl. לסנאהּ F Ex 20:5;

**§88e** III-y: /*rabe, rabəya?/ "boy": det. s. רביה F Lv 22:27, לרבייה F Lv 22:27;

§88f *III-w/y with a f. ending:* /*rabəya, rabita/[266] "girl": det. s. רְבִיתָא C Gn 34:12.

§89 *qātol*[267]

/*mazog, *mazoga/ "steward": det. pl. מן]זוגייה E Gn 40:9; מזוגייה E Gn 40:12; מזוגייה E Gn 40:12; /*nator, *natora/ "keeper": 3 m.s. נטורייה B Gn 4:9; /*marod, *maroda/ "rebel": abs. pl. מרודין F Ex 20:5; /paroq, paroqa?/ "redeemer": abs. s. פָרוֹק] Cd Ex 6:7, פרוק AA Dt 26:17; det. s. פרוקא Z Gn 49:17; /*qatol, *qatola/ "killer": abs. pl. קַטוֹלִין Cd Gn 37:22,[268] קטולין F Ex 20:13 (3x); /šalop, *šalopa/ "drawer": cst. pl. שלופי E Gn 31:26; /*tabo‘,[269] *tabo‘a/ "claimant": cst. s. ותב]וֹע A Ex 22:1, תבוֹע A Ex 22:2.

§90 *qutayl*[270]

§90a /zə‘er, zə‘era/[271] "small": abs. s. זעיר E Gn 30:15; det. s. זְעֵירָא Cd Gn 48:14, זְעֵירָא Cd Gn 48:19; abs. pl. זעירין AA₁ Ex 12:4; §90b *with a f. ending:* /*zə‘era, zə‘erəta?/ "small": det. s. זעירתה E Gn 29:18,26.

*Triconsonantal with Geminated Second Radical*

§91 *qattal*

§91a /*sawwar, *sawwəra/[272] "neck": 3 m.s. צוורֵיה Cd Gn 46:29, צוורידה F Lv 22:27, צוֹאחֵריה- Cd Gn 46:29;[273] §91b *with a f. ending:* /*yabbəša, yabbešta/[274] "dry land": det. s. בְּיַבֶּשְׁתָּא Bd Gn 7:22, ביבשתא W Ex 15:19.

§92 *qittal*

/'emmar, 'emməra?/ "lamb": abs. s. אֵימָר A Ex 21:37; אימר F Lv 22:27 (2x); det. s. אמרא F Nu 28:21; abs. pl. ואמרין E Gn 30:43; אִמְרִין F Nu 28:27; det. pl. באמרייה E Gn 30:32, אמרייה F Nu 28:21; /seppar?, *seppəra/[275] "bird": abs. s. צפר E Gn 7:14.

§93 *quttal*

/*‘orab?, ‘orəba/[276] "raven": det. s. עוֹרְבָא- Bd Gn 8:4.

§94 *qittol* (< *quttul?)[277]

§94a /*geyyor, geyyora?/ "proselyte": det. s. וגיורה A Ex 23:12; det. pl. גיוריא A Ex 22:20;[278] 2 m.pl. וְגִיוֹרֵכן F Ex 20:10; /*šeppol, *šeppola/[279] "extremity": 3 m.s. שְׁפוֹלוֹ- B Ex 39:24, שְׁפוֹלוֹ B Ex 39:26, בשפולוֹ F Ex 19:12, בְשְׁפוֹלוֹ F Ex 19:17;[280] §94b *with a f. ending:* /*šebbəla?, *šobbəla?, *šebbalta?, *šobbalta?/[281] "ear of corn": abs. pl. שבלין E Gn 41:22,[282] שבלין E Gn 41:23; det. pl.[283] שבלייה E Gn 41:7, שבלייה E Gn 41:24; /semmoqa?, *semmoqta?/ "red": abs. s. סמוקה AA Nu 19:2.

§95 *qattāl*

§95a /*'ettan, *'ettana/[284] "she-ass": 1 pl. אִיתָּנֶן C Gn 32:16; /*gebbar, *gebbara/[285] "strong": abs. pl. גברין AA₁ Ex 17:9; cst. pl. גיברי AA₁ Ex 17:9; /*gannab, gannaba?/ "thief": det. s. גנבה A Ex 22:6; abs. pl. גנבין F Ex 20:13; det. pl. גַנָּבַיָּא C Gn 31:39; /*dayyan, *dayyana/ "judge": det. pl. דַיָּנָא A Ex 21:22, דַיָּנָא Cd Gn 38:25, דינייה E Gn 38:25; /*dayyar, *dayyara/

154

"inhabitant": det. pl. or 3 f.s.? דיירה W Ex 15:14,15; /*ḥayyab, *ḥayyaba/
"guilty": det. pl. חַיָּבַיָּא Cd Ex 9:27, חַיָּבַיָּה F Ex 20:7;²⁸⁶ /ḥannan, *ḥannana/
"compassionate": abs. s. חַנָּן A Ex 22:22; /ḥaraš, ḥaraša/ "sorcerer": abs. s.
חֹרֵשׁ A Ex 22:17; det s. וְחֹרְשֵׁה A Ex 22:17; det. pl. וְלְחָרְשַׁיָּא Cd Ex 7:11; 3 m.pl.
חָרָשֵׁיהוֹן Cd Ex 7:22; /*paraš, *paraša/ "rider": 3 m.s. וּפרשׁוֹ W Ex 15:19;
/ṣayyar, *ṣayyara/ "embroiderer": abs. s. צַיָּיר B Ex 39:29;

§95b   with a f. ending: /*paraša, *parašeta/ "crossing": cst. s. בְּפָרָשַׁת Cd Gn
38:21; also the D Verbal Noun (§§126f, 132g);

§95c   III-w/y: /zakkay, zakkaya/²⁸⁷ "innocent, righteous": abs. s. זַכַּי A Ex
21:28,²⁸⁸ זַכַּי־ Cd Gn 37:22; det. s. זַכָּיָא Cd Ex 9:27;

§95d   III-': /*ḥaṭṭay, *ḥaṭṭaya/ "sinner": abs. s. וְחַטּ[אַ]ר Cd Gn 44:18,²⁸⁹ חטי Z
Gn 44:18;

§95e   III-w/y with a f. ending: /zakkaya, *zakkayəta/ "innocent, righteous":
abs. s. זַכָּיָא Cd Gn 38:26; זכייה E Gn 38:26.

§96   *qattīl

§96a   /*bakkir, *bakkira/ "early, first-ripening": cst. pl. בַּכִּירֵי־ B Gn 4:4; det.
pl. [וּב]כִּירֵיה E Gn 30:42; /bassim?, *bassima/ "sweet, pleasant": abs. s. בסם F
Ex 19:19;²⁹⁰ /*ḥabbib, *ḥabbiba/ "beloved": abs. pl. חביבין F Ex 19:5, חביבִין AA
Dt 26:18; /ḥakkim, *ḥakkima/ "wise": abs. s. חַכִּים Cd Gn 41:33; cst. pl. חַכִּימֵי־
C Gn 34:20; det. pl. וְחַכִּימַיָה D Dt 27:1; 2 m.pl. וְחַכִּימֵיכוֹן D Dt 5:20; 3 m.pl.
חכימיהון E Gn 41:8; /*yammin, *yammina/ "right hand": 1 s. ימיני W Ex 15:9; 3
m.s. בְּיַמִּינֵה Cd Gn 48:13,²⁹¹ יַמִּינָה־ Cd Gn 48:14; /*yaṣṣib, *yaṣṣiba/ "citizen":
det. pl. יציבייה F Lv 23:42;²⁹² /*yaššir, yaššira/ "honest": det. s. יְשִׁירָא F Lv
22:27; /*laqqiš, *laqqiša/ "late, late-born": abs. pl. לַקִּישִׁין Cd Ex 9:32; cst. pl.
ובלקישי E Gn 30:42; /*paṭṭir, paṭṭira?/ "unleavened bread": det. s. דפטירה AA₁
Ex 12:17; abs. pl. פטירין F Lv 22:27, 23:6; /ṣaddiq?, ṣaddiqa?/ "righteous": abs.
s. צדיק E Gn 7:1; det. s. צדיקא C Gn 35:9; abs. pl. צַדִּיקִין B Gn 4:10, צדקים E Gn
38:25;²⁹³ det. pl. צדיקיה F Ex 20:6; /qaddiš?, qaddiša/ "holy": abs. s. וְקֻ[דִּי]שׁ Cd
Ex 6:7; det. s. קַדִּישָׁא Cd Ex 6:3; abs. pl. קדישין C Gn 32:29; /qallil?, *qallila/
"little": abs. s. קליל E Gn 30:15; cst. s. וְקָלִיל Cd Gn 43:11;²⁹⁴ abs. pl. קלילין F Ex
19:4; /*qarib, *qariba/ "close, relative": 3 m.pl. וקָרִיבֵיהוֹן H Gn 15:1; /raḥiq?,
*raḥiqa/ "far": abs. s. רחיק F Ex 20:15;²⁹⁵ /rakkik?, *rakkika/ "soft": abs. s.
רכיך E Gn 30:37, F Lv 22:27; /*rašši', rašši'a?/ "wicked": det. s. רשיעא W Ex
15:9, רשיעה Z Gn 48:22; abs. pl. רַשִׁיעִין F Ex 20:5; /šalliṭ, šalliṭa?/ "ruler": abs.
s. וְשַׁלִּיט C Gn 34:19, יְשַׁלִּיט Cd Gn 44:18; det. s. or 3 m.s.? שליטה E Gn 39:1; cst.
pl. שליטי E Gn 40:7; /*šammin, *šammina/ "fat": 3 m.pl. שַׁמִּינֵיהוֹן־ B Gn 4:4;
/*šappir, *šappira/ "handsome, pleasing": abs. pl. שַׁפִּירִין C Gn 35:9; /*taqqip,
*taqqipa/ "strong": 3 m.s. וְתַקִּיפָה C Gn 31:42, בְּתַקִּיפָה C Gn 31:53; cst. pl.
תקיפי W Ex 15:15; /*tammim?, tammima?/²⁹⁶ "innocent": det. s. דתמימה F Lv
22:27; also /yattir?/ "in addition" (§158a);

§96b   with a f. ending: /bassima, *bassimeta/ "sweet, pleasant": abs. s. בַּסִּימָא־
B Gn 2:21;²⁹⁷ /*daqqiqa, *daqqiqəta/ "thin": abs. pl. דקיקן E Gn 41:23; det. pl.
דקיקתה E Gn 41:7, דקיקתה E Gn 41:20; /*bakkira, *bakkirəta/ "early, first-

155

ripening": abs. pl. בְּכִין Cd Ex 9:31; /qaddiša?, *qaddišəta/ "holy": abs. s.
קדישה F Ex 19:6, קדִישָׁה AA Dt 26:19; /*qallila, *qalliləta/ "little": abs. pl. קלִילָן
H Gn 15:1; /šappira?, *šappirəta/ "handsome, pleasing": abs. s. וּשפִירה E Gn
29:17; /taqqipa, *taqqipəta/ "strong": abs. s. תַּקִיפָּא Cd Ex 6:1; תַּקִיפָּא Cd Ex
6:1;

**§96c** *III-': /saggi, *seggi, *saggi'a?, *seggi'a?/*[298] "numerous": abs. s. וְסַגִּי Cd
Ex 9:28; abs. pl. סָגִין Cd Gn 37:34; סַגִּין Z Gn 48:4.

**§97** *qattūl
/*balluṭ, balluṭa/ "oak": cst. s. בְּלוֹט C Gn 35:8; det. s. בַּלּוֹטָא C Gn 35:8;
/*'ammud, *'ammuda/ "column, pillar": cst. s. עַמּוּד C Gn 32:25, עַמּוּד C Gn
32:27; 3 m.s.? וְעַמּוּדוֹן B Ex 39:33.

**§98** *quttāl
**§98a** /ḥollaq, *ḥollaqa/ "portion": abs. s. חוּלָק Cd Gn 44:18, חוּלָק Cd Gn
48:5; 3 m.s. חוּלְקֵהּ E Gn 43:34; abs. pl. חוּלְקָן E Gn 43:34; 3 m.pl. חוּלקהון E Gn
43:34; also /remmon/ "pomegranate" (§§18m, 119b)?
**§98b** *III-w/y:* /*ḥeppay, *ḥeppaya/*[299] "covering": cst. s. חֵיפָּיי B Ex 39:34,
חֵיפָי B Ex 39:34.

**§99** *qittāl
**§99a** /*kennar, *kennara/*[300] "harp": abs. pl. וּבכִינרִין E Gn 31:27; /*kettan,
kettana/ "flax": det. s. וְכִיתָּנָא Cd Ex 9:31; /leššan, *leššana/*[301] "tongue": abs.
s. לְשָׁן D Dt 27:8; cst. s. בְּלִישָׁן C Gn 31:47;[302] abs. pl. לִשָׁנִין D Dt 27:8; /'ešša,
'eššata/*[303] "fire": abs. s. אֶשָּׁא Cd Gn 38:26, בְּאֶשָּׁא Cd Gn 38:26; det. s. אֶשָּׁתה D
Dt 5:19; בְּאֶשָּׁתה D Dt 5:20;
**§99b** *with a f. ending:*
/ḥewwara?, *ḥewwarəta/*[304] "white": abs. s. חוורה E Gn 30:35; det.s. חוורתה E
Gn 30:37;[305] abs. pl. חוורין E Gn 30:37;[306]
**§99c** *III-w/y:* /*'ellay, 'ellaya?/ "high": det. s. עלִיא E Gn 40:17; abs. pl. עלָאִין
D Dt 26:19;[307] עלָין AA Dt 26:19.

**§100** *qittul (< *quttūl)
**§100a** /*bekkor, *bekkora/ "first fruits": det. pl. דִבכּוּרִיה F Nu 28:26; 2 m.pl.
בּבּוּרֵיכן D Dt 28:17; /seqqol, *seqqola/*[308] "mishap": abs. s. סְקֹל A Ex 21:22;
סְקֹל־ A Ex 21:23; סקל E Gn 42:38; /qeddom?, *qeddoma/ "east wind": abs. s.
דקדם E Gn 41:23; also /qettol/ the D Verbal Noun (§§126h, 132g);
**§100b** *III-w/y* /*šeroy?, šeroya?/ "beginning": cst. s. שירוי F Lv 23:10, וְשִׁירוּי
Z Gn 49:3; det. s. שירוֹיה E Gn 28:19; שִׁירוּיה E Gn 41:21.

**§101** *Triconsonantal with Geminated Third Radical*
/*'artak, *'artakka/*[309] "wagon": 3 m.s. אַרתַּבֵּיהּ Cd Gn 46:29; 3 m.s. דּאָרתְבּוֹ
W Ex 15:19;[310] /hədas?, *hədassa/ "myrtle": abs. s. הדס F Lv 23:40; /*ḥərak,
ḥarakka?/ "window":[311] det. s. or 3 f.s.? חַרכּה Bd Gn 8:6; cst. pl. חרכי E Gn
7:11.

**§102** *Reduplicated Nouns*
/lele?[312] lelya/ "night": abs. s. בְּלִילִי E Gn 41:11, לִילִי AA₁ Ex 12:42; cst. s. בלילי
AA₁ Ex 12:8,12; det. s. בְּלֵילִיָא C Gn 31:39, בְּלֵילִיָא C Gn 32:14; abs. pl.[313] לילוֹן E

156

Gn 7:4,12; /'erabrob?, *'erabrobba?/ "mixed multitude":[314] abs. s. עברוב AA₁
Ex 12:38.

§103   Quadriliteral Nouns

/*'oṣar, *'oṣəra/[315] "treasure, treasury": det. pl. לאוצרייה E Gn 41:47; /*gab'ul,
*gab'ula/[316] "bud": abs. pl. גִבְעוּלִין Cd Ex 9:31; /*'arpel, 'arpəla?, 'arpella?,
'arpela?/[317] "darkness, cloud": det. s. וְעַרְפֶּלָה D Dt 5:19, לערפלה F Ex 20:18;
/*səmal, *səmala/[318] "left hand": 3 m.s. שְׂמָאלֵיהּ- Cd Gn 48:13, שְׂמָאלֵיהּ F Ex
20:2;[319] /*šarbiṭ, šarbiṭa/[320] "staff": det. s. בְּשַׁרְבִיטֹהּ A Ex 21:20; abs. pl. שרביטין
E Gn 40:10; det. pl. שרביטייה E Gn 40:12.

Nouns with Prefixes

§104   *mV- prefix

§104a   /madbaḥ?, madbəḥa?/ "altar": abs. s. מדבח C Gn 35:7, מדבח AA Dt
27:5; det. s. or 3 m.s.? מדבחה AA Dt 27:6; 1 s. מדבחי F Ex 20:23 (2x); /*madbar,
madbəra/ "desert": det. s. בְּמדְבְּרָא Cd Ex 7:16;[321] במדברה E Gn 37:22, במדברא F
Ex 19:2; /*madmak?, *madməka/ "bed, couch": 3 m.s. מַדְמְכֵיהּ B Gn 2:24;
/madnaḥ, madnəḥa?/ "east": abs. s. מַדְנַח- B Gn 4:16; det. s. מדנחה E Gn 29:1;
/*mahlak, *mahləka/ "walk": cst. s מהלך E Gn 30:36, 31:23; /mertoq?,
mertuq?, *mertoqa?, *mertuqa?/ "fist": abs. s. בְּמֶרְתּוּק A Ex 21:18; /*meškan,
meškəna/ "tent": cst. s. משכן AA Nu 19:4; det. s. מִשְׁכְּנָה B Ex 39:33, מִשְׁכְּנָה- B
Ex 39:33; 3 m.s. מִשְׁכְּנֵיהּ C Gn 35:9; /mamlal, *mamləla/ "speech": abs. s. מַמְלַל
A Ex 4:10; also the G Verbal Noun /maqtal/ (§§126g, 131x) and the G
Infinitive /meqtol/ (§§126e, 131w);

§104b   with a f. ending:

/*maṣnəpa, maṣnapta/ "mitre": det. s. מִצְנַפְתָּה- B Ex 39:31; /mərahəqa,
*mərahaqta/ "abomination":[322] abs. s. מִרְחַקָא- C Gn 34:14; 3 m.pl. מְרַחֲקָתְהֹן- Cd
Gn 46:34; /*markəba, markabta?/ "vehicle": det. s. במרכבתה E Gn 41:43;
/*məṭalla, *məṭalləta/ "booth": abs. pl. למטלין AA₁ Ex 12:37; det. pl. דמטלייה F
Lv 23:34;

§104c   I-': /man, mana?/[323] "vessel": abs. s. מָן AA Nu 19:15; det. s. במנה AA₁,₂
Ex 12:22; abs. pl. מָאנִין A Ex 22:6, ומָנין AA₁ Ex 12:35; 3 m.s. מָאנֹי B Ex 39:33;
/*mesar, mesəra?/ "bunch": det. s. מִיסְרה AA₁ Ex 12:22, מיסרה AA₂ Ex 12:22;

§104d   I-y: /*mešar, *mešəra/ "plain": cst. pl. במשרֵ C Gn 35:9; det. pl.
במשרייה F Dt 34:8;

§104e   I-w: /*mo'ad?, *mo'ada?/[324] "appointed time": 3 m.s. מותדוי F Lv
23:37,44; 2 m.pl. מותדיכן F Lv 23:32;

§104f   with a f. ending: /*motəra, *motarta/ "remainder": 3 m.pl. מותרתהון
AA₁ Ex 12:34;

§104g   I-n: /*mabbo', *mabbo'a/[325] "spring": cst. pl. מַבּוּעֵי Bd Gn 8:2; 1 pl.
מבועינן E Gn 29:22; 3 m.pl. מַבּוּעֵינֹהֹן] Cd Ex 7:19;

§104h   I-n with a f. ending: /mattəna?, *mattatta/[326] "gift": abs. s. מתנה F Lv
23:20; 2 m.pl. מתנוותכן F Lv 23:38; /maṭṭəra?, *maṭṭarta/ "guard, prison": abs.
s. במטרֹה E Gn 41:10, למטרא AA Nu 19:9;

§104i   II-': /mal'ak, mal'əka?/ "angel, messenger": abs. s. מַלְאַךְ C Gn 32:25;

157

B בְּמַלְאָכִין‎ *abs. pl.*; E Gn 31:11 מלאכה‎ *det. s. or 3 m.s.?*; Z Gn 48:16 מלאבא‎ *det. s.*
C מַלְאָבַיָא‎ Gn 35:7; *det. pl.* C דְּמַלְאָבֵי‎ Gn 32:27; *cst. pl.* Gn 3:5;

§104j  *II-w/y:* /*məgir, *məgira/ "neighbor": 3 m.s. ומגירה‎ AA₁ Ex 12:4; also
/*mədor?/ "dwelling," /mazon/ "food," /*mərom/ "height," /*mahol?/
"dance," /*mamon/ "wealth" (§119d);

§104k  *II-w/y with a f. ending:* /*məgaza, *məgazəta/[327] "ford": 3 m.s. מְגַזְתֵּיה‎
C Gn 32:23; /*mədina, *mədinəta/ "city": 3 m.pl. ובמְדִינָתְהוֹן‎ H Gn 15:1;
/məkala, məkalta/[328] "measure": *abs. s.* מְכָלָא‎ Cd Gn 38:26; *cst. s.* בְּמְכָלַת‎ C
Gn 35:9; *det. s.* בְּמְכָלְתָּא‎ Cd Gn 38:26, מְכָלְתָה‎ F Nu 28:29;ˆ /*mənara,
mənarəta?/ "lamp": *det. s.* מנרתה‎ B Ex 39:37;ˆ /*məqama, *məqaməta/
"acquisition": 3 m.s. בְּקָמְתֵּה‎ A Ex 22:7;[329]

§104l  *III-w/y:* /mar'e, *mar'əya?/[330] "pasture": *abs. s.* מַרְעֵה‎ Cd Gn 47:4;
/*mVr'e?, *mVr'əya?/[331] "dung": 3 f.s. מריעֵיה‎ AA Nu 19:5;ˆ /*mašre?,
*mašrəya/ "dwelling": 3 m.s. מִשְׁרֵי‎ Cd Gn 46:28,[332] 3 m.pl. ומשרויְהוֹן‎ AA₁ Ex
12:40;[333]

§104m  *III-w/y with a f. ending:* /*mašri, mašrita/ "camp": *det. s.* בְּמַשְׁרִיתָא‎ C
Gn 32:22, משריתה‎ AA Nu 19:3,[334] משריתא‎ AA Nu 19:7; *abs. pl.* מַשְׁירִין‎ H Gn
15:1;[335] 3 m.s. בְּמשריתֵה‎ F Ex 19:16;ˆ[336] /*maštu, maštuta?/ "feast": *det. s. or 3
f.s.?* משתותה‎ E Gn 29:27;[337] /*morki?, *morkəta?/[338] "trough": 3 m.s.?
במורכיוותיה‎ E Gn 30:38, במורכיוות]תה[‎ E Gn 30:41.[339]

§105  *šV-prefix*

§105a  Š Verbal Noun (§130f);

§105b  *with a f. ending:* /*šalhabi, *šalhabita/ "flame": *cst. s?* בְּשַׁלְהֵבִית‎ F Ex
19:18.[340]

§106  *tV- prefix*

§106a  /*tašlom?, tašloma?/[341] "payment, exchange": *cst. pl.* תַּשְׁלוֹמֵי‎ A Ex
21:23,ˆ תֵּשְׁלוֹמֵי‎ A Ex 21:24, ]ת[שׁלוֹמֵי‎ A Ex 21:25; /tašmiš?, *tašmiša/
"copulation": *abs. s.* לתשמיש‎ F Ex 19:15;

§106b  *with a f. ending:* /tohmədа, *tohmadta/[342] "desire": *abs. s.* תּוֹחְמְדָה‎ B
Gn 3:6; /*telladu, telladuta/[343] "offspring": *det. s.* תֵּלְדוּתָה‎ Z Gn 48:6;[344] 2 m.s.
וְתֵּילַדּוּתָךְ‎ Cd Gn 48:6; *1 pl.* תלדותן‎ E Gn 43:7;ˆ 2 m.s. תלדוותך‎ E Gn 31:3,
13; /tešbəha, *tešbahta/[345] "praise": *abs. s.* לְתֵשְׁבְּחָה‎ D Dt 26:19;ˆ לתשבחה‎ AA
Dt 26:19; *abs. pl.* בתשבן‎ W Ex 15:11;[346]

§106c  *III-w/y with a f. ending:* /*taksi, *taksita/ "cover": 3 m.s. תכסיתה‎ A Ex
22:26;

§107  *yV- prefix*

/*yabruh, *yabruha/ "mandrake": *abs. pl.* יברוחין‎ E Gn 30:14; 3 m.s. ביברוחוֹי‎ E
Gn 30:16.ˆ

§108  *'a- prefix*

see /'aqtala, 'aqtalut-/ the C Verbal Noun (§§126f,i, 133f)[347]

§109  *hv- prefix*

see the C Verbal Noun (§§126f,i)

*Nouns with Suffixes*

§110  *-ān*

158

**§110a** *qaṭlān:* /raḥman, *raḥmana/ "merciful": abs. s. וְרַחֵם A Ex 22:22;
/*šedpan, šedpana/ "blight": det. s. וּבְשִׁדָּפ֑וֹן D Dt 28:22;^348 /*yarqan?,
yarqana?/ "mildew": det. s. וּבַיֵּרָק֑וֹן D Dt 28:22;

**§110b** *II-w:* /*motan, motana/ "plague": cst. s. מוֹתַן AA₁ Ex 12:13; det s.
בְּמוֹתָנָא AA Nu 20:3;^ מוֹתָנָה־ D Dt 28:21;^

**§110c** *qīlān*
/ 'ilan?,'ilana/^349 "tree": abs. s. אִילָן F Lv 23:40; cst. s. אִילַן־ B Gn 3:3;^ det. s.
אִילָנָא B Gn 3:6; cst. pl. אִילָנֵי B Gn 3:1;^350 det. pl. אִילָנַיָּא Cd Ex 9:25;

**§110d** *qillān*
/ 'eddan?, *'eddon?, *'eddana?, *'eddona?/^351 "time": abs. s. עִידָן F Lv 22:27,
23:14; cst. pl. לְעִדוֹנֵי E Gn 30:16, בְּעִידוֹנֵי F Ex 19:16;

**§110e** *qiṭlān*
*III-w/y:* /*menyan, menyana/^352 "number": cst. s. לְמִנְיַן F Nu 28:29, לְמִנְיָן HH
Ex 12:2; det. s. מִנְיָינָא־ C Gn 31:39; /*qenyan, *qenyana/^353 "possessions": 3
m.s. קִנְיָינֵיהּ E Gn 31:18;^354 3 m.pl. וְקִנְיָנְהוֹן C Gn 34:23; /*ḥezwan?,
*ḥezwana?/^355 "vision": cst. s. חֵזוּ E Gn 9:13;

**§110f** *quṭlān*
/*'oḥran, 'oḥəran, *'oḥrana, 'oḥərana/^356 "another": abs. s. דָּאחֳרָן A Ex 22:4;^357
אוּחֳרַן C Gn 31:50; det. s. אָחֳרָנָא Cd Gn 43:14; /*beṭlon, *beṭlona/^358 "idleness":
3 m.s. בְּטָלוֹנֵהּ A Ex 21:19;^ /'olpan?, *'olpana/ "teaching": abs. s. אוּלְפַן F Ex
19:3; cst. s. לְאוּלְפָן F Ex 19:4; /dokran?, dokrana?/ "remembrance": abs. s.
לְדָכְרַן AA₁ Ex 12:14; דּוּכְרַן AA₁ Ex 17:14; det. s. or 3 m.s. דּוּכְרַנָה? AA₁ Ex 17:14;^
3 m.s. דּוּכְרָנֵהּ AA₁ Ex 17:16; /pelḥan?, polḥan, pelḥana, *polḥana/^359 "worship":
abs. s. דְּפָלְחָן F Lv 23:35, פָּלְחַן F Nu 28:26; det. s. פָּלְחָנָא Cd Ex 6:9; 1 s. פָלְחִי E
Gn 30:26; 3 m.pl. פָּלְחָנְהוֹן Cd Ex 6:6; /por'an?, *por'ana/ "avenger":^360 abs. s.
וּפוּרְעָן F Ex 20:5;^ /perqon?, *porqan, perqona?, porqana?/^361 "redemption":
abs. s. לְפֻרְקַן AA₁ Ex 12:42;^ cst. s. פֻּרְקָ֑ן A Ex 21:30;^ det. s. פּוּרְקָנֵהּ Z Gn 49:1,
פּוּרְקָנֵה] Z Gn 49:2; /qorban?, *qorbana/ "sacrifice": abs. s. קוּרְבַּן F Lv 22:27; cst.
s. קֻרְבַּן F Lv 23:14; 1 s. קֻרְבָּנִי B Gn 4:8; 2 m.s. קוּרְבָּנָךְ B Gn 4:8; abs. pl. קוּרְבָּנִין F Lv
23:8; 1 pl. קוּרְבָּנִינָן F Lv 22:27; /*šolṭan, *šolṭana/ "ruler":^362 abs. pl. שֻׁלְטָנִין Z
Gn 49:11; 3 m.s. שֻׁלְטָנוֹי Cd Gn 41:37, שֻׁלְטָנֵהּ Cd Ex 7:10, שוּלטַנֵהּ F Dt 34:11;

**§110g** *quṭlaṭān:* /sokləṭan?, *sokləṭana/ "intelligent": abs. s. סוּכְלְתָן Cd Gn
41:33;

**§110h** *qaṭilān*
*II-y:* see /reqan/ "emptily" (§158a).

**§110i** *on Participles:*
G: /nagəšan?, *nagəšana/ "one who gores": abs. s. נַגָּשׁ A Ex 21:36;^363
D: /*malləpan, *malləpana/ "teacher": 3 m.pl. מְלַפָּנֵיהוֹן AA Nu 20:10;^364
/*məḥabbəlan, məḥabbəlana?/ "destroyer": det. s. לִמְחַבְּלָא AA₁ Ex 12:23; with
a f. ending: /*mərabbəyani, *mərabbəyanita/ "nurse": 3 f.s. מְרַבְּיָינִיתַהּ C Gn
35:8, מְרַבְּיָינִיתַהּ C Gn 35:9;^365

**§111** *-on*^366

**§111a** There is one diminutive of a Persian loanword—/zeggon/ "little bell"

(§117); also /bezyon/ "disgrace," /'arbon/ "pledge," /'esron/ "tenth," /petron?/ "interpretation" (§119e).

§112 *-ām: see /'imama/ "daytime" (§158b).

§113 *-āy suffix

§113a gentilic:[367] /*'ədomay, *'ədomaya/ "Edomite": det. pl. אדומייא W Ex 15:15; /*'ərammay, 'ərammaya?/ "Aramean": det. s. אֲרמייה E Gn 31:20, הארמייה E Gn 31:24;[368] /*kəna'ənay?, *kəna'ənaya/ "Canaanite": det. pl. דכנעאי E Gn 9:18,[369] דכנעאי E Gn 9:22; /*medyanay, *medyanaya/ "Midianite": abs. pl. [וּמִדִ]יָנָיִן Cd Gn 37:28; ^ /*mo'əbay, *mo'əbaya/ "Moabite": det pl.? דמואבי F Dt 34:5,6;[370] det. pl. מואבייא W Ex 15:15; /meṣray?, meṣraya?/ "Egyptian": abs. s. מצריי E Gn 39:1; det. s. מצרייה E Gn 39:2, דמצרייה E Gn 39:5; det. pl. דְמִצְרָאֵי Cd Ex 6:7, דמצריֵי Cd Ex 7:11, ולמצֻרֿאי E Gn 43:32;[371] /*sarqay, *sarqaya/ "Saracen": abs. pl. דְסֻרְקָאִין Cd Gn 37:25, דסרקאין E Gn 37:25; det. pl. לְסֻרְקָיֵי Cd Gn 37:28, דסרקאֵי E Gn 39:1; /'ebray, *'ebraya/ "Hebrew": abs. s. עִבְרֿאֵי A Ex 21:2; עְבְרָיֵי E Gn 41:12; det. pl. עבראי E Gn 43:32, דעבריא E Gn 40:15; /*'ədulləmay, 'ədulləmaya/ "Adullamite": det. s. עֲדֻלָמָיָא Cd Gn 38:20;

§113b other nouns: /*'oḥray?, *'aḥray?, *'oḥraya?, *'aḥraya?/[372] "last": det. s. אֲחֿרייָא A Ex 4:8; אחרייא F Lv 23:22; /*'artəlay?, *'artəlaya/ "naked": abs. pl. עֲרַטְלָיִין B Gn 2:25;[373] /*nokray, *nokraya/ "foreigner": abs. pl. כנוכריין E Gn 31:15; also the Greek loanword /gerday?/ "weaver" (§116), and the ordinal numbers (§48a).

§114 *-ūt

§114a III-w/y: /*'aṣu, *'aṣuta/ "trough": 2 m.pl. אַצְבָתְכוֹן D Dt 28:17;[374] /ba'u, *ba'uta/ "request": abs. s. בְּעֵוֹ Cd Gn 47:29; בעו Z Gn 47:29; /*galu, galuta?/ "exile": det. s. וגלותא F Ex 20:14; /dəmu?, *dəmuta/ "likeness": abs. s. דמו F Ex 20:4, בדמו E Gn 9:6; cst. s. בִּדְמוּת C Gn 32:25, בִּדְמוּת C Gn 32:29; /*zaku, *zakuta/ "merit": 1 s. בזכוותי E Gn 30:30,[375] בְזָכוּתִי Z Gn 48:22; 2 m.s. בזכוותך E Gn 30:27; /zənu?, *zənuta/ "prostitution": abs. s. דִזְנֻֿ Cd Gn 38:24; דזנו E Gn 38:24; /*ta'u, *ṭa'uta/ "idol": abs. pl. טעוֹן A Ex 22:19, טעוֹן Z Gn 49:2; det. pl. טעוותה E Gn 31:34; 1 s. טעוותי E Gn 31:32;[376] 3 m.pl. טעותהון AA₁ Ex 12:12; /*lə'u, *lə'uta/[377] "tiredness": cst. s. לְעֻת C Gn 31:42; also /ya'ut/ "properly" (§158a), /'asu/ "healing" (§118);

§114b other nouns:[378] /*'armlu, 'arməluta/ "widowhood": det. s. אַרְמְלוּתֵהּ Cd Gn 38:19, ארמלותה E Gn 38:19; /bišu?, *bišuta/ "illness": abs. s. לְבִישׁוֹ A Ex 21:18;[379] /*bəkoru, bəkoruta?/ "birthright": det. s. [ב]בורותה Z Gn 49:3, בבורותה] Z Gn 49:3;[380] /*zəbinu, *zəbinuta/ "purchase":[381] cst. s. זְבִינות A Ex 21:21; /*zə'eru, *zə'eruta/ "smallness": 3 m.s. כזעורתה E Gn 43:33, כָזְעֵירוּתֵהּ Cd Gn 43:33; /*ḥeru, ḥeruta?/ "freedom": det. s. לחירותה] A Ex 21:27; /ṭabu, *ṭabuta/ "goodness": abs. s. וטבו F Ex 20:6; /*ṭalyu, *ṭalyuta/ "youth": 1 pl. טַלְיוּתַן Cd Gn 46:34; /yəritu?, *yərituta/ "inheritance": abs. s. [וי]רֿיתו Cd Ex 6:8;[382] /*yašširu, *yašširuta/ "honesty": 2 m.s. וְיַשְׁרְתָךְ C Gn 35:9;[383] /malku?, malkuta?/ "kingdom": abs. s. ומלכוֹ Z Gn 49:7; det. s. מלכותה AA₁ Ex 12:29; det. pl. מלכוותא F Ex 20:14; /*sahədu, sahəduta/ "testimony": det. s. שָׂהֲדוּתָא C

Gn 31:47;ˊ *abs. pl.* סהדין F Ex 20:13, סהדותּ F Ex 20:13; /*sebu*, *sebuta/ *"old age"*: *abs. s.* סֵיב Cd Gn 48:10,[384] סֵיבוֹ Z Gn 48:10; /*'enwanu*, *'enwanuta/*[385] *"humility"*: 2 *m.s.* עִינְוָנוֹתָךְ C Gn 35:9, דְּעִינְוָנוֹתָךְ C Gn 35:9;ˊ /*ṣaddiqu*, *ṣaddiquta/ "righteousness"*: 2 *m.s.* וְצַדִּיקוּתָךְ C Gn 35:9; /*qɔpidu*, *qɔpiduta/ "shortness"*: *cst. s.* קְפִידוּתּ Cd Ex 6:9;ˊ /*qaribu*, *qaributa/ "proximity"*: *cst. s.* קְרֵיבוּתּ Cd Gn 37:27, קריבות E Gn 37:27; /*rabbu*, *rabbuta/ "greatness"*: 3 *m.s.* כרבוותהּ E Gn 43:33;[386] /*šeru?*, *šeruta/ "meal"*: *abs. s.* שֵׁירוּ E Gn 29:22; *det. s.* שֵׁירוּתָא Cd Gn 43:16;ˊ שֵׁירוּתָא Cd Gn 43:25;ˊ also /*maštu/ "feast"* (§104m), /*telladu/ "offspring"* (§106b); the fractions /*palgu/ "half"* (§49), /*rab'u/ "quarter"* (§49); the D, C, and Š Verbal Nouns (§§126f-g); /*babhilu?/ "hastily"* (§158b).

**§115 *-īt***

**§115a *III-y*:** /*bɔki*, *bɔkita/ "crying"*: *det. s.* בְּכִיתָא C Gn 35:8, בכיתה F Dt 34:8; /*rebbi*, *rebbita/ "usury"*: *abs. pl.* ורבּיין A Ex 22:24;

**§115b *other nouns*:** /*zar'i*, *zar'ita/ "family"*: *cst. pl.* לְזַרְעִיַת Cd Gn 48:4;[387] זַרְעִיַת Cd Gn 48:11; 2 *m.pl.* לזרעיתבון AA₁ Ex 12:21;ˊ[388] /*zehori*, *zehorita/*[389] *"crimson"*: *abs. s.* זְחוֹרִיˊ E Gn 38:28, דְּזְחוֹרִי AA Nu 19:6;ˊ /*šahpi*, *šahpita?/ "consumption"*: *det.s.* ובשׁוחפיתה D Dt 28:22;[390] /*dallaqi?*, *dallaqita/ "inflammation"*: *det. s.* ובדַלְקִיתָהּ D Dt 28:22;[391] /*hebri*, *hebrita/*[392] *"wound"*: *abs. s.* חֻבַרˊ A Ex 21:25, חָבָרְ A Ex 21:25;ˊ /*kopɔpit?*, *kopɔpita?/*[393] *"spelt?"*: *det. pl.* וכֻפָּפְיָתָא Cd Ex 9:32; /*peruki?*, *perukita?/*[394] *"grist"*: *abs. pl.?* ופירובּין F Lv 23:14; /*qɔlupi?*, *qɔlupita?/*[395] *"peel, husk"*: *det. s.?* קלֻוותה E Gn 30:37;[396] *abs. pl.* קלֻופּין E Gn 30:37; also /*mašri/ "camp"* (§104m), /*mɔrabbɔyani/ "nurse"* (§110i), /*šalhabi/ "flame"* (§105b), /*taksi/ "cover"* (§106c).

*Nouns of Foreign Origin*

**§116 *Greek***

Greek words (including Latin words via Greek) are common in these fragments, as is expected in a dialect from the Syro-Palestine region.[397] Examples of each loanword are ἀήρ *"air"*: *abs. s.* בְּאָיֵר F Ex 20:2; ὄχλος *"multitude, crowd, people"*: *abs. pl.* דְּאָכְלְסָין B Gn 4:10, אוכְלַסין Cd Gn 48:4; ὄγμος *"ploughed furrow"*: *det. s.* אומנא F Lv 23:22; ἀνάκη *"distress"*: *abs. s. or 1 s.?* אָניכִּי E Gn 38:25;ˊ στολή *"robe, garment"*:[398] *abs. s.* אוֹסטֹלִיˊ A Ex 22:8;[399] *det. s. or 3 m.s.?* אסטליתה E Gn 9:23, אָסְטְלִיתָהּ A Ex 22:26; ἐπίτροπος *"manager, guardian"*: *abs. s.* אפיטרופֹסˊ E Gn 39:4, אפטרפוֹסˊ E Gn 39:5; ἀννώνα, *Lat. annona "tax"*: *abs. pl.* ארתונין Z Gn 49:15; γέρδιος *"weaver"*: *abs. s.* גַּרְדִיˊ B Ex 39:27 (with Aramaic suffix /-ay/);[400] δῶρον *"gift"*: *abs. s.* דוֹרן B Gn 4:4; διπλᾶ, *Lat. dupla "double"*: *abs. s.* בְּדִיפְלָה A Ex 22:3,[401] בדיפלה A Ex 22:6;ˊ בְּדִיפְלָא A Ex 22:8; ζυγόν *"wife"*: *abs. s.* זוּג B Gn 2:18; 3 *m.s.* וְזוּגהּ C Gn 35:9; ζώνη *"belt, armor"*: *abs. s.* זוֹתׄˊ E Gn 41:44;ˊ κάλυξ, *Lat. calyx "goblet"*: *det. s.* כְּלִיתָא Cd Gn 44:12; 1 *s.* כְּלִידׄ E Gn 44:2;ˊ λεγεών, *Lat. legio "legion"*: *abs. pl.* לִיגְיוֹנִין H Gn 15:1; Λυβδικός, *Lat. Libycus "Libyan ass"*: *abs. pl.* ולובַּדְקָין C Gn 32:16; νόμος *"custom, manner"*: *cst. s.* כְּנִימֹוס A Ex 21:7; σημεῖον *"sign"*: *abs. s.* סֵימָן B Gn 4:15; *cst. s.* סימן E Gn 9:12; σπεκουλάτωρ, *Lat. speculator*

*"executioner": det. pl.* סְפִיקְלַטְרֵייה E Gn 39:1,ˆ[402] סְפִיקְלַטְרִיה E Gn 41:10,ˆ
ספקלטרִיה E Gn 41:12; πατροβουλή *"head of council":* פטיר בולי F Lv 22:27;[403]
φιάλη *"cup": det. s. or 3 m.s.?* פיילִיתה E Gn 40:12;ˆ πέλαγος *"sea": abs. s.*
ובּ]פליגוס W Ex 15:8; παλάτιον, *Lat. palatium "palace": abs. s.* פְּלָטִיןˆ Cd Gn
43:16, פְּלָטִין Cd Gn 43:16; πραιτώριον, *Lat. praetorium "palace": abs. s.*
לַפָּלָטוֹרִין Cd Gn 43:18; παραγαύδης, *Lat. paragauda "garment, tunic".*[404] *det. s.*
פְּרָגוֹדָאˆ Cd Gn 37:23, פרגודה E Gn 37:32; *3 m.s.* פְּרָגוּדֵ֫ה Cd Gn 37:23, פרגודה E
Gn 37:23;ˆ φερνή *"dowry": abs. s.* פְּרֵן C Gn 34:12; *cst. pl.* וכפרנֵי A Ex 22:16;[405]
πρόνος *"manager".*[406] *abs. pl.* פרתסין E Gn 40:12; πόρπη חח *"hook, clasp": 3 m.s.*
פָּרְפֵּז B Ex 39:33; κοιτών *"room, bedroom": det. s.* קיטוֹנָא Cd Gn 43:30, לקיטוֹנֵה
E Gn 43:30; κῆνσος, *Lat. census "fine, penalty".*[407] *abs. s.* קָנְסֵ A Ex 21:30; θήאח
*"sheath, receptacle": abs. s.* תֵּיקָה לְתֵיקָה Z Gn 44:18;[408] θυρεός *"shield": abs. s.*
תְּרִיס H Gn 15:1.

**§117** *Persian*

There are few nouns of Persian origin:[409] *Per. zen "arms": det. s.* זֵיְנֵהּ Z Gn
49:5; *Per. hamyan "belt, girdle": det. s.* הֶמְיָנָאˆ B Ex 39:29; *Per. zang "bell": abs.*
*s.* זֵיגוֹן B Ex 39:26, זֵיגוֹן B Ex 39:26 (with an Aramaic diminutive ending); *Per.*
*patigām "word, saying": abs. s.* פתגם H Gn 15:1; *det. s.* פִּתְגָמָא C Gn 32:20; *2*
*m.s.* כפתגמך E Gn 30:34; *3 m.s.* לפתגמֵיה Cd Ex 9:21; *cst. pl.* פִּתְגָמֵיˆ D Dt 27:8; *det.*
*pl.* פתגמייה E Gn 39:7; *Per. rāz "secret": det. pl.* חִיזוֹן] Z Gn 49:1; *Per. vātrang*
*"citron, orange": abs. pl.* תרוגין F Lv 23:40; *Per. šast-gōn "of sixty colors"; abs.*
*pl.* דסעטׂגוּגין B Ex 39:34, "multicolored,"[410] and *Per. drgš "bed": det. s.* דַּרְגְשָׁא
Cd Gn 47:31, *3 m.s.* דַּרְגְּשֵׁה Cd Gn 48:2.[411]

**§118** *Akkadian*

Nouns borrowed into Aramaic from Akkadian (including Sumerian words
via Akkadian)[412] are *Akk. /asū/, Sum. A.ZU "physician"* (> *Aramaic*
*"healing"):*[413] *abs. s.* אָסוּ D Dt 28:27; *Akk. /argamannu/ "purple": det. s.*
וארגְוונא B Ex 39:24, וְאַרְגְּוָנָא B Ex 39:29; *Akk. /nisannu/ "month of Nisan": abs.*
*s.* ניסן HH Ex 12:3; *Akk. /bel dabābi/ "enemy": det. s.* דבביא ובעיל W Ex 15:9; *2*
*m.s.* בעלי דבבֵיך H Gn 15:1; *3 m.pl.* דבביהון]בעלי Z Gn 49:6; *Akk. /zīmu/ "luster,*
*countenance": 3 m.pl.* זיוְהון F Dt 34:7; *3 f.pl.* זיוְהֵין B Gn 4:5, זוְהֵין B Gn 4:6; *Akk.*
*/zūzu/ "zuz": abs. pl.* זוזין E Gn 37:28; *Akk. /simānu/ "time".*[414] *abs. s.* זְמַןˆ Bd
Gn 8:7, זְמָןˆ D Dt 28:21; *cst. s.* זמן F Lv 23:14; *det. s.* זִמְנָהˆ B Gn 2:23, זִמְנָאˆ Cd
Gn 44:18; *abs. pl.* זְמִנִין C Gn 31:41; *cst. pl.* בִזְמְנֵי F Nu 28:26; *3 m.pl.* בזמניהון F Lv
23:4; *Akk. /kussū/, Sum.* ᵍⁱˢGU.ZA "chair":[415] *cst. s.* בורסי AA₁ Ex 12:29, כרסי
AA₂ Ex 12:29; *Akk. /manzaltu/ "star position, luck": det. s. or 3 m.s.?* במזלה E
Gn 29:17; *Akk. /muškēnu/ "destitute": det. pl.* מסכינייה A Ex 22:24, למסכינייא F
Lv 23:22; *Akk. /miksu/ "allotment": cst. s.* במכסת AA₁ Ex 12:4; *Akk.*
*/nuḫatimmu/ "baker".*[416] *abs. s.* נחתום E Gn 40:17; *det. pl.* נחתומייה E Gn 41:10;
*Akk. /nikassu/ "property": abs. pl.* נכסין AA₁ Ex 12:38; *cst. pl.* נכסי E Gn 31:18;
*2 m.s.* נכסיך E Gn 30:29;ˆ *3 m.s.* נכסו E Gn 31:9,18; *Akk. /qudāšu/ "earring":*
*abs. pl.* וְקדָשִׁין C Gn 34:12;[417] *Akk. /šutappu/, Sum. TAB.BA "partner": abs. pl.*
שותפין F Ex 20:13 (2x); *Akk. /tamkaru/ "merchant": abs. pl.* תַּגָרִין Cd Gn
37:28.ˆ Other nouns which may have entered Aramaic via Akkadian are *det. s.*

162

פָּתוֹרָא B Ex 39:36,ˆ "the table"[418] and *det. s.* וְשׁוֹשָׁפָא Cd Gn 38:25, "the cloak";[419] *2 m.s.* וְשׁוֹשָׁפָּךְ Cd Gn 38:18; *3 m.pl.* בשׁוֹשְׁפָּתְהוֹן AA₁ Ex 12:34; *det. s.* אַתּוֹנָ[א] F Ex 19:18, "the oven"; *abs. s.* ספר AA₁ Ex 17:14, "book."[420]

**§119 Hebrew**

There are a considerable number of nouns of ultimate Hebrew origin.[421]

**§119a** The following terms belong to the realm of religion and cultic observance: Heb. /bēt midrāš/ "*synagogue*": *det. pl.* בבתי מדרשׁייה E Gn 30:13; Heb. /bēt miqdāš/ "*Temple*": *abs. s.* בית מקדשׁ E Gn 28:22; *2 m.s.* בית מקדשָׁךְ W Ex 15:17; Heb. /dibbēr/ "*Commandment*": *det. s.* דִּבֵּירָה F Ex 20:2; *det. pl.* דִּבֵּירַיָה D Dt 5:19; *3 m.s.* דִּבֵּירוֹי D Dt 5:21; Heb. /ḥaṭṭat/ "*sin offering*": *det. s.* חטאתא AA Nu 19:9,17; Heb. /kəhunnā/ "*priesthood*": *det. s.* וכֹהֲנְתָה Z Gn 49:3; Heb. /kippurim/ "*atonement*": *det. pl.* כיפורייה F Lv 23:28,30, כיפוריה F Lv 23:27; Heb. /kətubbā/ "*marriage contract*": *1 pl.* כתובתן E Gn 31:15; Heb. /lulāb, lolāb/[422] "*palm branch*": *abs. pl.* לולבין F Lv 23:40;ˆ Heb. /nəbu'ā/ "*prophecy*": *abs. s.* נָבוּ H Gn 15:1;[423] *2 m.s.* בנבואתך F Ex 19:9; Heb. /məzuzā/ "*doorpost*": *det. pl.* מזוזיתה AA₁ Ex 12:7, מזוזִיתא AA₁ Ex 12:22; Heb. /minḥā/ "*meal offering*": *abs. s.* מִנְחָה F Nu 28:26; *3 m.s.* ומנחתיה F Lv 23:13; *3 m.pl.* ומנְחָתְהוֹן F Nu 28:28; Heb. /miṣwā/ "*command*": *abs. pl.* מִצְוַן H Gn 15:1; *det. pl.* מִצְוָתָה D Dt 27:1; *1 s.* מִצְוָתִי D Dt 5:26; *3 m.s.* מִצְוָתֵיה D Dt 26:18; *3 f.s.* מצְוָתָהּ F Ex 20:6; Heb. /solet/ "*fine flour*": *abs. s.* סלת F Lv 23:17, סוֹלֶת F Nu 28:28;[424] Heb. /pāroket/ "*curtain*": *det. s.* פָּרֻכ[תה] B Ex 39:34; Heb. /šabbāt/ "*Sabbath, week*":[425] *abs. s.* שׁבה F Lv 23:3 (2x), שׁוּבָה F Ex 20:10;[426] *cst. s.* שׁבת F Lv 23:24,32; *det. s.* דשׁוּבתָה F Ex 20:8; *abs. pl.* שׁבין F Lv 23:15; *2 m.pl.* שׁוֹביכן F Lv 23:32; Heb. /šabbāton/ "*Sabbath observance*":[427] *abs. s.* שׁבתן F Lv 23:24,32; Heb. /šopār/ "*horn*":[428] *det. s.* דשׁיפורא F Ex 19:13, דשׁיפורה F Ex 19:19; Heb. /šəkinā/ "*Divine Presence*": *abs. s.* שׁכינה W Ex 15:17;[429] *cst. s.* שׁכינת W Ex 15:17; *3 m.s.* שׁכינתֵיה C Gn 35:13; Heb. /šəlāmim/ "*peace offering*": *abs. pl.* שׁלמין AA Dt 27:7; Heb. /hattāmid/ "*the continual*":[430] *det. s.* תמידה F Nu 28:23,24.

**§119b** Other nouns of Hebrew origin are Heb. /'ēzob/ "*hyssop*":[431] *abs. s.* אזוב AA Nu19:18, דאיזוב AA₂ Ex 12:22; Heb. /da'at/ "*knowledge, mind*": *det. s.* דַּעְתָּא B Gn 3:3; *1 s.* דעתי E Gn 31:26; *3 m.s.* דעתיה E Gn 31:20: Heb. /hod/ "*glory*": *2 m.s.* וְהוֹדָךְ C Gn 35:9; Heb. /yəsod/ "*foundation*": *cst. pl.* יסדי E Gn 28:18; Heb. /kuttonet, kətonet, pl. kuttənot, kotnot/ "*shirt*":[432] *det. s.* כּוּתנתא Cd Gn 37:31; *3 m.s.* כָּתְנְתֵיה Cd Gn 37:31, כְּתוּנְתֵּיהּ Cd Gn 37:32,[433] כְּתָנְתיה Cd Gn 37:33, כֻּתְּנֵיה Cd Gn 38:26; Heb. /mə'il/ "*coat*": *det. s.* דַּמְעִילָא B Ex 39:24;ˆ דַּמְעִילָא B Ex 39:26; Heb. /māror/ "*bitter herb*":[434] *abs. pl.* מרורין AA₁ Ex 12:8; Heb. /marṣē'/ "*awl*": *det. s.* במרצעה A Ex 21:6;[435] Heb. /nā'im/ "*pleasant*": *abs. s.* וְנָעים F Ex 19:19; Heb. /səgullā/ "*property, wealth*":[436] *abs. s.* סְגֻלָּה D Dt 26:18, סגולה F Ex 19:5; Heb. /'ēṣā/ "*advice*":[437] *abs. s.* בְעֵיצָא C Gn 34:13, עצה E Gn 29:22; Heb. /nēs/ "*sign, miracle*":[438] *det. s.* נסא A Ex 4:8; *abs. pl.* ניסין H Gn 15:2; Heb. /pəsul/ "*blemish*":[439] *det. s.* פסלה Z Gn 49:2, פסולה Z Gn 49:2; Heb. /qiṭor/ "*thick smoke*": *cst. s.* כקיטור F Ex 19:18; Heb. /šir/ "*song*": *abs. pl.* ובשׁירין E Gn 31:27; Heb. /təhom/ "*abyss*": *abs. s.* תהוֹם E Gn 7:1; *det. s.* תְהוֹמָה

Bd Gn 8:2; *det. pl.* תהומיא W Ex 15:8; also *Heb.* /rāšim/ "heads" (§68c) and *Heb.* /rimmon/ "pomegranate"?[440]

§119c  Sporadic Hebraisms[441] are *Heb.* /'ēš/ "fire": *abs. s.* אֵשׁ A Ex 22:5 (§99a); *Heb.* /ben/ "son": *cst. s.* בֶן E Gn 29:5 (§60a); *Heb.* /ḥəmor/ "he-ass": *abs. s.* חמור A Ex 22:9 (§80a); *Heb.* /laylā/ "night": *abs. s.* בליילה E Gn 30:16 (§102).

§119d  The few examples of *maqol* and *məqol* nouns in Aramaic dialects may be due to the influence of the Hebrew class /māqol/ (the cognate Aramaic class is *məqāl*).[442] Examples of these noun classes in these fragments are *Heb.* /mādor/ "dwelling": *cst. s.* לְמדור W Ex 15:13; *2 m.pl.* מדוריכן F Lv 23:3, מדורכן F Lv 23:21; *Heb.* /māzon/ "food": *abs. s.* מָזון Cd Gn 43:20, מָזון Cd Gn 44:1; *Heb.* /mārom/ "height": *det. s.* מְרומָא C Gn 32:27, מרומא W Ex 15:11; *det. pl.* מרוממיה F Lv 22:27;[443] *Heb.* /māḥol/ "dance": *det. pl.* ובחולתא W Ex 15:20;[444] and /māmon/ "wealth" (II-w/y?)[445] *abs. s.* ודמומן A Ex 21:30; *3 m.pl.* ממונהון C Gn 34:23.

§119e  There are four nouns with suffixed /-on/[446] that have been borrowed from Hebrew. Three of the nouns belong to the Hebrew /qittālon/ pattern and have been Aramaized into *qVtlon* forms: *Heb.* /bizzāyon/ "disgrace": *abs. s.* לְבָזָיון Cd Gn 38:23; *Heb.* /'ērābon/ "pledge":[447] *abs. s.* עֶרְבֹּון Cd Gn 38:17, עֶרְבֹן E Gn 38:17 (*Heb. form) det. s.* עֶרְבֹונָה Cd Gn 38:18, עֶרְבֹונָא Cd Gn 38:20; *Heb.* /'issāron/ "tenth": *abs. s.* עֶשׂרון F Nu 28:29; *abs. pl.* עֶשׂרותין F Nu 28:28. The fourth example belongs to the Heb. /qitlon/ pattern—*Heb.* /pitron/[448] "interpretation": *cst. s.* כפתרון E Gn 41:11; *det. s. or 3 m.s.?* פֶּתְרונה E Gn 40:12, פתרונה E Gn 40:12;[449] *det. pl.* פתרוניה E Gn 40:8.

§119f  The class /qətela, qəteləta/ may be borrowed from Hebrew; however, even though some of the nouns belonging to this class have /qətēlā/ parallels in Hebrew, other nouns can be explained as the result of internal Aramaic developments (§77c, n.200).

§119g  The nouns /*bəkor, bəkora/ "first-born" and /*šəqop?, šəqopa?/ "threshold" may be Hebraisms in these fragments; however, here, too, internal Aramaic processes may have been at work. (§76a, nn.190,192)

§119h  In שבעיכון F Nu 28:26, "your weeks" and שמיא H Gn 15:1, "the heavens" (cf. שְׁמיָא Bd Gn 7:19) one cannot ascertain whether __ reflects /ə/,[450] a Hebraism on the part of the vocalizer, or a Hebraism in the language itself. Similarly, it is difficult to determine whether ותיישין C Gn 32:15, "and the he-goats" reflects a Hebraism only in pointing or also in speech (§67f, n.102). The same is true for the examples of גְּדִי "kid" (§§9i, 67h,n.104), באר, באיר "well" (§68c, n.116), and תאנין "figs" (§68d, n.119). Hebrew appears to have influenced the pointing of בְּלָשׁ C Gn 31:47, "tongue" (§99a, n.302) and may have been responsible for the final vowel of מִרעֶה Cd Gn 47:4, "pasture" (§104l, n.330), and the initial vowel of אִילָני B Gn 3:1, "trees" (§10d, n.69).

§119i  The *3 f.s.* וּשְׁלֶיוְתה Z Gn 49:1, "and her rest" appears to be a de-adjectival noun based on the Hebrew Participle /šālēw/.[451] The *det. s.* צְפִיתָא C Gn 31:49, "and the watch-post" reflects a Hebrew use of *ṣpy.[452]

164

§119j Note the nouns /mabbol?, mabbola/[453] "flood" and /*tebu, tebuta/ "ark," which have entered Jewish Targumim from Hebrew, but whose origins are uncertain:[454] abs. s. מבול E Gn 9:11; det. s. מַבּוּלָה Bd Gn 7:17; דְמַבּוּלָה Bd Gn 8:2; det. s. תֵּיבוּתָה Bd Gn 7:17, תֵּיבוּתָה Bd Gn 8:1. The nouns det. s. הינה F Lv 23:13, "hin," and the det. s. גוֹמְיָה E Gn 41:18, "reeds" have entered the Jewish Targumim from Hebrew but are of ultimate Egyptian origin.[455]

§120 Culture words

Nouns of wide geographical distribution and whose origins are obscure are 3 f.s. בּוּצִינֵיה B Ex 39:37, "candle, lamp";[456] abs. s. לטום Cd Gn 37:25, "ladanum," ולטום E Gn 37:25;[457] 3 m.s. סוסי E Gn 41:44, "horse";[458] det. s. לסוסיה Z Gn 49:17;[459] abs. pl. סוסותא W Ex 15:19; abs. s. דפרזל AA Dt 27:5, "iron";[460] det. s. פרזלא F Ex 20:22; פַּרְזְלָה D Dt 28:23.

§121 /rabbun/ "master"

The occurrences of /rabbun/ "master" (usually referring to God) merit special comment. This oft-discussed word[461] appears as /ribbon/ in Targum Onqelos (also /ribbun/ in the Editio Sabbioneta) and the Babylonian tradition of Rabbinic Hebrew. One finds, however, rabbon or rabbun in Palestinian sources—the Palestinian tradition of Rabbinic Hebrew, Samaritan Aramaic, and in Greek transcription in the New Testament. The Cairo Genizah form /rabbun/ derives from *rabbān/*rabbon, but appears to have gone over to the *qattūl class for morpho-semantic reasons—contamination with the divine epithets, /ḥannun/ "gracious" and /raḥum/ merciful.[462] Examples of /rabbun/ are cst. s. רבון C Gn 35:9, בְּרַבּוּן Cd Gn 38:25, בְּרַבּוּן Cd Gn 37:33; det. s. or 3 f.s.? דרבותה A Ex 21:8; 1 s. לְרַבּוּנִי C Gn 32:19, רַבּוּנִי Cd Gn 44:18; 2 m.s. וְרַבּוּנָךְ Cd Gn 44:8; 3 m.s. רַבּוּנֵה A Ex 21:4; לְרַבּוּנָה A Ex 21:32; 1 pl. לרבונן Cd Gn 44:20.

D. Verbs

§122 Inventory of Verbal Forms

The verbal system of the Cairo Genizah fragments is made up of the Perfect, Imperfect, Imperative, Infinitive, the Active and Passive Participles, an undeveloped Participial Conjugation, and Compound Forms containing an auxiliary verb, הוי, "to be." Capitalized terms refer to the morphological forms and not to their functions.

§123 Perfect

§123a The inflectional suffixes of the Perfect are

| 3 m.s. | Ø |
| 3 f.s. | /-at/ |
| 2 m.s. | /-t/ (/-ta/) |
| 2 f.s. | /*-t/ |
| 1 s. | /-et/ |
| 3 m.pl. | /-u/ (/-un/; III-w/y/' : /-on/) |
| 3 f.pl. | /-en/ |

| 2 m.pl. | /-ton/ |
|---|---|
| 2 f.pl. | /-ten/ |
| 1 pl. | /-nan/ |

On the pointing of the 3 m.pl. and 2 m.pl. suffixes, see §11t.

**§123b** There is only one example of the suffix /-ta/: אלִדְתָּ Z Gn 48:6, "you begat" (cf. אולְידְתָּ Cd Gn 48:6). This suffix is found alongside /-t/ in Biblical Aramaic, Targum Onqelos, the Genesis Apocryphon, and Samaritan Aramaic.[1] The fluctuation of *t* and *ta* in these sources need not be taken as Hebraisms, but rather as the reflexes of the *anceps* Proto-Aramaic vowel.

**§123c** *1 s.* As has long been observed for Biblical Aramaic and Syriac, the origin of /-et/ lies in the anaptyctic vowel that resolved the final consonantal cluster created after the loss of final short vowels, e.g., G *qatáltu > *qatált > *qatálit > qatlét.[2] Ma'lula[3] and Samaritan Aramaic[4] also demonstrate this Proto-Aramaic development. In Targum Onqelos (G /qətálit/) and Babylonian Talmudic Aramaic (G /qətálit/, /qətáli/), on the other hand, the 1 s. was remodeled on the pattern of the 3 m.s. /qətal/ to which the original anaptyctic vowel was re-added.[5]

**§123d** *1 s.* There are four examples of /-un/ on verbs: וְאֶתְגְּבָּרוּן Bd Gn 7:24, "they prevailed" (cf. וְאִגְּבָּרוּ Bd Gn 7:18); קמון W Ex 15:8, "they arose"; ואתקפון AA₁ Ex 12:33, "and they grew strong"; מיתון AA Nu 20:3, "they died." The /-n/ of this suffix was probably extended from the 3 m.pl. suffix of verbs III-w/y/', although it is also possible that it was extended from the 3 m.pl. suffix /-un/ on the Imperfect (strong verbs) and from the 3 m.pl. Independent Pronoun /'ennun?/.[6]

The 3 f.pl. suffix /-en/ was probably extended from the 3 f.pl. Independent pronoun /'ennen?/[7] and possibly from the 2 f.pl. /-ten/ of the Perfect.

**§123e** In verbs III-w/y/', the *n* of /-on/ of the Imperfect 3 m.pl. was extended to the Perfect 3 m.pl.[8] The 3 m.pl. suffix /-on/ with verbs III-w/y/' is first attested in the Genesis Apocryphon. It is well attested in both the Western and Eastern branches of Late Aramaic. Tal has argued that the forms ין and ין in Galilean Aramaic are the result of a phonetic process whereby a paragogic /n/ was suffixed to final long vowels.[9] This explanation, however, is unsatisfactory since it does not relate these suffixes to the evidence from other Late Aramaic sources, namely Syriac and Mandaic, in which the forms /qətalun/, /qətalen/ exist side by side with /qətal/ "they killed" (m. and f.), and which must be understood as /qetal/ + /-un/, and /qetal/ + /-en/. Further evidence is found in verbs III-w/y/' in Syriac. One finds the forms /rəma'un/, /rəmawun/ and /rəmayen/ (alongside original /rəmaw/ and /rəmay/) instead of the forms *rəmawn (> *rəmon?) and *rəmayn(> *rəmen?).

**§123f** The distribution in the Cairo Genizah fragments of /-u/ and /-en/ with strong verbs and /-on/ and /-en/ with verbs III-w/y/' is unique to Aramaic dialects.[10]

166

§123g *1 pl.* The suffix /-nan/ is also attested in the other Palestinian Targumim,[11] Galilean Aramaic,[12] Palestinian Syriac,[13] Samaritan Aramaic,[14] Syriac,[15] and Babylonian Talmudic Aramaic.[16] The final /-n/ (or /-an/) of this form may have been extended from the 1 pl. Independent Pronoun /'ənan/ and the 1 pl. pronominal suffix /-an/ with nouns.

§124 *Imperfect*

§124a The inflectional affixes of the Imperfect are

| | |
|---|---|
| *3 m.s.* | /yV-/ |
| *3 f.s.* | /tV-/ |
| *2 m.s.* | /tV-/ |
| *2 f.s.* | /*tV-...-in/ |
| *1 s.* | /'V-/, /nV-/ |
| *3 m.pl.* | /yV-...-un/ (III-w/y/':/-on/) |
| *3 f.pl.* | /yV-...-an/ |
| *2 m.pl.* | /tV-...-un/ (III-w/y/':/-on/) |
| *2 f.pl.* | /*tV-...-an/ |
| *1 pl.* | /nV-/, /nV-...-a/ |

The preformative vowel is /e/ in G,Gt,D,Dt and Ct; /ə/ in D; /a/ in /C/; /o/ in C verbs I-w.

§124b *1 s.* Nine of the eleven examples[17] of the 1 s. prefix /nV-/ are found in interpolated passages or with verbs that are interpolated into the text. All of the examples are in modal contexts: הא מני הינון בנייה דנתן ליך בנין E Gn 30:2, "are these sons from me that I should give you sons?"; [18] היא תילַד ואנה אֲרַבָּה [19] וּנֵתְבְּנֵי לְהֹד אנה מנה E Gn 30:3, "she will give birth so that I, too, shall raise and be built up by her"; הא מיתי[20] כען ונזדמן לוותיך E Gn 38:16, "come now and let me have intercourse with you"; טב לי נבהות בעלמה הֵן ולא נבהות בעלמה דאתי E Gn 38:26, "it is better that I should be ashamed in this world than in the world to come": טב לי יקד באשא טפייה בעלמה הדן ולא ניקד באשה אכלה אשא לעלמה דאתי E Gn 38:26, "it is better that I should burn in an extinguishable fire in this world than I should burn in a fire which devours fire in the world to come"; ואיך אעבד בישתה רובתה הדה ונתחייב ביה קדם י[°] E Gn 39:9, "and how can I commit this great evil and be guilty of it before God?"; אין לא אייתיית---נהוי מרחק E Gn 43:9, "If I do not bring back..., let me be banished"; נדי תשבּח W Ex 15:21, "I will thank and praise!"; בהדה זמנה אחדה תשבח קדם יֹי E Gn 29:35, "this time will I thank and praise the Lord!"

§124c The 1 s. prefix /'V-/, on the other hand, is found in both non-modal (65x) and modal (13x) contexts.[21] An example of a non-modal context is וְאֶפְרֹק יתכן Cd Ex 6:6, "and I shall save you"; an example of a modal context is וְאֶרְעֵי סְבַּר-אַפֹּי C Gn 32:21, "and I will appease his countenance" (see also אֲרַבָּה and אחדה above).

§124d The 1 s. prefix /nV-/ is known from other Aramaic sources in Syria-Palestine. It occurs occasionally in the other Palestinin Targumim and in Galilean Aramaic.[22] J. Lund has demonstrated that this prefix is used only to express modality in the non-translation portions of Targum Neophyti, whereas /'V-/ is used to express both modality and futurity.[23] Dalman pointed out that /nV-/ was modally conditioned, believing that the origin of the form was the 1 pl. prefix /nV-/: "Plural der selbstermunterung dessen häufiger Gerbrauch für die in ihm liegende Mehrzahl vollständig abgestumpft hatte."[24] Kutscher disagreed, regarding this form as a fusion of the Independent personal pronoun and the Imperfect, i.e., אנה אטקל.[25] /nV-/ functions as both the 1 s. and 1 pl. prefix in Ma'lula.[26] It has been argued that a 1 s. prefix /nV-/ also occurs in Biblical Aramaic: דְּנָה חֶלְמָא וּפִשְׁרֵהּ נֵאמַר Dn 2:36.[27]

§124e   This prefix is poorly attested in one Aramaic source outside of Syria-Palestine—Yemenite manuscripts of the Babylonian Talmud.[28]

§124f   The 1 s. prefix /nV-/ is also found in some mediaeval Arabic texts as well as certain modern Arabic dialects.[29] In these sources it stands in contast with the 1 pl. affixes /nV-...-u/. Two different explanations have been proposed as to the origin of this phenomenon in Arabic: 1) it is the fusion of the 1 s. Independent personal pronoun and the 1 s. Imperfect;[30] 2) it is the result of analogy to tqtlu (2 m.pl.) and yqtlu (3 m.pl.) yielding nqtlu (1 pl.), followed by a back-formation producing the s. nqtl. The second of these two proposals is most widely held.[31] It cannot, however, explain the phenomenon in Aramaic since no 1 pl. nqtlu is attested in Aramaic.

§124g   The 1 s. prefix /nV-/ is also attested in the Rabbinic Hebrew of Palestinian Amoraim where it is thought to be the result of Galilean Aramaic influence.[32] A few occurrences of nqtlu are also attested in Rabbinic Hebrew and are explained as either scribal errors or the influence of Judaeo-Arabic dialects.[33]

§124h   One possible explanation of the 1 s. prefix /nV-/ in Aramaic is related to the modal *lV- particle. Perhaps nqtl (1 s.) comes from *lV- (particle) + *'Vqtul (1 s. Imperfect) > *lVqtul > *nVqtul. There may be an exact parallel in Amharic where Ge'ez la (particle) + 'əqtal (subjunctive/jussive, 1 s.) becomes the 1 s. jussive form ləqtal in Amharic, whereas the jussive forms of other persons do not show the initial lV-.[34]

§124i   1 pl. There are three examples of what appears to be the Hebrew Cohortative נקטלה: וכדון אתן תקטל ויתיה ונטלקה יתה E Gn 37:20, "Come now let us kill him and let us throw him" (MT וְנַשְׁלִכֵהוּ וְנַהַרְגֵהוּ וּלְכוּ וְעַתָּה); אתון ונזבנה יתה E Gn 37:27, "Come let us sell him" (MT וְנִמְכְּרֶנּוּ לְכוּ); לֵית לן מה מה נקרבה F Lv 22:27, "we have nothing to sacrifice" (interpolated). Whereas the verbs in the first two passages have cohortative (i.e., modal) functions, the verb in the third passage does not.[35]

§124j   The more frequent 1 pl. prefix /nV-/ is used to express both modality (16x) and futurity (12x) in these texts. An example of the modal use is לא- נִקְטֹל יָתֵיהּ וְנִתְחַיַּב בְּאַדְמֵיהּ Cd Gn 37:21, "let us not kill him and be guilty of his blood" (MT לֹא נַכֶּנּוּ נָפֶשׁ); an example of a non-modal use is וְנִתֵּן יַת־בְּנָתַן לְכוֹן C Gn 34:16, "and we shall give our daughters to you" (MT וְנָתַנּוּ אֶת־בְּנֹתֵינוּ לָכֶם).

§124k This Cohortative form is also attested in the other Palestinian Targumim where it expresses modality,[36] which, however, is usually expressed by the regular Imperfect form.[37] There may also be Cohortative forms in Samaritan Aramaic.[38] The Cohortative form is clearly a borrowing from Hebrew in these sources.

§124l  *3 f.pl.* There are examples of the Imperfect 3 f.pl. with the prefix /tV-/ (as in Hebrew) in place of Aramaic /yV-/.[39] These examples are found in verses where the Masoretic text has *tiqtolnā* and clearly are in imitation of the underlying Hebrew form: תהוין F Lv 23:15, "they will be" (MT תִּהְיֶינָה); תהודין F Lv 23:17 (MT תִּהְיֶ֫נָה); תתאפיין F Lv 23:17, "they will be baked" (MT תֵּאָפֶ֫ינָה).

§125  *Imperative*
The inflectional suffixes of the Imperative are

|  |  |
|---|---|
| *m.s.* | ∅ |
| *f.s.* | /-i/ |
| *m.pl.* | /-u/ (III-w/y/':/-on/) |
| *f.pl.* | /*-en?/ |

As is the case with the suffixes of the Perfect, no other dialect shows the same distribution of /-u/ (strong verb) and /-on/ (III-w/y/').[40]

§126  *Infinitive, Verbal Noun*
§126a  The forms of the Infinitive are

|  |  |
|---|---|
| G | /meqtol/ (/meqtal/, /meqtel/) |
| D | /məqattala/ |
| C | /maqtala/ |
| Gt | /metqətala/ |
| Dt | /metqattala/ |
| Ct | /*mettaqtala/ |

§126b  A prefixed /lV-/ is found on these forms except when they are used to translate the Infinitive Absolute of the Masoretic text,[41] e.g., מִתקְנֹסָה יִתקְנֹס A Ex 21:20, "he shall surely be punished" (MT נָקֹם יִנָּקֵם). Object pronominal suffixes are not attested on the Infinitive, with one exception, וּלרוֹמָ[א]מֹ֫וְך D Dt 26:19, "to raise you up."[42]

§126c  The orthography למקבל אגרי E Gn 30:33, "to receive my wage" reflects the metanalysis of the sandhi pronunciation of the D Infinitive *lamqabbəla 'agri > lamqabbəlagri* into /lamqabbəl 'agri/.[43]

§126d  This inventory of forms appears to be identical to that reflected in the consonantal text of Galilean Aramaic manuscripts.[44]

§126e  The stem vowel of the G Infinitive /meqtVl/ corresponds to the vowel of the G Imperfect. /meqtol/ is the most frequent form.[45]

§126f  The following nouns function as verbal nouns in these fragments:

|  |  |
|---|---|
| G | /maqtal/ (/qətal?/-1x) (/maqtəlu?/-1x) |
| D | /qettol/, /qattalu, qattaluta/ |
| C | /'aqtala, 'aqtaluta/ (/haqtala/) |

§126g  /maqtal/ occurs with the prefixes /bV-/, /kV-/ (/lV-/ is restricted to the Infinitive /meqtol/).[46] There is one example of a *qitāl > /qətal?/ noun functioning as a G verbal noun: חצד ית ובחצדיכן F Lv 23:22, "in your harvesting";[47] and there is one example of a G verbal noun with the preformative /mV-/ and the suffix /-u/: במפקותהון Y Ex 19:1, "in their going forth."

§126h  /qettol/ is the most frequently attested D verbal noun.[48] /qattalut-/ is an archaic D infinitival bound form whose corresponding absolute form should be *qattala. The two attested unbound forms, however, have the shape /qattalu/, which is a back-formation from the bound form: ויבבו F Lv 23:24, "wailing," and דְרַמָיו C Gn 34:13, "of deceiving."

§126i  /'aqtala, 'aqtaluta/ is the archaic C infinitival form. Examples of an archaic C infinitival form with preformative /hV-/ are limited to the forms: הדיא AA Nu 19:9,13,20 "sprinkling" (root *ndy); הודייה F Lv 22:29, "thanksgiving" (root *wdy);[49] see also /haymanut?/ "believing" (§130i).

§126j  Three Š verbal nouns (§130e) are attested: שכלל "perfection," שעבד "enslavement," שעמימו "stupefaction." There is also one Poel verbal noun רוממו "raising" (§130e).

§127  *Active and Passive Participles*

The forms of the Participles are

|  |  | Active | Passive |
|---|---|---|---|
| G m.s. |  | /qatel/ | /qətil/ |
| D m.s. |  | /məqattel/ | /məqattal/ |
| C m.s. |  | /maqtel/ | /*maqtal/ |
| Gt m.s. |  | /metqətel/ |  |
| Dt m.s. |  | /metqattal/ |  |
| Ct m.s. |  | /*mettaqtal/ |  |

There are no examples of a D Passive Participle /məqottal/, which is attested regularly in Targum Onqelos (in the supralinear versions with the exception of verbs II-guttural), and infrequently in Galilean Aramaic, Babylonian Talmudic Aramaic, one manuscript of Babylonian Biblical Aramaic, and Eastern Neo-Syriac dialects.[50] Nor are there examples of a C Passive Participle /moqtal/, which is attested infrequently in Targum Onqelos and Galilean Aramaic.

§128  *Participial Conjugation*

The examples of a Participle with enclitic pronouns are limited to the form הוינא "I was" (/həwena/), which has taken the place of the Perfect 1 s. הוית*, and possibly הוית "you were" (/həwit?/) and הוינן "we were" (/həwenan/). See §§35, 151c.

§129  *Compound Forms*

Compound forms made up of the auxiliary verb הוה and other verbal forms are a salient feature of these fragments.

**§129a** הוי *Perfect* + *Participle:* This compound is frequent, expressing habitual and durative past action, e.g., דהווה אָכֵל E Gn 39:6, "which he used to eat": והוין רעיין E Gn 41:18, "and they (f.pl.) were grazing"; הֲוָה תָנֵן F Ex 19:18, "was smoking"; דהיינן נחתין Z Gn 44:18, "that we have been descending"; הֲוֵת מַשקֵי E Gn 40:13, "I used to give drink."

**§129b** הוי *Imperfect* + *Participle:* This compound is less frequent. It expresses habitual and durative action in the future, e.g., ויהיין מתיחמן E Gn 30:38, "they (f.pl.) will be in heat"; ויהוי כהנה מסָאב AA Nu 19:7, "the priest will be impure"; די יהוי ממני AA Dt 26:3, "who will be appointed"; תהוון צימין F Lv 23:32, "you shall be fasting"; תֶהֱוֵי שָׁלֵיט B Gn 4:7, "you shall rule."

**§129c** הוי *Imperative* + *Participle:* There are three examples of this compound, expressing a durative command: הֱוֹוֹ מזֻמָנין לתלתה יוֹמין F Ex 19:15, "Be prepared for three days" (MT הֱיוּ נכֹנים לשלֹשֶׁת יָמים; note also the periphrastic Imperative in Hebrew); הֲווֹן זְהִירין ית יומא דשובתה F Ex 20:8, "Keep the Sabbath day" (MT זָכוֹר אֶת-יוֹם הַשַּׁבָּת); and הַווּן זַהירין כל גבר מנכון באיקרה דאבוֹן] ודאמה F Ex 20:12, "Guard, each one of you, the honor of his father and his mother" (MT כַּבֵּד אֶת-אָבִיךָ וְאֶת-אִמֶּךָ).

**§129d** הוי *Infinitive* + *Participle:* The examples express durative action: למהווין מתיחמן E Gn 30:41, "so that they (f.pl.) will be in heat"; למהוי מדמיין Z Gn 44:18, "to be likened to"; למהוֵי-מְבָרְכִין C Gn 35:9, "to bless"; למהוֹוֹן-מְבַקרין C Gn 35:9, "to visit."

**§129e** הוי *Participle* + *Participle:* There is one example, expressing durative action in the future: וְתֶהֵי סָן גָלֵא וּמְטַלטַל B Gn 4:14, "and Cain will wander and move about."[51] Note, however, that הֲוֵי (Active Participle) + enclitic pronoun with another Participle expresses habitual or durative action in the past,[52] e.g., הַוֵינָא מְשַׁלֵם, "I used to pay," C Gn 31:39.

**§129f** הוי *Perfect* + *Perfect:* There is one example expressing the pluperfect in an interpolated passage: לא-הֲוָא אַתגֵייה C Gn 35:9, "he had not rested."

**§129g** /'ǝtid/ + *Infinitive or Participle:* Another compound form which occurs in these fragments, עתיד /'ǝtid/ + Infinitive or Participle, marks the future (+ הוה functions as Perfect Infinitive). This form contrasts with the Imperfect, which can mark futurity and modality.[53] There are ten occurrences of this compound in these texts: six with the Infinitive, three with the Participle, and one is followed by a *lacuna.* The following are the examples with the Infinitive: דַהֲווֹן עַתידִין לְמְקַם B Gn 4:10, "who were to arise"; ועתד] יד הוה עתיד למתב AA₁ F Lv 22:33, "who will, by my Word, redeem"; במֵמר למפרוק Ex 12:29, "who was to sit"; הוה עתיד למתב AA₂ Ex 12:29; דעתיד למקום AA₁ Ex 17:16, "who will arise." There is one example of an Infinitive without prefixed /IV-/: דעתיד] פרעה משתי E Gn 40:12, "which Pharoah will drink." The examples with a Participle are עתיד עָבֵד E Gn 41:25, "he will do"; עתידין משתעבדין E Gn 40:12, "they will be enslaved"; ועתידין מתפרקין E Gn 40:12, "and they will be redeemed." Note also ...ישראל דעֻתידין E Gn 40:18.[54]

§129h  Compounds consisting of הוי + Participle are attested from Official Aramaic on and increase in frequency in Late Aramaic dialects.[55] It is noteworthy that they are not a significant feature of Targum Onqelos.[56] The use of הוי + Participle to express habitual and durative action is poorly attested in Biblical Hebrew but is frequent in Rabbinic Hebrew. Compound forms with עתיד indicating futurity are also found in Syriac, Galilean Aramaic, Palestinian Syriac, Samaritan Aramaic, the other Palestinian Targumim, and Rabbinic Hebrew.[57]

§130  *Conjugations*

§130a  The inventory of conjugations consists of G, D, C, Gt, Dt, Ct, Pāel?, Ithpāal?, Poel, Ithpoal, Polel, Ithpolal, Š, Št, Q, Qt.

§130b  The prefix of C in the Perfect is /'V-/.[58] There are forms, however, in which it is difficult to distinguish an intransitive Perfect C verb from an intransitive G verb with prothetic *aleph*,[59] e.g., אַנְהַר Cd Gn 44:3, "(the morning) shone"; אנהרן E Gn 38:25, "(her eyes) shone"[60] (cf.-נְהַר Cd Gn 38:25);[61] אבאיש לְעַמָא Cd Ex 5:23, "it has been bad for the people";[62] וְאִסְתְּ נַהֲרָא Cd Ex 7:21,[63] "the river stank" (cf. וְסַ֫רַ נַהֲרָא Cd Ex 7:18);[64] אשלמו יומי פלחני E Gn 29:21, "the days of my service are completed."[65]

§130c  As a result of the merger of *ā and *a and the frequent absence of *daghesh forte* in the consonantal text, it is impossible to distinguish D, Dt from any original Pāel, Ithpāal forms. The forms מְזֻמָּן E Gn 28:17, "prepared" (Pss. Ptc.), and מְזַמְנִין F Ex 19:11 (Pss. Ptc. m.pl.) may be original Pāel or D. Similarly, תזדַמַּן E Gn 30:16, "prepare yourself!" (2 m.s.) may be either original Ithpāal or Dt.[66]

§130d  There are two verbs which consistently appear in the conjugations Poel and Ithpoal. The first is תוקף "*strengthen*," e.g., *Poel Perf. 3 m.s.* תוקף E Gn 41:52; *Act. Ptc.* מְתּקֵּף Cd Gn 48:4; and *Ithpoel Perf. 3 m.s.* וְאָתּוקַּף Cd Gn 48:2; *3 m.pl.* ואתּקפן AA₁ Ex 12:33 "and they grew strong."[67] This verb is also common in these conjugations in the other Palestinian Targumim.[68] It is possible that these forms arose from confusion with verbs I-w in Ct,[69] or it is possible that these are denominative verbs from the noun /təqop?, toqpa/ "strength."[70] The second verb is רוקן "*empty*." The *Poel Perf. 3 m.pl.* ורוקנו AA₁ Ex 12:36 is a denominative verb from /reqan/ "*emptily*"[71] (cf. *C Perf. 3 m.s.* וַאֲרַק C Gn 35:14, "he emptied out").

§130e  There are two roots attested in the Polel and Ithpolal conjugations, both of which are found in Targum Onqelos and the other Palestinian Targumim and are possible borrowings from Hebrew.[72] The first is גלל "*move, stir*" (root *gll): *Perf. 3 m.pl.* אתגוללו E Gn 43:30. The second is רומם "*raise, elevate*" (root *rwm): *Imperf. 3 m.s.* יְרֹומֵם E Gn 40:13; the verbal noun לרוממו AA Dt 26:19 and the Infinitive in the parallel passage וּלְרֹומָאמָ֫ךָ D Dt 26:19.[73]

§130f  The Š and Št verbal forms are all attested elsewhere in Aramaic and their origin is debated:[74] שיצי "*destroy*":[75] *Perf. 3 m.s.* וְשֵׁיצִיא Cd Ex 9:25, וְשֵׁיצִי

172

Bd Gn 7:23, שֵׁיצִי Cd Ex 9:25; *Imperf. 3 m.pl.* יְשֵׁיצוּן D Dt 28:21; *Inf.* מַשְׁצִיא AA₁
Ex 17:14; *Perf. 3 m.s.* וְאָשְׁתִיצִי Bd Gn 7:21; *Perf. 3 m.pl.* וְאָשְׁתְּצוּן Bd Gn 7:23;
שיזב "*save*": *Perf. 3 m.s.* וְשֵׁיזֵיב Cd Gn 37:21; *Inf.* לְמִשְׁיזבה E Gn 37:22; שכלל
"*complete, perfect*": *Perf. 3 m.s.* וְשַׁכְלֵל F Ex 20:22; *Perf. 3 f.pl.* שכללן W Ex
15:17; *Verbal Noun* שכלוליהן F Lv 22:27; שלחף "*change*": *Perf. 3 m.s.* שַׁלְחֵיף Cd
Gn 48:14; *Perf. 2 m.s.* וְשַׁלְחֵפְתְּ C Gn 31:41; שלהי "*tire*": *Imperf. 3 m.pl.* וְיְשְׁתַּלְהוּן
Cd Ex 7:18; שעבד "*enslave*": *Pss. Ptc. m.pl.* מְשַׁעְבְּדִין Cd Gn 44:16; *Ptc. m.pl.*
משתעבדין E Gn 40:12; *Ptc. f.pl.* מִשְׁתַּעְבְּדָן Z Gn 49:10; *Verbal Noun* שעבוד F Ex
20:2,[76] שעבודייה E Gn 40:18, שֶׁעְבְּדְהוֹן Cd Ex 6:7; שעמם "*stupefy*": *Verbal Noun*
וּבְשַׁעְמִימוּת D Dt 28:28.

**§130g** Q (Palpel) verbal forms are גלגל "*roll*": *Perf. 3 m.s.* וגלגל E Gn 29:10;
*Imperf. 3 m.pl.* ויגלגלון E Gn 29:3; הבהב "*roast*": *Pss. Ptc. m.s.* מהבהב AA₁ Ex
12:9; טלטל "*move about*": *Pss. Ptc. m.s.* וּמְטַלְטַל B Gn 4:12; משמש "*grope*":
*Imperf. 3 m.s.* יְמַשְׁמַשׁ D Dt 28:29; *Act. Ptc. m.pl.* מְמַשְׁמְשִׁין D Dt 28:29;[77] פשפש
"*search*": *Perf. 3 m.s.* וּפַשְׁפֵּשׁ Cd Gn 44:12; קדקד "*speckle*": *Pss. Ptc. m.pl.*
מקדקדין E Gn 30:39.

**§130h** There are three Qt (Ithpalpel) verbs: אזדעזע "*be shaken*": *Perf. 3 m.s.*
וְאָזדעזע F Ex 19:18; *Perf. 3 m.pl.* ואזדעזעו F Ex 20:15;[78] אתרברב "*contend*":[79]
*Perf. 2 m.s.* אתרברבת C Gn 32:29; אתערטל "*be denuded*":[80] *Perf. 3 m.s.* ואתערטל
E Gn 9:21.

**§130i** Other Q verbs are הימן "*believe*":[81] *Perf. 2 m.pl.* היימנתון AA Nu 20:12;
*Imperf. 3 m.pl.* יהדיימנון A Ex 4:8; *Act. Ptc. m.pl.* מהדיימנין E Gn 40:12;[82] *Verbal
Noun* [והיימנותא AA₁ Ex 17:12; שרג "*violate, rape*":[83] *Imperf. 3 m.s.* וְשַׁרְגֵג A Ex
22:15; see also verbs of foreign origin—משכן "*take a pledge*" (§154a), פרנס
"*provide*" (§153), פרסי "*make known, publicize*" (§153), תרגם "*translate*"
(§154b).

## Strong Verb

**§131** *G Conjugation*
The following verb classes are attested among strong triliteral roots:
**§131a** *(a,o)*: This is the largest class of verbs and includes many roots with
gutturals and /r/, e.g.,

| | Perfect | | Imperfect |
|---|---|---|---|
| קְטַל | B Gn 4:8 | יִקְטוֹל | B Gn 4:14, "kill" |
| וּפְרַס | Cd Ex 9:33 | אפרוס | E Gn 9:14, "spread out" |
| חֲזַר | Cd Gn 37:29 | יְחזוֹר | A Ex 21:34, "return" |
| וּטְעֲנוּ | Bd Gn 7:17 | וְתִטְעֲעוּן | Cd Gn 47:30, "bear" |
| וּפְתַח | Bd Gn 8:6 | יפתוֹח | A Ex 21:33, "open" |
| וּתְבַע | Cd Gn 43:30 | אתבע | E Gn 9:5, "demand" |

**§131b** *(a,a)*: This class is limited to the following examples before /'/ and
/r/:

| | | | |
|---|---|---|---|
| וּשְׁמַע | D Dt 5:25 | וְאָשְׁמַע | A Ex 22:22, "hear" |
| וַעֲבַר | C Gn 32:23 | אעבַר | E Gn 30:32, "pass, cross" |

The verb עבר is, however, more frequently attested in the (a,o) class, e.g., וְ‌אֶ‌עְ‌בּוּר- C Gn 31:52.[84]

§131c *(e,o):* This class contains intransitive and stative verbs. It is attested with the roots[85]

| דְּחֵלוּ | Cd Gn 43:18 | תִּדְחַל | H Gn 15:1, "fear" |
| קְרֵבוּ | Cd Gn 47:29 | יִקְרוֹב | F Ex 19:12 "approach" |
| תְּקֵף | Cd Gn 47:4 | יִתְקוֹף | A Ex 22:23 ˆ "be strong" |

The latter two verbs are attested less frequently as (e,a) verbs, e.g., וְ‌יִקְרַב A Ex 22:7;[86] יְתְקַף Cd Gn 48:19.[87]

§131d *(a,e):* This class is attested only in the following verb:

| עֲבַד | Bd Gn 8:6 | וְנַעְבְּיד | D Dt 5:24, "do" |

§131e Other examples of verbs in which \*a > /o/ as the vowel of the Imperfect are נבהות E Gn 38:26, "I should be ashamed";[88] וְ‌יִפְלַח A Ex 21:2, "he will work"; יַ‌חְפּ‌וֹר- A Ex 21:33, "he will dig." These verbs are not attested with pointing in the Perfect.

§131f The vowel of the Imperative agrees with the vowel of the Imperfect,[89] e.g., תְקוֹף C Gn 35:11, "be strong!"; עֲבוֹר C Gn 32:17; "cross!, pass!"; שְׁמַע D Dt 5:24, "hear!" The verb חזר, "return" is attested in the (a,o) class, but has Imperative forms with both /a/ and /o/, e.g., חֲזַר E Gn 43:2, חֲזוֹר E Gn 31:3.

§131g The stem vowel of the Infinitive also agrees with the vowel of the Imperfect.[90] Thus, one finds in (a,o) verbs, e.g., לְ‌מִקְטוֹל B Gn 4:15, "to kill"; למטען E Gn 44:1, "to bear"; למתבע F Ex 19:3, "to demand." For (e,o) verbs,[91] one finds לְ‌מִדְחַל D Dt 5:26, "to fear." For (a,e) verbs, one finds לְ‌מֶעְבַּד C Gn 34:14, "to do." Among (a,a) verbs, one finds, e.g., לְ‌מִשְׁ‌וּ‌מַע D Dt 5:22, "to hear" (cf. משמע F Ex 19:5).

§131h The form of the Active Participle (m.s.) is /qatel/ with strong verbs and /qatal/ with verbs III-guttural, /r/, e.g., בָּעֵר- D Dt 5:20; "burning"; פָּרַח F Ex 20:2, "flying"; וְ‌חָ‌זַ‌ר Bd Gn 8:7, "and returning"; תָּבַע C Gn 31:39, "demanding." The only exceptions are נָטַר F Ex 20:6, "guarding," and וּפְתַר E Gn 41:15, "and interpreting," where the e-vowel has been extended from the strong verb.

§131i The Passive Participle, /qǝtil/, is transitive in five examples:[92] הַוּון וְנַמְלַ‌יהֶ‌ן טְעִינִין שְׁ‌עָ‌בָ‌א Cd F Ex 20:8, "keep the Sabbath day": זְהִירִין יַת יוֹמָא דְשׁוּבְתָה Gn 37:25, "and their camels bearing tragacanth"; נפקו טעינ‌וֹן מן ארעה דמצרים חל‌ק דפטירין AA₁ Ex 12:39, "they went forth from the land of Egypt bearing unleavened cakes"; ואהרן וחור ה‌ת‌ן זקיפ‌ין ביד‌ו AA₁ Ex 17:12, "Aaron and Hur were raising his hands"; רְחִיצָא אֲנָא בְּרַבּ‌ך כָּל-עָ‌לְמַיָא Cd Gn 38:25; "I trust the Master of all worlds."

§131j A salient feature of this dialect is the vowel /a/ in the 1 s. and 3 f.s. Perfect: /qatlet/ and /qatlat/. There are no exceptions.[93] There are no examples of the 1 s. or 3 f.s. Perfect of verbs \*qatila among strong verbs; however, the pointing of the Proto-Aramaic I-w \*qatila verb יְ‌לֵ‌דֵת E Gn 30:20, "I bore" suggests that the 1 s. and 3 f.s. forms of intransitive and stative verbs were also /qatlet/, /qatlat/.[94]

174

G Conjugation—Historical and Comparative Discussion

**§131k** The classes attested in the strong verbs are related to the Proto-Aramaic verb classes in the following manner:

| Cairo Genizah | Proto-Aramaic |
|---|---|
| (a,o) | *(a,u) transitive |
| (a,a) | *(a,a) III-guttural, /r/ |
| (e,o) | *(i,a) intransitive, stative |
| (e,a) | |
| (a,e) | *(a,i) limited class (זבן "sell"; |

עבד "do"; נתן "give")[95]

**§131l** There are no reflexes in these fragments of a *(u,u) class.

**§131m** Of interest is the shift of verb classes in the following verbs: זבן (Proto-Aramaic a,i) > (?,o),[96] e.g., זבונו E Gn 43:2, "buy!" (m.pl.); למזבן E Gn 41:57; בשל (Proto-Aramaic i,a) > (a,?),[97] e.g., ובשלו E Gn 40:10, "and they ripened."

**§131n** The penetration of /o/ into the Imperfect, Imperative, and Infinitive of verbs originally *(a,a) and *(i,a) is also a prominent feature of Galilean Aramaic,[98] the other Palestinian Targumim,[99] and Palestinian Syriac.[100] There are also traces of this in Ma'lula.[101] It would appear that verbal forms with /a/ reflect a classical, archaizing style, whereas those forms with /o/ reflect a vulgar pronunciation.[102]

**§131o** The characteristic /a/ of the 1 s. and 3 f.s. Perfect /qatlet/ and /qatlat/ is also attested in Ma'lula (cf. 1 s. [zabnit], 3 f.s. [zabnat])[103] in active transitive verbs and in Tiberian Biblical Aramaic in verbs I-guttural (cf. /'abdet/ Dn 3:15, 6:23). A shift of *a > *i is thought to be responsible for the Syriac /qeθləθ/, /qeθlaθ/, and the Tiberian Biblical Aramaic strong verb /qitlet/, /qitlat/.[104] The Targum Onqelos forms /qətálit/ and /qətálat/ are not direct reflexes of the Proto-Aramaic forms, but rather new formations based on the 3 m.s. /qətal/.[105] Although the evidence is limited, it appears that a and not i is also the characteristic vowel in Samaritan Aramaic and Galilean Aramaic.[106]

**§131p** As mentioned above (§131j), there is reason to believe that *qatila verbs have reflexes of 1 s. /qatlet/ and 3 f.s. /qatlat/ in the Cairo Genizah fragments. Cf. the *qatila reflexes of Ma'lula 1 s. [dimḫit], 3 f.s. [dimḫat],[107] Syriac /qeθleθ/, /qeθlaθ/, and Tiberian Biblical Aramaic 1 s. /qitlet/, 3 f.s. /qitlat/, /qətélat/.[108]

**§131q** According to Kutscher,[109] the characteristic /a/ of the Cairo Genizah fragments is a direct reflex of Proto-Aramaic *a, whereas /i/ of Biblical Aramaic and /e/ of Syriac reflect a shift of *a > *i. In the case of Ma'lula, Spitaler[110] believes that the [a] of the 1 s. and 3 f.s. Perfect forms was extended from the 3 m.s. Perfect iqtal in order to differentiate active transitive forms iqtal, qatlat, qatlit from the intransitive forms iqtel, qitlat, qitlit. Kutscher's explanation of the origin of the /a/ of /qatlet/, /qatlat/ may, indeed, be

175

correct.[111] Spitaler's interpretation of the Maʻlula data, on the other hand, is not applicable to the Cairo Genizah fragments since the 1 s. and 3 f.s. intransitive forms appear to be /qatlet/, /qatlat/. Spitaler proposes and rejects another possibility, namely, that [a] was re-introduced into these verbal forms from verbs with object pronominal suffixes (e.g., *qatleh* "he killed him")[112] If one were to claim that this, too, was the case in the Cairo Genizah fragments, one would have to maintain that this took place before the object pronominal suffixes ceased to be affixed to finite verbs.[113]

Representative examples of the G conjugation are

§131r  *Perfect: 3 m.s.* וּקְטַל B Gn 4:8, "he killed"; וּפְשַׁט Cd Gn 48:14, "he stretched forth"; חֲזַר Cd Ex 5:22, "he returned"; וּקְרֵב C Gn 32:26, "he approached"; *3 f.s.* פָּתְחַת B Gn 4:11, "she opened"; וּבְלַעַת Cd Ex 7:12, "she swallowed"; יִטְלְקַת Cd Gn 38:25, "she threw"; וּלְבִשַׁת Cd Gn 38:19, "she wore"; *2 m.s.* הַעֲבָדְתְּ B Gn 4:10, "you did"; טְרַדְתְּ B Gn 4:14, "you drove out"; שְׁמַעַתְּ Cd Ex 7:16, "you heard"; *1 s.* מְסָרֵת B Gn 4:7, "I handed over"; פְּלַחֵת C Gn 31:41, "I worked"; וּקְבָרֵת Cd Gn 48:7, "I buried"; יַקְפִּיַת Cd Ex 6:8, "I raised"; *3 m.pl.* וּשְׁדַכּוּ Bd Gn 8:1, "they subsided"; עֲבָדוּ Cd Gn 31:46, "they did"; וּקְרֵבוּ Cd Gn 47:29, "they approached"; *3 f.pl.* ובלעין E Gn 41:7, "they swallowed"; E Gn 41:24; *2 m.pl.* וּקְרַבְתּוּן D Dt 5:20, "you approached";[114] הַעֲבָדְתּוּן Cd Gn 44:5, "you did"; *2 f.pl.* חכמתין E Gn 31:6, "you know"; *1 pl.* שְׁמַעְנָא D Dt 5:21, "we heard"; חֲזַרְנָ Cd Gn 43:10, "we returned"; וּפְתַחְנָ Cd Gn 43:21, "we opened";

§131s  *Imperfect: 3 m.s.* יִקְטוֹל B Gn 4:16, "he will kill"; יִקְרַב A Ex 22:7, "he will approach"; יִתְקֹל A Ex 22:16, "he will weigh"; *2 m.s.* תְּקַבּוֹר Cd Gn 47:29, "you will kill"; וְתִטְעַן Cd Gn 47:30, "you will bear"; תֵעֲבוֹר C Gn 31:52, "you will cross"; *1 s.* אֶעֱבּוֹר C Gn 31:52, "I shall cross"; וְאֶפְרַק Cd Ex 6:6, "I shall redeem"; אפרוס Cd Ex 9:29, "I shall spread out"; נבהות E Gn 38:26, "I should be ashamed," נבהות E Gn 38:26;[115] *3 m.pl.* וְיִתְקַפוּן Cd Gn 48:16, "may they be strong"; וְיִפְלְחָן Cd Ex 7:16, "that they may worship"; *3 f.pl.* וְיִשְׁלְטָן Cd Gn 37:27, "they will rule"; *2 m.pl.* וְתִכְתְּבוּן D Dt 27:8, "you will write"; תִּפְשְׁטוּן Cd Gn 37:22, "you will stretch forth"; תשפכן Cd Gn 37:22, "you will pour out"; *1 pl.* נֶקְטוֹל Cd Gn 37:21, "we shall kill"; נִגְנוֹב Cd Gn 44:8, "we shall steal"; וְנִשְׁמַע D Dt 5:24, "we will hear";

§131t  *Imperative: m.s.* תְּקוֹף C Gn 35:11, "be strong!"; קְרוֹב D Dt 5:24, "approach!"; שְׁמַע D Dt 5:24, "hear!"; *m.pl.* תְּקוֹפוּ C Gn 35:9, "be strong!"; וּשְׁמַעוּ D Dt 27:9, "hear!"; שֶׁרְצוּ E Gn 9:7, "swarm!";

§131u  *Active Participle: m.s.* דְּקָטֵל B Gn 4:15, "killing"; שָׁהֵיד C Gn 31:48, "witnessing"; שָׁלֵיט B Gn 4:7, "ruling"; *f.s.* וְשָׂהֲדָא C Gn 31:52, "witnessing";[116] *m.pl.* גָּנְבִין C Gn 31:39, "stealing"; וְחָסְרִין Bd Gn 8:5, "diminishing"; פָּסְקִין C Gn 35:9, "ceasing"; *f.pl.* צָמְחָן E Gn 41:23, "growing";

§131v  *Passive Participle: m.s.* גניב E Gn 30:33, "stolen"; צְעִיר C Gn 35:9, "pained"; *f.s.* וּקְטִילָה A Ex 21:36, "slain," קְטִילָא C Gn 31:39; רְחִיצָא Cd Gn 38:25, "trust";[117] *m.pl.* פְּרִיקִין Cd Ex 6:7, "redeemed"; קְטִילִין Z Gn 44:18,

176

"slain"; גִּזְרֵן C Gn 34:22, "circumcised";[118] *f.pl.* טְמִירָן Cd Gn 43:23, "hidden"; שדיפן E Gn 41:23, "blasted"; חצינָבָן F Ex 20:22, "hewn";

**§131w** *Infinitive:* לְמֶעֱבַּד C Gn 34:19, "to do"; לְמִגּוּר C Gn 35:9, "to circumcise";[119] מְקָסֵום Cd Gn 44:15, "divining"; לְמֶשְׁבַּק Cd Gn 44:22, "to leave";[120] לְמֶקְטַל Cd Ex 5:21, "to kill"; למחכום E Gn 38:25, "to know"; למקרוב F Ex 19:12, "to approach"; למפרוק F Lv 22:33, "to redeem";

**§131x** *Verbal Noun:* בְּמִגְזַר C Gn 34:15, "in circumcising",[121] בְּמִגְזַר־ C Gn 34:22; בְּמַשְׁמָעֵיהּ Cd Gn 44:18, "in his hearing", בְּמַשְׁמָעֲכֹון D Dt 5:20, "in your hearing"; בְּמֶעֱבָּרְכֹון D Dt 27:3, "in your crossing"; במכנשכן F Lv 23:39, "in your gathering together."

**§132** *D Conjugation*

Representative examples of the D conjugation are

**§132a** *Perfect: 3 m.s.* וּפַקֵּד Cd Gn 44:1, "he commanded"; וּבָרֵךְ C Gn 35:9, "he blessed"; וַחַכִּים־ Cd Gn 37:33, "he knew"; *3 f.s.* וְעַבְּרַת Cd Gn 38:18, "she conceived," תעברת E Gn 29:32; *2 m.s.* וּפַקֵּדְתְּ C Gn 35:9, "you commanded"; בָּרֵיכְתְּ C Gn 35:9, "you blessed", בָּרֵיכתְּ C Gn 32:27; *1 s.* וְשַׁלֵּחִית Cd Gn 38:26, "I sent"; הַקַבֵּלִית H Gn 15:1, "I received"; וקרבית F Ex 19:4, "I brought near"; *3 m.pl.* וְקַטִּלוּ Cd Gn 44:18, "they killed"; וּטְלַקּוּ Cd Ex 7:12, "they threw"; *3 f.pl.* תַּבִּלִן C Gn 31:38, "they miscarried"; *2 m.pl.* שלמתן E Gn 44:4, "you have repaid";

**§132b** *Imperfect: 3 m.s.* יְקַבֵּל־ C Gn 32:21, "he will receive"; יְבָרֵךְ Cd Gn 48:16, "he will bless"; יזֹבֵן A Ex 21:37, "he will sell"; *2 m.s.* ותקדש F Ex 19:10, "you will sanctify"; ותְתַחֵם F Ex 19:12, "you will mark a boundary"; *1 s.* הָאֶקְטִל A Ex 22:23, "I shall kill"; ואבריך Cd Gn 48:9, "I shall bless"; ואפלג W Ex 15:9, "I shall divide"; ונשבח E Gn 29:35, "I will praise";[122] *3 m.pl.*[123] וִיכַנְּשׁוּן Cd Gn 41:35, 'they will gather," יְקַבְּלֻן Cd Gn 48:5, "they will receive"; *3 f.pl.* יִצְלְחָן־ D Dt 28:29, "they will prosper";[124] *2 m.pl.* ותברכן AA₁ Ex 12:32, "you will bless"; תַצְעֲרֻן A Ex 22:22, "you will trouble"; וּתְקָרְבֻן D Dt 27:7, "you will draw near"; *1 pl.* וּנְזַבֵּן־ Cd Gn 37:27, "we shall sell";

**§132c** *Imperative: m.s.* תָּחֵם F Ex 19:23, "mark out a boundary!"; שמש E Gn 39:7, "have intercourse!"; *m.pl.* לַקִּיטוּ C Gn 31:46, "collect!"; וְכַבִּישׁוּ C Gn 35:9, "conquer!"; קַבִּילוּ־ Cd Gn 38:26, "receive!";

**§132d** *Active Participle: m.s.* מְשַׁלֵּם C Gn 3:39, "repaying"; וּמְקַבֵּל־ Cd Gn 44:18, "receiving"; מְפַקֵּד D Dt 27:10, "commanding,"; *f.s.* מְקַבְּלָא Cd Gn 44:18, "receiving";[125] מְתַבְּלָא C Gn 31:39, "miscarrying"; m.pl. מְבָרְכִין־ C Gn 35:9, "blessing";

**§132e** *Passive Participle: m.s.* מְבָרַךְ C Gn 35:9, "blessed";

**§132f** *Infinitive:* לְמְשַׁבָּחָא C Gn 32:27, "to praise"; לְמְחַזָּרָא Cd Gn 37:22, "to return"; לְמְעַבָּרָא Cd Gn 48:17, "to transfer"; לְמְקַדָּשָׁה F Ex 20:8,, "to sanctify";

**§132g** *Verbal Noun:*[126] בְּפַגְשׁוּתֵהּ C Gn 32:26, "in his meeting him"; בקטלותי AA₁ Ex 12:13, "in my killing"; also /ləqaddamut/ "towards" (§156y); B הַסְדּוֹרָא Ex 39:37, "arrangement"; בְּפַלוּג Cd Gn 44:18, "division," בְּפָלוּג Cd Gn 48:5, בְּפִילוּג Z Gn 44:18; פָּקֵדִין C Gn 35:9, "commands", ופקודיּ AA Dt 26:17;[127]

פירוש E Gn 31:13, "explanation"; שבֹיחֹה E Gn 30:13, "praise"; בְּשִׁיגֹעָה D Dt 28:28, "madness";

**§132h** /a/ alone is attested before gutturals and /r/. Examples are *Perf.: 3 m.s.* וּבַע Cd Gn 37:29, "he rent"; דַּבַּר Z Gn 48:15, "he led"; *2 m.s.* שַׁלַחְתְּ Cd Ex 5:22, "you sent"; *3 m.pl.* וְשַׁבָּחוּ Cd Gn 43:28, "they praised"; *Imperf.: 3 m.s.* וְיִשְׁלֹח A Ex 22:4, "he will send," וְיִשְׁלַח Cd Gn 43:14; *2 m.s.* תְּשַׁלַח Cd Gn 38:17, "you will send"; *Imper.: m.s.* שַׁלַח Cd Gn 43:8, "send!"; *Act. Ptc.: m.s.* וּמְשַׁקַּר F Ex 20:7, "lying."

**§133** *C Conjugation*

Representative examples of the C conjugation are

**§133a** *Perfect: 3 m.s.* אַמְלֵךְ- D Dt 26:18, "he enthroned"; וארעם E Gn 29:11, "he thundered"; *3 f.s.* אַשְׁכְּחַת- Cd Gn 38:25, "she found"; *2 m.s.* אַסְהֵדְתָּ F Ex 19:23, "you testified"; אסכלת E Gn 31:28, "you acted foolishly"; ארכינת W Ex 15:12, "you lowered"; *1 s.* אַשְׁכָּחֵית Cd Gn 47:29, "I found," אשכחת E Gn 38:22; *3 m.pl.* ואתקנו E Gn 43:25, "they prepared."

**§133b** *Imperfect: 3 m.s.* יַפְרֵשׁ B Gn 2:24, "let him separate"; יַדְבֵּק D Dt 28:21, "he will make cling"; *2 m.s.* ותחסן W Ex 15:17, "you will cause to inherit"; *1 s.* וְאַפְרֵשׁ Cd Ex 6:7, "I shall separate," אַפְרֵשׁ E Gn 28:22;

**§133c** *Imperative: m.s.* אַרְכֵּן Cd Ex 9:22, "lower!"; וְאַתְקֵן Cd Gn 43:16, "prepare!"; אַקְרֵב- Cd Gn 48:9, "bring near!"

**§133d** *Active Participle: m.s.* וּמְסַפֵּד C Gn 35:9, "lamenting"; *m.pl.* מסהדין F Ex 20:13, "testifying";

**§133e** *Infinitive:* לְמִפְרְשָׁא B Gn 3:5, "to separate"; למדכרה F Lv 22:27, "to remind"; למכעסה F Ex 20:20, "to anger";

**§133f** *Verbal Noun: abs. s.* וְאַחְסָנָה Cd Gn 48:5, "inheritance"; *cst. s.* אַחְסָנוּת Cd Gn 48:4;

**§133g** As is the case in the D conjugation, /a/ is attested before gutturals and /r/. Examples are *Perf.: 3 m.s.* אַשְׁכַּח Cd Gn 38:20, "he found"; *2 m.s.* אַשְׁכַּחְתְּ Cd Gn 38:23, "you found"; *3 m.pl.* וְשַׁלַחוּ "they stripped"; Cd Gn 37:23; *Imperf.: 3 f.s.* ותשכח A Ex 22:5, "it will find";[128] *Act. Ptc.: m.s.* מְשַׁכַּח B Gn 4:15, "finding." There is, however, one example in which /e/ of the non-guttural roots has penetrated: וְאַמְטַר Cd Ex 9:23, "he caused to rain."

**§134** *Gt Conjugation*

Representative examples of the Gt conjugation are

**§134a** *Perfect: 3 m.s.* אִתְקְטֵל Cd Gn 37:33, "he was killed"; וְאָתְרְכִין Cd Gn 46:29, "he bent down";[129] וְאִתְכַּנֵּישׁ Cd Gn 47:30, "he was gathered";[130] *3 f.s.* וְאִתְקְבְרַת C Gn 35:8, "she was buried"; *1 s.* אֶשְׁתְּמַעֵת E Gn 30:8, "I was heard"; אֶתְכְּלֵית- Cd Gn 43:14, "I was bereaved";[131] אתגנבֵית E Gn 40:15, "I was robbed";[132] *3 m.pl.* אתעבידו W Ex 15:8, "they were made into"; ואתבהלו W Ex 15:14, "they were agitated";[133] אתכנשו Z Gn 49:2, "they were gathered";[134]

**§134b** *Imperfect: 3 m.s.* וְיֶשְׁתְּבֵק B Gn 4:7, "he will be forgiven"; יתקטל Cd Gn 44:9, "he will be killed"; יִתְעֵבֵד- A Ex 21:31, "it will be done"; *3 m.pl.* יִתְמַנְעֻון

178

Cd Ex 9:29, "they will be held back";[135] וְיִתְהַפְּכָן Cd Ex 7:17, "they will turn into";[136]

**§134c** *Participle: m.s.* מְתְכְּנֵשׁ Cd Gn 48:21, "gathered";[137] מתעבד F Ex 20:22, "done"; משתפך E Gn 9:6, "poured out"; *m.pl.* דְמִתְכַּנְשִׁין H Gn 15:1, "gathered";[138]

**§134d** *Infinitive:* מִתקְטלה A Ex 22:18, "killing"; לְמֶתכְּנְשָׁא Cd Gn 47:29, "to be gathered";

**§134e** The characteristic /e/ of this conjugation is replaced by /a/ before gutturals and /r/. Examples are *Perf.: 3 m.s.* וְאִשְׁתְּבַע C Gn 31:53, "he swore"; וְאִתמְנַע Bd Gn 8:2, "it was held back"; *3 m.pl.* וְאִתמְנַעוּ Cd Ex 9:33, "they were held back";[139] *Imperf.: 3 m.s.* וַיִשׁתּבַח Cd Gn 44:9, "he will be found";[140] *Ptc.: m.s.* דְמִשׁתְּבַע F Ex 20:7, "swears."

**§134f** Note the possible assimilation of /t/[141] before /b/ and /g/ in איבהלו W Ex 15:15, "they were agitated" and וְיִגֹּנְבֹן A Ex 22:6, "they will be stolen."[142]

**§135** *Dt Conjugation*

Representative examples are

**§135a** *Perfect: 3 m.s.* אֶתקְבָּל B Gn 4:8, "it was accepted"; וְאִתפַּגַּשׁ C Gn 32:25, "he met"; אֶתבְּשַׂר C Gn 35:9, "he was informed"; *3 f.s.* ואטרפת E Gn 41:8, "she was agitated"; *3 m.pl.* אֶתגְבָּרוּ Bd Gn 7:19, "they prevailed"; אֶשׁתּלַּחוּ Cd Gn 44:3, "they were sent"; אתברכו E Gn 29:22, "they were blessed"; *2 m.pl.* אֶתחַשַּׁבתּוּן D Dt 27:9, "you were considered"; *1 pl.* אתחשבן E Gn 31:15 "we were considered";[143]

**§135b** *Imperfect: 3 m.s.* ייזדּבּן A Ex 22:2, "he will be sold"; ייתקדש F Lv 22:32, "he will sanctify himself"; *3 m.pl.* יִתעָרְבוּן C Gn 34:22, "they will intermingle"; יתקדשׁון F Ex 19:22, "they will sanctify themselves"; ישׁתתקן W Ex 15:16, "they will become still"; *3 f.pl.* יֶתפַּתּחָן B Gn 3:5, "they will be opened"; *2 m.pl.* וְתֶתעָרְבוּן C Gn 34:9, "you will intermingle"; *1 pl.* נִטַמַּר C Gn 31:49, "we shall be hidden";

**§135c** *Imperative: m.pl.* אזדָּהַרוּ F Ex 19:12, "be careful!"

**§135d** *Participle: m.s.* מְדַבַּר B Gn 4:8, "is lead"; מתקבל F Lv 23:13, "is received";

**§135e** *Infinitive:* לְמִסתַּכְּלה B Gn 3:6, "to look"; מִתחמדה E Gn 31:30, "longing for"; למתבשׂרא F Lv 22:27, "to be informed."

**§136** *Ct Conjugation*

The only examples not with weak roots are *Perfect 3 m.s.* וּוֹאִתְאָסְהד A Ex 21:29, "he has been warned";[144] *Imperative m.pl.* וְאִתּחְסָנוּ C Gn 34:10, "have possession!"

*Weak Verbs*

**§137** *Verbs I-n*

**§137a** Verbs I-n are characterized by the regular assimilation VnC > VCC. The only exceptions are attested in the forms of the root *nhr:[145] אַנהְר Cd Gn 44:3, "it shone";[146] אנהרין E Gn 38:25, "they shone";[147] דְאַנהָרוּתָה B Ex 39:37, "of shining."

**§137b** Initial /n/ usually is absent in G Imperative forms, e.g., טל E Gn 31:12, "take!" There are, however, three exceptions: וּנסבו AA₁ Ex 12:21, "take!" (cf. סבו AA₂ Ex 12:21; + 6x without /n/); וּנְבֹּח Cd Gn 43:16, "slaughter!" and וּנכסו AA₁ Ex 12:21.[148]

**§137c** (a,o) verbs make up the largest class. Cf., e.g.,

| Perfect | | Imperfect | |
|---|---|---|---|
| וְנֽפָלוּ | H Gn 15:1 | וִיפֹּל | A Ex 21:18, "fall" |
| וּנְפָק | B Gn 4:16 | תֽפֹּק | A Ex 22:5, "go forth" |
| וּנְבָסוֹ | Cd Gn 37:31 | יִכֹּס | A Ex 21:37, "slaughter" |

This last verb, however, is also attested with /e/ in the Perfect: וּנְבֵּיס C Gn 31:54 (cf. the forms of the Imperative above).

**§137d** There is one verb attested in the (a,a) class: נסב "take." Cf. *Perf. 3 m.s.* וּנְסָב Cd Gn 48:13; *Imperf. 1 pl.* -נֶסָב C Gn 34:16. Note the *qere/kethibh* distinction in נסֹיב A Ex 21:3 (pointing reflects Perf. /nəsab/; consonantal text reflects either Perf. /naseb/, Act. Ptc. /naseb/, or Pss. Ptc. /nəsib/).

**§137e** נתן "give" is well attested in the Imperfect and Infinitive with the characteristic /e/ vowel, e.g., *Imperf. 3 m.s.* יִתֵּן A Ex 21:22; *Inf.* לְמְתֵן A Ex 22:16 (+ 3x; but לְמָתֵן H Gn 15:2). This root is replaced by יהב in the Perfect, Participle, and Imperative (see §139).

**§137f** Two forms of נחת "descend" merit comment. The pointing of נָחֲתָה- Cd Ex 9:33 reflects a Perf. /nəhat/;[149] the consonantal text, however, reflects either a Perf. /nahet/ or an Act. Ptc. /nahet/. The Ct Perf. 3 m.s. אַתְחֵת E Gn 39:1 seems to have resulted from confusion with verbs I-w/y.

**§137g** The verb יִגֹּח A Ex 21:31, "he will butt" appears to have been inflected as if it were a verb II-w/y (cf. יְגוֹח A Ex 21:31).

Representative examples of I-n verbs are

**§137h** *Perfect: 3 m.s.* ונטל E Gn 31:17, "he took"; ונצב E Gn 9:20, "he planted"; ונחת E Gn 42:36, "he descended"; *3 f.s.* וּתְסָבַת B Gn 3:6, "she took"; ונפקת E Gn 30:16, "she went forth"; *1 s.* -דְּנְסָבֵית Cd Gn 38:26, "I took"; ונטלית E Gn 31:10, "I took"; *3 m.pl.* נְפָקוּ Cd Ex 5:20, "they went forth"; ונטלו Cd Gn 37:25, "they took"; וּנְסָבוּ C Gn 31:46, "they took"; *3 f.pl.* ונפקן W Ex 15:20, "they went forth"; -נֵהֹרֽן Cd Gn 38:25, "they shone" (see n.61).

**§137i** *Imperfect: 3 m.s.* -יְתֵּן D Dt 5:26, "he will give"; ויכס AA Nu 19:3, "he will slaughter"; יחות E Gn 42:38, "he will descend"; *2 m.s.* -תֵּתֵּין- Cd Gn 38:17, "you will give"; תֵּסָב Cd Gn 38:23, "you will take"; *1 s.* אֵתֵּן Cd Gn 38:18, "I shall give"; *3 m.pl.* יִפְקוּן C Gn 35:11, "you will go forth"; ויסבן HH Ex 12:3, "they will take";[150] ויכסן AA₁ Ex 12:6, "they will slaughter"; *2 m.pl.* -תֵּתְנוּן C Gn 34:9, "you will give"; תֵסְבוֹן A Ex 21:14, "you will take";[151] *1 pl.* נחות E Gn 43:4, "we shall descend"; וְנֶפּוּק B Gn 4:8, "we shall go forth"; וְנֵיסָב C Gn 34:17, "we shall take";

**§137j** *Imperative: m.s.* פוק E Gn 31:13, "go forth!"; חות Cd Gn 38:25, "descend!"; *m.pl.* טוּרו D Dt 27:1, "guard!"; פוקו AA₁ Ex 12:31, "go forth!"; סָבּו Cd Gn 43:12, "take!"

180

§137k *Active Participle: m.s.* נָפֵק B Gn 2:18, "going forth";[152] *f.s.* נָפְקָא Cd
Gn 38:25; *m.pl.* נָחֲתִין Cd Gn 44:18, "descending"; ונצחין AA₁ Ex 17:11,
"victorious";

§137l *Infinitive:* לְמֵיסַב Cd Gn 38:20, "to take"; וּלְמֵטוּר D Dt 26:18, "to
guard"; לְמִתֵּן B Ex 39:31, "to give"; למחות E Gn 37:25, "to descend";

§137m *Verbal Noun:* כְּמָפְקִי Cd Ex 9:29, "my going forth"; במפקותהון Y Ex
19:1, "their going forth";[153]

§137n *D Perfect: 3 m.s.* וְנַסֵּיךְ C Gn 35:14, "he poured a libation";

§137o *Passive Participle: f.s.* מְנַטְּלָא Cd Ex 6:6, "exalted"; *m.pl.* וּמְנַטְּלִין D Dt
26:19, "exalted";

§137p *Infinitive:* לְמִנְחֲמָה C Gn 35:9, "to comfort"; למנסיה F Ex 20:17, "to
test"; למנשקה E Gn 31:28, "to kiss";

§137q *Verbal Noun:* נִסּוּכִין C Gn 35:14, "libations";[154] ונסוכוי F Lv 23:13,
ונסוכיהון F Lv 23:18;

§137r *C Perfect: 3 m.s.* וְאַפֵּיק Cd Gn 48:12, "he brought forth"; *2 m.s.* אשיפת
W Ex 15:10, "you blew"; *1 s.* וְאַפְקִית F Ex 20:2, "I brought forth"; *3 m.pl.* אֲחִיתוּ
E Gn 39:1, "they brought down"; ואסיבו E Gn 29:22, "they gave in marriage";
*2 m.pl.* אַפֵּקְתּוּן Cd Ex 5:21, "you brought forth";

§137s *Imperfect: 3 m.s.* ויפק AA Nu 19:3, "he will bring forth"; *2 m.s.* ותפק
AA Nu 20:8, "you will bring forth"; *2 m.pl.* ותחתון E Gn 42:38, "you will bring
down"; *1 pl.* נפק AA Nu 20:10, "we shall bring forth";

§137t *Imperative: m.pl.* אֲחִיתוּ E Gn 43:7, "bring down!"; אפקו E Gn 38:24,
"bring forth!";

§137u *Active Participle: m.s.* מחית E Gn 7:4, "bringing down";

§137v *Passive Participle: m.s.* ומקף AA Nu 19:15, "surrounded";

§137w *Infinitive:* מַחֲתָה D Dt 28:23, "bringing down";

§137x *Verbal Noun:* בְּאַפְקוּתִי F Lv 23:43, "my bringing forth";

§137y *Dt Infinitive:* וּלְמִתְנַטְּלָא Cd Gn 43:18, "to exalt oneself";

§137z *Ct Perfect: 3 m.s.* אתּחת E Gn 39:1, "he was brought down."[155]

§138 *Verbs I-'*

Three classes are attested in G verbs: (a,o), (a,a), and (a?,e).

§138a The verb אכל "eat" belongs to both the (a,o) and (a,a) classes. The
examples of the Imperfect and Infinitive with /a/ reflect an older classical
stage of the language. The forms with /o/, on the other hand, reflect a newer,
vulgar pronunciation. Cf., e.g., *Perf. 3 m.pl.* וַאֲכָלוּ C Gn 31:46, *Imperf. 3 f.s.*
וְתֵיכוֹל A Ex 22:5 (+ 1x with /o/);[156] *Imperf. 2 m.s.* תֵּאכָל B Gn 2:17 (+ 2x with
/a/); *Inf.* למאכיל E Gn 28:20 (+ 1x with /o/),[157] *Inf.* לְמֵאכָל B Gn 3:6. The verbs
אסר "tie up" and אגר "hire" may also belong to this class; the evidence,
however, is limited to the forms of the Infinitive למיסור E Gn 41:44 and מיגור E
Gn 30:16.

§138b The (a,a) class is also represented by the verb אמר "say," e.g., *Perf. 3*
*m.s.* וַאֲמַר B Gn 4:10; *Imperf. 3 m.s.* וְיֵמַר Cd Gn 46:33, *Inf.* לְמֵימַר C Gn 32:20.

There is one example with /o/: *Imperf. m.s.* אֱמֹר Cd Ex 7:19. This may or may not be a Hebraism.[158]

**§138c**  The verb אזל "go" is the only example of the (a?,e) class. Cf. *Perf. 3 m.s.* וְאָזַל E Gn 29:21;[159] *Imperf. 1 s.* אֵיזֵל Cd Gn 37:30; *Inf.* לְמִיזַל Z Gn 49:2. There are two examples of the Imperative with /e/, but one with /a/: *m.s.* אֱזַל F Ex 19:10, אֱזֵל F Ex 19:24; *m.pl.* אזלו E Gn 41:55[160]

**§138d**  The quiescence of syllable closing /'/ is frequently represented in the consonantal text by the deletion of *aleph*.[161] It is possible that the pointing of forms such as וַאֲמַר C Gn 34:11 "and he said" reflects the elision of the /'/ and a realization of /wamar/; however, it is also possible that the vocalizers may have only partially pointed the word (cf. וַאֲמַר Cd Gn 38:25, וַאֲמַר C Gn 31:51).[162] Note the elision of /'/ in the *D Act. Ptc. m.pl.* דמלפין AA Nu 20:10, "teach"[163] (and in the *G Imperf. 3 m.pl.* וילפון F Ex 20:13 [4x]), as against the preservation of /'/ in the *D Pss. Ptc. f.s.* מְאֹרְסָה A Ex 22:15, "betrothed."

**§138e**  The only attested C verb is ואייכל F Lv 22:27, "he fed" (2x).[164]

**§138f**  There are five examples of I-' verbs in Gt. Medial /'/ is preserved in all of the examples, e.g. וְאִתְאֲמַר Cd Gn 48:1, "and it was said." There is only one poorly preserved I-' root in Dt: וְאִתְאַבַּל Cd Gn 37:34, "he mourned." Based on this limited evidence, it appears that /'/ was not elided in Gt and Dt verbs, as is often the case in Galilean Aramaic and the other Palestinian Targumim.[165]

**§138g**  The Proto-Semitic root *'rḍ has a reflex of 'r' "meet, befall" in these fragments.[166]

Representative examples of verbs I-' are

**§138h**  *G Perfect: 3 m.s.* וַאֲמַר B Gn 4:8, "he said," דֹּאכַל AA₁ Ex 12:19, "he ate";[167] דאזל E Gn 42:36, "he went"; *3 f.s.* וְאָזְלַת Cd Gn 38:19, "she went"; וְאָמְרַת Cd Gn 38:17, "she said"; אֲכַלַת Cd Gn 37:20, "she ate"; אחדת W Ex 15:14,15, "she grasped"; *2 m.s.* וַאֲמַרְתְּ Cd Gn 44:23, "you said"; אזלת E Gn 31:30, "you went"; *1 s.* אֲכַלִית C Gn 31:38, "I ate"; וַאֲמַרַת Cd Gn 38:26, "I said"; *3 m.pl.* אֲמַרוּ Cd Gn 38:22, "they said"; ואזלו AA₂ Ex 12:28, "they went"; *3 f.pl.* ואכלין E Gn 41:20, "they ate"; *2 m.pl.* וַאֲמַרְתּוּן D Dt 5:21, "you said"; *1 pl.* וַאֲמַרְן Cd Gn 44:20, "we said"; אכלנן AA Dt 26:13, "we ate";

**§138i**  *Imperfect: 3 m.s.* יֵאמַר A Ex 22:8, "he will say"; דיכל AA₁ Ex 12:15, "he will eat"; *3 f.s.* תיכל A Ex 23:11, "she will eat"; *2 m.s.* וְתֵימַר Cd Ex 7:16, "you will say", ותאמר E Gn 44:4; תֵּאכַל B Gn 2:17, "you will eat"; *1 s.* וְאֵמַר Cd Gn 46:31, "I shall say"; ואזל E Gn 30:26, "I shall go"; *3 m.pl.* יאכלן Cd Gn 43:16, "they will eat", יכלן E Gn 43:25, "they will eat"; יְאִזְלוּן H Gn 15:1, "they will go";[168] וילפון F Ex 20:14, "they will learn"; *2 m.pl.* וְתֵימְרֹן C Gn 32:21, "you will say"; וְתֵאכְלֹן D Dt 27:7, "you will eat"; ותיזלון AA Dt 26:2, "you will go"; *1 pl.* ונימר E Gn 37:20, "we shall say"; וְנֵאמַר Cd Gn 37:20; וְנֵזֵל C Gn 34:17, "we shall go";

**§138j**  *Imperative: m.s.* אֹזֵל Y Ex 19:10, "go!"; *m.pl.* וַאֲזֵלוּ AA₁ Ex 12:32, "go!";

182

**§138k** *Active Participle: m.s.* אָכֵל E Gn 39:6, "eating," אָזֵיל Bd Gn 8:7, "going," וְאָמַר B Gn 4:8, "saying," אָסַר Z Gn 49:11, "tying"; *f.s.* דְּאָכְלָא Cd Gn 38:26, "eating," אמרא W Ex 15:12, "saying"; *m.pl.* אָזְלִין Bd Gn 8:3, "going"; אָכְלִין Cd Gn 43:25, "eating"; וְאָמְרִין Cd Gn 43:28, "saying";

**§138l** *Infinitive:* מֵאמַר A Ex 21:5, "saying"; לְמִימָר C Gn 32:18; מיזל E Gn 31:30, "going"; למיכל E Gn 43:32, "to eat";

**§138m** *Verbal Noun:* מֵמְרִי- Cd Ex 6:7, "my Word"; מֵימְרֵהּ- Cd Ex 5:23; מֵאמְרֵהּ B Gn 4:4, "his Word"; מֵמְרֵהּ Cd Gn 48:11, "his Word"; מַאכְלה AA₁ Ex 12:4, "his eating";

**§138n** *D Perfect: 3 m.s.* וְאָרַע Cd Gn 44:6, "it befell"; ואלף F Lv 23:44, "he taught"; *3 f.s.* אָרְעִית- C Gn 35:9, "it befell";[169] *2 m.s.* אַלֵּיפת C Gn 35:9, "you taught";

**§138o** *Imperfect: 3 m.s.* וְיָאָרַע-C Gn 32:18, "he will meet"; *1 s.* אערע W Ex 15:9, "I will meet";[170] *3 m.pl.* וְיָאָרְעֻן D Dt 28:15, "they will befall"; *2 m.pl.* תָאָרְעֻן- C Gn 32:20, "you will meet";

**§138p** *Active Participle: m.pl.* דמלפין AA Nu 20:10, "teaching";

**§138q** *Passive Participle: f.s.* מְאָרְסָה A Ex 22:15, "betrothed";

**§138r** *Verbal Noun:* וְאַרְעַ F Nu 29:26, "festive meeting," [171] בירדע AA₁ Ex 12:16,[172] ואירועין F Lv 23:2;

**§138s** *C Perfect: 3 m.s.* ואייכל F Lv 22:27, "he fed" (2x).

**§138t** *Gt Perfect: 3 m.s.* וְאֶתְאֲמֵר Cd Gn 48:1, "it was said";

**§138u** *Imperfect: 3 m.s.* יתאכל A Ex 21:28, "it will be eaten,"[173] יתאכיל F Lv 22:30;

**§138v** *Dt Perfect: 3 m.s.* וְאֶתְלַאֲבַל Cd Gn 37:34, "he mourned."

**§139** *Verbs I-w/y*

**§139a** Only I-*y verbs are attested: יטב and ינק. The examples are *G Imperf. 3 m.s.* דְּייטַב E Gn 40:14, "it will be well'; *C Imperf. 2 m.s.* תַּיְיטִיב- B Gn 4:7, "you will do well," תַּיְיטֵב B Gn 4:7; *Act. Ptc. f.pl.* מֵינְקָן C Gn 32:16, "nursing";[174] *Inf.* לְמֵיטבה D Dt 5:26, "to deal kindly."

**§139b** It is difficult to ascertain the G verbal classes because of the absence of pointing in many forms. The verbs ילד "bear" and ירת "inherit" probably belong to the (e?,a) class. Cf. e.g., *Imperf. 3 f.s.* תֵּילַד E Gn 30:3, "she will bear"; *3 m.s.* [n]יֵירֻת H Gn 15:4, "he will inherit." ידע "know" probably belongs to the (a?,a) class, e.g., *Imperf. 2 m.s.* דְּתֶדַּע Cd Ex 9:29. There are no examples of the Perfect 3 m.s., 3 m.pl., or 3 f.pl. forms of these three verbs. Note that in the case of ילד, the *Perf. 1 s.* יָלֵדת E Gn 30:20 gives no indication of the characteristic vowel of the Perfect (as against Targum Onqelos /yəledat/).[175] The verb יתב "sit, dwell" appears to belong to both (e,e) and (a,e). Cf. *Perf. 3 m.pl.* וְיתִיבֻ Cd Gn 37:25 (+ 1x); *3 m.s.* וִיתַב C Gn 35:9 (+ 2x), *Imper. m.pl.* תִּיבֻ C Gn 34:10, *Inf.* למתב AA₁ Ex 12:29.

**§139c** Two verbs merit special attention. יכל "able, capable" is attested only in the Perfect, e.g., *3 m.s.* יְכִיל Cd Gn 48:10 and in the *Ptc. m.s.* יָכֵל C Gn 32:26. It is noteworthy that the root כהל is unattested in these fragments.[176] יהב

"give" is attested only in the Perfect, e.g., *3 m.s.* יְהַב Cd Ex 9:23, and in the Imperative, e.g., *m.pl.* וְהִיבוּ C Gn 34:12.[177] "Give" is expressed by the root נתן in the Imperfect and Infinitive (see §137).[178]

Some examples of verbs I-*w are

§139d  *G Perfect: 3 m.s.* יְהַב Cd Gn 48:2, "he gave"; יִתֵב C Gn 35:9, "he sat"; *3 f.s.* וילדת E Gn 29:34, "she bore"; ויהבת E Gn 30:9, "she gave"; *2 m.s.* יְהַבּת H Gn 15:2, "you gave"; וְיָכֵלְת C Gn 32:29, "you were able";[179] *1 s.* יְהָבֵית C Gn 35:12, "I gave"; *3 m.pl.* ויהבו E Gn 29:22, "they gave"; יְתֵבוּ Cd Gn 43:33, "they sat"; יְכִילוּ Cd Ex 7:21, "they were able"; *2 m.pl.* יְדַעתּוּן Cd Gn 44:15, "you know";

§139e  *Imperfect: 3 m.s.* יִירַת H Gn 15:4, "he will inherit"; *1 s.* ניקד E Gn 38:26, "I will burn";[180] *3 m.pl.* ידעון F Lv 23:43, "they will know"; *2 m.pl.* וְתִדְעוּן Cd Ex 6:7, "you will know";

§139f  *Imperative: m.s.* הב E Gn 29:21, "give!"; *f.s.* הבי E Gn 30:14, "give!"; *m.pl.* הבו E Gn 29:22, "give!";

§139g  *Active Participle: m.s.* יָהֵיב Cd Gn 38:16, "giving"; יָקֵד Cd Gn 38:26, "burning," יָרֵית H Gn 15:2, "inheriting"; יָדַע B Gn 4:9, "knowing"; *f.s.* ילדה E Gn 30:1, "bearing"; יָתְבָא Cd Gn 38:21, "sitting"; יְקֵדָא Cd Gn 38:25, "burning"; *m.pl.* יכלין C Gn 34:14, "able"; יָדְעִין B Gn 3:5, "knowing";

§139h  *Passive Participle: m.s.* יְתִיב C Gn 35:9, "seated"; *m.pl.* יהיבין Cd Gn 47:1, "given";

§139i  *Infinitive:* למתב AA₂ Ex 12:29, "to sit"; למילד E Gn 29:35, "to bear"; מדע E Gn 43:7, "knowing"; לְמֵירַת D Dt 28:21;

§139j  *Verbal Noun:* מֵלדה E Gn 38:28, "her giving birth"; מולדה E Gn 38:27, "her giving birth";[181]

§139k  *D Passive Participle: m.s. (det.)* מייקרא F Lv 22:32, "honored";

§139l  *Verbal Noun:* יחמות E Gn 30:41, "being in heat";

§139m  *C Perfect: 3 m.s.* וְאוֹכַח C Gn 31:42, "he reproved"; *2 m.s.* אוֹלֵידְת Cd Gn 48:6, "you begat," אולדתּ Z Gn 48:6;[182] *3 m.pl.* אוליִדו C Gn 31:43, "they begat";[183]

§139n  *Imperfect: 3 m.s.* יוקד AA Nu 19:5, "he will burn," יוקד AA Nu 19:5; *1 s.* אוסף E Gn 38:26, "I will add"; *2 m.pl.* תוזפן A Ex 22:24, "you will lend"; תוקדון AA₁ Ex 12:10, "you will burn";

§139o  *Active Participle m.s.* מוקד AA Nu 19:8, "burning";

§139p  *Gt Perfect: 3 f.s.* אתיהבּת Z Gn 49:3, "it was given"; *3 m.pl.* אֶתְיַלֵדו Cd Gn 48:5, "they were born";[184]

§139q  *Imperfect: 3 m.s.* יתילֵיד F Lv 22:27, "he will be born"; *3 m.pl.* יתיהבן F Lv 23:20, "they will be given";

§139r  *Dt Perfect: 3 m.s.* ואתיחם E Gn 30:39, "they were in heat";[185]

§139s  *Participle: f.pl.* מתיחמן E Gn 30:38, "in heat";

§139t  *Ct Perfect: 3 m.s.* אתידע E Gn 41:21, "it was made known"; *3 m.pl.* איתותבו Cd Ex 6:4, "they sojourned";

§139u  *Imperfect: 3 f.s.* ותתוקד E Gn 38:24, "let her be burned!";

184

**§139v** *Infinitive:* למתוקדה E Gn 38:25, "to be burned"; לְמֶתּוֹתָבָא Cd Gn 47:4, "to sojourn".

**§140** *Verbs II-'*

**§140a** Only two roots are attested in G: שאל "ask" belonging to the (a,o) class and באש "bad, ill" belonging to the (e,?) class. Cf., e.g., *Perf. 3 m.s.* שְׁאֵל Cd Gn 44:19, *Imperf. 3 m.s.* וְיִשְׁאָל C Gn 32:18,[186] *Perf. 3 m.s.* בְּאֵשׁ B Gn 4:6 (the Imperfect is not attested). Both of these roots are also attested in C.[187]

**§140b** Only two roots are attested in D and Dt: סאב "to make impure," אסתאב "be impure," and שאר, which has gone over to verbs II-w/y > שייר "leave," אשתייר "be left, remain,"[188] e.g., *D Imperf. 2 m.pl.* תשיירן F Lv 22:30, *Dt Perf. 3 m.s.* וְאֶשְׁתַּיַּר Bd Gn 7:23.

**§140c** The elision of medial /'/ is attested in two examples:[189] *G Perf. 3 m.pl.* וְשִׁילוּ AA₁ Ex 12:35, "they asked"[190] (as against /'/ preserved in G Perf. 7x) and *C Perf. 3 m.pl.* ואשלו AA₁ Ex 12:36, "they lent" (only occurrence of C). Note that both examples occur in the same manuscript.

Representative examples of verbs II-' are

**§140d** *G Perfect: 3 m.s.* וּבְאֵשׁ B Gn 4:5, "it was bad", ובאיש Z Gn 48:17; ושאל E Gn 38:21, "he asked", ושאל E Gn 40:7; *3 m.pl.* ושאלו E Gn 43:26,27, "they asked";

**§140e** *Imperfect: 3 m.s.* וְיִשְׁאָל C Gn 32:18, "he will ask";

**§140f** *Active Participle: m.s.* בָּאֵישׁ Cd Gn 48:1, "sick"; *m.pl. (det.)* בָּיְשַׁיָּא C Gn 35:9; "sick";[191]

**§140g** *Infinitive:* משאול E Gn 43:7,9, "asking";

**§140h** *D Perfect: 3 m.s.* סאב AA Nu 19:13,20, "he made impure"; *3 m.pl.* סָאֵיבוּ C Gn 34:13, "they made impure";

**§140i** *Imperfect: 2 m.pl.* תשירן AA₁ Ex 12:10, "you will leave";

**§140j** *Passive Participle: m.s.* מסאב AA Nu 19:7, "impure";

**§140k** *Infinitive:* מסאבה AA Nu 19:22, "making impure";

**§140l** *C Perfect: 2 m.pl.* אַבְאֶ[ו]שתון Cd Gn 44:5, "you did evil";

**§140m** *Infinitive:* לְמַבְאָשָׁה C Gn 31:52, "to do evil";

**§140n** *Dt Perfect: 3 m.s.* ואשתייַר C Gn 32:25, "he remained", דאשתייר E Gn 30:36;

**§140o** *Imperfect: 3 m.s.* ויסתאב AA Nu 19:8, "he will be impure"; ויסתאב AA Nu 19:10; *3 f.s.* תסתאב Nu 19:22, "she will be impure";

**§140p** *Participle: m.s.* דמשתייר AA₁ Ex 17:16, "remaining," דמשתיר AA₁ Ex 12:10;

**§141** *Verbs II-w/y*

**§141a** Three verbs are attested with consonantal /w/:[192] חור "clean" (D), כן "direct, intend" (D,Dt), and צוח "shout" (G). Examples are

**§141b** *G Perfect: 3 m.s.* וצבחו E Gn 41:55 , "they shouted";[193]

**§141c** *Imperfect: 3 m.s.* יְצוֹחַ A Ex 22:22, "he will shout," יצוח A Ex 22:26;

**§141d** *Active Participle: m.s.* צָוַח C Gn 35:9, "shouting," צָוַח Cd Gn 38:26; *m.pl.* צָוְחִין B Gn 4:10, "shouting";

185

§141e  *D Perfect: 3 m.pl.* וחוורו F Ex 19:14, "they cleaned"; וכוּוינוּ Y Ex 19:2, "they directed";

§141f  *Imperfect: 3 m.s.* יחוֹר AA Nu 19:7, "he will clean," יחוּר AA Nu 19:8; *3 m.pl.* ויחוורון F Ex 19:10, "they will clean";

§141g  *Passive Participle: m.s.* וּמְחוַר Z Gn 49:11, "cleaned"; דמכוּן E Gn 28:17, "directed";

§141h  *Dt Perfect: 3 m.s.* אתבוֹן A Ex 21:13, "he intended."

§141i  Two verb classes are fully attested in non-consonantal II-w/y verbs in the G conjugation: (a,o) and (i,u). Examples of (a,o) are וקם B Gn 4:8, "he arose," וִיקוֹם A Ex 21:21, "he will arise"; ח E Gn 30:6, "he judged," יְדוּנִן C Gn 31:53, "they will judge"; חסו Z Gn 49:6, "they had pity," יחוּס E Gn 43:29, "he will have pity." The only verb belonging to the (i,u) class is מות "die," e.g., דְּמִיתַת C Gn 35:9,[194] "she died" and וִימוֹת A Ex 21:20, "he will die." There are no examples of the (a,i) class.

§141j  Medial /aya/ (11x) is more frequent in G Active Participles than is medial /a'e/ (3x), e.g., קים AA₁ Ex 17:9, "standing," but קָאִים E Gn 41:17.

§141k  Confusion with geminate verbs may be seen in the Infinitive לְמֵיחָב B Gn 4:7, "to be guilty."[195] G Infinitives are attested with both /a/ (classical form) and /u?/ (vulgar form), e.g., לְמְקָם B Gn 4:10, "to arise," but למקום AA₁ Ex 17:16.

§141l  Although the evidence is limited, it appears that both /'ettəqil/ and /'ettəqal/ are attested in Gt/Ct.[196]

Representative examples are

§141m  *G Perfect: 3 m.s.* קָם Cd Gn 38:26, "he arose"; מֵ֫ית E Gn 42:38, "he died"; *3 f.s.*[197] מֵיתַת Cd Gn 48:7, "she died"; טפת E Gn 31:22, "it flooded"; וְקָמַת Cd Gn 38:19, "she arose"; *1 s.* מֵיתִת Cd Gn 46:30, "I died"; *3 m.pl.* וקמו E Gn 29:22, "they arose"; קמן W Ex 15:8;[198] מֵ֫יתוּ Cd Ex 7:21, "they died," מיתן AA Nu 20:3;[199] *1 pl.* מִיתְנַן AA Nu 20:3, "we died";

§141n  *Imperfect: 3 m.s.* יִקוֹם A Ex 21:19, "he will arise";[200] יְמוֹת A Ex 21:18, "he will die"; *3 f.s.* דתקם Z Gn 49:7, "she will arise"; *2 m.s.* תְּמוּת B Gn 2:17, "you will die"; *3 m.pl.* יְמוּתְן Cd Ex 7:18, "they will die"; יקומן F Ex 20:13, "they will arise"; *2 m.pl.* תְּמוּתְן B Gn 3:3, "you will die"; ותשֻׁועוּן D Dt 27:4, "you will plaster";[201] *1 pl.* נמות E Gn 43:8, "we shall die"; ונקום E Gn 43:8, "we shall arise";

§141o  *Imperative: m.s.* קום E Gn 31:13, "arise!"; *m.pl.* קומו AA₁,₂ Ex 12:31, "arise!'";

§141p  *Active Participle: m.s.* מָיֵית Cd Gn 44:22, "dying," מָיֵית–Cd Gn 46:30; דטאייס E Gn 7:14, "flying," וטָאיס F Ex 20:2; *f.s.* קָיְמָא Cd Gn 37:33, "standing";[202] צימה F Lv 23:29, "fasting"; *m.pl.* מָיְתִין D Dt 5:22, "dying," מיתין AA₁ Ex 12:33; צימן F Lv 23:32, "fasting"; דקיימין F Ex 19:22,20:23, "standing," קָאימַיָּא Bd Gn 7:23, "those existing" (det.);[203]

§141q  *Passive Participle: m.s.* לִיט B Gn 4:11, "cursed"; *f.s.* לִילָה F Nu 28:28, "soaked"; *m.pl.* לִיטִין D Dt 28:16, "cursed";

186

§141r   *Infinitive:* למצום F Lv 23:29, "to fast"; מְמַת B Gn 3:4, "to die"; למקֹם Z Gn 49:17, "to arise";

§141s   *D Perfect: 3 m.s.* ־וְקַיֵים Cd Gn 47:31, "he fulfilled"; *2 m.s.* קימת AA Dt 26:15, "you fulfilled"; *1 s.* קיימֹית E Gn 9:17, "I fulfilled";

§141t   *Imperfect: 2 m.pl.* וּתקַימוּן D Dt 27:10, "you will fulfill"; ותשיעון AA Dt 27:2, "you will plaster"; ותצימן F Lv 23:27,32, "you will make fast";

§141u   *Imperative: m.s.* ־קַיֵים Cd Gn 47:31, "fulfill!";

§141v   *Active Participle: m.s.* מקיים E Gn 9:9, "fulfilling," מְסָיֵיף Cd Gn 44:18, "finishing";

§141w   *Passive Participle: f.s.* מְצָיירָא Cd Gn 37:23, "ornamented";

§141x   *Infinitive:* למקיימה E Gn 6:19, 7:3, "to fulfill";

§141y   *C Perfect: 3 m.s.* וְאַקֵים Cd Gn 47:2, "he wet up"; וַאריק C Gn 35:14, "he emptied"; וַאבִית C Gn 32:14, "he spent the night";[204] *1 s.* ־אֲקִימֶת C Gn 31:51, "I set up";

§141z   *Imperfect: 3 m.s.* יֹוזד A Ex 21:14, "he will harm"; *2 m.pl.* תקימון AA Dt 27:4, "you will set up";

§141aa   *Imperative: m.s.* אדיק AA Dt 26:15, "examine!"; *m.pl.* צְיתוּ [א?] D Dt 27:9, "obey!"

§141bb   *Active Participle: m.s.* מְכִיל Cd Gn 38:26, "measuring"; *f.s.* מקימה E Gn 38:25, "setting up";

§141cc   *Infinitive:* ולמקמה F Lv 22:27, "to set up";

§141dd   *Gt/Ct Perfect: 3 m.s.* ואתעיר E Gn 41:7, "he woke up"; *1 s.* ואתעירת E Gn 41:21, "I woke up";

§141ee   *Imperfect: 3 m.pl.* יְתָּזָנֻן Cd Gn 41:40, "they will be fed";

§141ff   *Participle:* ־מִיתְּכִיל Cd Gn 38:26, "is measured";

§141gg   *Dt Perfect: 3 m.pl.* וְאֵדִינוּ AA Nu 20:3, "they contended"; *3 f.pl.* ואתקיימין H Gn 15:1, "they were fulfilled"; *1 pl.* וְאֵיתקַיֵמְנָ D Dt 5:23, "we endured";

§141hh   *Imperfect: 1 s.* ונתחייב E Gn 39:9, "I will be guilty"; *1 pl.* וְנֶתחַיֵיב Cd Gn 37:21;

§141ii   *Participle: m.pl.* מְדַיִינָן B Gn 4:8, "contending"; דמתגירן AA Nu 19:10, "adulterous";

§142   **Geminate Verbs**

§142a   The only verb attested in both the Perfect and the Imperfect of G is עלל "enter," which belongs to the (a,o) class, e.g., *Perf. 3 m.s.* וְעָאל Cd Gn 38:18, *Imperf. 2 m.s.* ־תֵּיעוֹל Cd Gn 38:16.

§142b   There are no examples of verbs of the type עֲיֵיל (G Active Participle) or עֲיֵיל (D perfect), as are infrequently attested in Galilean Aramaic and the Palestinian Targumim.[205]

§142c   The meager evidence in these fragments points to by-forms of the type *Act. Ptc. m.pl.* /'alǝlin/ עֲלְלִין D Dt 28:21) and /'allin/ (as reflected in the pointing of the f.pl.det. עֲלְלָתָא Cd Gn 41:35).[206]

Representative examples are

187

**§142d** *G Perfect: 3 m.s.* וְעָאל Cd Gn 43:26, "he entered," דיעאל Z Gn 49:7,[207] על E Gn 7:13; *1 s.* עַלֵּית- Cd Ex 5:23, "I entered";[208] *3 m.pl.* דְעָאלו Cd Gn 46:26, "they entered,"[209] עלו E Gn 7:15; *3 f.pl.* עלין E Gn 41:21, "they entered";

**§142e** *Imperfect: 3 m.s.* יֵעוֹל A Ex 21:3, "he will enter," יעול AA Nu 19:7; *3 f.s.* תעול E Gn 30:38, "she will enter"; *2 m.s.* ותיעול E Gn 6:18, "you will enter"; *1 s.* אִיעוֹל Cd Gn 37:30, "I will enter"; נ]אבח W Ex 15:9, "I shall plunder"; *3 m.pl.* יעלֹן A Ex 22:8, "they will enter," יעלן E Gn 6:20; *2 m.pl.* תעלן AA₁ Ex 12:25, "you will enter"; תחגן F Lv 23:39, "you will celebrate";

**§142f** *Imperative: m.s.* על E Gn 7:1, "enter!"

**§142g** *Active Participle: m.pl.* לבזזֶ E Gn 38:23, "plundering";[210] עָלְלין D Dt 28:21, "entering"; *f.pl.* עַלְלָתָא Cd Gn 41:35, "entering" (det.);[211]

**§142h** *Passive Participle: m.s.* חֲקִיק D Dt 27:8, "engraved"; *m.pl.* צרירין W Ex 15:8, "bound"; *f.pl.* צרימָ AA₁ Ex 12:34, "bound";

**§142i** *Infinitive:* למיעול AA₁ Ex 12:23, "to enter," למעל E Gn 31:18; למגיז E Gn 31:19, "to shear";[212]

**§142j** *Verbal Noun:* בְּמֵיחַם C Gn 35:9, "heat," בְּמֵיחם C Gn 35:9; מַעֲלֵ Cd Gn 48:5, "my entering"; מַעֲלָךְ Cd Gn 48:7, "your entering"; מעלה E Gn 43:25, "his (the?) entering"; במעלהון E Gn 30:38, "their entering"; מעלֹי- A Ex 22:25, "entering" ("setting of the sun");

**§142k** *D Perfect: 3 m.s.* מַלֵּיל D Dt 5:19, "he spoke," מַלֵּל- C Gn 35:13; *2 m.s.* מַלֵּלֹת A Ex 4:10, "you spoke,"[213] מללת E Gn 30:34; *1 s.* מללת F Ex 20:19, "I spoke"; *3 m.pl.* מַלֵּילו D Dt 5:25, "they spoke," מַלֵּילי-D Dt 5:25; *2 m.pl.* מללתון AA₁ Ex 12:32, "you spoke";

**§142l** *Imperfect: 3 m.s.* יְמַלֵּיל- D Dt 5:21, "he will speak," יְמַלֵּיל-Cd Gn 44:18, "let him speak"; *2 m.s.* תְּמַלֵּיל D Dt 5:24, "you will speak," תמלל E Gn 31:24; *2 m.pl.* תמללן C Gn 32:20, "you will speak";

**§142m** *Imperative: m.s.* מלל F Lv 23:10,34, "speak!"; *m.pl.* מללו AA₁ Ex 12:3, "speak!";

**§142n** *Active Participle: m.s.* ממלל E Gn 29:9, "speaking," ממלל F Ex 19:19;

**§142o** *Infinitive:* לַמְמַלָּא Cd Ex 5:23, "to speak," לְמְמַלָּלה Z Gn 44:19;

**§142p** *Verbal Noun:* במללותה E Gn 39:10, "her speaking"; בְּמַלָּלוּתְכוֹן D Dt 5:25, "your speaking";

**§142q** *C Perfect: 3 m.s.* וְאָעֵיל B Gn 2:22, "he brought in," אָעֵיל Cd Gn 43:16; ואגן AA₁ Ex 12:27, "he protected"; *2 m.s* אַפֶּסְתְּ F Ex 20:22, "you desecrated"; *3 m.pl.* ואעלו E Gn 43:26, "they brought in," וא]עֵילֹוֹ Cd Gn 37:32; *2 m.pl.* אָעֶלתוֹן AA Nu 20:5, "you brought in";

**§142r** *Imperfect: 3 m.s.* ויגן AA₁ Ex 12:13, "he will protect"; *2 m.s.* תעל E Gn 6:19, "you will bring in"; *1 s.* וְאָעֵל Cd Ex 6:8, "I shall bring in"; *2 m.pl.* ותעלן AA Dt 27:6, "you will bring in"; תפסן F Lv 22:32, "you will desecrate";

**§142s** *Imperative: m.s.* אָעֵיל Cd Gn 43:16, "bring in!";

**§142t** *Infinitive:* לְמָעֲלה AA Nu 20:5, "to bring in";

**§142u** *Gt Perfect: 3 f.s.* ואתרעת Z Gn 49:7, "it was ruined";

188

**§142v** *Participle: m.s.* וּמְתֻחֲקַק F Ex 20:2, "engraved";

**§142w** *Dt Perfect: 3 m.pl.* אֶתְקַלְלוּ ־ Bd Gn 8:8, "they were diminished";

**§142x** *Imperfect: 3 m.s.* וְיִתְחַלַל H Gn 15:1, "it will be desecrated";

**§142y** *Ct Perfect: 3 m.pl.* אֶתְעֲלוּ֬ Cd Gn 43:18, "they were brought up";

**§142z** *Participle: m.pl.* מְתַעֲלִין Cd Gn 43:18, "brought up."

**§143 Verbs III-w/y/'**

**§143a** As expected, verbs III-*' have fallen together with verbs III-*w/y. Verbs III-*', however, are almost always written with *aleph*, probably under the influence of Hebrew orthography,[214] e.g., one finds *aleph* in 51 out of the 59 attestations of the root קרא "call." On occasion, *aleph* is found with verbs III-*w/y, e.g., גְלָא B Gn 4:14, "wandering."[215]

**§143b** The only verbal class attested in G is (a,e), e.g., וּקְרָא C Gn 31:47, "he called," יְקַר־ Cd Gn 46:33, "he will call." Verbs *(i,a)[216] appear to have (a,e) reflexes, e.g., ושתה E Gn 9:21, "he drank"; ורבה E Gn 9:21, "he became drunk";[217] ושתתו E Gn 43:34, "they drank"; ורבו E Gn 43:34, "they became drunk";[218] וּסְגוֹ Bd Gn 7:17, "they increased"; יִסְגוֹן Cd Gn 48:16, "they will increase."

The following are salient features of verbs III-w/y/':

**§143c** *Perfect: G 3 m.s.* /-a/, but /-i/ in derived conjugations;[219] *G 3 f.s.* /-at/, but /-yat/ in derived conjugations;[220] *G 2 m.s.* /-et/; *1 s.* /-et/, but /-et/, /-yet/ in derived conjugations;[221] *3 m.pl.* /-on/ with one exception אֶתְגְּלוּן C Gn 35:7, "they revealed themselves";[222] *G 3 f.pl.* /-en/, but /-yen/ in derived conjugations;[223]

**§143d** *Imperfect: 3 m.pl.* /-on/; *3 f.pl.* suffix /-yan/

**§143e** *Imperative: m.s.* /-e/ or /-i/;[224] *m.pl.* /-on/

**§143f** *Participle: m.pl.* /-ayin/ with one exception שָׁנִין AA₁ Ex 12:12, "different";[225] *f.pl.* /-yan/

**§143g** *Infinitive:* /-aya/ of derived conjugations is preserved.[226]

Representative examples are

**§143h** *G Perfect: 3 m.s.* ובעה E Gn 43:30, "he sought"; וּשְׁרָא B Gn 4:16, "he dwelt"; בְּרָא D Dt 26:19, "he created"; וּקְרָא C Gn 35:7, "he called"; מְטָא־ C Gn 32:27, "it has arrived"; חַמָא C Gn 32:26, "he saw"; וּבְנָא C Gn 35:7, "he built"; *3 f.s.* בְּעַת Cd Gn 38:25, "she sought"; וּקְהַת C Gn 32:26, "it was dislocated? benumbed?";[227] חֲמָת־ Cd Gn 38:25, "she saw"; תְּלָת Cd Gn 38:26,ֿ "she lifted"; וּקְראת E Gn 29:32, "she called"; *1 s.* חֲמִית Cd Gn 46:30, "I saw"; חַטִית Cd Ex 9:27, "I sinned"; ברית E Gn 7:4,ֿ "I created"; *3 m.pl.* לְקוּן Cd Ex 9:31, "they were smitten"; קפו W Ex 15:8, "they congealed"; עֲנוֹ C Gn 34:13, "they answered"; ושרון F Ex 19:2, "they encamped"; וַחֲמוֹן Cd Gn 37:25, "they saw"; *3 f.pl.* כהין F Dt 34:7, "they grew dim"; *2 m.pl.* חמיתון F Ex 19:4, 20:19, "you saw"; *1 pl.* מְטֵינַן Cd Gn 43:21, "we arrived"; חֲמֵינַן D Dt 5:21, "we saw";

**§143i** *Imperfect: 3 m.s.* ויחמי AA₁,₂ Ex 12:23, "he will see"; יִמְחָא־ D Dt 28:22, "he will smite"; *2 m.s.* תֶּחֱמִי Cd Ex 6:1, "you will see"; *1 s.* אחמי C Gn 32:21, "I shall see"; אֶבְרָא־ B Gn 2:18, "I will create"; אֶרְעֵי C Gn 32:21, "I shall appease"; *3 m.pl.* וְיֶשְׁרְון C Gn 34:21, "they will dwell"; וְיָסְגון Cd Gn 48:16, "they will increase"; *2 m.pl.* וְתֶחְדֶון D Dt 27:7, "you will rejoice"; תֶּשְׁרְון C Gn 34:10, "you wil dwell"; דתמנון F Lv 23:16, "you will count"; תחוֹמַֿון E Gn 43:5, "you will see"; *1 pl.* וְנֶחְמֵי Cd Gn 37:20, "we shall see"; וְנִשְׁרֵ C Gn 34:16, "we shall dwell";

§143j    *Imperative: m.s.* חֲמֵי C Gn 31:50,ˆ "see!," חֲמִׂי Cd Gn 41:41ˀ סְגִּי C Gn 35:11, "increase!"; עֲנִי Cd Gn 38:25, "answer!"; שְׁרִ E Gn 29:19,ˆ "dwell!"; *m.pl.* סְגון C Gn 35:9, "increase!"; וּמְלַן C Gn 35:9, "fill!";

§143k    *Active Participle: m.s.* דֿחֹמֵי A Ex 22:9,ˆ "seeing," חָמֵי C Gn 31:43; וּבָכֵי C Gn 35:9, "crying," גְּלֵא B Gn 4:16,ˆ "wandering," יְסָגֵי⁻ Cd Gn 48:16, "increasing," שֶׁתֵי⁻ Cd Gn 44:5, "drinking," קָרֵא⁻ C Gn 31:46, "calling," קָרֵי⁻ B Gn 2:19, "calling"; בעי E Gn 31:15, "seeking"; שר E Gn 29:22, "dwelling"; *f.s.* טָעְיָא C Gn 31:39, "straying"; בכייה E Gn 29:17, "crying"; שָׁרְיָה F Ex 20:18,ˆ "dwelling";²²⁸ בעייה E Gn 30:15, "seeking"; *m.pl.* חֲמֵין F Ex 20:2, "seeing"; רָעֵין Cd Gn 46:32, "grazing"; בעיין E Gn 42:36, "seeking"; שָׁרֵין W Ex 15:9, "dwelling," שָׁרֵין Z Gn 49:7; *f. pl.* רעיין E Gn 41:18, "grazing";

§143l    *Passive Participle: m.s.* גְּלֵי C Gn 31:42, "revealed," גְּלֵא B Gn 3:5,ˀ²²⁹ רְעֵי C Gn 34:19, "enamored"; *m.pl.* עֲצִין D Dt 28:29,ˆ "oppressed";²³⁰ *f.pl.* מַלְיָן E Gn 41:22, "full";

§143m    *Infinitive:* לְמֶחְמֵי B Gn 2:19, "to see," למחמֵי E Gn 41:18; לְמִשְׁתֵּי Cd Ex 7:18, "to drink"; למרעי E Gn 30:31, "to graze"; למסֹגי E Gn 30:30, "to increase"; לְמִשְׁרֵ C Gn 34:22, "to dwell," לְמִשְׁרָא B Gn 4:13; לממני E Gn 41:49, "to count"; למבכי E Gn 43:30, "to cry";

§143n    *D Perfect: 3 m.s.* וְתַגִּי Cd Gn 47:1, "he told"; שָׁרֵ Cd Gn 44:12,ˆ "he began"; ומני E Gn 41:43, "he appointed"; ומאני E Gn 39:4, "he appointed";²³¹ וּבַנִּ B Gn 2:22, "he built"; שַׁהִי C Gn 34:19, "he tarried";²³² *3 f.s.* זַנִּיַת Cd Gn 38:24, "she whored"; ותנית E Gn 29:12, "she told"; *2 m.s.* תנית E Gn 31:27, "you told"; רבית E Gn 31:13, "you raised"; *1 s.* סַכַּיִֿת Cd Gn 48:11, "I awaited"; צלית E Gn 30:8, "I prayed"; *3 f.pl.* תשרין E Gn 41:54, "they began"; *1 pl.* ותנינן E Gn 41:12, "we told";

§143o    *Imperfect: 3 m.s.* יִכְסֵי A Ex 21:33, "he will cover"; *2 m.s.* ותתני F Ex 19:3, "you will tell"; *1 s.* וַאֲתַנִּי Cd Gn 46:31, "I shall tell";²³³ *3 m.pl.* ויתנון H Gn 15:1, "they will tell"; *2 m.pl.* ותצלון AA₂ Ex 12:32, "you will pray"; *1 pl.* וּנְכַסֵּי Cd Gn 37:26, "we shall cover";

§143p    *Imperative: m.s.* מַלִּי Cd Gn 44:1,ˆ "fill!"; *m.pl.* צלון Cd Ex 9:28, "pray!"; תנון E Gn 40:8 "tell!";

§143q    *Active Participle: m.s.* וּמְסַגֵּי Cd Gn 48:4, "increasing"; מגלי Z Gn 49:2, "revealing"; *f.s.* ומצלייה E Gn 29:17, "praying"; *m.pl.* מצליין F Ex 20:15, "praying"; מסכיין E Gn 31:22, "awaiting";

§143r    *Passive Participle: m.s.* מְמַנֵי Cd Gn 43:16, "appointed," מְמַנִּי-Cd Gn 44:1; מְדַמֵי Z Gn 49:22, "likened to"; *m.pl.* מדמיין Z Gn 44:18;²³⁴

§143s    *Infinitive:* למצליה AA₁ Ex 17:11, "to pray";²³⁵

§143t    *Verbal Noun:* וְשֵׁירוּי Z Gn 49:3, "beginning," שירה F Lv 23:10; שירוֿה E Gn 28:19,ˆ "the beginning," שירויה E Gn 41:21;

190

§143u   *C Perfect: 3 m.s.* וְאַשְׁקִי E Gn 29:10, "he watered"; אַשְׁקִי F Lv 22:27; *3 m.pl.* וְאַסְחוֹן E Gn 43:24, "they washed";

§143v   *Imperfect: 3 m.s.* וִיסַחֵי AA Nu 19:7, "he will wash"; וְיִסְרַח Cd Ex 7:18, "it will stink"; *2 m.s.* וְתַשְׁקִי AA Nu 20:8, "you will give drink"; *3 m.pl.* וְיַשְׁקוֹן E Gn 29:3, "they will water";

§143w   *Active Participle: m.s.* מַשְׁקִי E Gn 40:13, "giving drink";

§143x   *Imperative: m.pl.* אַשְׁקוֹן E Gn 29:7, "water!"; אָסְגוֹן C Gn 34:12, "increase!";[236] וּרְעוֹן E Gn 29:7, "graze!";

§143y   *Infinitive:* לְמַשְׁקְייָה E Gn 31:22, "to water"; לְמַשְׁרֵיא AA Dt 26:2, "to cause to dwell";

§143z   *Gt Perfect: 3 m.s.* אֶתְבְּרִיא B Gn 4:8, "it was created,"[237] אֶתְבְּרִי B Gn 4:8; אֶתְגְּלִי־ Cd Gn 48:3, "he revealed himself"; *3 f.s.* וְאִתְגְּלִיַת AA Nu 20:6, "it was revealed";[238] וְאֶתַּלְיִיַת Bd Gn 7:17, "it was suspended"; אֶתְבְּרִיַת־ B Gn 2:23, "she was created," אֶתְבְּרִיָה B Gn 2:23; אֶתְרְעִיַת Z Gn 49:6, "she was pleased";[239] *2 m.s.* אֶתְגְּלִית־ C Gn 35:9, "you revealed yourself," אֶתְגְּלִיַת C Gn 35:9, אֶתְגְּלִית C Gn 35:9; אֶתְגְּלִיַת C Gn 35:9; *1 s.* וְאִתְגְּלִית Cd Ex 6:3, "I revealed myself," אתגליית E Gn 31:13; *3 m.pl.* אֶתְחֲמוֹן Bd Gn 8:5, "they were seen"; אֶתְגְּלוֹן C Gn 35:7, "they revealed themselves";[240]

§143aa   *Imperfect: 3 m.s.* וִישְׁתְּבֵי A Ex 22:9, "he is taken captive"; יִתְלֵא־ B Gn 4:15, "it will be suspended";[241] יִשְׁתְּרֵי B Gn 4:7, "it will be forgiven"; וְיִתְקְרֵא Cd Gn 48:16, "he will be called," יתקרֵי C Gn 32:29; יִתְחֲמֵי F Ex 20:13, "he will be seen"; יִתְמְנֶה HH Ex 12:2, "he will be counted";[242] *3 f.s.* וְתִתְחֲמֵי E Gn 9:14, "it will be seen"; *3 m.pl.* יִתְקְרְאוּן Cd Gn 48:6, "they will be called," יִתְקְרוּן Z Gn 48:5; יִתְמְנוּן Cd Gn 32:13, "they will be counted";[243] *2 m.pl.* תִתְמְנוּן AA₁ Ex 12:4, "you will be counted";

§143bb   *Participle: m.s.* מִתְקְרֵא D Dt 27:8, "read," מתקרי AA Dt 27:8; מתגלי F Ex 19:9, "revealed"; *f.s.* מתמניה Z Gn 44:18, "counted"; *f.pl.* מתגליין E Gn 41:45, "revealed";

§143cc   *Infinitive:* לְמִתְקְרֵא B Gn 2:23, "to be called"; לְמֶתְבְּרֵיא B Gn 2:23, "to be created"; למתמנֵיה AA₁ Ex 12:4, "to be counted";

§143dd   *Dt Perfect: 3 m.s.* וְאִתֲּנֵי Cd Gn 48:2, "it was told," אתני E Gn 31:22; וְאִשְׁתְּהִי Cd Gn 43:31, "he tarried";[244] *3 m.pl.* וְאִתְכַּסוֹן Bd Gn 7:19, "they were covered"; *3 f.pl.* אשׁתּנין F Dt 34:7, "they were changed";[245] *1 pl.* דְּאִשְׁתְּהֵינַן Cd Gn 43:10, "we tarried";

§143ee   *Active Participle: m.s.* מְתַמַּנֵּי Cd Gn 44:18, "appointed";

§143ff   *Infinitive:* למשׁתּהיא AA₁ Ex 12:39, "to tarry."[246]

## Doubly Weak and Irregular Verbs

§144   *I-n, Geminate*

נדד: *G Perf 3 f.s.* וְנַדַּת C Gn 31:40, "it was restless."

§145   *I-y, Geminate*

§145a   יבב: *D Verbal Noun* וְ[י]בבו F Lv 23:24, "wailing";

§145b   ילל: *D Act. Ptc. m.pl.* מְיַלְלִין E Gn 42:34, "spying."[247]

§146   *Geminate, II-y, III-y*

191

חיי: *G Imperf. 3 m.s.* יֶחֱיֵ F Ex 19:13, "he will live," יְחֵיֻ° E Gn 41:43; יחיי E Gn 31:32;[248] *1 pl.* ונחי E Gn 43:8, "we shall live."

**§147 I-n, II-w**

**§147a** נוח: *G Perf. 3 f.s.* וְנָא[ח]ת Bd Gn 8:7, "she rested";[249] *C Imperf. 2 m.s.* הֶתְנִיח A Ex 23:12; "you will give rest"; *Gt Perf. 3 m.s.* אֶתְנֵייחֿ C Gn 35:9, "he rested,"[250] וְאִתְנֵייח F Ex 20:11;

**§147b** נוף: *C Imperf. 3 m.s.* יניף F Lv 23:11,20, "he will wave"; *2 m.pl.* תניפון F Lv 23:12, "you will wave"; *Verbal Noun:* דאנפותא F Lv 23:15, "of waving," אנפי F Lv 23:20;[251]

**§147c** *I-n, III-y* נצי: *Dt Imperf.: 3 m.pl.* יתנצון A Ex 21:22, "they will contend."

**§148 I-', III-y**

**§148a** אפי: *G Perf. 3 m.s.* אפה F Lv 22:27, "he baked"; *3 m.pl.* ואפון AA₁ Ex 12:39, "they baked"; *Gt Imperf. 3 f.pl.* תתאפיין F Lv 23:17, "they will be baked";[252]

**§148b** אתי: *G Perf. 3 m.s.* וַאתָא C Gn 34:20, "he came"; אֲתָה E Gn 30:11;[253] *3 f.s.* אתת E Gn 29:9, "she came"; *3 m.pl.* אֲתוֹן Cd Gn 46:31, "they came," אָתוֹן Cd Gn 47:1; *1 pl.* אֲתֵינַ Cd Gn 47:7, "we came"; *Imperf. 3 m.s.* ייתא A Ex 22:12, "he will come"; *3 f.s.* תיתי E Gn 41:50, "she will come"; *3 f.pl.* וְיִתְיָן D Dt 28:15; "they will come";[254] *Imper. m.s.* אֲתָא C Gn 31:44, "come!," אֲתָא B Gn 4:8; *f.s.* אתיי E Gn 30:2, "come!"[255] *m.pl.* אתון E Gn 37:20, "come!"; *Act. Ptc. m.s.* אָתֵי Cd Gn 48:2, "come," אתי F Ex 20:13; *f.s.* אתייה E Gn 37:25, "come," אתיה E Gn 29:6; *m.pl.* ואתיין H Gn 15:1, "come"; *Inf.* למיתי E Gn 41:54, "to come"; *Verbal Noun* בְמֵתָיִי Cd Gn 48:7, "my coming," במתיי Z Gn 48:7; בְמֵיתְיֵה C Gn 35:9, "his coming," במתייה C Gn 35:9; *C Perf. 3 m.s.* וְאַיְתֵי B Gn 2:19, "he brought," אייתי E Gn 30:14; *1 s.* אַיְיתֵיתִי C Gn 31:39, "I brought,"[256] אייתית E Gn 42:37; אייתיית E Gn 43:9, אֵיתֵיתֿ Z Gn 44:18; *3 m.pl.* אַיְתוּן Cd Gn 46:32, "they brought," ואייתון E Gn 37:32, אייתון E Gn 43:2; *2 m.pl.* אייתיתון E Gn 43:5, "you brought"; *1 pl.* אייתֵינַ AA Dt 26:10, "we brought"; *Imperf. 3 m.pl.* וְיֵיתוֹן AA Nu 19:2, "they will bring";[257] *2 m.pl.* ותייתון F Lv 23:10, "you will bring," תיתון F Lv 23:14.

**§149 I-w, III-y**

**§149a** ידי: *C Perf. 3 m.pl.* וְאוֹדוֹן Cd Gn 43:28, "they thanked," ואודו AA₁,₂ Ex 12:27;[258] *1 pl.* ואודינן AA Dt 26:10, "we thanked"; *Imperf. 1 s.* אודה E Gn 29:35, "I will thank,"[259] נודי W Ex 15:21;[260] *Verbal Noun* הודייה F Lv 22:29, "thanking";[261]

**§149b** יחי: *C Perf. 3 m.s.* אוחי F Lv 22:27, "he hurried";

**§149c** ירי: *C Verbal Noun:* אוֹרָיְתָה D Dt 27:3, "the teaching, law," אוֹרָיְתָה D Dt 27:8; דאוֹרָיְתֵי F Ex 20:6, "my teaching," דאורייתי F Lv 22:31.

**§150 II-', III-y**

גאי: *Gt/Dt? Imperf. 3 m.s.* וְיִתְגָאה Z Gn 49:17; "and he will be proud."[262]

**§151 II-w, III-y**

192

§151a הוי: *G Perf. 3 m.s.* וַהֲוָה B Gn 4:8, "it was," הֲוָה C Gn 31:42, הוֺא C Gn 34:19; הוֺא C Gn 34:19, *3 f.s.* הֲוֺת B Gn 4:16, "it was," ־דַּהֲוַת C Gn 31:39, דַּהֲוַת Cd Ex 9:24; *3 m.pl.* וַהֲווֺן B Gn 4:8, "they were," דַהווֺן C Gn 31:39; הֲוֺן B Gn 2:25, הוֺן AA₁ Ex 17:11; *3 f.pl.* הֲוֵין Cd Ex 9:32, "they were," דהוֵֺרין E Gn 41:21; *2 m.pl.* הוֺדֵתֻון A Ex 22:20, "you were"; *Imperf. 3 m.s.* וִיהוֵֺי A Ex 21:6, "it will be," יֶהֱוֵי C Gn 35:10, יהוה E Gn 28:20; *3 f.s.* תֶהוֵֺי A Ex 22:10, "it will be," תהוֵֺי A Ex 21:34, תֶּהֱוֵי C Gn 34:10; *2 m.s.* תֶהֱוֵי B Gn 4:7, "you will be," תֶּהֵֻוי B Gn 4:12; *1 s.* נהוֵֺי E Gn 43:9, "let me be!";[263] *3 m.pl.* וְיֶהֱוֺן Cd Ex 7:19, "they will be," יֶהֱוֺן D Dt 28:17; *3 f.pl.* וְיֶהֱוֻויֺן A Ex 22:23, "they will be," ויהיין E Gn 30:38;[264] *2 m.pl.* וְתֶהֱווֺן D Dt 28:29, "you will be," תהוֺון F Nu 28:29; *1 pl.* וְנֶהֱוֵי C Gn 34:16, "we shall be," נֶהֱוֵי Cd Gn 44:9, נהויה E Gn 38:23;[265] *Imper. m.pl.* הֱווֺן F Ex 20:8, "be!" *Act. Ptc. m.s.* וְהָוֵי B Gn 4:14, "being";[266] *m.pl.* וֺ]הָווֺין B Gn 2:24, "being"; *Inf.* לְמֶהֱוֵֺא B Gn 2:18, "to be," לְמֶהֱוֵי, Cd Gn 44:18, לְמֶהֱוֵי D Dt 26:18; למהווי F Lv 22:33; *Verbal Noun:* למהווין E Gn 30:41, "their being."

§151b There are two attestations of a shortened Imperfect יהי. The first is found in an interpolated passage and functions modally: יְהִי־שְׁמָךְ מְבָרַךְ C Gn 35:9, "May your name be blessed!" One expects a pointing of יְהֵי; יְהִי is probably a Hebraism.[267] The second attestation is found in a non-modal context: ויהי ממרי בסעדך E Gn 31:3, "and my Word will help you" (MT וְאֶהְיֶה עִמָּךְ). Note that the regular Imperfect /yehwe/ also functions modally, e.g., יֶהֱוֵי קָן ליט־ B Gn 4:11, "Cain shall be cursed!" Shortened Imperfect forms are attested alongside longer Imperfect forms in Syriac,[268] Galilean Aramaic,[269] Targum Onqelos,[270] and the other Palestinian Targumim.[271] The shortened Imperfect alone is attested in Palestinian Syriac[272] and Samaritan Aramaic.[273]

§151c There are four certain examples of a Participial conjugation[274] + הוי: הֲוֵינָא :אנה C Gn 31:39, ־הֲוֵינָא C Gn 31:39, הֲוֵינָא C Gn 31:40, הוֵיֺנֺה E Gn 29:33; Note that this form appears to have supplanted the Perfect 1 s. *הוית in the Palestinian Targum.[275] There are four possible examples of הוי: + את[276] הֲוֵית C Gn 31:39, הֲוֵית Z Gn 49:9, ־הֲוֵית Cd Gn 44:18, הֲוַת E Gn 40:13. There is one possible example of הוי: + אנן דַהֲוֵיֺן Cd Gn 44:18. Both הוית and הוינן can also be analyzed, however, as Perfect forms.

§151d חוי: *D Perf. 3 m.s.*[277] ־חַוִּי Cd Gn 48:11, "he showed," חַוִּי־ D Dt 5:21, חַוִּי E Gn 41:25; *Imper. m.s.* חווי E Gn 37:16, "tell!"; *Act. Ptc. m.s.* וֺ]מְ]חַוֶּה] Cd Gn 37:33, "showing," דמחווי E Gn 41:24; *Inf.* למחוויה E Gn 43:6, "to tell";
§151e שוי: *D Perf. 3 m.s.* וְשַׁוִּי B Gn 2:21, "he placed," וְשַׁוִּי B Gn 4:15; וְשַׁוִּי C Gn 32:17; *3 f.s.* ושוית E Gn 31:34, "she placed"; *1 s.* ושׁוּית E Gn 40:11, "I placed,"[278] ושוית E Gn 40:12; *3 m.pl.* וְשַׁוּוֺ B Ex 39:31, "they placed," ושוון E Gn 9:23, ושוון E Gn 43:32; *Imperf. 3 m.s.* יְשַׁוֵּה E Ex 21:22, "he will place," יְשַׁוֵּי A Ex 21:30; וְשַׁוֵּיר־ Cd Gn 48:20; [279] *2 m.s.* תשוֵֺי A Ex 21:1, "you will place," תשׁוֵֺ E Gn 44:2; *2 m.pl.* תשוון A Ex 22:24, "you will place," תְשַׁוֺּן C Gn 32:17, ותשׁון AA Dt 26:2; *Imper. m.s.* וְשַׁוֵּי Cd Gn 44:1, "place!," שַׁוִּי־ Cd Gn 47:29, שַׁוִּי E Gn 42:37; *m.pl.* שַׁוּוֺן Cd Gn 43:31, "place!," שׁוּוֺן E Gn 43:31; *Act. Ptc. m.s.* משווי E Gn 30:42, "placing"; *Inf.* לַ]נְ]מְשַׁוְיָא] Cd Ex 5:21, "to place," וְלַמְשַׁוְיָה D Dt 26:19;

ולמשׁויה AA Dt 26:19; *Dt Imperf. 1 pl.* נשׁתוה C Gn 34:15, "we shall agree," נשׁתוה C Gn 34:23.

**§152    *Irregular Verbs.***

**§152a**   הלך: *D Perf. 3 m.pl.* הליכו W Ex 15:19, "they walked"; *Imperf. 2 m.pl.* תהלכון E Gn 42:38, "you go"; *Act. Ptc. f.s.* דמהלכה C Gn 32:21, "going";[280] *m.pl.* דמהלכין C Gn 32:20, "going"; *Dt Imperf. 3 m.s.* יתהלך A Ex 21:19, "he will walk about";[281]

**§152b**   סלק: *G Perf. 3 m.s.* סלק- C Gn 32:27, "he went up," וסלק Cd Gn 46:29, סלק AA₁ Ex 12:38; *3 m.pl.* סלקו AA₁ Ex 17:10, "they went up"; *Imperf. 3 f.s.* תסק E Gn 29:17, "she will go up"; *2 m.s.* ותסוק F Ex 19:24, "you will go up"; *1 s.* אסק Cd Gn 46:31, "I shall go up"; *Act. Ptc. m.s.* וסליק Z Gn 49:11, "going up"; *m.pl.* דסלקין E Gn 31:10,12, "going up"; *f.pl.* סלקן E Gn 41:6, "going up," סלקן E Gn 41:18; *Inf.* למסק F Ex 19:12,13,23,24; *Verbal Noun:* מסק Cd Gn 32:25, "going up"; *C Perf. 3 m.pl.* ואסקו Cd Gn 37:28, "they brought up," ואסקו E Gn 37:28; *Inf.* למסקה- D Dt 28:23, "to bring up"; *Dt Perf. 3 f.* ואסתלקת C Gn 35:13, "it went away."[282]

### Verbal Forms of Foreign Origin

**§153    *Greek***

The following verbs go back to Greek forms: τάξις "arrangement" (τάσσω "to draw up, form): D Perf. 3 m.s.* וטבס Cd Gn 46:29, "he arranged"; παρρησία "outspokenness, freedom of speech": Qt. Act. Ptc. f.s.* מפרסיא- Cd Gn 38:25, "make known, publicize,"[283] מפרסייה E Gn 38:25; καλός "beautiful": D Act. Ptc. m.pl.* מקלסין E Gn 41:43, "praise"; κῆνσος, Lat. census "fine, penalty":[284] Gt Imperf. 3 m.s.* יתקנס A Ex 21:20, "he will be punished," יתקנס A Ex21:21; יתקנס A Ex 21:22; *Inf.* מתקנסה A Ex 21:20; מתקנסה A Ex 21:22; προνοέω "to provide".[285] D Inf. למפרנסה E Gn 30:30, "to provide"; φερνή "dowry":[286] C Imperf. 3 m.s.* יפרן A Ex 22:15, "he will provide the dowry"; [287] Inf. מפרנה A Ex 22:15.[288]

**§154    *Akkadian***

**§154a**   The following verbs go back to Akkadian nominal forms: *Akk. /asū/ "physician"* (< Sumerian A.ZU):[289] G Perf. 3 m.s.* דאסא A Ex 21:19, "he healed"; *Act. Ptc. m.s. (det.)* אסיא A Ex 21:19, "the healer, physician"; *D Inf.* למסיא C Gn 35:9, "to heal"; *Akk. /tamkaru/ "merchant":*[290] Dt Imperf. 3 m.pl.* ויתגרון C Gn 34:21, "they will trade"; *Imper. m.pl.* ואתגרו C Gn 34:10, "trade!"; *Akk. /maškanu/ "pledge": Qt. Imperf. 2 m.s.* תמשׁבן A Ex 22:25, "you will take as a pledge"; *Inf.* ממשׁבנה A Ex 22:25.

**§154b**   Although apparently not of Akkadian origin, the *Qt Pss. Ptc. m.s.* ומתרגם D Dt 27:8, "translated," ומתרגם AA Dt 27:8, may have entered Aramaic through Akkadian.[291] The Š and Št verbs (§130f) may or may not be of Akkadian origin.[292]

**§155    *Hebrew***

**§155a**   The Hebrew of the Masoretic text has been copied into the fragments in the examples ואבלו AA₁ Ex 12:8, "and they will eat" (cf. Targum Neophyti ויכלון); למות AA Nu 20:4, "to die" (cf. Targum Neophyti לממות).[293]

194

§155b  *ṣpy "watch" and *ṣly "roast," which, in Aramaic, are attested only in Jewish Aramaic and Samaritan Aramaic, have their origins in Hebrew: G Imperf. 3 m.s. יִצְפֶּי C Gn 31:49; "he will watch"[294] and the G Pss. Ptc. m.s. צלי AA₁ Ex 12:8,9, "roasted."[295] The same appears to be true for the G Pss Ptc. m.s. זקיק E Gn 30:30, "obligated," which is attested only in Jewish Aramaic sources.[296]

§155c  The following verbal forms reflect Hebrew influence: וַתֹּאמְרָ C Gn 32:19, "and you will say"[297] (cf. Targum Onqelos /wətemar/ Gn 32:18; MT וְאָמַרְתָּ); חוה E Gn 31:20, "he told" (it seems unlikely that this orthography reflects the D Perf. /ḥawwi/ as in Targum Onqelos; the orthography may well reflect a Hebrew D Perf. /ḥiwwā/);[298] תתאפיין F Lv 23:17, "they (f.) will be baked"[299] (cf. Targum Neophyti יתאפיין); תהוויין F Lv 23:17, "they (f.) will be"[300] (cf. Targum Neophyti יהוויין); תהוויין F Lv 23:15, "they (f.) will be"[301] (cf. Targum Neophyti יהוויין). In the case of זְבַן E Gn 41:56; "and he sold," the vocalizer has pointed a Hebrew D Perf.; the consonantal text, however, may reflect an Aramaic D Perf. /zabben/. The pointing of יְקוֹם A Ex 21:19; "he will arise" may be in imitation of the Hebrew יָקוּם;[302] the same may be true for יְהִי C Gn 35:9, "May it be!" (Hebrew וִיהִי),[303] and וְיָבֹלְת C Gn 32:29, "you were able" (Hebrew יָכֹלְתָּ).[304] The use of he to represent final /e/ in verbs III-w/y may also be the result of Hebrew influence[305]: יִמְחֶה D Dt 28:28, "he will strike";[306] נהוה E Gn 38:23; "we shall be"; אודה E Gn 29:35, "I will thank"; וְיִתְגָּאָה Z Gn 49:17; "and he will be proud"; יְתמנה HH Ex 12:2, "he will be counted"—as may be the prefixed he of the C verbal noun הוחדייה F Lv 22:29, "thanking."[307] וּלְרוֹמְאִמָךְ D Dt 26:19, "to raise you up"[308] would appear to be a Hebrew infinitival form; one expects in Aramaic either לרומותך or למרוממה יתך.

§155d  If the reading וְיָבָרְכוּ Cd Gn 48:20, "they will bless" by Kahle and Klein is correct, which is not certain,[309] then this verbal form is a Hebraism (for expected Aramaic יברכן). The pointing reflects a Hebrew pausal form.

§156  E. Prepositions

Representative examples of attested prepositions are

§156a  /bə'emṣa'/[1] "in the middle": בְּאֶמְצַע- B Gn 3:3; with pronominal suffixes: 3 m.s. בְּאֶמְצָעֵיה B Ex 39:23;

§156b  /'appe/ "before, in the presence of": בְּאַפֵּי B Gn 4:8; לְאַפֵּי B Gn 4:8 (2x); מן אפי E Gn 30:16; עַל-אַפֵּי Bd Gn 7:18; לקבל אפי AA Nu 19:4;

§156c  /bV-/ "in, by means of, with": בְּבֵיתָךְ C Gn 31:41, "in your house"; בְּשַׁבְתָּה B Gn 4:15, "in an oath"; בְּרַעֲוָה B Gn 4:8, "with pleasure"; with pronominal suffixes: 1 s. בי E Gn 29:25; 3 m.s. -בֵּיה Cd Gn 37:24, בֵּיה Cd Gn 44:5; 3 f.s. בָּה C Gn 34:10, -בָּה C Gn 34:21; 1 pl. בָּן F Ex 19:23; 2 m.pl. בכן Cd Gn 48:20; 3 m.pl. בהן F Ex 20:11; 3 f.pl. בהין E Gn 30:37;

§156d  /bəgen?/ "on account of": בגין F Lv 22:27. This is the only example.[2]

§156e  /ben/, /bene?/, /bet/ "between, among": /ben/ is attested 20x, e.g., בֵּין B Gn 4:7; בן E Gn 39:4; /bene/ is attested 4x: ביני A Ex 22:10, ביני AA₁ Ex

12:6,18 (2x). /bet/ is attested[3] in בֵית שֶׂפֶר חִקְלֵה ובית שֶׁפֶר בְּרמֵה A Ex 22:4, "from among the best of his field and from among the best of his vineyard," and possibly in בית קְרוחתה E Gn 30:40, "among the spotted ones" (or is this בֵית "house" > "at the place of"?).[4] With pronominal suffixes: *1 s.* בֵּינִי C Gn 31:44, בֵּינִי C Gn 31:48; *2 m.s.* וּבֵינֶך C Gn 31:44, וּבֵינֶך C Gn 31:48; *3 m.s.* בֵינה E Gn 30:36; *1 pl.* בֵּינֵינֶן C Gn 31:53, בינינן E Gn 29:22; *2 m.pl.* וּבֵינֵיכון E Gn 9:15, בֵּיניכן AA Nu 19:10,

**§156f** /bar men/, /ləbar men/ "except for, outside of":[5] בֵּר מן F Lv 23:38, בְּר מֶן Cd Gn 46:26; לבר מן AA Nu 19:3,9; with pronominal suffixes: *1 s.* בֵּר מנִי E Gn 41:16, בֵּר מנִי F Ex 20:3; *2 m.s.* וּבֵר וֹמֶנָּך E Gn 41:44;

**§156g** /batar/[6] "after": בָּתֵר C Gn 32:20; בָּתֵר Cd Gn 37:30, מן בתֵר E Gn 39:7; with pronominal suffixes: *2 m.s.* בָּתֵרֶך Cd Gn 48:4,[7] בֵּתרֶך C Gn 35:12; *3 m.s.* בתריה E Gn 39:6, לבתריה Z Gn 49:17; *3 f.s.* וֹבַ֨תרה W Ex 15:20; *1 pl.* בָּתֵר C Gn 32:19, בָּתֵר C Gn 32:21; *2 m.pl.* בתרכון E Gn 9:9, בתרכן F Ex 20:13; *3 m.pl.* בָּתֵריהון Cd Gn 48:6, בָּתְריהון Z Gn 48:6;[8] *3 f.pl.* בתרהֶן E Gn 41:6, בתרהֵין E Gn 41:19,

**§156h** /gab?/, /gabbe?/[9] "by": There are three examples of the preposition without pronominal suffixes: גב Z Gn 47:30; על גבי F Ex 20:23 (2x) "on"; with pronominal suffixes: *1 s.* גַּבִּי Cd Gn 43:16, גבי E Gn 29:19; *2 m.s.* גבך A Ex 22:25, גבך E Gn 30:29; *3 m.s.* גביה A Ex 22:11, גבה E Gn 29:30; *1 pl.* גבן E Gn 29:22, גֹבן E Gn 41:12; *2 m.pl.* לגבכון E Gn 42:36;

**§156i** /go/ "midst": בְּגוֹ B Gn 4:12; לגו Cd Gn 43:16; מֶן-גוֹ Cd Gn 47:29; בְּגוֹא Cd Gn 48:16,[10] with pronominal suffixes (base /goww-/, /gowwe-/);[11] *3 m.s.* בגֵיה Z Gn 49:7, בגֹה AA₁ Ex 12:9,[12] בגוה AA₁ Ex 12:30; *3 f.s.* בגווה E Gn 41:48; *3 m.pl.* בגווהון W Ex 15:15;[13] *3 f.pl.* לגֵּוֵּהֵין E Gn 41:21, לגֵּוֹהֵין E Gn 41:21;

**§156j** /hek/ "like":[14] הֵיך Cd Gn 44:18, הֵיך- D Dt 26:18, הֵך F Lv 23:21.

**§156k** /həlap/ "in place of, instead of": חולף A Ex 21:36, חולף E Gn 44:4; the seven examples of this preposition are all written *plene*.[15]

**§156l** /kV-/ "like, according to": כְּפֵירֵי- B Gn 4:16, "like the fruits of"; כְּחָלֵיה C Gn 32:13, "like its sand"; כַזְעֵירוּתֶה Cd Gn 43:33, "according to his youth";

**§156m** /kəwat/ "like, according to": All examples are with pronominal suffixes: *2 m.s.* כְּוָתֶר Z Gn 44:18, כוותך W Ex 15:11 (2x); *3 m.s.* כְּוָתֵיה Cd Ex 9:24; *1 pl.* כְּוָתַן C Gn 34:15, כְּוָתָן D Dt 5:23; *3 f.pl.* דכוותהֵין E Gn 41:19;

**§156n** /lV-/ "to, for, by": /lv-/ marks the indirect object, the direct object,[16] possession, agency (עֵבֵרת לֵיה E Gn 38:18, "she conceived by him"),[17] and possibly ingressive action[18] (וִיתֵב-לֵה C Gn 35:9, "he sat down," וִיתֵב לֵה C Gn 35:9; וִדְמַהֿ-לֵיהּ B Gn 2:21, "he fell asleep"; קמון וֹלֹחון W Ex 15:8, "they arose"); with pronominal suffixes: *1 s.* לִי- Cd Gn 47:31, לי E Gn 31:9; *2 m.s.* לָּך- B Gn 4:6, לָך- B Gn 4:7, *2 f.s.* לֵיך- Cd Gn 38:18; *3 m.s.* לֵה A Ex 22:16, לֵהּ- B Gn 4:15, לֵיהּ Cd Gn 47:29; *3 f.s.* לה E Gn 38:23, *1 pl.* לָן- C Gn 34:21, לָן- Cd Gn 44:20; *2 m.pl.* לְכון C Gn 34:9, לכון Gn 34:15; *3 m.pl.* לְהוֹן C Gn 34:21, לְהוֹן Cd Gn 37:22;

**§156o** /ləwat/ "to, towards": This preposition expresses direction, e.g., לְוָת Cd Ex 5:23, לְוָת- Cd Gn 37:30, לְוָתֿ HH Ex 12:1, מן-לְוָת Cd Gn 48:12. There

196

are two exceptional uses of /ləwat/ expresssing the indirect object (in place of /lV-/): מְלִילוּ לְבָת עַם בְּנִישְׁתָּה E Gn 40:16, "and he said to Joseph"; וֹאמר לוֹת יוֹסף HH Ex 12:3, [19] "Speak to the congregation!"; with pronominal suffixes: 1 s. לְוָתִי C Gn 31:52, לוותי Cd Gn 48:9; 2 m.s. לְוָתָךּ Cd Gn 44:18, לְוָתֶר Cd Gn 44:18; 2 f.s. לוותִּיך E Gn 38:16; 3 m.s. לְוָתֵיה Bd Gn 8:8; לותיה Z Cd Gn 44:18; 3 f.s. לְוָתַהּ Cd Gn 38:18, [20] לותה E Gn 30:4; 3 m.pl. לוותהוֹן E Gn 40:6, לוותֹךּ E Gn 37:18; [21]

**§156p** /men/ "from, by means of": מֶן B Gn 4:10 (2x), מֶן C Gn 35:9 (4x) וּמֶיךּ Cd Gn 47:2; with assimilated nun: [22] מעלֵי E Gn 29:8, "from on," מכל AA Dt 26:18, "from all"; /men/ combines frequently with other prepositions, e.g., מן בתר F Lv 23:16, מֶן־לְוָת Cd Gn 48:12, מֶן־עֶלָוֶ B Gn 4:14, מן־קדם C Gn 32:29, מֶן־תְּחוֹת C Gn 35:8, and also serves as part of compound conjunctions and adverbials; with pronominal suffixes: 1 s. וּמֵיִּי B Gn 4:8, מֶנִּי B Gn 4:8; 2 m.s. מֵיִּךּ B Gn 4:8, מנך Z Gn 44:18; 2 f.s. מנִיךּ E Gn 30:2; 3 m.s. מֵיִּה Cd Gn 48:19, מֶנֵּה Z Gn 49:1, מיניה Z Gn 49:2 (2x); 3 f.s. מֶנֵּה E Gn 30:3; [23] 2 m.pl. מנבון F Ex 20:12; 3 m.pl. מנהון A Ex 23:11, מיניהון W Ex 15:9 (2x);

**§156q** /səmik lV-?/ [24] "near to": סמיך לעלת תמידה F Nu 28:23, "near to the continuous burnt-offering," סמיך לעלת תמידה F Nu 28:24, סמיד לעֹלת...[ Y Nu 28:23;

**§156r** /'ad/ "until": עד־ B Gn 4:15, עד־ Bd Gn 7:23, עד AA₁‚₂ Ex 12:22. עד also serves in compound conjunctions; [25]

**§156s** /'al/ "on, upon, about": עַל־ B Gn 4:7, עַל־ C Gn 35:9; עַל Cd Ex 7:19; [26] על is part of the following compound prepositions: על ידי E Gn 40:12, "by means of"; עַל־עֵסָק Cd Gn 43:18, "on account of," על עסק E Gn 41:55; על פם F Dt 34:5, "according to"; על גבי F Ex 20:23 (2x), "on." על is also found in compound conjunctions; with pronominal suffixes: 1 s. עֲלָי Cd Gn 48:7, עליי E Gn 30:28; 2 m.s. עֲלָיךּ B Gn 4:10; עֲלָיִךּ E Gn 43:29; [27] 3 m.s. עֲלוֹי B Gn 4:7; עלוֹ A Ex 21:22; 3 f.s. עליה C Gn 35:14, עֲלָיהּ C Gn 35:14; 1 pl. [28] עֲלֵינַ Cd Gn 43:18; 2 m.pl. עֲלֵיכוֹן D Dt 28:15, עליכן A Ex 22:22; 3 m.pl. עֲלֵיהוֹן D Dt 27:3, עליהן A Ex 22:24;

**§156t** /men 'ellawe/ "from upon": [29] מֶן־עֵלָאהּ Bd Gn 8:3, מֶן־עֵלָאֵ Bd Gn 8:7, מן עלֹוֹי E Gn 7:4, מֶן עלוֹ E Gn 29:10, מעלֹוֹי E Gn 29:8; [30] with pronominal suffixes: 3 m.s. מֶן־עֵלָאוֹ C Gn 35:13; 3 f.s. מן־עֵלָוִיהַ Cd Gn 38:19, [31] מן עלה E Gn 38:19; 2 m.pl. וֹמֵעלָאֲרֵיכן D Dt 28:23;

**§156u** /'em/ "with": עֶם־ C Gn 34:20, עֶם־ D Dt 5:19, עם E Gn 31:24; with pronominal suffixes: 1 s. עֲמִי Cd Gn 43:8, עֲמִי D Dt 5:25; 2 m.s. עמך C Gn 31:41, עֲמָּך D Dt 5:25; 2 f.s. עמיך E Gn 30:15; 3 m.s. עֶמֵּה A Ex 22:14, עֲמֵיהּ C Gn 35:6, עֲמֵיהּ C Gn 32:25; 3 f.s. עֶמָה A Ex 22:15, עמהּ E Gn 39:10; [32] 1 pl. עֶמָן C Gn 34:22, עֶמָן C Gn 34:23; 2 m.pl. עֲמְבּוֹן C Gn 34:16, עמכן E Gn 31:29; 3 m.pl. עֲמְהוֹן Cd Gn 44:6, עמהן E Gn 29:9;

**§156v** /set?/ [33] "towards": עד צית E Gn 28:17. This is the only example.

**§156w** /qəbal/, /loqbal/, /kəloqbal/ [34] "in front of, before": כְּלָקְבַל Cd Gn 38:26, כְּלָקְבֵל Cd Gn 38:26, כלוקבל E Gn 30:38, לקבל F Ex 19:2,11; with

pronominal suffixes: *1 s.* לוקבלי E Gn 31:5; *3 m.s.* לְקָבְלֵיהּ Cd Gn 37:33, לקובלה E
Gn 31:2; *3 m.pl.* לקבלהון Z Gn 49:7;

**§156x** /qədam/[35] *"before, in the presence of":* קָדַם D Dt 27:7, קֳדָם־ Cd Gn
38:25, קֻדֹם F Nu 28:26,[36] מן קודם E Gn 30:2, מן קדם AA₁ Nu 20:6; with
pronominal suffixes: *1 s.* קָדָמַי D Dt 5:25, קֳדָמַי F Nu 28:29, קודמיי E Gn 30:30;
קֻודמוי E Gn 30:29,[37] קודמוי E Gn 31:12;[38] *2 m.s.* קָֽדָמֶיךָ B Gn 4:13; קֳדָמֵיך Cd Gn
44:18, קדמך Cd Ex 5:20; *3 m.s.* קֻודמֹוֹי E Gn 43:33, דקודמויי E Gn 31:2; *2 m.pl.*
קָדָמֵיכֹון C Gn 34:10, קָדָמְכֹון C Gn 34:11; *3 m.pl.* קָדָמְהֹון C Gn 34:21, קדמהון AA
Nu 20:8;

**§156y** /ləqaddamut/[39] *"towards":* לְקַדָמות־ Cd Gn 46:29, לְקַדָמוֹת F Ex 19:17;
with pronominal suffixes: *3 m.s.* לקדמותהּ E Gn 29:13, לקדמותיהּ E Gn 30:16;

**§156z** /taḥot/[40] *"under, in place of":* תחות A Ex 21:20, תְּחֹות Bd Gn 7:19, תְּחֹת
Cd Gn 47:29; with pronominal suffixes: *2 m.s.* תַּחְתֶּיךָ־ D Dt 28:23; *3 m.s.*
תָּחְתֵּיהּ B Gn 2:21,[41] תוחתוי F Lv 22:27, תחתוי AA₁ Ex 17:12;

**§156aa** There are two occurrences of the Hebrew preposition אל *"to"*:
מללו אל כל עם כנישתא דישראל AA₁ Ex 12:3, "Speak to the entire congregation of
Israel" (MT דַּבְּרוּ אֶל־כָּל־עֲדַת יִשְׂרָאֵל); ואמר משה אל יהושע AA₁ Ex 17:9, "and
Moses spoke to Joshua" (MT וַיֹּאמֶר מֹשֶׁה אֶל־יְהוֹשֻׁעַ).

**§156bb** There is one example in which one finds ל where ב is expected
(scribal error?): וימחי גבֹר ית חֹברֹה לאבֹן אֹו במֹרתֹוק A Ex 21:18, "and if a man
should strike his friend with a stone or a fist."[42]

**§157** *F. Conjunctions*
Representative examples of attested conjunctions are

**§157a** *Conjunctions of Time:* /'ərum?/ *"when":*[1] וארום A Ex 21:20, וֹ[ו]ארום A
Ex 21:26, ארום־ C Gn 32:18; /bəzemna dV-/[2] *"when":* בְּזִמְנָא דִי־ C Gn 32:20,
בזמנה דקם E Gn 41:46; /batar dV-/[3] *"after":* בָּתַר דִי־ Cd Gn 46:30; /kad/,
/kədi/[4] *"when":* כַּד־ B Gn 2:18, כַּד Cd Gn 43:21, כְּדִי־ B Gn 4:8, כְּדִי Cd Gn
37:23; /kewan dV-/ *"as soon as, when":* כֵּיוַן־דַחֲמָא־ Cd Gn 38:26, כון דאתא E
Gn 37:23, כיוון די E Gn 29:10; /men dV-?/ *"after":* מן די־ W Ex 15:9, מן דאתכנשו H
Gn 15:1;[5] /men šaʿəta dV-/ *"since":* וּמֶן־שַׁעֲתָ דִי־ Cd Ex 5:23; [6] מן שעתה דאזל E
Gn 42:36; /'ad dV-/ *"until":* עַד־דְּאָנָה Cd Gn 37:33; /'ad zəman dV-?/ *"until":*
עד־זמן די Cd Gn 38:17, עד זמן דיעברון W Ex 15:16; /'ad 'eddan dV-?/ *"until":* עד־
די F Lv 23:14; /'ad kewan dV-?/ *"until":* עד כיוון די E Gn 31:22; /qədam 'ad
dəla?/ *"before":* קדם עד דלא AA₁ Ex 12:34;[8]

**§157b** *Conjunctions of Cause:* /'ərum/ *"because":* ארום A Ex 21:21, אָרום B
Gn 4:12, ארוּם C Gn 35:7; /bəgen dV-?/ *"because":*[9] בגין דאת E Gn 39:9; /dV-/
*"because":* די E Gn 30:18; /ḥəlap/ *"because":*[10] חולף AA Nu 20:12, חֲלַף אֲרוּם B
Gn 3:1; /'al dV-/ *"because":* עַל־דְּנַסֵבִית־ Cd Gn 38:26, עַל־דְּי Cd Gn 44:18;
/həle/ *"because":* הֲלֹא D Dt 5:23;[11]

**§157c** *Conjunctions of Purpose:* /dV-/ *"so that, in order that":*[12] דנתן E Gn
30:2,[13] די E Gn 30:38; /dəla/ *"in order not to":* דלא F Ex 19:12, דלא Z Gn 49:2;
/kəmessat?/[14] *"in order that:* כמסד למתמנֵיה AA₁ Ex 12:4;[15] /kəmessat dəla?/
*"in order not to":* כמסת דלא E Gn 39:10;[16] /men baglal/, /men baglal dV-/ *"so*

198

that, in order that": מִן־בַּגְלַל לְמִיטבה D Dt 5:26; מן בגלל ישמעון F Ex 19:9, מִן־בַּגְלַל
מן בגלל די AA Dt 27:3; מן בגלל די Cd Ex 9:29, הֶתְדַע

**§157d** *Conjunctions of Condition and Restriction:* /'ellule/, /'ellule dV-/ "if
not": אֲלוּלֵי C Gn 31:42, אֱלוּלֵי דְאִשְׁתְּהִינָן Cd Gn 43:10, אלולי דאשתהינן E Gn 43:10;
/'en/[17] "if": אֶן C Gn 34:15, אֵין- B Gn 4:7, דְּאֵין- B Gn 4:8,[18] אֵין Cd Gn 46:30,
דְּאֵין Z Gn 44:18, אם F Ex 19:5;[19] /'ella/ "if not": אִילָא Cd Gn 44:18; /'en la/ "if
not": וְאֵן־לָא C Gn 34:17, אין לא E Gn 43:5; /'ap 'al gab dV-/ "although": אַף־עַל־
גַּב־דְּיָקְדָא Cd Gn 38:25, אַף עַל גַּב דִּי H Gn 15:1; /kə'ellu dəla/ "as if not": כְּאִילוּ
דְלָא Cd Gn 46:30; /ma dalma dV-/[20] "perhaps": מָה־דַּלְמָא דִּי־יָקַבֵּל C Gn 32:21,
עַל דַּלְמָא הֶגְבֵּלִית H Gn 15:1, דַּלְמָא דִי H Gn 15:1; /'al mənat?/ "even if":[21] עַל
מנת יקדה E Gn 38:25 (cf. אַף־עַל־גַּב־דְּיָקְדָא Cd Gn 38:25);[22]

**§157e** *Conjunctions of Comparison:* /hek dV-/, /hek ma dV-/ "as":[23] הֵיךְ־מָה
דִּפְרתה Cd Gn 44:18, הֵיךְ־מָה דִּי־מְלַיל D Dt 26:18, לא הך דאתמל E Gn 31:5; also
/kə'ellu dəla/ "as if not" above;

**§157f** *Conjunctions of Content:* /'ərum/ "that":[24] אֲרוּם- C Gn 32:26, אֲרוּם- Cd
Gn 44:15; /dV-/ "that": דְעֵינְוָנוּתָךְ C Gn 35:9, דְמִיתַת C Gn 35:9;

**§157g** *Conjunctions of Addition and Contrast:* /'o/ "or":[25] או A Ex 21:6, או C
Gn 31:43, או Cd Gn 44:8; /'o/.../'o/ "either...or": או...או AA Nu 19:16; /'ella
dV-/ "but, rather": אלא דְעָרְבֵית Z Gn 44:18; /'op ? 'up?/ "also, moreover":[26]
וְאוּף A Ex 21:35, ואוף E Gn 30:15, אוף AA Nu 20:5; /'ərum 'ellahen/ "but,
rather": אֲרוּם־אֶלָא־הֵן C Gn 32:27, ארום־אלא־הן Cd Gn 37:33, ארום אֵילָאהֵן H Gn
15:4; /bəram/ "but, rather": בְּרַם- B Gn 4:7, בְּרַם Cd Gn 48:19, ברם E Gn 38:25;
/bəram 'ellahen?/ "but, rather": ברם אלאהן E Gn 28:19, ברם אלא הן E Gn 39:6;
9; /wV-, u-/ "and, but":[27] וְהָא C Gn 31:43, תֵּעָא Cd Gn 31:43, וּלְקָן B Gn 4:5;
/'ərum 'ella'el/ "but, rather":[28] וְאֲר|וֹם אֶלָאֵל A Ex 22:19.

**§158**                        *G. Adverbials*

*Representative examples of attested adverbials are*

**§158a** *Adverbials of Quality:* /'epšar/[1] "possible": אֶפְשַׁר- B Gn 4:14;
/bədeppəla?, bədipla?/[2] "double": בְּדִיפְלָא A Ex 22:8, בְּדִיפְלָה A Ex 22:3,
בדיפלה A Ex 22:6; /ya'ut/ "properly": יָאוּת D Dt 27:8, יאות E Gn 30:34, יאות E
Gn 40:16; /yattir?/ "in addition": יתיר על Z Gn 48:22; /kahda?, kahədə?/
"together": כחדא W Ex 15:12, כחדה Y Ex 19:8, כחדה Z Gn 49:16; /lahda?,
lahədə/ "very": לַחֲדָה B Gn 4:5,[3] לַחֲדָה Bd Gn 7:18; לַחדא C Gn 34:12, לחד AA₁
Ex 12:38,[4] חדה לחדה B Gn 7:19; "very much"; /maggan?/ "freely": מַגָּן[ E Gn
29:15;[5] /saggi/[6] "much": וְסַגִּי Cd Ex 9:28; /reqan/ "emptily": רֵיקָן C Gn 31:42,
רֵיקָן Cd Gn 37:24; /bašlam/ "peacefully": בְּשְׁלָם Gn 37:22, בשלם Cd Gn 37:33;
בְּשְׁלָם Cd Gn 47:30;

**§158b** *Adverbials of Time:*
/kaddun/ "now":[7] וּכְדֵין B Gn 4:11, כַּדֵּין C Gn 31:42, וְכַדֵּין D Dt 5:22; /kə'an/
"now": כְּעַן B Gn 4:6, כְּעַן C Gn 31:44, כְּעַן- Cd Gn 37:27; /bəhada zemna/[8]
"now": בְּהָדָא־זְמְנָא- B Gn 2:23, בהדה זמנה E Gn 30:20;/bəhada ša'əta/[9] "now":
בְּהָדָא־שַׁעֲתָא[ Cd Gn 38:25; בהדה שעתה E Gn 38:25; /'od/ "still, yet": וְעוד- C Gn
35:9 (2x), עד E Gn 9:15; /tub/ "again": תּוּב Cd Gn 46:29,[10] תוב D Dt 5:22, תּוֹב

AA Nu 19:13; /tuban?/[11] "again": ותובן F Lv 22:27; /tədira?/ "always": תדירה
F Ex 20:17; /yoma haden/[12] "today": יומָה הָדֵן B Gn 4:14, יומָה הָדֵין C Gn 31:43,
יומא הדן C Gn 31:48; /'etmal/[13] "yesterday": דֿאתמל A Ex 4:10, דאתמל A Ex
21:36, דאתמל A Ex 21:29;[14] /lamḥar?/ "tomorrow": וֿלמחר F Ex 19:10, למחר
AA₁ Ex 17:9; /bəṣapra?/ "in the morning": בצפרה E Gn 28:18, בצפרֿה E Gn
29:25; /bə'eddone ṣapra?/[15] "in the morning": בעידוני צפרה F Ex 19:16;
/biṭVhra/[16] "at noon": בְטִיהְרָﬞה D Dt 28:29,ﬞ בשעת טהרֿה E Gn 43:25; /bene
šemšata?/ "at twilight": ביני שמשתה F Lv 23:5, ביני שימשתא AA₁ Ex 12:18 (2x);
/'ad maṭmə'e šemša?/ "sunset": עד מטמעי שֿﬞמשה AA₁ Ex 17:12; /'ad ma'ale
šemša?/[17] "sunset": עד־מעלﬞﬞי שמשה A Ex 22:25; /bəramša?, bəromša?/[18] "in the
evening": בְּרָמְשָׁא C Gn 31:42, ברמשה E Gn 29:23; /lə'eddone ramša?/[19] "in the
evening": לעדוני רמשﬞה E Gn 30:16; /bəlelya/ "at night": בְּלֵילְיָﬞא C Gn 31:39,
בליליה AA₁ Ex 12:31; /lelya haden?/ "tonight": ליליה הדן AA₂ Ex 12:42;
/bəpalgut lelya?/[20] "at midnight": בפלגות ליליה AA₁,₂ Ex 12:29; /bə'imama/[21]
"during the daytime": בְּאִימָמָﬞא C Gn 31:39; /bənohra?/[22] "during the daylight":
בנהרﬞה E Gn 44:3; /batar kəden?/[23] "later, afterwards": ובתר כדן AA Nu 19:7;
/men batar ken?/ "later, afterwards": וּמן־בתרﬞכֿן C Gn 32:21, ומן בתר כן E Gn
30:21, ומן בתר כן E Gn 38:30; /men šeroya?/ "from the beginning": מן שירֿוֿה E
Gn 28:19;ﬞ /lə'alam?/,/də'alam?/,/lə'aləme 'aləmin/ "forever": לעלם F Ex 19:9,
דעלם AA₁ Ex 12:14; /lə'aləmi 'aləmin/ C Gn 35:9, לְעָלְמֵי עלמֿין C Gn 35:9,ﬞ
/bəqadmayəta/ "at first":[24] בְּקָדְﬞﬞﬞמִיﬞﬞﬞﬞﬞﬞﬞﬞﬞﬞﬞﬞﬞﬞﬞﬞﬞﬞﬞﬞ Cd Gn 43:18, בְּקַֿﬞﬞﬞﬞﬞﬞﬞﬞﬞﬞﬞﬞﬞ Cd Gn 43:20;ﬞ
/qadmay?/ "first":[25] קדמיﬞ F Lv 22:27; /tenyan?/ "secondly":[26] תיניין F Lv
22:27; /təlitay?/ "thirdly":[27] תליתﬞﬞﬞﬞﬞﬞﬞﬞﬞﬞﬞﬞﬞﬞﬞﬞ F Lv 22:27; /men zemna qadmaya/ "since
the first time": מֶן־זְמְנָﬞﬞ־קָדְﬞמָיָﬞﬞﬞﬞﬞﬞﬞﬞﬞﬞﬞﬞﬞﬞﬞﬞﬞ Cd Gn 44:18; /zəman tenyanut?/ "second time":
זמן תניָﬞﬞﬞﬞﬞﬞﬞﬞﬞﬞﬞﬞﬞﬞ C Gn 35:9; /bah ša'əta/[28] "at that very moment": בַּה־שַׁﬞﬞﬞﬞﬞﬞ C Gn 35:9;ﬞ
בַּﬞﬞﬞﬞﬞﬞﬞﬞ Cd Gn 38:25;ﬞ /ləhal?/ "further": ולהל F Lv 22:27; /dəna/ "now,
already":[29] דנא עשרה זמנין C Gn 31:41, דְנָﬞﬞﬞﬞﬞﬞﬞﬞﬞﬞﬞ Cd Gn 43:10, דְנָﬞﬞﬞﬞﬞﬞﬞﬞﬞﬞﬞﬞﬞﬞﬞﬞﬞﬞ
E Gn 31:7; /yom batar yom?/ "daily": יום בתר יום E Gn 39:10; /kol yom?/
"daily": בכל יום F Nu 28:24; /babhilu?/ "hastily": בבהילו AA₁ Ex 12:11;

§158c *Adverbials of Place:*
/'appe bara?/ "outside": לְאַפֵּי בָרָﬞﬞ B Gn 4:8;ﬞ באפי בארﬞא Cd Ex 9:21, מן אפי ברהﬞ E
Gn 30:16; /haka?/ "here": הָכָﬞﬞﬞ Cd Gn 38:21;ﬞ הכﬞﬞﬞ Cd Gn 48:9, מן הכה E Gn
37:17; /ḥəzor ḥəzor/[30] "around": מֶן־חֲזֿﬞﬞﬞﬞﬞﬞﬞﬞ B Ex 39:26, חזור חזור F Ex 19:12;
/men lə'el/ "from above": מֶן־לְﬞﬞﬞ B Ex 39:31, מֶן־לֿﬞﬞﬞﬞﬞﬞ Bd Gn 7:20, מן לעל F Ex
20:4; /men raḥiq?/ "from afar": מֿﬞ רחיק F Ex 20:18; /men ləra'?/ "from
below":[31] מן לרע F Ex 20:4; /tamman/[32] "there": תמן C Gn 32:14, תמﬞﬞﬞ Cd Gn
43:30, לתמן E Gn 39:1;

§158d *Interrogative Adverbials:*[33]
/'ek?/ "how":[34] ואיך E Gn 39:9; /ha/ (interrogative particle):[35] הָﬞ B Gn 4:9,
הָﬞﬞ Bd Gn 8:8;ﬞ האית Z Gn 44:19,[36] העוד E Gn 31:14, אלית E Gn 39:9;[37] /han/[38]
"where": הן E Gn 37:16, הן E Gn 38:21; ולהן C Gn 32:18; /kəma?/ "how
many":[39] על חד כמה וכמה Z Gn 44:18 ("a fortiori"); /ləma/ "why": לְמָה־ B Gn
4:6, למה D Dt 5:22, למה E Gn 29:25; /men baglal ma/[40] "why": מֶן־בַּגְלַל־מָﬞﬞ
B מן בגלל מוﬞ] E Gn 40:7;

200

§158e  *Adverbials of Relationship:*
/bəgen ken?/, /men bəgen ken?/ "so, thus":[41] מִן בְּגִין כֵּן E Gn 29:35, בְּגִין כֵּן E Gn
30:6, מִן בְּגִין כֵּן E Gn 38:26; /bəgen kəden/ "so, thus": בְּגִין־כְּדֵין C Gn 31:48, ־בְּגִין
כְּדֵין C Gn 35:9; /kəden/ "so thus":[42] כְּדֵין Cd Ex 7:22, כְּדֵן Cd Ex 7:11; כֵּן E Gn
31:8; /ken?/ "so, thus": כֵּן E Gn 29:26, כֵּן E Gn 31:8, בְכֵן E Gn 31:22; /la/ "no,
not": ־לָא B Gn 4:5, ־לָא C Gn 31:52, הֲלָא B Gn 4:7; /ləhod/, /ləhod/, /ləhot?/,
/ləhot?/[43] "only, also": לְחוֹד Cd Gn 46:34, ־לְהוֹד Cd Gn 48:19, ־לְהוֹד Cd Gn
47:3 (2x), וְלַחוֹת F Ex 19:9, לַחוֹת F Lv 23:39, לַהוֹת E Gn 43:8;[44] /ləbalhod/
"alone": attested only with pronominal suffixes: 3 m.s. לְבַלְחוֹדֵי C Gn 32:17;
לְבַלְחוֹדַי E Gn 43:32; 3 f.s. לְבַלְחוֹדַהּ A Ex 22:26; 3 m.pl. לְבַלְחוֹדֵיהוֹן E Gn 43:32,
לְבַלְחוֹדֵיהוֹן E Gn 43:32.

§159  *H. Predicators of Existence*
/'it/ "there is": ־אִית B Gn 4:13; דְּאִית Bd Gn 7:22, ־דְּאִית C Gn 32:18; There
are no examples of pronouns suffixed to this particle.
/let/ "there is not": ־לֵית B Gn 4:14, ־לֵית C Gn 31:50, ־לֵית Cd Gn 47:4. There
are no examples of pronouns suffixed to this particle.
/ha/ "behold":[1] הָא B Gn 4:14, וְהָא C G 32:19, ־הָא Cd Gn 47:1.

§160  *I. Interjections*
The only attested interjections are
/way/ "woe": וָאִי H Gn 15:1;[1]
/ləway/ "if only":[2] לְוַי D Dt 5:26, לְוַי E Gn 30:34.[3] Note, however, הֲלַי AA
Nu 20:3.[4]
/ṭub-/ "happy is the": וְטוּבוֹי Cd Gn 38:26.[5]

201

Footnotes — Chapter VI

A. Pronouns

[1]אֲנוּן may be in imitation of the Tiberian Biblical Aramaic pointing. It is possible that the pronoun was realized as /'ennon/. The forms with *he* occur only in MSS E and F, although forms with *aleph* are also attested in both manuscripts.

[2]אִתְּיָן may also be in imitation of the Tiberian Biblical Aramaic form. It is also possible that the pointing reflects /'ennen/.

[3]For a comprehensive discussion and list of pronouns in Old Aramaic, Official Aramaic, and Middle Aramaic, see Tal, *Language*, pp. 1-5.

[4]See Bauer-Leander, *Grammatik*, pp. 69-71.

[5]The *kethibh* reflects /'antā/.

[6]See Dalman, *Grammatik*, pp. 107, 395.

[7]/naḥnā/ occurs where the Biblical text has נַחְנוּ.

[8]See Dalman, *Grammatik*, pp. 106, 395; H. Odeberg, *The Aramaic Portions of Bereshit Rabba with Grammar of Galilaean Aramaic* (Lund: Lund Universitet Årsskrift, 1939), II, p. 3; Kutscher, "Aramaic," *EJ*, 3, cols. 271-272; Kutscher, *Studies*, p. 31.

[9]This form is probably the result of Babylonian Talmudic Aramaic influence in printed editions containing Galilean Aramaic.

[10]See Kutscher, *Studies*, p. 31.

[11]See Dalman, *Grammatik*, pp. 107, 395; Levy, "Language," pp. 55-59; Foster, "Language," p. 69.

[12]This form probably entered the Palestinian Targumim through copyists and/or editors influenced by the Babylonian Talmudic Aramaic /'ant/ and the Biblical Aramaic /'ant/.

[13]Idem.

[14]On the distribution of these forms in the different Palestinian Targumim, see Foster, "Language," p. 69.

[15]See Targum Neophyti Gn 31:6.

[16]See Targum Pseudo-Jonathan Gn 31:6.

[17]See Schulthess, *Grammatik*, p. 32; Bar-Asher, *Palestinian Syriac Studies, passim*.

[18]See Macuch, *Grammatik*, pp. 131-132. These pronouns are represented graphically by 1 s. אנא,אנה, 2 m.s. את,אתה 2 f.s. אתי, 3 m.s. הו,הוא, 3 f.s. הי,היא, 1 pl. אנן,אנחנן, 2 m.pl. אתון, 2 f.pl. אתין, 3 m.pl. אנון,הנון, 3 f.pl. אנין,הנין.

[19]See Tal, *Samaritan Targum*, III, p.87.

[20]See Nöldeke, *Syriac Grammar*, p. 44.

[21]The *kethibh* reflects /'ant/.

[22]The *kethibh* reflects /'anti/.

[23]See Nöldeke, *Syriac Grammar*, p. 44.

[24]The *kethibh* reflects /'anton/.

[25]The *kethibh* reflects /'anten/.

[26]This form is used only as the copula.

[27]Idem.

[28]See Spitaler, *Grammatik*, pp. 50-51.

[29]See Spitaler, *Grammatik*, p. 28.

202

[30] E.g., Galilean Aramaic הוא > ד + הוא < דהוא < דו.

[31] Cf., e.g., וַאֲמַר Cd Gn 44:15, "and he said," whose pointing may point to the elision of the aleph. See §25a, n.131.

[32] Cf. הו and הי at Elephantine. See Leander, *Laut- und Formenlehre des Ägyptisch-Aramäischen* (Göteborg: Göteborgs högskolas årsskrift 34,4, 1928; reprint Hildesheim: Georg Olms, 1966), p. 25.

[33] See Brockelmann, *Grundriss*, I, p. 300.

[34] See §37h.

[35] מֵיתְאָנֶהֿ Cd Gn 46:30, "I die" is due to lack of spacing by the scribe. See also §§128, 151c.

[36] See Kahle's note on the pointing of this word (*Masoreten des Westens*, II, p. 8, n.2).

[37] Cf. Masoretic text הָיִיתִי בַיּוֹם אֲכָלַנִי חֹרֶב.

[38] The suffixing of /'att/ would appear to be the most reasonable explanation for this *daghesh*. For another possible explanation, however, see §151c, n.275.

[39] See Dalman, *Grammatik*, pp. 107, 289-291, 352.

[40] Ibid.

[41] Ibid.

[42] See Schulthess, *Grammatik*, pp. 18, 32.

[43] See Nöldeke, *Syriac Grammar*, pp. 44-46.

[44] See Nöldeke, *Mandäische Grammatik*, pp. 87-88.

[45] See Epstein, *Grammar*, pp. 20-22.

[46] See Kutscher, "Aramaic," *EJ*, col. 272.

[47] On the usual pointing of this morpheme with ‗‗, see §8e.

[48] There are six examples of this suffix; only one is pointed and five are attested on prepositions.

[49] As Kahle notes, ביך had been changed into ליך.

[50] All of the examples of /e/ are listed here. See also §25b.

[51] See n.47 above.

[52] ענהו E Gn 31:4 is a scribal error for עניה "his small cattle."

[53] See §25b.

[54] See §4h.

[55] This is the second of the two occurrences in the verse.

[56] For another possible example with /-oy/, see §81a, n.229.

[57] See §15i.

[58] אחיהו H Gn 15:1 "their brethren" is an error for אחיהון. (Or is it due to Babylonian Talmudic influence?) Cf. in the same verse וְקָרִיבֵיהוֹן "and their relatives" and בְקִרְוֵיהוֹן "and in their cities."

[59] See §16h.

[60] See Bauer-Leander, *Grammatik*, pp. 47-81.

[61] Cf. in the parallel passage יְדָךְ Cd Gn 47:29 (m.s.).

[62] Cf. Targum Pseudo-Jonathan and Fragment Targum (MSS P and V) תלת עיינהא "she lifted up her eyes" (Targum Onqelos suffix), but Targum Neophyti תלת עייני (3 f.s. suffix /'ayne/ < /'ayneh/ with apocopation of final /h/).

[63] Cf. Targum Pseudo-Jonathan אנהר עיינה; Fragment Targum (MS P) אנהרן עיינהא, (MS V) נהרין עינהא; Targum Neophyti ואנהרון עיינה. Cf. the parallel passage in the Cairo Genizah fragments (E Gn 38:25): אנהרין עייניה.

[64] This is the preposition עלוי /'ellawe/. See §156t.

203

⁶⁵For the pronominal suffixes attached to the m.s nouns אב "father" and אח "brother," see §59a.

⁶⁶See Bauer-Leander, *Grammatik*, pp. 71-81.

⁶⁷See Ben-Ḥayyim, "Third Feminine Plural in Old Aramaic," *EI*, 1 (1951), 135-139 (in Hebrew) for the difference between the *qere* /-hen/ and the *kethibh* /-hon/.

⁶⁸See Dalman, *Grammatik*, pp. 109-110, 202-206, 395.

⁶⁹See Odeberg, *Grammar*, p. 4; Kutscher, "Aramaic," *EJ*, col. 273, is based on the pointing in the Cairo Genizah fragments. One might speculate that these pronominal suffixes were realized as 1 s. *-i*, 2 m.s. *-ak*, 2 f.s. *-ek*, 3 m.s. *-eh/e*, 3 f.s. *-ah*, 1 pl. *-an*, 2 m.pl. *-kon*, 2 f.pl. *-ken*, 3 m.pl. *-hon/on*, 3 f.pl. *-hen/en*.

⁷⁰E.g., ליה "to me" in Svedlund, *Selected Passages*, p. 10.

⁷¹E.g., לי "to him" in Svedlund, *Selected Passages*, p. 17.

⁷²The pronominal suffixes attested in the Palestinian Targumim include Cairo Genizah-like forms alongside Targum Onqelos forms which have entered the Targum through copyists familiar with Targum Onqelos. See Dalman, *Grammatik*, pp. 109-110, 202-206, 395; Levy, "Language," pp. 61-70; Foster, "Language," pp. 73-74.

⁷³E.g., בייתי דאבוך Gn 12:1, "your father's house" (Targum Neophyti).

⁷⁴This appears to be a Targum Onqelos form. The orthography ך probably represents *-an* as in the Cairo Genizah fragments.

⁷⁵This pronominal form comes from Babylonian Aramaic and is the result of the copyists' familiarity with the Babylonian Talmud. See Dalman, *Grammatik*, p. 203.

⁷⁶See Schulthess, *Grammatik*, pp. 33, 50; Bar-Asher, *Palestinian Syriac Studies*, *passim*. In the light of Bar-Asher's work, Schulthess' vocalization of the pronominal suffixes must be used with extreme caution. One may conjecture that the forms on the chart reflect roughly 1 s. *i,∅*, 2 m.s. *-ak*, 2 f.s. *-ek,-eki*, 3 m.s. *-eh,-e*, 3 f.s. *-ah,-a*, 1 pl. *-an,-en,-nan,-nen,-ne*, 2 m.pl. *-kon,-kom*, 2 f.pl. *-ken*, 3 m.pl. *-hon*, 3 f.pl. *-hen*. One must keep in mind that the manuscripts of Palestinian Syriac do not come from one period.

⁷⁷According to Schulthess (*Grammatik*, pp. 16-17), this pronominal suffix was realized as ∅ but represented graphically under the influence of Syriac orthography. Bar-Asher, however (*Palestinian Syriac Studies*, p. 166), maintains that this pronominal suffix was, on occasion, realized as *-i*.

⁷⁸See Schulthess (*Grammatik*, p. 33) who believes that this orthography, as in Syriac, reflects *-ek*; Bar-Asher, on the other hand (*Palestinian Syriac Studies*, p. 326), is of the opinion that the use of diacritical marks points to a realization of *-eki*.

⁷⁹See Macuch, *Grammatik*, pp. 132, 299-307. These pronominal suffixes are represented graphically by 1s. יֽ-, 2 m.s. ך-, 2 f.s. יך-, 3 m.s. ה-, 3 f.s. ה-, 1 pl. נַנ-, 2 m.pl. כון-, 2 f.pl. כין-, 3 m.pl. הון-, 3 f.pl. יהין-.

⁸⁰See Nöldeke, *Syriac Grammar*, pp. 46, 87-91.

⁸¹The *kethibh* reflects /-i/.

⁸²The *kethibh* reflects /-exi/.

⁸³See Spitaler, *Grammatik*, pp. 52-56.

⁸⁴The *kethibh* reflects /-ayik/, /-ayk/, or /-ek/.

⁸⁵The *kethibh* reflects /-ayh/, /-ayah/, or /-eh/.

⁸⁶The *kethibh* reflects /-aynā/ or /-enā/.

⁸⁷The *kethibh* reflects /-ehon/. See n.67 above.

⁸⁸/-ayki/, however, is more frequent in the *Editio Sabbioneta*. See Dalman, *Grammatik*, p. 204. It seems unlikely that the *Editio Sabbioneta* has preserved the

204

Proto-Aramaic *aykī of the 2 f.s. on m.pl. and dual nouns. Rather, this may be an artificial form created under the influence of the *kethibh* of Syriac יכי-(with which editors were familiar) and the Biblical Hebrew /-ayki/ (e.g., חַיָּיְכִי Ps 103:4, "your life"). The diphthong /-ay/ may also have been created under the influence of the Biblical Aramaic *kethibh* of pronominal suffixes found on m.pl. nouns.

[89]The forms presented in the chart are only those found in reliable manuscripts of Galilean Aramaic and may possibly reflect 1 s. *-ay*, 2 m.s. *-ek*, 2 f.s. *-ek*, 3 m.s. *-oy,-ohi*, 3 f.s. *-eh*, 1 pl. *-enan*, 2 m.pl. *-ekon*, 2 f.pl. *-eken*, 3 m.pl. *-ehon*, 3 f.pl. *-ehen*. In printed editions one also finds 1 s. אי- (Babylonian Talmud), 2 f.s. ייכי- ,יייכי- (see n.59 above), 3 f.s. יהא- (Targum Onqelos), 3 m.pl. יהו- (Baylonian Talmudic).

[90]See Odeberg, *Grammar*, p. 155.

[91]As is the case with the pronominal suffixes added to m.s., f.s., and f.pl. nouns, the inventory of suffixes on m.pl. and dual nouns seems to consist of genuine Palestinian Aramaic forms as well as Targum Onqelos forms. One may conjecture that the original Palestinian forms were 1 s. יי- *(-ay)*, 2 m.s. יִךְ,-ָךְ- *(ek)*, 2 f.s. יִיךְ,-ָךְ- *(-ek)*, 3 m.s. וי- *(-oy)*, 3 f.s. יה,ה- *(-eh)*, 1 pl. ינן- *(-enan)*, 2 m.pl. יכן *(-ekon)*, 2 f.pl. יכן- *(-eken)*, 3 m.pl. יהון- *(-ehon)*, 3 f.pl. יהין- *(-ehen)*.

[92]For examples, see Levy, "Language," pp. 89-90; Díez Macho, "L'usage de la troisième personne au lieu de la première dans le Targum," in *Mélanges Dominique Barthélemy*, eds. P. Casetti, et al. (Fribourg: Éditions universitaires; Göttingen: Vandenhoeck & Ruprecht, 1981), pp. 62-85.

[93]Reflecting *ayik*? As is the case with 2 f.s. /ayki/ in the *Editio Sabbioneta*, this form appears to be a late artificial form which might be based on the Syriac as well as the Biblical Aramaic *kethibh* on m.pl. nouns.

[94]Reflecting /-eki/?

[95]See n.88 above.

[96]The *-h'* of יהא- and יהא- would appear to be the result of Targum Onqelos influence.

[97]The final *mem* is probably the result of Biblical influence.

[98]Idem.

[99]See Schulthess, *Grammatik*, p. 50; Bar-Asher, *Palestinian Syriac Studies, passim*. One also finds the pronominal suffixes on s. nouns occurring on pl. nouns in this dialect. The realization of these pronominal suffixes may have been roughly 1 s. *-ay*, 2 m.s. *-ek*, 2 f.s. *-eki*, 3 m.s. *-oy,-ohi*, 3 f.s. *-eh*, 1 pl. *-enan,-nen,-ene*, 2 m.pl. *-ekon*, 2 f.pl.- *eken*, 3 m.pl. *-ehon,-eyon*, 3 f.pl. *-ehen*.

[100]According to Schulthess (*Grammatik*, p. 50), an Arabic or Syriac dialectal form.

[101]Ibid.

[102]See Schulthess, *Grammatik*, p. 33, n.1.

[103]Represented graphically by 1 s. י-, 2 m.s. יך-, 2 f.s. יך-, 3 m.s. יו-, 3 f.s. יה-, 1 pl. ינן-, 2 m.pl. יכן-, 2 f.pl. יכין-, 3 m.pl. יהון,-ייהון-, 3 f.pl. יין,-ייהין-. See Macuch, *Grammatik*, pp. 132, 299-307.

[104]The *kethibh* reflects /ayki/.

[105]The *kethibh* reflects /awhi/.

[106]See Ben-Ḥayyim, *Studies*, pp. 56-57.

[107]The extension of the 2 m.s., 3 f.s., and 1 pl. suffixes on s. nouns (/-āk/, /-ah/, /-anā/) to m.pl. and dual nouns in Biblical Aramaic (and 2 m.s., 2 f.s., and 1 pl. in Targum Onqelos) is usually explained as having its origins in the suffixing of s. pronominal suffixes on s. nouns ending in *ay and the resulting confusion with s.

suffixes on m.pl. nouns. See Brockelmann, *Grundriss*, I, p. 480. For a different explanation, see Fassberg, "Topics in the Aramaic of the Palestinian Targum Fragments in the Light of Comparative Data," *Proceedings of the Ninth World Congress of Jewish Studies*, Jerusalem, 1985, Division D, Vol. 1, pp. 17-22 (in Hebrew).

[108]The grammar of the Aramaic-speaking inhabitants of Baḥ'a is similar to the Aramaic of its neighboring village, Ma'lula See C. Correll, "Materialien zur Kenntnis des neuaramäischen Dialekts von Baḥ'a" (Ph.D. thesis, Ludwig-Maximilians-Universität zu München, 1969).

[109]Odeberg was the first to suggest this sound shift in his *Grammar*, p. 155. Were, however, the examples with /-oy/ the result of a sound shift /ay/ > /oy/, one would not expect to find this shift limited only to one morphological category. Dalman cites a few isolated examples in other categories which he considers errors (*Grammatik*, pp. 90-91, 351). Ben-Ḥayyim has recently argued that final /ay/ > /oy/ in Western Aramaic as evidenced by the Palestinian Targumim, Galilean Aramaic, Palestinian Syriac, Ma'lula, and Baḥ'a. See Ben-Ḥayyim, "Third Masculine Singular in Place of First Singular?" in *Abraham Even-Shoshan Volume*, ed. Z. Ben-Ḥayyim, et al. (Jerusalem: Kiryat-Sefer, 1985), pp. 93-98 (in Hebrew). See also S. Friedman, "-Oy for -ay as First Person Singular Ponominal Suffix for Plural Nouns in Galilean Aramaic," *Language Studies*, II-III, pp. 207-215 (in Hebrew); Fassberg, "Topics," pp. 18-20.

[110]See Levy, "Language," pp. 89-90; Díez Macho, "L'usage," pp. 62-85. This argument is unable to explain the existence of the 1 s. /-oy/ in the non-Targumic sources. Golomb (*Grammar*, p. 51) considers the examples of /-oy/ to be spelling errors.

[111]Spitaler sees a different source for the [-ō] of these s. pronouns. He argues that this vowel is extended from the m.pl. determined ending which is realized as [-ōya], [-ōy], or [-ō] (*Grammatik*, pp. 53, 105). Although Spitaler's explanation is attractive for Ma'lula, it ignores the data from the Palestinian Targumim, Galilean Aramaic, and Palestinian Syriac. It seems more likely that the [-ōy] of the m.pl. determined forms is extended from the pronominal system where the origin of this form is easier to explain (see Fassberg, "Miscellanea," *Language Studies* II-III, pp. 200-202).

[112]See Ben-Ḥayyim, "Third Masculine Singular," pp. 96-97.

[113]Spitaler argues that there is no connection between the forms in Palestinian Syriac and Ma'lula (*Grammatik*, pp. 52-53). Bergsträsser, on the other hand (*OLZ* 49 [1926], 497), believes that the occurrences in the two dialects are related, although he does not explain.

[114]On the development of this pronominal suffix, see §15k.

[115]Muraoka explains the proliferation of ית with suffixes at the expense of object suffixes on the verb as a feature of popular speech that arose because speakers found it difficult to master the resulting changes in the vocalization of the verb ("Study," pp. 17-18).

[116]See §§16b, 130e, 155c. An ambiguous example is לית לן מה נקרבה F Lv 22:27; "we do not have anything to sacrifice." נקרבה may reflect /naqrəbeh/, "we shall sacrifice it" or it may reflect /naqrəba/, a Hebrew-type cohortative form. Cf. Targum Neophyti למקרביה (text) and ולית לן מה נקרבה (margin). There are no other examples of object pronominal suffixes on Aramaic infinitival forms. There are, however, subject pronominal suffixes on the Infinitive, e.g., בְּמִשְׁמָעֵיהּ Cd Gn 44:18, "in his hearing." On subject pronominal suffixes on Infinitives in these fragments, see

206

Kutscher, *Studies*, p. 4, n.14; Muraoka, "Morphosyntax," pp. 76-77. There are also no object pronominal suffixes on the Participle. Diez Macho's reading דפתריה E Gn 40:8, "who can interpret it" is not confirmed by an examination of the manuscript, which reveals דפתר יתה[ה].

[117]See Dalman, *Grammatik*, p. 362; Levy, "Language," pp. 75-76; Lund, "Descriptive Syntax," pp. 76-78. Object pronominal suffixes seem to be more common in Targum Pseudo-Jonathan than in the Fragment Targum and Targum Neophyti.

[118]See Schulthess, *Grammatik*, p. 78; Kutscher, "Aramaic Letters," p. 131, n.59a. Bar-Asher (*Palestinian Syriac Studies*, p. 209, n.195) points out that object pronominal suffixes on verbs are more frequent in later manuscripts than in early ones, perhaps under Syriac influence.

[119]For evidence of /yatkon/, see §32a.

[120]There are 83 pointed examples. There is only one example with ﹘ when bound by a pronominal suffix: יַתֵּיה E Gn 28:22, "him." יָת, when unbound or bound by a *maqqeph*, is pointed יָת, e.g., יָת־ B Gn 4:11. There are only three exceptions in 102 pointed occurrences: יָת B Ex 39:29, יָת־ B Ex 39:31, יָת־ D Dt 5:24.

[121]For a comprehensive discussion of the subject, see Kutscher, "Aramaic Letters," pp. 129-133; "Language of Genesis Apocryphon," pp. 20-21; Nöldeke, "Beiträge zur Kenntnis der aramäischen Dialekte," *ZDMG*, 22 (1868), 511.

[122]ית is used in Targum Onqelos wherever the Masoretic text uses את. See Dalman, *Grammatik*, pp. 110-111; W. B. Stevenson, *Grammar of Palestinian Jewish Aramaic*, 2nd ed. (Oxford: Clarendon Press, 1962), p. 17.

[123]The use of independent object pronouns is inversely related to the frequency of object pronominal suffixes on verbs. In the Fragment Targum and Targum Neophyti independent object pronouns are frequent and object pronominal suffixes on verbs are infrequent; in Targum Pseudo-Jonathan object pronominal suffixes on verbs are frequent and independent object pronouns are infrequent.

[124]See Schulthess, *Grammatik*, p. 33.

[125]See Macuch, *Grammatik*, pp. 325-326.

[126]See Dalman, *Grammatik*, p. 110. The independent object pronoun occasioally becomes suffixed to the verb in Galilean Aramaic and in Samaritan Aramaic. See Dalman, *Grammatik*, p. 360; Nöldeke, "Beiträge zur Kenntnis der aramäischen Dialekte," p. 104.

[127]See R. Degen, *Altaramäische Grammatik der Inschriften der 10-8 Jh. v. Chr.* (AKM 38,3; Wiesbaden: Deutsche Morgenländische Gesellschaft, 1969), p. 59.

[128]See Kutscher, "Aramaic Letters," pp. 129-133.

[129]See Dalman, *Grammatik*, p. 119; Levy, "Language," p. 84; Foster, "Language," p. 71.

[130]See Dalman, *Grammatik*, p. 118; Odeberg, *Grammar*, p. 5.

[131]Realized as [tid-]. See Spitaler, *Grammatik*, p. 59.

[132]See Epstein, *Grammar*, pp. 27-28.

[133]See Dalman, *Grammatik*, p. 119.

[134]See Schulthess, *Grammatik*, p. 33.

[135]Realized as [dill-]. See Ben-Ḥayyim, *Studies*, p. 134; *Literary and Oral Tradition*, III.2, p. 79, n.4; Macuch, *Grammatik*, p. 134.

[136]See Nöldeke, *Mandäische Grammatik*, p. 332.

[137]See n.130 above.

[138]See n.129 above. Perhaps דיל is the result of Targum Onqelos influence. Lund ("Descriptive Syntax," p. 49) shows that in Targum Neophyti דיד is found in translation and non-translation passages, whereas דיל is found only in translation passages.

[139]דיל occurs only in the speech of Palestinian speakers. See Epstein, *Grammar*, p. 27.

[140][ded-]. See Ben-Ḥayyim, *Literary and Oral Tradition*, III.2, p. 79, n.4; Macuch, *Grammatik*, p. 327. This particle, however, functions in Samaritan Aramaic as a preposition, "concerning, about."

[141]E.g., Brockelmann, *Grundriss*, I, p. 316; Dalman, *Grammatik*, p. 118; Ben-Ḥayyim, *Literary and Oral Tradition*, III.2, p. 79, n.4.

[142]ל + די.

[143]See Epstein, *Grammar*, p. 27.

[144]According to Ben-Ḥayyim (*Studies*, p. 149, n.3), דין = דאין in the syntagm מָא־דָאִיךְ דָא B Gn 4:8, "why is it?" Peri ("Morphology," p. 100) explains ד + אין = דאין "so what if..." or "even though." Klein translates, "How is it that...."

[145]Final /a/ is represented by *aleph* in all twelve occurrences of this pronoun.

[146]The underlying text, however, of בְהָדָה־זְמְנָה־ B Gn 2:23 is זאת הפֿעם.

[147]Other expressions of time include לירחה שביעייה הדין F Lv 23:27, "of this seventh month," and לְיֻרְחה שְׁבִיעֵייה הדן F Lv 23:34.

[148]Bauer-Leander reconstruct as *'ilay + n (*Grammatik*, p. 83).

[149]There are no occurrences of /'ellen/ in MS F.

[150]/ha'ellayin/ is spelled with double *yodh* 9x in unpointed manuscripts and only twice with a single *yodh:* קימיה האלין AA Dt 26:16, "these laws" and אבניה האלין AA Dt 27:4, "these stones" (there are no other examples of this demonstrative in MS AA).

[151]For a general discussion, see Tal, "Demonstrative Pronouns," pp. 43-65.

[152]See Bauer-Leander, *Grammatik*, pp. 81-84.

[153]See Dalman, *Grammatik*, pp. 113-114.

[154]See /dəyātah šabtā/ Dt 18:8 (MSS j,i,v dəyātah šabbətā).

[155]See Dalman, *Grammatik*, pp. 111-114, 396-397; Odeberg, *Grammar*, p. 7.

[156]E.g., ואילינון (= אינון + ואילין), in Svedlund, *Selected Passages*, p. 18.

[157]This is a Babylonian Talmudic Aramaic form. See Dalman, *Grammatik*, p. 111.

[158]Ibid.

[159]See Dalman, *Grammatik*, pp. 113-114, 396-397; Levy, "Language," pp. 76-81; Foster, "Language," pp. 70-71.

[160]This is a Targum Onqelos form.

[161]See Schulthess, *Grammatik*, pp. 33-34, 85.

[162]See Macuch, *Grammatik*, pp. 134-135. These demonstratives are represented graphically by "this" (m.) דן, הדן, אהן, האן, הן; "this" (f.) הזה, זה, זאה, האן, האן, זאת, ראה, דאה, דה, הדה, הדא; "these" הלין, אלין, האלין, אהלין; "that" (m.) ההוא, יתה; "that" (f.) ההיא, יתה; "those" הלין, אלין, האלין, אהלין, ההם. In some manuscripts one finds the orthographies זהיה, זייה, זיחה, עיה (reflecting [*zeyya?]).

[163]This is a Hebraism. See Macuch, *Grammatik*, p. 135.

[164]Ibid.

[165]Ibid.

208

[166]Ibid.

[167]Ibid.

[168]See Nöldeke, *Syriac Grammar*, pp. 47, 179-181.

[169]See Spitaler, *Grammatik*, pp. 56-57. The forms [hōt-], [hat-] are made up of the [h] of [hanna] "this" + ‏ית‏.

[170]See Tal, "Demonstrative Pronouns," pp. 46-51; Lund, "Descriptive Syntax," pp. 43-49.

[171]See Tal, "Demonstrative Pronouns," pp. 49-51. Tal (p. 51) ascribes this inverted word order to late Midrashic influence (i.e., Galilean Aramaic) which entered the Targumim through copyists.

[172]For other expressions, see Bauer-Leander, *Grammatik*, pp. 269-270.

[173]On the origin of this syntagm, see Rosenthal, *Grammar*, p. 40.

[174]See Cowling, "Notes," pp. 41-42.

[175]See §12f, n.132.

[176]‏רי‏ is never found in the genitive construction. See §161.

[177]See §33j.

[178]See Kahle, *Masoreten des Westens*, II, p. 7, n.6.

[179]The original ‏רי‏ was changed to a ‏ר‏ by erasing the *yodh* and lengthening the horizontal bar of the *daleth*.

[180]See §38a, n.116.

[181]The pointing ‏מֶן‏ is probably an error for ‏מָן‏.

[182]See §12f.

[183]See §134c, n.138.

[184]‏אנינקי‏ can be interpreted as either "my distress" or "distress." For this Greek loanword, see §116.

[185]For examples, see §157.

[186]See Cowling, "Notes," pp. 41-42.

[187]See Degen, *Altaramäische Grammatik*, p. 60.

[188]See Leander, *Laut- und Formenlehre*, p. 36, as well as the glossaries to Bresciani and Kamil, *Le lettere aramaiche*, and E. Kraeling, *The Brooklyn Museum Aramaic Papyri* (New York: Yale University Press, 1953). On the interchange of *zayin* and *daleth*, see Y. Lerner, "The Zayin/daleth Interchange in the Elephantine Documents: An Alternate Explanation," *Lesh*, 46 (1982), 57-64 (in Hebrew).

[189] See Bauer-Leander, *Grammatik*, pp. 85-86.

[190]See Fitzmyer, *Genesis Apocryphon*, p. 206; Fitzmyer and Harrington, *Manual*, pp. 313-314; Beyer, *Die aramäische Texte*, p. 425.

[191]See Dalman, *Grammatik*, pp. 116-118, and M. Z. Kadari, "The Use of ‏ר‏ Clauses in the Language of Targum Onkelos," *VT*, 3 (1963), 36-59. Professor T. O. Lambdin has gathered examples of ‏רי‏ which, he suggests, arose from the use of *yodh* as a *mater lectionis*, e.g., ‏רי כתיב > ריכתיב‏.

[192]See Schulthess, *Grammatik*, p. 34. *ðī is preserved in the independent possessive pronoun ‏ריל-‏. According to Schulthess, the form ‏רי‏ found in late manuscripts is an error.

[193]See Macuch, *Grammatik*, p. 136. The relative pronoun takes the forms [ad-], [da-], and [d-] depending on the environment. *ðī is preserved in the independent possessive pronoun [dill-].

[194]See Nöldeke, *Syriac Grammar*, pp. 47-48. *ðī is preserved in the independent possessive pronoun /dil-/.

[195]See Dalman, *Grammatik*, pp. 116-117.

[196]From *ðī. See Spitaler, *Grammatik*, p. 59. The shorter form (די) is preserved only in [miḏ] < [mā ḏ-].

[197]See Dalman, *Grammatik*, pp. 116-17. דהוא and דהיא often contract to די, דו.

[198]See Macuch, *Grammatik*, p. 136. Note the syncopation of [h] in [du] (דו) and [di] (די).

[199]See Dalman, *Grammatik*, p. 118.

[200]This pronoun is usually written מה even in texts where *aleph* is the predominant *mater lectionis* representing final /a/. In MS AA, however, one finds מא 8x and מה 7x. On the pointing of this pronoun, see s8f, n.22.

[201]See n.144 above. Is the *seghol* in imitation of the Tiberian Hebrew מֶה? See also s8f, n.22.

[202]See also n.181 above.

[203]See s16b, n.5.

[204]On וְהָלָא, see s157b, n.11.

[205]For a general survey, see Tal, *Language*, pp. 13-15.

[206]This phenomenon is attested in Galilean Aramaic (Dalman, *Grammatik*, p. 119), Samaritan Aramaic (Macuch, *Grammatik*, p. 137), Syriac (Nöldeke, *Syriac Grammar*, p. 47), and Ma'lula (Spitaler, *Grammatik*, pp. 57-58). It is also a salient feature of Babylonian Aramaic and Mandaic. See Tal, *Language*, p. 14.

[207]See Dalman, *Grammatik*, pp. 120-121.

[208]See Dalman, *Grammatik*, p. 121; Lund, "Descriptive Syntax," p. 50; Foster, "Language," p. 72.

[209]See Schulthess, *Grammatik*, p. 34.

[210]See Macuch, *Grammatik*, p. 137; Ben-Ḥayyim, *Literary and Oral Tradition*, III.2, p. 89.

[211]See Nöldeke, *Syriac Grammar*, p. 47.

[212]See Dalman, *Grammatik*, p. 121; Tal, *Language*, p. 13.

[213]See Dalman, *Grammatik*, pp. 44, 115-116.

[214]In this verse אחוי refers to "another" who is a fraternal brother.

[215]See Dalman, *Grammatik*, pp. 114-115.

[216]Ibid.

[217]See Bauer-Leander, *Grammatik*, p. 87.

[218]See Nöldeke, *Syriac Grammar*, pp. 187-188. Nöldeke remarks curiously that the use of /ḥavrā/ is "a somewhat childlike method." The Arabic /ba'ḍ/ is used as a reciprocal pronoun in Ma'lula (Spitaler, *Grammatik*, p. 59).

[219]See s12i for pointed examples of this form, all of which function as modifying adjectives.

[220]The pointing of כל generally agrees with that found in the Tiberian tradition of Biblical Aramaic: כָּל־ when bound by a *maqqeph* (36x), unbound כֹל (4x). Note, however, that there are three examples in which the *maqqeph* of the Masoretic text has been omittd in the Targum: וְכָל מָה Cd Gn 46:32; כָּל דְּרָעֵי Cd Gn 46:34; לְכָל בַּיְתתה HH Ex 12:3.ʿ When bound by pronominal suffixes, there is one pointing with ‿, one with ⁀, and one with _: כָּלָן C Gn 34:22 כּוּלָן C Gn 34:16; כָּלֵיה F Ex 19:2.ʿ

Note also the exceptional pointing כָּל־ל C Gn 34:24 (see s11f).

[221]On the pointing of מַן, see n.181 above.

210

[222]See §§20c, 28.

[223]See Schulthess, *Grammatik*, p. 34, who attributes the later orthography to Syriac influence.

[224]See Dalman, *Grammatik*, p. 124.

[225]Ibid.; Tal, *Language*, pp. 15-16.

[226]See Bauer-Leander, *Grammatik*, p. 200.

[227]See Dalman, *Grammatik*, p. 124.

[228]See Ben-Ḥayyim, *Literary and Oral Tradition*, III.2, p. 270; Macuch, *Grammatik*, p. 103.

[229]See Spitaler, *Grammatik*, p. 62.

[230]See Nöldeke, *Syriac Grammar*, p. 23.

[231]See Dalman, *Grammatik*, p. 122, and Díez Macho, "L'usage," pp. 62-63, for a discussion of ברנש and the suggestion that it stands for "I." See also G. Vermes, "The Use of *bar nash/bar nasha* in Jewish Aramaic" (Appendix E), in M. Black, *An Aramaic Approach to the Gospels and Acts* (Oxford: Clarendon Press), pp. 320-327.

[232]Ibid.

[233]See Spitaler, *Grammatik*, p. 61.

[234]This is a Babylonian Talmudic Aramaic form. See Dalman, *Grammatik*, p. 121.

[235]See Dalman, *Grammatik*, pp. 121-122. On מידי, see n.234 above. כל מן דעם is attested in Targum Neophyti (see Levy, "Language," p. 85).

[236]Ibid. Cf. /midda'am/ in the *Editio Sabbioneta*.

[237]See Macuch, *Grammatik*, p. 184.

[238]See Nöldeke, *Syriac Grammar*, p. 184.

[239]See Spitaler, *Grammatik*, p. 61.

B. Numerals

[1]Realized as /tərayn/? See §15c, n.4.

[2]One might have expected a pointing reflecting /təlatte/. Is the pointing תַּלְתִּי an error or was the number re-formed on the basis of /tarten/?

[3]This stem is pointed in "fourteen." See §47i.

[4]One finds the orthography שבע 9x as against שובע 2x. See §31a. Cf. Targum Neophyti Gn 41:2,3,5,6: שְׁבָע.

[5]Or does the one pointed example reflect /šoba'te/? Cf. Targum Neophyti Gn 41:4,7: שְׁבָעְתִי.

[6]This form is pointed in "twelve." See §47i.

[7]Figuratively, "in a short while."

[8]Díez Macho reads חֲדָה אֶל[ועא] and Klein reads חֲרָה אֶלְעֵויה[ן]; however, the absolute form, not the determined form, is expected in these fragments with חד, חדה.

[9]This form is written with double *yodh* 16x as against one occurrence with single *yodh*.

[10]One does not find the orthography תרן. Cf., however, the form with double *yodh* תריין. See n.9 above.

[11]See §15f.

[12]Also in "twelve." See §47i.

[13]This form is written *plene* 11x as against *defective* 1x.

[14]See §2e, n.33.

[15]Cf. also שרביטיה תלוחתין E Gn 40:12.

[16]See Kahle, *Masoreten des Westens*, II, p. 35, n.4.

[17]See §10d, n.70.

[18]On תורייה meaning "cows," see §54c.

[19]On the use of *he* to represent final /e/, see §16c.

[20]One finds עֲשַׂרְתִי in the manuscript. Final ָ is probably a sloppily pointed ָ

[21]See §28.

[22]See §§31a, 47a.

[23]See n.20 above.

[24]In both verses one finds 430 years—תלתין שנין וארבע מאון שנין.

[25]See §15i.

[26]The f.determined forms may all have been realized as /-ayta/. See §32a.

[27]One also finds ביומא תליתייתא F Ex 19:11. תליתייתא is clearly an error for תליתייא.

[28]See Lund, "Descriptive Syntax," pp. 34-37; Lund, "Syntax of the Numeral One," pp. 415-423; Fassberg, "Determined Forms of the Cardinal Number 'One' in Three Pentateuchal Targumim," *Sef,* 45 (1985), 207-215.

[29]This is not always the case. Cf., e.g., Ex 36:9,11,19,26 where חתה appears as an interlinear gloss.

[30]See §19b.

[31]This form may have arisen from the mis-analysis of /ḥadta/ as *ḥad + *ta (f. determined suffix).

[32]The influence of Targum Onqelos on the copyist of Targum Neophyti is well known. See, e.g., Tal, "Ms. Neophyti 1," pp. 38-42.

[33]One finds the m. absolute חד and f. absolute חדא following determined nouns in these sources.

[34]See, e.g., in Tal's edition of the Samaritan Targum, Ex 26:19, Ex 26:24, Lv 14:5, Lv 24:5, Nu 28:21. The orthographies with *aleph* are the influence of Hebrew orthographic practice. See Ben-Ḥayyim, *Literary and Oral Tradition,* III.2, pp. 244-245.

[35]See Ben-Ḥayyim, *Literary and Oral Tradition,* III.2, pp. 105, 224. Note that the f. absolute אחדה, חדה is realized as [ˈāda] (Ben-Ḥayyim, p. 54). Macuch, (*Grammatik,* pp. 311-312) and Vilsker (*Manuel,* pp. 45-47) transcribe both the m.s. determined and f. absolute forms as [ˈāda]. The m. absolute אחד, חד is realized as [ˈād] (Ben-Ḥayyim, p. 55).

[36]According to Vilsker (*Manuel, p. 47),* אחתה, חתה was realized as [ˈåtå] and אחדתה, חדתה as [ˈådtå].

[37]Ben-Ḥayyim (*Literary and Oral Tradition,* III.2, pp. 244-245) explains [ˈåddå] as arising from an older *aḥdā. If, however, [ˈåddå] < *ḥadtā, progressive assimilation of /t/ to /d/ took place.

[38]If arising from *ḥadtā, the regressive assimilation of /d/ to /t/ differentiated the m. form from the f. form.

[39]See Spitaler, *Grammatik,* pp. 113-114. /n/ is apocopated also in Babylonian Talmudic Aramaic. See Epstein, *Grammar,* p. 125.

[40]See Macuch, *Grammatik,* pp. 311-312. /n/ is preserved infrequently in the number "twelve." See, e.g., MS A Gn 49:28.

[41]See Dalman, *Grammatik,* pp. 124-125, and Kutscher, *Studies,* pp. 26-27. The apocopation of /n/ in Galilean Aramaic and Ma'lula is a conditioned sound change in which final /n/ was apocopated after /ayi/. See Kutscher, pp. 43-49; Spitaler, *Grammatik,* pp. 30, 104-105.

212

[42]See Dalman, *Grammatik*, p. 125.

[43]See Schulthess, *Grammatik*, pp. 52-53.

[44]See Nöldeke, *Syriac Grammar*, p. 186.

[45]See Dalman, *Grammatik*, p. 130. On the origin of this form, see Brockelmann, *Grundriss*, I, p. 259.

[46]See Kutscher, *Studies*, pp. 26-28.

[47]Ibid., p. 26. Both תריהון and תרייהון are attested in Palmyrene. See Rosenthal, *Die Sprache der palmyrenischen Inschriften* (Leipzig: J. C. Hinrichs, 1936), p. 81.

[48]See Dalman, *Grammatik*, p. 125. This numeral is also attested without the prothetic *aleph*.

[49]Ibid. See also Levy, "Language," p. 119.

[50]See Ben-Ḥayyim, *Literary and Oral Tradition*, III.2, p. 95; Macuch, *Grammatik*, p. 311. It is also attested without the prothetic vowel.

[51]See Nöldeke, *Syriac Grammar*, p. 95. This numeral also occurs without a prothetic vowel.

[52]See Dalman, *Grammatik*, p. 125; Levy, "Language," p. 119.

[53]See Dalman, *Grammatik*, p. 125; Kutscher, *Studies*, p. 28.

[54]See Macuch, *Grammatik*, p. 311.

[55]See Schulthess, *Grammatik*, p. 51. On the form שובע, see Bar-Asher, *Palestinian Syriac Studies*, pp 463-464, 491.

[56]See Spitaler, *Grammatik*, p. 113.

[57]See Bauer-Leander, *Grammatik*, p. 248.

[58]See Dalman, *Grammatik*, p. 125.

[59]See n.57 above.

[60]See Nöldeke, *Syriac Grammar*, p. 95.

[61]This orthography is due to Hebrew influence. See §16c.

[62]See Dalman, *Grammatik*, p. 126.

[63]See Levy, "Language," p. 120.

[64]See Dalman, *Grammatik*, p. 129; Levy, "Language," pp. 121-122.

[65]See Dalman, *Grammatik*, p. 129.

[66]See Schulthess, *Grammatik*, pp. 52-53.

[67]See Ben-Ḥayyim, *Literary and Oral Tradition*, III.2, pp. 95-96, n.24; Macuch, *Grammatik*, p. 313.

[68]See Nöldeke, *Syriac Grammar*, pp. 96-97. These forms occur only when bound by pronominal suffixes. Note that the Syriac form has a geminated /t/.

[69]תְּלָתֵּיהוֹן Dn 3:23. On the origin of these construct forms, see Brockelmann, *Grundriss*, I, p. 488; Nöldeke, "Beiträge zur Kenntniss der aramäischen Dialekte," pp. 483-484; Praetorius, review of F. Schwally's "Idioticon des christlisch-palästinischen Aramäisch", in *ZDMG*, 48 (1894), 365.

[70]See Spitaler, *Grammatik*, p. 114.

[71]See Levy, "Language," p. 118. Note also the conflated readings מאתוון (Gn 32:15) and מאוות (Gn 32:15). On expressing 300 and above, see Lund, "Problem."

[72]See Clarke, *Concordance*, pp. 332-333.

[73]E.g., Gn 11:19,21,23; 32:15; Ex 30:23; Nu 1:35; 2:21; 3:34,43; 4:44; 16:2,17,35; 26:10,14.

[74]*āyā > /aya/ also in the Infinitive of verbs III-w/y/' of the derived conjugations and in gentilic nouns. See §§113a-b, 143.

[75]See Dalman, *Grammatik*, p. 131.

[76]See Schulthess, *Grammatik*, p. 54. Note, however, the exceptional and late forms he cites.

[77]See Nöldeke, *Syriac Grammar*, pp. 27-28.

[78]See Bauer-Leander, *Grammatik*, p. 51. The Babylonian manuscripts of Biblical Aramaic show divergence in the treatment of *āyā. See Morag, "Biblical Aramaic," pp. 124-125.

[79]A comparison of the m. determined forms of the ordinal numbers in the Cairo Genizah fragments with parallel passages in the other Palestinian Targumim shows that *a'a* is the most frequent form in Targum Pseudo-Jonathan and that *aya* is the most frequent form in Targum Neophyti:

|      | Targum Pseudo-Jonathan | Fragment Targum | Targum Neophyti |
| ---- | ---------------------- | --------------- | --------------- |
| aya  | 1x                     | 1x              | 21x             |
| a'a  | 18x                    | 1x              | -               |

[80]See Dalman, *Grammatik*, pp. 131-132.

[81]See Macuch, *Grammatik*, pp. 315-316.

[82]See n.77 above.

[83]See n.78 above.

[84]See Dalman, *Grammatik*, p. 131.

[85]See Nöldeke, *Syriac Grammar*, p. 98.

[86]See Levy, "Language," pp. 122-123.

[87]See Foster, "Language," p. 78; Dalman, *Grammatik*, p. 131.

[88]See Dalman, *Grammatik*, pp. 103, 131; Odeberg, *Grammar*, p. 69. It is possible that some of the forms with assimilated /d/ are the result of Babylonian Talmudic influence (particularly those in which final *āy > /ā/, e.g., קמא).

[89]See Schulthess, *Grammatik*, p. 54.

[90]See Macuch, *Grammatik*, pp. 315-316; Vilsker, *Manuel*, p. 49.

[91]See Spitaler, *Grammatik*, p. 116.

[92]See Dalman, *Grammatik*, p. 132.

[93]Ibid.

[94]Cf. MSS P,V Ex 1:15.

[95]See Dalman, *Grammatik*, p. 132.

[96]See Macuch, *Grammatik*, p. 316.

[97]See Schulthess, *Grammatik*, p. 54. One finds תנינתא, but also תניניתא.

[98]Cf. תניינתא Gn 41:43 and תינייתה Gn 47:18.

[99]See Nöldeke, *Syriac Grammar*, p. 98. The attested forms are m. /tərayyānā/, f. /tərayyāniθā/ and m. /tenyānā/, f. /tenyāntəθā/.

[100]See Spitaler, *Grammatik*, p. 116. The Arabic ordinals have replaced the Aramaic forms. One finds for "second"—[tēni], [tēn].

[101]From *-āytā'.

[102]Prof. T. O. Lambdin suggests a parallel to the m. *-ān, f. *-āy contrast: Arabic m. adjectives ending in /-ān/ and their feminine forms ending in /-ā/ < *āy (e.g., m. /ġāḍbān/ "angry" and f. /ġaḍbā(y)/.

C. Nouns

[1]דיכרהה E Gn 31:10, "the rams," as noted by Kahle, is a scribal error for דיכרייה.

[2]On the pointing of the f.pl. absolute, see §8e.

[3]See §121.

214

⁴There are no examples of /tor/ with the f.pl. morphemes.

⁵As Kahle remarks, the manuscript reads שבע תוֹרִן בברייֹן. The additional *beth* is a dittograph.

⁶In Cd Gn 37:25 and E Gn 37:25 the participle modifying /gamlin/ is masculine. The gender cannot be determined in the two remaining occurrences, E Gn 30:43, E Gn 31:17. גמל is m. and f. in Biblical Hebrew and in Aramaic dialects.

⁷See Levy, "Language," pp. 95-96.

⁸For examples, see Clarke, *Concordance*, pp. 162, 377.

⁹I am indebted to Dr. D. Talshir for this parallel. See A. Cowley, *Aramaic Papyri from the Fifth Century B.C.* (Oxford: Clarendon Press, 1923; reprint Otto Zeller: Osnabrück, 1967), MS 15, lines 17-20; Kraeling, *Brooklyn Museum*, MS 7, line 34.

¹⁰I am indebted to Prof. M. Greenberg for this parallel. See F. Brown, S. R. Driver, C. A. Briggs, *Hebrew and English Lexicon of the Old Testament* (Oxford: Clarendon Press, 1907; reprint 1953), p. 121.

¹¹See §§16b, 19g.

¹²The forms with final *mem* may be backformations from the pl. construct מימי (for examples, see §61a).

¹³Ginsberg ("Notes," p. 383) suggested that Kahle's reading עזייה E Gn 38:20, "of the goats" may represent a reduplicated plural similar to the Palestinian Syriac פימשוי "his mouths" and the Samaritan Aramaic פממין. The correct reading of this word, however, is עזייה. Klein reads עזייה.

¹⁴Possibly also לזרעֳיָׂתְהן AA₂ Ex 12:21. From s. *zarʿit. See §115b.

¹⁵Is confusion with *ḥlw "sweet" responsible for the pl. forms with *waw*? See §15b, n.1.

¹⁶Also במורביריחתה E Gn 30:41. For a discussion of this form, see §104m, n.338.

¹⁷The pl. marker (/-awan/, /-awat/, /-awata/) distinguishes "springs" from "eyes" (with m.pl. suffix).

¹⁸Cf. the endings /-im/ and /-in/ in Rabbinic Hebrew, which are Hebrew dialectal variants. See Segal, *Grammar*, p. 126. The examples with /-in/ in Biblical Hebrew are usually understood as Aramaisms (e.g., Joüon, *Grammaire*, p. 216), although they, too, may be Hebrew dialectal variants (Ch. Rabin, *The Meaning of the Grammatical Forms in Biblical and Modern Hebrew* [Jerusalem: Academon, 1971], p. 77 [in Hebrew]).

¹⁹See Ben-Ḥayyim, "La tradition samaritaine," pp. 105-107.

²⁰See Macuch, *Grammatik*, p. 273.

²¹See Dalman, *Grammatik*, p. 195.

²²See Ben-Ḥayyim, *Literary and Oral Tradition*, II, p. 464.

²³Ibid., p. 511.

²⁴According to Blau ("Studies in Semitic Pronouns," in *Henoch Yalon Jubilee Volume*, pp. 40-4), there are a few examples of the weakening of the determined state in these fragments. The apparent loss of determination, however, can be explained away in the examples he cites.

²⁵See Schulthess, *Grammatik*, p. 35. The examples in Palestinian Syriac in which the determined form does not mark determination are due to Syriac influence. See Schulthess, p. 35, n.2, and Bar-Asher, *Palestinian Syriac Studies*, pp. 274, 310-311, 317.

²⁶See Macuch, *Grammatik*, pp. 282-288.

²⁷See Kutscher, *Studies*, pp. 7-8. Dalman believed that the determined form did not always retain the force of determination. His conclusion, however, was based on the

215

printed editions containing Galilean Aramaic. See Dalman, *Grammatik*, p. 188. See also Nöldeke, *Beiträge zur semitischen Sprachwissenschaft* (Strassburg: Trübner, 1904), p. 48.

[28]See Dalman, *Grammatik*, p. 188; Tal, *Language*, pp. 85-87.

[29]Ibid.; Tal, "Ms. Neophyti 1," pp. 36-37; Levy, "Language," p. 196.

[30]See Nöldeke, *Syriac Grammar*, pp. 151-168.

[31]See Spitaler, *Grammatik*, pp. 98-99; Blau, "Studies," pp. 17-45.

[32]E.g., Brockelmann, *Grundriss*, I, p. 147. If one applies both Philippi's Law and the attenuation of *a* to *i*, there is complete chaos in reconstructing *qall, *qill, *qatl, *qitl nouns (and with f. endings). For the most recent treatment of Philippi's Law and the attenuation of *a* to *i* in Hebrew, see T. O. Lambdin, "Philippi's Law Reconsidered," in *Biblical and Related Studies Presented to Samuel Iwry*, eds. A. Kort and S. Morschauser (Winona Lake: Eisenbrauns, 1985), pp. 135-145.

[33]From *p. See Bauer-Leander, *Grammatik*, p. 178.

[34]For a general discussion, see Kutscher, *Studies*, pp. 20-22. One finds an *e*-vowel in Palestinian Syriac (Schulthess, *Grammatik*, p. 45), reliable manuscripts of Galilean Aramaic (Kutscher, pp. 20-22, as against a *u*-vowel in printed editions), Samaritan Aramaic (but also an *a*-vowel, see Ben-Ḥayyim's glossary in Rosenthal, *An Aramaic Handbook*, II/2, p. 9), Ma'lula (Spitaler, *Grammatik*, p. 64), and in Targum Neophyti (Levy, "Language," p. 103). One finds the form פֻם, פּוּמָא in Targum Onqelos (Dalman, *Grammatik*, p. 201), Targum Pseudo-Jonathan (ibid.), the Fragment Targum (MS V, Ex 15:12, Nu 32:24) and Syriac (Nöldeke, *Syriac Grammar*, p. 62).

[35]This determined (vocative) form takes the place of the 1 s. pronominal suffix. On the vowel /e/, see §18c.

[36]אבוכן E Gn 31:5 is an error for אבוכין.

[37]These two examples are errors for אחה as the result of attraction to the following m. suffix on דאמה "his mother."

[38]Klein reads אחוי. As he notes, the second occurrence of אחוי in this verse has been corrected to אחה.

[39]This form reflects a conflation of אֲחָה "her brother" and אֲחֶיהָ "her brothers." One expects the latter.

[40]One finds the base forms /'aḥ-/ and /'ɔḥ-/ in Targum Onqelos with forms of the pl. See Dalman, *Grammatik*, pp. 198-199.

[41]See §26.

[42]Ibid.

[43]On *a > /e/, see §18h.

[44]See §8i.

[45]See, e.g., Gn 29:24. The Targum Onqelos form, however, is also attested, e.g., Gn 30:3.

[46]See Dalman, *Grammatik*, p. 199. S. forms without /h/ are also attested.

[47]See Clarke, *Concordance*, p. 36.

[48]Proto-Aramaic *bir ([bir] is attested in cuneiform transcriptions of Aramaic names) > /bar/ in Oficial Aramaic (see Bauer-Leander, *Grammatik*, p. 179). /ber/ in Western Aramaic dialects is probably the result of a sound shift /a/ > /e/, although one cannot rule out the possibility that the form with *i was preserved in some areas as a dialectal form. See §18g. The two pointed examples with *a*-vowels may have been in imitation of the Biblical Aramaic form. For the meaning "child," see §54b.

216

⁴⁹An e-vowel is also attested in Palestinian Syriac (Schulthess, *Grammatik*, p. 43), Samaritan Aramaic (with pronominal suffixes, see Macuch, *Grammatik*, p. 105; cf. [šam]), and Syriac (Nöldeke, *Syriac Grammar*, p. 91). A u-vowel is attested in Biblical Aramaic (Bauer-Leander, *Grammatik*, p. 179), Targum Onqelos (Dalman, *Grammatik*, p. 200), and the other Palestinian Targumim and Galilean Aramaic (ibid.), although the *scripto defectiva* may camouflage an e-vowel.

⁵⁰שְׁמֵהּ C Gn 32:28 is either an error for שְׁמָךְ or in imitation of the e-vowel of the Tiberian Hebrew שְׁמֶךָ-.

⁵¹One expects the s. אַנְתְּתִיהּ/אַתְתֵיהּ. Either this is an error (according to Klein, atraction to בְּנוֹ) or else the use of the pl. form to express the s. as attested at Elephantine. See Kraeling, *Brooklyn Museum*, p. 274.

⁵²See §§18g, 54b. Cf. Targum Onqelos cst. s. /bat/, 3 m.s. /bərateh/ (Dalman, *Grammatik*, p. 200), Syriac cst. s. /baθ/ (*kethibh* /barθ/), 3 m.s. /barθeh/, but 1 s. /bəraθ/ (according to the *qere*; /bəraθi/ according to the *kethibh*; see Nöldeke, *Syriac Grammar*, p. 91), Samaritan Aramaic abs. s. [bat] or [bɛ̄rrā̊], cst. s. [bat] or [bɛ̄rrat], 1 s. [berti] (Macuch, *Grammatik*, p. 309), Ma'lula det. s. [berča], 1 s. [birči] (Spitaler, *Grammatik*, p. 63). See also Sokoloff, "Notes on the Vocabulary of Galilean Aramaic," in *Studies in Hebrew and Semitic Languages Dedicated to the Memory of Prof. Eduard Yechezkel Kutscher*, ed. G. B. Sarfatti (Ramat-Gan: Bar-Ilan University Press, 1981), p. 168 (in Hebrew).

⁵³See §55h. See also Leander, *Laut- und Formenlehre*, pp. 69-70.

⁵⁴See §15i. Note that *mayyohi > /moy/.

⁵⁵According to Leander, *qatil (*Laut- und Formenlehre*, p. 77), but according to Nöldeke *qatal (*Mandäische Grammatik*, p. 108).

⁵⁶See §8i.

⁵⁷Cf. Syriac /šā'ā/; Tiberian Biblical Aramaic /šā'ā/ (qālat), /ša'tā/ (qalat) and Babylonian Biblical Aramaic /ša'ətā/ (see Bauer-Leander, *Grammatik*, pp. 178-179, 241, who consider Tiberian /šā'ā/ a Hebraism).

⁵⁸See §15i.

⁵⁹The forms with the diphthongs are attested only in the det. pl. An additional example which Kahle reads as בְּטוּרֵה and Klein as [וּבְ]טוּרֵה D Dt 27:4, should be read [וּבְ]טֻוֹרֵה. There are 22 examples of the forms of the s. unpointed, all written *defective*, probably reflecting /ṭur/. See §15f.

⁶⁰See §15f.

⁶¹See §24.

⁶²See §11r.

⁶³Cf. מל AA₁ Ex 12:5.ˆ See §30. /mum/ is attested in Jewish Aramaic sources, Syriac, and primarily Biblical Hebrew. One wonders whether it is a Hebrew loan into Aramaic. The *aleph* in the two occurrences of מאום in late Biblical Hebrew sources is best viewed as the result of contamination with the indefinite pronoun מְאוּמָה.

⁶⁴See §18c.

⁶⁵See §30.

⁶⁶The meaning "midwife" is attested in חַיְיתָהּ E Gn 38:28 (cf. Syriac /ḥayyəθā/, but Targum Onqelos /ḥāyətā/ < *qātilat).

⁶⁷See §55f.

⁶⁸See §§4i, 32a.

⁶⁹See §19h.

[70]Cf. Targum Onqelos /kissətā/, Syriac /kessəθā/. *Kaph* was written but erased, and *gimel* was written over it.

[71]From *qital.

[72]Cf. Targum Onqelos /bizzətā/, Syriac /bezzəθā/, but Tiberian Biblical Hebrew /baz/, /bizzā/.

[73]Cf. Targum Onqelos /pittā/, Syriac /pettəθā/, but Tiberian Biblical Hebrew /pat/, /pittot/.

[74]The scribe appears to have originally written דפתיה and corrected it to דפתה. Díez Macho reads דלֿיתה; Klein reads דפתיה.

[75]It is difficult to determine whether the absolute form of these nouns was /qol/ as in Tiberian Biblical Aramaic, or /qul/, as in Syriac. See §11r. The cst. form of /kol-/ "all" suggests /qol/.

[76]See §17g.

[77]See §55h.

[78]See §37k.

[79]See §19h.

[80]Ibid.

[81]Reflecting /ḥoqla/? See §11e.

[82]See §55f.

[83]Reflecting /ḥorba/? See §11e.

[84]Reflecting /yogra/? See §11d, n.73.

[85]The meaning "space" is also attested for this root in וּנְפֶּשׁ C Gn 32:17 (see §13a, n.163) translating the Masoretic רֶוַח. Cf. Gn 32:17 in Targum Neophyti ונפיש (margin ונפש), Targum Pseudo-Jonathan ונימש. Dalman (*Handwörterbuch*, p. 275) lists a form נְפָשָׁא, but does not cite an example. One finds נפש in the Samaritan Targum, and [nibboš] "relief" (*qittul) in the liturgy (see Ben-Ḥayyim, *Literary and Oral Tradition*, III.2, p. 322; Macuch, *Grammatik*, p. 253). Syriac has /nəfišā/ (Western), /nəfešā/ (Eastern) < *qutayl? (according to Brockelmann, *Grundriss*, I, p. 353).

[86]See §18e.

[87]See §11d, n.73. There is only one pointed example of this word with ‿,which can reflect either /a/ or /o/; there are eleven unpointed examples written *defective*.

[88]See §18c.

[89]See §8i.

[90]Ibid.

[91]See §18e.

[92]See §16b.

[93]This is the only attestaton of this cst. pl. form. A f.pl. is known from Syriac (examples in Palestinian Syriac are the result of Syriac influence, see Bar-Asher, *Palestinian Syriac Studies*, p. 320), and a f. cst. pl. form is attested in the Samaritan Targum (Dt 32:7), Targum Pseudo-Jonathan (Nu 12:6; Dt 29:14; 32:7), the Fragment Targum (MS V Dt 29:14, 32:7), and Targum Neophyti (Dt 32:7, margin to Dt 29:14). Note also the Biblical and Rabbinic Hebrew /yəmot-/.

[94]See §15f.

[95]See §54c.

[96]There are two examples of a *qayl noun in the absolute state: /ḥayil?/ and /ʿayin?/. See below.

[97]See §§15b,n.1, 55f.

218

[98]See §15b,n.1.

[99]See §§15b,n.1, 55f,n.17.

[100]Although Klein's reading עֵינֵיי appears to be verified by the published photograph, the final two dots make no sense.

[101]This orthography could also reflect /ˈebayya/. Kahle, Martínez, and Klein read בעבייה in the parallel passage in MS F, although the only letters that can be read with certainty are בייה[ ]. Cf. Targum Onqelos /ˈebā/ and Syriac /ˈaybā/.

[102]This pointing could be in imitation of the Hebrew pl. form /təyāšim/. One expects a pointing reflecting /tayšin/ as in Syriac (cf. Targum Onqelos /tešayyā/ Gn 32:14, but /teyāšayyā/ Gn 30:35).

[103]According to Bauer-Leander (Grammatik, p. 186), *qatil. Cf. Syriac /ḥaywā/.

[104]It is difficult to determine if the pointed examples of the absolute were intended to reflect /gəde/ or a Hebrew type /gədi/ (see §§9i, 119h).

[105]According to Brockelmann (Grundris, I, p. 166), *'aryayā > 'aryā. This was a quadriliteral noun in Proto-Semitic.

[106]See §19h.

[107]Cf. Targum Onqelos /ḥisdā/ "mercy, shame," Syriac /ḥesδā/ "mercy," /ḥesdā/ "shame"; Mandaic hizda; Tiberian Hebrew /ḥasdo/ "his mercy." The only example with the meaning "shame" is E Gn 30:23. The pointing with pathaḥ could be in imitation of the Tiberian form or could possibly reflect differentiation between "grace" (/ḥesda/) and "shame" (/ḥasda/).

[108]Cf. Syriac /mešḥā/, Targum Onqelos /mišḥā/, Tiberian Hebrew /mišḥā/, but Arabic /mash/.

[109]Cf. Syriac /neδrā/, Targum Onqelos /nidrā/. Mandaic nidra (variant nadra), Tiberian Hebrew (/nēder, neder/, but Arabic /nadr/.

[110]Cf. Syriac /nešrā/, Targum Onqelos /nišrā/, Tiberian Hebrew /nišr-/, but Arabic /nasr/, Akkadian /našru/.

[111]Cf. Syriac /seδrā/, Targum Onqelos /sidrā/, Mandaic sidra (variant sadarta), and Rabbinic Hebrew /sēder/.

[112]Cf. Syriac /setrā/, Targum Onqelos /siṭrā/, Mandaic siṭra, but Arabic /šaṭr/.

[113]See §47b, n.8.

[114]Klein's correction to פתרנה is unnecessary; פתר is also attested in Galilean Aramaic (Jastrow, Dictionary, p. 1256). On פתרון, see §119e.

[115]See §18a.

[116]Cf. Targum Onqelos /šiqrā/, Tiberian Hebrew /šiqrēhem/, Mandaic šiqra, but Syriac /šuqrā/ (*i > u / __ q?).

[117]The seven occurrences of this stem are all written with aleph, perhaps in order to distinguish "well" from its homonym ביר "son." It is also possible, however, that this is merely a historical orthography, or that this spelling reflects a Tiberian Hebrew realization (§119h). Cf. Targum Onqelos /berā/, Syriac /birā/, Samaritan Aramaic [ber], [bir] (see Rosenthal, An Aramaic Handbook, II,2, p. 2), and Ma'lula [bīra] (see Spitaler, Grammatik, p. 71).

[118]See §119b. The three pointed examples of the pl. all have ָ . Kahle's reading of a fourth example, רָאשֵׁי Bd Gn 8:5, is not borne out by an examination of the manuscript, which reveals ראשׁ. Klein reads רָאשֵׁׁי. Hebrew influence is responsible for the pointing with ָ . One finds a pl. base with an e or i vowel in all other Aramaic dialects. בְּרָאשֵׁיהֶם

Ezr 5:10 is usually also taken as a Hebraized form (see Bauer-Leander, *Grammatik*, p. 59). For a different view, see Garr, *Dialect Geography*, p. 36.

[119]The *aleph* could reflect a historical orthography or a Tiberian Hebrew realization (see §119h). Cf. Targum Onqelos /tenin/, Syriac /tittā/, Samaritan Aramaic תאנה, תינה (see Macuch, *Grammatik*, p. 276), Ma'lula [ṭēnča] (see Spitaler, *Grammatik*, p. 72).

[120]Cf. Targum Onqelos /ḥezu/ and Samaritan Aramaic חזו (see Rosenthal, *An Aramaic Handbook*, II/2, p. 4).

[121]The manuscript reads [בחזוו ורליליה] (proleptic suffix?). Cf. Targum Onqelos בחלמא דליליא; Targum Neophyti בחלמא בלליא; Targum Pseudo-Jonathan בחילמא דליליא; Peshiṭta בחלמא דלליא. See §25b.

[122]See Tiberian Hebrew /pele'/ (> *pil'), but Samaritan Aramaic [fāliyya], [fāl'yān], [fālyāta] (see Rosenthal, *An Aramaic Handbook*, II/2, p. 9). See §17i.

[123]This word appears to occur only in the pl. in this dialect as in Targum Onqelos.

[124]See Bauer-Leander, *Grammatik*, p. 184, who consider this word to be a Canaanism in Aramaic.

[125]Cf. Targum Onqelos /šiqyā/ Gn 24:20, Syriac /šeqyā/.

[126]According to Dalman (*Grammatik*, p. 143), this noun belongs to the *qitl class. Cf. Targum Onqelos /ḥiwwe, ḥiwyā/, Mandaic hiuia, Syriac /ḥewyā, ḥəwawwāθā/.

[127]The vocalizer seems to have pointed the Persian loanword דָּת "law" (or is this a *qatl noun? cf. Targum Onqelos and Tiberian Biblical Aramaic /dit'ā/). See also §25a.

[128]Proto-Aramaic *'udn > Proto-West Aramaic *'idn? Cf. Syriac /'eðnā/, Palestinian Syriac אידן (Syriac influence?), Samaritan Aramaic [idnå] (Macuch, *Grammatik*, p. 113), but Targum Onqelos /'udnā/, Mandaic 'udna. Cf. also Tiberian Hebrew /'ozen/, Arabic /'uðn/, Akkadian /uznu/. According to Sokoloff, the Jewish Palestinian Aramaic form is *qitl. See Sokoloff, "Notes," p. 169.

[129]Cf. Targum Onqelos /'orḥā/ Gn 38:16 and /'oraḥ/ Gn 24:18.

[130]See §31a.

[131]The *qutl class is suggested by Galilean Aramaic נהרה (in reliable manuscripts, see Kutscher, *Studies*, p. 23), Ma'lula [nohra] (Bergsträsser, *Glossar*, p. 62), and Syriac /nuhrā/. A by-form of *qvtūl is suggested by Biblical Aramaic /nəhorā/ (according to Bauer-Leander, *Grammatik*, p. 188, a Canaanism), Syriac /nəhurā/, Palestinian Syriac נהורא, Mandaic nhura, anhura, and Targum Onqelos /nəhorā/. Cf. Arabic /nahār/.

[132]Targum Onqelos, Syriac, and Arabic have reflexes of *qutl; Tiberian Biblical Hebrew, however, has a reflex of *qitl.

[133]See §§25b, 37g.

[134]Cf. Targum Onqelos /'utrā/ Gn 31:16 and /'otar/ Dt 32:14.

[135]The pl. form is used as "consecrated offerings."

[136]See §30.

[137]See §4f.

[138]Note the difference between the consonantal text (/qəšoṭ/ and the vocalized text /qəšeṭ/).

[139]Kahle and Martínez read מִיגַּה.

[140]Cf. Targum Pseudo-Jonathan דרוגזא, the marginal gloss in Targum Neophyti דרוגזי (his!).

[141]See §4f.

[142]See Dalman, *Grammatik*, p. 145.

220

[143]Cf. Targum Onqelos /sɔge/, and סוגי of Palestinian Syriac, Samaritan Aramaic, Targum Neophyti, and Syriac /soⱴā/ (Tal, *Language*, p. 57). See §§11g, n.88, 31a-b.
[144]Is this a scribal error for סוגי?
[145]Cf. Syriac /ḥaršā/, /ḥeršā/, Targum Jonathan /ḥaršin/, /ḥuršin/, Tiberian Hebrew /ḥərāšim/ (< *qatl? *qitl? *qatal?).
[146]Note the difference between the consonantal text (/ṭehra/) and the vocalized text (/ṭohra/ or /ṭahra/?). Cf. Targum Onqelos /ṭehrā/, Syriac /ṭahrā/, Samaritan Aramaic [ṭērayyå] (Macuch, *Grammatik*, p. 279), Tiberian Hebrew /ṣohar/, Arabic /ẓuhr/.
[147]Cf. Targum Onqelos /ṭaplā/, Arabic /ṭifl/ "child" (but /ṭafl/ "tender, soft"), Rabbinic Hebrew /ṭepel/, and Samaritan Aramaic [ṭefəl] (Macuch, *Grammatik*, p. 243).
[148]Cf. Targum Onqelos /yeṣrā/, Tiberian Hebrew /yiṣr-/, but Syriac /yaṣrā/.
[149]Cf. נגרוי in Targum Neophyti and Targum Pseudo-Jonathan, נגרוי in the Samaritan Targum (MSS A and J), /nēger/ in Rabbinic Hebrew (MS Parma, elsewhere /nāgār/, /naggār/—see Ben-Yehuda, *Dictionary*, IV, p. 3524). Dalman (*Handwörterbuch*, p. 263) lists נגרא, but cites no examples. Jastrow (*Dictionary*, p. 876), cites נגרא, but also נגרא. See also §4f.
[150]Cf. Syriac /savrā/, Targum Onqelos /sɔbar/, and Tiberian Hebrew /sēber/. Dalman (*Handwörterbuch*, p. 282) cites the forms /sibrā/, /subrā/.
[151]Cf. Syriac /salʿā/ and Targum Onqelos /silʿā/, /salʿin/.
[152]From *ʿnz. Cf. Syriac /ʿanzā/, Arabic /ʿanz/, but Targum Onqelos /ʿizzā/, Tiberian Hebrew /ʿēz/.
[153]See §55b.
[154]Cf. Syriac /pashā/, but Targum Onqelos /pishā/. See §18a.
[155]Cf. Syriac /reⱴlā/, Targum Onqelos /riglā/, /raglin/, Tiberian Hebrew /ragl-/, Arabic /rigl/.
[156]Cf. Rabbinic Hebrew /šizrā/, Arabic /šazar/. Dalman (*Handwörterbuch*, p. 419) cites /šizrā/. One finds שיזר in Targum Neophyti, Targum Pseudo-Jonathan and MS B of the Samaritan Targum (שזר in MSS A and J) to Ex 39:31.
[157]Cf. Syriac /savʿā/, Targum Onqelos /sibʿā/, Samaritan Aramaic [sāba] (Rosenthal, *An Aramaic Handbook*, II/2, p. 8), Tiberian Hebrew /sobaʿ/, /sābāʿ/.
[158]See Dalman, *Handwörterbuch*, p. 238.
[159]Cf. Syriac /ʿattəθā/, Akkadian /aššatu/, but Targum Onqelos /ʿittətā/, Samaritan Aramaic [ittå], [ittēta] (Rosenthal, *An Aramaic Handbook*, II/2, p. 2), Tiberian Hebrew /ʿiššā/.
[160]Cf. Tiberian Hebrew /biqʿā/, Targum Onqelos /biqʿā/, Arabic /buqʿat/, Syriac /pəqaʿtā/ (< *qVtalat).
[161]Cf. Syriac /neqbəθā/, Targum Onqelos /nuqbətā/, Mandaic *nuq(u)bta*, Arabic /nuqbat/, and Tiberian Hebrew /nəqēbā/ (< *qatilat). See §54a.
[162]See §11e. Cf. Targum Onqelos /pidʿā/, Targum Pseudo-Jonathan פדעא (Ex 21:25, 2x) and פידעא (Ex 15:25), Samaritan Aramaic פדאה (Ben-Hayyim, *Literary and Oral Tradition*, II, p. 460), Syriac /pəðʿā/ (contamination with /kəwāyā/ "burn"?).
[163]Cf. Syriac /ḥaðwā/ (abs.), /ḥədutā/ (det.), Tiberian Aramaic /ḥedwā/, Targum Onqelos /ḥadwā/ (abs.), *Editio Sabbioneta* /ḥidwā/, Targum Jonathan /ḥedu/ (abs.), /ḥadwətā/ (det.), Mandaic *haduta, hadua*, late Biblical Hebrew /ḥedwā/; Akkadian /ḥidūtu/. See Dalman, *Handwörterbuch*, p. 132; Jastrow, *Dictionary*, pp. 425-426.

221

[164]Cf. Targum Onqelos /'aryətā/, Tiberian Hebrew /'eryā/, /'erwā/, Arabic /'uryat/.

[165]Much has been written on the contradictory reflexes of *qatl, *qitl, and *qutl in the different Aramaic dialects. See Bauer-Leander, *Grammatik*, pp. 223-232; J. L. Malone, "Wave Theory, Rule Ordering, and Hebrew-Aramaic Segolation," *JAOS,*91 (1971), 44-66; Muraoka, "Segolate Nouns," pp. 226-235; Spitaler, "Zum Problem de Segolisierung im Aramäischen," in *Studia Orientalia in Memoriam Caroli Brockelmann,* ed. M. Fleischhammer; Wissenschaftliche Zeitschrift der Martin-Luther-Universität Halle-Wittenberg, Gesellschafts- und sprachwissenschaftliche Reihe, 273, 17 (1968), 193-199. See also Dalman, *Grammatik,* p. 136; Kutscher, "Language of the Genesis Apocryphon," pp. 12-13.

[166]See Bauer-Leander, *Grammatik*, pp. 223-232; Dalman, *Grammatik*, p. 136.

[167]See §31a.

[168]See n.143 above.

[169]See §§9i, 119h.

[170]See §54d.

[171]Or the f. abs? f. det.? It is found in the difficult phrase F Lv 23:16 מן חדתה [מנחדה] and F Nu 28:26 מִנְחָה מִן חַדְתָּה. Cf. Targum Onqelos מנחתא חדתה, Targum Neophyti מנחה מן חדתה, Targum Pseudo-Jonathan מנחתא דלחים חדת (Lv 23:16), דורונא מן עללתא עללתא מן דורונא (Nu 28:26), Syriac סמידא מן חדתא, and the Samaritan Targum מנחה חדתה (MS J), שליחה חדתה (MS A). The similarity in the construction מן חדתה is striking in the Cairo Genizah fragments, Targum Neophyti and Syriac. Has a noun like עללתא dropped out in these three Targumim? Díez Macho, in a note to Lv 23:16, suggests taking מן as "manna."

[172]The "correct" historical reflex of this word should be [ḥalva] and not [ḥalba].

[173]Cf. Tiberian Biblical Aramaic /hadrā/, Mandaic *hadra, hidra,* Tiberian Hebrew /hādār/, but Syriac /heðrā/. Is this an example of *a > /e/? See §18h.

[174]Cf. Targum Onqelos /tānan, tannā/, but Syriac /tennānā/.

[175]See §8i.

[176]Cf. Syriac /'əqar, 'aqrā/, Targum Onqelos /'əqar, 'aqqārā/, and Tiberian Hebrew /'āqār/.

[177]See Bauer-Leander, *Grammatik*, p. 185.

[178]Corrected from צלותיה. See Kahle, *Masoreten des Westens,* II, p. 37, n.7.

[179]See §55f.

[180]These nouns may have shifted to the *qital class as a result of confusion with other noun classes and/or a sporadic shift of *a > *i. See §§18a, 57.

[181]See §16h.

[182]Cf. Akkadian /zikar/ (according to Brockelmann, *Grundriss,* I, p. 202, *a > i,e in the environment of a sibilant). An *a* vowel is attested in Aramaic dialects only in Ma'lula ([dakra] Spitaler, *Grammatik,* p. 65), perhaps under the influence of Arabic /ðakar/. See also §54e.

[183]See §53, n.1.

[184]Cf. Syriac /'ezqəθā, 'əzaqtā/, Targum Onqelos /'izqətā/, Akkadian /izqātu/, /išqātu/. It is also possible to reconstruct a Proto-Aramaic *qitlat.

[185]See §§8f, n.23, 17d.

[186]Cf. Syriac /yəleð, yaldā/ and Tiberian Hebrew /yeled/, /yald-/ reflecting *qatl, Arabic /walad/, Biblical and Rabbinic Hebrew /wālād/ reflecting *qatal. Targum

222

Onqelos /wəlad, waldā/ may be a reflex of *qatl or *qatal. The form /wəlad/ in the Cairo Genizah fragments reflects *qatal (*qatl should yield /wəled/ in these texts).
[187]Cf. Mandaic ḥalṣa, Targum Onqelos /ḥarṣā/, Syriac /ḥaṣṣā/ /< *ḥalṣā?, *ḥarṣā?), and Tiberian Hebrew /ḥəlāṣayim/.
[188]Cf. Syriac /ṣəfar, ṣafrā/, Targum Onqelos /ṣaprā/, Samaritan Aramaic [ṣå̄far], [ṣå̄fårå] (Macuch, Grammatik, p. 242), and Mandaic ṣipra, Maʿlula [ṣofra] (Spitaler, Grammatik, p. 72, suggests that contamination with Arabic /ṣubḥ/ is responsible for the o vowel; assimilation to the labial, however, is also possible).
[189]This noun is attested in Targum Onqelos /qəbel, qablā/ and Targum Jonathan (see Tal, Language, p. 215), the Samaritan Targum (Dt 28:29), and Palestinian Syriac (Schulthess, Lexicon, p. 173).
[190]One expects a det. form /bokra/. Dalman (Grammatik, p. 144) attributes the form /bəkorayyā/ to Hebrew influence. It is also possible, however, to take this form as the extension of the abs. and cst. form /bəkor/. Cf. Targum Onqelos /bukrā/ but /bəkorayyā/, Syriac /buxrā/, Mandaic bukra, Samaritan Aramaic בכור, בכורה (Macuch, Grammatik, p. 251), Palestinian Syriac בכורא, בוכרא (Schulthess, Lexicon, p. 26). See also §119g.
[191]The consonantal text reflects /bokri/; the vocalized text reflects /bəkori/.
[192]Or from *qutūl? This word may be a borrowing from Rabbinic Hebrew (cf. /šəqop/) or influenced by Hebrew /mašqop/. See Kaufman, Akkadian Influences, p. 37. If this is a *qutul noun, the det. form /šəqopa/ for expected /šoqpa/ may be an extension of the abs. and cst. form /*šəqop/. See also §119g.
[193]Cf. Mandaic bukarta and Targum Neophyti בוכרת (Dt 26:10). The insertion of בוכרת in Gn 48:7 appears to be a Midrashic play on the underlying Biblical Hebrew כִּבְרַת- "distance." See also §4h, n.16.
[194]See §4h.
[195]Cf. Syriac /yittem, yaθmā/, Targum Onqelos /yitam, yatmā/, Mandaic iatim, iatma. The form /yetmin/ in the Cairo Genizah fragments may have been formed on the basis of an abs. *yetem (cf. the Syriac and Targum Onqelos forms in which *yətVm >yitVm).
[196]Syriac /ʿəqev, ʿeqvā/, Targum Onqelos /ʿiqbā/ ([ʿiqvā]), Tiberian Hebrew /ʿāqēb/, Arabic /ʿaqib/ point to *qatil. Tiberian Hebrew /ʿēqeb/ and Arabic /ʿiqbat/ reflect *qitl.
[197]A taw belonging to another hand is added above the line: רחלאָ.
[198]Cf. Targum Onqelos /taklā, təkilətā/, Syriac /texləθā/, Tiberian Hebrew /təkēlet/, Akkadian /takiltu/. On the bivalence of the ⏑ vowel sign, see §8a.
[199]See §4f.
[200]Dalman (Grammatik, p. 158) and Bauer-Leander (Grammatik, pp. 10, 186) view qətēlā nouns as Hebraisms in Tiberian Biblical Aramaic and Targum Onqelos. This is certainly possible for those nouns which are attested in either Biblical Hebrew or Rabbinic Hebrew (e.g., /gənēbā/, /gəzērā/). As for those nouns which are not attested in Hebrew, it is possible that this new "borrowed" class was extended to include other nouns. It is also possible, however, that some of these qətēlā nouns have different sources. Note the existence of qətēlā nouns in Syriac (Brockelmann, Grundriss, I, p. 353) for which Hebrew influence cannot be blamed. Possible sources of qətēlā nouns may be 1) *qutayl (as claimed by Brockelmann, p. 353), 2) nouns II-ʾ *qatilat (e.g., /šəʾela/); 3) *qatîlatā' > *qatiltā (shortening of vowel in closed syllable) > *qateltā (*i >

e before certain consonants?) and backformation of qətelā; 4) a new f. formation based on m. qətel nouns (< *qatl, *qitl); 5) a new f. noun formation based on G qətel verbs (e.g., /nəkesa/ "sacrifice" from verb /nəkes/ "slaughter"?—see n.204 below.
[201]Cf. Targum Onqelos and Syriac גנובתא (*i > u/‗b?). Gemination of /b/ may be reflected in MS i of Sperber's edition of Targum Onqelos to Ex 22:2 גְּנֻבְֿתֵּיהּ (/gənubbəteh/ or /gənubəteh/?).
[202]See s17i.
[203]Cf. Targum Onqelos /kəništā, kəneštā/, but Syriac /kənuštā/.
[204]Cf. Targum Onqelos /niksətā/, Syriac /nexsəθā/, Palestinian Syriac נביסא, נכסא (Schulthess, Lexicon, p. 124), Samaritan Aramaic נכיסה (Ben-Ḥayyim, Literary and Oral Tradition, II, p. 476). Is the Cairo Genizah (as well as that of Palestinian Syriac and Samaritan Aramaic) form /nəkesa/ based on the G Perfect /nəkes/, e.g., וּנְכֵיס C Gn 31:54? See n.200 above.
[205]See below s90, n.270.
[206]See s24.
[207]Cf. Targum Onqelos /ṭəme/, Tiberian Hebrew /ṭāmē'/, but Syriac /ṭəmā, ṭammā/.
[208]There appears to be a ḥireq beneath the he, which is puzzling.
[209]Cf. Tiberian Hebrew *qatul, which is used for colors (e.g., /šāḥor/ "black"). A det. form based on the abs./cst. form /qətol/ seems to have taken the place of the expected det. form /qatla/.
[210]See s19g, nn.71-72.
[211]Cf. the parallel passages to the verses cited here in the other Palestinian Targumim and in the Samaritan Targum.
[212]Cf. the parallel passages to the verses cited here in the other Palestinian Targumim and in the Samaritan Targum. See also s24.
[213]See s16h, n.26.
[214]Cf. Syriac and Targum Onqelos /'ənānā/, Arabic /'anān/, but Tiberian Hebrew /'ānān/ (<*qatal).
[215]This noun is assigned to the *qatāl class on the basis of Akkadian /qarābu/ (an Aramaism—see W. von Soden, "Aramäische Wörter in neuassyrischen und spätbabylonischen Text. Ein Vorbericht. II (n-z und Nachträge)," Or n.s., 37 (1968), 264.
[216]See s15i.
[217]Cf. Targum Jonathan and Rabbinic Hebrew /hənā'ā/, Arabic /hanā'/, but Syriac /hanniyutā/.
[218]This pointing, if read correctly, is puzzling.
[219]See s26.
[220]See s12h.
[221]See s119c.
[222]Cf. Arabic /ḥiṣād/.
[223]See s16h.
[224]Cf. Arabic /kitāb/ (Aramaic loan in Arabic?—see S. Fraenkel, Die aramäischen Fremdwörter im Arabischen [Leiden: E. Lokay, 1886; reprint Hildesheim: Georg Olms, 1962], p. 249; Bauer-Leander, Grammatik, p. 189).
[225]See ss12h, 33f.
[226]Cf. Arabic /kurā'/.

224

[227]See §12i.

[228]See §12i, n.155.

[229]Referring to God's works. Klein, on the other hand (Genizah Manuscripts, II, p. 17), takes בעבדוי as "by my deeds" (*ay > oy).

[230]See §19f. Cf. Syriac /'iqārā/, Targum Onqelos /yǝqārā/, but Tiberian Hebrew /yāqār/ (< *qatal).

[231]Cf. Syriac and Targum Onqelos /lǝqāṭā/.

[232]Cf. Syriac and Targum Onqelos /qǝhālā/, but Tiberian Hebrew /qāhāl/ (< *qatal).

[233]Cf. Syriac and Targum Onqelos /ṣǝrārā/, Mandaic ṣraria, and Tiberian Hebrew /ṣǝror/ (< qiṭāl? quṭāl?). A feminine form does not seem to be attested in other Aramaic dialects.

[234]Cf.Targum Onqelos /lǝwāṭā/. Syriac /lawṭǝθā/ and Mandaic luṭṭa indicate a by-form *qatlat.

[235]See §12k.

[236]Cf. Targum Onqelos /šǝ'ārā/ and Tiberian Hebrew /šǝ'ār/. According to Nöldeke, this noun belongs to the *quṭāl class (Beiträge, p. 30).

[237]The pointing of the two examples seems to reflect *qatlat (cf. Arabic /kayyat/), possibly realized as /kowya/ (see §11e). Cf. Syriac /kǝwāyā/, Targum Onqelos /kǝwā'ā/, Mandaic k(a)uaia.

[238]Note that this collective noun also has a pl. form in these fragments.

[239]See §16e.

[240]If the one occurrence of this noun, זבנְיָה, reflects /zǝbineh/, then this is one of the few examples in which medial /i/ is written defective (see §16e). Cf. Syriac /zǝvittā/ (kethibh /zǝvintā/), Targum Onqelos /zǝbin/ reflecting *qaṭīl, but also Syriac /zevnā/ (< qVtl? < *qatil?) and /zǝvānā/. See also Targum Neophyti zbnh (marginal zbwn'), and Targum Pseudo-Jonathan zbynwy to Gn 44:2.

[241]Cf. Syriac /hǝðir/. One finds in this verse /'addir/ in Targum Onqelos, אדיר in the Fragment Targum, and הדור in Targum Pseudo-Jonathan and Targum Neophyti.

[242]See §§10d, 32b.

[243]Ibid.

[244]*ba'īš > /biš/.

[245]See §32b.

[246]According to Dalman (Grammatik, p. 151), this noun belongs to the *qatil class. According to Kutscher, however, it belongs to *qatīl ("Mishnaic Hebrew," p. 273).

[247]Cf. Syriac /'ǝvurā/, Targum Onqelos /'ǝburā, 'ǝbor, 'ibbur/ (Dalman, Grammatik, p. 159), and Tiberian Hebrew /'ābur/.

[248]Cf. Akkadian /taḫūmu/. According to Kaufmann (Akkadian Influences, p. 105), this is not an Akkadian loanword.

[249]Cf. Akkadian /batūlu/ and Tiberian Hebrew /bǝtulā/. See also §11r.

[250]It is also possible to reconstuct a m.s. form (cf. Syriac, but Targum Onqelos f.s.). See §119h.

[251]Cf. Arabic /bāqūr/, Palestinian Syriac בקורתא (Schulthess, Lexicon, p. 30, lists it with בקר; a > o/__r?), and Galilean Aramaic בקורתה (Kutscher, Studies, pp. 22-23, assigns it to the qǝtullā class). One finds /baqrut/ in Rabbinic Hebrew.

[252]Targum Neophyti and the Fragment Targum (MSS P and V) read לבקרותיה; the marginal gloss in Targum Neophyti is לבקרותה.

[253]Cf. Arabic /dukūr/ and Tiberian Hebrew /dəkur/.

[254]Cf. Akkadian /lubūšu/ and Tiberian Hebrew /ləbuš/.

[255]The reconstruction of this word, which is attested in the Palestinian Targumim, Palestinian Syriac, Galilean Aramaic, Biblical Hebrew, and Akkadian, is difficult. Kaufman (*Akkadian Influences*, p. 59) does not believe this to be an Akkadian loan.

[256]Cf. Rabbinic Hebrew /səkum, səkom/, Targum Onqelos /sākom, sākum, səkum/ (Ex 5:8,18), and Samaritan Aramaic סכם (Ben-Ḥayyim, *Literary and Oral Tradition*, II, pp. 513-514, 581, 592).

[257]See ss11k, 32c.

[258]See s119h, n.450. Cf. Tiberian Hebrew /šəbu'ā/ (< *šabū'at?).

[259]For a different explanation of the origin of this stem in Hebrew and Aramaic, see Brockelmann, *Grundriss*, I, p. 474.

[260]This noun (based on a G Active Participle) is also attested in Targum Neophyti (e.g., Gn 31:51). Golomb (*Grammar*, p. 16) errs in assuming that the Targum Neophyti קיימא is an artificial noun formed under the influence of the frequent קיימא (/qəyama/) "covenant." Cf. Targum Onqelos and Targum Pseudo-Jonathan קמתא, קמא (also based on the G Active Participle).

[261]See s12k.

[262]Cf. Targum Onqelos cst. /māre/, Syriac abs. and cst. /māre/, det. /mārā, mārəyā/, Samaritan Aramaic [mār] (Rosenthal, *An Aramaic Handbook*, II/2, p. 7; also [māre]? (Ben-Ḥayyim, *Literary and Oral Tradition*, III.2, p. 95), Palestinian Syriac abs. and cst. מר, מאר (Schulthess, *Lexicon*, p. 115), det. מרא, מריא (in late sources), מרא (Syriac influence—see Bar-Asher, *Palestinian Syriac Studies*, pp. 298-299), and Rabbinic Hebrew /mār/ (< Aramaic).

[263]See s4k, n.24.

[264]See s9i.

[265]See s15i.

[266]For expected /rabyəta/.

[267]The Proto-Aramaic origin of this noun class is not certain. Barth reconstructs *qatūl (*Die Nominalbildung*, p. 176), but Brockelmann reconstructs *qātul (*Grundriss*, I, pp. 343-344). This class is attested in Aramaic dialects (in Syriac it can serve as the *nomen agentis* for any G verb), in late Biblical Hebrew, and in Rabbinic Hebrew (see Bar-Asher, "Rare Forms in the Language of the Tanna'im," *Lesh* 41 [1977-1987], 95-102, in Hebrew).

[268]See s11r.

[269]See s24.

[270]Brockelmann (*Grundriss*, I, p. 353) considers רתיתא "trembling" and נמש "space" to be *qutayl forms. See ss67a, n.85; 77c.

[271]Barth, however, assigns this noun to the *qatil class (*Die Nominalbildung*, p. 12). Kutscher pointed out that עיר usually is found in Eastern Aramaic dialects whereas עור is found in Western Aramaic dialects (*Studies*, pp. 23-25; see also Tal, *Language*, p. 55).

[272]Cf. Syriac and Targum Onqelos /ṣawwərā/, Mandaic ṣaura, and Tiberian Hebrew /ṣawwār/. Bauer-Leander (*Historische Grammatik*, p. 484) believe the root to be quadriliteral.

[273]The orthography is clearly in imitation of the Biblical Aramaic spelling, which itself is in imitation of the Tiberian Hebrew orthography.

[274]See s18d.

226

[275]From Proto-Semitic *quttul. See Brockelmann, *Grundriss*, I, p. 360; Bauer-Leander, *Historische Grammatik*, p. 478.

[276]See Nöldeke, *Syriac Grammar*, p. 72. Cf. Syriac /ʿurəvā/, Targum Onqelos /ʿorəbā/, but Tiberian Hebrew /ʿorēb/ and Akkadian /āribu/ (*qātil), and Arabic /ʿurāb/ (*qutāl).

[277]The origin of the *qiṭṭol* class is difficult to determine. The *quttul class of Akkadian, which marks intensive adjectives (also in Hebrew, e.g., /gibbor/ "strong' as suggested by Prof. T. O. Lambdin), leads one to wonder if Aramaic /geyyor/ "proselyte" and /semmoq/ "red" do not belong to an Aramaic *quttul class. The lack of vowel reduction in the second syllable (e.g., one expects /geyyəra/, /semməqa/ and not /geyyora/, /semmoqa/) may be due to contamination with another noun class. Many of the examples Dalman cites as *qiṭṭōl* nouns (*Grammatik*, p. 164) can be viewed as intensive adjectives.

[278]וּגְיּוֹרִיה A Ex 22:20 (Klein reads וּגְיּוֹרִיה) is a scribal error for וּגְיּוֹרֵיה. Aramaic dialects distinguish between *gāyor* / *gayyār* "adulterer" and *giyyor* "proselyte."

[279]Cf. Targum Onqelos /šippolā/, Rabbinic Hebrew /šippolim/, Samaritan Aramaic [afšibbūli] (Ben-Ḥayyim, *Literary and Oral Tradition*, II.2, p. 237), but Syriac /šəfolā/.

[280]§22.

[281]Cf. Syriac /šebbəlā/, šebbaltā/ (see Brockelmann, *Grundriss*, I, p. 202), Targum Onqelos /šublayyā/. See Brockelmann, p. 360; Bauer-Leander, *Historische Grammatik*, p. 478.

[282]See §10d, n.70.

[283]In E Gn 41:7 the scribe wrote שבלת but corrected it to שבלייה.

[284]See §18h, n.47.

[285]Cf. Syriac /gabbārā/, Mandaic *gabara*, Arabic /jabbār/. Targum Onqelos /gibbār/ has probably been influenced by Tiberian Hebrew /gibbor/ (see n.277 above), as has been the Cairo Genizah form (or is this an example of *qaṭqaṭ* > *qiṭqaṭ*? See §18).

[286]See §8i.

[287]Cf. Syriac /zakkāy/, but Targum Onqelos /zakkay/ (Dalman, *Grammatik*, p. 161).

[288]See §15i.

[289]See §15h.

[290]See §16e.

[291]See §12k.

[292]בגיורה ובits ציבה דארעה AA₁ Ex 12:19 is problematic. One expects either the det. pl. וּבִיצִיבָה or the 3 f.s. suffix on pl. nouns וּבִיצִיבָה.

[293]See §§16e, 55b.

[294]See §8i.

[295]See §158c.

[296]Cf. Syriac /tammim/. According to Dalman (*Handwörterbuch*, p. 444), a form *təmim* (*qaṭīl) also exists in Aramaic sources.

[297]See §4f.

[298]See §§18c, 29b.

[299]See §18m.

[300]M. Ellenbogen considers this a non-Semitic loanword (*Foreign Words in the Old Testament, Their Origin and Etymology* [London: Luzac, 1962], pp. 86-87). Nöldeke

(*Mandäische Grammatik*, p. 122) also questions the Semitic origin of this noun.

[301]Cf. Targum Onqelos /liššānā/ and Syriac /leššānā/. The Proto-Semitic form, however, appears to be *qitāl. See Brockelmann, *Grundriss*, I, p. 350.

[302]The first vowel (*qameṣ*) results from confusion with Hebrew לָשׁן (cf. Targum Neophyti לשׁן Gn 31:47).

[303]Cf. Targum Onqelos /'iššā, 'iššātā/, Syriac /'eššāθ, 'eššāθā/. According to Bauer-Leander (*Historische Grammatik*, p. 454), this noun belongs to the Proto-Semitic *qitāl class. The Proto-Aramaic form is *qittāl (*'iššāt) and the final *t has been misunderstood as the f. marker. See §28. If one were to treat this as a *qillat noun, one would expect a det. form /'eššəta/ and not /'eššata/. See also §119c.

[304]From Proto-Semitic *quttāl.

[305]See §17c, n.2.

[306]The suffix יין־ is due to attraction to the noun it modifies, ופירוכיין (see §§17c,n.2, 115b).

[307]See §16b.

[308]This meaning (< *"stoning"?) seems to be limited to Syria-Palestine and is attested, e.g., in Targum Pseudo-Jonathan (סקל Lv 10:19), Targum Neophyti (סקל Ex 21:23, Gn 42:38, but סקל Gn 21:22, Gn 47:2), Samaritan Targum אסקל MS A Gn 42:4, but אסקל MS J Gn 42:4,38; אסקל MSS A,J Ex 21:22, and MS J Ex 21:23), and the Fragment Targum (סקל MS V Gn 42:38). See also §11r.

[309]Cf. Targum Onqelos /rətikkā/ (Gn 41:43). This noun is common to Western Aramaic dialects (see Tal, *Language*, p. 118). See also §26.

[310]See §26, n.141.

[311]This noun is common to Western Aramaic dialects although the noun כה is usually used to denote "window" in all Aramaic dialects. See Tal, *Language*, p. 109.

[312]See also §119c.

[313]See §55f.

[314]Cf. Fragment Targum ערבוביך (MS V), the margin to Targum Neophyti ערבוביך, Samaritan Targum ערבוביך (Ben-Ḥayyim, *Literary and Oral Tradition*, II, p. 495), and Targum Onqelos /'erabrab/ to Ex 12:38.

[315]*qawtal? Cf. Syriac /'awṣərā/, Targum Onqelos /'oṣərā/, and Tiberian Hebrew /'oṣar/.

[316]Cf. Tiberian Hebrew /gib'ol/. Brockelmann believes the final /l/ to be a borrowed Indo-European diminutive ending (*Grundriss*, I, p. 402).

[317]The one pointed example could reflect any one of these realizations. Cf. Targum Jonathan /'arpilā/ (2 Sa 22:12), Samaritan Aramaic [larfīllā] (Ben-Ḥayyim, *Literary and Oral Tradition*, III.2, p. 54), Syriac /'arpellā/ and Tiberian Hebrew /'ərāpel/.

[318]From *śm'l.

[319]This pointing could reflect /səmaleh/ (see §12f); however, it may reflect /sammaleh/, in which case contamination with /yammin/ "right hand" is responsible.

[320]See §20d, n.111.

[321]See §12f.

[322]From a D Participle.

[323]From the root *'ny.

[324]Cf. Targum Onqelos /mo'ədā/, Syriac /mo'āðā/.

[325]See §§11r,x.

[326]See §55j.

228

327See Tal, *Language*, p. 111.

328Cf. Targum Onqelos /məkilətā/, Palestinian Syriac מכילתא (Schulthess, *Lexicon*, p. 92), Samaritan Aramaic מכלה, מכאלה (Ben-Ḥayyim, *Literary and Oral Tradition*, II, p. 471). See §32a.

329This appears to be a scribal error for במקמתה. See Klein, *Genizah Manuscripts*, II, p. 79.

330Cf. Syriac /marʿiθā/. Is /e/ influenced by Hebrew /mirʿe/? See §119h.

331This one attestation of the noun is problematic. Cf. the marginal notes of Targum Neophyti to Nu 19:5 (מרעייה) and Lv 16:27 (מרעיהון). A form רעייה, רעייה is also attested in Palestinian Targumim. Cf. Targum Neophyti רעייה (Nu 19:5), רעיהון (Lv 16:27), Targum Pseudo-Jonathan רעייה (Nu 19:5), רעיהון (Lv 16:27).

332See §4f.

333The *waw* is unexpected but is also attested in Targum Neophyti משרוייהון to this verse.

334See §10d.

335See §27.

336Ibid.

337משתותייה E Gn 29:28 is an error for משתותה.

338From *rkw? See Ben-Ḥayyim, *Literary and Oral Tradition*, II, p. 464, who equates it with the Arabic root /rkw/. This word is also attested in the other Palestinian Targumim (e.g., Targum Pseudo-Jonathan במורכייתא Gn 30:38, the Fragment Targum, MS V במרכוותא Gn 30:38, and Targum Neophyti במתרנכוותא Gn 30:38. Ben-Ḥayyim also relates this term to Targum Onqelos /ruqbā/ (Gn 21:14). It appears that *a > /o/ before /r/ (/*marki/ > /*morki/?) in the Palestinian Targum forms.

339See §55f.

340See §§25c, 161d.

341See §11r.

342Cf. Samaritan Aramaic [tēmmēde] (Ben-Ḥayyim, *Literary and Oral Tradition*, III.2, p. 259), Palestinian Syriac תחמדא (Schulthess, *Lexicon*, p. 66), Targum Neophyti תחמדא (Gn 3:6), Targum Pseudo-Jonathan תחמדא (Dt 9:22), and Targum Jonathan /taḥmude/ (Mi 7:3).

343See §18m.

344See §18m, n.54.

345Cf. Targum Onqelos /tušbaḥtā/, Syriac /tešbuḥtā/, Samaritan Armaic [attåšʾbān] (Ben-Ḥayyim, *Literary and Oral Tradition*, III.2, p. 58).

346See §30.

347For examples of nouns with prothetic *aleph, see* §26.

348If from *qatlan (cf. Targum Onqelos /šadpānā/, then *a >/e/(see §18). Or is /šedpana/, which is attested only in Western Aramaic sources (see Tal, *Language*, p. 147), an Aramaized form of Hebrew /šiddāpon/?

349See §10d, n.69.

350See §10d.

351According to Bauer-Leander (*Grammatik*, p. 196), *ʿid (< *wʿd) + ān. See §19h.

352See §9e.

353Ibid.

354It would appear that the scribe wrote the Hebrew pronominal suffix /-āw/; however, it is more reasonable to assume that he intended the Aramaic pronominal suffix /-oy/ and thus intended to write קיניווי. Kahle reads קיניניך (< קינינהון).

[355]The orthography could also reflect a Hebraism /ḥəzon/. Note also the puzzling לְחֶדְר־עֵינֶיהָ B Gn 3:6 (MT לְעֵינַ֫יִם). Is this a scribal error for חזון (/ḥezwan?/), חזין (Heb. /ḥezyon/), or חזו (/ḥezu?/—see s68e)?

[356]See ss12i, 46a.

[357]See s11f, n.87.

[358]Cf. Targum Onqelos /buṭlānā/, Mandaic buṭlana, but Syriac /beṭlānā/. See ss181, 19g.

[359]See ss181, 19g.

[360]The primary meaning is "payment, avenging." See Kutscher, "Articulation of the Vowels u,i," p. 249.

[361]See ss181, 19g.

[362]See Kutscher, "Articulation of the Vowels u,i," p. 249.

[363]Klein reads נגשׂ. The sign betwen the nun and gimel is unclear.

[364]From *'lp. See s25a.

[365]See s12k.

[366]See s19g.

[367]The m. det. pl. of gentilic nouns is represented by two dialectal by-forms: /aye/ and /a'e/. Cf. the breakdown in the fragments:

| | MS C | MS E | MS F | MS W | MS Y | MS AA |
|---|---|---|---|---|---|---|
| /aye/ | 2x | 1x | 0 | 2x | 0 | 13x |
| /a'e/ | 4x | 11x | 4x | 0 | 1x | 0 |

It is possible, although it seems less likely, that /a'e/ is the result of Targum Onqelos and Biblical Aramaic (qere) influence. A fluctuation of /ayin/ (1x) and /a'in/ (2x) is also attested (see "Midianite" and "Saracen" above; in s113b one finds two examples of /ayin/).

Cf. /āyē/ (Elephantine), /aye/, /a'e/ (Galilean Aramaic and Targum Neophyti), /a'e/ (Targum Pseudo-Jonathan), Samaritan Aramaic ā́il, ā́'il, and Eastern Syriac /ā'e/ (Western Syriac /āye/).

[368]See s56b.

[369]An error for דכנעאי.

[370]This appears to be either an error for דמואביי (Cf. Targum Neophyti דמואבי) or the use of the s. as a collective.

[371]This appears to be a conflated reading of the pl. forms מצרי and מצראי.

[372]See s11f.

[373]See s4f.

[374]See s4e.

[375]It appears from the published photograph that the scribe originally wrote בזכוותה but corrected it to בזכוותי.

[376]For expected 2 m.s. טעוותך.

[377]See s17h.

[378]Note וּבְסָמְיָה D Dt 28:28 "and with blindness" for expected /samyut/. Has the scribe confused the root *sm' "blind" with the root *smm "poison"?

[379]Klein reads לבשׁ.

[380]Was this word realized as /bekkoruta/? See s4h, n.17.

[381]This word is attested in Galilean Aramaic, Syriac, and in a Hebrew letter from Murabba'at. See Sokoloff, "Notes," p. 169.

[382]See s11n, n.95.

[383]See s11k.

230

[384]See §31b.

[385]*'nw + ān + ūt.

[386]Cf. the unexpected בְּרַבְתָּה Cd Gn 43:33.

[387]See §55f.

[388]See §12l.

[389]See §17f.

[390]Cf. Targum Neophyti שחפיתה, but Targum Onqelos /šaḥaptā/ and Targum Pseudo-Jonathan שחפותא.

[391]Cf. Targum Neophyti margin ובדלקיתה, but Targum Onqelos /dəleqətā/. The pointing of the Cairo Genizah form is unattested in other Aramaic sources.

[392]This form seems to be attested only in the Samaritan Targum in MS A (Ex 21:25). Cf. Syriac /ḥəvārəθā/, Tiberian Hebrew /ḥabburā/, and Galilean Aramaic חבורה.

[393]This word is puzzling. The only related form appears to be Mandaic kupa "sheaf, handful." The other Palestinian Targumim read כונתיא (cf. Targum Onqelos/kunātayyā/).

[394]This word is also difficult. Cf. Targum Onqelos /perukān/ (abs. pl., Lv 2:14), Syriac /parkuxā/ "morsel of bread," Targum Neophyti ופירוכין and Targum Pseudo-Jonathan ופירוכין to this verse.

[395]Or /qellopita/? Cf. Syriac /qallāfiθā/ ("scab"), Targum Onqelos /qilpā, qalpā/ or the D verbal noun /qillup/, Targum Neophyti קלפין, קלופיתא (text Gn 30:37), קלופין (interlinear gloss), קלופייתא (marginal gloss), and Targum Pseudo-Jonathan קליפין (Gn 30:37).

[396]See §17c, n.2.

[397]Works which deal with Greek loanwords in Aramaic dialects are S. Krauss, *Griechische und lateinische Lehnwörter im Talmud, Midrasch, und Targum*, 2 vols. (Berlin: Calvary, 1898-1899); A. Schall, *Studien über griechische Fremdwörter im Syrischen* (Darmstadt: Wissenschaftliche Buchgesellschaft, 1960); Tal, *Language*, pp. 175-185; Dalman, *Grammatik*, pp. 182-187, 412-416; Klein, *The Fragment-Targums*, I, pp. 252-260; Brock, "Greek Words in Syriac Gospels"; and most recently D. Sperber, *A Dictionary of Greek and Latin Legal Terms in Rabbinic Literature* (Jerusalem: Bar Ilan University Press, 1984).

[398]See §26.

[399]See §12c.

[400]See §113b.

[401]See §4d.

[402]a > i/—y?

[403]See §28.

[404]See §18f.

[405]Cf. Targum Neophyti כפרני. For examples of the denominative verb, see §153.

[406]For examples of the denominative verb, see §153.

[407]Ibid.

[408]The second occurrence of the word is superfluous and is due to dittography.

[409]Works which treat Persian loanwords in Aramaic dialects include P. de Lagarde, *Gesammelte Abhandlungen* (Leipzig: F. A. Brockhaus, 1866); S. Telegdi, "Essai sur la phonétique des emprunts iraniens en araméen talmudique," *JA* 226 (1935), 178-256; Rosenthal, *Grammar*, pp. 58-59; G. R. Driver, *Aramaic Documents of the Fifth Century B.C.*, 2nd ed. (Oxford: Clarendon Press, 1965); Tal, *Language*, pp. 186-190; Dalman, *Grammatik*, p. 183; Kutscher, "Aramaic," in *Current Trends in Linguistics*, Vol. 6, 393-

399; J. C. Greenfield, "Iranian Loanwords in Early Aramaic," *Encyclopaedia Iranica*, II, 3 (London: Routledge & Kegan Paul, 1986), pp. 256-259; S. Shaked, "Iranian Loanwords," pp. 259-261.

[410]See Shaked, "Iranian Loanwords," p. 261. See also §11s.

[411]See Telegdi, "Essai sur la phonétique," 218, 240; Brockelmann, *Lexicon*, p. 165; Shaked, "Iranian Loanwords," p. 261.

[412]Kaufman's *Akkadian Influences* replaces the out-of-date work of H. Zimmern, *Akkadische Fremdwörter als Beweis für babylonischen Kultureinfluss*, 2nd ed. (Leipzig: J. C. Hinrichs, 1917).

[413]For examples of the denominative verb, see §154.

[414]This word is considered by many to be of Iranian origin. On the dispute among Iranologists and Assyriologists as to the origin of זמן, see Kaufman, *Akkadian Influences*, pp. 91-92.

[415]See §20d.

[416]This word may be of Sumerian origin. See Kaufmann, *Akkadian Influences*, p. 79.

[417]Cf. Targum Onqelos /qǝdāšā/ (Gn 22:24).

[418]See Kaufmann, *Akkadian Influences*, pp. 81-82.

[419]Ibid., p. 104.

[420]Ibid., p. 29.

[421]For examples of Hebrew influence on other Aramaic *corpora*, see Rosenthal, *Grammar*, p. 57; Tal, *Language*, pp. 159-175; Brockelmann, *Lexicon, passim*; Dalman, *Grammatik*, pp. 78-79, 183-184; B. Jacob, "Das hebräische Sprachgut im Christlich-Palästinischen," *ZAW*, 22 (192), 83-113.

[422]For the most recent discussion of the word, see Steiner, "*Lulav*," pp. 121-122.

[423]See §25a.

[424]See §11s.

[425]See §28. It has been argued that the Hebrew /šabbāt/ is an Akkadian loanword (e.g., Brockelmann, *Lexicon*, p. 750) and even a Persian loanword (see Nöldeke, *Neue Beiträge zur semitischen Sprachwissenschaft* [Strassburg: Trübner, 1910], p. 37).

[426]See §11d.

[427]See §29c.

[428]The original meaning of this stem appears to be "ram" as attested in Akk. /sappāru, šappāru/ "wild ibex" and Biblical Hebrew /šopār/ "ram's horn." It is from the Hebrew "ram's horn" > "horn" that this word spread to Aramaic dialects where it is attested as שופרא or שיפורא *(qītōl? qittul? qittol?* The development of this form is not clear). See Nöldeke, *Mandäische Grammatik*, p. 126; Tal, *Language*, p. 165. Cf. also the Arabic /šabbūr/, which is a loanword from Aramaic (see Fraenkel, *Die aramäischen Fremdwörter*, p. 284).

[429]Baars reads שכינת אתקנת; Klein reads שכינת די אתקנת and believes שכינת is an error for שכינתך. The manuscript, however, reads שכינה די אתקנת.

[430]In the Biblical expression עֹלַת הַתָּמִיד, "the continual burnt offering" (Cairo Genizah fragments עלת תמידה).

[431]The form of this word is undeniably Hebrew. Cf. Akkadian /zūpu/, Syriac /zufā/, Arabic /zūpā(y)/.

[432]Cf. Targum Onqelos /kittunā/, Syriac /kuttinā/. For the relationship to Akkadian, see Kaufman, *Akkadian Influences*, p. 28. The form /kettuna/ is not attested in the Cairo Genizah fragments. Díez Macho's reading כתונה is not borne out by an examination of the manuscript, which shows ה[ כת] (= כתנתה?).

232

[433]See Kahle, *Masoreten des Westens*, II, p. 17, n.4.

[434]Cf. Syriac and Targum Onqelos /mərārā/, Mandaic *mrara*. It is possible, although it seems less likely, that *ā > o/‗r in the Cairo Genizah form.

[435]See §12c.

[436]See Kaufman, *Akkadian Influences*, p. 93, for a discussion and references.

[437]The Aramaic form should be /'eṭa/.

[438]The fact that this noun is found only in Jewish Aramaic sources and in Syriac (only in the pl.—/nesse/, /nāse/) suggests that it was borrowed from Hebrew where it is well attested.

[439]See Tal, *Language*, p. 170.

[440]*Abs. s.* וְרְמֹז B Ex 39:26; *abs. pl.* רמונין AA Nu 20:5; *cst. pl.* רְמוֹנֵי B Ex 39:24. רמן is attested in Western Aramaic sources as against רומנא in Eastern Aramaic (see Tal, *Languages*, p. 121, who does not consider רמן a Hebraism in Western sources). It is also possible to view /remmon/ as the result of internal Aramaic Developments. See §§181, 19g.

[441]The following words usually occur in these fragments in their expected Aramaic form.

[442]See Bauer-Leander, *Grammatik*, p. 42. Brockelmann (*Grundriss*, I, p. 203), on the other hand, would attribute some of the examples to *ā > o/‗r. Note that /o/ occurs before a liquid in all of the examples.

[443]Note the dittography for expected מרומייה.

[444]Baars does not read anything here; Klein reads אַ ]ׂלַ ﭏ ].

[445]The etymology of this noun, which is found in Rabbinic Hebrew, Targum Onqelos, Syriac, Palestinian Syriac, Samaritan Aramaic (Ben-Ḥayyim, *Literary and Oral Tradition*, II, p. 597), and Mandaic (Nöldeke, *Mandäische Grammatik*,, p. 50) is unknown. Jastrow (*Dictionary*, p. 794) derives it from המן, Dalman (*Grammatik*, p. 171) from מאמן, and Barth (*Die Prominalbildung in den semitischen Sprachen* [Leipzig, J. C. Hinrichs, 1912], p. 40) from מן + מן.

[446]For additional examples of /-on/, see §§19g-h, 111. For the suffixes /-on/, /-ān/ in Hebrew, see B. Gross, "Noun-formations with the Afformatives *ōn, ān* (Comprising only Words of Semitic Origin) and Their Meanings in Biblical and in Mishnaic Hebrew" (Ph.D. thesis, Hebrew University of Jerusalem, 1971, in Hebrew).

[447]See Kutscher, review of Ben-Ḥayyim, *Literary and Oral Tradition*, III.2, p. 409.

[448]Cf. /*pətar, petra?/ "interpretation" (§68a).

[449]Note also ותרוה E Gn 40:12, which is clearly a scribal error for ופתרונה.

[450]Cf. Targum Onqelos /šābu'in/ (e.g., Dt 16:9). According to Dalman, the vocalization with *qameṣ* arose in order to distinguish "week" from "oath" (*Grammatik*, p. 159). Cf. also Syriac /šabbu'ā/ (note that the /a/ and gemination distinguish "week" from "oath"). See §§12f, 84b.

[451]Also attested in Targum Jonathan /šəlewā/ (Ez 16:49). It belongs to the /qətela/ noun class. See §77c.

[452]Also attested in Targum Neophyti, but as a cst. form צפית. Or do both the Cairo Genizah fragments and Targum Neophyti interpret this form as a D Perfect 2 m.s. /ṣappit(a)/? See also §155b.

[453]See §11r,x.

[454]See, e.g., Brown-Driver-Briggs, *Lexicon*, pp. 550, 1061.

[455]See Lambdin, "Egyptian Loan Words in the Old Testament," *JAOS*, 73 (1953), 145-155. בוץ "byssus" (§63a) is a possible loan.

[456]See Kaufman, *Akkadian Influences*, p. 45.

[457]See §11s.

[458]See Baumgartner, *Lexikon*, III, p. 794, for bibliography on this possible Indo-European loan, and M. Dietrich-O. Loretz, "Ug. SSW/ŚŚW 'Pferd,' SSWT "stute" und Akk. *sisîtu "stute," *UF,* 15 (1983), 301-302. See also §55f.

[459]See §12k.

[460]See Baumgartner, *Lexikon*, I, pp. 148-149. According to Rosenthal (*Grammar*, p. 57), this word entered Aramaic via Akkadian.

[461]See H. Yalon, "The Reasoning behind the Pointed Mishnayot," *Lesh,* 24 (1960), 162 (in Hebrew); Yalon, *Inroduction*, p. 29; Kutscher, "Mishnaic Hebrew," *Henoch Yalon Jubilee Volume*, pp. 269-271; Kutscher, *Archive of the New Dictionary of Rabbinical Literature* I (Ramat-Gan: Bar-Ilan University, 1972), p. 44 (in Hebrew); N. Wider, "Concerning רבון in Hebrew Sources," *Lesh,* 27-28 (1963-64), 214-217 (in Hebrew); Ben-Ḥayyim, *Literary and Oral Tradition,* III.2, pp. 37-38; Kahle, *Cairo Geniza,* p. 129. See also §11v.

[462]See Fassberg, "Miscellanea," pp. 204-205.

D. Verbs

[1]See Bauer-Leander, *Grammatik*, p. 101; Dalman, *Grammatik*, p. 254; Fitzmyer, *Genesis Apocryphon,* p. 210; Macuch, *Grammatik*, p. 210.

[2]See Brockelmann, *Grundriss*, I, p. 573.

[3]See Spitaler, *Grammatik*, p. 146.

[4]See Kutscher, review of Ben-Ḥayyim, *Literary and Oral Tradition*, II.2, p. 401.

[5]See Kutscher, "Aramaic," *EJ,* 3, col. 280.

[6]Unless the pronoun was realized as /'ennon/. See §34, n.1.

[7]See §34, n.2.

[8]The C Perf. 3 m.pl. ואחדו AA[1,2] Ex 12:27, "they thanked" is the result of attraction to the 3 m.pl. forms of the strong roots in תעקדו עמה ואחדו ושבחו "the people bowed, thanked, and praised" (the same is true in Targum Neophyti Ex 12:27). Cf. וְאַחִדוּ תְעַקְדוּ וְשַׁבַּחוּ Cd Gn 43:28.

[9]See §29.

[10]Cf.

| | Masculine | Feminine |
|---|---|---|
| Proto-Aramaic | *-ū | *-ā |
| Old Aramaic | ־ו | unattested |
| III-w/y/' | ־ו | unattested |
| Official Aramaic | | |
| Biblical Aramaic | /-u/ | kethibh /-u/; qere /-ā/ |
| III-w/y/' | /-o/ | unattested |
| Middle Aramaic | | |
| Genesis Apocryphon | ־ו | ־ה |
| III-w/y/' | ־ון | unattested |
| Targum Onqelos | /-u/ | /-ā/ |
| III-w/y/' | /-o/ | /-a'ā/ |
| Late Aramaic-Western | | |
| Galilean Aramaic | ־ון | ־יִן, ־ן |
| III-w/y/' | ־ון | ־יין, ־יִן |

| | Masculine | Feminine |
|---|---|---|
| Palestinian Syriac | חֵ, חֵ | יֵן |
| III-w/y/' | חֵ, חֵ | יֵ |
| Samaritan Aramaic | [-u], [-on] | [-i] |
| III-w/y/' | [-u] | [-i] |
| Late Aramaic-Eastern | Masculine | Feminine |
| Syriac | kethibh /u/,/-un/; qere Ø, /-un/ | kethibh Ø, /-ay/, /-en/; qere Ø, /-en/ |
| III-w/y/' | /-aw/, /-a'un/ | /-ay/, /-ayen/ |
| Babylonian Aramaic | /-u/ | /-ā/, /-ān/ |
| III-w/y/' | /-o/ | /-ayān/ |
| Mandaic | Ø, יֵן, יוּן | Ø, יאָן |
| III-w/y/' | יֵן | יֵ |
| Modern Aramaic | | |
| Ma'lula | Ø | Ø |
| III-w/y/' | Ø | Ø |

It is difficult to go behind the consonantal text and recover the pronunciation of some of the 3 m. and f.pl. Perfect suffixes in the Palestinian Targumim. A writing of יֵ, e.g., could reflect /-an/ or /-en/, just as a writing of יֵ could reflect /-en/, /-yan/, or /-ayen/. It appears that the m. suffix was /-u/ on the strong verb in Targum Pseudo-Jonathan, the Fragment Targum (infrequently /-un/), and Targum Neophyti (infrequently /-un/), and was /-on/ on verbs III-w/y/' in the Fragment Targum and Targum Neophyti (infrequently /-o/), but /-o/ in Targum Pseudo-Jonathan.

It should be added that there is one example in the Cairo Genizah fragments of a writing reflecting /-un/ on a verb III-w/y/': אֶתְגְלָן C Gn 35:7, "they revealed themselves,". See §11y.

[11]See Dalman, *Grammatik*, p. 255, and Tal, "Ms. Neophyti 1," p. 40. The few examples of נגא are the result of Targum Onqelos influence.

[12]See Dalman, *Grammatik*, p. 255.

[13]See Schulthess, *Grammatik*, p. 62. One also finds יֵ, נֵיה־, נֵה־.

[14]See Macuch, *Grammatik*, pp. 143, 147.

[15]See Nöldeke, *Syriac Grammar*, p. 104. One also finds /-n/.

[16]See Epstein, *Grammar*, p. 35; Tal, *Language*, p. 77.

[17]Kahle's reading of another example, נְהֵר חֲטָאִ־ Cd Gn 44:18 is not supported by an examination of the manuscript,which shows חטא(נהור. The two verbs which are not interpolated occur in E Gn 30:3 and E Gn 39:9.

[18]See §12g, n.141.

[19]See §9d, n.42.

[20]One expects the f.s. Imperative מיתי. אתיי may be the G Infinitive functioning as a polite command.

[21]J. W. Wesselius in "A Subjunctive in the Aramaic of the Palestinian Targum," *JJS*, 35 (1984), 197, on the other hand, contends that '*eqtol* is limited to non-modal contexts.

[22]See Dalman, *Grammatik*, pp. 265-266; Tal, *Language*, p. 75; Wesselius, ibid.

[23]See Lund, "Descriptive Syntax," pp. 22-24.

[24]See Dalman, *Grammatik*, pp. 265-266. N. Braverman also views /nV-/ as the 1 pl. form used in place of the 1 s. in "Targum Neophyti—A Syntactic Examination" (Masters thesis, Hebrew University of Jerusalem, 1978, in Hebrew), pp. 91-92. Ginsberg, "Notes," p. 383, n.14, argued that /nV-/ was the authentic form in the

Palestinian Targumim and Galilean Aramaic and that /'V-/ was the result of Hebrew influence.

[25]See Kutscher, "Aramaic," *EJ*, 3, col. 272.

[26]See Spitaler, *Grammatik*, p. 148.

[27]See Dalman, *Grammatik*, p. 265, n.6; Lund, "Descriptive Syntax," p. 24.

[28]See Kara, *Babylonian Aramaic*, p. 150. These isolated examples are probably the result of confusion with the Imperfect 3 m.s. prefix /nV-/ and thus are not related to the /nV-/ 1 s. prefix in Syro-Palestinian sources.

[29]See J. Blau, *The Emergence and Linguistic Background of Judaeo-Arabic: A Study of the Origins of Middle Arabic* (Jerusalem: Ben-Zvi Institute, 1981), pp. 119-120; H. Blanc, "The nekteb-nektebu Imperfect in a Variety of Cairene Arabic," *IOS*,4 (1974), 206-222.

[30]E.g., Blau, *Emergence*, pp. 119-120.

[31]See A. Fischer, *Mitteilungen des Seminars für orientalische Sprachen*, 1 (Berlin, 1898), 216; Brockelmann, *Grundriss*, I, p. 567; Bergsträsser, *Einführung in die semitischen Sprachen* (München: Max Hüber, 1928; reprint Darmstadt: Wissenschaftliche Buchgesellschaft, 1977), p. 164.

[32]See Sokoloff, "The Hebrew of Bereshit Rabba According to MS Vat. Ebr. 30," *Lesh*,33 (1969), 28-32 (in Hebrew); Kutscher, "Mishnaic Hebrew," *EJ*, 16, col. 1607.

[33]See M. Mishor, "Anomalies in Verb Formation," *Lesh*,41 (1977), 291-293 (in Hebrew).

[34]Prof. T. O. Lambdin suggests this possibility and parallel. For a discussion of the Ge'ez and Modern South Ethiopic verbal forms with the *la- particle, see J. Huehnergard, "Asseverative *la and Hypothetical *lu/law in Semitic," *JAOS*,103 (1983), 579-580.

[35]Wesselius ("Subjunctive," p. 198), on the other hand, does assign this verb a modal function. On the form נקרבה, see §38a, n.116.

[36]See Dalman, *Grammatik*, p. 265; Lund, "Descriptive Syntax," 20-21; Wesselius, "Subjunctive," pp. 197-199. There are also rare examples of a 1 s. Cohortative אקטלה in the Palestinian Targumim.

[37]The use of the Imperfect to express modality in Galilean Aramaic was pointed out by Odeberg (*Grammar*, p. 93) and in Palestinian Syriac and Samaritan Aramaic by Kutscher (review of Ben-Ḥayyim, *Literary and Oral Tradition*, III.2, p. 402). Lund has also demonstrated this in Targum Neophyti ("Descriptive Syntax," pp. 15-16). Whereas indicative futurity is usually expressed by the Participle in these sources, there is evidence that the Participle can also express modality in the Cairo Genizah fragments. Cf. the parallel passages: MS Cd Gn 38:26: טָנֻ לִיֹ בָּהֵית בְּעָלְמָה הָדֵן וְלֹאْ[נֶ]בָהֵית ‎ MS E Gn 38:26: טב לי נבהות בעלמה הדן ולא נבהות בעלמה דאתי לְעָלְמָא דְאָתֵי‎ "it is better that I should be embarrassed in this world than in the world to come."

[38]See Ben-Ḥayyim, *Literary and Oral Tradition*, III.2, p. 195; Macuch, *Grammatik*, p. 169.

[39]There are infrequent examples of this in Galilean Aramaic and the Palestinian Targumim. See Dalman, *Grammatik*, p. 266.

[40]Cf.

| | Masculine | Feminine |
|---|---|---|
| *Official Aramaic* | | |
| Biblical Aramaic | /-u/ | unattested |
| III-w/y/' | /-o/ | unattested |

236

*Middle Aramaic*

| | | |
|---|---|---|
| Targum Onqelos | /-u/ | /-ā/ |
| III-w/y/' | /-o/ | /-a'ā/ |

*Late Aramaic, Western*

| | | |
|---|---|---|
| Galilean Aramaic | ־וֹ | ־יִ |
| III-w/y/' | ־וֹ | ־יִ |
| Palestinian Syriac | ־וֹ,־ןַ,∅ | ־וֹ,־ןַ,(־יֹ-?) |
| III -w/y/' | ־וֹ | |
| Samaritan Aramaic | ־יַ | ־נה, ־ןַ |
| III-w/y/' | ־יַ | ? |

*Late Aramaic, Eastern*

| | | |
|---|---|---|
| Syriac | *kethibh* /u/, *qere* | *kethibh* /-e/, *qere* |
| | ∅,/-un/ | ∅,/-en/ |
| III-w/y/' | /-aw/, /-a'un/ | /-ayen/ (/-a'en/) |
| Babylonian Aramaic | /-u/ | /-in/ |
| III-w/y/' | /-o/,/-u/ | ? |
| Mandaic | ∅,־ןַ,־יון | ∅ |
| III-w/y/' | ־וֹ | ־יאן |

*Modern Aramaic*

| | | |
|---|---|---|
| Ma'lula | [-un] | [-en] |
| III-w/y/' | [-on] | [-en] |

Tal has shown ("Layers," p. 174) that one finds, in general, ־יַ on strong verbs and ־ןַ on verbs III- w/y/' in Targum Neophyti. Targum Pseudo-Jonathan follows Targum Onqelos on the whole; there are, however, examples of ־ןַ on verbs III w/y/'.

⁴¹There is one exception following עתיד. See §129g.

⁴²See §§16b, 38a, 162.

⁴³See §28.

⁴⁴For a thorough discussion of the forms of the Infinitive and the verbal nouns in Galilean Aramaic, Palestinian Syriac, and Samaritan Aramaic, see Tal, "Forms of the Infinitive in Jewish Aramaic." See also Muraoka, "On the Morphosyntax of the Infinitive."

⁴⁵As pointed out by Kutscher in *Studies*, p. 29. See also Tal, "Infinitive," pp. 202-204; Muraoka, "Morphosyntax," p. 78.

⁴⁶Also noted by Kutscher in his review of *Literary and Oral Tradition*, III.2, p. 402. See also Tal, "Infinitive," pp. 202-203; Muraoka, "Morphosyntax," pp. 78-79.

⁴⁷Targum Onqelos, Targum Neophyti, and Targum Pseudo-Jonathan all read ובמחצדכן. The Samaritan Targum (MSS A and J) read ובחצדכן. See also §§16h, 80a.

⁴⁸The cognates of /qettol/ are widely attested as D verbal nouns in Samaritan Aramaic and Rabbinic Hebrew.

⁴⁹Hebrew influence may be responsible for the latter example. Cf. Rabbinic Hebrew /hodāyā/, /hodā'ā/.

⁵⁰See Dalman, *Grammatik*, pp. 253, 283; Morag, "Biblical Aramaic," pp. 127-128. According to Morag, these are remains of an Aramaic *pu''al*, and not Hebraisms. Kahle and Martínez read a D Passive Participle וּמְפֹרַשׁ D Dt 27:8. An examination of the manuscript, however, shows וּמְפֹ[רַשׁ.

⁵¹Klein believes the Participle is an error and the Imperfect was intended. Cf. Targum Neophyti יהוה.

⁵²For additional examples, see §§35, 151c.

237

[53]See §124.

[54]ישראל is the last word on the page. Cf. Targum Neophyti דעתידין ישראל למשתעבדא and the marginal note משתעבדין.

[55]Greenfield has collected the material in "The 'Periphrastic Imperative' in Aramaic and Hebrew," *IEJ*, 19 (1969), 199-210. There appears to be one example in Old Aramaic. See Fitzmyer, *Aramaic Inscriptions of Sefire*, p. 118. See also Golomb, *Grammar*, pp. 188-208.

[56]See Stevenson, *Grammar*, p. 57.

[57]See Kutscher, review of Ben-Ḥayyim, *Literary and Oral Tradition*, III.2, p. 402. See also Lund, "Descriptive Syntax," p. 17.

[58]There are, however, a few verbal nouns with /hV-/. See §126i.

[59]The appearance of prothetic *aleph* is common in Syriac, Samaritan Aramaic, and Ma'lula and can lead to confusion between G *qatila verbs and C verbs. See Nöldeke, *Syriac Grammar*, p. 37; Macuch, *Grammatik*, p. 144; Spitaler, *Grammatik*, p. 143; see also Bar-Asher, *Palestinian Syriac Studies*, pp. 474-478. For a G intransitive verb which has gone over to C, see §141y, n.204.

[60]See §37e, n.63.

[61]The pointing appears to reflect a Perfect 3 f.pl. with *a > /e/. This root is attested with the meaning "to shine" in both G and C in Palestinian Syriac. See Schulthess, *Grammatik*, p. 139. For the evidence in the Palestinian Targumim, see §37e, n.63.

[62]Or is this a C transitive verb (Pharoah is the subject)? Cf. Targum Onqelos and Targum Pseudo-Jonathan אתאבש, Peshitta באש, Targum Neophyti אבאש, and the Samaritan Targum (MSS A and J) אבאש. This root does not seem to be attested with an intransitive meaning in C in the lexica.

[63]This root is related to סרח. It, too, is unattested in the C with an intransitive meaning in the lexica. Cf. Targum Onqelos סרי, Targum Pseudo-Jonathan and Peshitta וסרי, Targum Neophyti ואסרה (אסרי in the margin), and Samaritan Targum אסרי (MS A), אסרה (MS J).

[64]This is clearly a C verb.

[65]Cf. Targum Onqelos שלימו, Peshitta דשלמו, Targum Pseudo-Jonathan אשלימו, and Samaritan Targum אשלמו (MS A). It is possible that the C 3 m.pl. form is used to express the passive.

[66]If gemination were marked consistently in all the pointed manuscripts, one could differentiate D and Dt verbs from Pāel and Ithpāal verbs. On Pāel and Ithpāal in Aramaic, see Dalman, *Grammatik*, pp. 89, 90, 251, 329. See also Morag, "Pā'ēl and the Nithpā'ēl: on the Elucidation of Forms in the Traditions of Rabbinic Hebrw," *Tarbiz* 26 (1957), 348-356 (in Hebrew); also "More on Pā'ēl and Nithpā'ēl," *Tarbiz*,27 (1958), 556 (in Hebrew).

זמן is attested in Targum Onqelos in Pāel and Ithpāel. In Biblical Aramaic the verb is attested once; the *qere* suggests a Gt verb, but the *kethibh* a Dt. See Rosenthal, *Grammar*, p. 46. The Samaritan Aramaic cognate can be taken as Gt or Ithpāal. See Ben-Ḥayyim, *Literary and Oral Tradition*, III.2, p. 189. On the evidence for Pāel and Ithpāal in Palestinian Syriac, see Bar-Asher, "Two Grammatical Phenomena," pp. 117-125. Does the pointing of שְׁהִי C Gn 34:19 and וְאֶשְׁתֵּהִי Cd Gn 43:31 reflect an original Pāel and Ithpāal? See §143n, n.232.

[67]See §123d.

[68]See Dalman, *Grammatik*, p. 250.

238

[69]This stem is well attested in these fragments in G but is not at all attested in C or Ct. The Poel and Ithpoal forms have replaced them.

[70]See §69a.

[71]See §158a. See Dalman, *Grammatik*, p. 250; Tal, *Language*, p. 118. One also finds נִתְרֹקֵן, רֹקֵן, רֵק in Rabbinic Hebrew. See Segal, *Grammar*, p. 67.

[72]These conjugations, which are a salient feature of Biblical Hebrew, are also attested in two Aramaic *corpora* which were influenced by Hebrew—Biblical Aramaic and Targum Onqelos. A Polel?/Pālel? form knn is also attested in the Old Aramaic Tell Fekherye inscription and can be interpreted as either an Old Aramaic feature which died out in later Aramaic, or as a Canaanite influenced form. See, e.g., J. C. Greenfield and A. Shaffer, "Notes on the Akkadian-Aramaic Bilingual Statue from Tell Fekherye," *Iraq*,45 (1983), 111.

[73]See §§16b, 38a, 155c, 162c.

[74]See §11r, n.104.

[75]See §§10d, 16e.

[76]See §11r.

[77]See §4f.

[78]See §16b.

[79]G. Vermes translates "you have conducted yourself as a prince," in "The Archangel Sariel," in J. Neusner, ed., *Christianity, Judaism and Other Greco-Roman Cults, Studies for Morton Smith at Sixty* (Leiden: E. J. Brill, 1975), p. 165.

[80]For the related adjective, see §113b.

[81]Brockelmann viewed הימן as a borrowing from Hebrew /he'əmin/) into Aramaic (*Grundriss*, I, p. 592); Bauer-Leander considered it an internal Aramaic development (*Grammatik*, p. 139; C verb from *'mn).

[82]Díez Macho reads מְהֵימְנִין; Klein reads מְהֵימְתִין. An examination of the manuscript shows מְהֵימְנִין, which must be an error.

[83]See §20c, n.112.

[84]Cf. תֵּעֲבֹד־ C Gn 31:52 and the Imperative עֲבוּרוּ C Gn 32:17.

[85]Also in the irregular verb סלק "ascend." See §152b.

[86]This is the only example of the Imperfect with /a/. There are three examples with /o/.

[87]There are seven examples with /o/ in the Imperfect and Imperative as against two examples with /a/.

[88]See §124b.

[89]As noted by Kutscher in *Studies*, pp. 29-30.

[90]Ibid.

[91]See also סלק §152b.

[92]For a discussion of Passive Participles with active meaning in different periods of Hebrew, see Blau, "The Passive Participle with Active Meaning," *Lesh*,18 (1953), 67-81 (in Hebrew). Blau cites the pertinent Aramaic parallels in n.1.

[93]There are 23 pointed examples. On the pointing of the first syllable in /qatlet/ and /qatlat/, see §8k, n.34.

[94]Cf. Tiberian Biblical Aramaic 3 f.s. /tiqpat/ (Dn 5:20), /bətelat/ (Ezr 4:24); Targum Onqelos (*qatila) 1 s. /qətelit/, 3 f.s. /qətelat/.

[95]Note, however, that the root *yhb supplanted the Perfect and Participles of the root *ntn already in a stage of Proto-Aramaic. See §§137, 139.

[96]Cf. Syriac /zəvan, yezven/, but Targum Onqelos /zəban, yizbon/. There are no examples of the Perfect.

[97]There are no examples of the Imperfect. This verb is attested in the (i,a) class in both Targum Onqelos and Syriac.

[98]See Kutscher, *Studies*, p. 29-30.

[99]Ibid; Dalman, *Grammatik*, pp. 269-274.

[100]See Schulthess, *Grammatik*, p. 61.

[101]See Spitaler, *Grammatik*, p. 145.

[102]The occurrence of verbs belonging to more than one class is also attested in Syriac (Nöldeke, *Syriac Grammar*, pp. 111-112).

[103]See Spitaler, *Grammatik*, p. 152.

[104]On the differences between Tiberian Biblical Aramaic and the Babylonian tradition of Biblical Aramaic, see Morag, "Biblical Aramaic," pp. 126-127. (Cf. n.50 for an example of /qatlet/ in a Babylonian manuscript.)

[105]See §123c.

[106]See Kutscher, review of Ben-Ḥayyim, *Literary and Oral Tradition*, III.2, pp. 408-409. Ben-Hayyim, however (p. 75), believes that the *qətalat* type form is found in Samaritan Aramaic.

[107]See Spitaler, *Grammatik*, p. 152.

[108]See n.94 above.

[109]See Kutscher, "Aramaic," *EJ*, 3, col. 272.

[110]See Spitaler, *Grammatik*, p. 151.

[111]It is curious, however, that elsewhere in the Cairo Genizah fragments *a frequently is replaced by /e/. See §§18a-k.

[112]See n.110 above.

[113]See §38.

[114]See §11t.

[115]See §124b.

[116]See §32a.

[117]See §131i.

[118]See §16e.

[119]See §4f.

[120]Ibid.

[121]See §13b.

[122]See §124b.

[123]See also §155d.

[124]One expects either a G or C verb. The D meaning is usually "split" (cf. Targum Onqelos and Syriac). The consonantal text could reflect either G or C.

[125]See §12f.

[126]See §11r.

[127]See §15j.

[128]See §18d.

[129]See §12f.

[130]Ibid. See also §157a, n.5.

[131]From *tkl. One expects the pointing תִּתְכְּלִית-ֹ. Cf. the Gt in Targum Pseudo-Jonathan איתכלית, Samaritan Targum אתכלת (MS J), but the G in Targum Onqelos /təkolit/, Targum Neophyti תכלת (however, in same verse למתכלה); Fragment Targum תכלית (MSS P,V), Samaritan Targum תכלית (MS A). Or does the verb belong to C with a > e?

240

[132]This orthography could also reflect Dt.

[133]Idem. See also §19c.

[134]Although the orthography could also reflect a Dt verb, the pointed examples of this root in the Perfect, Participle, and Infinitive all point to the Gt conjugation. See also §157a, n.5.

[135]Although the orthography could be interpreted as reflecting a Dt verb, the pointed example of the Perfect 3 m.s. verb (§134e) reflects the Gt conjugation. See also §11t.

[136]Or did the vocalizer not fully point the word (i.e., daghesh forte) and intend a Dt verb? See also §11k.

[137]See §12f.

[138]One expects דְּמִתְכַּנְשִׁין. Is this an example of anaptyxis /*metkanšin/ > /metekanšin?/ or an error?

[139]See n.135 above.

[140]See §12f.

[141]See §19c.

[142]See §4d.

[143]Or does this unpointed example belong to Gt as does the verb in Targum Onqelos and Syriac?

[144]On the shift of *a to /e/, see §18d. One expects /'ettashad/. Does this form reflect a by-form (artificial?) Ith'aphal of Ittaphal?

[145]The /n/ does not assimilate because of the following guttural /h/. On the lack of assimilation of /n/ before gutturals in Semitic languages, see Brockelmann, Grundriss, I, p. 595. In Syriac /n/ does not assimilate to a following /h/ (Nöldeke, Syriac Grammar, p. 115). /n/ does assimilate in the Cairo Genizah fragments, however, before /ḥ/ in the verb נחת "descend" (see below).

[146]See §130b.

[147]Ibid.

[148]Note that two of the three exceptions occur in the same verse and may be the result of scribal confusion (with the Perfect?).

[149]See §3k.

[150]See §12f.

[151]See §12c.

[152]See §31b.

[153]See §126g.

[154]See §11r, n.102.

[155]See §137f.

[156]There is also one unpointed example written defective.

[157]There are also two unpointed examples written defective.

[158]There are no other examples of the Imperative. See §155c for a form of אמר that is clearly a Hebraism.

[159]There are no pointed examples of this form.

[160]The vocalizer may have confused this form with the Perfect.

[161]See §§16d, 25a.

[162]See §§25a, 33f.

[163]Cf. also מלְפָנֵיהוֹן AA Nu 20:10.ʼ See §110h.

[164]This form results from confusion with verbs I-y.

[165]See Dalman, *Grammatik*, p. 298. /'/ is frequently elided in Dt in Targum Onqelos, but never in Gt.

[166]See §20a.

[167]The *yodh* was inserted between the *daleth* and the *aleph* by a different hand from that which wrote דאכל.

[168]See §16d.

[169]See §162d, n.4.

[170]See §20a.

[171]See §§11r, 24.

[172]See §25a.

[173]See §12c.

[174]See §12f.

[175]See §131j.

[176]On the distribution of יכל and כהל in Aramaic dialects and in Semitic in general, see Leander, *Laut- und Formenlehre*, p. 60.

[177]This form is also attested (as a late form) in Palestinian Syriac (see Schulthess, *Grammatik*, p. 75). /e/ may have been extended from the Imperfect and Infinitive of נתן (e.g., /yetten/, /ləmetten/) or from verbs I-w/y of the class *(a,i) such as יתב (cf. Imperative /teb/).

The Imperative forms of הב appear unpointed 7x *defective*. These examples could reflect /heb/ or /hab/. Kahle's reading הַב־ Cd Gn 38:25 is not borne out by an examination of the manuscript, which shows הב־.

[178]יהב and נתן form a suppletive paradigm in Aramaic dialects: יהב in the Perfect, Imperative, Participles; נתן in the Imperfect and Infinitive. יהב, however, is also attested in the Imperfect in Galilean Aramaic. See Dalman, *Grammatik*, p. 308, n.1.

[179]See §§12f, 155c.

[180]See §124b.

[181]The *waw* may be a scribal error for *yodh*, although it is possible that confusion with the C conjugation is responsible.

[182]See §123b.

[183]One expects the G form and not the C (m.!) when the subject is female. Cf., e.g., Targum Neophyti ילדן (but margin ילדו, ילידו). Does this example and the previous (n.181) suggest that the semantic distinction between G and C in the root *wld was breaking down?

[184]See §12f.

[185]The subject is the collective noun ענה "the small cattle."

[186]There is no need to assume that this is a Hebrew form. Cf. the infinitival form below.

[187]See also §130b.

[188]The same phenomenon occurs in the other Palestinian Targumim, Galilean Aramaic, and Samaritan Aramaic. See Dalman, *Grammatik*, p. 304; Macuch, *Grammatik*, p. 175. /'/ is preserved in the noun /šə'ar/ "remainder" (§82d).

[189]Note /'/ is preserved in the noun /*sə'ela/ "question" (§77e). Medial /'/ is elided in the *qatîl* adjective /biš/ "bad" (§83c).

[190]This elision is regular in verbs II-' in Syriac and apparently in Palestinian Syriac. See Nöldeke, *Syriac Grammar*, pp. 112-113; Schulthess, *Grammatik*, pp. 66-67.

[191]See §12k.

242

[192]These verbs are well attested in Aramaic with consonantal /w/. See, e.g., Dalman, *Grammatik*, pp. 315, 318-319.

[193]See s4e.

[194]See s31c.

[195]Confusion between verbs II-w/y and geminate verbs also occurs, e.g., in Targum Onqelos. See Dalman, *Grammatik*, pp. 315-316.

[196]For the examples, see below ss141dd-ff. The Gt forms of the root *nwḥ, however, are formed on the pattern of the strong verb ('etqǝyal). See s147a. Many scholars assign *'ettǝqīl*, *'ettǝqāl* to Gt (e.g., Brockelmann, *Grundriss*, I, p. 616; Bauer-Leander, *Grammatik*, pp. 145-146); however, others (e.g., Nöldeke, *Syriac Grammar*, p. 125; Ben-Ḥayyim, "Comments on the Inscriptions of Sfire," *Lesh*, 35 [1971] 249 [in Hebrew]) have argued that the Ct form has supplanted the Gt form.

[197]See s31c.

[198]See s123d.

[199]Ibid.

[200]See ss12a, 155c.

[201]This verb is also attested in D. See below s141t.

[202]See also the de-adjectival noun /qayǝma/ "pillar" (s88c).

[203]This det. pl. form may have been remodelled on the m.s. form /qa'em/ (see s141j); it may, however, be in imitation of the Tiberian Biblical Aramaic /qā'ǝmayyā/ Dn 7:16.

[204]Cf. Samaritan Targum (MS J) and Targum Neophyti ואבית, and Targum Onqelos, Peshitta, and Targum Pseudo-Jonathan ובת. This is an example of a G intransitive verb going over to the C conjugation. See also ss130b, 139m,n.183.

[205]These verbs are formed on the pattern of verbs II-w/y. See Dalman, *Grammatik*, p. 328; Stevenson, *Grammar*, p. 79. They are also found in Mandaic (see Nöldeke, *Mandäische Grammatik*, p. 253) and Babylonian Talmudic Aramaic (see Epstein, *Grammar*, pp. 83-84).

[206]Cf. the different forms found in the Babylonian pointed Yemenite manuscripts of Targum Onqelos and the Tiberian pointed manuscripts. See Dalman, *Grammatik*, p. 328; Stevenson, *Grammar*, pp. 79-81. Cf. also Biblical Aramaic *kethibh* /'ālǝlin/, but *qere* /'āllin/ in עֶלְלִין Dn 4:4, 5:8, and עֵל Dn 2:16, but דָּקוּ Dn 2:35.

[207]For expected די עאל. On the *plene* orthography, see s16b.

[208]One might have expected the orthography עֵלִּית. The consonantal text seems to reflect /'alǝlet/. Cf. Biblical Aramaic עַלְלַת Dn 5:10 (*kethibh* /'alǝlat/, *qere* /'allat/).

[209]See s42e.

[210]One finds לְבֵזָין in the parallel passage in MS Cd (see s119e; also לביזין in Targum Neophyti), which makes better sense. One wonders if the reading לבזין has its source in an orthographic confusion of *waw, yodh*, and *zayin*, which are all similar in this manuscript.

[211]The pointing reflects /'allata/, but the consonantal text reflects /'alǝlata/.

[212]Although one expects למגו, the reading למגיו is certain. See *Masoreten des Westens*, II, p. 41, n.2.

[213]See s4d.

[214]As is the case in Samaritan Aramaic. See Macuch, *Grammatik*, p. 202. See also s16a.

[215]See s16c.

[216]Cf. Targum Onqelos /šəti/, /rəwi/, /səgi/ (see Dalman, *Grammatik*, pp. 337-345). G Perfect forms with /-i/ are also attested in Biblical Aramaic (see Bauer-Leander, *Grammatik*, pp. 161, 164) and in Syriac (see Nöldeke, *Syriac Grammar*, pp. 121-123).

[217]See §4e.

[218]Ibid.

[219]One finds /-a/ as well as /-i/ in Targum Onqelos, Galilean Aramaic, and the other Palestinian Targumim. See Dalman, *Grammatik*, p. 338.

[220]Cf. Targum Onqelos /-i'at/ (see Dalman, *Grammatik*, p. 338), Syriac /-yaθ/ (See Nöldeke, *Syriac Grammar*, p. 124), Samaritan Aramaic [-iyyåt] (see Macuch, *Grammatik*, pp. 211-212), Galilean Aramaic ייר־ (see Dalman, *Grammatik*, p. 339), and Ma'lula [-aṭ] (see Spitaler, *Grammatik*, pp. 165-169).

[221]On the possibility of a realization of 1 s. [-eθ] vs. 2 m.s. [-et], see §151g, n.275. For examples of both /-et/ and /-yet/, see §§148b, 151e.

[222]See §11y.

[223]There is only one example of the 3 f.pl. in a derived conjugation: (D) ושׂרׂין E Gn 41:54, "they began." See §151a for examples in G.

[224]One finds the same fluctuation in Tiberian Biblical Aramaic and in Targum Onqelos.

[225]The consonantal text could reflect /-ayin/. The vocalizer has pointed the Act. Ptc. m.pl. of the strong verb. Cf. Targum Onqelos /-an/ (see Dalman, *Grammatik*, p. 340), Syriac /-en/ (see Nöldeke, *Syriac Grammar*, p. 123), Samaritan Aramaic [-en] (see Macuch, *Grammatik*, p. 209), Ma'lula [-i] (see Spitaler, *Grammatik*, p. 165-169), and Galilean Aramaic /-ay/ (in reliable manuscripts; see Kutscher, *Studies*, pp. 43-49). One finds, however, /-ayin/ in Tiberian Biblical Aramaic (one also finds /-an/ in the Babylonian tradition—see Morag, "Biblical Aramaic," pp. 128-129). For Palestinian Syriac, Schulthess (*Grammatik*, p. 74) cites a form לאין = *lā(j)ēn*.

[226]Cf. ייה־ in Galilean Aramaic (see Dalman, *Grammatik*, p. 340), /-āyā/ in Tiberian Biblical Aramaic (in the Babylonian tradition one also finds /-ā'ā/; see Morag, "Biblical Aramaic," pp. 124-125) One finds /ā'ā/ in Targum Onqelos (see Dalman, *Grammatik*, p. 340), אה־ in Samaritan Aramaic (see Macuch, *Grammatik*, pp. 210-216).

[227]See §8e, n.20.

[228]See §§4f, 32a.

[229]See §9i.

[230]See §4f.

[231]See §16b.

[232]This verb is usually attested in G, Gt, or Dt. (See also §130c, n.66.) Cf. Targum Neophyti אשׁתחי and the Samaritan Targum שׂאי (MS A) and שׂחו (MS J) to this verse. It is also possible to take this form as a G Active Participle, although the MT and the other Targumim have a Perfect form here. This root is also attested in Dt in these fragments. For examples, see below.

[233]See §9i.

[234]The consonantal text could also represent a Gt or Dt Participle with assimilated /t/: /meddəmayin/ or /meddammayin/.

[235]למ is written at the end of one line, צליה at the beginning of the next.

[236]See §18d.

244

[237]See §16e.

[238]This form, as well as others from the stem גלי that appear below, could also be taken as Dt forms. In pointed forms without a *daghesh forte* in the *lamed* but with a *pathaḥ* under the *gimel*, the *pathaḥ* could merely reflect the pronunciation of the *shewa mobile*, and thus a Gt form (see §12f).

[239]One expects the pointing אֶתְרָעִית. Cf. Targum Neophyti אתרעיית.

[240]See §11y.

[241]See §16c, n.7.

[242]See §§12f, 16c.

[243]See §12f.

[244]See n.232 above.

[245]In אשתינין זיהון דאפו. The verb agrees with דאפו in number (cf., however, וְאֶשְׁתַּנִּי זִיהֵן דָּאפוֹי B Gn 4:5). One expects אשתנין reflectin /'eštannen/ (or אשתני agreeing with זיו). See also Dn 2:19.

[246]For expected למשתחיא. Is this a scribal error, contamination with the verb /'oḥi/ "hurry" (see §149b), or an example of /a/ > /o/? See n.232 above.

[247]From *'ll. The root ילל is found in the other Palestinian Targumim (see Dalman, *Grammatik*, p. 98) and in Mandaic. One finds אלל in Targum Onqelos and Syriac. Note that *wll (*yll?) means "lament."

[248]If this form is not an error, the scribe appears to have intended /yeḥye/ (Hebrew יחיה?). A /yeḥe/ type form is found in other Aramaic sources (Targum Onqelos, Palestinian Syriac, the other Palestinian Targumim, Syriac) with the exception of [yeḥ] in Ma'lula (see Spitaler, *Grammatik*, p. 187) and יתחי (Ct conjugation) in Samaritan Aramaic (see Macuch, *Grammatik*, pp. 219-220).

[249]See §16b.

[250]Cf. Targum Onqelos /'ittənāḥ/. See §§12k, 14ll.

[251]For expected אנפו. A form with *yodh* is also attested in דאנפי F Lv 23:17. Scribal confusion of *waw* and *yodh* is responsible for both of these examples.

[252]See §124l.

[253]See §8f.

[254]One expects the m.pl. וייתון (subject לוטיה-) as in Targum Onqelos and Targum Neophyti (וימטון in Targum Pseudo-Jonathan). Either לוטיה is f. (cf. Peshitta נאתין עליך הלין כלהין לוטתא) or the scribe has been influenced by the gender of the MT הקללות (cf. Samaritan Targum וייעלון עליך כל קללאתה where the verb does not agree in gender with the MT form, which has been borrowed).

[255]See §15i.

[256]See §12k.

[257]The *ṣere* is unexpected. One expects a diphthong. The consonantal text, however, could reflect /yayton/.

[258]See §123e, n.8.

[259]See §16c.

[260]See §124b.

[261]See §126i.

[262]See §16c.

[263]See §124b.

[264]One expects an orthography reflecting /yəhəwan/. Is this form due to scribal error (confusion of *waw* and *yodh*) or does the orthography reflect a spoken form

/yehəyan/?

[265]See §16c.

[266]See §129e, n.51.

[267]See §155c but also §§9i, 143e, 143j.

[268]See Nöldeke, *Syriac Grammar*, p. 134.

[269]One finds יהו, יהא and יי. See Dalman, *Grammatik*, pp. 352-354.

[270]Shorter forms are the rule except in the 1 s. and f.pl. See Dalman, *Grammatik*, pp. 353-354.

[271]See Dalman, *Grammatik*, pp. 352-354; Levy, "Language," pp. 165-166.

[272]See Schulthess, *Grammatik*, p. 74.

[273]See Macuch, *Grammatik*, p. 218. This root is unattested in Ma'lula.

[274]See §35.

[275]Although it seems more likely that the *daghesh* reflects the suffixing of את, one cannot rule out the possibility that the 1 s. ended in [-eθ], but the 2 s. ended in [-et] in order to distinguish the two inflectional categories. Cf. Targum Onqelos verbs III-w/y/' 1 s. [-eθi] but 2 m.s. [-etā] (Dalman, *Grammatik*, p. 406), and Syriac *qatila verbs III-w/y/' 1 s. /-iθ/ but 2 m.s. /-it/ (Nöldeke, *Syriac Grammar*, p. 121). See also Muraoka, "Study," p. 8.

[276]See Kaufman, review of *A Grammar of Targum Neophyti* by D. Golomb, *JAOS* 107 (1987) 142, and Lund, "First Person." The same is true for Galilean Aramaic. See Sokoloff *apud* Levias, *Grammar*, pp. XXIII, XXV. הות is attested (influence of Targum Onqelos?) in Targum Pseudo-Jonathan, e.g., Gn 40:11.

[277]On תוה E Gn 31:20, see §155c.

[278]The realization /šawwet/ is suggested by the orthography without the supralinear *yodh*. /šawwəyet/ is suggested with the supralinear *yodh*.

[279]See §38a.

[280]See §12f, n.132.

[281]See §33d. Klein (*Genizah Manuscripts*, II, p. 56) is probably correct in viewing מִתְבְּלָא Cd Ex 9:23 as an error for מְתַלְּבָא (<מִתְהַלְּבָא). Cf. Targum Onqelos and Peshiṭta ומהלכא, Targum Neophyti הלכת.

[282]Although the pointing may reflect a Targum Onqelos type form, it is preferable to take the *pathaḥ* under the *lamedh* as representing /ə/. See §12f.

[283]See §12k. Le Déaut prefers to view this verb as Aramaic *prs* in the *Pali* conjugation (cf. Syriac *prsy*). See Le Déaut, review of *Genizah Manuscripts of Palestinian Targum*, by M. L. Klein, *Bibl,*68 (1987),574.

[284]For examples of the noun, see §116.

[285]Ibid.

[286]Ibid.

[287]This verb is attested in C in both Rabbinic Hebrew and Aramaic dialects.

[288]One expects a pointing that reflects a C Inf. /maprana/.

[289]For an example of the noun, see §118.

[290]For the relationship of *tgr* and *'gr*, see Kaufman, *Akkadian Influences*, p. 107. For examples of the noun, see §118.

[291]See Kaufman, *Akkadian Influences*, p. 107; I. J. Gelb, "The Word for Dragoman in the Ancient Near East," *Glossa,*2 (1968), 93-104.

[292]See §11r, n.104.

[293]It is less likely that this is an example of an Aramaic G Infinitive without preformative *mem*; such forms are unattested in these fragments (? - see §126g).

246

<sup>294</sup>For examples in Jewish Aramaic sources, see Jastrow, *Dictionary*, p. 1297; for examples in Samaritan Aramaic, See Ben-Ḥayyim, *Literary and Oral Tradition*, II, pp. 574, 590, 591. Cf. MT וְהַמִּצְפָּה...יְצֶף; Cairo Genizah fragments רצפיתא...יצפי; Targum Neophyti רצפית...יתגלי; Samaritan Targum (MS J) יצף...וקעמתה, (MS A) יצפי...ומצבתה; Targum Onqelos יסך...וסכותא; Targum Pseudo-Jonathan יסתכי...וסכותא; Peshiṭta נחזי. See also §119i.

<sup>295</sup>Translating MT /ṣāli/ "roasted." צלי is also attested in Ex 12:8,9 in Targum Neophyti and the Samaritan Targum (one finds the root *ṭwy in the Targum Onqelos, Targum Pseudo-Jonathan, and the Peshiṭta; *hbhb in the Fragment Targum). The root *ṣlw/y usually has the meaning in Aramaic of, in G, "turn, incline," and, in D, "pray." The meaning "roast" is found, in addition to Hebrew, in Arabic and Ethiopic.

<sup>296</sup>For examples, see Jastrow, *Dictionary*, p. 410.

<sup>297</sup>See also §138b.

<sup>298</sup>If חוזה reflects /ḥawwi/, this is the only example in these fragments in which final /i/ is represented by *he* (see §16e). *ḥwy is attested in Biblical Hebrew (as a D verb; in Biblical Aramaic as a D and C verb) in poetry and late sources. חוזה could, in theory, reflect a G Perf. /ḥəwa/. This stem, however, is attested only in D or C in Aramaic dialects.

<sup>299</sup>See §124l.

<sup>300</sup>Ibid.

<sup>301</sup>Ibid.

<sup>302</sup>See also §12a.

<sup>303</sup>See also §§9i, 151b.

<sup>304</sup>See also §12f.

<sup>305</sup>See §16c.

<sup>306</sup>Ibid. The use of *seghol* to mark the final /e/ may also be in imitation of Hebrew.

<sup>307</sup>See also §126i.

<sup>308</sup>See §§16b, 38a, 130e, 162c.

<sup>309</sup>Kahle reads יְבָרֵכבּד־בישראל; Klein reads יְבָרֵיכוּ יִשְׂרָאֵל. It is difficult to ascertain what follows the *waw* of the verb.

E. Prepositions

<sup>1</sup>See §26.

<sup>2</sup>This form is frequent in an adverbial construction. See §158e.

<sup>3</sup>Also in Syriac (Nöldeke, *Syriac Grammar*, p. 102), Mandaic (Nöldeke, *Mandäische Grammatik*, pp. 194-195), Babylonian Talmudic Aramaic (Epstein, *Grammar*, p. 137, ביַת < בי), and perhaps in Biblical Hebrew (Brown-Driver-Briggs, *Lexicon*, p. 108).

<sup>4</sup>See Nöldeke, *Syriac Grammar*, p. 102, n.1. Klein takes בית as "place of." See *Genizah Manuscripts*, II, pp. 19, 79.

<sup>5</sup>There is one occurrence of בר that is not followed by מן: בר שובי קדשׁוּ F Lv 23:38. The absence of מן is also attested in the Samaritan Targum (e.g., מלבר שבי MSS J,A, Lv 23:38).

<sup>6</sup>*Aleph* is elided regularly: בתר < באתר. See also §158b.

<sup>7</sup>One expects בָּתְרַךְ־.

<sup>8</sup>The consonantal text reflects /batərehon/; the vocalized text reflects /batarhon/.

<sup>9</sup>In some Galilean Aramaic texts one finds the s. base with s. pronominal suffixes and the pl. base with pl. pronominal suffixes (see Kutscher, *Studies*, pp. 31-32). This is

not the case, however, in the most reliable of Galilean Aramaic manuscripts, MS Vatican Ebr. 30 (containing Bereshit Rabba). גבן (as against גבין) and the *scriptio defectiva* of לגבכן show that the s. base is used with pl. pronominal suffixes in the Cairo Genizah fragments.

גב also functions as part of a compound conjunction. See §157d.

[10]See §16f.

[11]It appears that /goww-/ is the base with s. pronominal suffixes and /gowwe-/ is the base with pl. pronominal suffixes.

[12]The sign above the *waw* usually marks lack of gemination or spirantization. In this example it serves to distinguish /gowweh/ from /gabbeh/ (§156i).

[13]Baars and Klein read בגייהן. The *yodh* and *waw*, however, are often similar in this manuscript. If their reading is correct, this is the only example of the preposition /gew/.

[14]היך also functions as a conjunction. See §157e. The prepositional use appears to be limited to the Palestinian Targumim (Dalman, *Grammatik*, p. 226-227) and Palestinian Syriac (Schulthess, *Grammatik*, p. 58).

[15]There is one example of חלף (written *defective*) functioning as a conjunction. See §157b. For the vowel of this preposition, see §12i.

[16]See §162.

[17]Cf. the parallel passage וְעֶבְרַת מִנֵּה Cd Gn 38:18.

[18]See Lund, "Descriptive Syntax," pp. 24-26; Sokoloff, "Hebrew of Bereshit Rabba," pp. 135-317. Against this interpretation of the preposition, see Muraoka, "The So-Called Dativus Ethicus in Hebrew," *JTS,* 29 (1978), 495-498 (he designates this the "centripetal *lamedh*"); Dalman, *Grammatik*, p. 226; Nöldeke, *Syriac Grammar*, p. 177.

[19]See §4e.

[20]The final *heth* is an error for *he*. See Kahle, *Masoreten des Westens*, II, p. 18, n.1.

[21]See §25b.

[22]See §19a. On the form מִי H Gn 15:2, see §28.

[23]See §9d, n.42.

[24]Originally a G Passive Participle. It is attested in Targum Onqelos and the Palestinian Targumim. See Dalman, *Grammatik*, p. 232.

[25]See §157a.

[26]See §8i.

[27]See §§9c, 12g. For a Tiberian Biblical Aramaic *qere* form, see §37e.

[28]One finds עליין in E Gn 43:7, which must be a scribal error for עלינן.

[29]/ᶜellawe/ is always preceded by /men/, /me-/ in these fragments. On the orthography, see §16b.

[30]See §§19a, 156p.

[31]See §37e.

[32]The vocalizer appears to have confused the preposition /ᶜem/ with the noun /ᶜam/ "people."

[33]See §19b.

[34]Cf. Syriac /luqval/ (Nöldeke, *Syriac Grammar*, p. 102), Targum Onqelos /qəbel/, /loqəbel/ (Dalman, *Grammatik*, p. 231), Galilean Aramaic קבל, בלוקבל (Kutscher, *Studies*, pp. 18-19), Palestinian Syriac לקבל, לקביל, לקובול, לקבול (Bar-Asher, *Palestinian Syriac Studies*, p. 453), Samaritan Aramaic [alqåbål], [malqubål] (Macuch,

248

*Grammatik*, p. 321), Ma'lula [luqbel] (Spitaler, *Grammatik*, p. 128), and Biblical Aramaic /loqǝbel/, /kolqǝbel/ (Bauer-Leander, *Grammatik*, p. 262). See also §12i, n.150.

[35]See §12i. Note that the by-form with assimilated /d/ (*qadm > *qVmm), which is found in Galilean Aramaic (Dalman, *Grammatik*, p. 230), Samaritan Aramaic (Macuch, *Grammatik*, p. 324), Palestinian Syriac (Schulthess, *Grammatik*, p. 56), Ma'lula (Spitaler, *Grammatik*, p. 131), Babylonian Talmudic Aramaic, and Mandaic (Nöldeke, *Mandäische Grammatik*, p. 194), is not attested in these fragments.

[36]See §12i, n.152.

[37]See §37d,k.

[38]Ibid.

[39]This is an old D Infinitive. See §§126, 132g.

[40]See §19g.

[41]Díez Macho reads תחתיה, Klein reads תַּחְתֵּיהּ. The orthography תחתיה may reflect either /taḥteh/ or /toḥteh/. ‗ in the pointed examples with pronominal suffixes reflects /toḥt-/ as can be seen in the *scriptio plena* of the unpointed examples. The by-forms with suffixes /toḥt-/ and /tǝḥot-/ are attested in Galilean Aramaic. See Dalman, *Grammatik*, pp. 94, 229.

[42]Cf. the occasional interchange of the two prepositions in Samaritan Aramaic (Ben-Ḥayyim, *Literary and Oral Tradition*, III.2, p. 154), the Genesis Apocryphon (Kutscher, "Language of the Genesis Apocryphon," pp. 29-30), and Rabbinic Hebrew (Epstein, *Introduction*, p. 1110).The other Palestinian Targumim all read באבן.

F. Conjunctions

[1]In the following examples ארום can also be taken as a conjunction of condition "if." It also functions as a conjunction of cause. See below. ארום is a salient feature of Palestinian Targumim. See Foster, "Language," p. 78.

[2]See §§18a, 118.

[3]See §156g, n.6.

[4]On the distribution of כד and כדי, see §42l.

[5]If the reading is correct, both the word division and the pointing are puzzling. The supralinear vowel sign seems to point to a Gt verb while the sublinear signs seem to point to a Dt form. See §134a.

[6]See §§16a, n.1, 25c, 161d.

[7]See §19h.

[8]It appears that the vocalizer confused the Aramaic /qǝdam/ with the Hebrew cognate /qódem/.

[9]This form also functions as a preposition (§156d) and as part of an adverbial construction (§158e).

[10]For examples as a preposition, see §156k. See also §12i.

[11]This conjunction is also attested in Targum Neophyti and in Samaritan Aramaic. See Tal, "Language of Ms. Neophyti 1," p. 43.

[12]On the distribution of -ד and די as relative pronouns, see §42.

[13]See §124b.

[14]See §19j.

[15]There is one other occurrence of כמסת: F Lv ארום כל [נפש] די כמסת למצום ולא צימה 23:29, "because any soul that is capable of fasting, but does not fast..." (also in the Fragment Targum, MS V and in the margin of Targum Neophyti [body of text די ותאכל למצום]).

[16]Cf. Targum Neophyti דלא למהי and the Fragment Targum (MS V) דלא למיהוי.

[17]The form הן is found in the conjunction אלא־הן "but, rather." See §157g below. On the usual *plene* orthography, see §16d.

[18]See §41a, n.144.

[19]See §19e for the probable *sandhi* origin of this form. It seems less likely that this one example is a Hebraism or is the result of Targum Onqelos influence. Golomb (*Grammar*, p. 34) believes that אם in Targum Neophyti is in imitation of the Masoretic text; one could, however, also argue that Targum Onqelos influence is responsible in Targum Neophyti.

[20]Cf. the exceptional אודלמא H Gn 15:1, "or perhaps" (if the reading is correct).

[21]The more common use of this conjunction in Rabbinic Hebrew and the Palestinian Targumim "on condition that" is not attested in these fragments.

[22]Cf. the other Palestinian Targumim to Gn 38:25: Fragment Targum (MS P) על מנת, (MS V) אף על גב דאנא, Targum Neophyti אף על גב דאנה, Targum Pseudo-Jonathan ואף על גב דאנא.

[23]הין also functions as a preposition (see §156j). The form איך functions as an adverb (see §158d).

[24]For other functions of ארום, see §§157a-b.

[25]See n.20 above.

[26]On *a > o/u, see §19h. The form /ʾap/ is attested only in the conjunction /ʾap ʿal gab dV-/ "although" (see §157d).

[27]On /u-/, see §33e. On ב representing /wV-/ as a conjunction, see §4e.

[28]This conjunction is also attested in Klein's MS KK Gn 24:4. It is not known elsewhere in Aramaic.

G. Adverbials

[1]See §26, n.137. See also Tal, *Language*, p. 54, who notes that this adverb is not attested outside of Jewish Aramaic sources.

[2]See §§4d, 12c, 21b, 116.

[3]See §4f.

[4]This form appears to be a scribal error for לחדה.

[5]The reconstruction is based on the parallel passage in Targum Onqelos, Targum Pseudo-Jonathan, the Fragment Targum, and Targum Neophyti.

[6]On /saggi/ vs. /seggin/, see §29b. See also §18c.

[7]On the distribution of כדן and כען in Palestinian Targumim, see Foster and Lund, *Variant Versions*, p. 170, n.5; Tal, *Language*, pp. 51, כה.

[8]See §§41e,l-m.

[9]Ibid.

[10]Klein translates "for a long while."

[11]See §29a.

[12]Cf. the orthography יומדן found in reliable manuscripts of Galilean Aramaic, יומדין in Palestinian Syriac, and [imōd] in Maʿlula. See Kutscher, *Studies*, p. 18; Tal, *Language*, p. 50.

[13]See §26.

[14]This is a Hebraism.

[15]See §19h.

[16]See §70a, n.146.

250

[17]The realization of the verbal noun is /ma‘al/ in these fragments (see §142j); cf., however, Targum Onqelos /me‘āl šimšā/ (Ex 22:25).

[18]See §§11d, n.73, 67a.

[19]See §19h.

[20]See §49.

[21]See §§19f, 112.

[22]See §69a, n.131.

[23]See §156g, n.6.

[24]See §§48a,c.

[25]Ibid.

[26]Ibid.

[27]Ibid.

[28]See §41m.

[29]In imitation of /ze/ of the Masoretic text.

[30]See Tal, *Language*, p. 57.

[31]Se §25a.

[32]See §29a.

[33]See also §41a, n.144.

[34]Cf. הָיִךְ in §§156j, 157e.

[35]One finds הא 25x as against -ה 11x. Cf. also הא "behold" (§159).

[36]Cf. הָא אִית Cd Gn 44:19.

[37]See §25b.

[38]Kahle's reading אָךְ B Gn 4:9 is corrected to הן by Klein.

[39]Also [וכמה] חַד־בַלְמָה Cd Gn 44:18.` See §12f, n.129.

[40]See also §157c.

[41]See also §156d.

[42]On בְּדֵין Z Gn 44:19, see §12f.

[43]See §§17e, 19j.

[44]Cf. in the same verse ולהוד and להוד.

H. Predicators of Existence

[1]Cf. /ha-/ (interrogative particle). See §158d.

I. Interjections

[1]See §15h.

[2]On the possible origin of this interjection, see Huehnergard, "Asseverative *la and Hypothetical *lu/law in Semitic," p. 572.

[3]See §15i.

[4]__ is a scribal error for __

[5]See §15i.

## VII TWO SYNTACTIC FEATURES

**§161**              *A. The Genitive Relationship*

**§161a**   There are three ways of expressing the genitive relationship in these fragments, as in many Aramaic dialects:[1] 1) the construct chain (noun + noun), e.g., אֱלָהּ שְׁמַיָּא Cd Gn 48:3, "the God of the Heavens"; 2) noun (det. or abs.) + /dV-/ + noun, e.g., מִטְרָה דְּמַבּוּלָה Bd Gn 8:2, "the rain of the flood"; מְשַׁח דְּבָטְמִין וּדלוּזִין Cd Gn 43:11, "oil of pistachios and almonds"; 3) noun + proleptic suffix + /dV-/ + noun, e.g., בְּנוֹי־דְיוֹסֵף Cd Gn 48:8, "Joseph's sons." Where the text is unpointed and one finds *scriptio defectiva*, it is often impossible to determine which construction is employed,[2] e.g., לביתה דיוסף E Gn 43:24, "to Joseph's house" may reflect /bayta dəyosep/ or /bayteh dəyosep/. As can be seen in the following chart, the construct chain is the most common construction:[3]

|          | A    | B    | C     | D    | E     | F     | H     | W    | Y    | Z    | AA   | HH  |
|----------|------|------|-------|------|-------|-------|-------|------|------|------|------|-----|
| *cst.*   | 20x  | 32x  | 108x  | 27x  | 159x  | 111x  | 7x    | 19x  | 6x   | 22x  | 91x  | 4x  |
| /dV-/    | 2x   | 15x  | 32x   | 2x   | 47x   | 56x   | 2x    | 3x   | 10x  | 7x   | 61x  | 1x  |
| *prolep.*| 7x   | 27x  | 89x   | 7x   | 70x   | 39x   | 1x    | 5x   | 5x   | 14x  | 24x  | 1x  |

**§161b**   All 22 pointed examples of the syntagm ממרה דיי "the Word of the Lord" reflect the construction with proleptic suffix, e.g., מֵאמְרֵהּ דַּאדֹנָי B Gn 4:9, מֵימְרֵהּ דַּאדֹנָי D Dt 5:25. There are 14 unpointed examples in which the *scriptio plena* also reflects the proleptic suffix, e.g., וממריה־ד־יׇ Cd Ex 9:23, ממרה דיי F Lv 23:23. In 29 other unpointed examples, the *scriptio defectiva* is ambiguous and could be taken as reflecting either /memareh dadonay/ (which seems most likely in the light of the pointed examples) or /memara dadonay/, e.g., מימרה דיׇ Cd Ex 9:23. Cf. Targum Onqelos /meməra dadonāy/.

**§161c**   The syntagm "the children of Israel" is regularly expressed by the construct chain, with only one exception: בנו דשירׇאל AA Ex 12:42 (cf. in the same verse בני ישראל). The pointed examples of the syntagm "the land of..." are regularly expessed by /dV-/, e.g., בְּאַרְעָא־דַכְנַעַן Cd Gn 46:31, "in the land of Canaan," בְּאַרְעָא דְגֹשֶׁן Cd Gn 47:4, "in the land of Goshen," בְּאַרְעָא דמצרֵם Cd Gn 48:5, "in the land of Egypt."

252

**§161d** It should be noted that there are a few exceptional syntagms expressing the genitive relationship, some of which may be scribal errors or may reflect certain phonetic processes. The examples are

*construct form before /dV-/:*[4] בְּשַׁלְהָבִית דְּאֵשָׁה F Ex 19:18, "in a flame of fire":[5] בְּחַיֵי דְרִשִׁי דְאבא Z Gn 44:18, "by the life of my father('s head)";[6]

*construct form before /di/:* וּמְן־שָׁעַת דִּי־עַלְלִית Cd Ex 5:23, "and from the moment I entered";[7] נפשת די הוון AA Nu 19:18, "the souls that were";[8]

*omission of /dV-/:* בְּאַפֵּי בעלה E Gn 29:31, "in the countenance of her husband";[9] מלוֹיי בנוי דלבן E Gn 31:1, "the words of Laban's sons";[10] בארעה מצרים E Gn 41:48, "in the land of Egypt."

**§162** *B. Marking of the Direct Object*

**§162a** The undetermined direct object is unmarked in these fragments, e.g., וּנְסַב יַעֲקֹב אֶבֶן C Gn 31:45, "and Jacob took a stone."

**§162b** The determined direct object may be either marked by the particle /yat/ or the particle /1V-/, or unmarked (frequently when the direct object in the Masoretic text is unmarked). Cf., e.g., וקרא ית שמיה E Gn 38:29, "and he called his name," but וקרא שמיה E Gn 38:30; וְקַבֵּל מֵאמְרֵהּ דַּאדֹנָי בְּרַעֲוָה יַת־הֶבֶל וְיָת־דּוֹרוֹן דִּידֵהּ B Gn 4:4, "and the Word of the Lord accepted Abel and his gift with favor," but וּלְקָיֵן וּלְדוֹרוֹן־דִּידֵהּ לָא־קַבֵּל בְּרַעֲוָה B Gn 4:5, but he did not accept with favor Cain and his gift"; וברך ממר דַיֵּית ביתה דמצריה E Gn 39:5, "and the Word of the Lord blessed the house of the Egyptian," but למהוֵי־מברכין לחתנא ולכלתָא C Gn 35:9, "to bless the bridegroom and the bride"; וּפְקַד ית־גוברא Cd Gn 44:1, "and he ordered the man," but in the parallel passage וּפְקַד לדן E Gn 44:1, "and he ordered him" (lit. "this one"). As can be seen from the following chart, the determined direct object is most frequently marked by /yat/:[1]

| | A | B | C | D | E | F | H | W | Y | Z | AA | HH |
|---|---|---|---|---|---|---|---|---|---|---|---|---|
| /yat/ | 15x | 30x | 83x | 21x | 123x | 41x | – | 4x | – | 12x | 62x | – |
| /1V-/ | – | 3x | 2x | – | 2x | 5x | – | – | – | – | – | – |
| Ø | 5x | 1x | 26x | – | 45x | 7x | 3x | 3x | 1x | 1x | 10x | – |

**§162c** When the direct object is represented by a pronominal suffix, /yat-/ alone is employed, e.g., וּבָרֵיךְ יַתְהוֹן C Gn 35:9, "and he blessed them." There are, however, two exceptions: יְשַׁוֵּי־יָתַךְ יְיָ Cd Gn 48:20, "May the Lord make you (like Ephraim and Manasseh!)";[2] וּלְרוֹמָ֫א֫מָ֫ךְ D Dt 26:19, "to raise you up."[3]

**§162d** There are no examples of /yat/ + pronominal suffix attached to verbs[4] as in Galilean Aramaic (e.g., חמתיה = חמה יתיה "he saw him"),[5] Palestinian Syriac,[6] and Samaritan Aramaic.[7]

**§162e** There are two examples of the Hebrew *nota accusativi* את embedded in the Aramaic text in imitation of the translated Hebrew text: ויהב ליה את [אס]נת ברת פוטיפרע E Gn 41:45, "and he gave him Asenath, the daughter of Potiphera" (MT וַיִּתֶּן־לוֹ אֶת־אָסְנַת בַּת־פּוֹטִי פֶרַע), and ואת בנימן אתון בעיין למסב E Gn 42:36, "and you seek to take Benjamin" (MT וְאֶת־בִּנְיָמִן תִּקָּחוּ).

**§162f** The Biblical Hebrew preposition /'et/ "with" is misunderstood by the translator as the direct object marker[8] in E Gn 31:25

וְיַעֲקֹב [פרס י]ת משכנה בטורה ולבן פרס ית אחוי בטור גלעדה (וְיַעֲקֹב תָּקַע אֶת־אָהֳלוֹ בָּהָר וְלָבָן תָּקַע אֶת־אֶחָיו בְּהַר הַגִּלְעָד MT)

# Footnotes — Chapter VII

## A. Genitive Relationship

[1]See, e.g., M. Z. Kadari, "Studies in the Syntax of Targum Onqelos," *Tarbiz*, 32 (1963), 232-251 (in Hebrew); "Construct State and di- Phrases in Imperial Aramaic," in *Proceedings of the International Conference on Semitic Studies* (1965), pp. 102-115; Muraoka, "Notes on the Syntax of Biblical Aramaic," *JSS*, 11 (1966), 152-155; Lund, "Descriptive Syntax," pp. 215-217; Golomb, "Nominal Syntax in the Language of Codex Vatican Neofiti 1: The Genitive Relationship," *JAOS*, 102 (1982), 297-308; *Grammar*, pp. 218-227.

[2]Except when the det. state is represented by *aleph*.

[3]Although inalienable possession is usually expressed by the construction with proleptic suffix, there are several exceptions.

[4]See also §§4k, n.24, 16a, n.1.

[5]See §25c.

[6]See §25b.

[7]See §§16a, n.1, 25c.

[8]See §25c.

[9]Cf. the marginal gloss in Targum Neophyti: באפי בעלה.

[10]מלווה is an error for מלוי. Cf. Targum Neophyti מלוי דבני דלבן.

## B. Marking of the Direct Object

[1]The marking of the direct object by /yat/, /lV-/, and Ø is known elsewhere in Aramaic. Cf. Lund's discussion of the interpolated material in Targum Neophyti in "Descriptive Syntax," pp. 76-78. Lund shows that /lV-/ is restricted to marking human beings, angels, and God. This is true in the Cairo Genizah fragments with one exception in which /lV-/ marks an animal: דְּמָחֵי לְסוּסְיָה Z Gn 49:17; "who strikes the horse" (§§8i, 12k). Cf. Targum Neophyti דנכת לסוסיא (MT הַנֹּשֵׁךְ עִקְּבֵי־סוּס).

[2]See §38. According to Klein, the *kaph* of ישויך is a scribal error in anticipation of the *kaph* of יתך (*Genizah Manuscripts*, II, p. 56).

[3]See §§16b, 38a, 130e, 155c.

[4]Díez Macho's reading דערביתֹהֹ E Gn 43:9, "who vouches for him" is not borne out by an examination of the manuscript, which reveals דיערב יתה; nor is Kahle's וגנבית דעתי E Gn 31:27, "and you stole my mind" (read וגנב ית דעתי, haplography for וגנבת ית דעתי; cf. Targum Neophyti וגנבת ית דעתי [margin]). In אורחיה־דְעָלְמָה כָּד־אָרְעִית לִדְבוּרָה C Gn 35:9, "when the way of the world happened to Deborah," the scribe may have conflated the Perf. 3 f.s. ארעת לדבורה and ית דבורה or may have conflated the Perf. 3 m.s. ארע לדבורה and ארע ית דבורה (cf. the Fragment Targum [MS V] ארעית לדבורה, and Targum Neophyti ארעת לדבורא).

[5]See Dalman, *Grammatik*, p. 360; Kutscher, "Aramaic Letters," p. 132, n.62b; Nöldeke, *Mandäische Grammatik*, p. 390, n.2.

[6]See Schulthess, *Grammatik*, p. 78.

[7]See n.5 above.

[8]See Klein, *Genizah Manuscripts*, II, p. 22.

•163    A. VOCALIC PHONEMES AND THEIR GRAPHIC REPRESENTATION

|  | /a/ | /e/ | /i/ | /o/ | /u/ | /ə/, /ʔ/ |
|---|---|---|---|---|---|---|
| **Palestinian Vowel Signs** MS A |  |  |  |  |  |  |
| MS E |  |  |  |  |  |  |
| MS H |  |  |  |  |  |  |
| **Tiberian Vowel Signs** MS A |  |  |  |  |  |  |
| MS B |  |  |  |  |  |  |
| MS C |  |  |  |  |  |  |
| MS D |  |  |  |  |  |  |
| MS E |  |  |  |  |  |  |
| MS F |  |  |  |  |  |  |
| MS H |  |  |  |  |  |  |
| MS ʒ |  |  |  |  |  |  |
| MS Y |  |  |  |  |  |  |
| MS Z |  |  |  |  |  |  |
| MS AA |  |  |  |  |  |  |
| MS HH |  |  |  |  |  |  |

¹with non-gutturals and gutturals.

256

§164   B. PRONOUNS

*Independent Personal Pronouns*

| | |
|---|---|
| 1 s. | /'əna/ |
| 2 m.s. | /'att/ |
| 2 f.s. | /'att?/ |
| 3 m.s. | /hu/ |
| 3 f.s. | /hi/ |
| 1 pl. | /'ənan/ |
| 2 m.pl. | /'atton/ |
| 2 f.pl. | /'atten?/ |
| 3 m.pl. | /'ennun?,hennun?/, /'ennon?,hennon?/ |
| 3 f.pl. | /'ennin?,hennin?/, /'ennen?,hennen?/ |

*Pronominal suffixes on Nouns*

| | *m.s., f.pl. nouns* | *m.pl., dual nouns* |
|---|---|---|
| 1 s. | /-i/ | /-ay/ (/-oy/) |
| 2 m.s. | /-ak/ | /-ek/ |
| 2 f.s. | /-ek/ | /*-ek/ |
| 3 m.s. | /-eh/(/-e/) | /-oy/ |
| 3 f.s. | /-ah/ | /-eh/ |
| 1 pl. | /-an/ | /-enan/ |
| 2 m.pl. | /-kon/ | /-ekon/ |
| 2 f.pl. | /*-ken/ | /*-eken/ |
| 3 m.pl. | /-hon/(/-on/) | /-ehon/ |
| 3 f.pl. | /-hen/ | /-ehen/ |

( ) contain infrequent forms

## §165. C. STRONG VERB

| | *G* | *D* | *C* | *Gt* | *Dt* | *Ct* |
|---|---|---|---|---|---|---|
| **Perf.** | | | | | | |
| 3 m.s. | /qatal/ | /qattel/ | /ʾaqtel/ | /ʾetqetel/ | /ʾetqattal/ | /ʾettaqtal/ |
| 3 f.s. | /qatlat/ | /qattəlat/ | /ʾaqtəlat/ | /ʾetqatlat/ | /ʾetqattəlat?/ | /ʾettaqtəlat?/ |
| 2 m.s. | /qatalt/ | /qattelt/ | /ʾaqtelt/ | /ʾetqatalt/ | /ʾetqattalt/ | /ʾettaqtalt/ |
| 2 f.s. | /*qətalt/ | /*qattelt/ | /*ʾaqtelt/ | /*ʾetqatalt/ | /*ʾetqattalt/ | /*ʾettaqtalt/ |
| 1 s. | /qatlet/ | /qattelet/ | /ʾaqtəlet/ | /ʾetqatlet/ | /ʾetqattəlet/ | /ʾettaqtəlet/ |
| 3 m.pl. | /qatalu/ | /qattelu/ | /ʾaqtelu?/ | /ʾetqatelu?/ | /ʾetqattalu/ | /ʾettaqtalu/ |
| 3 f.pl. | /qatlen?/ | /qattəlen/ | /*ʾaqtəlen?/ | /*ʾetqatlen?/ | /*ʾetqattəlen?/ | /*ʾettaqtəlen?/ |
| 2 m.pl. | /qətalton/ | /qattelton?/ | /*ʾaqtelton/ | /*ʾetqatelton/ | /*ʾetqattalton/ | /*ʾettaqtalton/ |
| 2 f.pl. | /qətalten?/ | /*qattelten/ | /*ʾaqtelten/ | /*ʾetqatelten/ | /*ʾetqattalten/ | /*ʾettaqtalten/ |
| 1 pl. | /qətalnan/ | /*qattelnan/ | /*ʾaqtelnan/ | /*ʾetqatelnan/ | /*ʾetqattalnan/ | /*ʾettaqtalnan/ |
| **Imperf.** | | | | | | |
| 3 m.s. | /yeqtol/ | /yəqattel/ | /yaqtel/ | /yetqetel/ | /yetqattal/ | /yettaqtal/ |
| 3 f.s. | /*teqtol/ | /*təqattel/ | /*taqtel/ | /*tetqetel/ | /*tetqattal/ | /*tettaqtal/ |
| 2 m.s. | /teqtol/ | /təqattel/ | /taqtel?/ | /tetqetel/ | /tetqattal/ | /tettaqtal/ |
| 2 f.s. | /*teqtəlin/ | /*təqattəlin/ | /*taqtəlin/ | /*tetqatlin/ | /*tetqattəlin/ | /*tettaqtəlin/ |
| 1 s. | /ʾeqtol/ | /ʾəqattel/ | /ʾaqtel/ | /ʾetqetel/ | /ʾetqattal/ | /ʾettaqtal/ |
| 3 m.pl. | /yeqtəlun/ | /yəqattəlun/ | /*yaqtəlu/ | /yetqatlun/ | /yetqattəlun/ | /*yettaqtəlun/ |
| 3 f.pl. | /yeqtəlan/ | /yəqattəlan/ | /*yaqtəlan/ | /yetqatlan/ | /yetqattəlan/ | /*yettaqtəlan/ |
| 2 m.pl. | /teqtəlun/ | /təqattəlun/ | /*taqtelu/ | /tetqatlun/ | /*tetqattəlun/ | /*tettaqtəlun/ |
| 2 f.pl. | /*teqtəlan/ | /*təqattəlan/ | /*taqtəlan/ | /*tetqatlan/ | /*tetqattəlan/ | /*tettaqtəlan/ |
| 1 pl. | /neqtol/ | /nəqattel/ | /naqtel/ | /netqetel/ | /netqattal/ | /nettaqtal/ |
| **Imper.** | | | | | | |
| m.s. | /qətol/ | /qattel/ | /ʾaqtel/ | /ʾetqetel/ | /ʾetqattal/ | /ʾettaqtal/ |
| f.s. | /*qətoli/ | /*qatteli/ | /*ʾaqteli/ | /*ʾetqatli/ | /*ʾetqattali/ | /*ʾettaqtali/ |
| m.pl. | /qətolu/ | /qattelu/ | /*ʾaqtelu/ | /*ʾetqatelu/ | /ʾetqattalu/ | /ʾettaqtalu/ |
| f.pl. | /*qətlen?/ | /*qattəlen?/ | /*ʾaqtəlen?/ | /*ʾetqatlen?/ | /*ʾetqattəlen?/ | /*ʾettaqtəlen?/ |
| **Act. Ptc.** | | | | | | |
| m.s. | /qatel/ | /məqattel/ | /maqtel/ | /metqetel/ | /metqattal/ | /*mettaqtal/ |
| f.s. | /qatəla/ | /məqattəla/ | /*maqtəla/ | /*metqatla/ | /*metqattala/ | /*mettaqtəla/ |
| **Pss. Ptc.** | | | | | | |
| m.s. | /qətil/ | /məqattal/ | /maqtal/ | | | |
| f.s. | /qətila/ | /məqattəla/ | /maqtəla/ | | | |
| **Inf.** | /meqtol/ | /məqattala/ | /maqtala/ | /metqatala/ | /metqattala/ | /*mettaqtala/ |

/*/ unattested and reconstructed phonemic transcription
/?/ attested but either unpointed, only partially pointed, or the phonemic transcription is uncertain
/*?/ reconstructed and uncertain phonemic transcription

References are to paragraphs.

139e, 157g
Gn 21:4    47a, 47e
Gn 28:17    11j, 16f, 19b, 67a, 72a,
72d, 130c, 141g, 156v
Gn 28:18    75a, 119b, 158b
Gn 28:19    11r, 100b, 143t, 157g,
158b
Gn 28:20    68a, 69a, 85a, 138a,
151a
Gn 28:22    16c, 39a n.120, 47a, 49,
133b
Gn 29:1    67a, 68a, 104a, 138c
Gn 29:2    41h, 46a, 64b, 68c
Gn 29:3    67c, 130g, 143v
Gn 29:5    119c
Gn 29:6    148b
Gn 29:7    69a, 86a, 143x
Gn 29:8    19a, 67a, 68c, 156p,
156t
Gn 29:9    42c, 142n, 148b, 156u
Gn 29:10    9d, 42a, 59a, 67a,
130g, 143u, 156t, 157a
Gn 29:11    61a, 133a
Gn 29:12    60a, 143n
Gn 29:13    15h, 41g, 59b, 60a,
68a, 156y
Gn 29:14    67a
Gn 29:15    158a
Gn 29:17    4e, 67f, 68e, 96b, 118,
143k, 143q, 152b
Gn 29:18    31a n.3, 47a, 60b, 90b
Gn 29:19    143j, 156h
Gn 29:20    47a
Gn 29:21    130b, 139f
Gn 29:22    31a, 47a, 68a, 72a,
104g, 114b, 119b, 135a, 137r,
139d, 139f, 141m, 143k, 156e,
156h
Gn 29:23    60b, 67a, 158b
Gn 29:24    59c
Gn 29:25    156c, 158b, 158d
Gn 29:26    64b, 72a, 90b, 158e
Gn 29:27    41a-b, 47a, 47g, 104m
Gn 29:28    47g

Gn 29:29    59c
Gn 29:30    156h
Gn 29:31    72b, 161d
Gn 29:32    67a, 132a, 143h
Gn 29:33    35a, 41a, 151c
Gn 29:34    47a, 139d
Gn 29:35    16c, 124b, 132b, 139i,
149a, 155c, 158e
Gn 30:1    59b,139g
Gn 30:2    15i, 19a, 34, 37b, 69a,
74a, 75a, 124b, 148b, 156p, 156x,
157c
Gn 30:3    9d, 12g, 59c, 124b, 124b
n.17, 139b, 156p
Gn 30:4    70b, 156o
Gn 30:5    60a
Gn 30:6    61a, 81a, 141i, 158e
Gn 30:7    48a, 59c
Gn 30:8    9d, 59b, 72d, 134a, 143n
Gn 30:9    139d
Gn 30:10    18g, 60a
Gn 30:11    8f, 12g, 64a, 148b
Gn 30:12    48a, 60a
Gn 30:13    11r, 60b, 67f, 119a,
132g
Gn 30:14    37b, 67d, 68b, 80a,
107, 139f, 148b
Gn 30:15    37b, 90a, 96a, 143k,
156u, 157g
Gn 30:16    67a, 107, 110d, 119c,
130c, 137h, 138a, 156b, 156y,
158b-c
Gn 30:17    15i, 60a
Gn 30:18    157b
Gn 30:19    26, 48a, 60a
Gn 30:20    41e, 47a, 47e, 86a,
131j, 139b, 158b
Gn 30:21    16a, 31b, 54b, 60a-b,
70b, 158b
Gn 30:22    72d
Gn 30:23    15i, 68a n.107, 68a
Gn 30:25    42a, 67a
Gn 30:26    31b, 60a, 110f, 138i
Gn 30:27    55f, 114a

Gn 38:19   8e, 31c, 37b, 37e, 83a,
85a, 114b, 131r, 138h, 141m, 156t
Gn 38:20   8b, 8e, 9d, 9i, 16d, 18d,
19a, 19f, 37d, 55e n.13, 59a, 67h,
70b, 77a, 113a, 119e, 133g, 137l
Gn 38:21   8e, 8e n.17, 53a, 64a,
69a, 88b, 95b, 139g, 140d, 158c-d
Gn 38:22   8e, 88b, 133a, 138h
Gn 38:23   9d, 16c, 67h, 119e,
133g, 137i, 142g, 142g n.210,
151a, 155c, 156n
Gn 38:24   114a, 137t, 139u, 143n
Gn 38:25   8i, 9d, 11s, 11v, 12f-g,
12i, 12k, 16b, 16e, 18a, 25a, 33f,
34a, 37d-e, 40a, 41e, 41h, 41m,
42h, 42l, 47a, 47e-f, 55b, 61b,
63a, 67a, 67f, 69a, 70a-b, 72d,
73b, 95a, 96a, 116, 118, 121,
130b, 131i, 131r, 131v-w, 133a,
137a, 137h, 137j-k, 138d, 139c
n.177, 139g, 139v, 141bb, 143h,
143j, 153, 156x, 157d, 157g, 158b
Gn 38:26   3h, 6b, 9f, 12a, 12h,
12k, 15i, 18c, 18e n.38, 32a, 33f-
g, 41a, 46a, 47a, 47f, 59a, 60a,
62a, 63a, 67f, 68a, 70a, 81a, 83a,
88a, 95e, 99a, 104k, 119b, 124b,
124k n.37, 131e, 131s, 132a, 132c,
137h, 138h, 138k, 139e, 139g,
139n, 141d, 141m, 141bb, 141ff,
156w, 157a-b, 158e, 160
Gn 38:27   19g, 37d, 55a, 74a,
138j
Gn 38:28   17f, 41b, 48a, 59a, 64b,
75a, 115b, 139j
Gn 38:29   162b
Gn 38:30   158b, 162b
Gn 39:1   4j, 15b, 64a, 96a, 113a,
116, 137f, 137r, 137z, 158c
Gn 39:2   67a, 113a
Gn 39:4   4j, 16b, 116, 143n, 156e
Gn 39:5   16b, 113a, 116, 162b
Gn 39:6   9c, 42f, 46a, 68e, 129a,
138k, 156g, 157g

Gn 39:7   41d, 117, 132c, 156g
Gn 39:8   6b, 12g, 20b, 28, 46a
Gn 39:9   13a, 19a, 19h, 25b, 34,
46a, 64b, 67f, 70b, 124b, 124b
n.17, 141hh, 157b, 157g, 158d
Gn 39:10   41d, 142p, 156u, 157c,
158b
Gn 40:5   86a
Gn 40:6   156o
Gn 40:7   31b, 67a, 96a, 140d,
158d
Gn 40:8   38a n.116, 42f, 119e,
143p
Gn 40:9   67a, 68a, 89
Gn 40:10   37d, 47f, 65a, 67a, 103,
131m
Gn 40:11   74, 151e
Gn 40:12   8f, 12a, 42g, 47f, 61a,
68a, 69a, 77a, 89, 103, 116, 119e,
119e n.449, 129g, 130f, 130i,
151i, 156s
Gn 40:13   8d, 12g, 35b, 61a, 68c,
129a, 130e, 143w, 151c
Gn 40:14   86a, 139a
Gn 40:15   16c, 46a, 67a, 113a,
134a
Gn 40:16   65b, 68c, 77g, 156o,
158a
Gn 40:17   68c, 81a, 99c, 118
Gn 40:18   8f, 47f, 68a, 77f, 129g,
130f
Gn 41:6   152b, 156g
Gn 41:7   8f, 47g, 68a, 94b, 94b
n.283, 96b, 131r, 141dd
Gn 41:8   19c, 68a, 96a, 135a
Gn 41:9   37d
Gn 41:10   104h, 116, 118
Gn 41:11   68a, 102, 119e
Gn 41:19   9d, 12g, 15i, 37d, 67a,
68a, 77f, 113a, 116, 143n, 151e,
156h
Gn 41:13   9c, 72a
Gn 41:15   8d, 131h
Gn 41:16   8d, 13b, 79a, 156f

Ex 6:4    139t
Ex 6:5    10d, 32b, 83b
Ex 6:6    18l, 26, 39a, 55e, 62a, 64a, 68a, 80a, 110f, 124c, 131s, 137o
Ex 6:7    11r, 33c, 60a, 89, 96a, 113a, 130f, 131v, 133b, 138m, 139e
Ex 6:8    9d, 11n, 33c, 37b, 59a, 114b, 131r, 142r
Ex 6:9    11m, 24, 63a, 65b, 77f, 110f, 114b
Ex 7:10    68e, 110f
Ex 7:11    16c, 37d, 70a, 95a, 113a, 158e
Ex 7:12    9f, 11d, 68e, 69a, 131r, 132a
Ex 7:14    8b
Ex 7:16    12f, 12h-i, 80a, 104a, 131r-s, 138i
Ex 7:17    11k, 13b, 72a, 134b
Ex 7:18    4h, 11l, 53a, 63a, 130b, 130f, 143m, 143v
Ex 7:19    8e, 8i, 9g, 11d, 11t, 12h, 26, 37b, 37d, 59a, 61a, 67a, 69a, 72a, 77d, 104g, 138b, 151a, 156s
Ex 7:20    72a
Ex 7:21    10b, 26, 55b, 59a, 61a, 63a, 130b, 139d, 141m
Ex 7:22    9d, 37b, 65a, 70a, 95a, 158e
Ex 9:21    16b, 16e, 83a, 117, 158c
Ex 9:22    5e n.6, 37b, 72a, 133c
Ex 9:23    61a, 72a, 133g, 139c, 152a n.281, 161b
Ex 9:24    8e, 151a, 156m
Ex 9:25    10d, 12k, 16e, 68a, 110c, 130f
Ex 9:26    60a
Ex 9:27    95a, 95c, 143h
Ex 9:28    4j, 25a, 96c, 143p, 158a
Ex 9:29    4h, 11t, 37d, 61a, 131s, 134b, 137m, 139b, 157c
Ex 9:30    12g-h, 37b, 80a

Ex 9:31    82b, 96b, 99a, 103, 143h
Ex 9:32    29e, 68b, 96a, 115b, 151a
Ex 9:33    3k, 12f, 67i, 69a, 131a, 134e, 137f
Ex 12:1    4e, 5e n.5, 8e, 12g, 67a, 156o
Ex 12:2    8e, 9e n.44, 12f, 15i, 16c, 19a, 41e, 48a, 59b, 67a, 68c, 110e, 143aa, 155c
Ex 12:3    4e, 8d, 12f-g, 33b, 46a n.220, 47a, 77c, 118, 137i, 142m, 156o, 156aa
Ex 12:4    19j, 30, 58, 90a, 104j, 118, 138m, 143aa, 143cc
Ex 12:5    30, 67h, 70a
Ex 12:6    47i, 137i, 156e
Ex 12:7    47d, 76a, 119a
Ex 12:8    63a, 73a, 102, 119b, 155a-b
Ex 12:9    81a, 130g, 155b, 156i
Ex 12:10    75a, 139n, 140i
Ex 12:11    59a, 67a, 69a, 70a, 75a, 114b, 158b
Ex 12:12    62a, 102, 114a, 143f
Ex 12:13    34, 110b, 132g, 142r
Ex 12:14    110f, 158b
Ex 12:15    83a, 138i
Ex 12:16    4e, 15i, 25a, 138r
Ex 12:17    15b n.1, 55f, 67f, 96a
Ex 12:18    68a, 156e, 158b
Ex 12:19    12k, 83a, 96a n.292, 138h
Ex 12:20    83a
Ex 12:21    8e, 55f, 55f n.14, 61a, 67c, 70a, 115b, 137b
Ex 12:22    104c, 119a-b, 156r
Ex 12:23    67a, 110h, 142i, 143i
Ex 12:25    142e
Ex 12:27    123e n.8, 142q, 149a
Ex 12:28    138h
Ex 12:29    20c, 49, 76a, 114b, 118, 129g, 139b, 139i, 158b
Ex 12:30    76a, 156i

Nu 19:19    48a

Nu 19:20    9i, 41h, 82a, 126i, 140h

Nu 19:22    140k, 140o

Nu 20:3    9d, 15g, 59a, 110b, 123d, 141m, 141gg, 160

Nu 20:4    11t, 34, 83a, 155a

Nu 20:5    8b, 11t, 16c, 19h, 67a, 68d, 72a, 119b, 119b n.440, 142q, 142t, 157g

Nu 20:6    67a, 82a, 143z, 156x

Nu 20:8    15i, 61a, 77d, 83a, 137s, 143v, 156x

Nu 20:9    69a

Nu 20:10    25a, 77d, 110h, 137s, 138d, 138d n.163, 138p

Nu 20:11    15i, 50, 77d, 83a

Nu 20:12    130i, 157b

Nu 28:16    18a, 47i, 48b, 70a, 77c

Nu 28:17    19j, 28, 47a, 47i, 64a

Nu 28:18    20a, 25a

Nu 28:20    47a, 47c, 49, 73a

Nu 28:21    16c, 47c, 47g, 49, 68a, 92

Nu 28:23    41a, 41g, 72d, 119a, 156q

Nu 28:24    16c, 47g, 119a, 156q, 158b

Nu 28:26    8e, 9d, 11r, 12i, 18l, 24, 61a, 64a, 67d, 72a, 72a n.171, 83b, 84b, 100a, 110f, 118, 119a, 119h, 138r, 156x

Nu 28:27    8e, 11d, 13b, 15c, 19h, 24, 47a, 47g, 55a, 55f, 59b, 67b, 67d, 72d, 73a, 77d, 92

Nu 28:28    11s, 19b, 37b, 47a, 47c, 49, 67d, 73a, 119a, 119e, 141q

Nu 28:29    9d, 9e n.44, 12h-i, 13b, 16c, 47a, 47c, 47g, 49, 53a, 68a, 104k, 110e, 119e, 151a, 156x

Dt 5:19    9d, 9g, 13b, 15c, 15f, 41c, 47d, 61a, 63a, 79a, 82a, 82c, 99a, 103, 119a, 142k, 156u

Dt 5:20    6b, 9d, 11t, 15f, 19g, 33f, 61a, 63a, 68a, 68c, 78a, 96a, 99a,

131h, 131r, 131x

Dt 5:21    9d, 9g, 11d, 11t, 12h, 69a, 80a, 82a, 119a, 131r, 138h, 142l, 143h, 151d

Dt 5:22    29a, 131g, 141p, 158b, 158d

Dt 5:23    11d, 43a, 43c, 53a, 66b, 141gg, 156m, 157b

Dt 5:24    6b, 9j, 39a n.120, 42f, 46a, 131d, 131f, 131s-t, 142l

Dt 5:25    9d, 9f-h, 12g-i, 24, 37d, 61a, 64a, 65b, 131b, 142k, 142p, 156u, 156x, 161b

Dt 5:26    6b, 12i, 43a, 60a, 65a, 67d, 119a, 131g, 137i, 139a, 157c, 160

Dt 26:2    138i, 143y, 151i

Dt 26:3    129b

Dt 26:8    83b

Dt 26:9    72a, 77f

Dt 26:10    76b, 148b, 149a

Dt 26:11    16c, 61b

Dt 26:12    48a

Dt 26:13    47a, 77a, 138h

Dt 26:15    59a, 64a, 67a, 68a, 69a, 72a, 77f, 141s, 141aa

Dt 26:16    41g n.150, 62a, 65a, 82c

Dt 26:17    11r, 11t, 15i, 62a, 69a, 89, 132g

Dt 26:18    9h, 11r, 33c, 41c, 42a, 53a, 66b, 96a, 119a-b, 133a, 137l, 151a, 156j, 156o, 157e

Dt 26:19    16b, 30, 33a, 38a, 42a, 61a, 66b, 96b, 99c, 106b, 126b, 130e, 137o, 143h, 151e, 155c, 162c

Dt 27:1    5b n.2, 8f, 9h, 11g, 53a, 96a, 119a, 137j

Dt 27:2    8d, 12k, 19h, 55e, 62a, 64b, 141t

Dt 27:3    12h, 41c, 59a, 67a, 68a, 68e, 77f, 131x, 149c, 156s, 157c

Dt 27:4    39a, 41g n.150, 62a, 63a n.59, 141n, 141z

# Index of Words

This index contains words found in the Cairo Genizah fragments and cited in this grammar. References are to paragraphs. Verbs are listed alphabetically by root; verbs III-w/y/' are listed as III-y. Nouns, including verbal nouns, are listed alphabetically in the absolute state according to *scripta defective* (with the exception of some loanwords), followed by attested examples of *scripta plene*. Final *a* is represented by *he*. Parentheses contain noteworthy forms or etymologies. Only selected occurrences of the frequently attested particles ו, ל ב, ד/די, are cited.

א interrogative particle: 25b; see also ה

אב (איבה) "father": 8d-e, 12g, 15f, 16g, 18c, 25b, 37b, 42c, 43c, 46a, 47f, 55c, 59a, 59a n.36, 129c, 161d

אבל *Dt* "mourn": 138f, 138u

אבל "mourning": 68a

אבן "stone": 12c, 12g, 41g n.150, 55b, 67a, 156bb, 162a

אבק "dust": 72a

אבר/איבר "lead": 16h, 18h n.47, 79a

אגר *G* "hire": 138a

אגר "wage": 12b, 28, 33f n.7, 67a, 126c

אדומי/אדמי "Edomite": 113a

אדם (דם) "blood": 4k, 8e, 19a, 26, 59a, 124j

אדן "ear": 69a

אדני "Lord": 2e, 25b, 37b, 161b, 162b

אדרע "arm": 26, 80a

אהרן/אהרון "Aaron": 5e n.5, 12g, 16i, 131i

או "or": 11j, 156bb, 157g

אויר "air": 116

אומן "ploughed furrow": 116

אוף (אף, אף על גב) "also": 19h, 42g, 42k, 157d, 157g

אוצר "treasure, treasury": 103

אוריה "law, teaching": 41d, 149c

אזוב "hyssop": 119b

אזל *G* "go": 8j, 16d, 36, 138c, 138h-l, 157a

אח "brother": 3i, 6b, 15f, 15i, 16e, 16g, 25b, 37d n.58, 45b, 59a, 162f

אחד *G* "grasp": 138h

אחה "sister": 59b

אחסנה "inheritance": 13b, 16a, 133f; see also חסן

אחר/אחרי "last": 11f, 11f n.86, 113b

אחרן/אוחרן "another, other": 8e n.19, 11f, 12i, 13c, 46a, 54c, 110f

איבר "lead": see אבר/איבר

איד "hand"; see יד

איזה "that, which": 42j, 43c; cf. הידה "which?"

איך "how?": 124b, 158d; cf. היך "like, as"

אילן "tree": 19d, 110c, 119h

אימה "fear": 67g

אימם "daytime": 35a, 112, 158b

איקר "honor"; see יקר

אית "there is": 4h, 29b, 29b n.159, 41b, 42c, 46a, 158d, 158d n.36, 159

אכל G "eat": 9g, 16d, 35a, 124b, 129a, 138a, 138h-i, 138k-l, 155a; C "feed": 138e, 138s; Gt "be eaten": 12c, 42a, 138u

אבלסין/אובלסין "multitude, crowd, people": 116

אל "to" (Heb.): 156aa

אלאל "but, rather": 157g

אלה "God": 12h, 33i, 37b, 53a, 80a, 161a

אלה/אילה "if not": 157d, 157g

אלה־הן/אלאהן/אילהן/אלא הן "but, rather": 157g

אלולי "if not": 42k, 157d

אלין/אליין "these": 34a, 41a-b, 41g; see also האלין/האליין

אלע (עלע >) "rib": 12g, 20a, 47b, 68a

אלף G "learn": 138d, 138i; D "teach": 9h, 25a, 138d, 138n, 138p; see also מלפן

אלפן/אולפן "teaching": 110f

אלף "thousand": 47m, 67a

אם "if"; see אן

אם "mother": 9d, 65a, 129c

אמה "cubit": 47j, 64b

אמהא "handmaiden": 8i, 12b, 59c

אמה "people"; see עם

אמה/אומה "nation": 11d, 43c, 53a, 66b

אמן see הימן

אמצע "middle": 26, 156a

אמר G "say": 2e, 11t, 12f-h, 16d, 25a, 25a n.131, 33f, 34d n.31, 35b, 42f-g, 138b, 138d, 138h-i, 138k-l, 155c, 156o, 156aa; Gt "be said": 138f, 138t; see also מאמר

אמר/אימר "lamb": 16c, 47c-d, 47g, 92

אין/ין (אם) "if": 5g, 9k, 16d, 19e, 41a n.144, 124b, 157d

אנה "I": 5b n.2, 8f, 12g, 16a, 34, 34a, 34d, 35a n.35, 42i, 43c, 124b, 131i, 157a

אנהרו "shining": 137a; see also נהר "shine"

אנן (הנן) "they" (m.): 3j, 9d, 29b, 34, 34a, 41b, 124b

אנין/אינין (הינין) "they" (f.): 34, 34a

אנינקי "distress": 42h, 42h n.184, 116

אנן "we": 29d, 34, 34d, 34g

אנפו (אנפי) "waving": 147b; see also נוף

אנש "man": 8d, 12h, 12h n.147, 33f-g, 46a, 81a

אנתה "woman"; see אתה/איתה

אסו "healing": 11n, 16f, 114a, 118; see also אסי

אסטלי/אוסטלי "garment, robe": 9c, 9c n.38, 11e, 12c, 26, 116

אסי G "heal": 154a; D "heal": 154a; see also אסו

אסנת "Asenath": 162e

אסר G "tie up": 138a, 138k; see also מיסר

אף see אוף

אף (אנף >) "nose, face": 15e, 19a, 37d, 43c, 67a, 124c, 143dd n.245, 161d

אפי G "bake": 148a; Gt "be baked": 124l, 148a, 155c

אפי "before, in the presence of" (על אפי, באפי, לאפי, מן אפי, לקבל אפי): 42c, 156b, 158c

אפיטרופוס "guardian, manager": 4j, 116

אפסד "loss": 4k, 12c, 12m, 26 n.137

אפקו "bringing forth": 137x; see also נפק

אפרת "Ephrat": 16i

אפשר "possible": 26 n.137, 158a

אצבה "trough"; see אצחה

אצבע "finger": 26 n.137

אצחה (אצבה) "trough": 4e, 114a

ארבע "four" (f.): 16c, 26 n.137, 47a, 47i-j, 47l, 471 n.24

ארבעה "four" (m.): 47a, 47e, 47i, 48b

ארבעין "forty": 47k-l

ארגן/ארגון "purple": 118

ארום "because, when, that": 2e, 11m, 12g, 41b, 157a-b, 157f-g

ארע/אירע (בירתע) "festive meeting": 4e, 11r, 20a, 24, 25a, 138r; see also ארע

ארז "cedar": 67a

ארח/אורח "way": 11d, 53a, 69a, 71a, 162d n.4

אריה "lion": 67h

ארמי/ארמיי "Aramean": 56b, 113a

ארמלה "widow": 12c, 26 n.137, 53a

ארמלו "widowhood": 37b, 114b

ארנך "tax": 116

ארס D "betroth": 8f, 138d, 138q

ארע "land": 8b, 37b, 41d, 42b-c, 46a, 67a, 96a n.292, 131i, 161c-d

ארע (ערע) D "befall, meet, come upon": 20a, 138g, 138n-o; see also ארע

ארתך (רתך) "wagon": 26, 101

אשה "fire": 9d, 25c, 28, 30, 99a, 119c (אש), 124b, 161d

אשן "season, time": 86a

אשתה "six"; see שתה

את (אנת) "you" (m.s.): 19a, 34, 34e, 36, 43b

את (אנת) "you" (f.s.): 19a, 34, 34e, 157b

את "sign": 72c

את direct object marker (Heb.): 162e

אתה (אנתה) אתה/איתה "woman": 9d,

12c, 16d, 18a, 21b, 42h, 70b

אתן (אנתן) "you" (m.pl.): 19a, 34, 34e, 162e

אתן "furnace": 118

אתי G "come": 8f, 9d-e, 9e n.44, 12g, 12k, 124b, 124i, 124k n.37, 148b; C "bring": 3k, 4c, 12h, 12k, 15b, 15i, 124b, 148b, 157a; see also מתי

אתמל "yesterday": 8e, 26, 157e, 158b

אתן (אנתן) "you" (f.pl.): 19a, 34, 34e

אתן/איתן "she-ass": 18h, 95a

אתר "place": 12g, 72a

ב "in, by means of, with": 156c

באר/באיר "well": 42h, 68c, 119h

באש G "be bad, sick": 130b n.59, 140a, 140d, 140f; C "do evil": 140l-m; see also ביש/בייש, בישו ביש, ביש,

בגין "on account of, because": 12a, 42k, 156d, 157b, 158e

בגלל "in order to": 42k, 157c, 158d

בהילו "haste": 114b, 158b

בהל Gt (Dt?) "be agitated, be hurried": 19c, 134a, 134f

בהת G "be ashamed, embarrassed": 124b, 124k n.37, 131e, 131s

בהתה "shame": 18e, 67b

בוץ "byssus": 63a

בוצין "candle, lamp": 120

בזה/ביזה "booty": 18a, 65b

בזז G "plunder": 142e, 142g

בזיון "disgrace": 119e, 142g n.210

בזע D "rend, tear": 132h

בטלן "idleness": 18l, 19h, 110f

בטם "pistachio": 69a, 161a

בין (ביני, בית) "between, among": 156e, 158b

ביש "bad, evil" (m.): 83c

בישה "bad, evil" (f.): 32b, 42h, 83d, 124b

ביש/בייש "sick, ill": 12k, 140f

בישו "illness": 114b

בית C "spend the night": 141y

בית (בתי, בייתה) "house": 4k, 9c, 15b, 15h, 16a n.2, 46a, 46a n.220, 67f, 156c, 162b; בית מקדש "Temple": 119a; בתי מדרשייה "synagogues": 119a

בית "between, among": see בין

בכור "first born": 41b, 76a, 119g

בכור "first fruit": 11r, 11x, 100a

בכורו "birthright": 4h, 114b

בכי G "weep": 143k, 143m

בכי "weeping": 115a

בכיר "early, first ripening" (m.): 96a

בכירה "early, first ripening" (f.): 96b

בכרה/בוכרה "first, beginning": 4h, 76b, 76b n.193

בלוט "oak": 97

בלחוד "alone": 15i, 17e, 158e

בלע G "swallow": 131r

בן "son"; see בר

בני G "build": 143h; D "build": 143n; Gt "be built": 9d, 124b

בנימן "Benjamin": 162e

בנין "building": 9e n.43

בסים (בסם) "sweet, pleasant" (m.): 4f, 16e, 96a

בסימה "sweet, pleasant" (f.): 96b

בסר "flesh"; see בשר

בעו "request": 114a

בעי G "seek, request": 143h, 143k, 162e

בעיר (בער) "cattle": 4d, 9i, 10d n.70, 12c-d, 16e, 83a

בעל "husband, master": 67a, 161d; בעיל דבבה "enemy": 118

בער G "burn": 131h

בקעה "valley": 70b

בקר D "visit": 129d; D "clear (with fire)": 21b

בקרה/בקורה "herd of cattle": 84b

בר (ביר, בנין) "son, male": 4d, 8j, 9g, 11i, 12c, 12f, 15b, 15d, 15h, 16b, 18g, 31a, 33b, 37b, 47d, 47e-f, 47j, 54b, 60a, 119c (בן), 124b, 161a, 161c-d

בר מן (בר) "except for": 156f, 156f n.5

בר (בארא) "field": 16b, 64a, 158c

ברה (בנתא) "daughter, female": 16a, 18e, 18e n.38, 54b, 60b, 124j, 162e

ברד "hail": 72a

ברי G "create": 16a, 42a, 143h-i; Gt "be created"; 16e, 143z, 143cc

ברי "healthy" (f.): 8f, 54c, 54c n.5

בריה "creature": 83f

ברך D "bless": 9h, 129d, 132a-b, 132d-e, 151b, 155d, 162b-c; Dt "be blessed": 135a

ברך "knee": 68a

ברכה "blessing": 12f, 18a, 73b

ברם "but, rather": 157g

ברנש "someone": 46a

ברק "lightning": 72a

בשר Dt "be informed": 135a, 135e

בשר (בסר, ביסרה) "flesh": 4j, 16h, 18a, 33a, 37b, 37d, 46a, 47b, 73a

בשל G "ripen": 131m

בתולה "virgin": 11r, 11r n.99, 84b

בתר "after": 8e, 42k, 156g, 156p, 157a, 158b

גאי Gt/Dt? "be proud": 16c, 150, 155c

גב (גבי, על גבי, אף על גב "back, by": די): 42g, 42k, 156h, 156s, 157d

גב/גוב "pit": 8f, 11d-e, 11r, 66a

"remember, be reminded": 19c

דכר (דיכרה) "male": 8e, 9d, 18h, 47c-d, 53a n.1, 54a-c, 54e, 73a

דכן/דוכן "remembrance": 110f

דלווי see דלבי

דלבי (ודלווי) "plane-tree": 4e

דלמה "lest": 42k, 157d

דלקי "inflammation": 115b

דם "blood"; see אדם

דמו "likeness": 11n, 33c, 114a

דמי D "liken to": 129d Gt/Dt?), 143r

דמך G "sleep": 156n; see also מדמך

דן/דין "this" (m.): 6b, 12f, 41a-b, 41f, 41l, 158b, 158e, 158e n.42, 162b; see also דה, דן/הדין, הדה

דנה "already": 41i, 158b

דעת "knowledge, mind": 119b, 162d n.4

דקיק "thin" (m.): 54c, 96b

דקיקה "thin" (f.): 96b

דר "generation": 8e, 9i, 37d, 47m, 61a

דרג "step": 67a

דרגש "bed": 53a, 117

דרמסק "Damascus": 20b

דתי "vegetation": 68f

דתן/דותן "Dothan": 16i

ה interrogative particle: 25b (א), 43c, 158d-e, 160

הא interrogative particle: 124b, 158d, 158d n.36

הא "behold": 6b, 124b, 157g, 159

האלין/האליין "these": 9d, 15c, 34a, 41c, 41g; see also אלין/האליין

הבהב Q "roast": 130g

הבל "Abel": 162b

הדה "this" (f.): 41c, 41e, 41e n.146, 41f, 41l-m, 42h, 124b, 158b; see also דה, דן/דין, הדה

הדיה "sprinkling": 9i, 126i

הדן/הדין "this" (m.): 8d, 8j, 9h, 41c-e, 41e n.147, 48b, 124b, 124k n.37, 158b; see also הדן/הדין דה, דן/דין,

הדיר "adorned": 83a

הדס "myrtle": 101

הדר "glory": 18i, 72a

ההוא "that" (m.): 41h

ההיא "that" (f.): 41h

הוא "he": 6b, 34, 34a, 34f, 42h

הוד "glory": 119b

הודיה/הודייה "waving": 126i, 149a, 155c; see also ידי

הוי G "be": 3k, 4e, 8e, 8e nn.17-18, 9d, 9g, 9i, 11t, 12b, 12g-h, 12h n.148, 13b, 16a, 16c, 21c, 25c, 29e, 33f, 35a-b, 42, 42d, 42f, 42i, 42j, 42l, 122, 124b n.17, 124l, 128, 129a-129g, 131i, 151a-c, 155c, 161d, 162b

היא "she": 6b, 34, 34a, 34f, 42h, 124b

הידה "which?": 15b, 42, 43a, 43c; cf. אידה "that, which"

היך (הך) "like, as": 42a, 42k, 156j, 157e

הילן "which?": 15b, 43a, 43c

הימן Q "believe": 12c, 15h, 130i

הימנו "believing": 126i

הין "hin": 49, 119j

הינין see אנין/אינין

הכה "here": 158c

הל "further": 158b

הלא "because, for": 157b

הלך D "walk, go": 12f, 33d, 42b, 152a; Dt "walk about": 152a

המין "belt, girdle": 117

הן "where?": 158d, 158d n.38

הנן "they": see אנין

הנייה/הנייה "pleasure": 79d

הפך Gt/Dt? "turn into": 11k, 134b

ו "and, but": 4e (ב), 157g

וי/ואיי "woe": 15i, 160
ולד "child": 75a
זבד "gift": 86a
זבינו "purchasing": 11m, 114b
זבן G "buy": 131m; D "sell": 12a, 124i, 132b, 155c; Dt "be sold": 23, 135b
זבן "purchase": 83a, 83a n.240
זגן/זיגן "bell": 18f, 111a, 117
זהר G "be careful, keep": 129c, 131i; Dt "be careful": 19i, 23, 135c
זוג "wife": 116
זוד C "harm": 12c, 141z
זוז "zuz" (coin): 118
זון Gt/Ct "be fed": 141ee
זוע G "be shaken, moved": 16b; see also זעזע
זיו (זו) "luster": 16e, 37b, 118, 143dd n.245
זחור/זיחורי "crimson": 17f, 115b
זין "weapons, arms": 117
זיק "water skin, comet": 62a
זית "olive": 67f
זכו "merit": 55f, 114a
זכי G "be innocent": 4c
זכי/זכיי "innocent, righteous" (m.): 15i, 95c
זכיה/זכייה "innocent, righteous" (f.): 95e
זמן D/Pael? "prepare": 129c, 130c; Dt/Ithpaal? "have intercourse": 124b, 130c
זמן "time": 18a, 41e, 41e n.146, 41l-m, 42k, 47d-e, 50, 53a, 118, 124b, 157a, 158b
זנו "prostitution": 114a
זני D "whore": 143n
זעזע Qt "be shaken, moved": 16b, 130h; see also זוע
זעיר "small" (m.): 90a
זעירה "small" (f.): 90b
זעירו "smallness": 114b

זקף G "raise": 131i, 131r
זקק G "be obligated": 155b
זרע "seed": 67a
זרעי "family": 12l, 53a, 55f, 55f n.14, 115b
חבש "imprisonment": 86a
חביב "beloved": 96a
חבר "friend": 8b, 9c, 45a-b, 77a, 156bb
חברי "wound": 10r, 115b
חג "feast": 64a
חגג G "celebrate, feast": 142e
חד "one" (m.): 12f, 47a-b, 47i-j, 49, 52f, 72a, 158d, 158d n.39; see also חתה, כחדה, לחדה, להוד/לחוד, בלחוד.
חדה "one" (f.): 47a-b
חדו (וחדוה) "joy": 70c
חדי G "rejoice": 143i
חדת "new": 72a
חדתה "the one"; see חתה
חוב G "be guilty": 141k; Dt "be guilty": 124b, 124j, 141hh
חוב "guilt, sin": 29b, 37d, 67d
חובה "guilt, sin": 37b, 67e
חוי D "tell": 16e, 151d, 155c
חוי "serpent": 9d, 68e
חוס G "have pity": 141i
חור D "clean": 141a, 141e-g
חור/חוור "white": 17c n.2, 99b
חור "Hur": 131i
חזו (וחזוה) "vision, appearance": 25b, 68e, 110e n.355
חזן "vision": 110e, 110 n.355
חזור "around": 158c
חזר G "return": 8c, 33f, 131a, 131f, 131h, 131r; D "return, bring back": 132f
חטאת "sin offering": 119a
חטה (וחנט) "wheat": 68b
חטר/חוטר (וחוטרה) "staff": 11d-e, 13a, 31a, 34a, 37b, 69a, 71a
חטי G "sin": 143h

ירך "thigh": 77a

ירקן "mildew": 110a

ירת G "inherit": 139b, 139e, 139g, 139i; see also ירותו

ישראל "Israel": 3j, 33d, 46a, 129g, 155d n.309, 156aa, 161c

ישיר "honest": 96a

ישירו (ישרו) "honesty": 11k, 114b

ית direct object marker: 4k, 8e, 9c, 11i, 12k, 32a, 35a, 38a, 39a, 39a n.120, 41b, 45a-b, 124c, 124i-j, 126g, 129c, 131i, 156bb, 162b-c, 162f

יתב G "sit, dwell": 9f, 33d, 129g, 139b, 139d, 139g-i, 156n; Ct "sojourn": 139t, 139v

יתיר "in addition": 96a, 158a; see also מותרה

יתם "orphan": 77a

כ "like, as, according to": 12f, 19j, 42k, 47m, 156l, 156q, 156x, 157c, 158b, 158e

כבש D "conquer": 9f, 132c

כד/כדי "when": 42l, 157a, 162d n.4

כדן "now": 29a, 124i, 158b

כהי G "grow dim": 143h

כהן "priest": 88a, 129b

כהנה/כהונה "priesthood": 119a

כויה/כווייה "burn": 11e, 82e

כול C "measure": 141bb; Gt/Ct "be measured": 141ff; see also מכלה

כון D "direct": 141a, 141e, 141g; Dt "intend": 141a, 141h

כופפי "spelt": 115b

כורסי "chair": 20c, 118

כות "like, according to": 43c, 156m

כחדה "together": 158a

כין/כוון "as soon as, when": 42a, 42g, 42k, 157a

כיף "stone": 77d

כל/כול "all, every, any": 11d, 11f, 19a, 20b, 42e-f, 46a, 46a n.220, 66a, 129c, 131i, 156aa, 158b

כלה "bride, daughter-in-law": 8e, 18e n.38, 53a, 64b, 162b

כליד "goblet": 116

כמה "how many": 12f n.129, 43b, 158d, 158d n.39

כן "thus, so": 158b, 158e

כנשה/כנישה "assembly": 3j, 53a, 77c, 156o, 156aa; see also מכנש כנש,

כנען "Canaan": 8c n.16, 8j, 33j, 42b, 161c

כנעני "Canaanite": 113a

כנף "wing": 72a

כנר/כינר "harp": 99a

כנש D "gather": 142l; Gt "be gathered": 9d, 12f, 42g, 134a, 134c-d, 157a; see also מכנש כנשה/כנישה,

כס "cup": 8d, 61a

כסי D "cover": 143o; Dt "be covered": 8i, 8i n.29, 11t, 143dd

כסף "silver": 12m, 37b, 67a, 71a

כען "now": 29a, 124b, 158b

כעס C "anger": 133e

כף "palm": 64a

כפור/כיפור "atonement": 119a

כפן (כיפנה) "famine": 18c, 47g, 53a, 67a

כרך "city": 37d n.58, 72a

כרם "vineyard": 67a, 156e

כרע "leg": 81a

כתב G "write": 131s

כתב "writing": 80a

כתבה/כתובה "marriage contract": 119a

כתן/כיתן "flax": 99a

כתנה/כותנה/כתונה "shirt": 3i, 119b

כתף "shoulder": 77a

ל "to, for, by": 156n

לא "no": 42k, 43c, 124b, 124j, 129f, 157a, 157c-e, 158e, 162b

לב/ליב (לבביכן) "heart": 9d, 37b, 65a

לבן "Laban": 161d, 162f

לבש G "wear": 131r

לבת "to, towards"; see לות/לוח

לבש "cloth": 111, 85a

לגין/ליגין "legion": 116

להב "flame": 13b

לובדק "Libyan ass": 116

להד/לחד (להות) "only, also": 17e, 19j, 41b, 41f, 124b, 158e

לח "almond": 4f, 63a, 161a

לוח (לווחי/ליוחי) "tablet": 15f, 47d, 63a

לוט G "curse": 82c, 141q, 151b

לוי/לוח "if only": 15i, 160

לוי/ליח "Levite": 16c

לולב "palm branch": 119a

לות/לוח (לבת) "to, towards": 4e, 8e, 25b, 37b, 43c, 124b, 156o-p

לחד "only, also": see להוד, בלחוד

לחד (לחה) לחדה/חדה "very": 4f, 8d, 158a

לחש "reddish? blackish?": 78a

לחם "bread": 9h, 67a

לטום "ladanum": 11s, 120

לילי (ליילה) "night": 25b, 41h, 49, 55f, 102, 119c, 158b

ליש "dough": 15b n.1, 67f

לית "there is not": 25b, 38a n.116, 42f, 42i, 43c, 46a, 124i, 158d, 159

למה "why": 43b, 158d

למפד "torch"; see לפד

לעי (לאי) G "labor": 17h

לעו (לאו) "labor": 17h, 114a

לעל/לעיל "above": 158c

לפד (למפד) "torch": 30

לקט D "collect": 132c

לקט "gleaning": 82a

לקי G "be smitten": 143h

לקיש "late, late born": 96a

לרע (לארע) "below": 25a, 158c

לשן "language, tongue": 9d, 47b, 99a, 119h

מאה "hundred": 47l, 47l n.24, 47m, 48b, 52g, 55f, 60b

מאכל "eating": 138m; see also אכל

מאמר (מימר, ממר) "Memra, Word": 3j, 9h, 25b, 37b, 41b, 129g, 138m, 151b, 161b, 162b; see also אמר

מאן (מן) "vessel": 104c

מבל "flood": 11r, 119j, 161a

מבע "spring": 11r, 104g

מגזה "ford": 104k

מגזר "circumcising": 13b, 131x; see also גזר

מגיר "neighbor": 104j

מגן "freely": 158a

מדבח "altar": 104a

מדבר "desert": 12f, 104a

מדור "dwelling": 104j, 119d

מדין "why?": 16b n.5

מדינה "city": 104k

מדיני "Midianite": 113a

מדמך "bed, couch": 104a; see also דמך

מדנח "east": 104a

מדע "knowing": 139i; see also ידע

מדרש "study"; see בתי מדרש

מה "what": 8f, 8f n.22 34a, 38a n.116, 41a, n.142, 42, 42a, 42f, 42i, 43a, 43a n.200, 43b, 46a, 46a n.220, 124i, 157d-e, 158d

מהלך "walk": 104a

מואבי/מואביי "Moabite": 113a

מול "blemish"; see מום

מום (מול) "blemish": 30, 63a, 63a n.60

מועד "appointed time": 104e

מות G "die": 10b, 11l-m, 31c, 35a n.35, 123d, 141i, 141m-n, 141p, 141r, 155a, 157f

מותן "plague": 15g, 110b

מותרה "remainder": 104f; see also יתיר

מזוג "steward": 89

מזוזי "doorpost": 47d, 119a

מזון "food": 11h, 104j, 119d; see also זן

מזל "star position, luck": 118

מחלה "dance": 119d

מחי G "strike": 8i, 8i n.30 (D?), 9i, 16c, 143i, 155c, 156bb (D?), 162b n.1 (D?)

מחם/מיחם "heat": 142j

מחר "tomorrow": 72a, 158b

מטי G "arrive": 42l, 143h

מטלה "booth": 104b

מטמע "setting": 158b

מטר C "cause to rain": 133g

מטר "rain": 73a, 104h, 161a

מין "kind": 31d, 62a

(מים, מימיהון, מוי) מין/מיין "water": 8i, 8i n.27, 9g, 9i, 15i, 15i n.10, 37d, 55b, 61a

מיסר "bunch": 104c; see also אסר

מית "corpse": 62a, 141q; see also מות

מכלה "measure": 32a, 53a, 104k; see also כל

מכנש "gathering together": 131x; see also כנש, כנשה/כנישה

מכסה "allotment": 118

מלאך "messenger": 53a, 104i

(מולד) מלד "giving birth": 139j; see also ילד, תלדו/תילד

מלה "word": 9d, 9g, 37d, 65b, 161d; see also מלל, ממלל

מלי G "be full, fill": 143j, 143l; D "fill": 143p

מלך C "enthrone": 11t, 133a

מלך "king": 2e n.33, 47e, 67a

מלכו "kingdom": 55f, 114b

מלל D "talk": 4d, 9f, 41b, 42a, 142k-o, 156o, 156aa, 157e

מלל "speech": 70a

מללו "speaking": 142p

(מאלף<) מלפן "teacher": 110h, 138 n.163; see also אלף, אלפן

ממון "wealth": 104j, 119d

ממלל "speech": 104a

מן/מאן "who, whom": 6b, 16b, 34a, 41b, 42f, 42f n.181, 43a-b, 46a

מן/מין/מ "from": 6b, 8e, 9a n.35, 9d, 9h, 16a n.1, 16b, 16d, 19a, 25a, 25c, 26, 28, 29b, 37b, 42b, 42f n.181, 42j-k 46a, 49, 124b, 129c, 131i, 156n n.17, 156o-p, 156p n.22, 156t, 157a, 157c, 158b-e, 161d

(מן דעם) מן דעם "anything": 20b, 28, 46a

מנחה "meal offering": 37b, 72a n.171, 119a

מני G "count": 143i, 143m; D: "appoint": 16b, 42d, 129b, 143n, 143r; Gt "be numbered, counted": 9d, 12f, 16c, 19j, 143aa-cc, 155c; Dt "be appointed": 143ee

מנין/מניין "number": 9e, 9e n.44, 12f, 42j, 110e

מנע Gt "be held back": 11t, 11y, 12f, 134b, 134e

מנרה "lamp": 104k; see also נור

מנת "even if": 157d

מסד see מסת

מסכן/מסכין "destitute": 118

מסר G "hand over": 42g, 131r

מסת (מסד) "in order to": 19j, 42k, 157c, 157c n.16 (able)

מעבר "crossing, passing over": 131x; see also עבר

מעה "womb": 37d, 74a

נטור "keeper": 89; see also נטר

נטל G "take": 137b, 137h; D "lift up": 137o; Dt "exalt oneself": 137y

נטר G "guard, keep": 11g, 131h, 137j, 137l; D "guard": 33c; see also נטור

ניח "rest": 82c; see also נוח

ניסן "Nisan": 118

ניר "yoke": 62a

נכסה/נכיסה "sacrifice": 77c

נכס G "slaughter": 137b-c, 137i

נכס "property": 118

נכרי/נוכרי "foreigner": 113b

נמוס/נימוס "custom, manner": 116

נמור "speckled" (m.): 11i, 78a

נמורה "speckled" (f.): 78b

נס/ניס "miracle": 119b

נסב G "take": 3h-i, 8c, 9d, 11o, 11t, 11y, 12c, 12f, 16d, 21b, 42a, 137b, 137d, 137h-j, 137l, 162a, 162e; C "give in marriage": 137r; see also נסיבה

נסי D "try, test": 137p

נסיבה "free-will offering": 83b; see also נסב

נסוך "libation": 11r, 137q; see also נסך

נסך D "pour a libation": 137n; see also נסוך

נעים "pleasant":119b

נפל G "fall": 8c, 12f, 42g, 137c

נפק G "go forth": 3g n.8, 4c, 8d, 9h, 9k. 11i, 11o-p, 12c, 21a-b, 31b, 31b n.9, 31a, 33d-e, 41b, 42l, 131i, 137c, 137h-k; C "bring forth": 11t, 137r-t; see also מפק מפקו, אפקו,

נפקה "whore": 88b

נפש "soul, person": 25c, 37b, 41h, 42b, 46a, 47d, 53a, 67a, 71a, 161d; "space": 67a n.85

נץ "blossom": 65a

נצב G "plant": 137h

נצח G "be victorious": 137k

נצי Dt "contend": 147c

נקבה "female": 8e, 31b, 53a, 54a-e, 70b

נקי "clean, pure" (m.): 77f

נקיה/נקייה "clean, pure" (f.): 77g

נקף C "surround": 137v

נשין "women": 12c, 12m, 37d, 47f, 60a (wife)

נשמה "soul": 18a, 53a, 73b

נשף C "blow": 137r

נשק C "kiss": 137p

נשר "eagle": 68a

נתן G "give": 9d, 9h, 19a, 21b, 29b n.159, 41b, 124b, 124j, 137e, 137i, 137l, 157c; see also מתנה

סאב D "make impure": 9f, 129b, 140b, 140h, 140j-k; Dt "be impure": 140b, 140o

סאובה "uncleanness": 69c

סב "old, elder": 4j, 61a; see also סיבו

סבר "countenance": 4j, 70a, 124c

סגול "bunch of grapes": 37d

סגלה/סגולה "property, wealth": 53a, 119b

סגי G "increase": 143b, 143i-k, 143m; D "increase, make great": 143q; C "increase, make great": 18d, 143x

סגי "many, much": 4c, 15i n.10, 18c, 18i, 25a, 29b, 29b n.159, 96c, 158a

סוגי "multitude": 9i, 11g, 31a-b, 69d, 71a, 71c

סדור "arrangement": 11r, 132g

סדר "row, order": 4j, 9d, 9i, 68a, 71b

סהד G "witness": 4j, 32a, 47f, 88a, 131u; C "testify": 133a,

n.28, 157b ("because" ד על), 157d, 158d

עלה "sacrifice": 55f, 72d, 119a n.430, 156q

עלוי/עלאוי "over": 16b, 19a, 37e, 156p, 156t

עלי/עלאי "high": 16b, 16b n.3, 99c

עלל G "enter": 16a n.1, 16b, 25c, 42e, 43c, 142a, 142c-g, 142i, 161d; C "bring in, up": 8b, 9f n.48, 11t, 142q, 142r-t; Ct "be brought up"; 142y-z; see also מעל

עללה "harvest": 8i, 12g, 72b

עלם "world" 8j, 16a, 41d, 46a, 47f, 53a, 87, 124b, 124k n.37, 131i, 158b, 162d n.4

עם (אמה) "people": 12c, 21b, 30, 47b, 64a, 123e n.8, 156o, 156aa

עם "with": 37b, 41f, 42d, 156u

עמד "column, pillar": 11m, 97

עמל "labor": 72a

עמק "depth": 25b, 37b, 69a

עמר (עומרה) "sheaf": 69a

ענב "grape": 74

ענונו/עינוונו "humility": 114b, 157f

עני/עאני G "answer": 13b, 16b, 143h, 143j, 157g

ענן "cloud": 79a

עסק "affair": 68a, 156s

עפר "dust": 72a

עצה/עיצה "advice": 119b

עצי G "be oppressed": 4f, 143l

עקב "heel, end": 77a

עקד G "bow": 123e n.8

עקה "distress": 8i, 61b

עקרה "barren": 72b

ערב D "vouch": 157g, 162d n.4; "intermingle": 41f, 135b

ערבן "pledge": 8b, 111a, 119e

ערברוב "mixed multitude": 102

ערד "onager": 79a

ערטל Qt "be denuded": 130i

ערטלי "naked": 4f, 113b

עריה "nakedness": 70c

ערים "sly": 83a

ערלה "foreskin": 69b

ערמה/עורמה "pile": 69b

ערס "bed": 67a

ערע "befall, meet"; see ארע

ערפל "darkness, cloud": 103

עשב "grass": 68a

עשירי "tenth": 8d;, 21c, 48a

עשר "ten": 13b, 19j, 28, 47i-j, 48b, 72a

עשרה "ten" (m.): 47a, 47e, 49-50, 158b

עשרון "tenth": 47d, 49, 11a, 119e

עשר/עשרה "teen": 16c, 18a, 47i-j, 52e

עשרין "twenty": 18a, 47k-l

עשרתי "the ten": 47a, 47h-j, 52f

עתיד "destined, future": 4c, 83a, 126b n.41, 129g

עתר (עותרה) "wealth": 69a

פגש Dt "meet": 135a

פגשו "meeting": 132g

פדעה "wound": 11e, 70b

פוטיפרע "Potiphera": 162e

פל G "soak": 141q

פטיר "unleavened bread": 96a, 131i

פטיר בולי "head of council": 28, 116

פיילי "cup": 116

פירוכי "grist": 17c n.2, 99b n.306, 115b

פלג D "divide": 12c, 21b, 132b; see also פלוג/פילוג

פלגו "half": 49, 114b, 158b

פלגוס/פליגוס "sea": 116

פלוג/פילוג "division": 11r, 132g; see also פלג

פלח G "work, worship": 131e, 131s

צפי   G "watch": 155b

צפי   "watch-post": 119i

צפיר   "he-goat": 83a

צפר   "morning": 75a, 158b

צפר   "bird": 92

צרף   Dt "join": 19i, 23

צרד   G "bind": 8e, 142h

צררה   "bundle": 82b

קבל   D "receive": 9f, 12f, 28, 126c, 132a-d, 157d, 162b; Dt "to be received": 4f, 135a, 135d

קבל/לקבל/כלקבל   "in front of, before": 156w

קבורה (קברתה)   "burial place": 11k, 32c, 37b, 86b

קבילה (קבלתה)   "cry": 10d, 32b, 83b

קבלה   "darkness": 75a

קבר   G "bury": 131r-s; Gt "be buried": 134a

קבר   "grave": 67a

קדם   "east wind": 100a

קדם/קדם   "before, in the presence of": 8d-e, 12c, 12i, 15e, 15h, 29b, 29b n.159, 31a, 37d, 41b, 42k, 81a, 124b, 156p, 156x, 157a

קדמות   "towards": 156y

קדמי/קדמיי   "first" (m.): 4f, 15h-i, 41b, 48a, 158b

קדמייה   "first" (f.): 48a, 158b

קדש   D "sanctify": 132b, 132f; Dt "sanctify oneself": 135b

קדש (קודשה, קושא)   "holiness": 4f, 30, 69a, 156f n.5

קדש   "earring": 118

קדיש   "holy" (m.): 4e, 96a

קדישה   "holy" (f.): 96b

קדקד   Q "speckle": 130g

קהי   G "be dislocated? benumbed?": 8e, 143h

קהל   "congregation": 33b, 53a, 82a

קום   G "arise": 8e, 11m, 11p, 12a, 31c, 33d, 42b, 123d, 129g, 141i-k, 141m-p, 141r, 157a; D "fulfill": 141s-v, 141x, 155c, 156n; C "set up": 9j, 10b, 141y-z, 141bb-cc; Dt "be fulfilled, endure": 16d, 43c, 141gg; see also מקמה קים/קיים, קימה/קיימה, קימה,

קרץ   "thorn": 55d

קושא   see קדש

קטב   "balsam"; see קטף

קטול   "killer": 11r, 89

קטל   G "kill": 3h, 10b, 10d n.70, 11i, 12c, 42e, 42g, 124i, (D?) 124j, 131a, 131g, 131r-s, 131u-w; D "kill": 9f, 12c, 132a-b; Gt: "be killed": 12c, 134a-b, 134d

קטלו   "killing": 132g

קטם   "ashes": 54c, 68a

קטף/קטיף (קטב)   "balsam": 17a

קיטון   "room, bedroom": 116

קיטור   "thick smoke": 119b

קים/קיים   "covenant, law": 12k, 15i, 41g n.150, 47d, 82c

קימה/קיימה   "pillar": 88c, 141p n.200

קין   "Cain": 129e, 151b, 157g, 162b

קירוש   "frost": 12f, 16h

קיס   "wood": 77d

קל   "voice": 61a

קלווי   see קלופי

קלופי (קלוותיה?)   "peel, husk": 17c, 17c n.2, 115b

קליל   "little" (m.): 8i, 96a

קלילה   "little" (f.): 96b

קלל   Dt "diminish": 142w

קלס   D "praise": 153

קמח   "flour": 67a

קנאה   "jealousy": 68f

קני   "cane, reed": 77f

קנין   "possessions": 9e, 110e

קנס   Gt "be fined, be punished": 9c-d, 12c, 126b, 153

קנס "fine, penalty": 12c, 12m, 116

קסם *G* "divine": 131w

קפי *G* "congeal": 143h

קפידי "shortness": 11m, 114b

קץ "end": 65a

קצת "part, end": 72d

קרב *G* "draw near, approach": 6b, 9r, 11t, 11y, 131c, 131r-t, 131w; *D* "bring near": 132a-b; "sacrifice": 38a n.116, 124i; *C* "bring near": 133c

קרב "battle": 79a

קרבן/קורבן "sacrifice": 11d, 37d, 110f

קרדו "Ararat": 11j

קרח "spotted" (m.): 24, 78a

קרחה "spotted" (f.): 78b, 156e

קרי *G* "call": 8f, 16c, 143b, 143h, 143k, 162b; *Gt* "be called, read": 9d, 16c, 41b, 143aa-cc

קריב "close, relative": 37d n.58, 96a

קריבו "proximity": 114b

קריה (קרתה, קורייא) "city": 4k, 11e, 11e n.75, 19h, 67i

קש "straw": 64a

קשוט (קשיט) קשט/קשוט "truth": 69a, 71

קשי "hard" (m.): 77f

קשיה "hard" (f.): 77g

קשת "bow": 59b

ראש (ריש) "head": 18d, 26b, 37b, 53a, 68c, 68c n.118, 119b, 161d

רב (רברבני, רברבין) "great, chief" (m.): 55d-e, 64a

רבה (רובתה, רברבן) "great" (f.): 19h, 64b, 124b

רבו "greatness": 114b

רבן "master": 9h, 11l, 11v, 25b, 31b, 37b, 42h, 121, 131i

רבי "interest": 115a

רבי *D* "increase, make great, raise": 12g, 124b-c, 143n

רבי "be saturated, drunk"; see רוי

רבי "boy": 88e

רביה "girl": 88f

רביעי/רביעיי "fourth" (m.): 48a

רבע *G* "lie, crouch": 8g, 24

רבעו "quarter": 49, 114b

רברב *Qt* "contend" ("act as a prince?"): 130h

רגז/רגו (רוגזה) "anger": 4f, 11e, 69a

רגל "foot": 37d, 70a

רדיד "veil": 8e, 37b, 83a

רו/ריו "appearance": 9c, 68e

רוח "wind, spirit": 24, 63a

רוי (רבי) *G* "be saturated, drunk": 4e, 143b

רום *Polel* "to raise": 16b, 38a, 126b, 126j, 130e, 155c, 162c; see also רם, רמה/ראמה, מרום

ח "secret": 117

רחיק "far": 96a, 158c; see also רחק, מרחקה

רחל "ewe": 18e, 77a

רחם *G* "love": 35a

רחמין/ריחמין "mercy": 13b, 18e, 18i, 37d, 67a

רחמן "merciful": 110a

רחץ *G* "trust": 131i, 131v

רחק *D* "make distant, banish": 124b; see also רחיק, מרחקה

רחש *G* "crawl": 42b

ריח "smell": 24, 77d

ריק *C* "empty": 130d, 141y; see also רוקן

ריקן "emptily": 110f, 130d, 158a

רכיך "soft": 96a

רכן *C* "lower": 133a, 133c; *Gt* "bend down": 12f, 134a

רם "high": 61a; see also רום, מרום

רמה/ראמה "hill": 16b, 61b; see also רום, מרום

רמון "pomegranate": 18l, 19g-

302

שיצי Š "destroy": 10d, 16e, 130f;
Št "be destroyed": 10d, 130f

שיר "song": 119b

שכח C "find": 13a, 18d, 19d,
(G? Gt?), 46a, 133a, 133g; Gt
"be found": 4d, 12c, 12f, 19d,
33d, 134e

שכינה "Shekhina": 3j, 119a,
119a n.429

שכלל "completion, perfection":
126j, 130f

שבלל Š "complete, perfect":
130f

שכם "Shechem": 5e n.5

שלהבי "flame": 25c, 105b, 161d

שלהי Št "tire": 130f

שלח D "send": 8e, 132a, 132h;
C "strip": 133g; Dt "be sent"
135a

שלחף S "change": 130f

שלט G "rule": 16e, 129b, 131s,
131u

שלטן/שלטן "ruler": 110f

שלוה/שליוה "rest": 119i

שליט "ruler": 96a

שלם G/C? "be completed": 9f,
42, 130b; D "pay": 12a, 35a,
129e, 132a, 132d; see also תשלום

שלם "well-being, peace": 8d,
53a, 79a, 158a

שלמין "peace offering": 119a

שלוף "drawer": 89

שם "name": 8e, 9k, 33c, 37b,
55c, 60a, 60a n.47, 151b, 162b

שמין "fat": 96a

שמין/שמיין "heavens": 12f, 33a,
119h, 161a

שמע G "hear": 8c, 19e, 24, 131b,
131f-g, 131r-t, 157c; Gt "be
heard": 9d, 134a

שמע "fame": 68a

שמש D "have intercourse": 132c

שמש "sun": 18a, 68a, 158b

שן/שין "tooth": 16d, 65a

שנה (שתה) "year": 19a, 47e, 47g,
47j, 47l n.24, 48b, 59b

שנה (שנתה) "sleep": 60b

שני G "differ": 143f; Dt "be
changed": 143dd, 143dd n.245

שעבד S "enslave": 3k, 130f; St
"be enslaved": 129g, 130f

שעבה "balsam": 8f, 13b, 17d,
75a, 131i

שעבוד (שעבד) "enslavement":
11r, 47f, 126j, 130f

שעה "hour, time": 16a n.1, 25c,
41e, 41h, 41l-m, 42h, 42k 47b,
61b, 157a, 158b, 161d

שעמימו "stupefaction": 126j,
130f

שפל "extremity": 22, 94a

שפור/שיפור "horn": 119a

שפי G "be favorable": 17c

שפיר "handsome, pleasing"
(m.): 96a

שפירה "handsome, pleasing"
(f.): 96b

שפך G "pour out": 11t, 131s; Gt
"be poured out": 134c

שפר G "be pleasing": 11o; 12a
and 156e (noun?)

שקוף "threshold": 76a, 119g

שקי C "give drink, water": 35b,
129a, 143u-y

שקי "irrigation": 68e

שקר D "lie": 132h

שקר "lie": 68a

שרב "heat": 35a

שרביט "staff": 20c, 47f, 47f n.15,
103

שרגג Q "violate, rape": 9h, 20c,
130i

שרה/שירו "meal": 114b

שרי G "dwell": 4f, 15c, 32a,
143h-k, 143m; "forgive": 29b; D
"begin": 143c n.223, 143n; C

304

תרגם‎ *Qt* "be translated": 19c,
130i, 154b

תרוג‎ orange, citron": 117

תרין/תרין‎ (תרי)‎ "two" (m.): 4c,
15c, 47a, 47d, 47i-j, 49-51, 52b,
55a, 158b

תריס‎ "shield": 116

תרע‎ "door, gate": 13a, 33b, 67a

תרתין‎ "two" (f.): 47a, 47d, 47l,
52b, 52g

תשבחה‎ (תשבן)‎ "praise": 30, 106b

תשבן‎ see תשבחה‎

תשלום‎ "payment, exchange":
11r, 106a; see also שלם‎

תשמיש‎ "copulation": 106a

תשע‎ "nine" (f.); 12a, 47a, 68a

תשעה‎ "nine" (m.): 47a, 47e, 68b

# BIBLIOGRAPHY

Allony, N. "What is הנקח שלנ in the Vitri Maḥzor?" *Beit Miqra*, 17 (1964), 135-144 (in Hebrew).

_____ *Geniza Fragments of Rabbinic Literature: Mishna, Talmud and Midrash with Palestinian Vocalization.* Facsimile Edition. Jerusalem: Makor, 1973 (in Hebrew).

Arlotto, A. *Introduction to Historical Linguistics.* Boston: Houghton Mifflin, 1972.

Baars, W. "A Targum on Exod. XV 7-21 from the Cairo Genizah," *VT,* 11 (1961), 340-342.

Bacher, W. "Targum," *Jewish Encyclopedia.* New York: Funk and Wagnalls, 1906, 12, 57-63.

Bar-Asher, M. "The Mishnah of Ms. Parma B of the Order Ṭohorot." Introduction to the *Facsimile Edition of Ms. Parma B.* Jerusalem: Makor, 1971 (in Hebrew).

_____ *Palestinian Syriac Studies: Source Texts, Traditions and Grammatical Problems.* Jerusalem, 1977 (in Hebrew).

_____ "Rare Forms in the Language of the Tanna'im," *Lesh,* 41 (1977-1978), 95-102 (in Hebrew).

_____ *The Traditions of Mishnaic Hebrew in the Communities of Italy According to Ms. Paris 328-329.* Jerusalem: Hebrew University Language Traditions Project, VI, 1980 (in Hebrew).

_____ "Two Grammatical Phenomena in Palestinian Syriac" *Language Studies* II-III, ed. M. Bar-Asher. Jerusalem: Hebrew University, 1987, 111-126 (in Hebrew).

_____ "Le syro-palestinien—études grammaticales," *JA,* 276 (1988), 28-59.

Barr, J. "St Jerome and the Sounds of Hebrew," *JSS,* 12 (1967), 11-36.

Barth, J. *Die Nominalbildung in den semitischen Sprachen.* 2nd ed. Leipzig: J. C. Hinrichs, 1894.

_____ *Die Pronominalbildung in den semitischen Sprachen.* Leipzig: J. C. Hinrichs, 1912.

Bassfreund, J. "Das Fragmenten-Targum zum Pentateuch, sein Ursprung und Charakter und sein Verhältnis zu den anderen pentateuchischen Targumim," *MGWJ,* 40 (1896), 1-14, 49-67, 97-109, 145-163, 241-252, 353-365, 396-405.

Baumgartner, W. et al. *Hebräisches und aramäisches Lexicon zum alten Testament.* Leiden: E. J. Brill, 1967–.

305

306

Bauer, H. and Leander, P. *Historische Grammatik der hebräischen Sprache.* Halle: Max Niemeyer, 1922; reprint Hildesheim: Georg Olms, 1965.

―― *Grammatik des Biblisch-Aramäischen.* Halle: Max Niemeyer, 1927; reprint Hildesheim: Georg Olms, 1981.

Beit-Arie, M. "The Vocalization of the Worms Maḥzor," *Lesh*, 29 (1965), 27-46, 80-102 (in Hebrew).

―― *Hebrew Codicology.* Jerusalem: The Israel Academy of Sciences and Humanities, 1981.

Ben-Ḥayyim, Z. "The Third Feminine Plural in Old Aramaic," *EI*, 1 (1951), 135-139 (in Hebrew).

―― *Studies in the Traditions of the Hebrew Language.* Madrid-Barcelona: Consejo Superior de Investigaciones Científicas, 1954.

―― "The Samaritan Vowel-System and Its Graphic Representation," *ArOr,* 22 (1954), 515-530.

―― *The Literary and Oral Tradition of Hebrew and Aramaic amongst the Samaritans.* 5 vols. Jerusalem: The Academy of the Hebrew Language, 1957-1977 (in Hebrew).

―― "La Tradition samaritaine et sa parenté avec les autres traditions de la language hebräique," *MélPhLJ,* 3-5 (1958-1962), 89-128.

―― "Concerning the Originality of the Penultimate Stress in Hebrew," in *Henoch Yalon Jubilee Volume,* ed. S. Lieberman et al. Jerusalem: Kiryat Sefer, 1963, 150-160 (in Hebrew).

―― "Reflections on the Hebrew Vowel System," in *Studies in Bible and the Ancient New East Presented to Samuel E. Loewenstamm on His 70th Birthday,* ed. J. Blau and Y. Avishur. Jerusalem: E. Rubinstein, 1968, 95-105 (in Hebrew).

―― "Comments on the Inscriptions of Sfire," *Lesh,* 35 (1971), 243-253 (in Hebrew)

―― "Third Masculine Singular in Place of First Singular?" in *Abraham Even-Shoshan Volume,* ed. Z. Ben-Ḥayyim et al. Jerusalem: Kiryat-Sefer, 1985, 93-98 (in Hebrew).

Ben-Yehuda, E. *Thesaurus totius hebraitatis et veteris et recentioris.* 8 vols. New York: Thomas Yoseloff, 1959.

Bergsträsser, G. *Hebräische Grammatik.* 2 vols. Leipzig: Vogel, 1918-1929.

―― *Glossar des neuaramäischen Dialekts von Ma'lula.* AKM 15,4. Leipzig: Deutsche Morgenländische Gesellschaft, 1921: reprint Nendeln: Krauss, 1966.

―― *OLZ,* 29 (1926), 497.

―― *Einführung in die semitischen Sprache.* München: Max Hüber, 1928; reprint Darmstadt: Wissenschaftliche Buchgesellschaft, 1978.

Berliner, A. *Targum Onkelos.* 2 vols. Berlin: Gorzelanczyk, 1884.

Beyer, K. *Die aramäischen Texte vom Toten Meer samt den Inschriften aus Palästina, dem Testament Levis aus der Kairoer Genisa, der Fastenrolle und den alten talmudischen Zitaten.* Göttingen: Vandenhoeck & Ruprecht, 1984.

———. "The Pronunciation of Galilean Aramaic According to the Geniza Fragments with Palestinian and Tiberian Pointing," *Proceedings of the Ninth World Congress of Jewish Studies*. Jerusalem, 1985. Division D, Vol. 1, 17-22.

———. *The Aramaic Language: Its Distribution and Subdivisions*. Göttingen: Vandenhoeck & Ruprecht, 1986.

Birkeland, H. "The Syriac Phonematic Vowel Systems," in *Festskrift til Professor Olaf Broch*. Avhandlinger utgitt av det norske videnkaps-Akademi i Oslo. II. Historik-Filosofisk Klasse (1947), 13-39.

Birnbaum, S. A. *The Hebrew Scripts*. 2 vols. Leiden: E. J. Brill, 1954-1971.

Blake, F. R. "The Apparent Interchange Between a and i in Hebrew," *JNES,* 9 (1950), 76-83.

Blanc, H. "The nekteb-nektebu Imperfect in a Variety of Cairene Arabic," *IOS,* 4 (1974), 206-222.

Blau, J. "The Passive Participle with Active Meaning," *Lesh*, 18 (1953), 67-81 (in Hebrew).

———. "Studies in Semitic Pronouns," in *Henoch Yalon Jubilee Volume,* ed. S. Lieberman et al. Jerusalem: Kiryat Sefer, 1963, 17-45 (in Hebrew).

———. *The Emergence and Linguistic Background of Judaeo-Arabic: A Study of the Origins of Middle Arabic*. Jerusalem: Ben Zvi Institute, 1981.

Bloch, R. "Note sur l'utilisation des fragments de la Geniza du Caire pour l'étude du Targum Palestinien," *REJ,* 14 (1955), 5-35.

Braverman, N. "Targum Neophyti—A Syntactic Examination." Masters thesis, Hebrew University of Jerusalem, 1978 (in Hebrew).

Bresciani, E. and Kamil, M. *Le lettere aramaiche di Hermopoli*. Rome: atti della Accademia Nazionale dei Lincei, Memorie, classe di Scienze morali, storiche e filologiche, ser. VIII, Vol. XII, 5 (1966), 361-428.

Brock, S. P. "Greek Words in the Syriac Gospels (VET and PE)," *MUS,* 80 (1967), 389-426.

Brockelmann, C. *Grundriss der vergleichenden Grammatik der semitischen Sprache*, 2 vols. Berlin: Reuther und Reichard, 1908-1913.

———. *Lexicon Syriacum*. 2nd ed. Halle: Max Niemeyer, 1928; reprint Hildesheim: Georg Olms, 1982.

Brønno, E. *Studien über hebräische Morphologie und Vokalismus auf Grundlage der mercatischen Fragmente der zweiten Kolumne der Hexapla des Origenes*. AKM 28. Leipzig: Deutsche Morgenländische Gesellschaft, 1943.

Brown, F., Driver, S. R., and Briggs, C. A. *Hebrew and English Lexicon of the Old Testament*. Oxford: Clarendon Press, 1907; reprint 1953.

Ceriani, A. M. *Translatio syra pescitto Veteris Testamenti ex Codice Ambrosiano*. 2 vols. Milan, 1876-1883.

Chiesa, B. *L'Antico Testamento Ebraico secondo la tradizione palestinense*. Torino: Bottega d'Erasmo, 1978.

Clarke, E. G. "The Neofiti 1 Marginal Glosses and the Fragmentary Targum Witnesses to Gen VI-IX," *VT,* 22 (1972), 257-265.

308

—— *Targum Pseudo-Jonathan of the Pentateuch: Text and Concordance.* Hoboken, New Jersey: Ktav, 1984.

Cook, E. M. "Rewriting the Bible: The Text and Language of the Pseudo-Jonathan Targum." Ph.D. thesis, University of California at Los Angeles, 1986.

Correll, C. "Materialien zur Kenntnis des neuaramäischen Dialekts von Baḫ'a." Ph.D. dissertation, Ludwig-Maximilians-Universität zu München, 1969.

Cowley, A. *Aramaic Papyri of the Fifth Century B.C.* Oxford: Clarendon Press, 1923; reprint Otto Zeller: Osnabrück, 1967.

Cowling, G. "The Palestinian Targum: Textual and Linguistic Investigations in Codex Neofiti I and Allied Manuscripts." Ph.D. thesis, University of Aberdeen, 1968.

—— "Notes, Mainly Orthographical, on the Galilaean Targum and 1Q Genesis Apocryphon," *AJBA*,2 (1972), 35-49.

Cross, F. M., and Freedman, D N. *Early Hebrew Orthography.* American Oriental Series 36. New Haven: American Oriental Society, 1952.

Dalman, G. *Grammatik des jüdisch-palästinischen Aramäisch.* 2nd ed. Leipzig: J. C. Hinrichs, 1905; reprint Darmstadt: Wissenschaftliche Buchgesellschaft, 1960.

—— *Aramäisch-Neuhebräisches Handwörterbuch zu Targum, Talmud und Midrash.* 2nd ed. Göttingen: Vandenhoeck & Ruprecht, 1938; reprint: Hildesheim: Georg Olms, 1967.

Degen, R. *Altaramäische Grammatik der Inschriften der 10-8 Jh. v. Chr.* AKM 38,3. Wiesbaden: Deutsche Morgenländische Gesellschaft, 1969.

Dietrich, M. *Neue palästinisch punktierte Bibelfragmente.* Leiden: E. J. Brill, 1968.

Díez Macho, A. "Nuevos fragmentos del Targum Palestinense," *Sef,* 15 (1955), 31-39.

—— "Onqelos Manuscript with Babylonian Transliterated Vocalization in the Vatican Library (MS Eb. 448)," *VT,* 8 (1958), 113-133.

—— "The Recently Discovered Palestinian Targum: Its Antiquity and Relationship with the Other Targums," *SVT,* 7 (1959), 222-245.

—— "Un Manuscrito Babilonico de Onqelos en el que se confunden los timbres vocalicos Pataḥ y Qameṣ," *Sef,* 19 (1959), 273-282.

—— "A New List of So-called 'Ben Naftali' Manuscripts Preceded by an Inquiry into the True Character of These Manuscripts," in *Hebrew and Semitic Studies Presented to G. R. Driver,* ed. D. Winton Thomas and W. D. McHardy. Oxford: Clarendon Press, 1963, 16-52.

—— "Deux nouveaux fragments du Targum palestinien à New York," in *Studi sull' Oriente e la Bibbia offerti a P. Giovani Rinaldi.* Genova: Studio e Vita, 1967, II, 175-178.

—— *Neophyti 1: Targum Palestinense MS de la Biblioteca Vaticana.* 6 vols. Madrid-Barcelona: Consejo Superior de Investigaciones Científicas,1968-

1979.

——. "Un nuevo fragmento del Targum palestinense a Génesis," *Aug,*9 (1969) 120-123.

——. *Biblia Polyglotta Matritensia.* Series IV: Targum Palestinense in Pentateuchum. Madrid: Consejo Superior de Investigaciones Científicas, 1977–.

——. "L'usage de la troisième personne au lieu de la première dans le Targum," in *Mélanges Dominique Barthélemy,* ed. P. Casetti et al. Fribourg: Éditions universitaires; Göttingen: Vandenhoeck & Ruprecht, 1981, 62-85.

Dodi, A. "The Grammar of Targum Onqelos According to Geniza Fragments." Ph.D. thesis, Bar-Ilan University, 1981 (in Hebrew).

Dotan, A. "Masorah," *EJ.* Jerusalem: Keter; New York: Macmillan, 1971, 16, 1402-1482.

Doubles, M. C. "The Fragment Targum: A Critical Re-examination of the Editio Princeps, Das Fragmententhargum by Moses Ginsburger, in the Light of Recent Discoveries." Ph.D. thesis, University of St. Andrews, 1962.

Driver, G. R. *Aramaic Documents of the Fifth Century B.C.* 2nd ed. Oxford: Clarendon Press, 1965.

Drower, E. S. and R. Macuch. *A Mandaic Dictionary.* Oxford: Clarendon Press, 1963.

—— and O. Loretz. "Ug. *SSW/ŚŚW* 'Pferd,' *SSWT* 'Stute' und Akk. *\*sisītu* 'Stute'," *UF,*15 (1983), 301-302.

Eldar, I. *The Hebrew Language Tradition in Medieval Ashkenaz (ca. 950-1350 C.E.), I: Phonology and Vocalization.* Jerusalem: Hebrew University Language Traditions Project, IV, 1978 (in Hebrew).

Ellenbogen, M. *Foreign Words in the Old Testament, Their Origin and Etymology.* London: Luzac, 1962.

Epstein, J. N. *Introduction to the Text of the Mishnah.* 2 vols. Jerusalem: Magnes Press, 1948 (in Hebrew).

——. *A Grammar of Babylonian Aramaic.* Jerusalem: Magnes Press, 1960 (in Hebrew).

Fassberg, S. "Topics in the Aramaic of the Palestinian Targum Fragments in the Light of Comparative Data," *Proceedings of the Ninth World Congress of Jewish Studies.* Jerusalem, 1985. Division D, Vol. 1, 17-22 (in Hebrew).

——. "Determined Forms of the Cardinal Number 'One' in Three Pentateuchal Targumim," *Sef,*45 (1985) 207-215.

——. "Miscellanea in Western Aramaic" in *Language Studies* II-III, ed. M. Bar-Asher. Jerusalem: Hebrew University, 1987, 199-206 (in Hebrew).

Fischer, A. *Mitteilungen des Seminars für orientalistische Sprachen.* Berlin, I, 1898.

310

Fischer, W. and Jastrow, O. *Handbuch der arabischen Dialekte*. Wiesbaden: Harrassowitz, 1980.

Fitzmyer, J. *The Genesis Apocryphon of Qumran Cave I: A Commentary*. Rome: Biblical Institute Press, 1966.

——— *The Aramaic Inscriptions of Sefire*. Rome: Biblical Institute Press, 1967.

———, and Harrington, D. *A Manual of Palestinian Aramaic Texts*. Rome: Biblical Institute Press, 1978.

——— "The Phases of the Aramaic Language," *A Wandering Aramean: Collected Aramaic Essays*. Missoula: Scholars Press, 1979.

Foster, J. "The Language and Text of Codex Neofiti I in the Light of other Palestinian Aramaic Sources." Ph.D. thesis, Boston University, 1969.

Fraenkel, S. *Die aramäischen Fremdwörter im Arabischen*. Leiden: E. Lokay, 1886: reprint Hildesheim: Georg Olms, 1962.

Friedman, S. "-Oy for -ay as First Person Singular Pronominal Suffix for Plural Nouns in Galilean Aramaic" in *Language Studies*, II-III,ed. M. Bar-Asher. Jerusalem: Hebrew University, 1987, 207-215 (in Hebrew).

Garr, W. R. *Dialect Geography of Syria-Palestine, 1000-586 B.C.E.* Philadelphia: University of Pennsylvania Press, 1985.

Geiger, A. *Urschrift und Übersetzung der Bibel in ihrer Abhängigkeit von den inneren Entwicklung des Judenthums*. Breslau: Hainauer, 1857.

Gelb, I. J. "The Word for Dragoman in the Ancient Near East," *Glossa*, 3 (1968), 93-104.

Ginsberg, H. L. "Zu den Dialekten des Talmudisch-Hebräischen," *MGWJ*, 77 (1933), 423-475.

——— "Notes on a Palestinian Targum," *Tarbiz*, 5 (1934), 381-383 (in Hebrew).

Ginsburg, C. D. *Introduction to the Massoretico-Critical Edition of the Bible*. London: Trinitarian Bible Society, 1897.

Ginsburger, M. *Das Fragmententhargum*. Berlin: Calvary, 1899.

——— *Pseudo-Jonathan: Thargum Jonathan ben Usiël zum Pentateuch*. Berlin: Calvary, 1903.

Ginzberg, L. *Yerushalmi Fragments from the Genizah*. New York: Jewish Theological Seminary, 1909.

——— *Genizah Studies in Memory of Dr. Solomon Schechter*, I. New York: Jewish Theological Seminary, 1928.

Golomb, D. "Nominal Syntax in the Language of Codex Vatican Neofiti 1: The Genitive Relationship," *JAOS*,102 (1982), 297-308.

——— *A Grammar of Targum Neofiti*. Harvard Semitic Monographs 34. Chico: Scholars Press, 1985.

Goshen-Gottstein, M. H. "The Rise of the Tiberian Bible Text" in A. Altmann, ed., *Biblical and Other Studies*. Philip W. Lown Institute of Advanced Judaic Studies, Brandeis University, Studies and Texts, I. Cambridge: Harvard University Press, 1963, 79-122.

——— "Linguistic Structure and Tradition in the Qumran Documents," *ScrHier*,4 (1965), 101-137.

———. "The 'Third Targum' on Esther and Ms. Neofiti 1," *Bib*, 56 (1975), 301-329.

———. "The Language of Targum Onqelos and the Model of Literary Diglossia in Aramaic," *JNES*, 37 (1978), 169-179.

———. *Fragments of Lost Targumim*, I. Ramat-Gan: Bar-Ilan University, 1983 (in Hebrew).

Greenfield, J. C. "The 'Periphrastic Imperative' in Aramaic and Hebrew," *IEJ*, 19 (1969), 199-210.

———. "Standard Literary Aramaic" in A. Caquot and D. Cohen, eds., *Actes du premier congrès international de linguistique sémitique et chamito-sémitique*. The Hague: Mouton, 1974, 280-289.

———. "Iranian Loanwords in Early Aramaic," *Encyclopaedia Iranica*. London: Routledge & Kegan Paul, 1986. II, 3, 256-259.

———, and A. Shaffer. "Notes on the Akkadian-Aramaic Bilingual Statue from Tel Fekherye," *Iraq*, 45 (1983), 109-116.

Gross, B. "Noun-formations with the Afformative 'on, ān' (Comprising only Words of Semitic Origin) and Their Meanings in Biblical and in Mishnaic Hebrew." Ph.D. thesis, Hebrew University, 1971 (in Hebrew).

Grossfeld, B. "Bible: Translations," *EJ*. Jerusalem: Keter; New York: Macmillan, 1971, 4, 842-851.

———. *A Bibliography of Targum Literature*. 2 vols. Cincinnati: Hebrew Union College; New York: Ktav, 1972-1977.

Haneman, G. *The Morphology of Mishnaic Hebrew According to the Tradition of MS Parma (de Rossi 138)*. Tel-Aviv: Tel-Aviv University, 1980 (in Hebrew).

Harviainen, T. *On the Vocalism of the Closed Unstressed Syllables in Hebrew: A Study Based on the Evidence Provided by the Transcriptions of St. Jerome and Palestinian Punctuations*. Studia Orientali 48:1. Helsinki, 1977.

Huehnergard, J. "Asseverative *la and Hypothetical *lu/law in Semitic," *JAOS*, 103 (1983), 569-593.

Jacob, B. "Das hebräische Sprachgut im Christlich-Palästinischen," *ZAW*, 22 (1902) 83-113.

Janssens, G. *Studies in Hebrew Historical Linguistics Based on Origen's Secunda*. Orientalia Gandensia 9. Leuven: Peeters, 1982.

Jastrow, M. A. *A Dictionary of the Targumim, the Talmud Babli, and Yerushalmi, and the Midrashic Literature*. London: Luzac; New York: G. P. Putnam's Sons, 1903; reprint New York: Judaica Press, 1975.

Joüon, P. *Grammaire de l'hébreu biblique*. Rome: Institute Biblique Pontifical, 1923; reprint 1965.

Kadari, M. Z. "The use of -ד Clauses in the Language of Targum Onqelos," *VT*, 3 (1963), 36-59.

———. "Studies in the Syntax of Targum Onqelos," *Tarbiz*, 32 (1963), 232-251 (in Hebrew).

———. "Construct State and di-Phrases in Imperial Aramaic," *Proceedings of the International Conference on Semitic Studies held in Jerusalem, 1965*. Jeru-

312

salem: The Israel Academy of Sciences and Humanities, 1969, 102-115.

Kahle, P. *Masoreten des Ostens.* Leipzig: J. C. Hinrichs, 1913; reprint Hildesheim: Georg Olms, 1984.

——. *Masoreten des Westens*, II. Stuttgart: W. Kohlhammer, 1930; reprint Hildesheim: Georg Olms, 1967.

——. *The Cairo Geniza.* 2nd ed. Oxford: Basil Blackwell, 1959.

Kara, Y. *Babylonian Aramaic in the Yemenite Manuscripts of the Talmud: Orthography, Phonology, and Morphology of the Verb.* Jerusalem: Hebrew University Language Traditions Project, X, 1983 (in Hebrew).

Katz, K. *The Hebrew Language Tradition of the Djerba Community (Tunisia).* Jerusalem: Hebrew University Language Traditions Project, II, 1977 (in Hebrew).

——. *The Hebrew Language Tradition of the Aleppo Community: Phonology.* Jerusalem: Hebrew University Language Traditions Project, VII, 1981 (in Hebrew).

Kaufman, S. *The Akkadian Influences on Aramaic.* The Oriental Institute of the University of Chicago, Assyriological Studies No. 19. Chicago: University of Chicago Press, 1984.

——. "Aramaic Vowel Reduction," in *Arameans, Aramaic and the Aramaic Literary Tradition,* ed. M. Sokoloff. Ramat-Gan: Bar-Ilan University Press, 1983, 47-55.

——. Review of *A Grammar of Targum Neofiti* by D. Golomb, *JAOS,*107 (1987), 142-143.

Kautzsch, E. *Grammatik des Biblisch-Aramäischen mit einer kritischen Erörterung der aramäischen Wörter im Neuen Testament.* Leipzig: Vogel, 1884.

Klein, M. "The Extant Sources of the Fragmentary Targum to the Pentateuch," *HUCA,*46 (1975), 115-137.

——. "A Genizah Fragment of Palestinian Targum to Genesis 15:1-4," *HUCA,*49 (1978), 73-87.

——. "Nine Fragments of Palestinian Targum to the Pentateuch from the Cairo Genizah," *HUCA,*50 (1979), 149-164.

——. *The Fragment-Targums of the Pentateuch According to Their Extant Sources.* 2 vols. Analecta Biblica 76. Rome: Biblical Institute Press, 1980.

——. "Bibliography of Manuscripts and Editions of Palestinian Targum to the Pentateuch from the Cairo Genizah," *Studies in Bibliography and Booklore,* 13 (1980), 20-25.

——. "New Editions of the Palestinian Targumim to the Pentateuch," in *Arameans, Aramaic and the Aramaic Literary Tradition,* ed. M. Sokoloff. Ramat-Gan: Bar-Ilan University Press, 1983, 89-96.

——. *Genizah Manuscripts of Palestinian Targum to the Pentateuch.* 2 vols. Cincinnati: Hebrew Union College Press, 1986.

Kohut, A. *Aruch Completum.* 8 vols. 2nd ed. Wien: Menorah, 1926.

Kraeling, E. *The Brooklyn Museum Aramaic Papyri.* New Haven: Yale University, 1953.

313

Krauss, S. *Griechische und lateinische Lehnwörter im Talmud, Midrasch und Targum*. 2 vols. Berlin: Calvary, 1898-1899.

Kuiper, G. *The Pseudo-Jonathan Targum and Its Relationship to Targum Onkelos*. Rome: Institutum Patristicum Augustinianum, 1972.

Kutscher, E. Y. "The Language of the Genesis Apocryphon: A Preliminary Study," *ScrHier*, 4 (1958), 1-35.

——. "Das zur Zeit Jesu gesprochene Aramäisch," *ZNW*, 51 (1960), 46-54.

——. "The Language of the Hebrew and Aramaic Letters of Bar Koseba and His Contemporaries. Part I: The Aramaic Letters," *Lesh*, 25 (1961), 117-133 (in Hebrew).

——. "Mishnaic Hebrew," in *Henoch Yalon Jubilee Volume*, ed. S. Lieberman et al. Jerusalem: Kiryat-Sefer, 1963, 246-280 (in Hebrew).

——. "Marginal Notes to the Mishnaic Lexicon and A Grammatical Note," *Lesh*, 31 (1967), 107-117 (in Hebrew).

——. Review of *The Literary and Oral Tradition of Hebrew and Aramaic amongst the Samaritans*, III.2, by Z. Ben-Ḥayyim, *Tarbiz*, 37 (1968), 379-419.

——. "Articulation of the Vowels u,i in Transcriptions of Biblical Hebrew, in Galilean Aramaic, and in Mishnaic Hebrew" in *Benjamin de Vries Memorial Volume*, ed. E. Melamad. Jerusalem: Tel-Aviv University and Stichting Fronika Sander Fonds, 1968, 218-251 (in Hebrew).

——. "Aramaic," in *Current Trends in Linguistics: Vol. 6: Linguistics in South West Asia and North Africa*, ed. T. A. Sebeok. The Hague: Mouton, 1971, 347-412.

——. "Aramaic," *EJ*. Jerusalem: Keter; New York: Macmillan, 1971, 3, 260-287.

——. "Mishnaic Hebrew," *EJ*. Jerusalem: Keter; New York: Macmillan, 1971, 16, 1590-1607.

——. "The Hermopolis Papyri," *IOS*, 1 (1971), 103-119.

——. *A History of Aramaic*, I: *Old Aramaic, Jaudic, Official Aramaic (Biblical Aramaic excepted)*. Jerusalem: Academon, 1972 (in Hebrew).

——. *Studies in Galilean Aramaic*, trans. M. Sokoloff. Ramat-Gan: Bar-Ilan University, 1976.

——. *A History of the Hebrew Language*, ed. R. Kutscher. Jerusalem: Magnes Press; Leiden: E. J. Brill, 1982.

Lagarde, Paul de. *Gesammelte Abhandlungen*. Leipzig: F. A. Brockhaus, 1866.

Lambdin, T. O. "Egyptian Loan Words in the Old Testament," *JAOS*, 73 (1953), 145-155.

——. *Introduction to Biblical Hebrew*. New York: Charles Scribner's Sons, 1971.

——. "Philippi's Law Reconsidered," in *Biblical and Related Studies Presented to Samuel Iwry*, ed. A. Kort and S. Morschauser. Winona Lake: Eisenbrauns, 1985, 135-145.

314

Lasry, G. "Some Remarks on the Jewish Dialectal Aramaic of Palestine During the 1st Centuries of the Christian Era," *Aug*,8 (1965), 468-476.

——. "Gramitica del arameo dialectal de Palestina en tiempo de Jesus según el ms. Neofiti I (Deuteronomio)." Ph.D. thesis, University of Barcelona, 1974.

Le Déaut, R. *Introduction à la littérature targumique.* Première partie. Rome: Institut Biblique Pontifical, 1966.

——. "Levitique XXII 26—XXIII 44 dans le Targum Palestinien. De l'importance des gloses du Codex Neofiti 1," *VT,* 18 (1968), 458-471.

——. Review of *Genizah Manuscripts of Palestinian Targum to the Pentateuch* by M. L. Klein, *Bibl,*68 (1987) 568-576.

Leander, P. *Laut- und Formenlehre des Ägyptisch-Aramäischen.* Göteborg: Göteborgs högskolas årsskrift 34,4, 1928; reprint Hildesheim: Georg Olms, 1966.

Lerner, Y. "The Zayin/daleth Interchange in the Elephantine Documents: An Alternate Explanation," *Lesh,* 46 (1982), 57-64 (in Hebrew).

Levias, C. *A Grammar of Galilean Aramaic.* New York: Jewish Theological Seminary, 1986 (in Hebrew).

Levy, B. "The Language of Neofiti 1: A Descriptive and Comparative Grammar of the Palestinian Targum." Ph.D. thesis, New York University, 1974.

Levy, J. *Wörterbuch über die Talmudim und Midraschim.* 4 vols. 2nd ed. Berlin: 1924; reprint Darmstadt: Wissenschaftlich Buchgesellschaft, 1963.

Lisowsky, G. "Die Transkription der hebräischen Eigennamen des Pentateuch in der Septuaginta." Ph.D. thesis, Basel, 1940.

Lund, J. "A Descriptive Syntax of the Non-Translational Passages according to Codex Neofiti I." Masters thesis, Hebrew University of Jerusalem, 1981 (in Hebrew).

——. "On the Interpretation of the Palestinian Targumic Reading *WQHT* in GEN 32:25," *JBL,*105 (1986), 99-103.

——. "The Syntax of the Numeral 'One' as a Noun Modifier in Jewish Palestinian Aramaic of the Amoraic Period," *JAOS,*106 (1986), 413-423.

——. "The First Person Singular Past Tense of the Verb הוה in Jewish Palestinian Aramaic," *Maarav,*4 (1987), 191-199.

——. "The Problem of Expressing 'Three Hundred' and the Like in the Language of Codex Neofiti 1," *Sef,*4 (1987), 149-157.

Lund, S. and Foster, J. *Variant Versions of Targumic Traditions within Codex Neofiti I.* Society of Biblical Literature Aramaic Studies, No. 2. Missoula: Scholars Press, 1977.

Macuch, R. *Handbook of Classical and Modern Mandaic.* Berlin: Walter de Gruyter, 1965.

——. *Grammatik des samaritanischen Aramäisch.* Berlin: Walter de Gruyter, 1982.

315

Malone, J. L. "Wave Theory, Rule Ordering, and Hebrew-Aramaic Sego-lation," *JAOS*,91 (1971), 44-66.

Maman, A. "The Reading Tradition of the Jews of Tétouan: Phonology of Biblical and Mishnaic Hebrew," *Mass*, 1 (1984), 51-120 (in Hebrew).

—— "La position de l'hébreu des juifs de Tétouan parmi les traditions dites séfarades," *Mass*, 2 (1986), 93-102.

Marmorstein, A. "Einige vorläufige Bemerkungen zu den neuentdeckten Fragmente des jerusalemischen (palästinensischen) Targums," *ZAW*, 49 (1931), 231-242.

Melamed, R. H. "The Targum to Canticles According to Six Yemen Mss. Compared with the 'Textus Receptus' (ed. de Lagarde)," *JQR* n.s., 10 (1919-1920), 377-410; 11 (1920-1921), 1-20; 12 (1921-1922), 57-117.

Merx, A. "Bemerkungen über die Vocalisation der Targume," *Verhandlungen des fünften Internationalen Orientalisten-Congresses.* Berlin: Asher, 1882, 142-225.

—— *Chrestomathia Targumica.* Berlin: Reuther, 1888.

Milik, J. T. *The Books of Enoch: Aramaic Fragments of Qumran Cave 4.* Oxford: Clarendon Press, 1976.

Miller, J. "A Grammar of the Type II Marginalia within Codex Neofiti I with Attention to other Aramaic Sources." Ph.D. thesis, Boston University, 1978.

Mishor, M. "Anomalies in Verb Formation," *Lesh*, 41 (1977), 291-293 (in Hebrew).

Morag. S. "The Conjugation Pā'ēl and the Conjugation Nithpā'ēl: On the Elucidation of Forms in the Traditions of Rabbinic Hebrew," *Tarbiz*, 26 (1957), 348-356 (in Hebrew).

—— "More on Pā'ēl and Nithpā'ēl," *Tarbiz*, 27 (1958), 556 (in Hebrew).

—— "The Vocalization of Codex Reuchlinianus: Is the 'Pre-Masoretic' Bible Pre-Masoretic?" *JSS* 4 (1959), 216-237.

—— "The Babylonian Aramaic Tradition of the Yemenite Jews," *Tarbiz*, 30 (1961), 120-129 (in Hebrew).

—— *The Vocalization Systems of Arabic, Hebrew, and Aramaic: Their Phonetic and Phonemic Principles.* 's-Gravenhage: Mouton, 1962.

—— *The Hebrew Language Tradition of the Yemenite Jews.* Jerusalem: The Academy of the Hebrew Language, 1963 (in Hebrew).

—— "Biblical Aramaic in Geonic Babylonia," in *Studies in Egyptology and Linguistics in Honour of H. J. Polotsky*, ed. H. B. Rosén. Jerusalem: Israel Exploration Society, 1964, 117-131.

—— "Comments on the Description of the Pointing System of the Worms Mahzor," *Lesh*, 29 (1965), 203-209 (in Hebrew).

—— "The Phonology of Babylonian Aramaic According to the Pointing of MS Sasson הלכות פסוקות," *Lesh*, 32 (1968), 67-88 (in Hebrew).

—— "Pronunciations of Hebrew,' *EJ*. Jerusalem: Keter; New York: Macmillan, 1971, 13, 1120-1145.

316

_____ *The Hebrew Language Tradition of the Baghdadi Community: Phonology.* Jerusalem: Hebrew Language Traditions Project, I, 1977 (in Hebrew).

_____ "Bamme Madliqin in Two Cairo Geniza Manuscripts," in *Studia Orientalia Memoriae D. H. Baneth Dedicata,* ed. J. Blau et al. Jerusalem: Magnes Press, 1979, 111-123 (in Hebrew).

_____ "On Processes of Transformation and Transplantation in the Traditions of Hebrew," *Proceedings of the Sixth World Congress of Jewish Studies.* Jerusalem, 1980. Division D, 141-156 (in Hebrew).

_____ Review of *On the Vocalism of the Closed Unstressed Syllables in Hebrew* by T. Harviainen, *JSS,* 27 (1982), 288-291.

_____ "De la tradition au dialecte: problèmes d'enquête linguistique," *Mass,* 2 (1986), 103-110.

_____ *Babylonian Aramaic: The Yemenite Tradition.* Jerusalem: Ben Zvi Institute, 1988 (in Hebrew).

Muraoka, T. "Notes on the Syntax of Biblical Aramaic," *JSS,* 11 (1966), 152-155.

_____ "Concerning שני לחות," *Lesh,* 40 (1976), 290 (in Hebrew).

_____ "Segolate Nouns in Biblical and other Aramaic Dialects," *JAOS,* 96 (1976), 226-235.

_____ "The So-Called Dativus Ethicus in Hebrew," *JTS,* 29 (1978), 495-498.

_____ Review of *Palestinian Syriac Studies* by M. Bar-Asher, *JSS,* 24 (1979), 287-290.

_____ "On the Morphosyntax of the Infinitive in Targumic Aramaic," in *Aramaeans, Aramaic and the Aramaic Literary Tradition,* ed. M. Sokoloff. Ramat-Gan: Bar-Ilan University Press, 1983, 75-79.

_____ "A Study in Palestinian Jewish Aramaic," *Sef,* 45 (1985) 3-21.

Murtonen, A. *Materials for a Non-Masoretic Hebrew Grammar,* I. Helsinki, 1958.

Nöldeke, T. "Beiträge zur Kenntnis der aramäischen Dialekte," *ZDMG,* 22 (1868), 443-527.

_____ *Mandäische Grammatik.* Halle: Waisenhaus, 1875; reprint Darmstadt: Wissenschaftliche Buchgesellschaft, 1974.

_____ *Die semitischen Sprachen.* 2nd ed. Leipzig: Tauchnitz, 1899.

_____ *Beiträge zur semitischen Sprachwissenschaft.* Strassburg: Trübner, 1904.

_____ *Compendious Syriac Grammar,* trans. J. Crichton London: Williams and Norgate, 1904.

_____ *Neue Beiträge zur semitischen Sprachwissenschaft.* Strassburg: Trübner, 1910.

Odeberg, H. *The Aramaic Portions of Bereshit Rabba with Grammar of Galilaean Aramaic.* Lund: Lunds Universitet Arsskrift, 1939.

Peri, Y. "The Morphology of Galilean Aramaic According to the Palestinian Targum Fragments." Masters thesis, Tel-Aviv University, 1977 (in Hebrew).

Peshiṭta Institute. *The Old Testament in Syriac According to the Peshiṭta Version* Leiden: E. J. Brill, 1977–.

317

Porath, E. *Mishnaic Hebrew as Vocalized in the Early Manuscripts of the Babylonian Jews.* Jerusalem: Bialik Institute, 1938 (in Hebrew).

Porten, B. and Greenfield, J. "The Aramaic Papyri from Hermopolis," *ZAW*, 80 (1968), 216-231.

_____ and Yardeni, A. *Textbook of Aramaic Documents from Ancient Egypt, I: Letters.* Jerusalem, 1986.

Praetorious, F. Review of *Idioticon des christlich-palästinischen Aramäisch* by F. Schwally, *ZDMG*,48 (1894), 361-362.

Qimron, E. "Medial Aleph as a Mater Lectionis in Hebrew and Aramaic Documents from Qumran in Comparison with Other Hebrew and Aramaic Sources," *Lesh*, 39 (1975), 133-164 (in Hebrew).

_____ *The Hebrew of the Dead Sea Scrolls.* Harvard Semitic Studies 29. Atlanta: Scholars Press, 1986.

_____ "לוחות, לוחיים," *Lesh*, 40 (1976), 147 (in Hebrew).

Rabin, C. "The Nature and Origin of the Shaf'el in Hebrew and Aramaic," *EI*, 9 (1969), 148-158 (in Hebrew).

_____ *The Meaning of the Grammatical Forms in Biblical and Modern Hebrew.* Jerusalem: Academon, 1971 (in Hebrew).

Revell, E. J. *Hebrew Texts with Palestinian Vocalization.* Toronto: University of Toronto Press, 1970.

_____ "Studies in the Palestinian Vocalization of Hebrew," in *Essays on the Ancient Semitic World*, ed. J. W. Wevers and D. B. Redford. Toronto: University of Toronto Press, 1970, 51-100.

_____ "The Placing of the Accent Signs in Biblical Texts with Palestinian Pointing," in *Studies on the Ancient Palestinian World*, ed. J. W. Wevers and D. B. Redford. Toronto: University of Toronto Press, 1972, 34-45.

_____ *Biblical Texts with Palestinian Pointing and Their Accents.* Society of Biblical Literature Masoretic Studies No. 4. Missoula: Scholars Press, 1977.

Rieder, D. *Pseudo-Jonathan: Targum Jonathan ben Uziel on the Pentateuch Copied from the London MS.* Jerusalem: Salomon, 1974.

Roberts, B. J. *The Old Testament Text and Versions.* Cardiff: University of Wales Press, 1951.

Rosenthal, F. *Die Sprache der palmyrenischen Inschriften und ihre Stellung innerhalb des Aramäischen.* Leipzig: J. C. Hinrichs, 1936.

_____ *Die aramäistische Forschung seit Th. Nöldeke's Veröffentlichungen.* Leiden: E. J. Brill, 1939.

_____ *An Aramaic Handbook.* 2 vols. Wiesbaden: Harrassowitz, 1967.

_____ *A Grammar of Biblical Aramaic.* Porta Linguarum Orientalium 5. Wiesbaden: Harrassowitz, 1974.

Sassoon, J. M. "A Note on šarbiṭ," *VT*,22 (1972), 111.

Schall, A. *Studien über griechische Fremdwörter im Syrischen.* Darmstadt: Wissenschaftliche Buchgesellschaft, 1960.

318

Schelbert, G. "Exodus XXIII 4 im palästinischen Targum," *VT*,8 (1958), 253-263.

Schulthess, F. *Lexicon Syropalaestinum*. Berlin: Reimer, 1903.

—— *Grammatik des christlisch-palästinischen Aramäisch*. Tübingen: J. C. B. Mohr, 1924.

Schlatter, D. *Die hebräischen Namen bei Josephus*. Gütersloh: Bertelsmann, 1913.

Segal, M. H. *A Grammar of Mishnaic Hebrew*. Oxford: Clarendon Press, 1923.

Shaked, S. "Iranian Loanwords in Middle Aramaic," *Encyclopaedia Iranica*, London: Routledge & Kegan Paul, 1986, II, 3, 259-261.

Siegfried, C. "Die Aussprache des hebräischen bei Hieronymus," *ZAW*, 4 (1884), 34-83.

Sixdenier, G. "La langue du targum samaritain," *JA*,272 (1984) 223-235.

Soden, Wolfram von. "Aramäische Wörter in neuassyrischen und neu- und spätbabylonischen Texten. Ein Vorbericht," *Or*, n.s., 35 (1966), 1-20; 37 (1968), 261-271.

Sokoloff, M. "The Hebrew of Bereshit Rabba According to MS Vat. Ebr. 81," *Lesh*, 33 (1969), 25-42, 135-149, 270-279 (in Hebrew).

—— *The Geniza Fragments of Bereshit Rabba*. Jerusalem: The Israel Academy of Sciences and Humanities, 1982 (in Hebrew).

—— "Notes on the Vocabulary of Galilean Aramaic"in *Studies in Hebrew and Semitic Languages Dedicated to the Memory of Prof. Eduard Yechezkel Kutscher*, ed. G. B. Ṣarfatti et al. Ramat-Gan: Bar-Ilan University Press, 1981, 166-173 (in Hebrew).

—— and Y. Yahalom. "Aramaic Piyyutim from the Byzantine Period,"*JQR*, 75 (1985) 309-321.

Speiser, E. A. "Secondary Developments in Semitic Phonology: An Application of the Principle of Sonority," *AJSL*,42 (1926), 145-169.

Sperber, A. "Hebrew Based upon Greek and Latin Transliterations,"*HUCA*, 12-13 (1937-1938), 103-274.

—— *A Grammar of Masoretic Hebrew: A General Introduction to the Pre-Masoretic Bible*. Copenhagen: Ejnar Munksgaard, 1959.

—— *The Bible in Aramaic*. 4 vols. Leiden: E. J. Brill, 1959-1968.

Sperber, D. *A Dictionary of Greek and Latin Legal Terms in Rabbinic Literature*. Jerusalem: Bar-Ilan University Press, 1984.

Spitaler, A. *Grammatik des neuaramäischen Dialekts von Maʿlula* [Antilibanon]. AKM 23,1. Leipzig: Deutsche Morgenländische Gesellschaft, 1938.

—— "Zum Problem der Segolisierung im Aramäischen," in *Studia Orientalia in Memoriam Caroli Brockelmann*, ed. M. Fleischhammer. Wissenschaftlicher Zeitschrift der Martin-Luther-Universität Halle-Wittenberg, Gesellschafts- und sprachwissenschaftliche Reihe, Heft 2/3, 17 (1968), 193-199.

Steiner, R. C. "*Lulav* versus \*lu/law: A Note on the Conditioning of \*aw>ū in Hebrew and Aramaic," *JAOS*,107 (1987), 121-122.

Stevenson, W. B. *Grammar of Palestinian Jewish Aramaic*. 2nd ed. Oxford: Clarendon Press, 1962.

Svedlund, L. *Selected Passages in Galilean Aramaic*. Jerusalem: Academon, 1967.

——— *The Aramaic Portions of the Pesiqta de Rab Kahana*. Uppsala: Acta Universitatis Upsaliensis, 1974.

Tal, A. "Ms. Neophyti 1: The Palestinian Targum to the Pentateuch, Observations on the Artistry of a Scribe," *IOS* , 4 (1974), 13-43.

——— *The Language of the Targum of the Former Prophets and Its Position within the Aramaic Dialects*. Tel-Aviv: Tel-Aviv University, 1975 (in Hebrew).

——— "The Samaritan Targum to the Pentateuch, Its Distinctive Characteristics and Its Metamorphosis," *JSS* , 21 (1976), 26-38.

——— "Layers in the Jewish Aramaic of Palestine: The Appended Nun as a Criterion," *Lesh*, 43 (1979), 165-184 (in Hebrew).

——— "Studies in Palestinian Aramaic: The Demonstrative Pronouns," *Lesh*, 44 (1980), 43-65 (in Hebrew).

——— *The Samaritan Targum. A Critical Edition*. 3 vols. Tel-Aviv: Tel-Aviv University, 1980-1983.

——— "The Forms of the Infinitive in Jewish Aramaic" in *Hebrew Language Studies Presented to Professor Zeev Ben-Ḥayyim*, ed. M. Bar-Asher et al. Jerusalem: Magnes Press, 1983, 210-218 (in Hebrew).

Teicher, J. "A Sixth Century Fragment of the Palestinian Targum?" *VT*, 1 (1951), 125-129.

Telegdi, S. "Essai sur la phonétique des emprunts iraniens en araméen talmudique," *JA*, 226 (1935), 178-256.

Vaux, R. de and Milik, J. *Discoveries in the Judaean Desert*, VI. Oxford: Clarendon Press, 1977.

Vermes, G. "The Use of *bar nash/bar nasha* in Jewish Aramaic." Appendix E in M. Black, *An Aramaic Approach to the Gospels and Acts*. Oxford: Clarendon Press, 1967, 320-327.

——— "The Archangel Sariel" in *Christianity, Judaism and other Greco-Roman Cults, Studies for Morton Smith at Sixty*, ed. J. Neusner. Leiden: E. J. Brill, 1975, 159-166

Vilsker, L. H. *Manuel d'araméen samaritain*, trans. J. Margain. Paris: Centre National de la Recherche Scientifique, 1981.

Wesselius, J. W. "A Subjunctive in the Aramaic of the Palestinian Targum," *JJS*,35 (1984), 196-199.

Wider, N. "Concerning רבק in Hebrew Sources," *Lesh*, 27-28 (1963-1964), 214-217 (in Hebrew).

Wright, W. *A Grammar of the Arabic Language*, 2 vols. 3rd ed., ed. R. Smith and M. J. de Goeje. Cambridge: University Press, 1896-1898; reprint 1971.

320

Yahalom, Y. "The Palestinian Pointing in the קדשתות הדותה למשמרת and the Linguistic Phenomena Reflected in It," *Lesh*, 34 (1969-1970), 25-60 (in Hebrew).

—— Review of *Neue palästinisch punktierte Bibelfragmente* by M. Dietrich, *KirSef*, 45 (1970), 388-389 (in Hebrew).

Yalon, H. *Introduction to the Vocalization of the Mishnah.* Jerusalem: Bialik Institute, 1964 (in Hebrew).

—— "The Reasoning behind the Pointed Mishnayot," *Lesh*, 24 (1960), 157-165, 253 (in Hebrew).

Yeivin, I. *The Hebrew Language Tradition as Reflected in the Babylonian Vocalization.* 2 vols. Jerusalem: The Academy of the Hebrew Language, 1985 (in Hebrew).

Zimmern, H. *Akkadische Fremdwörter als Beweis für babylonischen Kultureinfluss.* 2nd ed. Leipzig: J. C. Hinrichs, 1917.

Zunz, L. *Die gottesdienstlichen Vorträge der Juden.* 2nd ed. Kaufmann: Frankfurt a. Main, 1892.

Zurawel, T. "The Sheva in Maimonides' Commentary to the Mishna (Autograph)" in *Language Studies* II-III, ed. M. Bar-Asher. Jerusalem: Hebrew University, 1987, 217-233 (in Hebrew).

321

## Addenda and Corrigenda

pp. 1-2 See also M. H. Goshen-Gottstein, "Aspects of Targum Studies," *Proceedings of the Ninth World Congress of Jewish Studies*, Jerusalem, 1985, Panel Sessions: Bible Studies and Ancient Near East, pp. 35-44.

p. 10 note 39 add: M. Goshen-Gottstein, *Fragments of Lost Targumim*, II (Ramat-Gan: Bar-Ilan University Press, 1989, in Hebrew).

p. 11 n.54 add: A. Tal, "The Aramaic Dialects of Palestine and the 'Yerushalmi' Targum to the Pentateuch," *Proceedings of the Ninth World Congress of Jewish Studies*, Jerusalem, 1985, Panel Session: Bible Studies and Ancient Near East, pp. 13-22 (in Hebrew); "The Dialects of Jewish Palestinian Aramaic and the Palestinian Targum of the Pentateuch," *Sef*, 46 (1988), 441-448.

p. 12 n.57 add: T. Muraoka, "Segolate Nouns in Biblical and Other Aramaic Dialects," *JAOS*, 96 (1976), 230.

p. 26 §4k line 2 read: Final consonant *he*.

p. 33 §8f lines 6-7 read: the only other exceptions

p. 55 §14n For the most recent analysis of a text with the "Palestinian-Tiberian" pointing system, see Y. Bentolila, *A French-Italian Tradition of Post-Biblical Hebrew* (Beer Sheva: Hebrew University Language Traditions Project, XIV, 1989 in Hebrew).

p. 71 §24 next to last line: The two examples from E Gn 30:32 should be deleted.

p. 83 n.57 On the fluctuation of *e* and *i* in the Tiberian and Babylonian pointing traditions of Biblical Aramaic and Targum Onqelos (as well as *o* and *u* in Targum Onqelos), see now A. Dodi, "Pausal Forms in Aramaic," in *Studies in the Hebrew Language and the Talmudic Literature*, ed. M. Z. Kaddari and S. Sharvit (Ramat-Gan: Bar-Ilan University Press, 1989), pp. 63-74 (in Hebrew).

pp. 89-90 n.189 add: and its English translation in *Sef*, 46 (1988), 41-84.

p. 90 n.190 add: Yahalom, "The Palestinian Vocalization—Its Investigation and Achievements," *Lesh*, 52 (1988), 112-143 (in Hebrew).

p. 119 §38a Tal ("Infinitive," p. 213 n.33) views both forms as errors.

p. 142 8th line: יְגַר C Gn 31:46 is an *abs. s.* noun.

p. 157 add to §106a: /*tapšil,*tapšila/ "cooked food": abs.pl. תפשילין F Lv 22:27; *3 m.s.* תפשילוי F Lv 22:27 (§17b).

p. 194 add to §155b: The verbal forms of the root חזר "return" in Palestinian Aramaic sources (cf. Eastern Aramaic הדר, אהדר) are the result of Hebrew influence. See Tal, *Language*, pp. 108, 163. Examples of this root in the Cairo Genizah fragments are *G. Perf. 3 m.s.* וְחַזַר Cd Gn 37:29, וְחַזַר Cd Ex 5:22; *Imperf. 3 m.s.* יֶחֱזוֹר A Ex 21:34; *Imper. m.s.* חֲזוֹר E Gn 31:3; *m.pl.* חִזְרוּ E Gn 43:2; *Act. Ptc. m.s.* וְחָזַר Bd Gn 8:7; *D Inf.* לְמֶחֱזָרָא Cd Gn 37:22.

322

p. 205 n.109 add: S. Sharvit, "Evidence for פעו״פעאי in Rabbinic Hebrew," *Lesh*, 53 (1988-1989), 54-59 (in Hebrew).

p. 215 n.32: On Philippi's Law, see now also E. Qimron, "Interchanges of e and a Vowels in Accented Closed Syllables in Biblical Hebrew," *Lesh*, 50 (1985-1986), 77-102 (in Hebrew), and Z. Ben-Hayyim, "Remarks on Philippi's Law," *Lesh*, 53 (1988-1989), 113-120 (in Hebrew).

p. 221 n.182: Cf. Ugaritic *dakaru*. See J. Huehnergard, *Ugaritic Vocabulary in Syllabic Transcription* (Harvard Semitic Studies 32, Scholars Press: Atlanta, 1987), pp. 43, 96.

p. 227 n.303: For a Proto-Semitic *'iš*, see J. Blau, "Marginalia Semitica II," *IOS*, 2 (1972), 62-65; Huehnergard, *Ugaritic Vocabulary*, p. 63.

p. 239 n.106 add: Bar-Asher, *Palestinian Syriac Studies*, p. 378 n.66.

p. 239 n.111: If *qatlet > *qitlet* and *qatlat > *qitlat* already in a stage of Proto-Aramaic, then the /a/ of Cairo Genizah /qatlet/, /qatlat/ may have been reintroduced into G from the 1 s. and 3 f.s. of the derived conjugations: D /qattəlet/, /'aqtəlat/, Gt /'etqatlet/, /'etqatlat/, Dt /'etqattəlet/, /'etqattəlat/.

p. 257: The only fully pointed example of the G Perfect 3 f.pl. /qatlen/ belongs to the I-n class in which *a > /e/:-נְהֵרֶן Cd Gn 38:25. See §130 n.61.

p. 278 under Fragment Targum add: Gn 30:32 78a nn.211-212; Gn 30:38 55j, 104m n.338; Gn 31:39 19f n.65; Gn 35:9 20a n.104, 162d n.4; Gn 38:25 37e nn.60-61, 157d n.22; Gn 39:10 157c n.16; Gn 42:38 100a n.308.

M. L. Klein as just published additional Genizah material in "New Fragments of Palestinin Targum from the Cairo Genizah," *Sef*, 49 (1989), pp. 123-133. One can now add to MS D: CUL T-S AS 68.83 (Gn 37:8-11,13-14,16-17), CUL T-S AS 64.27 (Gn 48:10-11), CUL T-S AS 64.239 (Ex 5:6-7,18-19), CUL T-S AS 66.187 (Ex 7:15-16,20), CUL T-S AS 68.234 (Dt 29 : 13-15); to MS E: CUL T-S AS 68.224 (Ex 36:8-13,22-29) and CUL T-S AS 68.144 (Ex 39:32-40; 40:2-12); and to MS H: CUL T-S B 9.11 (Gn 15:11-16:16). Klein now classifies MS H as Fragment Targum (see §2e, n.32). He points out that חתת as a det. f.s. cardinal number ("the one") is now attested in CUL T-S AS 68.224 (MS E Ex 36:9,11). See §52a.